LANDSCAPE, MONU
AND SOCIETY

The prehistory of Cranborne Chase

JOHN C. BARRETT,
RICHARD BRADLEY
and
MARTIN GREEN

with contributions from Mark Bowden, S. G. E. Bowman, Andrew Brown, S. Butcher, Rosamund Cleal, Mark Corney, Roy Entwistle, Jill Fisher, Peter Fisher, Julie Gardiner, Martin Jones, A. J. Legge, Barry Lewis, Brendan O'Connor, Jill Parker, Mark Robinson, Juliet Rogers, Bill Startin and Jameson Wooders

The right of the University of Cambridge to print and sell all manner of books was granted by Henry VIII in 1534. The University has printed and published continuously since 1584.

CAMBRIDGE UNIVERSITY PRESS

Cambridge
New York Port Chester
Melbourne Sydney

CAMBRIDGE UNIVERSITY PRESS
Cambridge, New York, Melbourne, Madrid, Cape Town, Singapore, São Paulo, Delhi

Cambridge University Press
The Edinburgh Building, Cambridge CB2 8RU, UK

Published in the United States of America by Cambridge University Press, New York

www.cambridge.org
Information on this title: www.cambridge.org/9780521109222

First published 1991
This digitally printed version 2009

A catalogue record for this publication is available from the British Library

Library of Congress Cataloguing in Publication data

Barrett, John C.
Landscape, monuments, and society : the prehistory of Cranborne
Chase / John C. Barrett, Richard Bradley and Martin Green.
p. ca.
Includes bibliographical references.
ISBN 0 521 32128 X
1. Neolithic period–England–Cranborne Chase. 2. Bronze Age–
England–Cranborne Chase. 3. Cranborne Chase (England)–
Antiquities. 4. England–Antiquities. I. Bradley, Richard. 1946– .
II. Green, Martin, 1955– . III. Title.
GN776.22.G7B37 1990
036.2′33–dc20 89–22083 CIP

ISBN 978-0-521-32128-0 hardback
ISBN 978-0-521-10922-2 paperback

CONTENTS

ILLUSTRATIONS

TABLES

ACKNOWLEDGEMENTS

A volume of this size is the work of many people, and we must begin by thanking all those who have contributed to the text. Behind these are a large number of people who have made equally important contributions.

Our fieldwork was funded by grants from a variety of sources: the British Academy; the Dorset Archaeological Committee; Glasgow University Excavation Fund; the Historic Buildings and Monuments Commission; Leeds University Research Fund; the Prehistoric Society; Reading University Research Board; and the Society of Antiquaries. Research on the Pitt Rivers archive in Salisbury was supported by the Carnegie Fund for the Universities of Scotland, and Mark Bowden's post-excavation work on the Down Farm ring ditch by the Historic Buildings and Monuments Commission. Two grants from the British Academy allowed the project to employ Martin Cook to prepare many of the illustrations. Our departments in Glasgow and Reading also provided considerable help in kind. Radiocarbon dates were provided by the British Museum Research Laboratory and the Science and Engineering Research Council.

We must thank Michael Pitt Rivers for allowing us to excavate at South Lodge Camp and the Historic Buildings and Monuments Commission for permission to work on a scheduled ancient monument. We also received much practical help from the staff of the Rushmore Estate, in particular K. and I. Burt. Thanks are due to Peter Saunders for access to the Pitt Rivers Collection in the Salisbury and South Wiltshire Museum, where Clare Coneybeare and Mark Bowden were of invaluable assistance during this research. In Dorchester Roger Peers provided similar help with material in the Dorset County Museum.

Many people have helped in the preparation of this volume. In Reading a major contribution was made by Mark Bowden, whilst Martin Cook was responsible for many of the illustrations. Julie Carr, Steve Ford and Juliet Foulkes helped to analyse the flintwork from South Lodge Camp, and Averil Culverhouse processed many of the soil samples from the excavation. In Glasgow work was carried out on the drawings by A. McGie, L. McEwan and K. Barrett. We have also benefited from the care taken with the production of this volume at Cambridge University Press.

We are grateful to John Boyden for the frontispiece and to Claire Halpin, Julian Thomas, Nicholas Thomas and the Royal Commission on the Historical Monuments of England for allowing us to include unpublished material in the figure drawings. We also thank the executors of the Virginia Woolf estate and the Hogarth Press for permission to reproduce material from Woolf's *Diary*.

Many people contributed to the excavations described in this volume, and the successful outcome of this work is largely due to their enthusiasm and good humour and to the excellence of the cooks. Particular responsibilities were taken by John Arnold, Mark Bowden, Steve Cogbill, H. Duncan, Margaret Ehrenberg, Peter Fisher, Steve Ford, Julie Gardiner, K. McAnally, J. McDougall, Barry Mead, Lorraine Mepham, Helen Patterson, Frances Raymond, Kirstie Shedden, Jennie Stopford, Robin Taylor and Julian Thomas. The majority of the workforce was drawn from Glasgow, Leeds and Reading Universities and from the East Dorset Antiquarian Society.

Lastly, we must thank many professional colleagues for their help, support and advice, but we owe a still greater debt to Kathryn and Katherine who will know why.

INTRODUCTION

Cranborne Chase: the stunted aboriginal forest trees, scattered, not grouped in cultivations; anemones, bluebells, violets, all pale, sprinkled about, without colour, ... for the sun hardly shone. Then [the] Vale; a vast air dome and the fields dropped to the bottom; the sun striking, there, there; a drench of rain falling, like a veil streaming from the sky, there and there; and the downs rising, very strongly scarped (if that is the word) so that they were ridged and ledged – and all the cleanliness of [the] village, its happiness and well-being, making me ask ... still this is the right method, surely?

Virginia Woolf, *Diary*, 30 April, 1926

The title and subtitle of this book have been selected with special care, and this is the obvious point at which to explain why they were chosen. This volume presents the main results of a project which took its own authors by surprise. Our fieldwork in Cranborne Chase, on the edge of the southern English downland, began as a contribution to landscape archaeology, and also owed something to the tradition of culture history. The subtitle of this volume sums up the original intention of that research, but as the project developed, our work took a different course.

Although the title reflects this change in the character of our research, this work was never intended as a comprehensive regional study. The original nucleus was the excavation of a Bronze Age site at South Lodge Camp, which began in 1977. This site was selected, not because it was situated in Cranborne Chase, but because work in the 1890s had documented a large body of diagnostic material (*Excavations* IV, 1–41). This allowed us to approach the excavation with fairly clear objectives in mind, but no sooner had the project got under way than we realised that a full understanding of the South Lodge complex would involve analysis of other contemporary sites in the area. Our growing acquaintance with the archaeology of Cranborne Chase suggested that this would not be possible unless those sites were viewed in relation to a longer sequence of change. Having embarked on a modest programme of excavation and museum work, we realised that we were caught. Our research became steadily more ambitious, and when, in 1981, we published a provisional report (Barrett, Bradley, Green and Lewis 1981), we found it necessary to review the entire prehistoric sequence in the area. Since then our concern has been with the development of Cranborne Chase from the beginning of the Neolithic period to the end of the Iron Age.

Such changes in the scope of our research took place at a time that saw significant changes in the nature of archaeology itself, so that what had started as an investigation of landscape history almost inevitably extended into a study of social change. As this happened, our attention turned to the role of more spectacular field monuments in Cranborne Chase. Because of our existing work on landscape history in that area, an immediate objective was to consider their relationship to the contemporary pattern of settlement. This encouraged us to bring together parts of the archaeological record which normally were studied quite separately. The scale of the project widened once again.

Many projects must have gone through a similar development during those years, but few have been published at any length. By the 1970s prehistorians had become quite skilled at investigating the relationship between settlement and the natural environment. Specialists in soils, seeds, plant remains and animal bones had all developed new ways of looking at the archaeological record, and, not surprisingly, these played a major part in our fieldwork in Cranborne Chase. This was only right since some of these approaches were pioneered on General Pitt Rivers' excavations in the same region. On the other hand, as the project extended beyond South Lodge Camp and came to concern itself with earlier material, it became obvious that ecological features had not played a dominant role in the sequence that we were observing. They may have presented certain constraints, but from the outset the main influence over the changing configuration of the landscape was the existence of large, apparently non-utilitarian monuments. Their interpretation posed a major challenge to archaeological theory. Not only did these earthwork monuments exercise a decisive influence over the character of contemporary settlement; their very existence determined the way in which the landscape was used for a long time after their construction. Older monuments attracted new monuments around them, and the fabric of everyday life seems to have been affected by their presence. In short, it became apparent that the *past* itself, and the features which represented it in the life of later generations, was a crucially important resource. For almost two millennia it exercised an influence over the ways in which the landscape of Cranborne Chase was used. By this point it was obvious that traditional economic explanations had little to do with the evidence that we were collecting, and we found ourselves obliged to think more clearly about the nature of prehistoric *society* in this area, and the role played by monuments in the overall pattern of change. This gave us an added flexibility, but the more integrated approach that we now adopted meant that those parts of the archaeological record which are studied by different specialists would now need to be united in the same interpretative framework. This book is an attempt to put that programme into practice.

At the risk of some simplification, the development of the Cranborne Chase Project can be divided into two stages. Between 1977 and 1981 it focused mainly on the Bronze Age enclosures at South Lodge Camp and Down Farm, together with their associated cemeteries. This work involved excavation by all three of the authors. Once it was complete, the emphasis shifted to the Neolithic period, and in particular to the largest and most mysterious monument of that date, the Dorset Cursus. This could hardly be interpreted in terms of economic or ecological factors and yet it provided the focus for a dense distribution of burial mounds and other earthworks. The Cursus therefore became the main subject of a second stage of fieldwork, which ran between 1982 and 1984. This also involved the excavation of several small monuments close to the Cursus and detailed analysis of material collected in field survey. Like most of the excavation, this survey was carried out by Martin Green, whilst Richard Bradley investigated the Cursus itself.

The same twofold division is reflected in the structure of this book. Part I (Chapters 2 to 4), entitled 'The dead and the living', concerns the establishment of a social landscape dominated by the Dorset Cursus and the non-utilitarian field monuments which developed around it. As we shall see, even the character of domestic activity was influenced by the proximity of these sites. Part II (Chapters 5 to 6), entitled 'The living and the dead', concerns the dissolution of that structure and the very different system which took its place. It traces the development of first-millennium settlement and its growing concern with land and food production. It also documents the modification and destruction of the earlier monuments. Whilst parallel developments can be recognised in many other areas of Britain (Barrett and Bradley 1980; Bradley 1984), the peculiar richness of the archaeological record in Cranborne Chase makes it ideally suited to a study of social change on a local scale over more than three thousand years.

We have tried to show how this project developed under the influence of current debates in British archaeology, but the decisive factor was undoubtedly the quality of this archaeological record, which provided an almost unparalleled opportunity to put ideas to work. Its high quality raises certain problems, however, for whilst fieldwork and subsequent analysis have taken on a strongly thematic character, it would be unprofessional to confine our treatment of the primary data to those aspects of the work that we now find most informative. We should not forget that this project began as an exercise in landscape studies of a type which still enjoys a general currency. Our study area is also of some importance for traditional cultural archaeology, as it provides a particularly full and varied sequence of artefacts. It is not possible to cater for all tastes in a single monograph, and our attempts to give the same weight to every class of material proved to be quite indigestible. For this reason, the present volume is a selective account of our excavation and survey work, together with certain analyses of the artefacts and ecofacts. We make no apology for structuring it around what seem to be the most important issues. For an extended account of all the categories of excavated material, the reader is referred to a companion volume of essays, published by Oxbow Books (Barrett and Bradley in prep.). That volume does not duplicate the detailed site reports presented here, but considers each class of excavated material as it runs through the sequence as a whole, including pottery, worked flint, seeds and animal bones. This ancillary publication is intended to complete the definitive record of this project, leaving nothing hidden in microfiche. Meanwhile the present volume contains sufficient information on the nature, context and chronology of the finds to stand or fall on its own merits.

The component parts of our title, *Landscape, monuments and society*, are arranged in that particular order because they reflect the archaeologist's experience in dealing with them – landscape studies, for example, are better established than social archaeology. They do not represent any kind of 'hierarchy of inference'; nor are they successive steps in a single programme of research. They make up a unified whole, and their separation may tell us more about our own society than those that we are studying. 'Landscape' is an entirely subjective concept, and carries different connotations for different members of society (see Cosgrove 1984). Monuments may be one element in these views of the world, and sometimes it seems as if their builders were trying to merge them into the natural order. On the other hand, the particular emphasis of this study is on the *social* rather than the natural landscape, and for this reason our discussion of monuments and their role in society takes up more space than is normal in a volume of this kind. This needs detailed justification before we can proceed. It is equally important to understand the changing character of our study area. Thus our first chapter has two main tasks to fulfil. First, we must explain in greater detail the theoretical framework within which our analysis was conducted; and, secondly, we have to describe the distinctive character of the landscape where those processes were played out.

The first part of the volume is concerned with the third and second millennia bc, in conventional terminology the Neolithic and Early Bronze Age periods. It is divided into four chapters. The first three describe the major developments in the study area, whilst the fourth also provides a more thematic overview of the sequence as a whole. Although the three chronological divisions happen to correspond to traditional archaeological periods, they are used here because they mark major changes in the occupation of Cranborne Chase. There is so much information to consider that it may be helpful to summarise the main outlines at this point.

After an initial chapter, setting out the main aims of the project and the character of the study area, *Chapter 2* considers the establishment of agricultural communities in the region. Earlier Neolithic activity may have started as little more than a seasonal extension to a settlement pattern with its emphasis in lowland areas. It was towards the end of this phase that complex monuments were built, and at much the same time there are indications of increased settlement of the Wessex downland. In Cranborne Chase, however, the Dorset Cursus and its accompanying long barrows dominate the archaeological record completely.

Chapter 3 continues the sequence into the Later Neolithic period when the intensity of upland settlement increased dramatically. Non-utilitarian monuments continued to be built, but now their locations were influenced by the prominent earthworks of the previous phase. Not only did newer monuments make reference to those already in existence; the whole character of contemporary settlement may have been structured by the presence and operation of those sites.

Chapter 4 completes the descriptive element in the first part of the book by tracing the sequence into a period in which again there is less evidence of domestic settlement in Cranborne Chase than there is in lowland parts of Wessex. On the other hand, the distinctive area around the earlier monuments retained its specialised character and includes one of the densest concentrations of barrows on the chalk. This remained important into the period of agricultural reorganisation considered in Part II.

The second part of this book carries our analysis into the later prehistoric period, a time when the landscape became dominated by the remains of field systems and settlements, representing a distinct contrast with the earlier forms of monument.

Chapter 5 describes our own excavations on two Middle Bronze Age settlements and cemeteries, before reconsidering Pitt Rivers' earlier excavations on similar sites. In the light of this work, we are able to offer an explanation for the transformation of the settlement record at this time.

Chapter 6 then examines the apparently discontinuous sequence of settlement extending from the end of the Middle Bronze Age to the Late Iron Age. Drawing upon the considerable amount of field survey evidence now available, we describe the sequence in terms of a continuous history of settlement evolution, leading to the complex of enclosures around the Late Iron Age settlement on Gussage Hill.

Radiocarbon chronology[1]

A good chronological framework is essential for any regional analysis. It was with this in mind, and with the ready co-operation of the British Museum Research Laboratory, that a large number of radiocarbon dates was obtained for material recovered during our fieldwork. Problems have arisen with some of these data, however, and Dr Sheridan Bowman has provided the following commentary on the use of the Cranborne Chase (British Museum) date list.

The British Museum radiocarbon laboratory has now issued revised, and in some cases new, results for the great majority of samples which were originally measured between 1980 and 1984. This was necessary because of the identification of a systematic error in BM radiocarbon results issued during that period (Tite *et al.* 1987, 1988). In the absence of new results for all previously dated samples or the availability of new samples, the revised results for the Cranborne material must be taken as definitive, and the previously published dates in *Radiocarbon* should be ignored.

This is not the appropriate place to describe how the error was identified and the revisions evaluated; a full account of these is in preparation and will be published by the present author, together with Janet Ambers and Morven Leese. It is, however, worth briefly discussing the cause of the problem. The British Museum employs liquid scintillation counting to evaluate the radiocarbon content in a sample and to facilitate this the sample is converted to benzene. Counting of the beta particles from the radioactive decay of the radiocarbon takes place quasi-simultaneously with counting of one or more reference standards, referred to as moderns, which have the radiocarbon activity of a zero-age sample. Similarly 'dead' samples (i.e. having no radiocarbon activity) are counted to measure the number of counts induced by sources of radioactivity other than radiocarbon (e.g. cosmic rays or natural radioactivity in the immediate environment of the counter). These moderns and backgrounds have a long residency time in the counter, whereas samples for dating are present for relatively short periods.

Benzene is a fairly volatile liquid and even apparently small levels of evaporation will give significant shifts in the radiocarbon result. Both modern and background evaporation losses contribute to give ages that are too young. A 1% loss of modern benzene is equivalent to an eighty-year reduction in age, and a 1% loss of background to a twenty-year reduction if the sample age is 5570 years (i.e. equal to the ^{14}C half-life). Such evaporation losses can therefore readily account for discrepancies of several hundred years. It is important to note that evaporation losses in the standards give rise to systematic errors, i.e. the results will be consistently biased relative to the true result, in this case too young. Biased results are inaccurate, though not necessarily imprecise. Precise, but inaccurate, data are those where repeated evaluations, under the same experimental conditions, will give very nearly the same value, but that value will not be close to the true one. In radiocarbon dating, a measure of reproducibility, i.e. precision, is experimentally evaluated and given as the error term. Since the true value is rarely known, a radiocarbon result with a small associated error term can give a false impression of validity. A difficulty can arise in attempting to evaluate biases. Assuming two independent results are available, one of which can be taken to be accurate, they will both have errors associated with measurement (i.e. precision errors). While the difference in the results should be a measure of the bias of the inaccurate one, it might not be possible to prove this bias differs from zero because of the poor precision of the individual results.

To investigate the scale of the problem, the BM counting system was first upgraded. The measures adopted are summarised in Bowman and Ambers (1988) and were designed to remove any biases, ensure that they do not recur, and to obtain a realistic measure of precision. In particular a sample of *accurately* and *precisely* known radiocarbon age is counted quasi-simultaneously with all samples to be dated. These reference samples are groups of ten or twenty rings of bog oak dated by Gordon Pearson's high-precision radiocarbon laboratory in Belfast. The samples were kindly supplied by Mike Baillie, who, together with Jon Pilcher, performed the dendrochronology for the Belfast high-precision calibration curve (Pearson *et al.* 1986). The first four samples, representing three different ages, that were run by the BM differed on average by fourteen years from the Belfast results (standard error of ± 9: Bowman and Ambers 1988). From these comparisons it is clear that no significant systematic errors exist in the upgraded BM counting system, and this has provided a firm basis from which to investigate the earlier problem. The precision on BM results for a full-sized sample is typically ± 40 to 50 years at the one sigma level (note that this is substantially less precise than the Belfast data, but part of this difference is due to sample size).

It will be noted that the Cranborne datelist contains two types of new BM reference number: those with the letter R appended and those with the letter N appended. These refer to revised and new results respectively. The latter are measurements on samples where enough material remained to enable them to be redated completely from scratch. Each revised date has been calculated from the original result using a combination of other data. Given that the evaporation losses were to some extent time dependent and that two counters were involved, the amount by which results are revised is not necessarily the same from sample to sample. The error terms associated with the revised results are larger than the original ones, since the corrections themselves have error terms and, in addition, the original errors were underestimated (the method now used to evaluate total precision on BM dates is outlined in Ambers *et al.* 1987). Clearly increased error terms affect the 'sensitivity' with which these revised results can be used, i.e. how different two radiocarbon dates need to be in order for them to be statistically distinguishable. For one site of the Cranborne series, Handley Barrow, only one new date was feasible and no revisions could be issued for the other results. These non-revised data must be used with caution.

It is perhaps appropriate to discuss at this stage two other forms of bias, leaving aside questions of residuality and inadequate contextual control, that can affect radiocarbon results and their interpretation. Contamination of sample material by carbon of a different age is an obvious source of bias. Pretreatment procedures are used by all radiocarbon laboratories, and are designed to eliminate carbon-containing materials that have entered a sample *post mortem*. Samples that have been stored for long periods, in a museum for example, should not present any additional difficulties unless they have undergone certain types of conservation treatment. Impregnation, for example, introduces chemicals which, being difficult to remove, are unlikely to be entirely eliminated by pretreatment.

A second type of bias is inherent to the sample material itself. Samples of marine origin are an extreme example (see for example Olsson, 1983). Equally tree-rings cease to exchange carbon with the biosphere soon after they are laid down, and it is well known that long-lived species such as oak, and hence oak charcoal, give radiocarbon results that can be several centuries older than the event of usage. As part of the procedure of revising the discrepant BM results, it was necessary to redate a selection of samples. In many cases, the only material available was charcoal. The likelihood of bias entering the revision process therefore had to be investigated. Two samples were chosen which were sufficiently large to enable several dates to be measured from scratch. One was bone: the vertebrae of a single ox from Badshot (submitted by Jon Cotton; original reference BM-2273, Ambers *et al.* 1987). The other was charcoal from Down Farm (part of the Cranborne series submitted by Richard Bradley; original reference BM-1852, Burleigh *et al.* 1982). The results are shown below.

The N1, N2 ... etc. appended to the original BM reference numbers indicate new results on different aliquots of sample, i.e. replications of the dating process from scratch. In the case of the Badshot bone it is accepted that a sub-sample of material of the same age is being selected in each case. For the Down Farm charcoal this is not necessarily the case. Four sub-samples were taken without any particular selection of size or type of charcoal fragments (BM-1852N1 to BM-1852N4). These data might appear rather more scattered than the bone results, but given the estimated precision it cannot be proven statistically that these charcoal samples are not of the same radiocarbon age. However, one further sub-sample was very carefully chosen. This has been given a different reference (BM-2577), since it was selected to represent young, i.e. 'twiggy', material. On a one-sided significance test, BM-2577 is statistically younger, at the 99% level of confidence, than the mean result for the non-selected material. The validity of taking a mean of these four results might be questionable since a charcoal sample, as discussed, is not necessarily all of the same age. However, a more conservative test of the youngest individual sample, 1852N3, against the 'twiggy' material also confirms the possibility of a difference, though at a lower level of confidence (significance tests have been based on the estimated precisions). From the point of view of the revision of the discrepant BM results, the reasonable reproducibility of the replicates on non-selected charcoal is encouraging and necessary for the success of the procedure adopted. For archaeological interpretation, however, the difference relative to 'twiggy' material is a bias that must be continually borne in mind in comparison of results.

Site	New reference	New result (years BP)
Down Farm	BM-1852N1	3120 ± 50
	BM-1852N2	3270 ± 50
	BM-1852N3	3100 ± 50
	BM-1852N4	3150 ± 60
	BM-2577	2980 ± 50
Badshot	BM-2273N1	4780 ± 40
	BM-2273N2	4710 ± 50
	BM-2273N3	4730 ± 50

Returning now to the Cranborne data as a whole, for the revised results, although the precision has decreased, the purpose of the revision was to increase accuracy, i.e. to reduce systematic bias. Overall, the results have consistently moved back in age by some 250 radiocarbon years or more. Calibration of these data (Pearson and Stuiver 1986; Pearson *et al.* 1986) should give age ranges which represent better the true dates of usage of the sites. In particular this affects the interpretation of the Wessex Deverel-Rimbury complex (see chapter 5), which was previously a chronological anomaly relative to other localities: this anomaly has now been removed. The Cranborne series serves to emphasise the point made in the opening paragraph of this discussion, that the previously published BM results (for samples measured between 1980 and 1984) should not be used.

Note

1 S. G. E. Bowman

1. TIME AND PLACE

1.1 The archaeology of social reproduction[1]

The main themes of our title, *Landscape, monuments and society*, often appear to be specific areas of archaeological interest. Monuments, for instance, are analysed in terms of their form and structural history, and the landscape provides a context for the distribution of monuments, revealing their spatial organisation and ecological setting. But what of society? If anything, society appears as the ghost in the machine, whose archaeologically verifiable existence is still contested. Let us therefore look at the relationship between society, the landscape and the monument.

Since the work of Gordon Childe, archaeologists have tended to treat 'society' as a system of institutions which are mapped by their material remains. Cultural archaeologists defined the social realm as a relatively closed set of shared beliefs. It was the acceptance of those beliefs which established cohesion between a society's members and the practical application of belief systems which produced regular patterns of material association (Childe 1956). The application of this rather straightforward idea has led to the chronological and geographical ordering of artefacts and monuments. Such ordering has appeared to reflect the nature, history and extent of a given belief system; and the categorisation and mapping of archaeological material in these terms remains part of the conceptual framework of British archaeology.

By now there have been numerous criticisms of such an approach to archaeology. One of the more sustained critiques has been developed by Renfrew (1977). He notes that the definition of cultural types has depended upon norms, arbitrarily drawn from rich assemblages of material. An example relevant to our present work would be the vaguely defined 'Wessex Culture', based upon a group of poorly recorded but exotic Early Bronze Age grave assemblages.

Renfrew also accuses Childe of muddling questions of ethnicity with questions of social organisation. This seems another way of arguing that the organisation of any society is difficult to understand when all available data are interpreted in terms of the normative principles of a cultural tradition. An alternative approach is to seek the organisation of the various institutions which comprise the social system in the spatial organisation of sites and artefacts. A classic application of this approach is Renfrew's own model for the Neolithic and Early Bronze Age of Wessex (1973). Here the sequence of monuments, their spatial distribution and the labour demands estimated for their construction are used to deduce a sequence of increasingly centralised 'polities' (Renfrew 1973 and 1986). However, such models tell us little about the history of these social systems. Just as in cultural archaeology, where all available data are used to map cultural norms, all the information is now being used to expose the systemic and functional arrangement of social institutions. We have no information about the processes which generated those particular systems. Consequently their genesis seems entirely mysterious, arising either from some adaptive necessity, and therefore determined by ecological conditions, or the result of largely abstract processes inherent in earlier social relations. Ultimately such an archaeology has had to rely heavily upon models of social evolution to breathe life into static representations.

Social archaeology confronts several historical problems. It considers how people reproduce (1) their material conditions through their actions upon the environment; (2) the social system by maintaining the demands, and meeting the obligations, of social discourse; and (3) their knowledge and understanding of how to proceed in such practices. The emphasis here is upon *reproduction* in the sense of the routine maintenance of social practices, rather than upon discovering descriptive terminologies for entire social systems, such as band, tribe, chiefdom, state etc. These routines are daily and traditional practices, and historical analysis should reveal the means by which such practices were maintained or transformed. Archaeological evidence is not simply a material record of social processes: it is part of the material resources employed in past social practices.

Social practices are maintained by people's *practical knowledge* of the specific cultural and social conditions they experience. This is the practical competence of knowing how to proceed in daily and seasonal activities. It is how the world is comprehended in order to allow action that is meaningful and effective. People have some control over the available cultural resources through which they respond to obligations, enter alliances or make demands. The way in which that control is exercised is part of the practical strategy of daily life, routines which draw upon available resources of authority and respond to demands and obligations. Thus social practices reproduce structures of authority. But alternative strategies are available and modes of authority may be transformed during the execution of such practices. Material conditions do not remain constant: they are worked and reworked, and history is made under these changing conditions.

Practical knowledge and *discursive knowledge* (the latter called to mind to explain the world) are likely to be created under different conditions. There has been considerable debate in the recent archaeological literature concerning the nature, role and origin of ideological systems (Miller and Tilley 1984). We take ideology in non-capitalist societies to have a quite specific role and specific means of reproduction. Ideologies are those forms of discursive knowledge which explain the world or its cultural values in a particular and functionally coherent way. Because ideologies preserve key sets of cultural values which recur in routine practices, they maintain social conditions rather than transform them. They therefore appear to serve the interests of dominant groups. Ideology is not a 'false consciousness' but a dominant discursive reading of key cultural values.

A discursive knowledge which gives this dominant reading to the elements of the symbolic system is reproduced through *ritual*. It is through ritual that particular conditions are given precise cultural definitions because ritual controls transitions between those conditions. Burial rituals enable the transition from life to death and by so doing they give an explicit cultural definition to the symbolism associated with this life:death opposition. Similarly rituals may be employed to deal with those moments when culturally defined categories appear to be transgressed as in cases of illness or infertility. Such a transgression can only be contemplated by employing the symbolism used to define 'normality'. This approach follows the work of Turner (1967) and Bloch (1985), and preserves ritual as a distinctive form of practice, reproducing a particular form of discursive knowledge. It is through the highly formalised drama of ritual that dominant readings of cultural symbols are constructed.

We can now confront the means of reproducing not only material conditions but also forms of knowledge. Both are necessary components of human action (Godelier 1986). We can recognise that different forms of knowledge will be created under specific cultural and historical conditions.

In archaeological terms these approaches raise two quite fundamental issues. Firstly, social systems are reproduced by people who are knowledgeable because of their ability to monitor the conditions under which they act. Different forms of knowledge are reproduced under different conditions. We cannot treat the social system as a machine with specific organisational properties which function in cross-culturally consistent ways. Instead the ecological or material conditions which people experience are given a specific cultural meaning by people's actions: such conditions constitute *resources* which both guide and result from those actions. Social systems are therefore reproduced by internalising material conditions in a culturally and historically specific manner.

Secondly, all social actions are culturally meaningful and find their expression in a symbolic medium. Ritual cannot be equated with symbolism without losing its analytical value (Goody 1961). This would mean equating ritual with all communicative action, rather than restricting it to the particular kinds of strategy discussed above. Consequently archaeologists cannot recognise ritual activity simply as having resulted in those deposits or monuments which they believe to be 'symbolic'. Routine activities are likely to preserve symbolic values of 'cleanliness' or 'order', or to be executed with a practical reference to gods or ancestors. This does not make them ritual actions.

As we have seen, in archaeology time and space are normally employed to describe sequences of sites and material, and their overall distribution. Time and space also become the matrix within which social practices take place. This forces us to consider the frequency with which certain actions are repeated or certain *locales* are occupied. It also allows us to recognise that locales have different roles, separated in time, in the reproduction of social conditions. No site is permanent, but sites and monuments are locales within a landscape at which people have congregated and through which they have passed. They were foci of human interaction, occupied for a matter of hours in daily or seasonal cycles. Only prisoners and the infirm occupy the same place twenty-four hours a day and for weeks or months at a time.

Landscape archaeology, as it is practised, involves the study of systematic relationships between sites. Sites are assigned one or more functions in the working of a regional system, primarily functions concerned with the extraction and redistribution of material forces, or as 'ritual sites'. A time–space perspective, on the other hand, is concerned with the routine movement of people through landscapes, constituted by the locales in which they came into contact. Around and within these sites social practices routinely maintained the obligations and affinities which marked out people's position and status, and ritually controlled moments of social transition. Not only did the landscape provide the necessities of life: it was culturally defined, and people's practical experience of that world allowed them to monitor their own place within it. The monuments that archaeologists study within the landscape 'participated' actively in the structuring of social conditions.

Landscape is thus the entire surface over which people moved and within which they congregated. That surface was given meaning as people acted upon the world within the context of the various demands and obligations which acted upon them. Such actions took place within a certain *tempo* and at certain *locales*. Thus landscape, its form constructed from natural and artificial features, became a culturally meaningful resource through its routine occupancy. Scattered forests, ploughed fields, earthworks and hedges all contributed towards structuring the movement and communication of people.

Monuments therefore take on an ambiguity through time. They may be the locales of ritual observance, where models of social order may be made explicit, or, silent and almost unnoticed, encountered in the routines of daily life, but each time a new mark was made on the landscape, those who came after might accommodate that scar into their own understanding of the world.

In this book we shall make an attempt to convince the reader of the usefulness of this approach through a detailed study of such processes at work over three millennia in one of the most intensively studied landscapes in prehistoric Europe.

1.2 The study area[2]

Cranborne Chase is better known for its place in the development of archaeology than it is for its own prehistory. It owes its position in the archaeological literature to the happy accident that a large part of the region was once the property of General Pitt Rivers, for it was here that he established many of the ground rules of modern excavation and publication (see Barker 1977, 13–14). The existence of so much well-documented material from his excavation at South Lodge Camp was an obvious incentive to renew work on that site, but we must make it clear that the widening scope of the project did not grow out of any wish to review the General's achievement. His collection did provide an invaluable basis for some of our research, but its main importance lay in its sheer extent and variety. An equally strong inducement to extend our interests in Cranborne Chase was the extraordinary body of material already collected by Martin Green during a programme of solo fieldwork. It was when we decided to join forces on the publication of that material that the wider project really took shape.

There were, however, two aspects of Pitt Rivers' legacy that played a significant part in the planning of our research. There is the existence of a large body of well-recorded material from his excavations. Although this was familiar from published sources, the artefacts and those records that still survived had not been available since his private museum closed in the 1960s.

It was only when his archaeological collection was transferred to the Salisbury and South Wiltshire Museum that it could be studied again. Our work at South Lodge Camp soon showed that the General's published reports could not be interpreted to any effect without access to this material (cf. Barrett, Bradley, Bowden and Mead 1983).

The General's legacy was important in another way, for large parts of his collection relate to periods and types of site which have not received enough attention from later generations of archaeologists. This was the reason for resuming work at South Lodge Camp. At the same time, much of the interest of Pitt Rivers' excavations arises from the fact that he was exploring an area which had largely escaped agricultural damage. The Chase had been medieval hunting forest, and it preserved a variety of prehistoric monuments of types which rarely survive above ground. If we were to obtain a balanced view of the prehistory of this region, it would be necessary to make some use of what was available already.

Pitt Rivers' inheritance was a stroke of good fortune because it gave him the resources with which to indulge his penchant for archaeology. He was still more fortunate in the location of his new property on the borders of Hampshire, Dorset and Wiltshire (Fig. 1.1). His estate occupied one edge of the great expanse of chalkland that contains so many of the most famous prehistoric sites in Wessex. Such dramatic monuments as Stonehenge and Durrington Walls are only 22 km to the north of our study area (Atkinson 1956; Wainwright and Longworth 1971). Thirty-five km to the south, rivers rising in Cranborne Chase discharge into the English Channel in another area with a rich archaeological record. The Pitt Rivers estate bridged the uplands and lowlands of Wessex and was flanked by two of the rivers that communicated between these different areas. The eastern limit of the Chase was marked by the Hampshire Avon, which ran past Durrington Walls. To the west its boundary was marked by the River Stour, which gave access to the equally important Neolithic site of Hambledon Hill

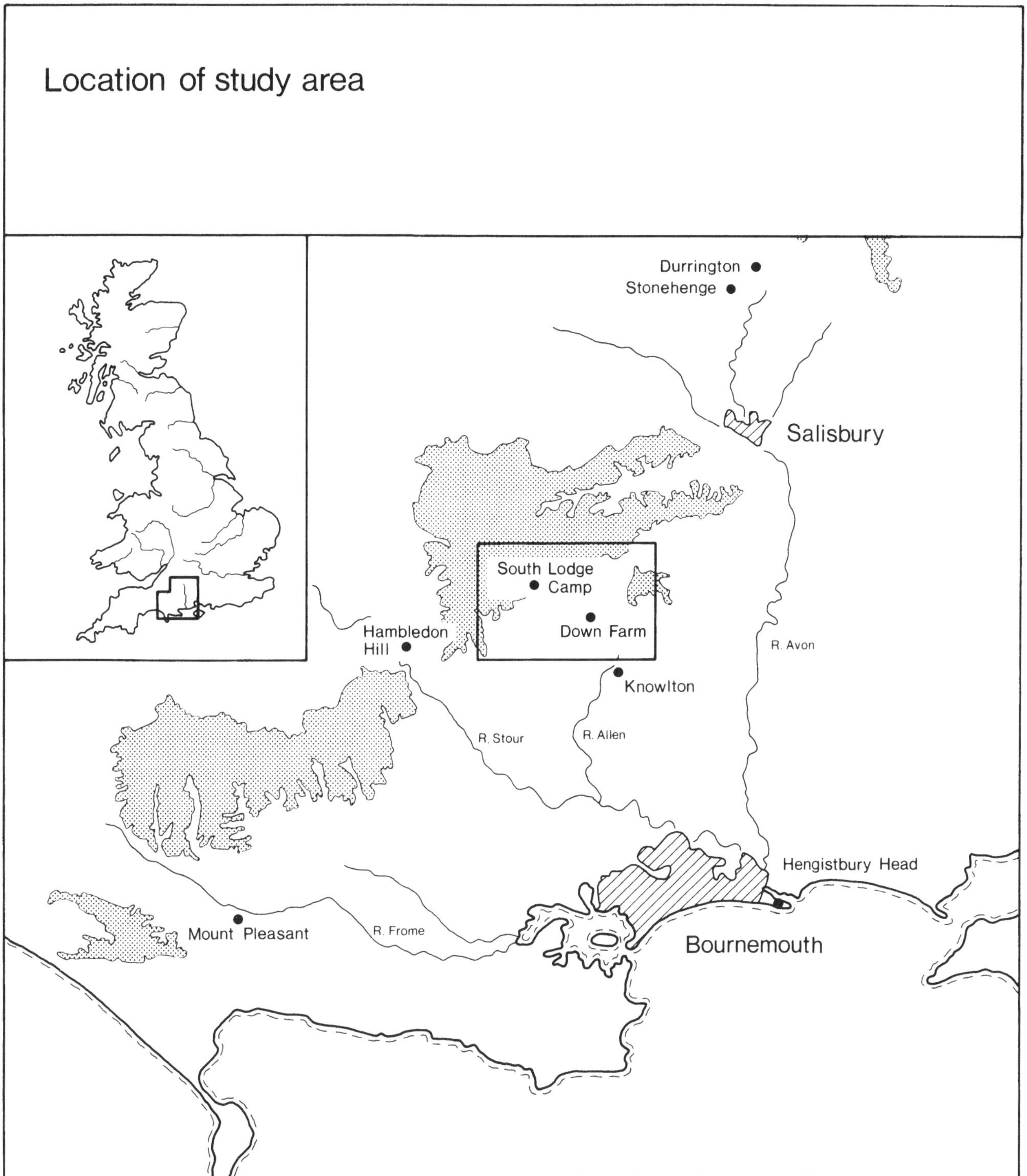

Fig. 1.1 The location of the study area in relation to major sites mentioned in the text

(Mercer 1980). Tributaries of both these rivers rise in the study area.

At a more detailed level, the essential features of this area are summarised in the epigraph to this chapter. The topography of the Chase itself has four main elements (Fig. 1.2), three of which are referred to in Virginia Woolf's brief description. As she noted, the most striking feature is the surviving remnant of the hunting forest which gave the region its name. A large area of Cranborne Chase is still wooded, with Pitt Rivers' estate at Rushmore towards its centre. It was here that the General undertook so much of his fieldwork. The topography is relatively even and most of the wooded area is capped by deposits of clay with flints, overlying chalk (Fig. 1.3). To the north, these superficial deposits are absent, and the ground rises to a maximum of 275 m. Here an open chalk ridge overlooks the valley of the River Ebble, one of the tributaries of the Avon that separate the Chase from the rim of Salisbury Plain. At the north-western edge of the study area, the same expanse of downland gives way to the Vale of Wardour, which has a more mixed geology, dominated by deposits of greensand. Apart from the higher ground, all three of these regions are heavily cultivated today. To the south of the clay with flints, at an elevation of between 50 and 150 m, there is a further expanse of chalk downland, broken by a series of valleys running towards the south-east. Again this area is largely free of superficial deposits and is under the plough. The springline is at 75 m and feeds a number of streams and rivers, the most important of which, the River Allen, is a tributary of the Stour. Their valleys contain quite extensive deposits of gravel. Some of these areas are in permanent pasture today, although others have recently been ploughed for the first time. The streams and rivers rising in this part of the study area run southwards into the Hampshire Basin, where the chalk gives way to a more varied series of clays and sandy soils.

The area selected for detailed study covers about 80 square km, centred on Pitt Rivers' Rushmore Estate, but extending south-eastwards along the valley of the River Allen towards the famous henge monuments at Knowlton (Royal Commission on Historical Monuments 1975, 113–15). In the opposite direction it reaches to the edge of the Vale of Wardour, where a recent field survey has already been published (Gingell and Harding 1983). Apart from the topographical features already mentioned, we should note the position of the Dorset Cursus, which follows the springline for almost 10 km and crosses the full extent of the study area (Fig. 1.2).

In other respects, the limits of the study area have been chosen on pragmatic grounds. They enclose all the major sites excavated by Pitt Rivers and the principal concentrations of field monuments in the area. This is also the part of the region which has seen extensive field-walking. The details of this work will be considered in due course, but the extent of the areas which it has been possible to examine on the ground are mapped in Figure 1.3. They cover practically all the cultivated land to which we could gain access. The same area has also been examined from the air.

1.3 The development of fieldwork in the study area[2]

We must now turn to the work of our predecessors, which did so much to influence our choice of study area. We need to consider the development of archaeological research in Cranborne Chase, and the excavated material that was available for analysis when this project started. Earlier fieldwork was of three main kinds: research excavation of monuments surviving above ground; rescue excavation of sites levelled by the plough; and analytical field survey undertaken on standing earthworks. Our one innovation is the sample excavation of a lithic scatter whose contents were confined to the ploughsoil.

The research excavations are probably the best known. These were mainly concerned with earthwork monuments surviving above ground in the areas of medieval forest. Contrary to general opinion, this development did not start with Pitt Rivers, for a number of barrows in the well-preserved cemetery on Oakley Down were investigated by Sir Richard Colt Hoare (1812, 236–44). The General did not conceal his low opinion of this work, but some details can still be rescued from the published account. His own work was entirely confined to the period between 1880, when he inherited the Rushmore Estate, and his death in 1900, by which time the results of all but one of his excavations were in print (*Excavations* I–IV). It is hard to comprehend the scale of this work, but the basic statistics are daunting. In those twenty years Pitt Rivers investigated thirty barrows, an urnfield, three Bronze Age enclosures, two Iron Age settlements and a hill fort, as well as other, minor features of the pre-Roman landscape. Not all of these sites have the same importance for modern archaeology, and in this book we shall pay special attention to only a dozen (Table 1.1). In the Neolithic period our main concern will be with the Wor Barrow complex and with the nearby pits on Handley Hill. In the following period, we shall be concerned with a small number of the General's barrow excavations, together with a group of Beaker pits at Martin Down. Our main interest, however, is in the large-scale excavations that he carried out on the Middle Bronze Age enclosures at South Lodge Camp, Martin

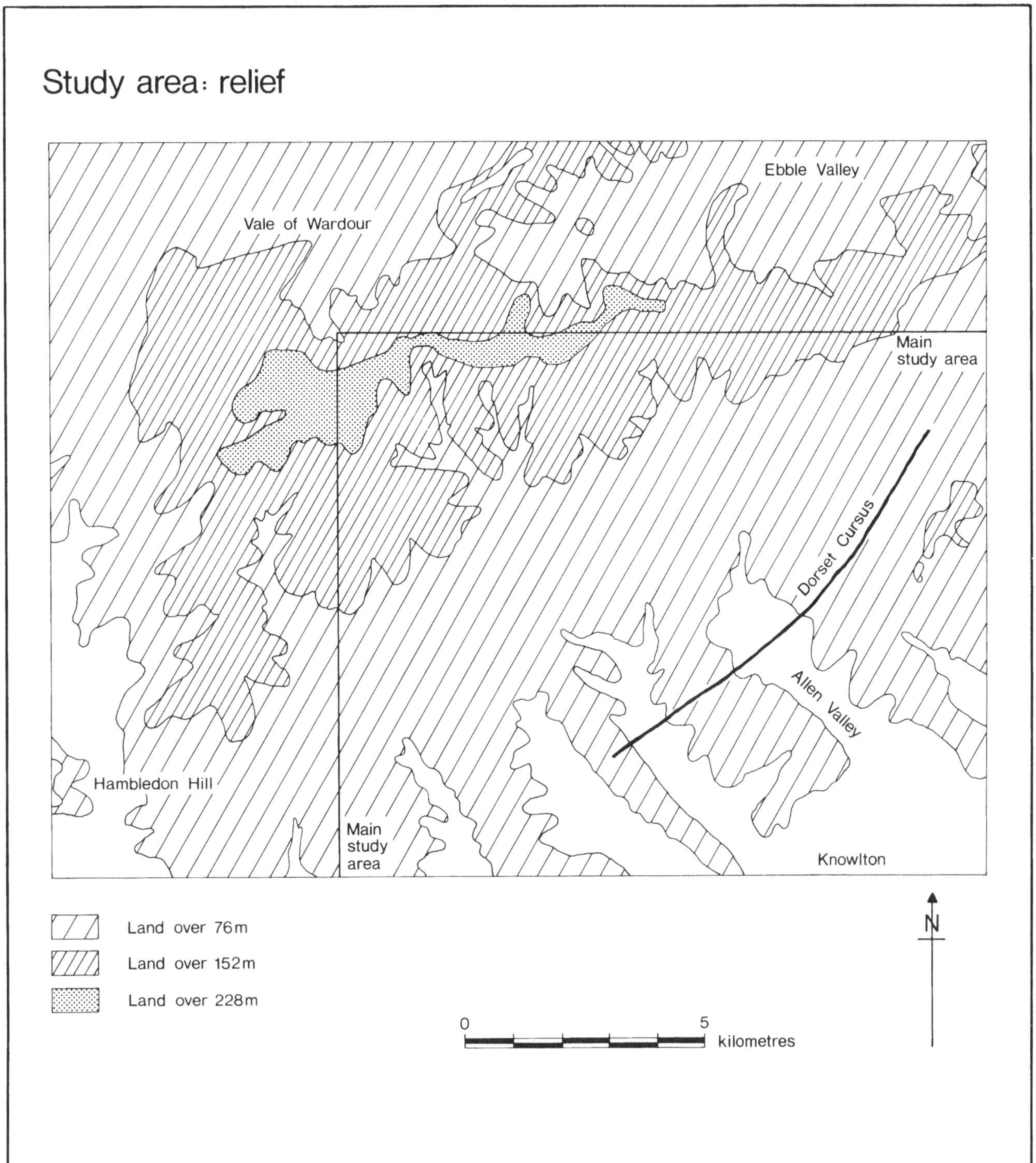

Fig. 1.2 The topography of the study area, in relation to the area studied in greatest detail, and the location of the Dorset Cursus

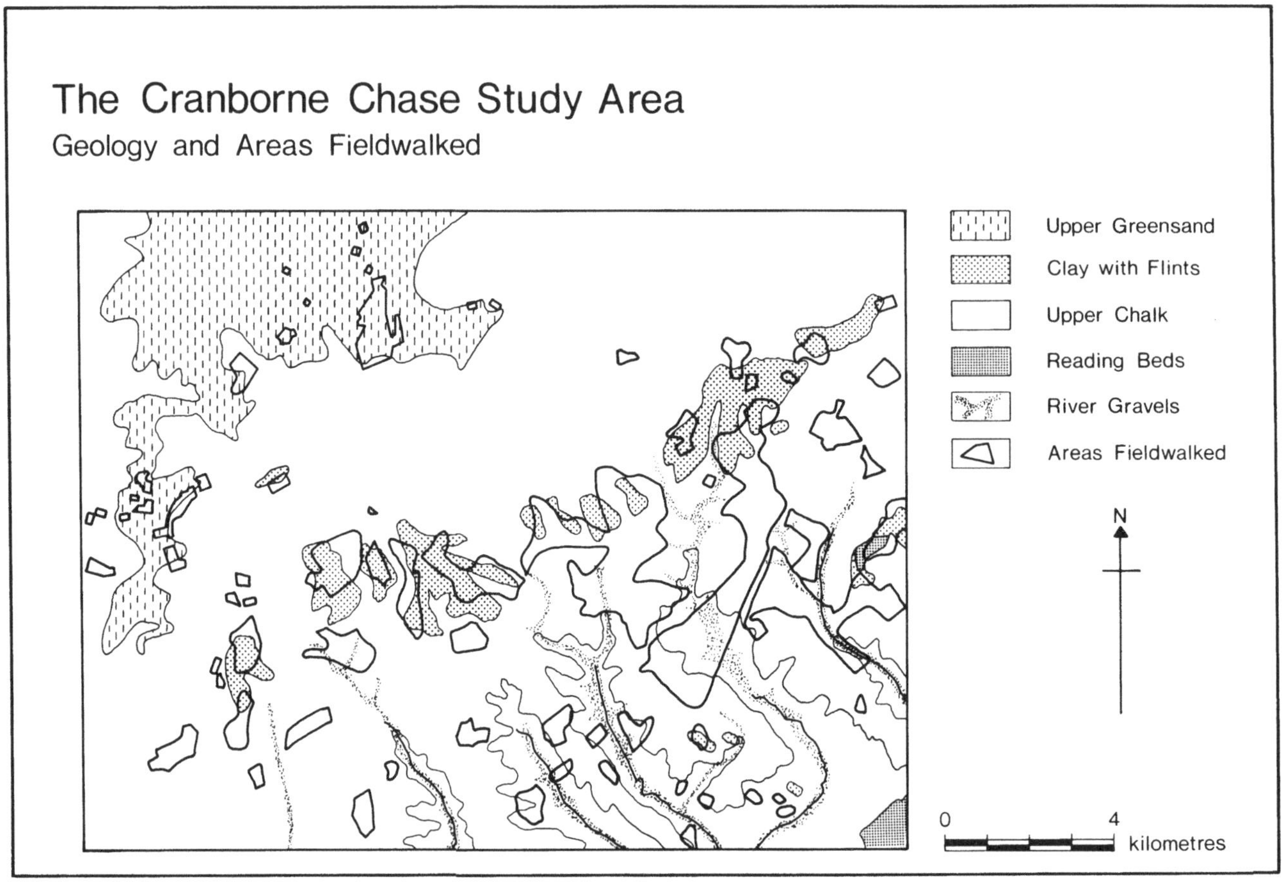

Fig. 1.3 The geology of the study area in relation to the areas examined by fieldwalking

Down and Angle Ditch, and on two cremation cemeteries very near to these earthworks. We shall make less use of the Iron Age material excavated by the General, since its interpretation has already been considered in an influential paper by Hawkes and Piggott (1947). Only certain aspects of his work on the settlements of Rotherley and Woodcutts will be reconsidered in this monograph.

After so much activity during the nineteenth century, it is hardly surprising that the pace of work has slackened. Apart from any other consideration, there are significantly fewer standing earthworks left to investigate. One research excavation carried out more recently was the investigation of Thickthorn Down long barrow (Drew and Piggott 1936). We shall offer a new interpretation of that monument. Outside the study area itself, there have been important excavations on two Iron Age sites – Hod Hill, 12 km to the south-west (Richmond 1968) and Hengistbury Head, 35 km to the south (Cunliffe 1987) – but in the Chase itself sites with standing earthworks were rarely examined until we returned to South Lodge Camp in 1977.

Rescue excavation is a feature of recent years, and Cranborne Chase has seen a number of important projects of this type. The main work on a Neolithic site was at Hambledon Hill (Mercer 1980). This is 12 km south-west of the study area but the results of that excavation have a direct bearing on our discussion of the Dorset Cursus. Bronze Age sites are sparsely represented, mainly by piecemeal excavation on outliers of the Oakley Down cemetery (summarised by Royal Commission on Historical Monuments 1975, 102–4, updated by Grinsell 1982), although we can learn more about this type of site from larger-scale excavations at Crichel and Launceston Downs, 3 km south of the study area (Piggott and Piggott 1944; Green, Lynch and White 1982). The Iron Age, however, has been much better served. Berwick Down, close to Pitt Rivers' site at Rotherley, was one of the first area excavations of an Iron Age settlement to appear in print (Wainwright 1968), whilst 2 km to the south of the study area was the still more ambitious excavation of an enclosed settlement at Gussage All Saints (Wainwright 1979a). Another important rescue excavation took place on an Iron Age barrow at Gussage Cow

Down (White 1970). Although our programme of excavation has been directly integrated with our other research, the great majority of the sites investigated had already been levelled by the plough. The Neolithic sites comprised the Dorset Cursus, a ring ditch, a henge monument and two settlements; we also examined a group of Beaker pits, an Early Bronze Age flat cemetery and a Middle Bronze Age enclosed settlement and its nearby burials (cf. Table 1.2).

Generally speaking, earthwork survey is another twentieth-century development in Cranborne Chase. With the exception of Colt Hoare's plans of Oakley Down and Gussage Cow Down (1812, facing p. 236 and 1819, facing p. 31), little work took place until after Pitt Rivers' death. Despite his experience of surveying, the General had a poor eye for earthworks and failed to recognise some of those close to his excavated sites. That task was left to the next generation, whose key figures were Herbert Toms and Heywood Sumner. Toms is a neglected pioneer in the development of field archaeology and had been one of the General's assistants, before taking a post at Brighton Museum (Holleyman 1987). His own work in Cranborne Chase took place in the 1920s and resulted in the identification of early field systems around South Lodge Camp and Angle Ditch (Toms 1925). He surveyed both groups of fields, and through careful observation established their chronological relationship to the two enclosures. He also recorded a profile of the Dorset Cursus before it was ploughed out (Fig. 2.12). His contemporary, Heywood Sumner, published an entire book on the earthworks of Cranborne Chase, and this provides valuable plans of further monuments which no longer survive (Sumner 1913). A new generation of field survey began in 1955 with the publication of Atkinson's account of the Dorset Cursus, and in more recent years the study area has been considered in greater detail in an inventory published by the Royal Commission on Historical Monuments (1975) and concerned with field monuments in Dorset. This has been of particular value in this research. Our own contribution to this genre has been limited, consisting of additional work on the Dorset Cursus and nearby monuments, and earthwork survey, combined with excavation, in the field system around South Lodge Camp.

Most of this work presents little problem. The finds from the various excavations are well curated, and the sites are published in detail. The major complications concern the Pitt Rivers Collection. We must comment on this material before we can put it to use. Two issues are particularly important here: its recovery and documentation by the General himself, and its subsequent history. Both can be considered rather briefly, as a fuller discussion is to be found in the companion volume.

We must appreciate that the General's excavation and recording methods became steadily more detailed as he grew accustomed to working on a large scale. His later publications contain a growing amount of information (Barrett, Bradley, Bowden and Mead 1983); the same applies to the annotation on the labels accompanying his finds (Burleigh, Bradley, Barrett and Kinnes 1982). At the same time, Pitt Rivers had his biases, and it is important to appreciate what they were. His excavation methods were guided by two ideas which can be traced to his anthropological reading (Bradley 1983a). First, he was convinced that prehistoric buildings would have taken a similar form to those familiar to him from the ethnographic record. Thus he did not adopt suitable techniques for recognising postholes, although he was aware of their existence. His settlement excavations were carried out by narrow trenching, which affected his ability to identify subsoil features. This was more difficult in some excavations than others. Thus he could find smaller features on chalkland sites than he did on clay with flints. This distinction is illustrated in Figure 1.4, which also shows the dimensions of the subsoil features on the more recently excavated site at Berwick Down, Tollard Royal, which has much in common with Rotherley. Smaller features were present at Berwick Down than were found at Rotherley. This suggests one reason why four-post structures were identified in both excavations, whilst house plans were entirely absent on the latter site.

The second point concerns the General's conception of *sequence*. Later scholars have found it difficult to understand why he never worked out the phasing of his settlement sites, leaving his successors to carry out the work (cf. Hawkes and Piggott 1947). They can also be puzzled by the way in which he combined his detailed observations of site stratigraphy into what he called 'average sections'. In fact one of the General's original reasons for undertaking excavation was to further his studies of the evolution of material culture, an interest which had guided the formation of his ethnographic collection and which continued to dominate his priorities in the field. His limited appreciation of sequence, as we think of it today, was rooted in his individual reading of evolutionary theory (see Barrett, Bradley, Bowden and Mead 1983; Bradley 1983a).

At a more empirical level, there are problems to be overcome in using the museum material. Again this is a collection with certain biases, only some of them of the General's making. More attractive or 'diagnostic' artefacts may be best represented because of Pitt Rivers' practice of rewarding his workmen for outstanding finds (C. M. Guido pers. comm.). On the other hand, our work

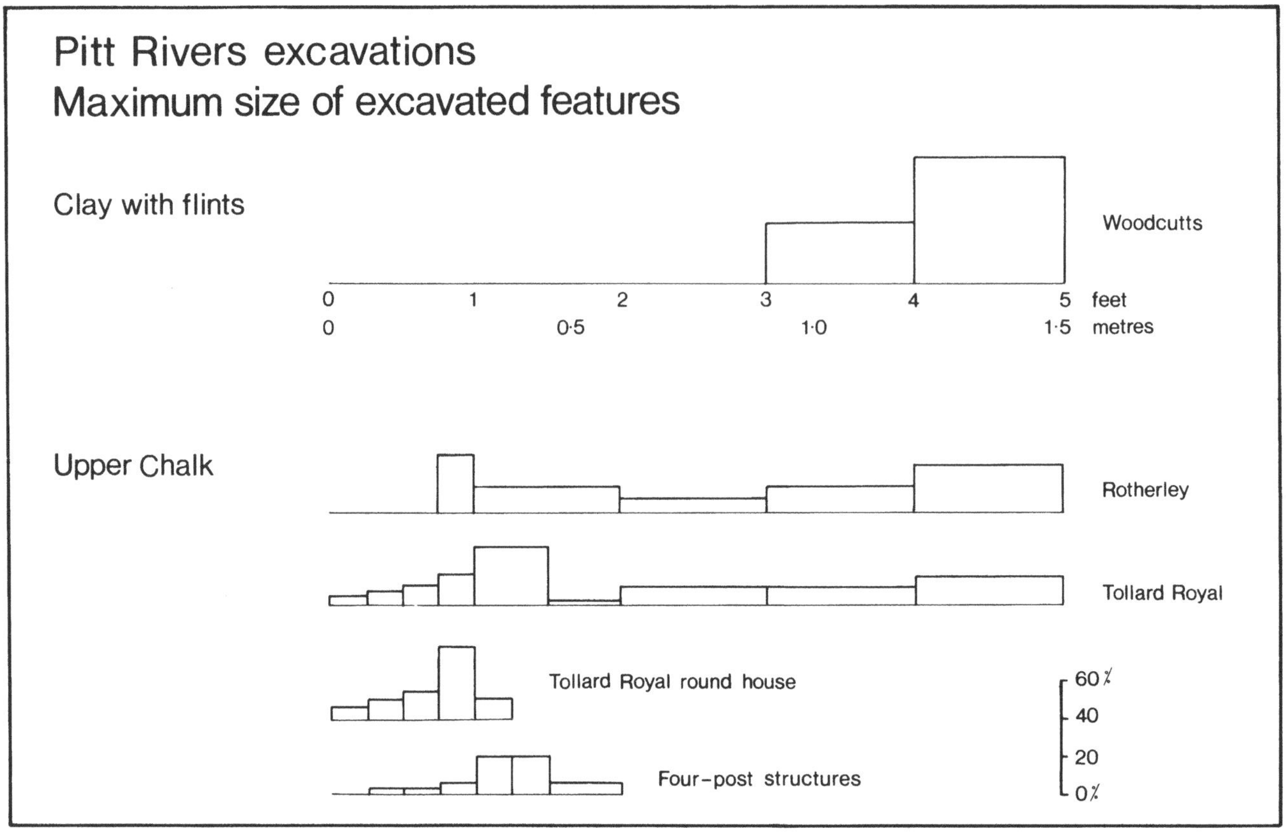

Fig. 1.4 The maximum dimensions of the excavated features on Pitt Rivers' sites at Woodcutts and Rotherley, compared with those on the contemporary site at Tollard Royal. The detail shows the maximum dimensions of the postholes belonging to two types of structure at Tollard Royal. This analysis suggests that only the largest subsoil features were recognised in Pitt Rivers' excavations on the clay with flints and that he may have identified only some of the postholes at sites on the Upper Chalk

at South Lodge Camp has shown that they found it difficult to recognise worked flints, especially those of later prehistoric date. Similarly, he did not retain all the human bones from his sites, limiting himself to the skulls and long bones that could further his interest in physical anthropology and racial history (Bradley 1983a). For the same reason, damaged or incomplete skeletons were discarded or left in the ground. He took a broader view of the value of animal bones and recorded these in great detail, but unfortunately the faunal remains from the sites considered in this volume seem to have been discarded after his death.

Lastly, we must say something about the documentation which accompanies this collection. Again rather little survives. A certain number of field drawings have been catalogued by Thompson (1976), and two site notebooks have been traced in the Dorset County Museum (Bradley 1973), but for the most part this material adds little to the published accounts of the General's fieldwork, which drew on these sources directly. The main exceptions concern the excavations at Wor Barrow and South Lodge Camp. The General's unpublished plans of the latter site have played an important part in our work, since they indicate the precise positions of many of the artefacts found in the enclosure; sometimes these can be identified by the labels attached to individual finds. Where field plans no longer survive, the detailed information on these labels can still provide useful information; for example, this is how we were able to reconstruct the pottery sequence at Wor Barrow and the ditch sequence at South Lodge Camp. In the case of the Bronze Age Handley Barrow 24, the original finds bags survive, providing detailed information about the contexts of pottery, charcoal and cremated bone (Burleigh, Bradley, Barrett and Kinnes 1982). In other cases, however, Pitt Rivers' labels are less informative, and we have experienced considerable difficulty in reconstituting individual pit groups. The remaining source is most unusual. This consists of three-dimensional models of the sites before and after excavation. These were made by the estate carpenter using a complicated procedure described by the General (*Excavations* III, 297–8). These models repro-

Table 1.1. *The main sites excavated in the study area before the project began showing the principal categories of material found*

Main period:	Pottery	Flint-work	Metal-work	Grave goods	Human bone	Animal bone	Cereals	Samples used for ¹⁴C dating
Neolithic:								
Wor Barrow long barrow (1893)	X	x	–	X	X	x	–	X
Handley Hill pits (1893)	X	x	–	–	x	x	–	–
Handley 26 round barrow (1894)	X	–	–	X	x	–	–	–
Handley 27 round barrow (1894)	X	–	–	–	x	–	–	–
Thickthorn Down long barrow (1933)	X	X	–	–	–	X	–	X
Early Bronze Age:								
Scrubbity Coppice barrow cemetery (1882–3)	X	X	–	X	x	x	–	–
Middle Bronze Age:								
Barrow Pleck barrow cemetery (1880 & 84)	X	x	X	–	–	–	–	–
South Lodge Camp (1893)	X	X	X	–	–	x	–	–
Handley 24 barrow and urnfield (1893)	X	x	X	X	X	x	–	X
Angle Ditch enclosure (1893–4)	X	x	X	–	–	x	–	–
Martin Down enclosure (1895–6)	X	X	X	–	–	x	–	–
Iron Age:								
Winklebury hillfort (1881–2)	X	–	–	–	–	x	–	–
Woodcutts settlement (1884)	X	–	X	–	–	x	–	–
Rotherley settlement (1885–6)	X	–	X	–	–	x	x	–
Berwick Down settlement (1965)	X	–	X	–	–	X	X	–
Gussage Cow Down barrow (1969)	X	–	–	–	X	–	–	–

X: material available for study.
x: material published but no longer surviving.

duce the original contour surveys so faithfully that in one case they even depict earthworks that were not recognised as such until later. Sometimes they provide details which are not shown in the published plans, and in one case, Handley Barrow 26, where no plan was ever published, a scale model is our only evidence of the appearance of an important site.

None of these problems is insuperable, and they have certainly not prevented us from studying a number of the monuments excavated by the General, in particular Wor Barrow and South Lodge Camp. It would be a mistake, however, to treat the General's publications as the only source of information. Used critically, the surviving material from his excavations is of such importance that its existence was an incentive to mount the project described in this book.

This section has covered a considerable amount of ground, and has referred to a large number of separate sites and monuments. These have produced very different kinds of material for study. Before turning to the past development of Cranborne Chase, it may be helpful to provide a summary of those sources. Table 1.1 provides an overview of the material which was available for analysis when this project started. Table 1.2 then brings the account up to date by summarising the fieldwork carried out by the writers between 1977 and 1984. Information collected during that work forms the basis for the closing section of this chapter.

1.4 The development of the landscape in the study area[2–8]

As we mentioned earlier, the Cranborne Chase Project is being published in two parts. This volume is concerned mainly with social developments in the study area, and particularly with the role of monuments. The companion volume traces the subsistence economy, the development of the landscape and the changing material culture of its inhabitants. Environmental factors do not play a large role in our analysis in this volume, but it is impossible to consider more theoretical issues as if the landscape had remained unaltered throughout the prehistoric period. Before we can turn to the main focus of this study, we must review the principal changes in that landscape. This section draws together the results of some of the specialist studies to be found in the companion volume, where the evidence is documented in detail by those responsible for the work (Barrett and Bradley in prep.).

Our description of Cranborne Chase highlights two important contrasts: the distinction between the area of the forest and the more open parts of the downland; and the equally important division between the chalk and the clay with flints. In both cases there is a danger

Table 1.2. *The excavations undertaken during recent fieldwork and reported in this volume, showing the main categories of material analysed*

Main period	Pottery	Flint-work	Metal-work	Grave goods	Human bone	Animal bone	Cereals	Charcoals	Land snails	^{14}C samples
Neolithic										
Firtree Field (1977–8) pits	X	X	–	–	–	X	X	–	–	X
Firtree Field (1980) ring ditch	X	X	–	–	–	X	–	–	X	–
Firtree Field (1982) Dorset Cursus	X	X	–	–	–	–	–	–	X	–
Wyke Down (1983–4) henge monument	X	X	–	–	X	X	–	X	X	X
Chalkpit Field (1984) Dorset Cursus, settlement and pits	X	X	–	–	X	X	–	–	X	X
Early Bronze Age										
Barrow Pleck (1980–81) settlement	X	X	–	–	–	–	–	–	–	–
Firtree Field (1981–82) pits and flat cemetery	X	X	X	X	X	X	–	X	–	X
Middle Bronze Age										
Firtree Field (1977–79) enclosure	X	X	X	–	–	X	X	X	X	X
South Lodge Camp (1977–81) enclosure and fields	X	X	–	–	–	X	–	X	X	X
Firtree Field (1980) cemetery	X	X	X	X	X	X	–	X	X	X
Barrow Pleck (1980–81) cemetery	X	X	X	X	X	–	–	X	X	X

of allowing our perception of the modern landscape to colour our interpretation of the past.

This danger is lessened when we consider the area of forest, for one of the most striking features of Pitt Rivers' work is the sheer extent of prehistoric and Roman settlement found there. This is so considerable that it provides a *terminus post quem* for the development of the medieval Chase. At the same time, Peter Fisher's study of the natural environment of the region reminds us that we need to consider not only the solid geology but also the soils that it supports, for it is the soils that may have changed under the pressures of human occupation. As he points out, there is considerable evidence that the Wessex downland was once covered by loess. This may have attained a depth of between one and four metres before erosion started in the late glacial and early postglacial periods. By now such deposits may be as little as 0.1 m thick. Their reduction must be due partly to erosion caused by human activity. This process is well documented through studies of alluvial and colluvial deposits in southern England. Although relatively few of these have remained *in situ*, on some sites it is possible to correlate episodes of soil loss with signs of prehistoric farming in the vicinity (Bell 1983). It has been noted that loess makes a major contribution to some of these deposits. Two substantial deposits of colluvium have been observed in Cranborne Chase. In Chalkpit Field at Down Farm a metre of hillwash sealed a layer containing Early Iron Age pottery, whilst an even greater depth of colluvium was observed by Martin Green during the construction of the Blandford Forum bypass (Green 1985). This covered a massive deposit of burnt flints, very similar to those found in Middle Bronze Age contexts in this area.

Loess was of great importance to early farmers, as it was light, fertile and easily tilled (Catt 1978). Unfortunately, it was also vulnerable to erosion. The critical point of our study is that it seems to have mantled *the whole of the downland*, so that initially there would have been no real difference between conditions on the chalk and those on the clay with flints. Of course other factors may have been very important in the latter area – the underlying clay could have made it easier to conserve water, and there would have been abundant good-quality

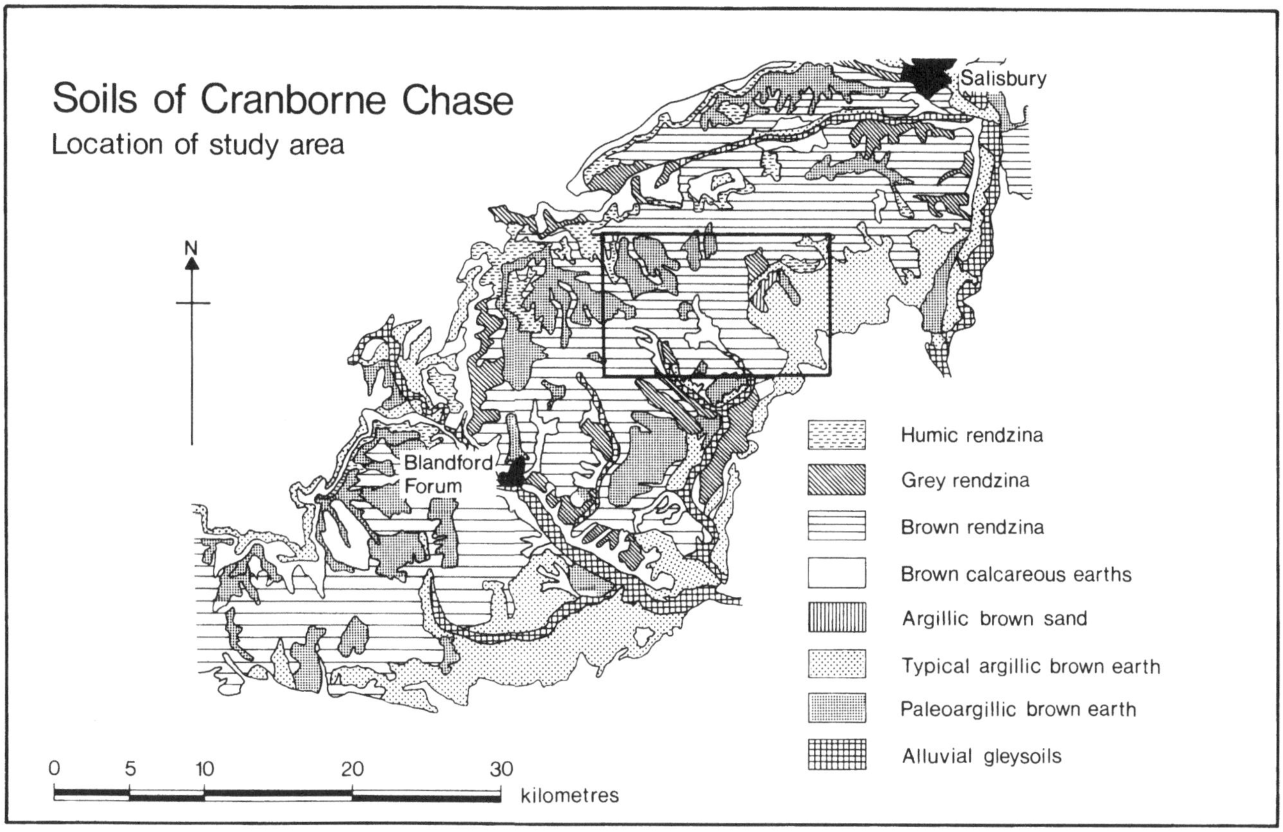

Fig. 1.5 The soils of Cranborne Chase, showing the location of the study area (published by permission of the Soil Survey of Great Britain)

stone – but reconstructions based on the medieval and modern patterns of settlement cannot be sustained.

In Fisher's opinion major changes would have come about with the final erosion of the loess as a result of human land use. This would have caused significant changes in the local soils, until they assumed their present distribution, with rendzinas covering the chalk and paleoargillic brown earths on the clay with flints (Fig. 1.5). Only at that stage would calcareous material be likely to come to the surface in the course of ordinary land use. For present purposes the most significant point is that this would affect the base status of different parts of the study area. The argillic soils, for instance, are acid and so would not be able to support a barley crop, although wheat would flourish. It also seems that once the surface cover was lost from the clay with flints, the ground may have become rather heavy for primitive cultivation. Roy Entwistle suggests that such changes of base status might explain why Mesolithic finds from sites on the clay with flints are generally unpatinated, whilst Later Neolithic implements found on the same sites do show this phenomenon.

At its simplest this scheme is consistent with the changing distribution of human activity in the study area. During the Mesolithic period this concentrated mainly on the clay with flints, where good-quality raw material could be found, but during the Neolithic it is also evidenced on the Upper Chalk. The second millennium presents something of a problem, but by the Middle Bronze Age there seems to have been much less use of the clay with flints. That area was not reused to any extent until the Late Iron Age and Roman periods. A very similar sequence can be recognised elsewhere in Wessex (Bonney 1968; Gardiner 1984). Whilst it would be tempting to suggest that changes in settlement distribution were due to the increased base status of the rendzinas, additional evidence is needed to confirm this. Again, the renewed occupation of the clay with flints suggests that there were growing pressures on other parts of the landscape, but this is another hypothesis that has to be tested. The remainder of this section attempts to do exactly that, using the evidence of land snails, seeds, charcoals and animal bones from a number of different sites (Fig. 1.6). Taken together, this evidence should allow us to identify the main periods of activity in the landscape and the changing character of its two major components. What

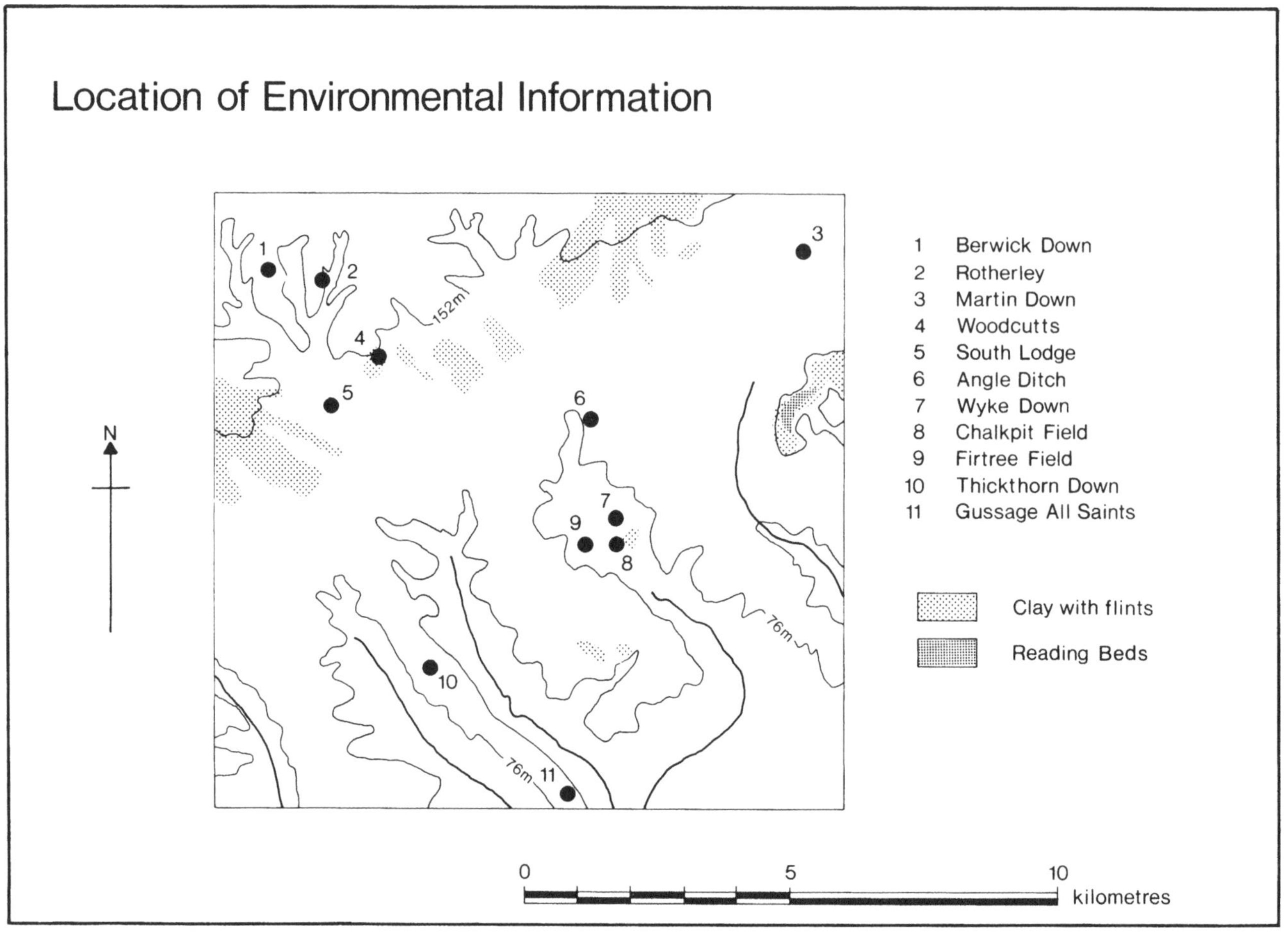

Fig. 1.6 The location of sites in and close to the study area producing environmental evidence discussed in the text

follows is a synthesis of information published in detail in the companion volume.

Molluscan analysis can provide information at two different scales. As an indication of the local environment its main value is in site-based studies (Evans 1972), but by using diversity indices we can also say something about the nature of the wider ecosystem (Evans 1984). A large number of molluscan samples have been examined as part of this project, and the detailed results appear in the companion volume. Two areas were considered: a group of sites on the Upper Chalk at Down Farm, Woodcutts, and a more limited area around South Lodge Camp, which is on the edge of the main area of clay with flints.

The earliest samples analysed belong to the period of the construction of the Dorset Cursus around 2600 bc and suggest an environment more or less dominated by woodland. There were localised differences within this landscape, but open conditions may have been rather restricted, and the evidence for the rapid return of shaded conditions in the secondary filling of the earthwork suggests that woodland refugia were never far away. There was some opening of the landscape during the Later Neolithic, and in two cases this seems to be associated with excavated settlement sites. The same is true of an excavated henge monument belonging to the same period. There was a further episode of clearance beside the Cursus during the Beaker period, but there is still some evidence of residual woodland at this time.

The next group of samples from the Upper Chalk is associated with a Middle Bronze Age field system and an enclosed settlement which was established within its area. By this time open conditions were more firmly established, although some of the fields around the enclosure may have gone out of use and could have been colonised by scrub. Finally, many of the excavated monuments were levelled by Iron Age ploughing and an open landscape is evidenced on virtually all the sites investigated.

The value of these results is limited by the very local

habitats which they reflect. For example, the increasing amounts of shade represented in practically every ditch sequence may be affected by the distinctive nature of that type of context. Diversity indices have been introduced into molluscan analysis as a way of overcoming these local effects (Evans 1984; Gordon and Ellis 1985). They measure the complexity of the molluscan population from which the individual samples were drawn. A low diversity index should reflect a fairly homogeneous environment, whilst a higher figure indicates a more complex and varied ecosystem. Diversity indices from the sites on the chalk show a reasonably consistent trend, suggesting that these are indeed monitoring more general developments in the landscape.

The overall trend seems to be from a fairly simple ecosystem dominated by woodland towards a more varied environment in the Later Neolithic, associated with the clearance phases mentioned earlier. From the Middle Bronze Age onwards this evidence suggests an increasing impact on the landscape until a more uniform ecosystem, dominated by open conditions, was established during the Iron Age. By this stage it is clear that large areas were under cultivation, including many of the monuments built during earlier phases. Thus the major changes suggested by the molluscan evidence from the Upper Chalk were in the Later Neolithic, possibly in the Later Bronze Age and certainly in the Iron Age.

We can compare this evidence with the less complex sequence at the Middle Bronze Age site of South Lodge Camp on the edge of the clay with flints. Shaded conditions are indicated throughout this sequence, with a high proportion of woodland snails and very few that require an open habitat. There was a sharp increase in molluscan diversity in the filling of a barrow ditch, one of the first features on the site, but samples from a later field system suggest a rather slower rate of change. A useful check on this evidence was provided by a sample taken from the ground surface preserved by one of Pitt Rivers' spoil heaps. This showed a similar fauna to both groups of samples, but had a higher diversity index. This information is important since we know from contemporary photographs that the sample location had been on the edge of a clearing in the midst of an expanse of woodland. All the Bronze Age samples showed a similar range of land snails, but their diversity indices suggest that the local ecosystem was rather less varied during that period; presumably the area was more extensively wooded at that time. At the beginning of the Middle Bronze Age, then, the diversity indices from this part of the study area were lower than those for samples from the Upper Chalk.

Although wet sieving was undertaken at South Lodge Camp, no carbonised seeds were recovered, with the result that our botanical evidence is confined to the Upper Chalk. This has its drawbacks, as only two excavations have produced any material: a Later Neolithic settlement and a Middle Bronze Age enclosure, both on the same site (Firtree Field). Although each produced a limited number of cereals, Martin Jones, who undertook the analysis, has recognised a striking contrast among the other plant remains. The Neolithic samples contain hazelnut and crab apple, whilst the Bronze Age samples include elderberry, onion-couch tuber and a variety of weeds. These suggest that the two sites had been located in different settings from one another. The Neolithic material was derived from a woodland environment, whilst the Middle Bronze Age samples came from disturbed, open habitats. Equally open conditions are indicated by the carbonised plant remains from the Iron Age site of Gussage All Saints, just south of the study area (Evans and Jones in Wainwright 1979a, 172–5). As Martin Jones points out, a similar contrast is found elsewhere in southern England.

The evidence of prehistoric charcoals is still more limited, but it does help to compensate for the paucity of environmental evidence from the Earlier Bronze Age. Samples have been identified from four sites: three on the Upper Chalk (a Later Neolithic henge monument, an Early Bronze Age pond barrow and a Middle Bronze Age cemetery) and the Middle Bronze Age complex at South Lodge Camp on the edge of the clay with flints.

In general terms the charcoal identifications agree well with the results of molluscan analysis, although they must be biased by the fact that particular woods had been deliberately selected for use as fuel. The earliest of these sites does not seem to have occupied a particularly open landscape and there is little evidence of scrub species. By contrast the charcoal from the Pond Barrow, one of the few indicants of the Early Bronze Age environment, suggests to Mark Robinson a rather more open landscape, with some scrub species whose presence might indicate the proximity of abandoned agricultural land; a similar chronological development is suggested by molluscan analysis. The last site on the Upper Chalk is a Neolithic barrow, reused as a cemetery during the Middle Bronze Age. The charcoals from the earlier of the Bronze Age levels give the impression of a less open landscape, and are dominated by finds of oak. The burials, which may be later in date, contain charcoal with rather more scrub species, although these may have been collected especially for use in the pyre. Even so, land-snail assemblages belonging to the same period still contain a significant proportion of woodland species.

The charcoals from South Lodge Camp cover a similar

range to those from the neighbouring cemetery and are dominated by ash rather than oak. The rarity of scrub species is consistent with the results of molluscan analysis. The high proportion of ash is perhaps a little unexpected, but Mark Robinson suggests that this could be explained if the timber had been collected in secondary woodland. If so, one would expect oak to have taken over as the dominant species within two centuries of an earlier episode of land use. The hypothesis is consistent with the molluscan sequence mentioned earlier.

Lastly, we can contrast the results of all these analyses with the larger body of charcoal identifications from Gussage All Saints, where oak was joined by hazel and ash as the dominant species and where a wider range of scrub species was represented (Wainwright 1979a, 188). Again this suggests that there were much greater pressures on the landscape during the Iron Age.

Finally, we can turn to the evidence of animal bones, where similar contrasts occur. Here we have a larger body of information, but it comes from sources of varying degrees of reliability. The animal bones from our recent fieldwork have been analysed by Anthony Legge, whose detailed report appears in the companion volume. There are also modern bone reports on the Iron Age material from Berwick Down and Gussage All Saints (Bird in Wainwright 1968, 146–7 and Harcourt in Wainwright 1979a, 150–60). The bones from Thickthorn Down long barrow were published in 1936, but have been examined more recently by Julian Thomas (1986). We cannot re-examine the faunal remains excavated by General Pitt Rivers, for these no longer survive in their entirety. In this case we must work from his published identifications. We cannot tell whether all of these were correct, but at least we are comparing like with like. For this reason, we are obliged to rank the species represented at different sites by the number of individual bones, grouping these together only where there is evidence that they had belonged to a single individual. These collections also vary in size, with small numbers of identifications from all sites earlier than the Iron Age. Since we are concerned with only the broadest patterning, these problems are not insuperable. We need to use this material to investigate two major questions: the principal periods of change in the character of the study area; and the origins of the present-day contrast between the chalk and the clay with flints.

The species represented in these collections show very clear chronological patterning. The Neolithic fauna are completely dominated by species which are suited to a woodland habitat, particularly cattle and pig. These collections also contain a proportion of wild animals, especially red deer, roe deer and wild cattle. Sheep are poorly represented in all the collections dating from the third millennium bc. There may be hints of a change during the Early Bronze Age, when two sheep burials were deposited in the flat cemetery at Down Farm, but there is no clear evidence for a change to more open conditions before the Middle Bronze Age. The enclosed settlements of that period contain rather fewer cattle and pigs and a slightly higher proportion of sheep, but at Down Farm Legge's study of the mandibles suggests that sheep accounted for 58% of the animals on the site. Wild species are less often found, except at South Lodge Camp (*Excavations* IV, 39–41). Horse bones are also present in small numbers. Finally, there are indications of still more open conditions in the Iron Age when sheep bones outnumber cattle on two of the four sites for which information is available. Horses are better represented, but with the exception of the fauna from Woodcutts (*Excavations* I, 189–239), pig bones are infrequent and wild species are rare. Taken together, these observations reveal a contrast between the fauna from the Neolithic sites and those from the Bronze Age enclosures, and a still sharper distinction between the latter material and the evidence from two of the Iron Age sites, Rotherley (*Excavations* II, 67–110) and Gussage All Saints (Harcourt in Wainwright 1979a, 150–60). In the latter case the proportions of the different species do not vary greatly across a sequence lasting five hundred years.

There is also evidence of a growing contrast between the fauna from sites on or close to the clay with flints and those found on the chalk. This first becomes apparent in the Bronze Age enclosure at South Lodge Camp, where an unusually high proportion of the bones were of deer (*Excavations* IV, 39–41). This site is situated on the edge of the clay with flints. By contrast, the broadly contemporary site at Down Farm on the chalk contains a high proportion of sheep bones. In the Iron Age there is a still sharper contrast between the faunal remains from different parts of the study area. Sheep are the commonest species at Rotherley and Gussage All Saints, and dominate large tracts of chalkland (*Excavations* II, 67–110; Harcourt in Wainwright 1979a, 150–60), whilst the settlement at Woodcutts, on the clay with flints, contained fewer sheep bones and a higher proportion of pig and deer (*Excavations* I, 189–239); only the material from the pits at Woodcutts was used in making this estimate, as these seem to be limited to the Iron Age occupation of the site.

Some of the estimates used in this exercise are crude, but if they can be taken at face value, they suggest two rather striking patterns. First, the major periods of change in the landscape of the study area seem to have been the Middle Bronze Age and, more particularly, the

Iron Age. Exactly the same pattern was suggested by molluscan analysis and by the carbonised plants from Down Farm. At the same time, the first evidence for contrasts between the chalk and the clay with flints appears in the Middle Bronze Age, although faunal samples of earlier date were not available from the latter area. That contrast gains added definition in the Iron Age, with a greater representation of deer and pig on the clay with flints site at Woodcutts and a much higher proportion of sheep on two sites on the Upper Chalk. These observations are enough to suggest that the character of the chalkland may have changed by the first millennium bc. This is entirely consistent with the distribution of settlement in the study area.

These specialist studies all support Fisher's idea that significant changes took place in the prehistoric landscape of Cranborne Chase. They provide a broad environmental framework within which to approach the specific problems treated in this volume. In particular, they reveal a basic distinction between the earlier and later prehistoric landscape in this area, with a significant change towards the beginning of the first millennium bc. That twofold division will be followed in the remaining parts of this study.

Notes

1 John C. Barrett
2 Richard Bradley
3 Mark Bowden
4 Roy Entwistle
5 Peter Fisher
6 Martin Jones
7 A. J. Legge
8 Mark Robinson

PART I
THE DEAD AND THE LIVING

Though grave-diggers' toil is long,
Sharp their spades, their muscles strong,
They but thrust their buried men
Back in the human mind again.
W. B. Yeats, 'Under Ben Bulben'

2. THE EARLIER NEOLITHIC

2.1 Introduction[1]

Three issues have seemed important for our understanding of activity in Cranborne Chase. Each will run throughout this study, and each, we believe, has implications for work in other parts of the country (Figs. 2.1 and 2.2). First, we have to consider the position of our study area in the wider pattern of settlement. Recent research has emphasised the way in which human activities may be structured over vast areas of the landscape. Very often what archaeologists call 'sites' are simply locations in which a higher density of activity has been recognised than elsewhere (Foley 1981). A 'site'-based archaeology often carries an implication of permanence and self-sufficiency and excludes the seasonal aspect which features so prominently in human settlement. Earlier Neolithic settlement may have been fairly mobile, and in any case we have to remember that Cranborne Chase is at the boundary of upland and lowland Wessex. Analogy with the historical period would certainly suggest that the main focus of settlement might have been in the river valleys and other low-lying areas, with the downland providing supplementary resources on a seasonal basis. Very much this interpretation has been sug-

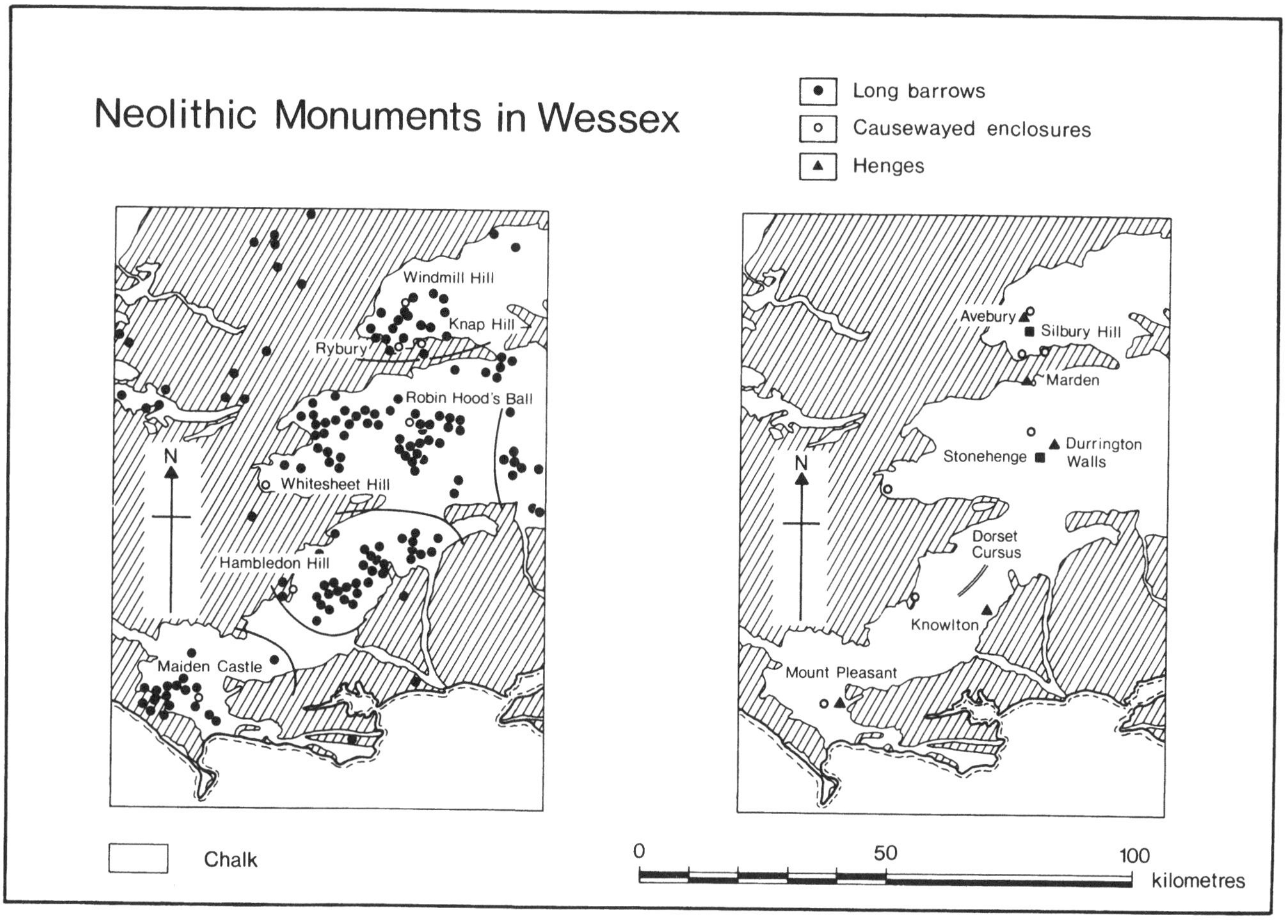

Fig. 2.1 The distribution of major monuments in Neolithic Wessex in relation to the chalk downland (unshaded) (after Renfrew 1973)

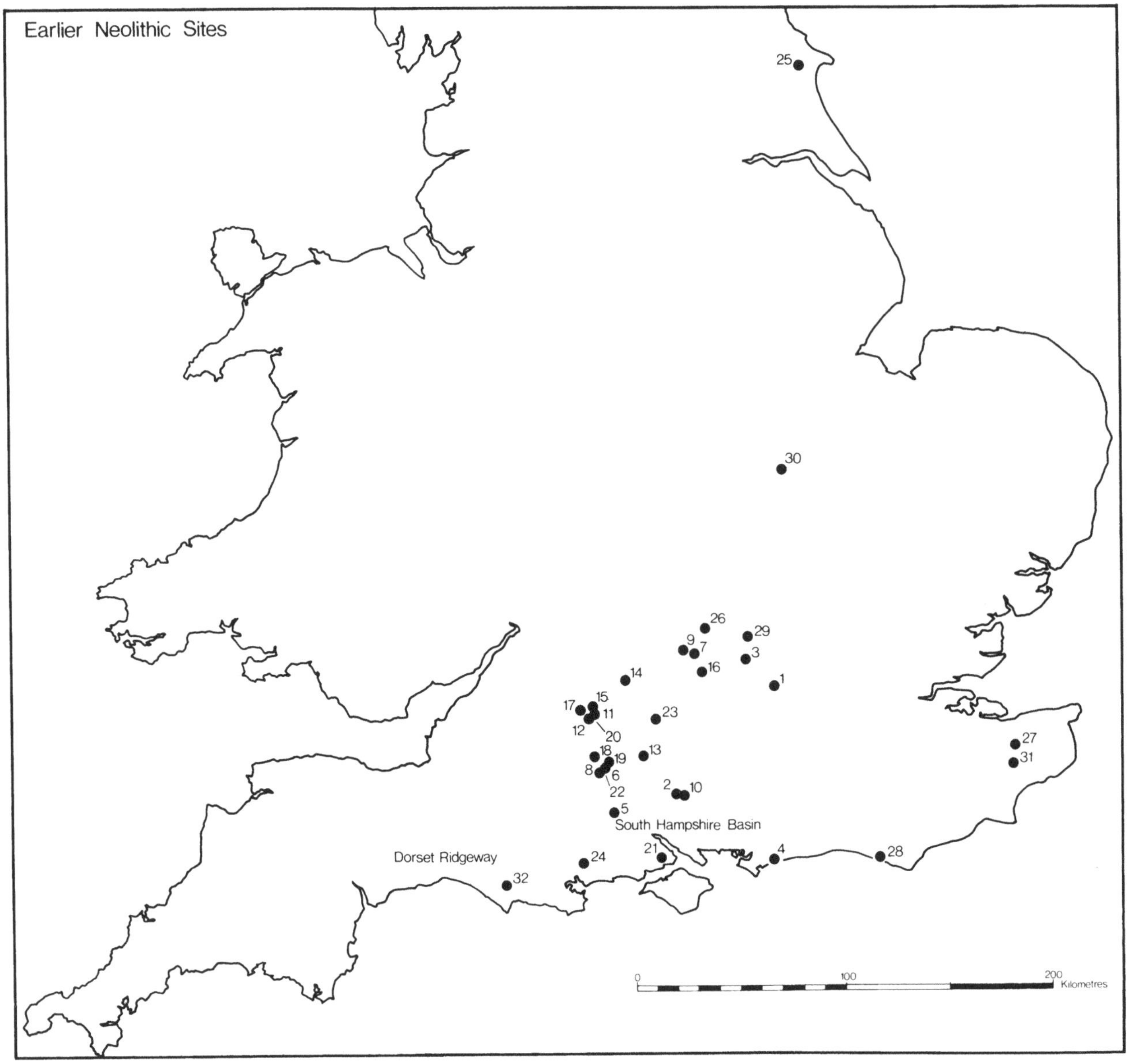

Fig. 2.2 The distribution of Earlier Neolithic sites outside the study area which are considered in this chapter. Key: 1 Blashenwell; 2 Winchester; 3 Rimsmoor; 4 Launceston Down; 5 Downton; 6 Stonehenge Cursus; 7 Dorchester on Thames; 8 North Marden; 9 Barrow Hills; 10 Winnall Down; 11 South Street, Avebury; 12 Beckhampton Road, Avebury; 13 Nutbane; 14 Wayland's Smithy; 15 Windmill Hill; 16 Rowden; 17 Cherhill; 18 Marden; 19 Durrington Walls; 20 Hemp Knoll; 21 Bishopstone; 22 Normanton Down; 23 Kennet Valley; 24 Moortown; 25 Rudston; 26 North Stoke; 27 Julliberries Grave; 28 Alfriston; 29 Whiteleaf; 30 Aldwincle; 31 Brook; 32 Maiden Castle

gested by Schofield's analysis of the flintwork from the East Hampshire Survey and the Avon valley (1987). In what follows we shall often refer to the archaeological record in the Hampshire Basin, and in particular to the river valleys flanking the study area.

This emphasis on the interrelationship of upland and lowland is by no means new in the archaeology of this region. Much research has been devoted to the character of lowland settlement. In particular, Bob Smith's research has emphasised its distinctive place in Wessex prehistory. His analysis suggests that activity on the downland took place discontinuously, with substantial periods in which occupation retreated onto lower ground (Smith 1984). Cranborne Chase is located on the southern edge of the Wessex chalk and provides an excellent opportunity to map the changing 'tide mark' of human settlement. At the same time, it also permits us to review specific reconstructions of the place of earthwork monuments in the landscape. Barker and Webley, for example, have suggested that Neolithic causewayed enclosures, among them Hambledon Hill, were used in the course of summer grazing from settlements in lowlying areas (1978). Similarly, Fleming (1971) considers that the distinctive clusters of Bronze Age barrows on the chalk may also have been located in areas of seasonal pasture. One of the main groups of barrows considered in his paper is located in the study area.

A second theme arises from this contrast between upland and lowland Wessex, for Cranborne Chase is notable for its profusion of non-utilitarian monuments (Fig. 2.4). Despite a long history of observation, very few sites of similar character have been identified in the Hampshire Basin, with its concentration of earlier prehistoric findspots around Bournemouth and Christchurch (Fig. 2.5). There are no causewayed enclosures, cursuses or henges, elaborate round barrows are uncommon, and only one long barrow has been found. This distinction between the upland and lowland areas is particularly important since it is emphasised in the location of the most striking monument in the study area, the Dorset Cursus, which runs for 10 km midway between the headwaters of two rivers discharging into Christchurch Harbour. This earthwork also links up a series of the long barrows and endows the distinction between uplands and lowlands with a lasting cultural significance. For this reason the Cursus is at the heart of our discussion of the earlier prehistoric landscape.

Again this specific discussion allies our work with broader issues in modern archaeology, where the existence and operation of monumental structures poses a whole series of problems. For the most part these have been concerned with the place of these monuments in the sequence of settlement. The establishment of monuments to the dead is sometimes considered as one way in which societies lay claim to restricted but critical resources; in this interpretation ancestry and land tenure are very closely connected (Chapman 1981). Such ideas require us to consider the changing place of specialised monuments in the wider landscape – at what stage in the sequence did they come into being? How far can we find regularities in the locations of monuments and settlement areas? This is particularly important when so often the distribution of non-utilitarian monuments is treated as a clue to the settlement pattern as a whole.

Our last theme also concerns the monuments, for it seems likely that they exerted a decisive influence over the activities of contemporary and later populations. This is easily overlooked in favour of environmental and topographical factors, which are easier to identify. We shall be concerned with the *cultural* landscape which formed around these prominent earthworks. This discussion has two main aspects. First, it seems as if the nature of domestic activity varied according to the proximity of the Cursus and its attendant monuments, so that we have to consider the changing character of occupation in different parts of our study area. This approach links our work with research in a number of other areas of the country, and in particular with the Stonehenge Environs Project which has identified rather similar spatial patterning in relation to the major monuments on Salisbury Plain (Richards 1984). Such work touches upon a second question of wider interest, the explanation of those collections of elaborate objects found in the vicinity of large earthwork monuments. This is a pattern which extends through many of the 'core areas' of the Later Neolithic (see Bradley 1984, 41–67). Our analysis will assess the status and context of such finds, without resorting to the assumption that the distribution of complex monuments necessarily marks areas of the landscape which were reserved for 'ritual' activities.

Finally, if the existence of major monuments influenced the character of later settlement, the same also applies to the process of monument building. In many areas lengthy sequences of special-purpose monuments have been identified, extending from long barrows and causewayed enclosures to complex cemeteries of the Early Bronze Age (e.g. Fig. 2.1). We need to investigate the nature of these apparent continuities. Do they really imply a pattern of continuous activity? And why was the planning of later monuments influenced so strongly by the character and location of earthworks which were already centuries old? We have referred to Colin Renfrew's discussion of such continuities in the Wessex landscape (1973); it is now possible to examine this much-quoted interpretation in a region where a full range of monuments has been studied alongside the evidence of settlement – something that was not possible in 1973. We can also ask further questions of this material. To what extent did the building of successive monuments in the study area involve an explicit acknowledgement of the achievements of the past? And how far did the activities of later generations gain authority by referring to long-established structures in the landscape? Discussion of the broader issues is reserved for later chapters, but even at the most empirical level these questions affect the ways in which our account of this region has been organised.

2.2 The nature of the evidence[2.1]

We must now cast a critical eye over the types of material used in describing this sequence. Very similar kinds of data are employed in the three chapters that follow, and to avoid unnecessary repetition they are best considered at this point.

The evidence of pottery plays a prominent part in this account, and Chapters 2 to 4 each include an overview of the ceramic sequence (cf. Fig. 4.4, p. 115). We have to stress that, except where radiocarbon dates have been obtained in the course of this project, most of the chronological evidence depends on comparison with work outside the study area; few of the excavations reported here have detailed stratigraphic sequences. This applies particularly to those sites dug by Pitt Rivers. We should also emphasise that virtually all the pottery discussed in Part II comes from excavation rather than survey.

The evidence of lithics plays the dominant role in our discussion of earlier prehistoric settlement. This is virtually our only source of domestic evidence until the development of enclosed settlements in the Bronze Age, and for this reason we must start our account with a review of the role that it plays in our analysis. The main questions to be considered are the ways in which this material has been recovered, the possible biases affecting this process, and the evidence on which the main chronological divisions are founded.

Although a large quantity of flintwork has been excavated, this material rarely plays much role in building the detailed sequence, which depends largely on ceramics and radiocarbon dates. Where it does play a decisive role is in our interpretation of surface finds. Although Pitt Rivers did collect some flintwork, we are chiefly concerned with the material found in recent years. Field survey has proceeded since 1968 and began long before a methodology for collecting lithic artefacts had been established nationally. Collection did not take place on a grid, except on one site (Chalkpit Field), where this was done as a preliminary to excavation, but the distributions of different types of artefact were noted in the field and the major concentrations of flintwork were recorded. Not all locations were investigated in the same detail, and this is made clear in tabulating the results (Table 3.4, p. 73). In two cases it has been possible to check the completeness of surface collection against the results of subsequent excavation. On a Mesolithic site, not reported here, it can be shown that the frequency of the major artefact types found by survey shows no significant difference from the composition of the excavated assemblage (Lewis and Coleman 1982). The same exercise was carried out on a Later Neolithic flint scatter with similar results (p. 72).

For the most part debitage was not collected systematically, but fortunately Barry Lewis' work in the study area does provide some information on the amounts of

Table 2.1. *The changing composition of 'off-site' flint industries in different parts of the study area (data collected by Barry Lewis), compared with evidence from the Avon gravels. The figures for the Avon valley are from Schofield (1987)*

	Clay with flints[1]	Edge of clay	Upper Chalk	Knowlton area	Avon gravels
Cores: flakes	1:18	1:21	1:26	1:23	1:27
Tools: flakes	1:107	1:74	1:63	1:59	1:29
Tools: cores	1:6	1:4	1:4	1:3	1:3

[1]Sample based on single location not collected previously.

'off-site' flintwork along a transect extending from the clay with flints, across the Upper Chalk to the Knowlton complex (Table 2.1). His results can be compared directly with similar figures for 'off-site' flintwork on the Avon gravels (Schofield 1987). This information is presented in the form of three ratios – cores:flakes; tools:flakes; and tools:cores. All three seem to emphasise similar features of the study area. The intensity of stoneworking appears to have declined with distance from the main raw-material sources on the clay with flints, whilst tools seem to have been curated to an increasing extent in the same areas. Flint was used far more wastefully where it was naturally abundant, but even allowing for the ready supply of raw material on the higher ground, the amount of material found in the study area is very much greater than it is on the Avon gravels, which Schofield considers to be one of the more intensively exploited environments in the region (1987).

Debitage was not collected from the main series of lithic scatters. On the other hand, the recovery of regular implement types has been extremely thorough in Cranborne Chase and results in one of the largest provenanced collections of this material in the country. The finds from the Hampshire Basin seem to cover an equally wide range of types, including the less 'attractive' pieces, but much less is known about the conditions under which they were found.

Thirty-one surface assemblages have been identified in this part of Cranborne Chase, and their contents can be compared with the material from eight major excavations in the same area, including those of two long barrows. In addition, some information can be drawn from smaller-scale excavations carried out by Pitt Rivers. It hardly needs to be added that the quantity and variety of tool types recovered as surface finds is far in excess of anything encountered in excavation. At the same time, examination of the finds from field survey does not suggest any obvious bias in collection apart from the under-representation of debitage, already noted.

Table 2.2. *The extent of the main geological deposits in the area examined by fieldwalking and in the study area as a whole*

	Percentage of each deposit in the study area	Percentage of each deposit in the area fieldwalked
Clay with flints	8.0	17.5
Upper Chalk	84.0	68.8
Valley Gravel	5.2	2.8
Other	2.8	10.4

The contents of the Pitt Rivers Collection raise more problems. There is little doubt that the General's recovery of worked flint in excavation was unsatisfactory, although it may have been at its weakest when he was dealing with crude Bronze Age industries of the type found at South Lodge Camp. This weakness extends to his collection of surface finds, few of which were noted in print. The finds from his collection show a bias towards the recovery of heavy-duty pieces – axe roughouts, polished axe fragments and tranchet axes in particular; there are some arrowheads but very few scrapers or other lightweight pieces. This contrasts with the results of more recent collection on the same sites. Even combining excavated and surface material, however, the Pitt Rivers Collection accounts for less than ten per cent of the flintwork currently available for examination.

Most of Pitt Rivers' surface finds do have reasonable provenances, but it is difficult to integrate this material with the results of more recent work. The areas of Cranborne Chase which have been examined by *systematic* fieldwalking are indicated in Figure 1.3 and total 85 km^2. They cover most of the cultivated land on the geological deposits considered earlier (Table 2.2). There are too few finds of Earlier Neolithic date for statistical analysis to be warranted, but analysis by Dr Peter Fisher, using the Kolmogorov–Smirnov Test, has shown that the distributions of both Mesolithic and Later Neolithic findspots were significantly different from the distribution of geological deposits in the study area. This test omits findspots known only from the Pitt Rivers Collection.

The methods of studying large surface collections described by Gardiner (1987) are followed here. They involve reducing the seventy or so lithic artefact types identified in the literature to a relatively small number of major groups, based on similarities in tool morphology, size and techniques of production; they do not depend on the 'functions' of different tools. The list includes a number of types which are known in surface collections elsewhere but which have not been encountered in excavation. With this exception, the chronology of these types depends on their discovery in dated contexts, often outside the study area. This allows only three major divisions: Earlier Neolithic, Later Neolithic and a less well-defined group which contains a few types associated with Beaker pottery. By no means all these types are restricted to one group. Analysis is also complicated by the fact that a wider range of retouched artefacts was used in the Later Neolithic than in the preceding period (see Bradley 1987a). Nevertheless, there seems to be no contradiction between the artefact sequence suggested on the basis of work throughout southern England and the dating of individual forms from sealed contexts in Cranborne Chase (Gardiner 1988).

These complications must be kept in mind in the account of the earlier prehistoric sequence here and in the following two chapters.

2.3 The Mesolithic background[1]

The study area has been occupied on a large scale by hunter-gatherers, but it seems likely that this phase of settlement was over well before the Neolithic settlement of the Chase. For this reason, it has no *direct* bearing on the sequence of change studied in this book. The Mesolithic material collected in field survey is published separately (Arnold, Green, Lewis and Bradley 1988) and only a few results of that analysis are relevant here.

There seems no doubt that the areas of clay with flints were the major focus for Mesolithic land use in this area (Fig. 2.3). They offered an important source of raw material, but study of the tool types represented in the surface collections shows that these parts of Cranborne Chase also provided the basis for a much wider range of activities. To some extent this also applied to the main river valleys. By contrast, occupation of the greensand was a late development and involved a more restricted tool kit. Spatial analysis suggests that activity was quite tightly structured on the clay with flints and may have taken place within a series of fairly long-lived clearings. There were no finds of Mesolithic material from the Upper Chalk.

The Mesolithic background is important for three reasons. Firstly, it confirms the significance of the clay with flints, and in this respect provides strong support for the sequence of soil development suggested by Peter Fisher: not until the Neolithic period were areas of Upper Chalk brought into use. Secondly, it seems likely that in some places occupation was sufficiently intensive to have affected the landscape settled during later periods. Even if 'cultural' continuity was lacking, the impact of earlier populations may have left its mark. Lastly, Meso-

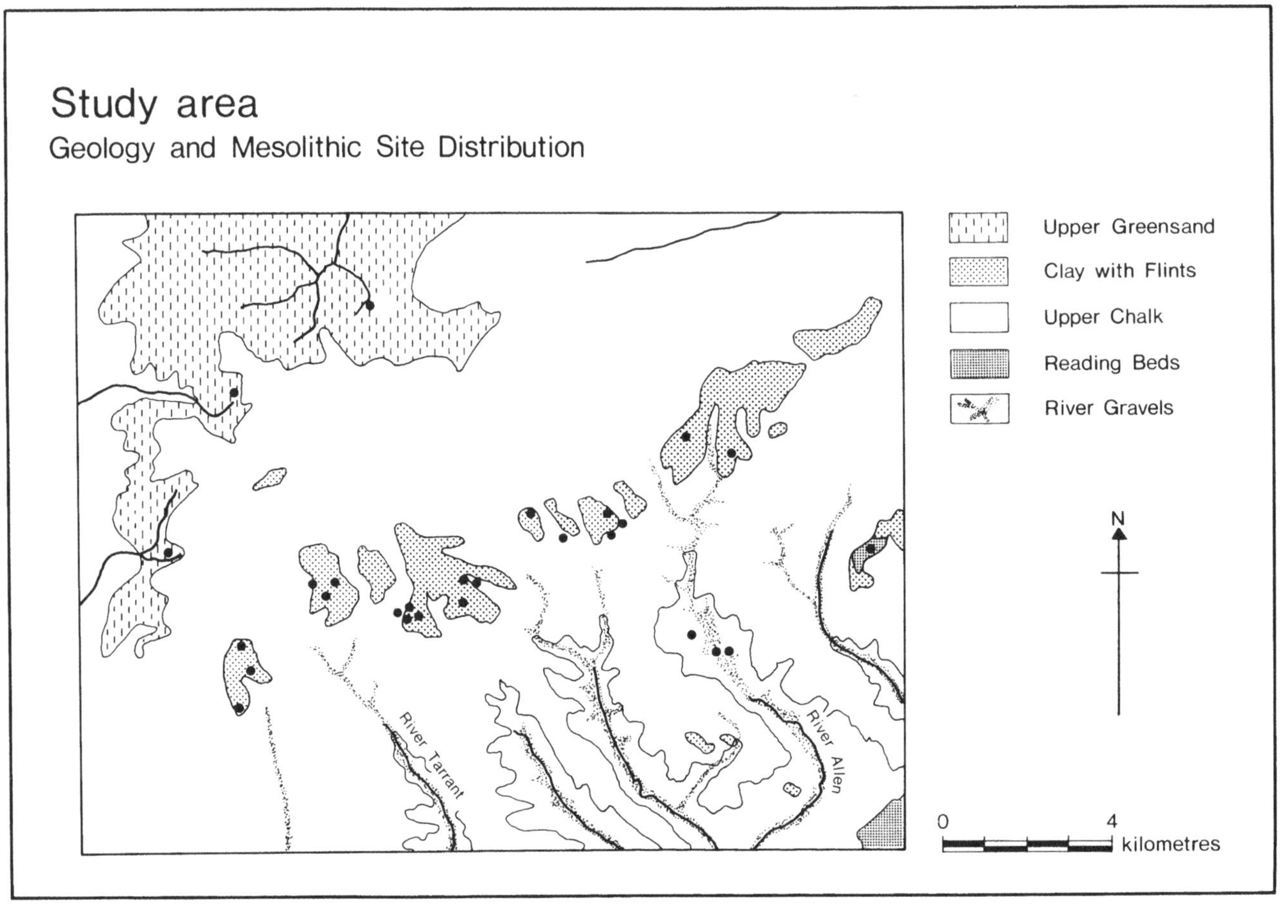

Fig. 2.3 The location of Mesolithic flint scatters in the study area in relation to the drift geology

lithic activity is significant because it set in motion an oscillation between upland and lowland settlement which was to continue throughout the prehistoric period.

For our purposes it is most important to pinpoint the end of the Mesolithic use of this area. Typological evidence suggests that the microlith sequence in Cranborne Chase came to an end no later than 4000 bc (Arnold, Green, Lewis and Bradley 1988); what indications there are of even later material in Wessex come from lower-lying areas away from the chalkland, either in the Kennet Valley or in the coastal basin. In one case, at Blashenwell in Dorset, there is evidence for the use of marine resources during this period (Preece 1980), but as the shoreline itself has been lost, it is impossible to say with any confidence whether the Late Mesolithic period saw increased exploitation of the coast, as may have happened in other parts of the country. This is suggested, however, by pollen analysis from the coastal basin, which shows increasing clearance in the later Meolithic period, in two cases accompanied by evidence of cereal pollen (Haskins 1978). The Wessex downland offers one other clue to the sequence of change. The two pollen analyses from the Wessex chalk, those from Winchester and Rimsmoor, indicate that forest cover may have *increased* just before the Elm Decline (Waton 1982). This could have taken place during the interval between the use of the downland by hunter-gatherers and its re-use in the Neolithic period.

2.4 The Earlier Neolithic: the evidence of domestic activity

The monuments of the downland have played such a prominent part in the development of Neolithic studies that it is worth reminding ourselves how few of them can be dated to the early part of this period. There is little archaeological material of any kind between 4000 bc and 3300 bc, but in southern England developments on the higher ground seem to be even longer retarded. For this reason they are best discussed in relation to a wider geographical area. This account will begin with the direct evidence of settlement in the study area and will compare this with the information, first from the Hampshire Basin, and then from the southern chalkland as a whole. Finally, the evidence of domestic activity will be combined with an account of the earthwork monuments of the study area. This will entail a reconsideration of the Cranborne Chase long barrows and a new account of the Dorset Cursus.

2.4.1 The flint industries in the study area[2]

The existence of complex monuments in Cranborne Chase might lead us to believe that the area was an important focus of Earlier Neolithic settlement. In fact, despite extensive fieldwork and excavation, the study area has produced only a handful of leaf-shaped arrowheads and just one narrow flake assemblage (Fig. 2.4).

The narrow flake industry was excavated from Thickthorn Down long barrow (Clark in Drew and Piggott 1936, 88–91). In Pitts' and Jacobi's scheme this material would be placed firmly in the Earlier Neolithic (1979). In addition, the industry is associated with a leaf-shaped arrowhead and with sherds from a plain Neolithic bowl. It also includes a number of large cores from which blade-like flakes had been removed, possibly *in situ*. By contrast, the finds from the primary levels of the Dorset Cursus, which should be of approximately the same age, have a lower proportion of narrow flakes and seem to result from the preliminary knapping of material encountered in the construction of the monument (cf. Ford 1987a). This contrast suggests that the Thickthorn Down barrow had covered an occupation site. The large flint industries from the Hambledon Hill complex have yet to be published, and too few flints survive from Pitt Rivers' sites to be considered here.

Apart from the two well-recorded groups from major monuments, we are left with an 'earlier' Neolithic component of just fifty leaf-shaped arrowheads from the study area. Other types regularly found in industries of this date have not been identified in this area. The finds of arrowheads are widely dispersed (Fig. 2.4) and most of the major flint scatters have produced between one and three examples. Their actual frequency appears to vary with the total number of items recovered during fieldwork, even though the great majority consist of diagnostic Later Neolithic forms, and it seems likely that groups belonging to the earlier period are so ephemeral that they have only been identified during the most intensive fieldwork; the same conclusion has been reached by workers in other parts of southern England (cf. Richards 1984; Bradley 1987a; Ford 1987b and Healy 1987). The arrowhead distribution is almost equally divided between the clay with flints, already used in the Mesolithic, and a strip of Upper Chalk around the headwaters of the main streams and rivers. This group includes finds from the primary levels of the two excavated long barrows (Wor Barrow and Thickthorn Down). Although the finds from the Upper Chalk are sometimes close to individual long mounds, there seems to be no direct link between the two distributions. Recent work on surface industries from the Sussex Downs has demonstrated that leaf-shaped arrowheads in that area cluster towards the funerary monuments (Gardiner 1984, 21), but in Cranborne Chase, whilst 50 per cent of these artefacts do occur within 2 km of a long barrow, this is hardly surprising when so many of these earthworks are known.

A more appropriate comparison may be made with the coastal plain around Bournemouth, and with the lower Stour Valley (see Gardiner in Cunliffe 1987, 329–30). Only one long barrow (Holdenhurst) is known, but many more leaf-shaped arrowheads and small amounts of Earlier Neolithic flintwork have been recovered. These are largely concentrated towards the west end of Christchurch Harbour, where some tight clusters of leaf-shaped arrowheads occur, for instance at Latch Farm, Thistlebarrow and Hengistbury Head (Fig. 2.5). Again many of these are surface finds. This raises problems, since Frances Healy (1987) has shown how commonly Earlier Neolithic occupation debris is found in subsoil features and how little of it may be represented in the ploughsoil. The greater extent of quarrying in the Hampshire Basin would have provided more opportunities for the discovery of material in pits, and this means that we cannot rely too strongly on comparison between the finds from this area and those from Cranborne Chase. On the other hand, it is surely revealing that, of at least fifteen leaf-shaped arrowheads recorded from Hengistbury Head, only one was actually recovered during excavation. It is true that to a large extent the distribution of arrowheads reflects the positions of gravel pits favoured by local collectors, but whilst the recovery of artefacts seems to have been haphazard compared with work in Cranborne Chase, the number of leaf-shaped arrowheads known from the Bournemouth area is more than *three times* that in the study area. The contrast between these two regions is easier to assess when we turn to the distribution of pottery and pits.

2.4.2 The ceramic evidence[3]

A minimum of twelve vessels belonging to Earlier Neolithic ceramic traditions are present in the study area, although most are represented only by a small number of sherds (for the Neolithic sequence as a whole see Fig. 4.4, p. 115). These come from five locations, including

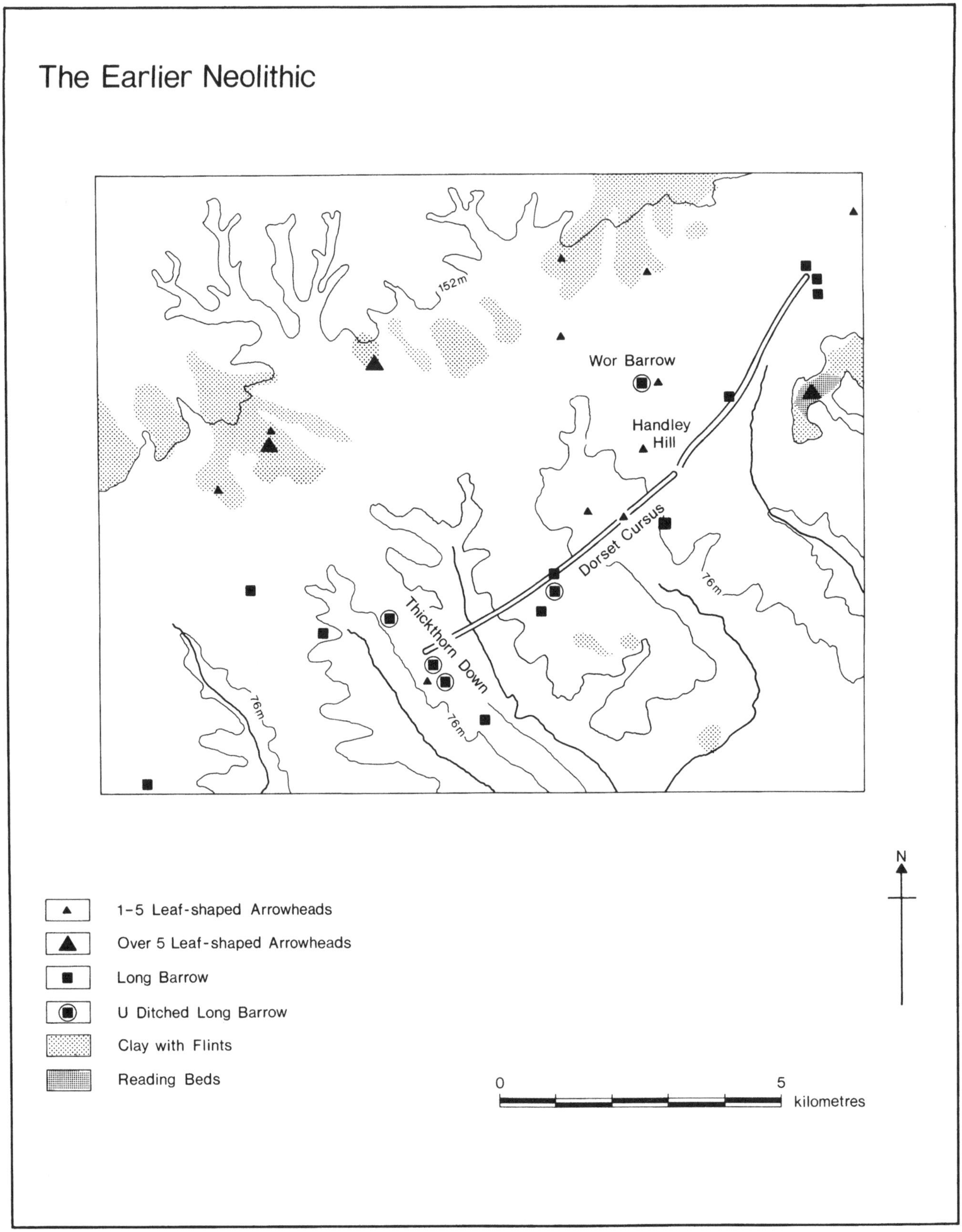

Fig. 2.4 The distribution of Earlier Neolithic flintwork and monuments in the study area

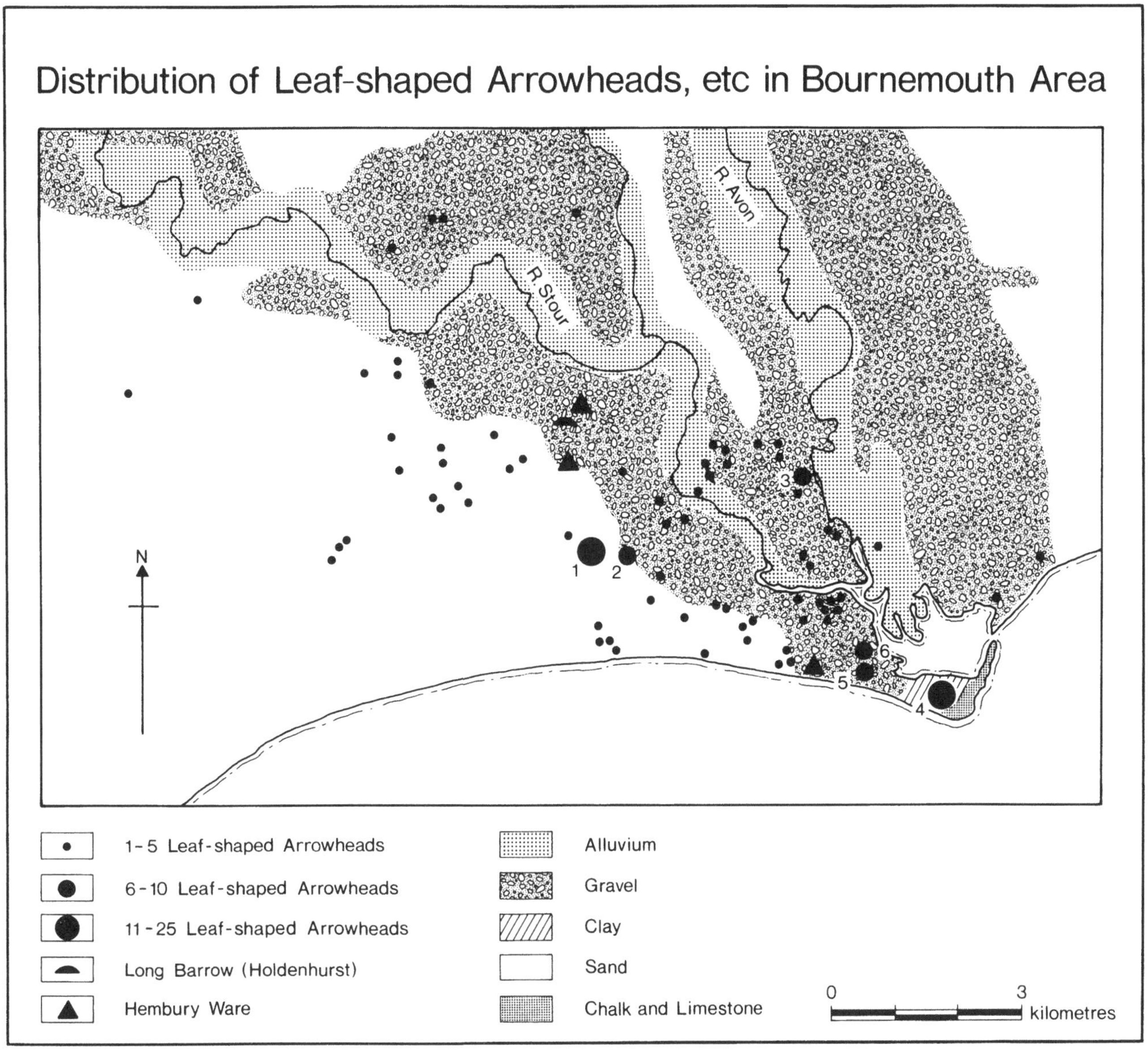

Fig. 2.5 The distribution of Earlier Neolithic artefacts and monuments around the confluence of the Rivers Avon and Stour. Key: 1 Thistlebarrow; 2 King's Park; 3 Latch Farm; 4 Hengistbury Head; 5 Whitepits (Southfield); 6 Roebury (Northfield)

three monuments (the long barrows at Thickthorn Down and Wor Barrow and the lower levels of the Dorset Cursus). The remaining pottery comes from two parts of Pitt Rivers' excavations on Handley Hill: the interior of a medieval enclosure and a pit outside this earthwork. The latter site is located near to Wor Barrow and will be considered in the following section. Only five vessels from the study area are sufficiently complete to be assigned to particular ceramic styles, in four cases Whittle's South Western style (Hembury Ware), and in one to his Eastern Style (Grimston Ware) (see Whittle 1977). This material is considered in detail in the companion volume.

Pottery of similar character is more abundant on the coastal plain and has been published from six locations (five sites with pits and the ditch of Holdenhurst long barrow). The most extensive of the domestic sites is at present under excavation at Moortown on the Stour gravels and includes material in the South Western style (Horsey and Jarvis 1984).

2.4.3 The results of excavation[1]

There is little other evidence of human activity before the later third millennium bc. We have summarised the molluscan data from three locations (two sections through the west ditch of the Dorset Cursus and the buried soil beneath Thickthorn Down long barrow) and two points need to be emphasised here: the low diversity of molluscan species represented and the strongly contrasting environments revealed by these analyses (Fig. 1.7). The long barrow seems to have been built in open grassland, perhaps on the site of an earlier settlement, but the two samples from equivalent positions in the Cursus ditch provide very different results. Whilst one location seems to have been in a fairly open area, the other, a mere 700 m away, appears to have been in closed woodland which remained unaltered until the Later Neolithic. It is well known that molluscan analyses reflect events within a very restricted catchment, but as these results come from sites which should be virtually contemporary with one another, they emphasise the small scale of human activity at this time.

In spite of a large number of excavations, Earlier Neolithic pits have been found at only two sites: Thickthorn Down and Handley Hill. The pits at Thickthorn Down were sealed by the turf line under the long barrow and contained a small number of worked flints (Drew and Piggott 1936, 81). A microlith from one of these features was so eroded that the excavators considered it to be residual. The irregular character of these features suggests that they might have been tree holes. The pits at Handley Hill were much more regular and contained pottery and flintwork, the latter including a leaf-shaped arrowhead. There were at least three of these features, occurring in an area about 200 m across (*Excavations* IV, 49–51). They were found during excavation of a medieval enclosure and may form only part of a rather wider spread of activity; for example, further flintwork, which no longer survives, was sealed beneath the mound at Wor Barrow, 800 m away (*ibid.*, 63–5). It is not always possible to reconstruct the contents of these pits but one contained a disarticulated human burial and an arrangement of cattle bones. This was also the source of a large vessel of Grimston Ware. This particular pit seems to have been marked by an upright post, a feature which is found at two other sites in Cranborne Chase. At Hambledon Hill similar posts marked the positions of some of the pits inside the main causewayed enclosure (Mercer 1980, 23), whilst at Launceston Down a similar post marked the position of a crouched burial underneath a Neolithic round barrow (Piggott and Piggott 1944, 74–5). There is no evidence to show that these developments were contemporary with one another.

Again this evidence is rather different from the pattern around Bournemouth and Christchurch, although we have already seen that there would have been more opportunities for the discovery of subsoil features in that area. One contrast is worth noting, however, for preliminary accounts of the current work at Moortown suggest that the density of subsoil features there may have been much greater than on open sites on the Wessex chalk (Horsey and Jarvis 1984).

2.4.4 Discussion[1]

We have considered three different kinds of evidence for Earlier Neolithic settlement in the study area, and in each case the material has been extremely limited. Whilst the rarity of surface finds could reflect biases in the fieldwork, comparison with the Mesolithic picture suggests that these can hardly account for such a striking contrast between the finds belonging to the two periods. Comparisons with the lower ground have also been illuminating. It is not known how much Earlier Neolithic material might have been masked by colluvium, but whatever allowance we make for sample bias, the abundance of finds of this date towards the coast is very striking. It is true that there were more chances of finding subsoil features in that area, but few of the all-important arrowheads seem to have been found in pits. Either the study area was not settled to any extent during this period or it was used sparingly, and by communities who retained a significant element of mobility. Indeed, this may be the implication of the lightweight and adaptable tool industry in general use during this period (Bradley 1987a; Edmonds 1987). We have already suggested that the Mesolithic sequence on the downland was truncated. It seems possible that settlement contracted into lowland areas by the end of the fifth millennium bc; perhaps we should envisage the re-use of parts of the study area from more lasting settlements on the lower ground.

If the quantity of Earlier Neolithic material is slight in comparison with the Mesolithic pattern, there are still some contrasts to observe. Roughly half the arrowheads were found on the Upper Chalk, an area completely shunned during the previous phase, and it is the *Later* Neolithic distribution that more closely resembles the Mesolithic pattern. For these reasons, we must envisage some land clearance during this phase, even if this was effected through the pressure of grazing animals.

The most important contrast, however, is between developments in Cranborne Chase and those in the Hampshire Basin, where more artefacts and more subsoil features have been found. It may be significant that the

Table 2.3. *Radiocarbon dates from Earlier Neolithic occupation sites on the chalk of southern England*

Site	Radiocarbon date(s)	Location
Wessex sites:		
Windmill Hill, Wiltshire	2960 ± 150 bc (BM 73)	Hilltop, sealed by causewayed enclosure
Rowden, Dorset	2990 ± 70 bc (Har 5247) 2910 ± 70 bc (Har 5248) 2740 ± 70 bc (Har 5245)	Ridgetop
South Street, Avebury, Wiltshire	2810 ± 130 bc (BM 356)	In valley, sealed by long barrow
Cherhill, Wiltshire	2765 ± 90 bc (BM 493)	In valley, below colluvium
Marden, Wiltshire	2654 ± 59 bc (BM 560)	In valley, sealed by henge monument
Durrington Walls, Wiltshire	2634 ± 80 bc (Gro 901) 2625 ± 50 bc (Gro 901a) 2450 ± 150 bc (NPL 191)	In valley, sealed by henge monument
Hemp Knoll	2630 ± 80 bc (Har 2997)	Spur overlooking dry valley
Outside Wessex		
Brook, Kent	2590 ± 105 bc (BM 254)	Finds from colluvium in valley
Bishopstone, Sussex	2510 ± 70 bc (Har 1662)	Hilltop, overlooking coast

pollen analyses which show the impact of Neolithic agriculture in the fourth millennium come from low-lying areas at or beyond the southern limit of the chalkland. A massive phase of land clearance took place at Winchester at about the time of the Elm Decline, although the one radiocarbon date of 3680 ± 90 bc (Har 4342) is anomalously early if the Elm Decline is to be regarded as a synchronous phenomenon (Waton 1982, 77). A second site, at Rimsmoor in south-east Dorset, also shows signs of agricultural activity at, or even before, the Elm Decline, which this time has a radiocarbon date at the end of the fourth millennium bc (3200 ± 70 bc: Har 3919; *ibid.*, 84–5). Further clearance phases are recorded close to Poole Harbour (Haskins 1978).

When we consider the purely archaeological evidence from the chalk itself, we are faced by a paradox, for there is no lack of settlement sites with the styles of pottery and flintwork attributed to the Earlier Neolithic. However, the radiocarbon dates associated with them are not evenly distributed but are clustered in the later part of this period (Table 2.3). All fall within the third millennium bc. The same probably applies to the date of the earliest valley bottom occupation at Downton in the Avon valley, which was associated with a mixture of plain bowls and Ebbsfleet Ware (ApSimon in Rahtz 1962, 128–38).

At the same time, these dates are significantly later than those for early agriculture in the pollen record of southern Wessex. They are also later than those from the first long barrows on the chalk. It is noticeable that none of these sites has much domestic material in the buried soil underneath the mound. By contrast, the majority of the long barrows in Wessex which *are* known to postdate 3000 bc do overlie settlement material, perhaps suggesting that more intensive settlement was taking place by the time they were built.

These arguments suggest that the evidence from Cranborne Chase probably can be taken at face value, and that full-scale settlement of the chalkland may have started extremely slowly. Indeed, in Cranborne Chase there is little sign of large-scale occupation until the Later Neolithic period. This has serious consequences for our understanding of the field monuments of the area, and it is to these that we must turn our attention now.

2.5 The evidence of earthwork monuments[1]

2.5.1 Introduction

In this section the term 'monument' is used to refer to three types of earthwork built on an elaborate scale – long barrows, causewayed enclosures and the Dorset Cursus. Long barrows represent an investment of about 7,000 worker-hours (Startin 1982), whilst Startin's estimate for the Dorset Cursus is a minimum figure of 450,000 worker-hours. Mercer's preliminary estimate for the Hambledon Hill complex is approximately twice as high (1980, 59–60). Although it seems likely that earthworks of all three types were built and enlarged in stages, the scale of these sites must always have been the main consideration. It is unhelpful to embark on a one-dimensional classification of these monuments. For example, some parts of the Hambledon Hill complex were probably inhabited, whilst others are thought to have been used for exposing the dead. At this stage it is enough to say that none of the occupation sites in the study area, or on the coastal plain, appear to have been defined by earthworks.

Mercer's current work on the Hambledon Hill complex is a separate project, but its relevance cannot be overemphasised, as the site lies on the western edge of Cranborne Chase, only 10 km beyond our study area (Fig. 1.1). Although we shall often refer to the development of the Hambledon complex (Mercer 1980), our main concern will be with another enormous monument, the Dorset Cursus, and with the nearby long barrows. Earlier drafts of this chapter attempted to treat these two 'types' of monument separately, but so close are the relationships between them that this created confusion. The more we study the Cursus and the long barrows which accompany it, the more obvious it is that they represent a single phenomenon.

2.5.2 The character of the Dorset Cursus complex

It is difficult to treat these types of monument separately because the Cursus follows the full extent of the barrow distribution. The study area contains sixteen long barrows (Fig. 2.4.), roughly half the monuments of this type in Cranborne Chase (Ashbee 1984, 162–4). Like similar monuments in Hampshire, the distribution of long barrows follows the headwaters of streams and rivers running southwards into the English Channel (Fig. 2.6). The mounds in the study area are all on Upper Chalk at heights of between 80 and 120 m. Eleven of the sixteen mounds are within 2 km of permanent water today, and only three are more than 3 km away. Nearly all the barrows occupy a strip of land 2 km wide following the present springline. The longest of the mounds tend to lie towards the limits of this zone, suggesting some order in their distribution. In addition, as many as five crop marks in the vicinity of the Cursus could represent 'long mortuary enclosures'. None has been excavated and their date is uncertain. They are mapped in Figure 2.7, together with causewayed ring ditches.

The Cursus follows the group of long barrows for nearly 10 km, but unlike the individual mounds it ignores the local topography, crossing a river and several major valleys (Fig. 2.4). Like most of the barrows, the Cursus follows the springline, but once it had been completed its earthwork would have cut off the higher ground of the Chase, and in particular the clay with flints so much favoured in the Mesolithic. The Cursus was built in stages and can be thought of as two self-contained monuments, the earlier running from Thickthorn Down to a terminal on Bottlebush Down, whilst its northern extension, which is butted on to the Bottlebush terminal, took the earthwork a further 4 km to Martin Down (Fig. 2.8). The main distribution of long barrows is to the south of the Cursus, although a few individual mounds lie directly in its path. The distribution of long barrows and possible mortuary enclosures broadens out at the ends of the Cursus, and opposite the early terminal on Bottlebush Down, where Wor Barrow and a crop mark site, possibly another mortuary enclosure, are located. Otherwise the Cursus seems to have emphasised the distinction between upland and lowland areas which loomed so large in our discussion of Earlier Neolithic settlement.

2.5.2.i Structural details of the long barrows

This is not the first study to treat these barrows as a group, as Paul Ashbee has already argued that some of the mounds belong to a distinctive 'Cranborne Chase type' (1984, 15). Such earthworks are chiefly distinctive because the ditches have been carried around one or both ends. This also applies to the crop marks suggested as long mortuary enclosures, which are similar in size to these mounds.

Three members of this group have been excavated, two within the study area and the third as part of the Hambledon Hill project. All have unusual features. The most recent excavation has been of a damaged long barrow set between the main enclosure and the outworks on Hambledon Hill (Mercer 1980, 42–4). Little remained *in situ*, although it was clear that this had been a relatively short mound, flanked by two side ditches. The distinctive deposits in these ditches matched those in the main causewayed enclosure ditch, and the two should be contemporary. Radiocarbon dates from this enclosure fall between 2890 ± 150 bc (Har 1886) and 2530 ± 130 bc (Har 1885). No trace of the primary burial remained in position but all the bones bulldozed out of the mound some years earlier could have come from an adult male.

The second site is one of a pair of U-ditched long barrows on Thickthorn Down (Figs. 2.9–2.11), which share much the same alignment as the southern terminal of the Dorset Cursus, 10 and 200 m away respectively (Drew and Piggott 1936). Its Earlier Neolithic date is confirmed by undecorated pottery in the primary levels of the ditch and a narrow flake industry in its lower layers. In addition, there is a radiocarbon date of 3210 ± 45 bc for red deer antler found on the old land surface beneath the mound (BM 2355).

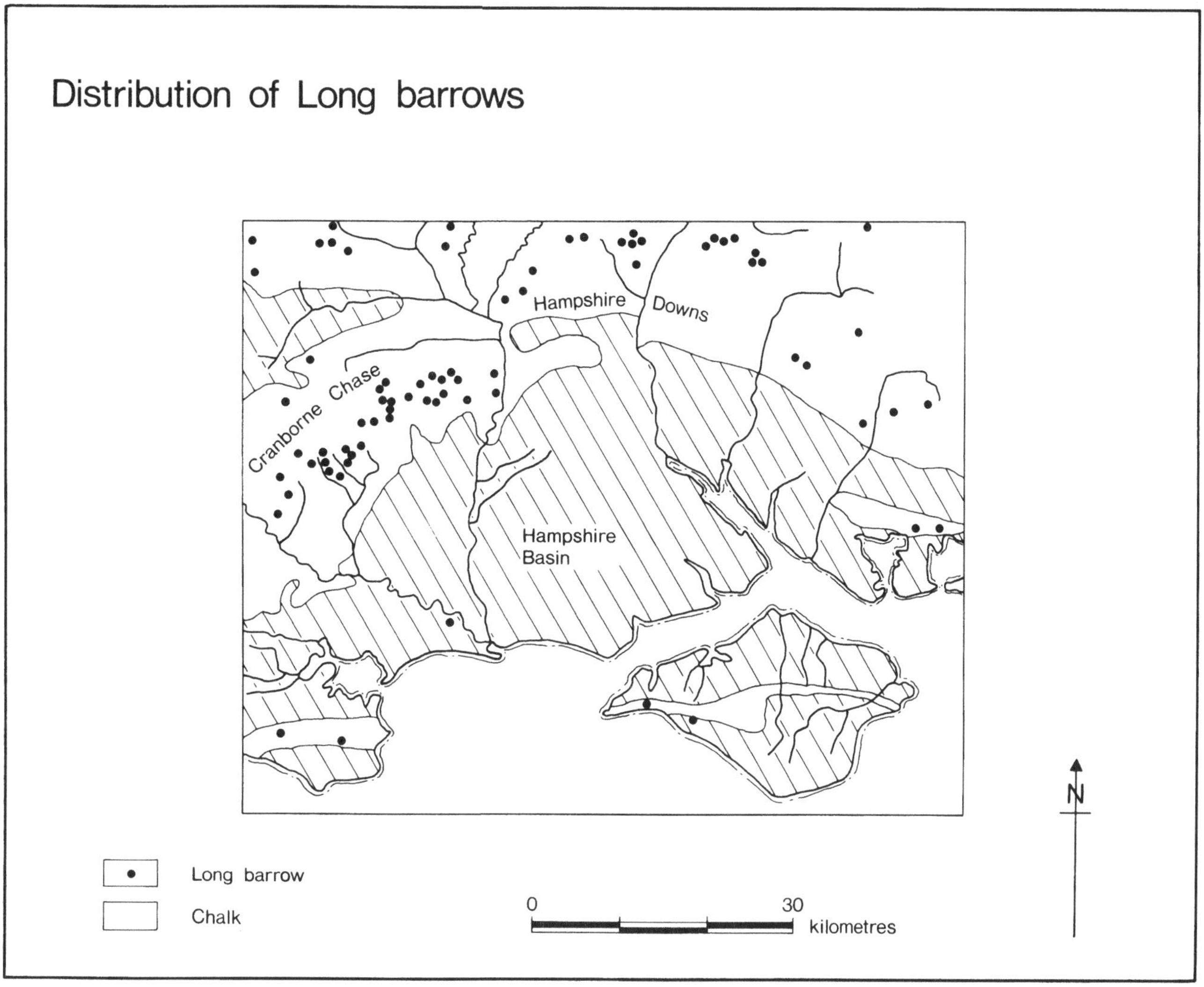

Fig. 2.6 Distribution of long barrows in relation to the chalk downland and the rivers discharging into the Hampshire Basin

The nature of this mound has always given problems, for no contemporary burials were found in or under the barrow. On the other hand, the excavators identified a turf 'mortuary structure' towards the south-eastern end of the mound, whose vertical walls showed up clearly in section. Their interpretation raises a number of problems, for this was by no means the only vertical break in the stratigraphy along the main axis of the mound. Photographs of this excavation show another break about 2 m further into the mound, whilst the drawn section reveals up to eight such breaks at intervals of between 1.7 and 3 m (Fig. 2.10). When this site was excavated, little was known about the structure of non-megalithic long barrows, but subsequent work has shown that a number of mounds had been constructed in a series of bays defined by rows of hurdles, one following the main axis of the mound and the others running off it at right angles. The best examples of this pattern are two long barrows at Avebury, which also lack any burials (Fig. 2.10; Ashbee, Smith and Evans 1979). Had upright stakes been set in the buried soil at Thickthorn Down, it is most unlikely that they could have been seen in excavation. This alternative interpretation is consistent with the excavators' own comment that 'construction proceeded by successive additions . . . from the original turf structure' i.e. the 'mortuary house' (Drew and Piggott 1936, 81). Reinterpretation of that 'mortuary house' as one of a series of infilled bays may explain the absence of human bones. Indeed, their place may have been taken by a series of intentional deposits of pottery and animal bone in the barrow ditch. These have been studied by Julian Thomas (1986), whose analysis of their distribu-

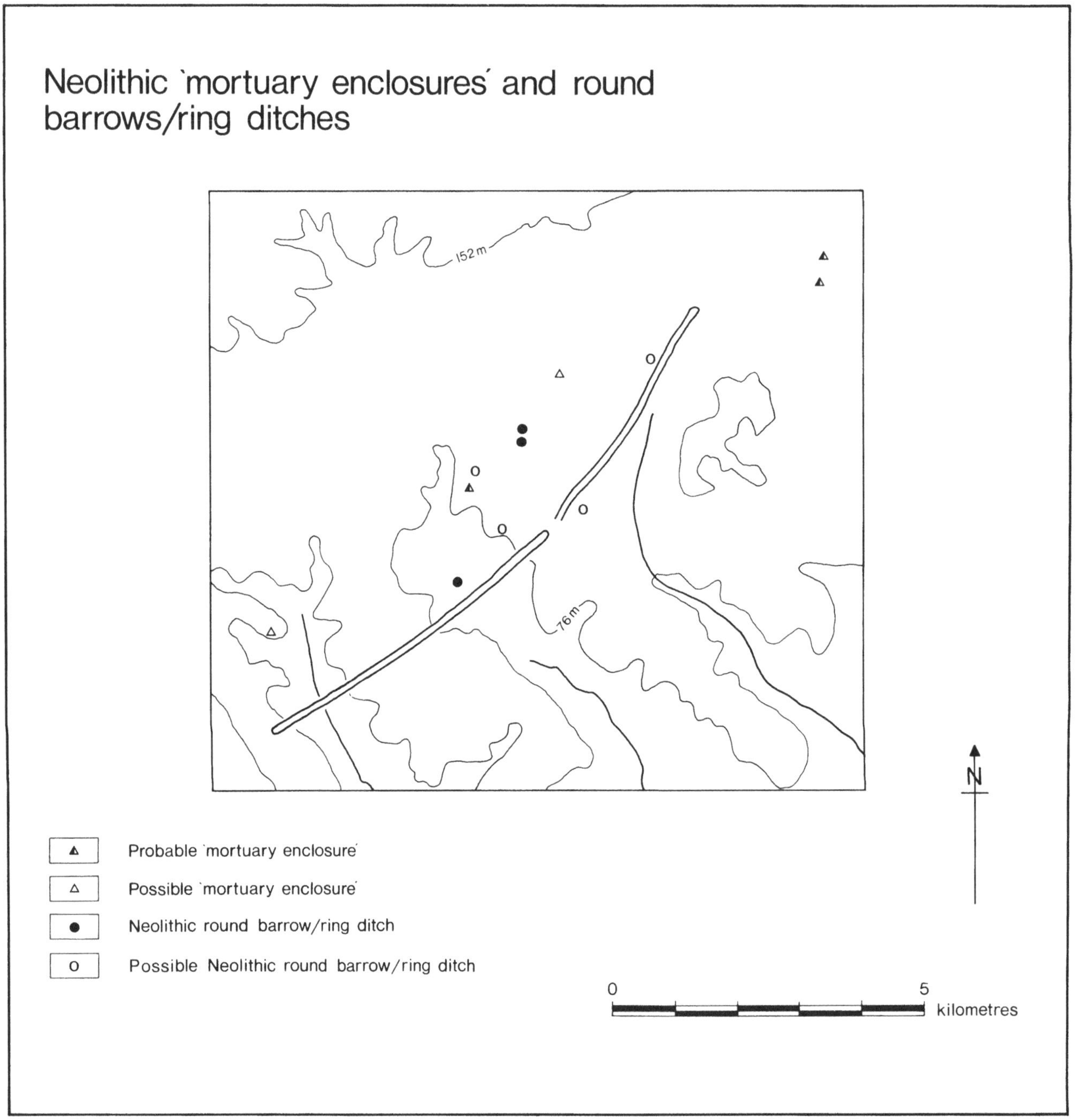

Fig. 2.7 The location of the Dorset Cursus in relation to possible 'mortuary enclosures' and Neolithic round barrows or ring ditches

tion is reproduced in Figure 2.11. This also draws attention to the continued use of the site for intentional deposits in later periods.

The third excavated site, Wor Barrow (Fig. 2.9), has been the subject of considerable discussion since its excavation in 1893, although the discovery of the site notebook in 1971 has provided additional information (*Excavations* IV, 62–133; Bradley 1973). The excavated structures must belong to at least two phases, for the mound covered a smaller post-built enclosure which it sealed entirely. Similarly, the ditch which surrounded this mound had cut through a much smaller feature on the same line. At first it seemed likely that the post trench had defined a free-standing enclosure and that the material excavated from the earlier ditch had been banked against its outer face. This now seems improbable

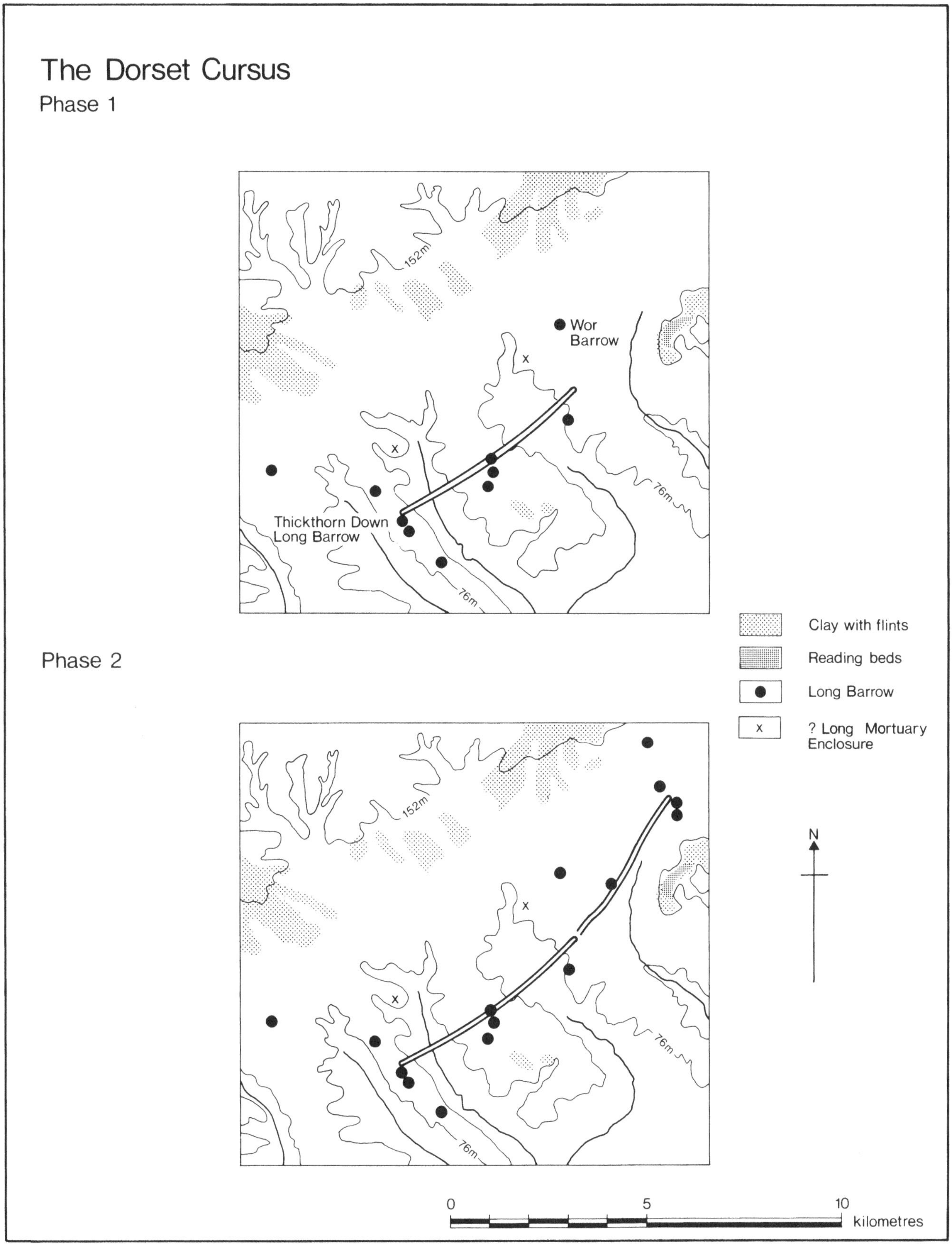

Fig. 2.8 The successive phases in the building of the Dorset Cursus in relation to other monuments of the period

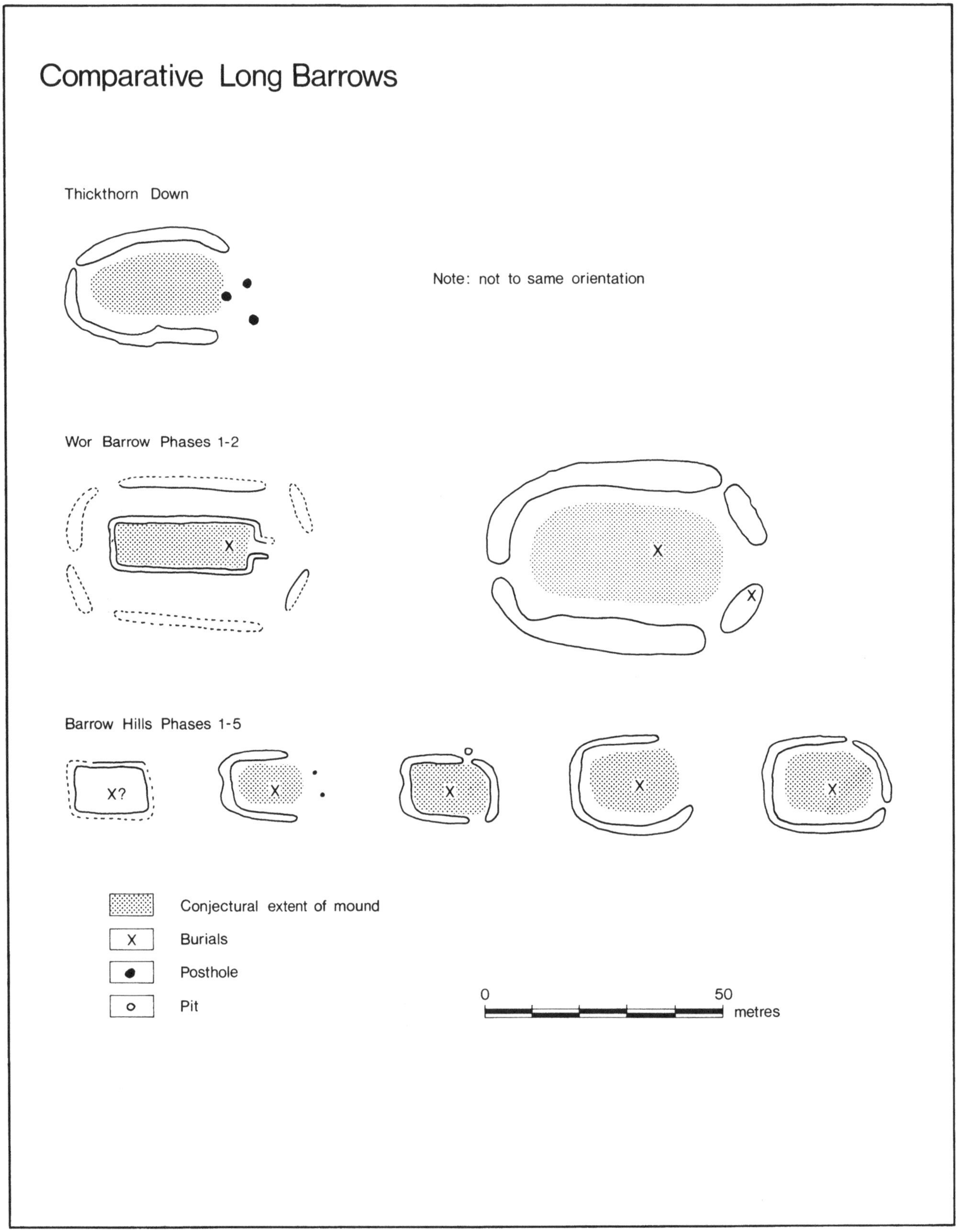

Fig. 2.9 Outline plan of Thickthorn Down long barrow in relation to the likely structural sequence on similar monuments at Wor Barrow and Barrow Hills

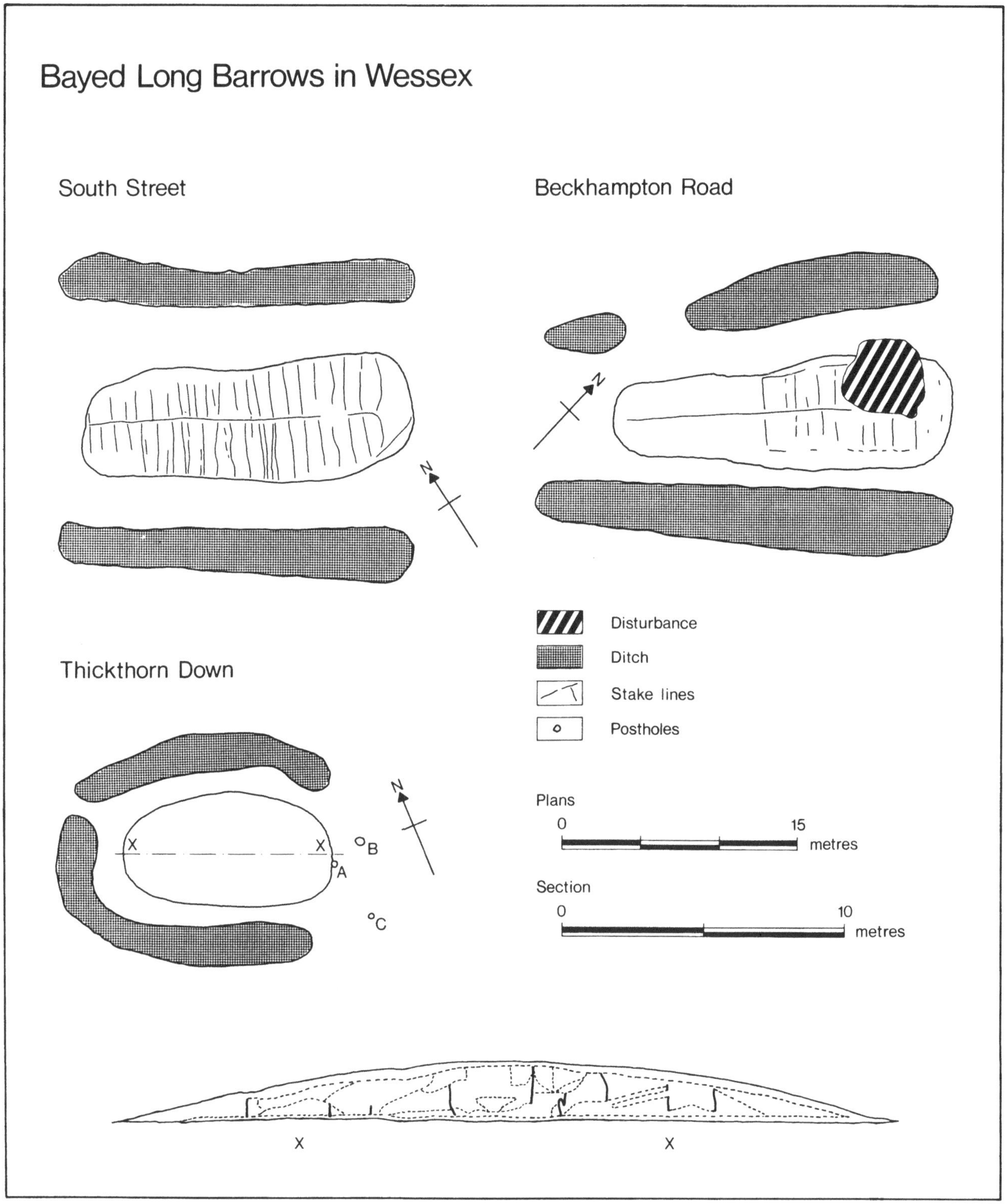

Fig. 2.10 (Above) Outline plans of the excavated long barrows at South Street and Beckhampton Road, showing the construction of the mound in bays (below) outline plan and longitudinal section of Thickthorn Down long barrow. The vertical breaks in the stratigraphy suggest the position of similar divisions.

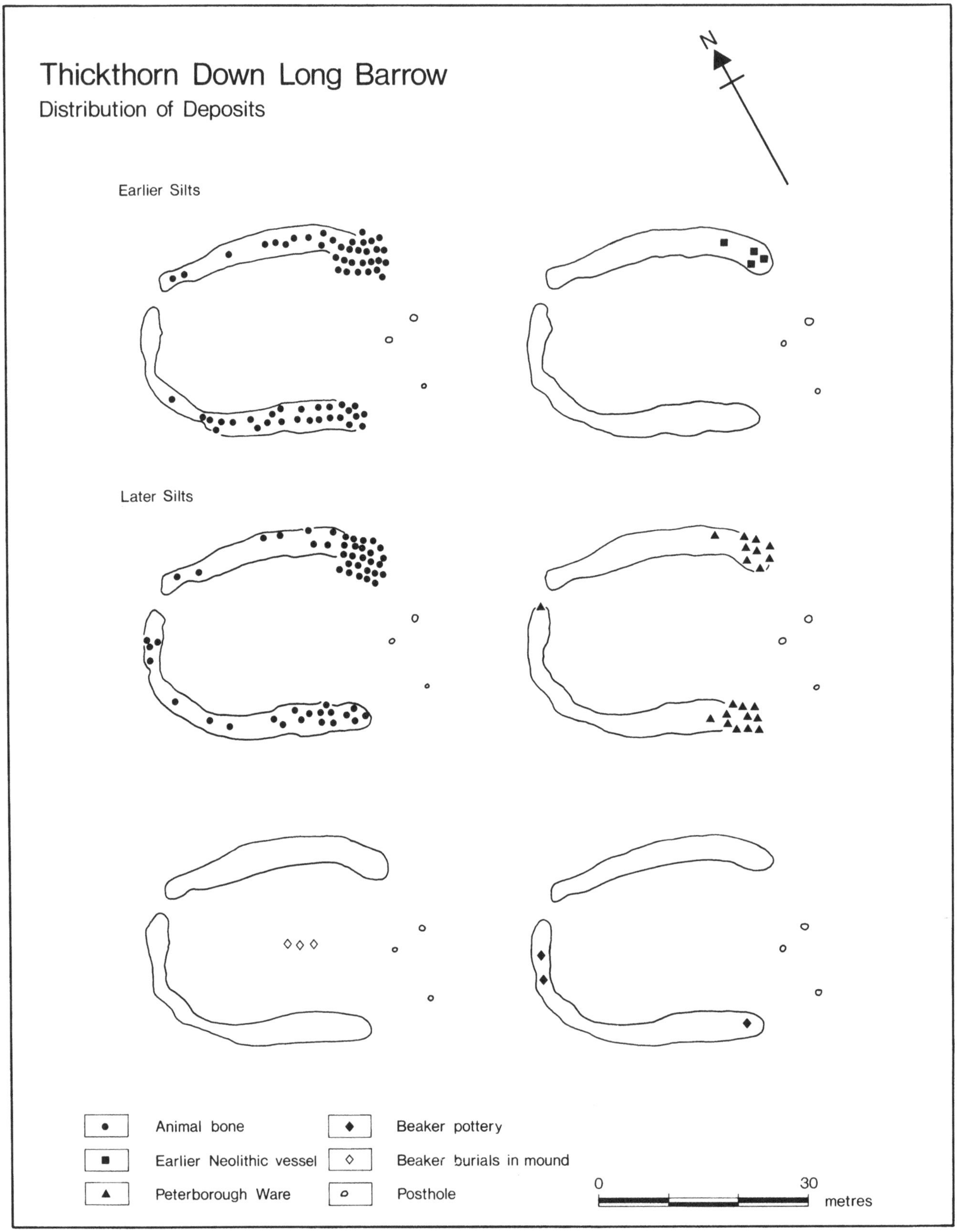

Fig. 2.11 The distribution of deposits of artefacts and animal bones at Thickthorn Down long barrow (from an unpublished analysis by Julian Thomas)

because the excavation notebook shows that this trench was more substantial than was originally supposed. Its excavation could have produced all the spoil required by this interpretation, in which case the first ditch on the site could have provided material for a small mound revetted by the wooden uprights. This early mound seems to be shown in some of the excavation photographs (e.g. Piggott 1954, Pl. 2b), and extrapolation from Pitt Rivers' cross section of the early ditch suggests that it could have provided enough material for a barrow 1.5 m high. In that case the second ditch would have been dug in order to replace the early mound with a more impressive structure. The latter would have covered a larger surface area and would have been at least twice as high as its predecessor (Fig. 2.9).

The early revetment trench had a 'porch' at its south-eastern end, one arm of which was probably missed during Pitt Rivers' excavation. Just inside this feature was the burial area. This seems to have been bracketed by two D-shaped pits. A stone bank was also recorded, flanking the burial deposits. The description of these features recalls the mortuary structures identified by Kinnes (1975). On the old ground surface between these three features were a series of skeletal remains. These were recorded as the disarticulated bones of three males and the articulated skeletons of three others. All the bones were covered by a low mound of soil, but it is not clear whether their deposition was immediately followed by the building of the barrow. We shall return to later developments at Wor Barrow in Chapter 3, but a word is necessary on the dating of the early phases of this site. None of the burials described above was found with any artefacts, but undecorated Neolithic pottery was present in the early layers of the main barrow ditch. An antler pick found on the bottom of this ditch has a radiocarbon date of 2790 ± 130 bc (BM 2284R), whilst another deposited within the primary silts of the same feature has a date of 2710 ± 130 bc (BM 2283R).

The wider relations of all three excavated sites will be considered with the development of the Cursus complex as a whole.

2.5.2ii Structural details of the Dorset Cursus

Little of the Dorset Cursus remains intact and the best-preserved earthwork, its southern terminal on Thickthorn Down, provides a rather misleading impression since it appears to have been built on a more massive scale than the remainder of this monument. A more representative view is provided by an unpublished profile recorded by H. S. Toms south of the Bottlebush terminal before the area came under the plough; the manuscript original is in the Dorset County Museum and was brought to my attention by Jo Draper. This drawing shows a rather unimpressive earthwork, with a ditch 7 m wide and 0.3 m deep and a low bank on the inside (Fig. 2.12). It is not surprising that in Toms' day the earthwork was interpreted as a trackway. Although we now know more about the extent of the Cursus, excavation shows an earthwork of rather modest proportions.

The Cursus has been examined at two points where surface finds were encountered in fieldwalking, one on either side of the source of the River Allen in the early section of the earthwork (Figs. 2.12 and 2.13). These locations were 700 m apart and in both cases the western side of the Cursus was examined in most detail. In spite of the contrasting topography at these points, its ditch took a similar form (Fig. 2.12). It was steep-sided and flat-bottomed, and where it crossed level ground it was 3 m wide at the top and 2 m wide at the bottom and had been dug 1.2 m into the chalk. At the other site, it abutted a Pleistocene river cliff, and was of rather similar proportions. In both cases the primary filling was fairly symmetrical and consisted of loose chalk rubble derived from the faces of the ditch (Fig. 2.13 – 1982 section, 1.10 and 1984 section, 1.5). On each site this was sealed by a denser chalk wash and then by a thin level of partly sorted humus, which may represent the initial stabilisation of the early silts (1982, 1.9 and 1984, 1.4). The later levels of the Cursus will be considered in relation to subsequent settlement in its vicinity, but it is worth noting that they did not show any signs of a collapsed bank. However, in both cases there were indications of where an internal bank had been. In the 1982 excavation there were traces of a protected surface about 3 m wide, located 1 m inside the ditch and standing 0.17 m above the level of the surrounding chalk. This feature was not found in the other excavation, but a decalcified area running parallel to the ditch 4 m inside the Cursus may mark the inner edge of an area protected by the bank; in this case the existence of a former river cliff just beyond the Cursus means that none of the spoil could have been placed outside the ditch. It is clear that the protected surface was so narrow and so near to the ditch that the bank must have been revetted.

Less can be said about the eastern ditch, which was sectioned at only one location. Its excavation had been discontinued at a depth of 0.84 m, perhaps because the natural chalk was unusually hard. This ditch may have filled in quite rapidly, and had been recut twice, at least one of the later cuts terminating at a causeway (Fig. 2.12). The innermost cut, which was one of the deepest, had an asymmetrical primary filling, perhaps including material from an internal bank. The earthwork had been

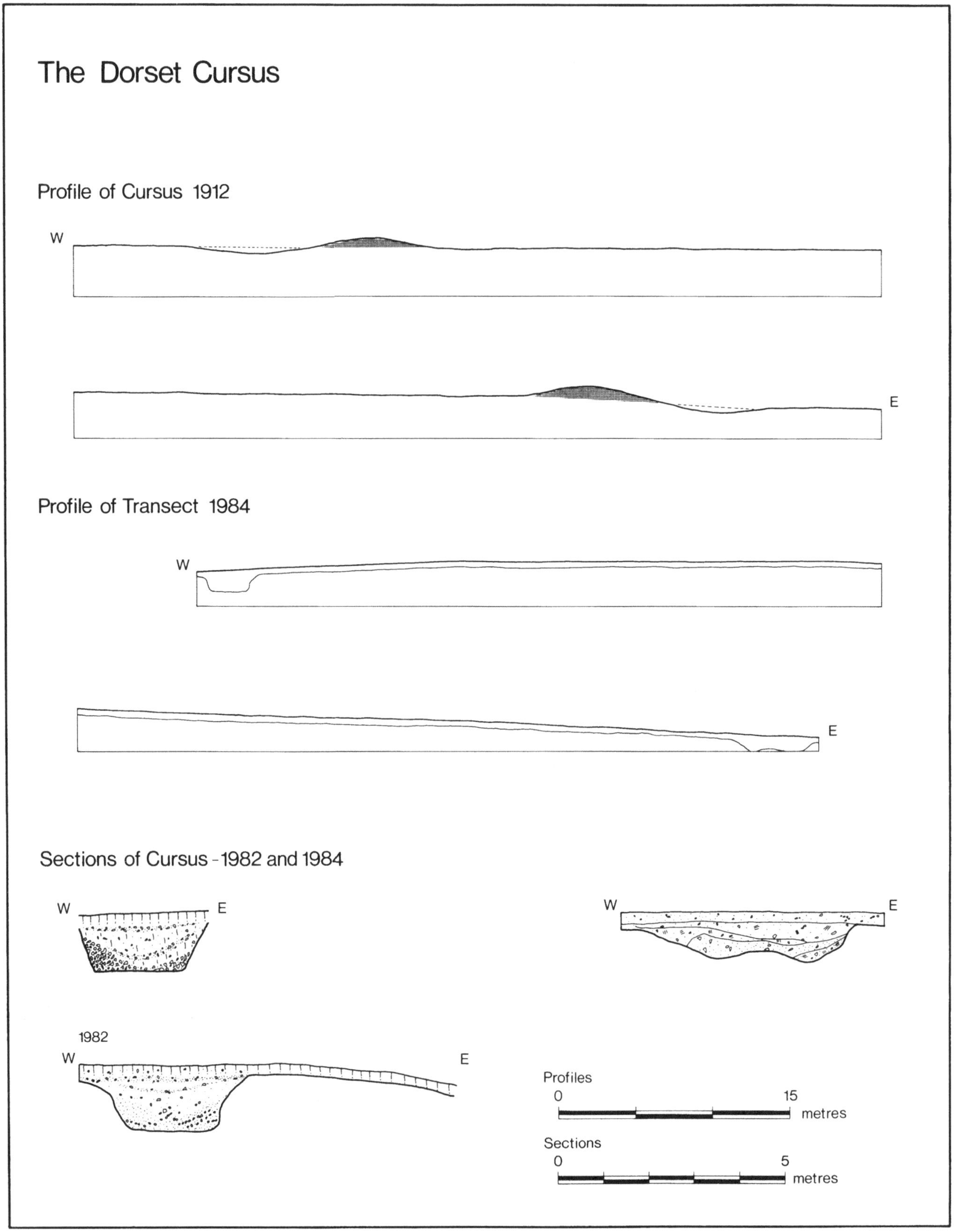

Fig. 2.12 (Upper) The profile of the Dorset Cursus on Bottlebush Down before it came under the plough (from an unpublished drawing by Herbert Toms in Dorset County Museum) (centre) the profile of the Dorset Cursus on its excavation in 1984 (lower) outline sections of the Cursus ditches in the 1982 and 1984 excavations

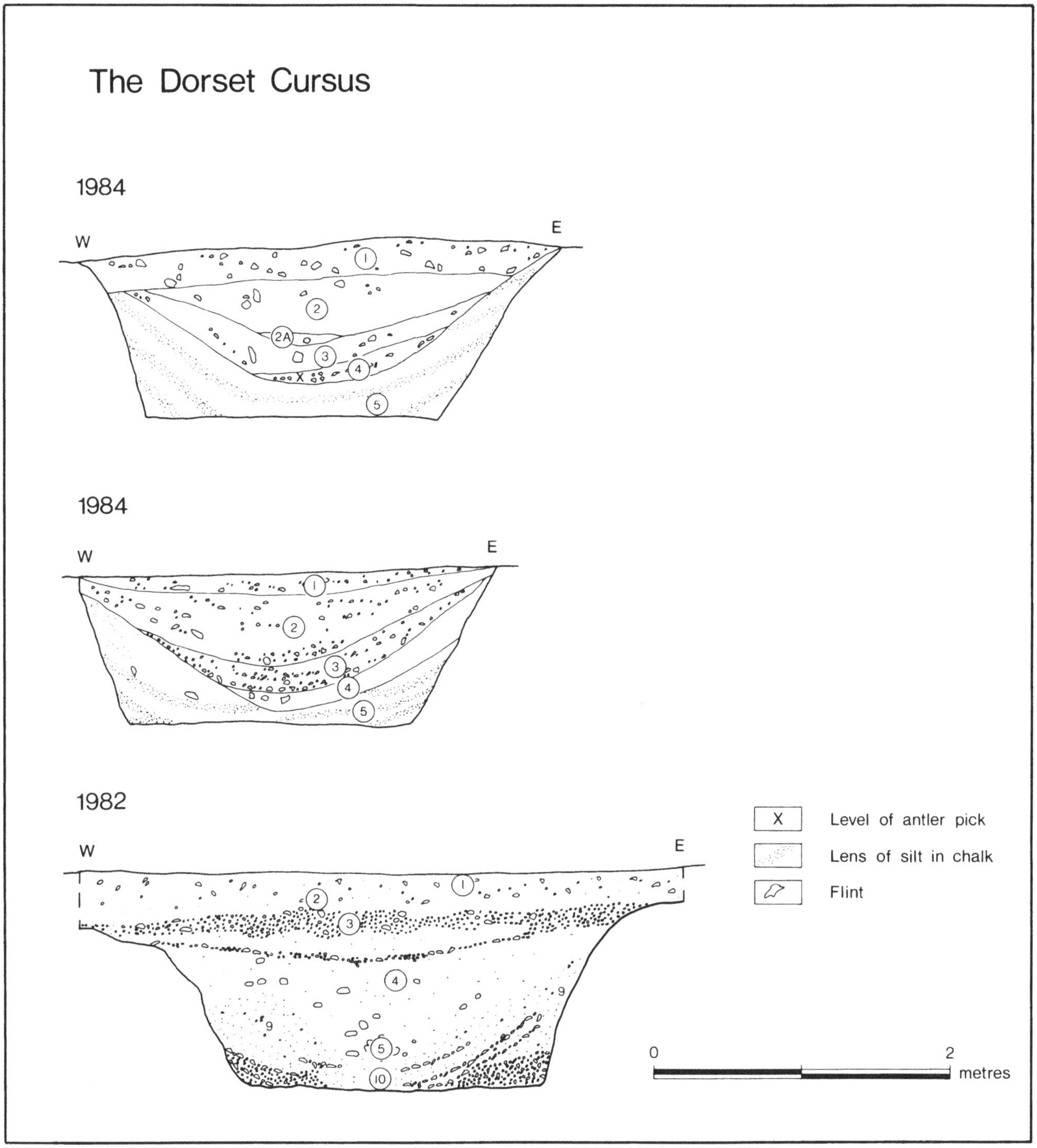

Fig. 2.13 Detailed sections of the Cursus ditches in the 1982 and 1984 excavations

severely truncated during Early Iron Age ploughing, but as it was following a break of slope it would have appeared more prominent than was actually the case.

It is worth considering the original appearance of this monument and the amount of human effort devoted to its building. The following discussion of these questions is contributed by Bill Startin:

We can assume that the original cross-section of the ditch corresponded to a trapezoid 3 m wide at the top, 2 m wide at the bottom and 1.4 m deep (allowing for the loss of about 0.20 m of chalk through ploughing). Thus the cross-sectional area of the ditch was 3.5 m^2. It is normal to allow an expansion factor of 1.45 for quarried chalk and an angle of rest of 35 degrees. Thus the cross-sectional area of bank upon construction would have been 5.01 m^2. Assuming that its cross-section resembled an isosceles triangle with a basal angle of 35 degrees, a simple dump rampart would have been 1.7 m high and 5.95 m wide at the base. Since there is evidence that the bank had been only 3 m wide, we must assume that originally it had been revetted. A revetment on only one side would have produced a bank with a basal width of 4.2 m and a height of 2.4 m. Again this seems to be too wide. A fully revetted bank 3 m wide at the base would have been 1.7 m high, whilst a partly revetted bank would have had to be supported to a height of 1.26 m and would have been 2.12 m high.

The full length of the Cursus, including the terminals, would require the excavation of about 232,000 m^3 of chalk. This figure is based on the west ditch of the Cursus and ignores the shallower section of its east ditch recorded in 1984 and the greater scale of the southern terminal.

We can estimate that, using prehistoric tools, a picker and shoveller can excavate 1.67 m^3 of chalk per hour (Startin and Bradley 1981; Startin 1982). Merely to dump the spoil created by this team need not involve more than one basketer; indeed, for much of the time the shoveller could have thrown the spoil into place. The estimate for the entire monument therefore assumes a team of three. On that basis the construction of the ditch and bank would have taken 416,766 worker-hours.

Experiments carried out by Erasmus (1965) demonstrated that one person could shift about 1.48 m^3 per hour over a distance of 50 m. In the calculation made earlier the basketer would have been left idle for part of the time. Seven metres of drystone wall, roughly 2 m high and 0.4 m wide, can be constructed by one person in a day. One picker and one shoveller could have produced enough spoil for about 1.5 m of bank in the same time. If the bank was partially revetted using quarried chalk blocks, the basketer could spend perhaps a quarter of his or her time building the revetment. If so, there is no need for a basic team of more than three people, although we do not know how many teams of this size were working at the same time.

In conclusion, we can estimate the total investment of labour at roughly 450,000 worker hours, of which about 250,000 would have been involved in building the original length of the Cursus from Thickthorn Down to Bottlebush Down. We should stress that these are minimum figures, however, and turf revetment of the bank would require more labour – perhaps a team of five rather than three, since the turf has to be cut as an additional exercise.

The *chronology* of the Cursus complex will be pursued in a later section but we must refer to the dating evidence from these two excavations. Work in 1982 produced one sherd in an Earlier Neolithic fabric from the primary silt of the west Cursus ditch (Fig. 2.13 – 1982 section, 1.10) and further pieces, attributed to another two vessels of similar date, from a lens of humus on the surface of this deposit (1.9). It could also be shown that the ditch had filled completely before a Beaker settlement was established just outside the earthwork. Pits belonging to that settlement have given radiocarbon dates of 1920 ± 50 bc and 1950 ± 120 bc (BM 2325 and 2191R). Excavation of the same ditch 700 m further to the north-east was still more informative (Fig. 2.13). The early layers of the ditch contained a small quantity of knapping debris, but after the secondary silts had started to form, the interior of the Cursus was occupied by a settlement associated with Mortlake and Fengate Wares; sherds in both these styles were found in the upper part of the ditch filling. (A full account of this material appears in the following chapter.) The east ditch was less informative but had been refilled before a barbed and tanged arrowhead was deposited. More important is a series of radiocarbon dates obtained on samples from the west Cursus ditch. Five were accelerator dates on small fragments of cattle bone, whilst the sixth was on an antler pick found on the partially stabilised surface of the primary silts. Two samples were apparently of residual material, perhaps originating during Late Mesolithic occupation of the nearby valley floor. These provided dates of 4510 ± 140 bc and 4950 ± 100 bc for bones from the primary silts and from the partly stabilised surface of this layer respectively (OxA 628 and 627 – Fig. 2.13, 1984 section, ls. 5 and 4). The antler pick from the latter context gave a date of 2540 ± 60 bc (BM 2438). Two further pieces of animal bone from the lower part of the secondary silts (1984, 1.3) gave dates with a weighted mean of 2625 ± 77 bc (OxA 625 and 626) and a final sample from the middle of this layer was dated to 2620 ± 120 bc (OxA 624). This evidence is entirely consistent with the ceramics from these excavations.

We must now consider how this monument was built. It is often supposed that it represents a major achievement of prehistoric surveying, but there is little to support this view. Despite its extraordinary length, the Cursus need not have been built in a particularly open landscape. There is evidence of open grassland from Thickthorn Down long barrow (Bradley and Entwistle 1985), but neither of the excavated sections of the Cursus was built in a similar environment, and in one case it appears to have run through an area of closed woodland. Atkinson's study suggested that only one of its ditches maintained a precise alignment, whilst the other was laid out by offsets (1955, 9). There is evidence of this arrangement at a number of points, although on either side of the Allen Valley the roles of the two ditches seem to have been reversed. This may be reflected by their contrasting character on excavation. The same interpretation is supported by air photographs, which show that at one point the east ditch of the Cursus was dug continuously whilst its west ditch ran in a series of slight arcs, separated by wide causeways. At this point the main earthwork seems to have replaced a slighter ditch on the same line; this can be observed again about a kilometre north of the Bottlebush terminal.

The earthwork follows a rather irregular course. This is emphasised in Figure 2.14, which combines the ground plan of the monument with its longitudinal profile. It is clear that the changes of course observed during survey are all located at breaks in the surface topography and reflect the difficulty of establishing long alignments in such a dissected landscape. The one apparent exception is a curious 'dogleg' where the earlier section of the Cursus crosses Gussage Cow Down. Here the earthwork changes course twice within 230 m, as if to link together two longer alignments. This might suggest that this was the junction between two separate monuments built end to end, but close study of these alignments on the ground favours an alternative view: the length of Cursus running south from the Bottlebush terminal was aligned exactly on a long barrow on the crest of Gussage Cow Down, but seems to have drifted off course in the lee of the hill *where that landmark could not be observed* – the change of direction was needed to enclose the barrow within the monument. Its importance as a skyline feature is emphasised by the positioning of the Bottlebush terminal *below* the crest of the hill; it seems to have been located on rather lower ground so that the barrow would appear on the horizon.

There is a certain symmetry in the layout of the Cursus, particularly in its first phase. The long barrow on Gussage Cow Down occupies a prominent location towards the midpoint of this earthwork and is visible from both terminals, even though those terminals cannot be seen from one another. At the same time, the monument runs through a wide tract of lower ground and would not be visible from far away. It would provide an unsuitable setting for processions as it crosses two small rivers, but like the cursuses at Rudston in Yorkshire (Kinnes 1984), the layout of the monument does emphasise the visual effect felt by those *inside* it. The northern length of the Dorset Cursus, which runs between Bottlebush Down and Martin Down, has features in common with this layout. The Martin Down terminal is not sited at a particularly prominent location and would not have been visible from any distance outside the monument. At the same time, like the Bottlebush terminal, it would have allowed spectators to view a considerable *length* of the monument. In doing so they could also have seen some of the long barrows which cluster around it. It is to the relationship between these two types of monument that we turn next.

2.5.2.iii The relationship of the long barrows to the Cursus

We have stressed the close relationship between the Dorset Cursus and the nearby long barrows: now we must consider this question in detail. We shall start by examining the placing of the entire system of long barrows in relation to the Cursus and then analyse the spatial and chronological relationship between this monument and individual mounds. This should also allow us to discuss the development of the Cursus complex as a whole.

We have already commented on the way in which the longest mounds in Cranborne Chase lie at either end of the distribution of the shorter barrows. The Dorset Cursus fits neatly into that pattern. Its northern terminal at Martin Down is emphasised by one of the longest mounds, and another mound of unusual length is located quite close to its southern limit. The three remaining mounds of unusual length are found some way beyond either end of the Cursus.

At a rather more detailed level we can consider the relationship of individual mounds to the position of the Cursus. Figure 2.15 plots the lengths of all the barrows, together with their distance from this monument. This diagram highlights the distinctive mounds with a ditch around one or both ends and also shows which barrows seem to be directly related to the Cursus. This analysis reveals that most of the Cranborne Chase long barrows were built within 2.5 km of the Cursus, with a second, less coherent group of mounds between 5 and 7.5 km away. The barrows near to the monument include a higher proportion of U-ditched and completely ditched mounds than the rest of Cranborne Chase (33 per cent compared with 15 per cent). The barrows which share this feature are among the smaller examples in this region. Moreover, whilst 33 per cent of the long barrows within 2.5 km of the Cursus had U ditches or encircling ditches, 43 per cent of those linked more directly to the monument possessed this distinctive ground plan.

Having considered the patterning visible at this scale,

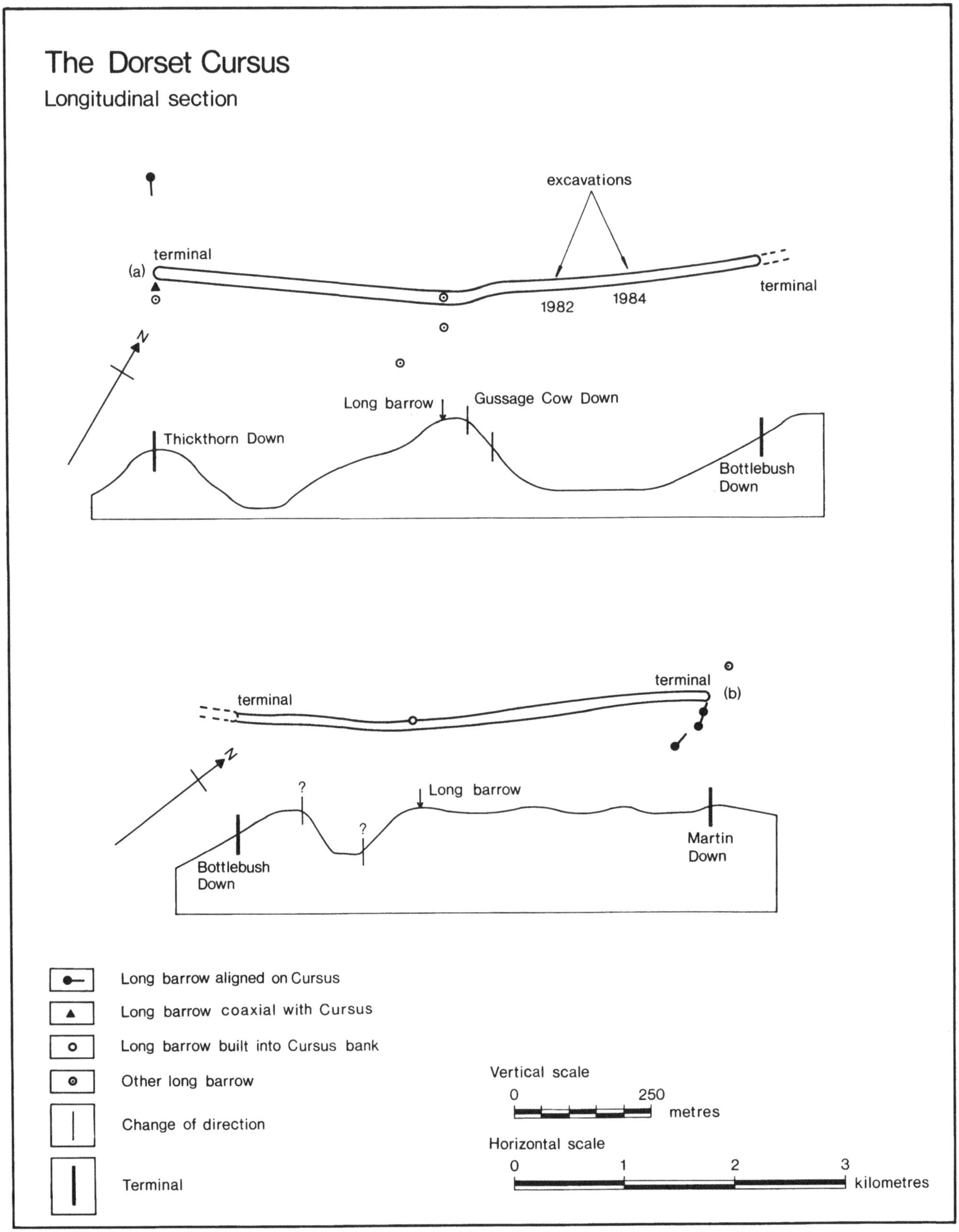

Fig. 2.14 Outline plan of the Dorset Cursus in relation to the axis of nearby long barrows. Its layout is compared with a longitudinal profile of the monument drawn at an exaggerated vertical scale, stressing how frequently it alters course when it crosses breaks of slope

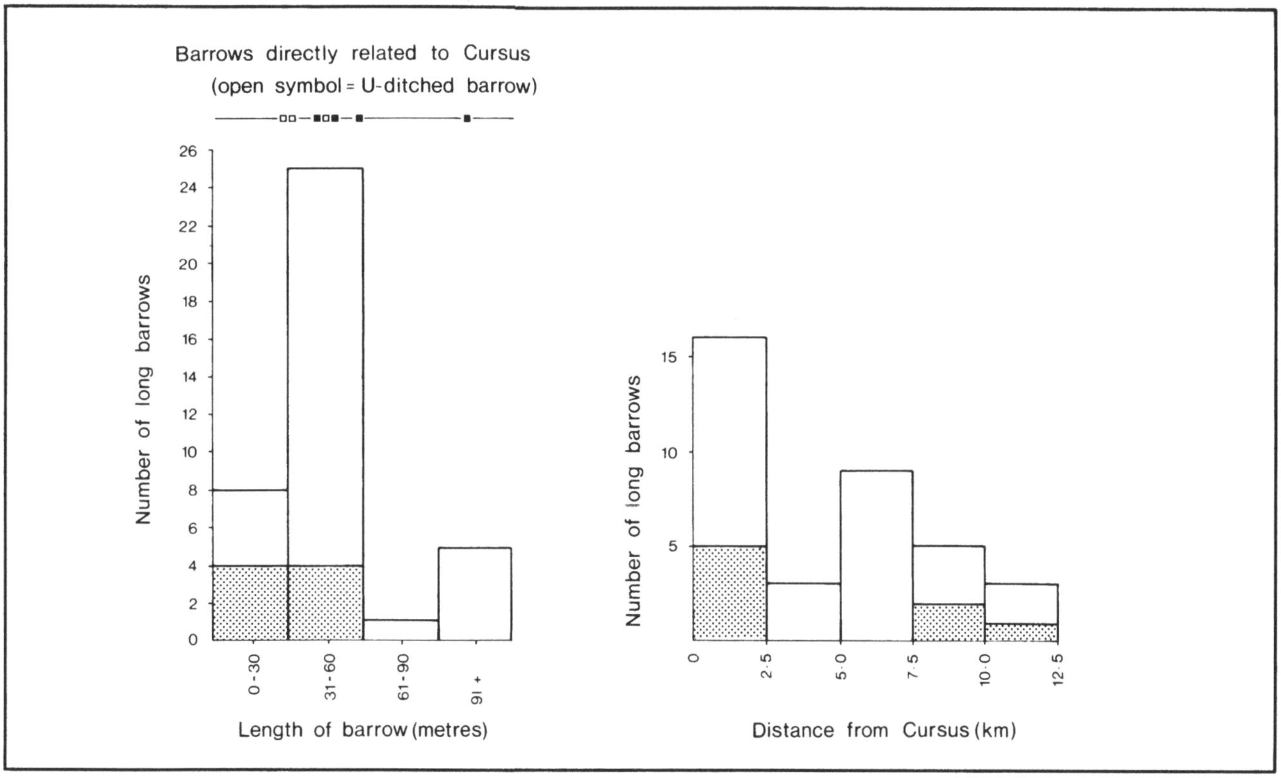

Fig. 2.15 (Left) The lengths of the long barrows in the Cranborne Chase group. The lengths of U-ditched or completely enclosed barrows are shaded. The diagram also distinguishes the lengths of those barrows in direct relationship to the Dorset Cursus (right) the frequency of long barrows in the Cranborne Chase group in relation to their distance from the Cursus. Again U-ditched and completely enclosed barrows are shaded

we must focus on the barrows nearest to the Cursus (Fig. 2.16). We can identify a number of characteristic relationships between these two types of monument: in order of descending reliability, they can be described as incorporation, alignment and imitation.

There are two cases in which the Cursus takes in the position of an existing long barrow. The best known is Pentridge 19, whose mound was incorporated into the west bank of the Cursus, but the sequence of events is far from straightforward. The mound departs from the usual alignment of long barrows in this area and is on a slightly different axis from the Cursus itself; for that reason it cannot have established the alignment of the latter monument. Nor does it seem likely that the barrow was built in anticipation of the Cursus as it does not command a sufficiently extensive view of that earthwork. Since it appears that the west ditch of the Cursus might have replaced a slighter feature on the same line, it is possible that this barrow was built *alongside* an early phase of the Cursus and only incorporated in its bank when that earthwork was enlarged.

The second case of incorporation has been discussed already. This concerns the prominent long barrow inside the Cursus on Gussage Cow Down. We cannot be certain that the length of earthwork running north from Thickthorn Down was also aligned on this long barrow, but I have already argued that the corresponding section proceeding south from Bottlebush Down was intended to incorporate this feature. This may be why the builders corrected the line of the earthwork where it drifted off course in the lee of the hill, and may also explain the positioning of the Bottlebush terminal where the long barrow could be seen on the skyline. The reasons for this arrangement will be considered later in this chapter.

Questions of alignment are less easy to establish and the reader must judge whether chance plays a part. The line of the Cursus may either have been established between a series of existing long barrows, or some of the barrows themselves may have been aligned on prominent features of the Cursus. Where both earthworks share the same axis no sequence can be established, but where one appears to be aligned directly on the other, either the relationship is fortuitous or an obvious sequence is involved. Apart from the cases mentioned earlier, there is only one instance in which the Cursus appears to have been aligned on an earlier barrow. This

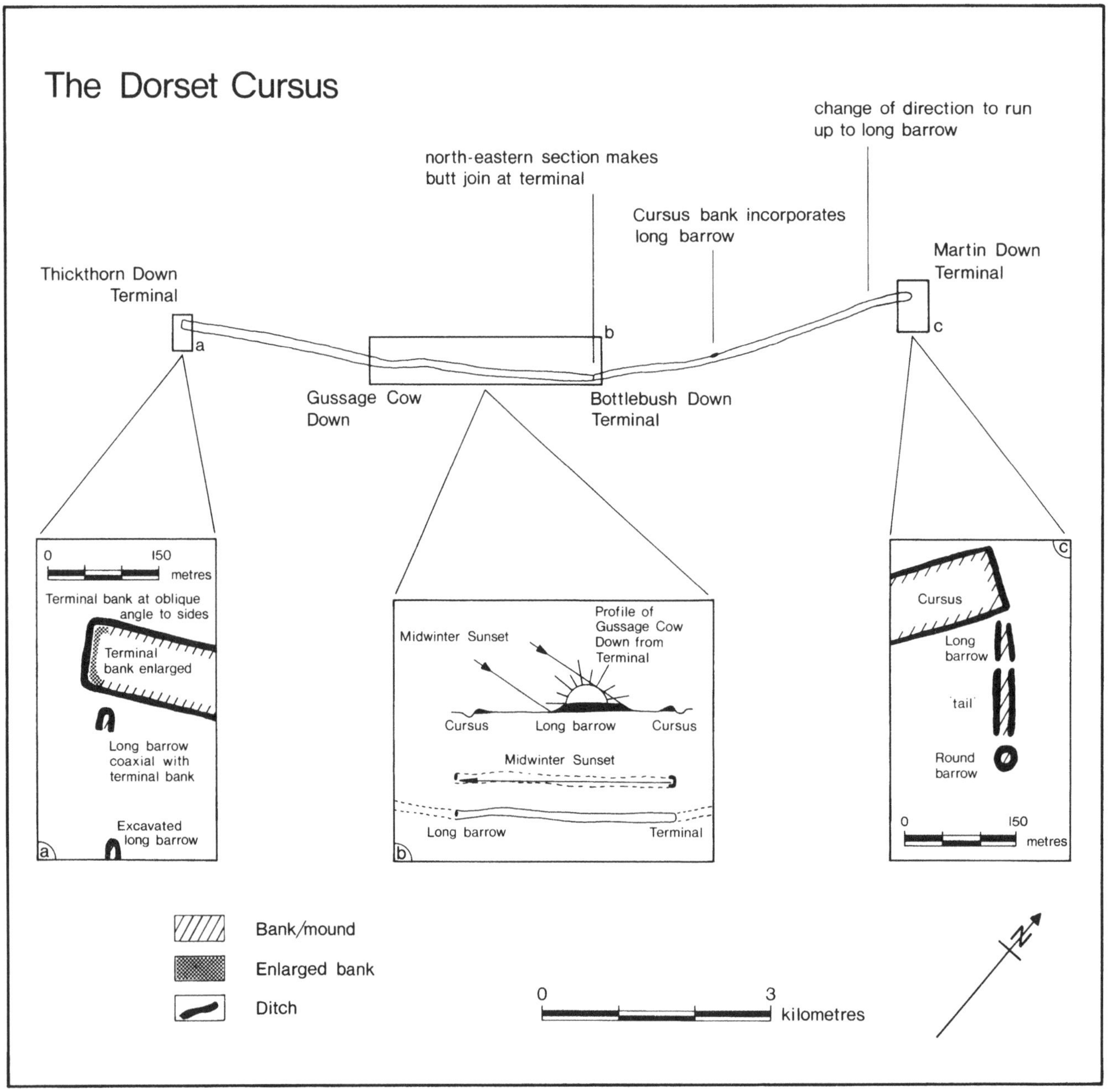

Fig. 2.16 (Upper) Outline plan of the Dorset Cursus illustrating the principal relationships with other monuments discussed in the text (lower) insets illustrating the three key relationships and the axis of the midwinter sunset

happens about 600 m short of the Martin Down terminal, where the earthwork changes direction by about 7° so that it ends alongside a conspicuous mound (Fig. 2.16). I owe this observation to Roy Loveday.

Other relationships seem to be less complicated. In two cases we find long barrows which share the same axis as parts of the Cursus. This applies to one of the two long barrows beside the Thickthorn terminal, and to a second long barrow on Gussage Cow Down, which shares the same axis as the barrow discussed already. There may be some evidence of sequence at Thickthorn Down, where the nearest long barrow shares the same axis as the southern terminal of the Cursus. The latter is rather unusual in lacking the squared-off end normal on this type of monument. Instead the end bank of the Cursus runs at an oblique angle to the sides, and since this is not demanded by the topography it may be a deliberate design feature, intended to link the southern end of the Cursus to the axis of an existing monument (Fig. 2.16).

In three other cases long barrows point straight at the ends of the Cursus. In the circumstances we must either dismiss these alignments as fortuitous, or accept that those long barrows postdate elements of the Cursus (Figs. 2.14 and 2.16). All three examples concern the northern and southern terminals of the completed monument, and if we accept them as deliberate they should bracket the period of its construction.

A more complicated problem is encountered at the northern end of the Cursus on Martin Down. We have suggested that the line of the Cursus was altered so that it ran up to an existing long barrow. That barrow now appears to point at the terminal of the Cursus, which is only about ten metres away. At the same time this mound is sometimes claimed to be one of a pair built end to end – Pentridge 2a and b. This curious arrangement has led to considerable discussion: do the two mounds represent one massive linear monument – a bank barrow – or were they really two quite separate features (see Ashbee 1984, 15)? Recent fieldwork, combined with analysis of air photographs taken before and after the area came under the plough, shows clearly that the more westerly mound was a classic long barrow with its higher, broader end to the east. This abutted the Cursus. Its ditches were not continuous with those of its neighbour, which shows no gradation of height or width and appears to be a bank or 'tail' *added* to this mound (Fig. 2.16). Such an arrangement is known elsewhere, but in other cases in which a long barrow had been extended the addition was made at the distal end and not where any burials would occur – in this case the tail has been added to the 'wrong' end of the mound. Since the terminal of the Cursus blocks expansion in the expected direction, it seems likely that the long barrow was embellished after the Cursus was in place. This sequence implies that a typical long barrow, probably predating the Cursus, was turned into a bank barrow after the latter earthwork had been completed (cf. Bradley 1983b).

The other relationship between the long barrows and the Cursus is imitation. Here we must return to the terminal on Thickthorn Down. The bank which closes off the Cursus seems to have been built on a disproportionately large scale, compared with the sides of this monument. At the same time, we have seen how it shares the same general alignment as two U-ditched long barrows. Its unusual size would be explained if the terminal had been intended to imitate their characteristic appearance. A similar arrangement has been recognised on two other sites. Amesbury 42 long barrow seems to have been built as a monumental backdrop to the east terminal of the Stonehenge Cursus (Richards 1984, 182), whilst the western end of that monument had also been built on a disproportionate scale (Christie 1963). Similarly, the southern terminal of Cursus A at Rudston was so massive that it was excavated by Canon Greenwell under the impression that it was a long barrow. Indeed, he even found human remains of uncertain date within it (Greenwell 1877, 253–7).

These detailed observations may appear tedious but all have implications for our understanding of the chronology and function of the Cursus complex. Few of these relationships can be tested by excavation or even by radiocarbon dating: the case for a close connection between these elements must stand or fall on the sheer number of links which have been suggested between the barrows and the Cursus. These involve no fewer than half the long barrows within a kilometre of that monument. In some cases more than one link can be suggested between these different types of earthwork; in fact our discussion has considered no fewer than ten possible connections between these features. It seems reasonable to insist that this is more than a coincidence.

2.5.2.iv *The date of the Dorset Cursus complex*

It follows from these arguments that the Cursus must have been completed within the lifespan of non-megalithic long barrows and perhaps whilst bank barrows were also in use. We must also accept that at least three of the long barrows were established before parts of the Cursus had been built. We shall consider the absolute dating evidence for these elements, before turning briefly to comparative material from neighbouring areas of southern Britain.

First, a *terminus ante quem* for two of the long barrows and for two points on the earlier section of the Cursus is provided by the occurrence of Peterborough Ware and Beaker pottery in secondary positions on these monuments. This applies to the long mounds at Wor Barrow and Thickthorn Down and to the west ditch of the Cursus. At the same time, all three contained undecorated Neolithic pottery in primary contexts. The same general date is suggested by the finds of leaf-shaped arrowheads from early levels at Thickthorn Down and at Wor Barrow.

Secondly, nine radiocarbon dates are available from the study area, in addition to the important series from Hambledon Hill. With two exceptions, which seem to be of Later Mesolithic date, those from the Cursus itself agree in setting its construction, or more exactly the end of its active maintenance, at around 2600 bc. Although the best dating evidence comes from the surface of the primary silts, molluscan analysis suggests that they had formed extremely rapidly. The dates from Wor Barrow are not much earlier, with the crucial radiocarbon determination of 2790 ± 130 bc on an antler from the bottom of the ditch (BM 2284R). This is important for the dating of the Cursus since the barrow is almost opposite the original northern end of this monument. The position of Wor Barrow may have influenced the builders of the Cursus, but the mound would have been inaccessible *after* that earthwork was extended. Thus the date for the long barrow also provides a *terminus post quem* for the completion of the Cursus.

Other long barrows in Cranborne Chase may belong to the same general period, and Mercer argues that the example at Hambledon Hill was used at the same time as the adjacent causewayed enclosure (1980, 42–4). Although the barrow itself has not been dated, radiocarbon dates for the enclosure extend from 2890 ± 150 bc (Har 1886) to 2530 ± 130 bc (Har 1885).

So far the evidence seems to be consistent, but the date obtained from antler found under Thickthorn Down long barrow is significantly earlier than the rest: 3210 ± 45 bc (BM 2355). There may not be a problem in accepting this date for the long barrow as it is not related directly to the Cursus. On the other hand, long barrows of similar form in southern England produce significantly later dates (see below). There is a possibility of contamination here, since it was discovered during processing of the samples that the material from Thickthorn Down had been impregnated with PVA. It is believed that this has been removed successfully, but if any of this material had remained its effect would be to increase the apparent age of the sample (Janet Ambers pers. comm.). It is impossible to resolve the problem on the available evidence.

There are problems in comparing the dates from the study area with those from other regions, since different local sequences may not have been precisely equivalent. On the other hand, some of the structural details of the long barrows are so similar that it would be unnecessarily restrictive to ignore this evidence entirely. There are very few dates from cursus monuments in other areas, but almost all of these fall in the first half of the third millennium bc (Bradley 1987b). In particular the primary level of the Lesser Cursus near Stonehenge has dates of 2600 ± 120 bc and 2690 ± 100 bc (OxA 1404 and 1405 – Julian Richards pers. comm.), and a similar context in the Dorchester on Thames cursus has a date of 2560 ± 100 bc (BM 2443 – Bradley and Chambers 1988); an antler from a less satisfactory context in the ditch of the Stonehenge Cursus (Stone 1947) is dated to 2150 ± 90 bc (OxA 1403 – Julian Richards pers. comm.) The two dates currently available from bank barrows are of a similar order of magnitude: 2790 ± 100 bc from Maiden Castle (BM 2456 – Niall Sharples pers. comm.) and 2722 ± 49 bc from North Stoke (BM 1405 – Case 1982).

This is not the occasion to engage in elaborate discussion of the chronology of long barrows in other areas. Our best course may be to highlight the most striking features of the monuments in our study area and to consider the available dates for sites with similar characteristics (Table 2.4). All of these features have been discussed on other occasions, and some authorities already consider them to be characteristic of later long barrows (see Thorpe 1984).

We should consider five such features. The most striking is the characteristic ground plan of Ashbee's 'Cranborne Chase' type long barrows, which they share with a number of freestanding enclosures found near to the Cursus. This arrangement is also found at eight or nine sites in central-southern England with reasonable dating evidence. In particular, different constructional phases at Barrow Hills in Oxfordshire strongly resemble the sequence suggested at Wor Barrow (Fig. 2.9; Bradley 1986). The monument at Barrow Hills also shares its ground plan with Thickthorn Down long barrow (Fig. 2.9), and both sites contain a series of distinctive deposits in the ditch (Fig. 2.11). Those at Barrow Hills match the deposits in an adjacent causewayed enclosure in a way that recalls the evidence from Hambledon Hill (*ibid.*) With the sole exception of the sample from Thickthorn Down, the available dates extend from 2850 ± 80 bc at Winnall Down in Hampshire (Har 2196 – Fasham 1982, 19–24) to 2550 ± 60 bc at Barrow Hills (BM 2392).

The second feature is the absence of burials or mortuary structures on thoroughly investigated sites. This is a notable feature of Thickthorn Down, but is also found at both long barrows at Avebury with which it shares its distinctive construction (Ashbee, Smith and Evans 1979, 228–46 and 250–67). Their dates run from 2750 ± 135 bc (BM 357) to 2517 ± 90 bc (BM 506b). This is also consistent with the age of an imported flint axe from Julliberries Grave in Kent, another site without any human remains (Jessup 1939).

By contrast, it seems that the long barrow at Hambledon Hill contained the remains of only one individual. There is no direct dating for this monument, but the long barrow seems to have been used at the same time as the adjacent enclosure; the mound at Barrow Hills, which accompanies another causewayed enclosure, has a date of 2550 ± 60 bc from an early phase (Bradley 1986). Again a long barrow with a single burial at Alfriston is dated to 2360 ± 110 bc (Har 940 – Drewett 1975).

In the study area the two sites with burials seem to

Table 2.4. *The dating evidence for long barrows in Cranborne Chase and for sites with similar characteristics elsewhere in southern England*

Site	'U' ditch or encircling ditch	No burial	One burial	Burials all or mainly male	Burials all or some articulated	Dating evidence
Cranborne Chase						
Wor Barrow	X			X	X	2790 ± 70 bc (BM 2284R)
Thickthorn Down	X	X				After 3210 ± 45 bc (BM 2355)
Hambledon Hill			X?	X	unknown	Ditch sequence matches that of adjacent enclosure with its dates of 2890 ± 150 bc to 2530 ± 130 bc (HAR 1886 and 1885)
Wessex Sites						
Wayland's Smithy 1					X	Before 2820 ± 130 bc (I 2328)
North Stoke (enclosure)	X					Before 2722 ± 49 bc (BM 1450)
Winnall Down	X					2850 ± 80 bc; 2730 ± 90 bc; 2700 ± 110 bc (HAR 2196; 2201; and 2202)
South Street		X				2750 ± 135 bc; 2670 ± 90 bc; 2580 ± 110 bc (BM 357; 358a; and 358b)
Normanton Down (enclosure)	X					2560 ± 150 bc (BM 505)
Nutbane				X	X	Before 2730 ± 150 bc (BM 49)
Beckhampton Road		X				2517 ± 90 bc (BM 506b)
Other published sites						
North Marden	X	X?				2760 ± 110 bc (HAR 5544)
Barrow Hills	X				X	2550 ± 60 bc (BM 2392) Belt slider, polished knife and probably arrowhead in grave
Aldwincle	?			X	X	Before 2610 ± 70 bc (HAR 1411)
Alfriston			X		X	2360 ± 110 bc (HAR 940)
Whiteleaf Barrow	X		X	X		Ebbsfleet Ware
Julliberries Grave	X	X				Scandinavian flint axe – early to mid third millennium bc

have produced only males, although we should be cautious of early identifications. This feature is repeated at three well-dated sites in southern England. One of these, Whiteleaf Barrow, was associated with Ebbsfleet Ware, which probably emerged by about 2700 bc (Childe and Smith 1954); the other two sites have only a *terminus ante quem*: 2730 ± 150 bc for Nutbane (BM 49 – Morgan 1959) and 2610 ± 70 bc for Aldwincle (Har 1411 – Jackson 1976).

Finally, the burials from Wor Barrow include a distinctive mixture of articulated and disarticulated remains. This has been found elsewhere in southern England; in other cases all the bones were articulated. Apart from the dates from Wor Barrow itself, the evidence extends from a *terminus post quem* of 2820 ± 130 bc for Wayland's Smithy 1 (I 2328 – Atkinson 1965) to a date of 2360 ± 110 bc from Alfriston (Har 940 – Drewett 1975).

Taken together, the characteristic features of long barrows in the study area can be paralleled at sites in southern England whose dates fall between about 2800 and 2500 bc (cf. Thorpe 1984). This evidence is also consistent with the artefact associations and is set out in full in Table 2.4. It is worth stressing that few of the features highlighted in this discussion occur in isolation, any more than they do in Cranborne Chase. Twelve of the sixteen sites listed in Table 2.4 have more than one of these features, and out of a possible score of four elements (two of these are mutually exclusive) they show a mean of 1.7 ± 0.8. It only remains to add that with the exception of the single date from Thickthorn Down, this evidence is consistent with the other indications of the age of the Cursus complex.

2.5.3 Concluding discussion

Earlier in this chapter we suggested that the building of some of the monuments on the Wessex chalk might precede the general establishment of settlement in that area. Our work revealed a disparity between the abundance of large earthwork monuments and the paucity of lithics, ceramics and excavated features indicating Earlier Neolithic settlement. This contrasted sharply with their greater representation in the lowlands, where earthwork monuments were rare. Our discussion of the first monuments established on the chalkland sheds some light on these problems. It seems that the components of the Dorset Cursus complex were not established until relatively late in the sequence of occupation, so that settlement of the downland and the building of those monuments might have been different aspects of the same period of expansion. The development of a local form of long barrow in the study area may be particularly relevant to this process, for whilst some of its characteristic features are found in other regions, the distribution of these monuments in Wessex divides itself between Cranborne Chase and the coastal fringe (Fig. 2.17). It recalls the complex connections already suggested between these two areas.

If developments in the study area were an offshoot of more intensive and long-lived settlement in the coastal basin, it is striking how the building of the Cursus complex emphasised that process. The main concentration of 'Cranborne Chase'-type long barrows is along the springline between two major rivers discharging into Christchurch Harbour, the Avon and the Stour. Indeed, the upper reaches of the Stour are further emphasised by the situation of the Hambledon Hill complex. The Dorset Cursus itself is midway between the headwaters of these rivers, so that in effect the distribution of these three types of monument marks the upper boundary of an enormous triangular territory (Fig. 2.17). The Cursus also forms a major cultural monument, emphasising what may have been an important division in contemporary land use. To the south were the streams and rivers feeding into the coastal basin, whilst to the north, on the clay with flints plateau, were the areas most heavily settled during earlier phases and the sources of the best flint. Although there may have been a close relationship between the expansion of settlement and the construction of monuments, it would be too simple to see so much earthwork building as a side effect of land tenure. On the other hand, we must also stress that the Dorset Cursus was not alone in forming, or even following, a major boundary. Further to the north, the Stonehenge Cursus seems to separate two major groups of long barrows, each bounded by an important enclosure (Richards 1984).

Whilst such monuments may have emphasised important divisions in the landscape, this does not account for their distinctive symbolism. At one level cursus monuments may be greatly elaborated versions of the 'mortuary enclosures' occasionally found beneath long barrows, although it would be idle to pretend that their interpretation as exposure areas for the dead is based on very much evidence (cf. Megaw and Simpson 1979, 94). Far more important, the Cursus links together a whole series of mounds associated with the dead and sometimes gives them a stronger visual impact. At the same time, long barrows around the Cursus could be used to focus attention on the terminals of that extraordinary monument; one was even extended into a bank barrow after the northern end of the Cursus had been built. Each form of monument, then, gained emphasis by its association with the other. This process is especially clear at Thickthorn Down, the southern limit of the Cursus, where the terminal may have been built to imitate the appearance of two nearby long barrows, at least one of which was without any human remains. As John Barrett stresses in Chapter 4, the emphasis was on the dead – the ancestors – and not just on the act of burial, for the disposal of the dead and the construction of earthwork monuments are very different matters.

At the same time, we must remember that the sheer scale of the Cursus complex is unparalleled. In its final form the Dorset Cursus was the longest example of its type in Britain and was defined by an earthwork which was built on an unusually large scale for this type of monument. For instance, its closest neighbour, the Stonehenge Cursus, itself a considerable undertaking, required an investment of less than a twentieth of the labour devoted to this remarkable earthwork (Burl 1987, 44). In particular, there are signs that the bank of the Dorset Cursus might have been revetted and could have stood nearly two metres high. Even the excavation of the ditch would have taken nearly half a million worker-hours; and none of this makes any allowance for all the long barrows associated with the Dorset Cursus. Only one monument was being built on a larger scale at this time. This was Hambledon Hill, only 10 km to the west (Mercer 1980). Indeed, the analogy goes further, for both sites really consist of a series of freestanding monuments, linked together by one unusually considerable earthwork. The Dorset Cursus unites a whole series of separate mounds, whilst excavation at Hambledon has shown that what began as a series of distinct enclosures, supplemented by a pair of long barrows, was eventually bound together by a massive defensive scheme. Mercer's estimate of the magnitude of the task is about a million worker-hours (1980, 59–60).

Even so, there is a striking difference between these sites. The Hambledon complex occupies a prominent landmark and in its later phases the site was provided with impressive defences, which were surely intended to be seen from far away. The Dorset Cursus may be

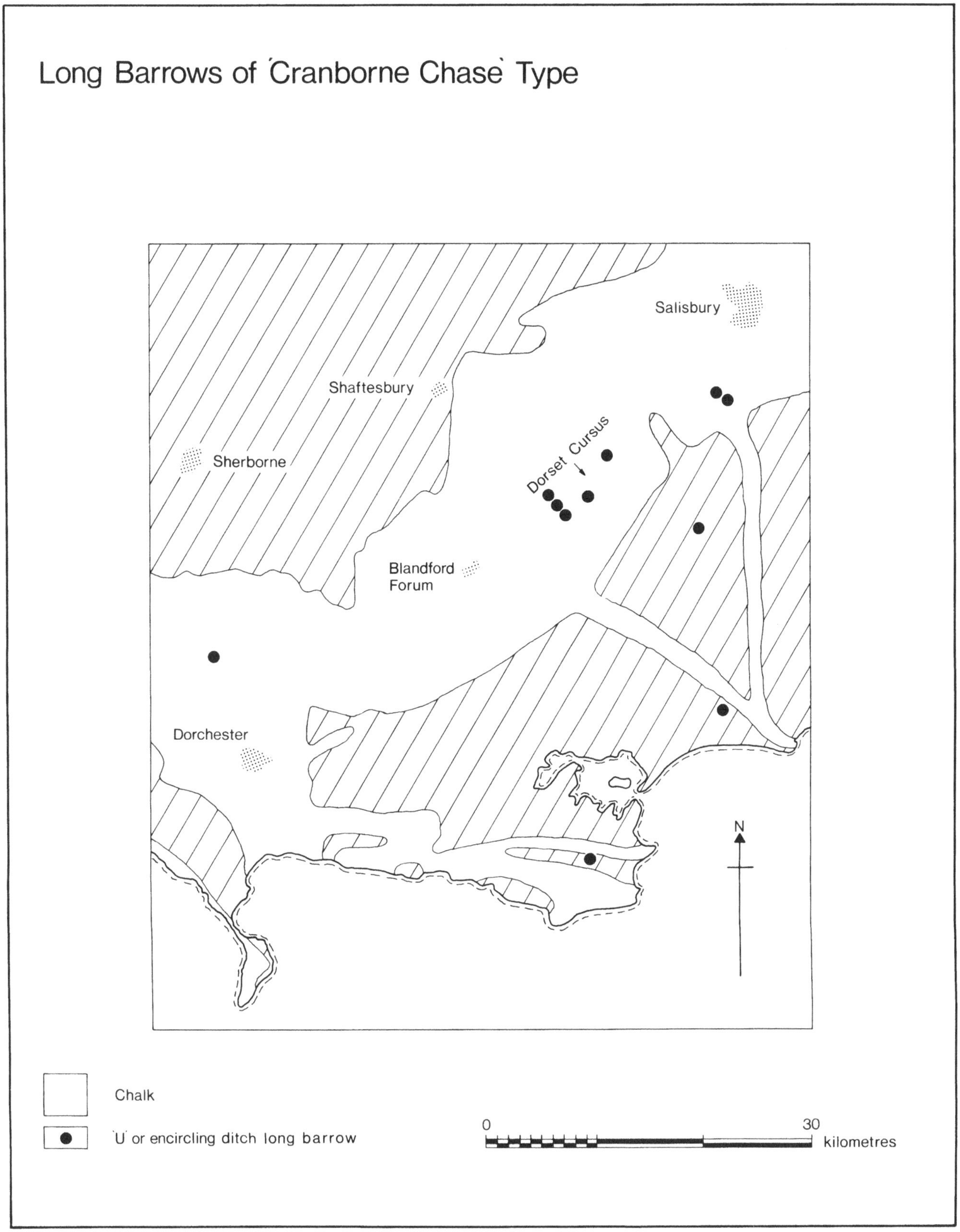

Fig. 2.17 The distribution of long barrows of Ashbee's 'Cranborne Chase type'

another elaborate and costly monument, but its overall design makes little sense except to those *inside* it. Its progress across the countryside would not be apparent from any distance. This is true of the other major cursuses on the chalk, and in particular the Stonehenge Cursus (Richards 1984) and the monuments at Rudston (Kinnes 1984). The main impact of the Dorset Cursus would have been experienced from its terminals, especially those built during its earlier phase; this would also be true of the long barrow on Gussage Cow Down, which forms such an integral feature of the whole design. Although some lengths of the earthwork were less impressive than others, the conception effectively *excludes outsiders*. This is also indicated by the lack of formal entrances through the earthwork.

The Dorset Cursus creates its most impressive visual impact between the Bottlebush terminal and the long barrow on Gussage Cow Down, if only because this includes the longest stretch which can be seen from one vantage point. This alignment is important for another reason. In 1973, Penny and Wood suggested that the Dorset Cursus had been built as an astronomical observatory, claiming to have identified a number of alignments between the Cursus and particular mounds, or between the mounds themselves. They suggested that five of these alignments were of astronomical significance and that the northern terminal of the Cursus had been positioned where two of these alignments crossed. Most of their field evidence is unconvincing, but there is every reason to accept the most basic of the alignments suggested in their paper. This extends from the Bottlebush terminal to the long barrow which forms a prominent skyline feature on Gussage Cow Down. We have already accepted the argument that the position of the Bottlebush terminal was chosen to obtain that visual effect: Penny and Wood argue that this was done so that the midwinter sun could be observed setting behind the mound. Although they underestimated the age of the Cursus by about five hundred years, an appropriate correction does not weaken their argument, the alignment changing by only 4 minutes of arc (Clive Ruggles pers. comm.). Indeed, the effect that they describe can still be observed today (Fig 2.16).

This is not to say that the Dorset Cursus was built as an observatory. It is more likely that, by relating such an enormous monument to the movements of the heavenly bodies, its builders were making the Cursus appear part of nature itself and freeing its operation from any challenge. It is not difficult to find a precedent for this arrangement; the Dorchester on Thames cursus seems to be aligned on the midsummer sunset (Bradley and Chambers 1988), whilst Aubrey Burl has suggested that the alignment of the Stonehenge Cursus could have marked the equinoctial sunrises midway between the solstices (1987, 44). Ritual is sometimes described as employing a different concept of *time* from everyday affairs: surely it was the nature of this great monument to deny the attrition of time altogether. More important, it made the dead seem part of the unchanging world of nature and appeared to confirm their status in perpetuity. That may be why it was so important for the Dorset alignment to be established by the Cursus and a long barrow in combination.

The relationship between these two types of monument is important for another reason. We have seen how the Dorset Cursus links up a whole series of barrows distributed along the springline of Cranborne Chase, but, with only one exception, this monument has a completely different orientation from any of these mounds. This may have happened because the barrows were aligned with the prevailing topography, but there is another possibility to consider. Burl has suggested that the long barrows on Salisbury Plain were aligned on the rising moon and show a wider range of orientations than could be explained by their alignment on the sunrise (1987, 27–9). The same is true of the long barrows in Cranborne Chase: only seven of these could have been directed towards the contemporary sunrise, whilst 87 per cent of the mounds would have pointed towards the rising moon. This compares with a figure of 90 per cent for Salisbury Plain and is unlikely to be fortuitous.

If there is any significance in these observations, the construction of the Dorset Cursus must have marked a particularly significant point in the development of the study area. It would have entailed the imposition of a massive solar alignment on a series of separate monuments which were orientated towards the rising moon. In this respect the change could have been as drastic as the conversion of Stonehenge from a lunar to a solar alignment some centuries later (Burl 1987, 65–71). We do not need to translate this potent symbolism to appreciate its importance for the contemporary population. On the other hand, it may be no accident that at about the same time other major sites were making significant use of the midwinter or midsummer sun. The great passage tombs at Newgrange and Maes Howe relate the movements of the midwinter sun to the commemoration of the dead in very much the same manner as the Cursus (Patrick 1974; Burl 1981, 124–6). Radiocarbon dates from Newgrange indicate that this was happening about 2450 bc. The date of Maes Howe is more contentious, although it could have been built at about that time (Sharples 1985, 63–5). Direct links between these phenomena are not impossible, but it is more important to

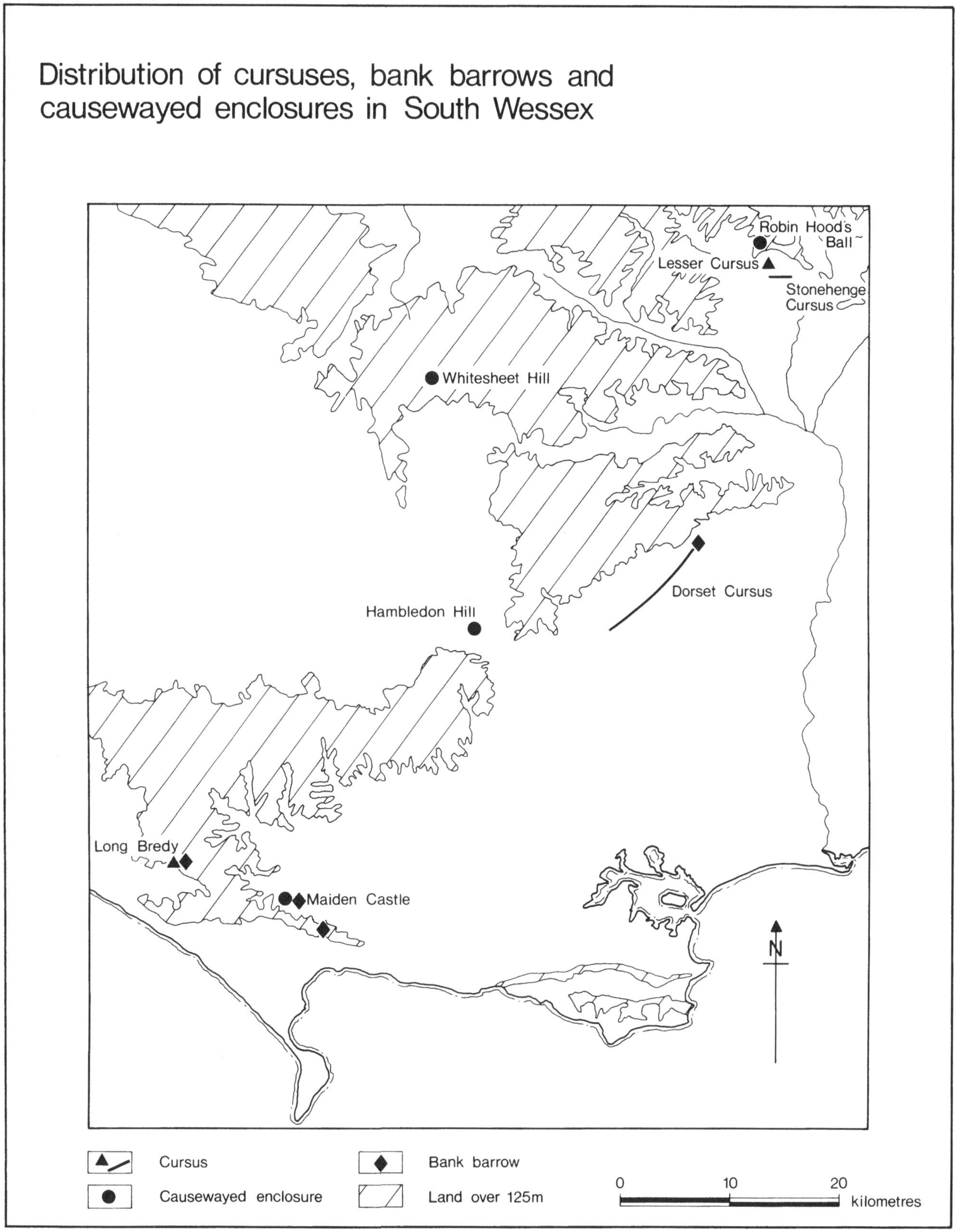

Fig. 2.18 The distribution of major Earlier Neolithic monuments in southern Wessex

understand that a rather similar process may have been operating in all three cases.

Having stressed the possibility of long-distance links, we should say more about the local importance of the Cursus complex. Southern Wessex seems to evidence an unusually strong emphasis on the dead during this period, reflected by the construction of large monuments (Fig. 2.18). Such a combination of different types does not occur on this scale anywhere else. The Hambledon Hill complex is not only the largest group of causewayed enclosures to have been discovered in Britain: its evidence for the complex treatment of the dead is so far unmatched in detail on such a site. The Dorset Cursus is also the largest monument of its type known at present. At the same time, southern Wessex also includes the most complex non-megalithic long barrows – the earthworks described as bank barrows (Bradley 1983b). Such monuments are extremely rare in other parts of the country, but Dorset includes no fewer than four examples. We have already stressed the way in which the Dorset Cursus is flanked by the larger long barrows in the area, and the identification of a bank barrow marking one end of this monument recalls the evidence of the Dorset Ridgeway cemetery. Not only is that great chain of barrows delimited by a bank barrow at either end: part way along, but offset from the ridge itself, was a third bank barrow, built across the site of the Maiden Castle causewayed enclosure (Royal Commission on Historical Monuments 1970, 420–1). This stresses the close interrelationship between these different types of monument. The same is shown by the pairing of a bank barrow and another cursus at the west end of the Ridgeway cemetery (Bradley 1983b).

Having stressed the regional aspects of this question, we must end by stressing the element of sequence, for a number of writers have argued that attitudes to the dead changed significantly during the Earlier Neolithic period: deposition beneath large mounds became more restricted and the later long barrows emphasise the deposition of articulated skeletons rather than the mixture of bones seen at earlier sites. More emphasis was placed on the burial of males, sometimes only one per site, and occasionally these deposits could be accompanied by grave goods (Thorpe 1984). Although the evidence from the study area is very limited, comparison with the evidence from neighbouring regions seems to indicate that the deposition of human remains beneath long barrows was being restricted to certain groups or individuals. In very much the same way the entire layout of the Cursus seems to be intended to *exclude* outsiders: only for those inside the great enclosure was the design of the monument apparent. It may be that the building of the Dorset Cursus was the ultimate expression of these changes in attitudes to the dead. It integrated the separate long barrows scattered along the upper limits of the settlement pattern, and at the same time, it bound them together in a complex design which could only be appreciated by those who had access to *certain specific points inside the monument*. By incorporating into its structure an important astronomical alignment, those who built it made those developments appear to be part of the functioning of nature.

If the middle years of the third millennium bc were a period of drastic change, this way of naturalising relations between the living and the dead may have been one sphere in which those changes were played out. Not far away, at Hambledon Hill, events took a different course and the final enclosure complex seems to have been attacked and destroyed (Mercer 1980, 65). It is striking that from the middle of the third millennium, activity in Cranborne Chase shifted towards the Cursus and that this part of the south Wessex landscape dominated the settlement pattern until about 2000 bc. During that entire period there is no evidence for the refurbishment of the monument itself, yet it continued to influence the ways in which the landscape was used. We shall trace that complicated process in Chapter 3.

Notes

1 Richard Bradley
2 Julie Gardiner
3 Rosamund Cleal

3. THE LATER NEOLITHIC

3.1 Introduction[1]

The Later Neolithic can be considered as the period between the last long barrows in the study area and the development of henge monuments. It has a most distinctive flint industry and at least two traditions of decorated pottery: Peterborough Ware and Grooved Ware. It begins around the middle of the third millennium bc and extends to about 1800 bc, when this material began to be replaced by elements of the Beaker complex. At the same time, the tradition of individual burial in round barrows gained considerably in importance. The situation is so complex, however, that the period division must depend on the general currency of Beaker material, rather than its first appearance.

We ended the last chapter with the building of the Cursus complex. This chapter investigates the ways in which that monument and its associated long barrows influenced later developments, for the Cursus seems to have been as important in its relict state as it was when newly built. In the first part of this chapter we consider the distribution of settlement in relation to the sequence in the Hampshire Basin, and investigate how far everyday activity was influenced by the existence of this zone of complex monuments (Fig. 3.1). Then we report the results of two excavations undertaken close to the Cursus. One site overlay the Cursus itself, and its spatial organisation seems to have been determined by the position of the earlier earthwork; a second site alongside this earthwork contained two groups of pits, whose rather specialised contents may again reflect the importance of this monument.

The second part of this chapter investigates the development of new monuments in the study area, and in particular within the Cursus complex. We begin with the emergence of a distinctive tradition of individual burials, best exemplified by Later Neolithic developments at Wor Barrow, and then report the recent excavation of a ring ditch close to the Cursus. Lastly, we turn to the development of the henge tradition and present an account of a recently excavated monument, which is aligned on a conspicuous section of the Cursus. Here it is possible to show how the position of the earlier monument may have influenced the spatial organisation of the deposits in the henge.

3.2 The evidence of domestic activity

3.2.1 Introduction[1]

In Chapter 2 the evidence of monuments completely overshadowed the traces of domestic activity. Now the balance is redressed, and more space can be devoted to the evidence of contemporary settlement. For the first time the study area shows a range of artefact assemblages comparable in extent and variety with those in the Hampshire Basin. In addition, more is known about some of the findspots as a result of excavation. For this reason our accounts of the surface finds and pottery are followed by a discussion of two excavated sites close to the Dorset Cursus, one associated with Peterborough Ware and the other with Grooved Ware. This chapter stresses their relationship to that monument. In one case a more detailed analysis of the excavated material has been published elsewhere (Gardiner 1985). Otherwise our presentation of the settlement evidence follows the same format as in Chapter 2.

3.2.2 The flint industries of the study area[2]

The rather meagre scatter of leaf-shaped arrowheads emphasised two areas: the Upper Chalk around the long barrows and the Cursus, and the clay with flints. These two zones also dominate artefact distributions during the Later Neolithic, although the amount of material is vastly greater (Fig. 3.2). Its distribution is summarised in Table 3.1. Analysis by Peter Fisher shows that at the 95 per cent significance level the geological and site distributions are different.

Although the relationship between lithic industries and monuments will be considered later, one preliminary point should be emphasised. The construction of the Dorset Cursus had cut off access to the upland area, and for this reason it seems likely that the activity described in this section may belong to the period when that earthwork was no longer an obstacle. Our information on the later history of the Cursus is limited, but it is consistent with this idea. At one point its active maintenance was over by the time that Mortlake Ware was in use, whilst further to the south, the ditch had silted up completely by the Beaker period.

Most of the flintwork from the study area is Later Neolithic, and transverse arrowheads outnumber leaf forms by nearly three to one. Many of the surface industries are very large, both in their extent on the ground and in the number of artefacts (Table 3.3, p. 67). For example, one of the largest, at Farnham, covers at least 28 hectares and has so far produced over 600 retouched implements.

Virtually all the major flint scatters are on clay with flints in the northern part of the study area; the two notable exceptions are on the greensand at Rowberry and Donhead. Since the clay with flints covers a quite limited area, the distribution of sites seems to show some clustering. The average distance between surface scatters

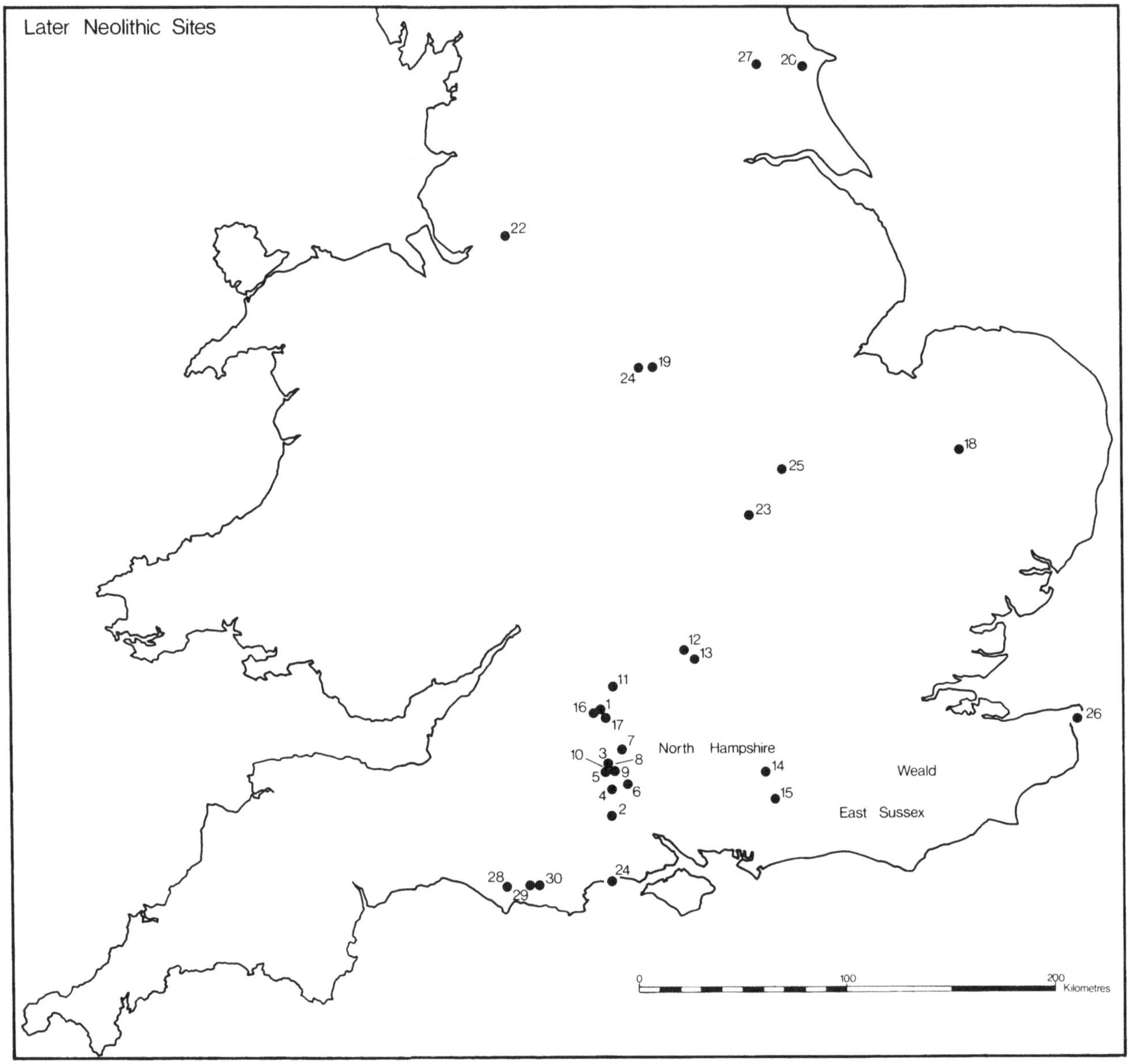

Fig. 3.1 The distribution of Later Neolithic sites outside the study area which are considered in this chapter. Key: 1 Avebury; 2 Downton; 3 Durrington Walls; 4 Winterbourne Dauntsey; 5 King Barrow Ridge; 6 Easton Down; 7 Snail Down; 8 Woodhenge; 9 Ratfyn; 10 Stonehenge; 11 Christchurch; 12 Barrow Hills; 13 Dorchester on Thames; 14 Sutton Veney; 15 Tisbury; 16 Silbury Hill; 17 The Sanctuary; 18 Grimes Graves; 19 Swarkestone; 20 Rudston Wold; 21 Willington; 22 Trelystan; 23 Ecton; 24 Hengistbury Head; 25 Aldwincle; 26 Ramsgate; 27 Duggleby Howe; 28 Maiden Castle; 29 Maumbury Rings; 30 Mount Pleasant

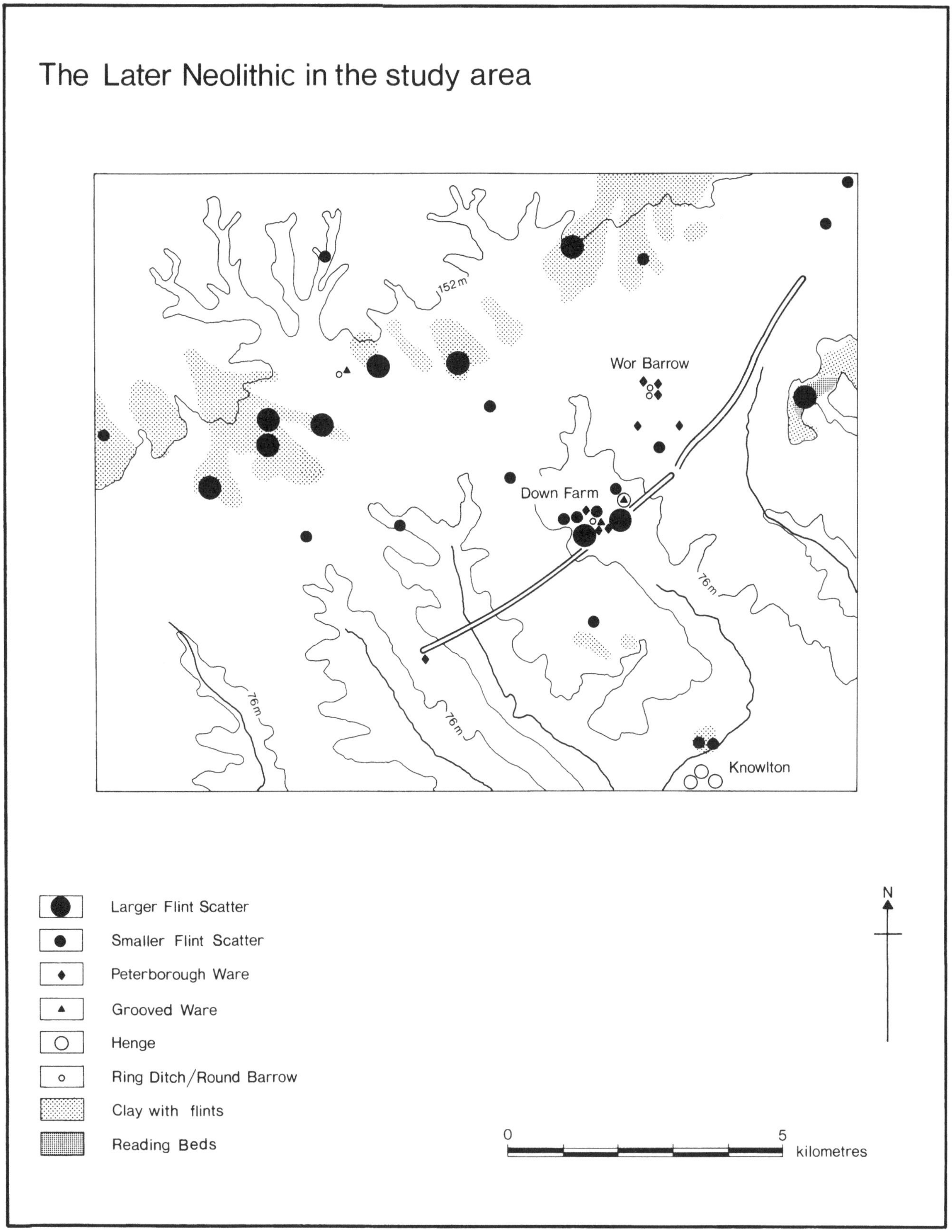

Fig. 3.2 The distribution of Later Neolithic artefacts and monuments in the study area

Table 3.1. *The distribution of Later Neolithic flint scatters in relation to the extent of the main geological deposits in the study area and in the parts examined by fieldwalking*

Deposit	Percentage of each deposit in the study area	Number of flint scatters found by fieldwork	Percentage of each deposit in the area examined by fieldwork
Clay with flints	8.0	13	17.5
Upper Chalk	84.0	5	68.9
Valley Gravel	5.2	–	2.8
Other	2.8	1	10.4

is 0.95 km, with a tendency for them to occur on south or south-east-facing slopes. At present, however, the boundaries of the scatters are determined by the extent of arable land, and the general feeling is that there may have been an almost continuous spread of Later Neolithic material across the clay with flints, spilling over onto the chalk. Precisely the same locations were favoured on the downland of east Sussex and north Hampshire, where findspots on the clay with flints are spaced at intervals of 1.2 km and 1.1 km respectively (see Gardiner 1984).

All the clay with flints scatters in the study area have produced some Mesolithic material, notably tranchet adzes, but also 'microlithic' pieces. Care has suggested that from the Mesolithic period onwards this deposit was used mainly as a source of raw material (Care 1979 and 1982). It now appears that the situation is more complex. Cranborne Chase is not alone in producing an admixture of Later Neolithic and Mesolithic material. The same is seen on the chalk of east Sussex and in parts of Hampshire (Gardiner 1984). It also occurs on the sandstone ridge of the high Sussex Weald and in the Avon/Stour basin, where Calkin (1951) remarked on the occurrence of both microliths and transverse arrowheads at a number of specific locations. In each case the distribution of the Mesolithic material tends to be tightly clustered and only small amounts may be present, whilst the later component has a much wider distribution, involving many hundreds of artefacts. Such contrasts are so striking that, rather than assume the continued exploitation of specific flint resources, we might envisage the reuse of particularly favourable areas which had experienced a phase of clearance and partial regeneration.

This interpretation is supported by the detailed composition of these industries. One feature of the clay with flints assemblages is the presence of large numbers of very rough, heavy artefacts (Fig. 3.3). There are now about 800 of these pieces in the study area, of which perhaps a quarter may be classified as axe roughouts. Picks, 'Y-shaped' tools and hammers are also common, but several hundred other pieces cannot be classified according to normal typological conventions. For the most part these non-specific heavy-duty implements do not seem to be 'roughouts', since they are generally so crudely worked and so irregular that it is difficult to envisage any 'finished' form.

The best parallels for this group come from the Sussex flint mines and from Grimes Graves in Norfolk, where large numbers of utilised but wholly unclassifiable artefacts occur within the mineshafts (see Saville 1981). We can envisage a whole range of functions for these pieces, from use as wedges to crude fabricators, but their basic association must have been with the extraction and primary trimming of flint nodules. They were probably made to meet immediate requirements and then discarded. The presence of similar implements in the study area seems to confirm the suggestion that the clay with flints provided a source of good raw material.

We must be careful not to place too much emphasis on these artefacts. Despite their abundance in strictly numerical terms, picks, adzes and non-specific heavy-duty implements account for quite a low proportion of the whole assemblage. On average, the heavy industry (excluding axe roughouts) accounts for only 7.2 per cent of the implements in collections from Cranborne Chase, compared with twice this figure for sites in different areas of east Sussex, where it has been suggested that the production of axes from surface flint was an important activity (Gardiner 1984). The nodules available in Cranborne Chase are just as suitable for making axes, and there is no doubt that some were used in this way, but barely 2 per cent of the artefacts in the surface scatters can be classified as flaked or roughout axes. We may conclude that the extraction of nodules for use in their production was not the predominant activity on these sites.

Most of the implements are small, lightweight flake-tools, which could as easily have been made of flint derived from the chalk, although most appear to have been made and used on the clay with flints (Fig. 3.3). All the scatters are dominated by convex scrapers, which account for between 60 per cent and 84 per cent of the total tool component. Transverse arrowheads are common, occurring in both 'chisel' and 'oblique' forms in most locations; in the study area as a whole the ratio of chisel to oblique forms is 1:1.45. There is evidence for local production of these types, and numerous unfinished examples have been found, as well as a few

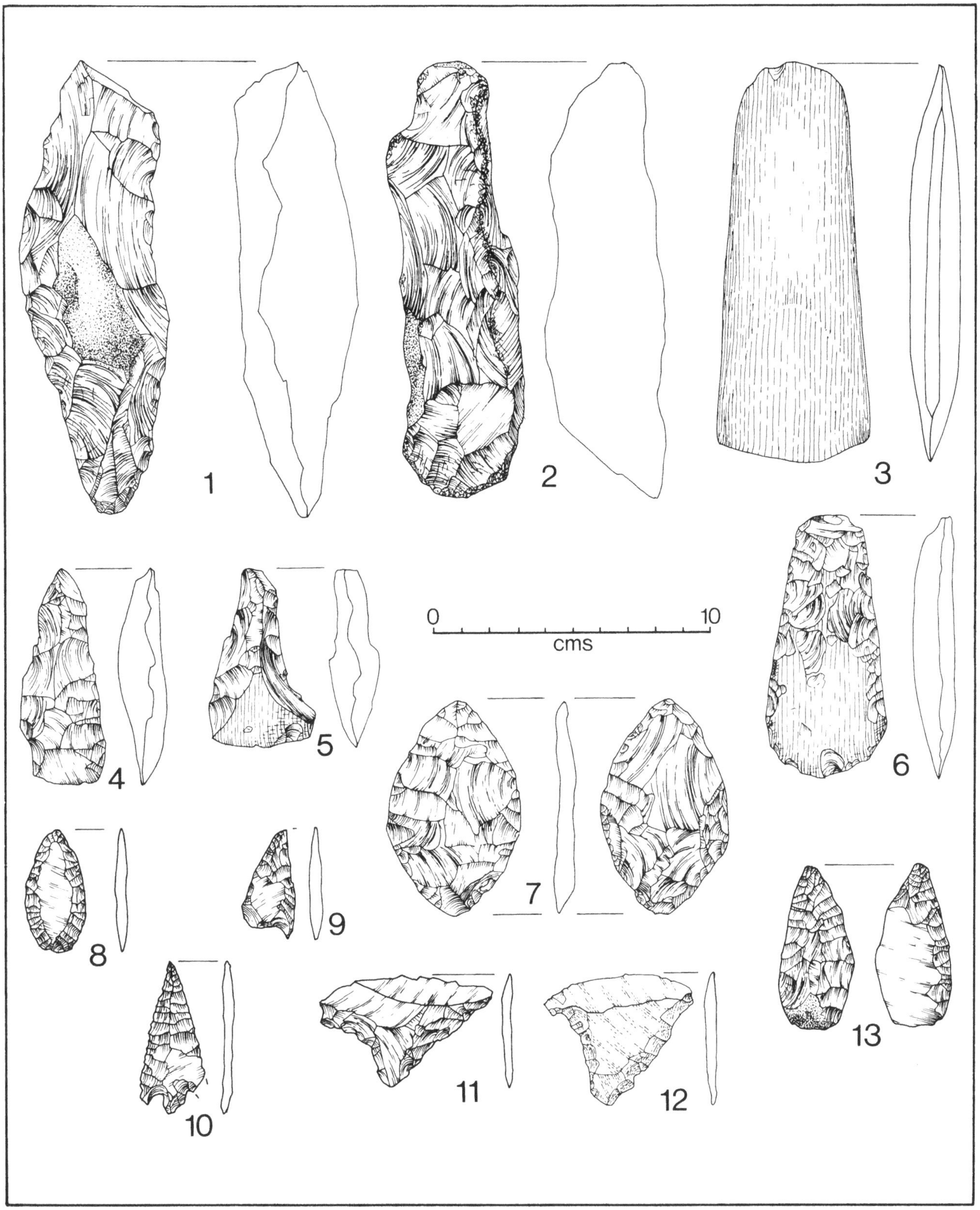

Fig. 3.3 Selected flint artefacts from Cranborne Chase. 1 Pick (Bussey Stool); 2 Heavy-duty implement (Down Farm, Barn Field); 3 Polished axe (Woodyates); 4 Tranchet tool (Woodcutts Common); 5 Tranchet tool on polished axe fragment (Woodcutts Common); 6 Partly polished miniature axe (Wor Barrow); 7 Laurel leaf (Woodyates); 8 Leaf arrowhead (Stonedown); 9 Oblique arrowhead (Farnham); 10 Barbed-and-tanged arrowhead (Farnham); 11 Chisel arrowhead (Woodcutts Common); 12 Chisel arrowhead in Portland chert (Bussey Stool); 13 Plano-convex knife (Handley Common)

'discoidal' cores of the form best described by Manby (1974, 83). Borers, fabricators and miniature axe forms are all represented in relatively high percentages, along with knives, burins, chisels and other lightweight pieces. Small, tanged versions of the so-called 'Y-shaped' or 'tranchet' tools also occur, and these are occasionally manufactured on fragments of polished axe. Nearly all the 128 polished axes examined from the study area are either broken or damaged. Most fragments are chipped for rehafting, resharpened or are worked down into other tool forms. Although some examples are clearly made from the local raw material, well over half are in a fine, probably mined, grey flint. The origin of this material is not known at present, but axes in closely similar flint occur in the Bournemouth area and at Maiden Castle.

Polished axes occur in a wide variety of shapes and forms, but it is extremely difficult to date them. Thirteen examples from Cranborne Chase, however, are of a distinctive Late Neolithic/Early Bronze Age type (Gardiner 1988). They constitute just 10 per cent of the total sample, but only eight examples of this type are known from the rest of Dorset, and forty (about 3 per cent) from the whole of Hampshire and Sussex. By contrast, only one example is obviously early, and this probably originates from one of the Sussex mines. There is every reason to suppose that the vast majority of the polished axes are contemporary with the rest of the lithic material.

The heavy utilisation of polished axe fragments is mirrored in other types of implement. Use-polish is present on numerous fabricators and borers, whilst scrapers are generally heavily abraded and may have crushed and polished areas on the working edge. Utilised pebbles of sarsen and quartzite are also common, and many of the small 'Y-shaped' pieces have damaged working edges and abraded tangs.

The predominant forms on the clay with flints sites are scraping, boring and lightweight processing tools, often with signs of heavy wear. It seems as if the surface scatters in this area mark a major focus of Later Neolithic settlement. At one time this would have been difficult to explain, because of the rather marginal character of the clay with flints today. This problem is considered by Peter Fisher in the companion volume, where he suggests that the present status of this area may result from environmental change. Initially, the clay with flints would have combined large tracts of fertile, well-drained soil with an excellent supply of raw material.

Not all the surface scatters in this part of the Chase are on the main deposit of clay with flints. There is a whole series of generally smaller scatters, which also need to be considered. These are broadly contemporary with the larger scatters and contain many of the same elements, but there are noticeable differences in composition and location, which need to be considered. Whereas the major scatters seem to have been located with regard to 'economic' considerations, the smaller scatters focus on a feature of the cultural landscape, the Dorset Cursus, although some do occupy small patches of rather similar subsoil. In some ways this is the opposite of what we might have expected. It would seem logical for such a massive structure to be linked closely with the main areas of settlement, but instead the flint assemblages found near to the Cursus are often smaller than the others in the study area (Fig. 3.4). Only two substantial surface scatters occur very near to that monument, and these are discussed separately below.

The range of tool types in these industries is generally much smaller than in the clay with flints assemblages, whilst the standard of workmanship and overall finish of the implements is considerably higher. Scrapers dominate again, but transverse arrowheads and polished axe fragments are more common. The arrowhead types show minor differences with distance from the Cursus. In assemblages within 3 km of the monument chisel arrowheads account for an average of 1.01 per cent of the implement types and oblique arrowheads account for 1.52 per cent, but on sites further away the figures are 1.23 per cent and 0.41 per cent respectively. A notable feature of the groups found near the Cursus is the increased proportion of polished flint tools (Fig. 3.4). Apart from polished axe fragments, there are polished-edge knives, chisels and miniature axe forms. In addition, there are a number of elaborate flint and stone tools, such as plano-convex knives, imported stone axes and fragments of macehead, including one in polished flint. Most of the industries contain at least one of these items, and usually more. Several of the stone axes originate from Cornwall, representing Groups I, III, IIIa and IVa, with one example from Wales (Group VII). Other non-local stones include greenstone, rhyolite and limestone.

We can test this division by means of discriminant analysis. This has been carried out by Jill and Peter Fisher, who provide the following note: 'To test whether the tool assemblage at lithic scatters in the vicinity of the Cursus is different from those elsewhere, discriminant analysis was conducted using the number of tool types present. Ward's method was used to select those variables with most discriminatory power. The analysis used all the tool types recorded during fieldwork. The actual discriminant functions are listed below and provide a perfect division of the sites into those close to the Cursus and those distant from it. According to a multivariate Chi-squared test this was significant at the 95 per cent level. The discriminant functions in Table 3.2 show the relative

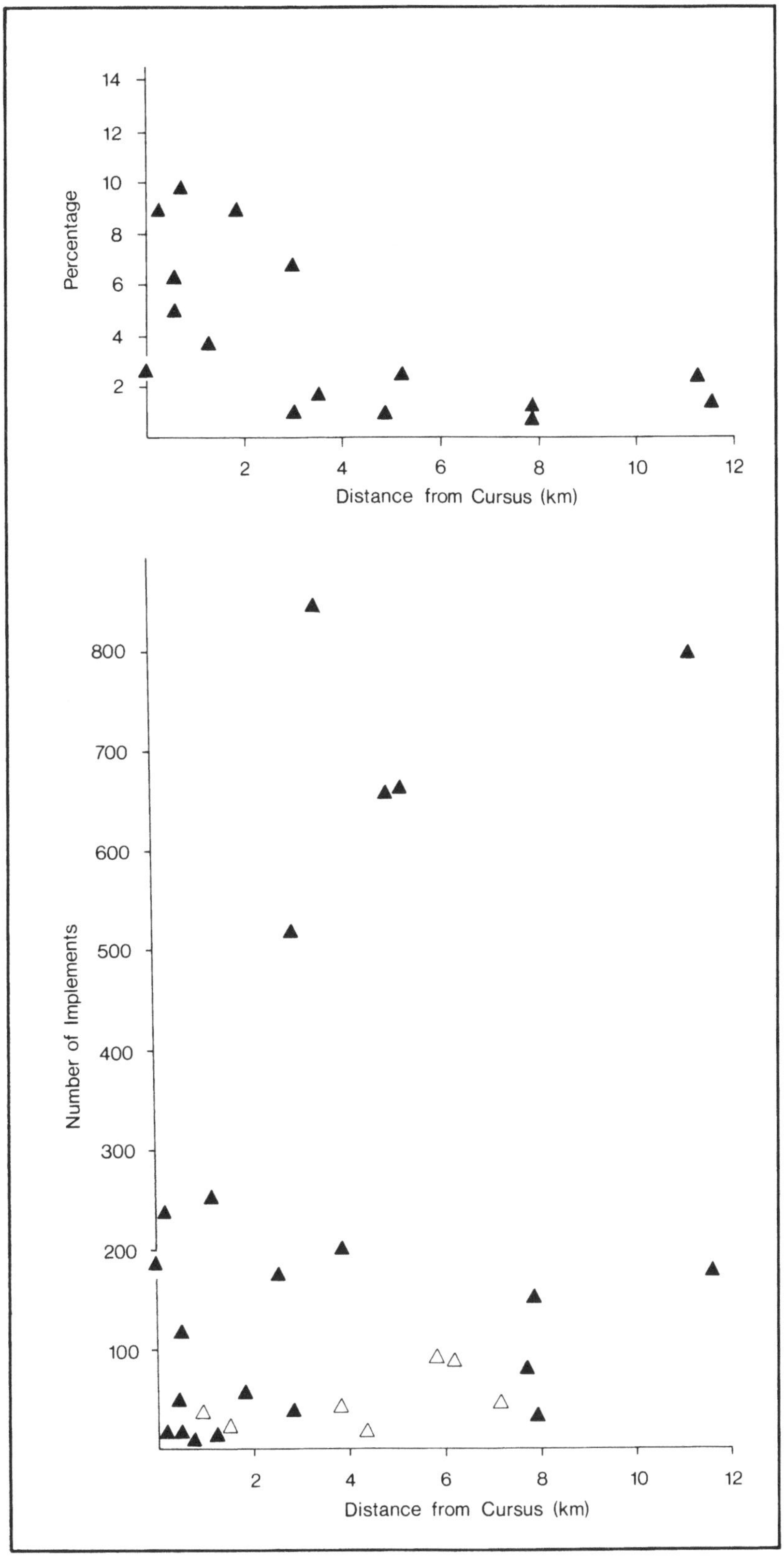

Fig. 3.4 (Upper) The percentage of polished flint artefacts in the lithic scatters in relation to their distance from the Cursus (lower) The number of retouched artefacts in the lithic scatters in relation to their distance from the Cursus. Open triangles represent groups of material in the Pitt Rivers Collection

Table 3.2. *Discriminant functions for the different tool types found on the clay with flints and beside the Dorset Cursus*

Tool type	Discriminant function
Transverse arrowheads	29.7500
Chisels	28.4953
Heavy duty tools	28.1959
Leaf-shaped arrowheads	7.7064
Plano-convex knives	− 2.9834
Polished axe flakes	− 6.3020
Scrapers	−13.4399
Picks	−18.5108
Borers	−25.8227

importance of major types in distinguishing between these two groups of sites.' (Leaf-shaped arrowheads are included here as some may run on into this period.)

Not unexpectedly, a plot of the distribution of polished items against distance from the Cursus (Fig. 3.4) shows a marked concentration within 2 km of the monument.

Two of the lithic scatters close to Down Farm, Woodcutts, are of particular interest because in each case the surface material has been supplemented by excavation. As we shall see, they present a basic problem of interpretation, containing as they do a mixture of 'ordinary' artefacts and more specialised types. For example, the flint scatter overlying the Cursus in Chalkpit Field included six transverse arrowheads, two miniature axes, pieces of at least two polished axes, a plano-convex knife and part of a macehead. By contrast, the Neolithic surface finds from Firtree Field do not stand out so sharply, although excavations revealed a series of chalk-cut pits with a much wider range of contents, including polished flint axe fragments, stone axes and polished-edge knives. Such sites again emphasise the distinctive nature of the finds made close to the Cursus. These questions were pursued in the excavations reported later in this chapter.

The contents of the surface collections from the study area are summarised in Table 3.3, which also indicates the intensity with which different locations were investigated. Too little is known for useful discussion of the finds from other deposits, but the figures from the Cursus area and the clay with flints highlight the contrasting features of these two collections. During his fieldwork Martin Green divided the findspots on the clay with flints into 'larger' and 'smaller' lithic scatters. Although a number of these were investigated with the same thoroughness, it is clear that the smaller collections contained a less varied tool assemblage, although the density of implements was higher than it was in the other group. At the same time, the *smaller* scatters on the clay with flints were of roughly the same extent as those around the Cursus and contained a similar range and density of tool types. This observation would repay more investigation in the field. At present it does not seem likely that the contrasts between the two groups on the clay with flints result from the presence or absence of 'industrial' material.

We must now investigate the relationship between the study area and the coastal plain around Bournemouth and Christchurch (see Gardiner in Cunliffe 1987, 330–3). There is a considerable body of Later Neolithic flintwork in this area (Fig. 3.5), although much of the material studied by Calkin (1951) cannot be traced today. Information from his reports can, at least, be combined with the results of more recent research.

Calkin suggested that there were several major concentrations within the general scatter of lithic material in this region. These are mostly on the gravels and alluvial deposits associated with the river floodplains. He does not discuss the more mundane aspects of the flintwork, but sufficient material survives for us to suggest the presence of at least eight concentrations which could represent settlement sites. These are about 2 km apart, and five of them are within 1 km of a major river (Fig. 3.5).

The outstanding group is that from Hengistbury Head (Gardiner in Cunliffe 1987, 22–47). This site has produced a very large collection of Late Neolithic/Early Bronze Age flintwork, which has been largely overlooked until recently. This material comes from the high part of the Head (Warren Hill) and from the low ground on the harbour side, mostly from the area known as the Nursery Garden. It was recovered partly during excavation and fieldwork early in this century by St George Gray and Bushe-Fox, partly by local collectors and partly during recent excavations. Small amounts of flintwork and fragments of at least three vessels of Grooved Ware were recovered by Cunliffe from the main Iron Age occupation area, particularly in 1984, and further Grooved Ware and a comprehensive sample of flint were obtained in 1984–5 from the Nursery Garden during excavations by the present author and Amanda Chadburn (*ibid.*).

The assemblage is dominated by small flake tools, including over 1,200 scrapers, borers, fabricators, knives and other retouched pieces. There are also a large number of arrowheads, including at least forty-eight transverse forms (sixteen chisel and thirty-two oblique), whilst eight or more polished axes are recorded by Calkin; three flakes from a single polished axe were excavated in 1984. Many of these implements show signs of heavy wear.

There is some reason to believe that Hengistbury might have been rather a special location. The composition of the assemblage indicates extensive settlement here during

Table 3.3. *The main characteristics of the lithic scatters examined by surface survey, omitting finds of diagnostic Mesolithic flintwork and of leaf-shaped, barbed and tanged, and triangular arrowheads*

Clay with flints:	
Areas of 'larger' lithic scatters	32.1 ± 14.4 hectares (N = 5)
Areas of 'smaller' lithic scatters	8.7 ± 7.4 hectares (N = 8)
Density of implements in all intensively investigated 'larger' lithic scatters	19.0 ± 6.3 implements per hectare (N = 4)
Density of implements in all intensively investigated 'smaller' lithic scatters	29.8 ± 12.1 implements per hectare (N = 3)
Range of implement types in 'larger' lithic scatters	16.0 ± 1.5 types
Range of implement types in 'smaller' lithic scatters	12.5 ± 1.5 types
Reading Beds (one site):	
Area	6.0 hectares
Density of implements	41.6 implements per hectare
Range of implement types	17 types
Greensand (two intensively investigated scatters)	
Mean area of lithic scatters	4.25 hectares
Mean density of implements	105.1 implements per hectare
Mean range of implement types	12 types
Lithic scatters around the Dorset Cursus	
Area of lithic scatters	7.1 ± 3.8 hectares (N = 5)
Density of implements	30.9 ± 24 per hectare
Range of implement types	11.2 ± 2.4 types

the Later Neolithic, and there are some indications of the status of this site. For the most part, the quality of the industry is exceptionally high, and even the scrapers are beautifully worked. Some of the arrowheads and knives are particularly finely pressure-flaked. Most pieces are manufactured on local pebbles, but it is clear from some of the cores and large implements that much larger nodules of good-quality material were being imported to the site in quantity, probably from the clay with flints. One of the nearest sources for this flint would be Cranborne Chase.

There is a marked concentration of stray finds of arrowheads and plano-convex knives on, and just to the west of, the Head itself, and on a wider scale the area to the south of the Stour shows a general increase in the number of finds, particularly of polished axes, towards Hengistbury. This does not seem to be the result of collection bias, since the distribution of later artefacts extends over a much wider area. As we shall see, finds of Later Neolithic decorated pottery focus on this same area.

Finally, we should remember that Hengistbury Head is a major landmark, commanding a dominant and easily defended position at the entrance to Christchurch Harbour and the mouths of the Avon and Stour. It seems to have provided the focal point for the Later Neolithic artefact distributions and remained a focus of activity during the second millennium bc. The evidence from the Bournemouth area suggests that the coastal plain may have experienced a longer phase of Neolithic activity than Cranborne Chase, and one which did not involve the construction of many monuments. By contrast, the evidence of flintwork from the study area suggests that much of the identifiable activity was confined to a relatively short period which also saw the creation of a whole landscape of specialised earthworks. It may be no accident that some of the artefact distributions in that area echo the distribution of the monuments themselves.

The key to understanding the relationship between these two areas may lie in the belt of chalkland between the coastal plain and the Chase. This area contains several long barrows and the group of henge monuments known as the Knowlton Circles (RCHM 1975, 113–15). Unfortunately, little fieldwork has been undertaken here. A few stray finds have been reported, including polished flint and stone axes, but very little can be made of their distribution. Martin Green has only recently identified surface flint scatters close to the Knowlton henges. These

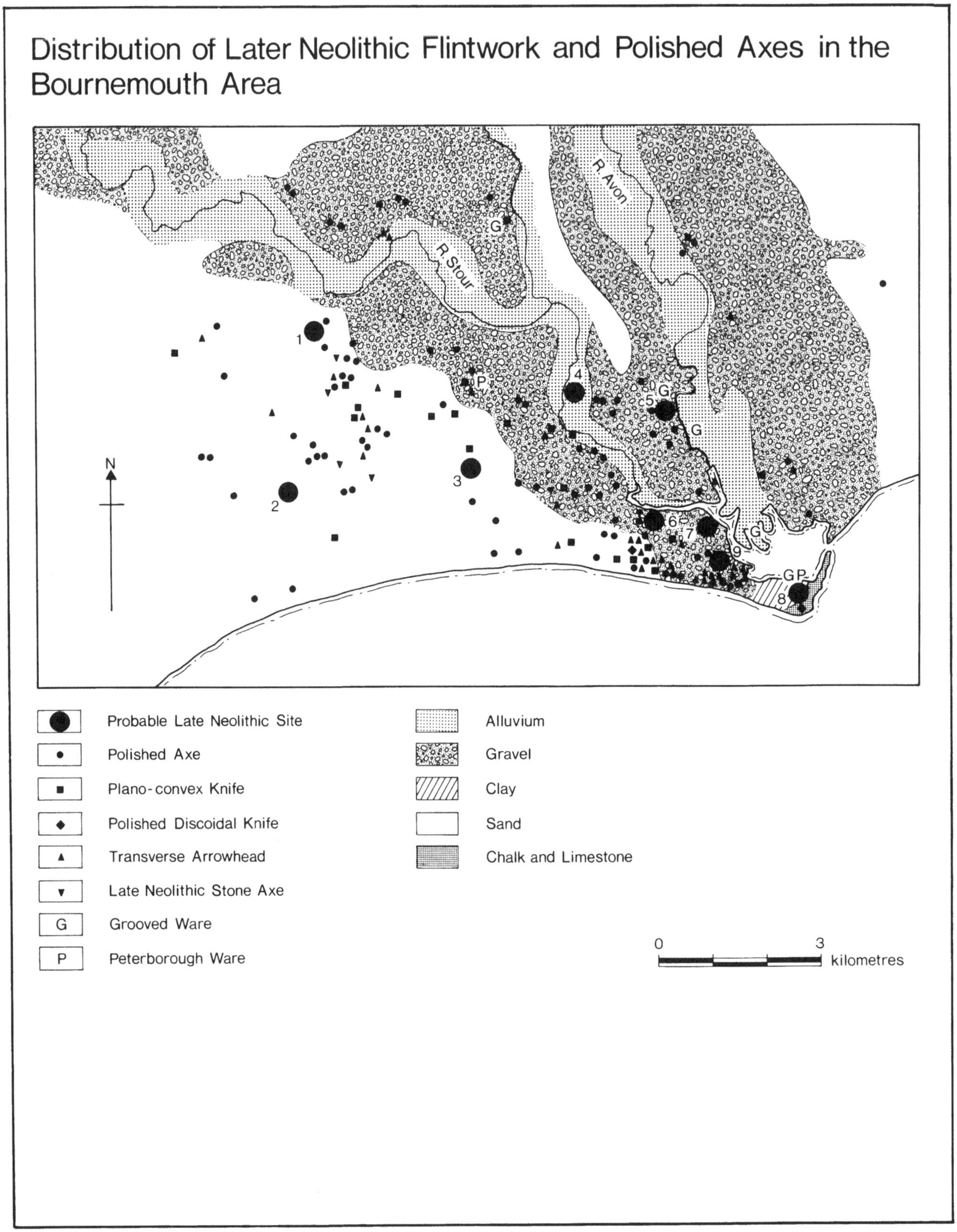

Fig. 3.5 The distribution of Later Neolithic artefacts around the confluence of the Rivers Avon and Stour. Key: 1 Redhill Common; 2 Talbot Woods; 3 King's Park; 4 Grove Farm; 5 Latch Farm; 6 Tuckton Road; 7 Barrow Plot; 8 Hengistbury Head; 9 Roebury and Whitepits (North and South Field)

are on the opposite side of the Allen valley to the monuments and are located on small patches of clay with flints. Like many other sites in Cranborne Chase, they face south-east. One of these scatters produced an oblique transverse arrowhead. At present they would appear to be smaller versions of the industries from the clay with flints described earlier.

Although some of the evidence is unsatisfactory, a few broader observations can be made. There seems to be a general distribution of Later Neolithic flintwork extending across the Dorset chalk and the coastal plain. Where research has been undertaken, the flint assemblages present at least two facets. There appear to be areas of fairly intensive settlement, although their actual extent may prove to be much wider than their present distribution suggests. In Cranborne Chase settlement is primarily associated with clay with flints, and on the coastal plain most evidence comes from the well-drained gravels and the light alluvial soils. Some distortion is likely as a result of the more erratic nature of collection in the latter area, but in combination this evidence suggests that the Later Neolithic inhabitants of Dorset were very selective in the areas that they chose to occupy.

At the same time, there is evidence of variations in the lithic material that seem to be independent of environmental factors. The distribution of certain elaborate and exotic artefacts reveals distinct concentrations. In Cranborne Chase, and probably in the Maiden Castle/Mount Pleasant area, these concentrations are associated with a series of major earthwork monuments, for which a specialised role has been suggested (Gardiner 1984). In Cranborne Chase we seem to be looking at two separate zones of activity, each with very different emphases. The coastal plain lacks similar monuments, but the clustering of elaborate or attractive objects around Hengistbury Head could suggest the position of an important focal point, joined to the study area by the rivers discharging into Christchurch Harbour. The implications of these suggestions are far-reaching and will be discussed later in this chapter.

3.2.3 The ceramic evidence[3]

A considerable increase in the quantities of pottery has been recorded for the Later Neolithic period in the study area (cf. Fig. 4.4, p. 115). In the earlier period a minimum of twelve vessels has been recorded, but the Later Neolithic, as defined above, accounts for at least 102 vessels, fifty-nine pots probably belonging to the Peterborough tradition and thirty-five of Grooved Ware. Apart from twenty vessels of indeterminate character, the Peterborough Ware can be subdivided as follows: one vessel possibly of Ebbsfleet Ware, twenty-six vessels of Mortlake Ware and ten of Fengate Ware. Mortlake Ware has been found on nine sites and Fengate Ware on six. Indeterminate vessels of Peterborough Ware have been recorded from ten findspots. Taken together, the Peterborough vessels have been recorded from fourteen separate sites, if the two Cursus excavations are counted separately. The Grooved Ware, on the other hand, came from only four locations, two of which contained just three vessels between them. The distribution of these vessels is summarised in Figure 4.4 (p. 115), and, with only one exception, two vessels of possible Grooved Ware discovered close to South Lodge Camp, all were found near the Dorset Cursus. The virtual absence of Later Neolithic pottery from the clay with flints may be due partly to poorer conditions for preservation in that area.

The contexts of this material can be divided into five groups. Four of the sites contain pits and may represent settlement locations. Another four are burial monuments, probably built during the Later Neolithic; in addition, pottery of this date appears as residual material on the sites of three barrows of Bronze Age date. Three more groups of pottery were found in the secondary fillings of monuments constructed during the Earlier Neolithic and may be intentional deposits; this is particularly clear at Thickthorn Down long barrow, where all the finds came from the ditch terminals (Fig. 2.11, p. 42). In the same way the Grooved Ware from Wyke Down comes from formal deposits in the filling of a contemporary henge monument.

A few direct associations between these different styles should be noted here, although they will be discussed in detail in the companion volume. With one exception, Peterborough and Grooved Wares do not occur together. Only in Firtree Field was Peterborough Ware found in the same features as Grooved Ware, and even here only three Peterborough vessels, both Mortlake and Fengate Ware, are involved. The sherds of these two Peterborough styles did not occur in the same pits, however, but Mortlake and Fengate Wares were found together in the same general deposits at four sites: the secondary ditch fillings of the Cursus and Thickthorn Down long barrow and the early ditch silts of Handley Barrows 26 and 27. However, in all these cases they may result from different episodes of occupation and have been incorporated in the ditch fills long after their original use and discard. More doubtfully, there is possible Peterborough Ware from the pits on Handley Hill, excavated in 1893. This may have been associated with Beaker pottery but the surviving documentation is not sufficient to establish this relationship.

In this case the amount of Later Neolithic pottery from

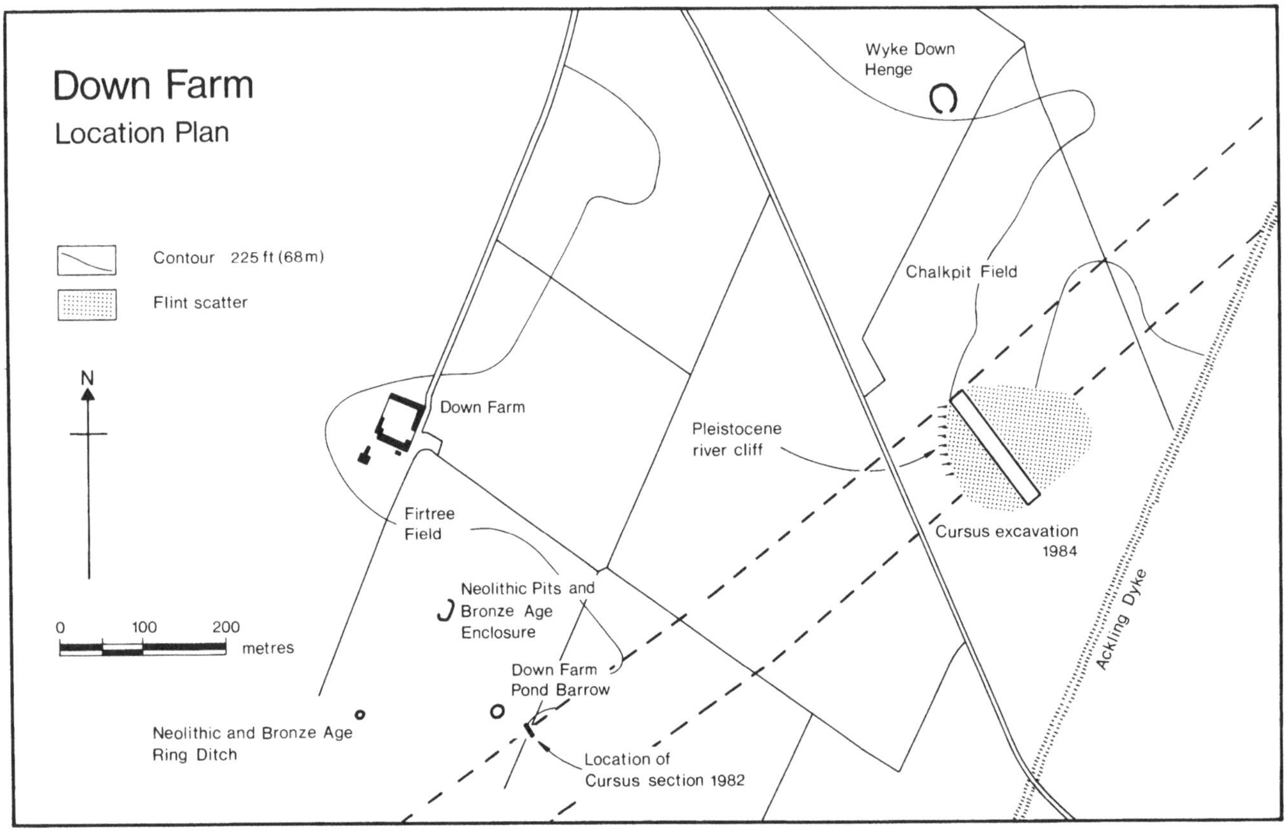

Fig. 3.6 The locations of the excavated sites at Down Farm, Woodcutts

the study area seems to be greater than the quantity recorded from the Bournemouth/Christchurch region, where Peterborough Ware is recorded on only two sites, Hengistbury Head and Holdenhurst long barrow. On the other hand, Grooved Ware is more common than Peterborough Ware and is recorded from five separate sites, again including Hengistbury Head (Gardiner in Cunliffe 1987, 38–47 and 330–3). The connections between this material and the Grooved Ware from Cranborne Chase will be considered later in this chapter.

3.3 The evidence of domestic activity: the results of excavation[1]

Although the study area contains so much Later Neolithic pottery, its detailed context is not always clear. Nothing can be added to our earlier account of the pits on Handley Hill, at least two of which contained Peterborough Ware, but recent excavation on other sites has done something to make good the deficiency. One site, associated with Peterborough Ware, was located over the Dorset Cursus, whilst the second, which was associated with Grooved Ware, was situated beside that monument (Fig. 3.6). This work provided an opportunity to investigate the character of the finds from this area of the landscape. We wished to discover whether this material reflected a phase of domestic settlement, or whether it resulted from more specialised deposits of non-utilitarian character. If some or all of this material *did* come from occupation sites, had their nature and organisation been influenced by the proximity of the Cursus? In each case these questions were investigated by considering spatial patterning. The two sites are treated in chronological order, before the evidence of both excavations is combined in a more general discussion.

3.3.1 The Peterborough Ware-associated site at Chalkpit Field (Figs. 3.6–3.8)[1]

The existence of this site was first noted in print in 1981 as an artefact scatter with a range of distinctive contents, whose position overlapped that of the Dorset Cursus (Barrett, Bradley, Green and Lewis 1981, 213). The site occupied a low spur running roughly south-west, overlooking the source of the River Allen and bounded by a Pleistocene river cliff. The subsoil was a mixture of Coombe Rock, Upper Chalk and clay with flints. The whole area was crossed by the Cursus running roughly north-east, with the larger ditch to the west just above the cliff. We have already reviewed the character of its earthwork as revealed by excavation.

Since our major objectives were to examine the spatial relationship of the artefact scatter to the Cursus and to obtain stratified samples of flintwork, pottery and animal bones, excavation was preceded by extensive surface survey. After Martin Green had defined the apparent limits of the scatter in his own fieldwork, it was decided to confine investigation to a transect 150 m long and 20 m wide, crossing the site at the only point where we could observe the full width of the flint scatter and both ditches of the Cursus. Pre-excavation analysis consisted of total surface collection within the transect, all worked and burnt flint being left *in situ* once its density had been recorded. Magnetic susceptibility analysis, phosphate analysis and geophysical survey were also undertaken at this stage. In combination, these different approaches suggested the existence of a series of separate zones within the ploughsoil and the presence of a number of pits.

One aim of this work was to assess how far the organisation of Later Neolithic activity was constrained by the character of the Cursus, and for this reason excavation was intended to investigate the spatial patterning in the ploughsoil and to relate such variations to the contents of subsoil features. It was also designed to examine any stratified deposits surviving in the excavated sample. The excavation was laid out in a series of short transects dug in sample units measuring 2 m × 2 m. These 'sectioned' the apparent boundaries between the zones defined by surface survey, but were sometimes offset in order to cross the positions of subsoil features suggested by geophysical analysis. Finally, surface survey had been accompanied by auger sampling of the subsoil, with the result that it was clear that the best preservation of bone and pottery could be expected in the western Cursus ditch, the eastern ditch being in an area with an acid base. Accordingly, a length of 8 m of the western ditch was cleared, whilst the eastern ditch was merely sectioned to relate finds in the ploughsoil to the ditch stratigraphy. A fuller account of the methodological aspects of this project is published separately (Bradley 1987b). For our purposes we are concerned with only three aspects of the work: the stratification and environmental context of the Later Neolithic artefacts; the character of the parent assemblage; and the extent of recognisable spatial patterning in relation to the pre-existing monument.

3.3.1.i The context of the Later Neolithic artefacts[1]

Apart from the flintwork in the primary silts, mentioned on p. 31, virtually all the stratified finds came from the three uppermost levels of the western Cursus ditch (Fig. 2.13, 1984 section, ls. 1, 2 and 3). These layers consisted of symmetrical brown chalky silts, with variable densities of chalk fragments and flint nodules. It does not seem likely that any of them represent collapsed bank material. The uppermost layer in the ditch (*ibid.*, 1.1) may have been slightly disturbed in later ploughing and contained a few sherds of Iron Age date. There are minor differences in the stratification of the different finds. Animal bones occurred mainly in layers 2 and 3, although material in layer 1 may not have survived so well. Pottery was confined to layers 1 and 2, and sherds of similar form and fabric were distributed throughout these deposits without convincing signs of an internal sequence. Wet sieving and flotation of samples from these layers showed no sign of carbonised plants. Apart from occasional animal bones, there was a complete break between the finds from the primary filling (*ibid.*, 1.5) and the distribution of Later Neolithic material.

This separation is less apparent in the eastern ditch, where the earthwork had been recut several times, but in this case its filling had been disturbed by burrowing animals. Here worked and burnt flint extended almost to the lowest silts. The surface of this material produced a barbed and tanged arrowhead, but because this section was so disturbed, no weight can be placed on this evidence.

The only environmental evidence comes from molluscan analysis of the western ditch silts. Analysis by Roy Entwistle and Jill Parker suggests that the ditch

> had been dug in a predominantly shaded environment, perhaps local woodland. Open country species were present in very small numbers, but it is possible that similar evidence could be created by scrub or long undisturbed grass. At the same level as the finds of pottery there seems to have been a restricted episode of clearance, but this was not followed by an increase in the abundance of the open country species which might accompany arable or pastoral land use, and in the upper part of layer 2 the samples were again dominated by shade-loving species, although in smaller numbers. There was also a slight reduction in species diversity.

Such evidence suggests that this episode had only a limited impact on the contemporary environment.

Apart from the two ditches, the only geophysical features of archaeological significance were difficult to inter-

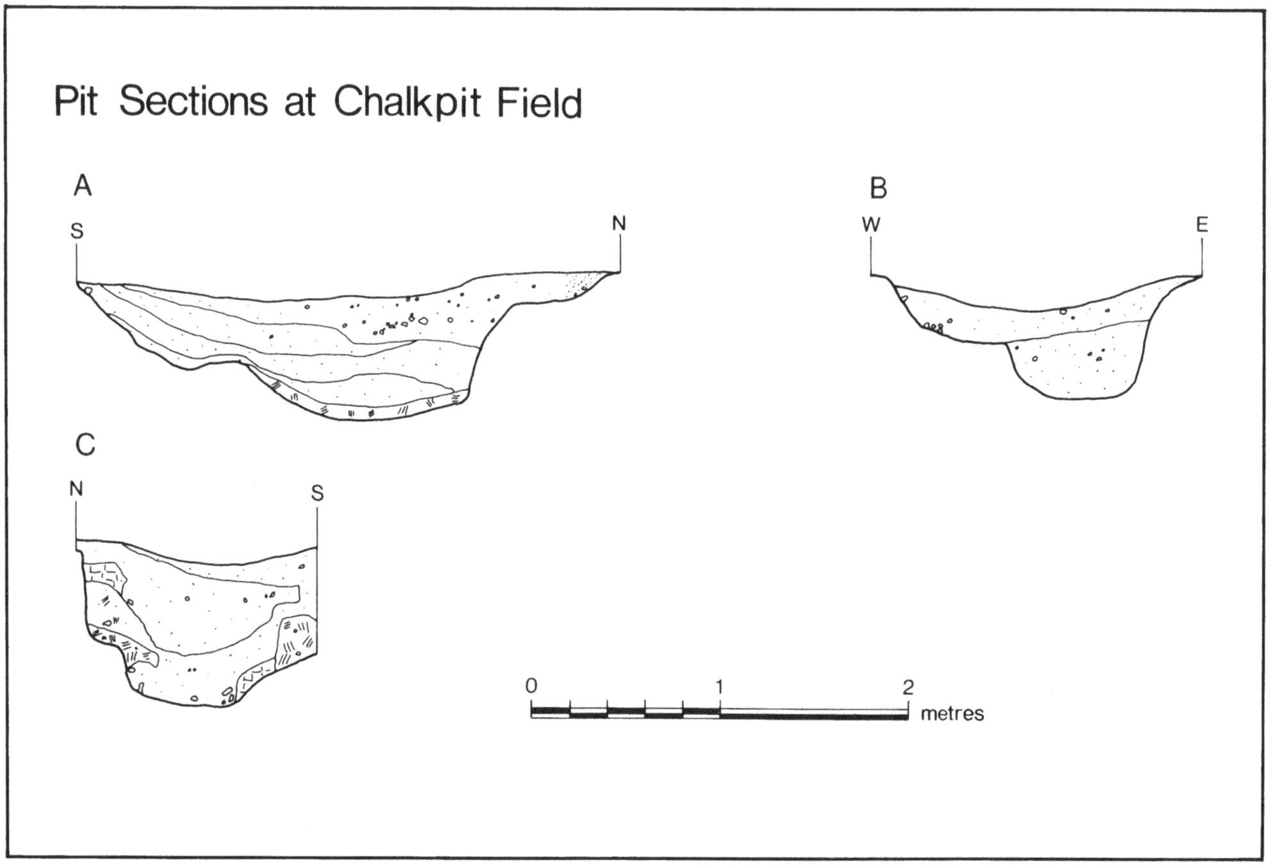

Fig. 3.7 Sections of the Later Neolithic pits in Chalkpit Field

pret. These were three pits, between 1.1 and 2.9 m in maximum dimensions and up to 0.9 m deep (Figs. 3.6 and 3.7). Like the eastern Cursus ditch they had been disturbed by burrowing animals. Enough could be recovered to show that they belonged to the Later Neolithic occupation of the site. One pit contained a blunted axe, of a rare type known on other Later Neolithic sites (Curwen 1939), and a second pit included a polished axe flake; the remaining flintwork was of similar character to the material in the ploughsoil.

3.3.1.ii The artefact assemblage[2–4]

All the excavated material consists of pottery, worked flint and bone. Three Peterborough sherds were discovered in later layers sealing the pits described earlier; otherwise all this material comes from layers 1 and 2 of the western Cursus ditch and consists of Mortlake and Fengate Wares, with a slight predominance of the latter style. There are no indications of an internal ceramic sequence in the ditch silts and the material was widely scattered along its length.

Similarly, all the bone recovered during excavation came from the filling of the western Cursus ditch. A small amount of this material comes from layer 3, underlying the Peterborough Ware. There were also two human long bones, probably from different individuals. There was some patterning in the distribution of different body parts. Layer 3 contained six fragments of limb and vertebrae accompanied by only one *Bos* tooth, whilst layer 2 included parts of at least four tooth rows of cattle and one of pig, as well as six limb bones. Such a contrast need not be a result of differential survival, since extremely friable pottery survived in layer 2.

Now that a representative sample of flintwork has been obtained by excavation, it also shows the features which distinguish groups found around the Cursus from those on the clay with flints (Table 3.4). Classifiable tool types amount to only 2.2 per cent of the assemblage, with a further 2 per cent of obviously retouched or utilised flakes. 2.6 per cent of the material consisted of cores or core fragments, including six of the discoidal cores thought to be associated with arrowhead production. 75 per cent of the classifiable tool forms were scrapers.

Table 3.4. *The proportions of different tool types amongst the surface finds from Chalkpit Field, compared with those in the excavated sample*

Implement type	Surface sample	Excavated sample
Scrapers	71.0%	68.0%
Hollow scrapers	–	6.6%
Borers	2.2%	6.6%
Chisel arrowheads	3.6%	6.6%
Oblique arrowheads	0.7%	–
Leaf-shaped arrowheads	0.7%	–
Barbed & tanged arrowheads	–	1.3%
Fabricators	10.2%	1.3%
Polished edge knives	–	2.7%
Polished axe (broken)	1.5%	–
Polished axe flakes	1.5%	1.3%
Picks	–	1.3%
Blunted axe-like implement	–	1.3%
Plano-convex knife	0.7%	–
Flaked axe/roughout	5.0%	–
Miniature axe	1.5%	–
Y-shaped tool	0.7%	–
Notched flake	–	1.3%
Denticulate	–	1.3%
Macehead	0.7%	–
Number of implements	75	137

Apart from one flake from a polished axe, all the raw material seems to have been local to the site.

In the light of our earlier discussion, four implement types from the excavation may be noted: a long narrow blade with shallow bifacial flaking and worn or polished edges; a finely polished knife of plano-convex section found in the secondary filling of the western Cursus ditch; a bifacially retouched blade, found in one of the pits, which resembles the 'blunted axe-like implements' recorded by Curwen (1939) in Sussex; and six arrowheads. Five are of the chisel form associated with Peterborough Ware, whilst the sixth is a barbed and tanged arrowhead of Green Low type and was found in the highest level of the eastern Cursus ditch (cf. Green 1980, 51 and 140). Comparison of the excavated implements with the finds from surface collection shows that the more mundane items are only slightly under-represented on the surface (Table 3.4).

3.3.1.iii Spatial analysis: the lithic scatter and the Cursus (Fig. 3.8)[2]

Detailed examination of the 3,393 worked flints found in the ploughsoil has suggested that the excavated transect may be divided into four zones numbered from west to east. These have the following characteristics:

Zone 1 is the most distinct. It coincides with the position of the western ditch of the Cursus. The area outside the monument was occupied by the Pleistocene river cliff and must have formed one boundary to the site, whilst the number of flints falls off markedly to the east. The ratio of implements to unretouched flakes in this area is quite low, but some *in situ* flint knapping seems to be in evidence. This also took place within the ditch, where good-quality nodules outcropped. Here fresh knapping debris was recovered in primary contexts (Fig. 2.13, 1984 section, 1.5), but it was distinct from the main group of flintwork in the secondary silts (*ibid.*, layers 1 to 3). 12 per cent of the sixty-six retouched pieces in the topsoil were recovered from the first 10 m of the excavated transect, whereas only 3.5 per cent came from the next 60 m.

Zone 2 occupies the highest part of the excavated transect and is completely contained within the Cursus. The density of worked flint was about the average for the site as a whole, but the only implements were three scrapers and three edge-retouched flakes. The source of the raw material appears to have been a very local patch of clay with flints, and there was quite a high proportion of cortical and broken flakes in this area. Whilst this might suggest that flint knapping had taken place here, the absence of cores is unexpected. However, the small size of the flakes and the high proportion of broken pieces would be explained if they had been trampled into the ground surface, when the rest of the area was cleared of debris. This is consistent with ethnoarchaeological observations (cf. Schiffer 1983, 679–80) and might also explain why the highest part of the site gave enhanced magnetic readings but lacked any burnt flints. Since this zone is central to the Cursus, it may have been kept clean for domestic activities or for some more specialised purpose.

Zone 3 extends from the high ground to the eastern ditch of the Cursus. It had been badly disturbed by Iron Age ploughing, which may have caused some down-slope movement of artefacts. It also led to some blurring of boundaries in the vicinity of the ditch itself. This was the most sheltered part of the site and contained all three Neolithic pits. Zone 3 included a few sherds of Mortlake Ware and had the highest density of burnt flint on the site. This part of the excavated transect contained ten of the thirteen tool types, including convex and hollow scrapers, borers and a variety of edge-retouched pieces. Subject to our comment about the clearance of debris from Zone 2, this suggests that a wider range of activities took place here than on other parts of the site.

Zone 4 was outside the Cursus to its east. This produced fewer worked flints than expected for the area excavated, but had the highest ratio of cores and

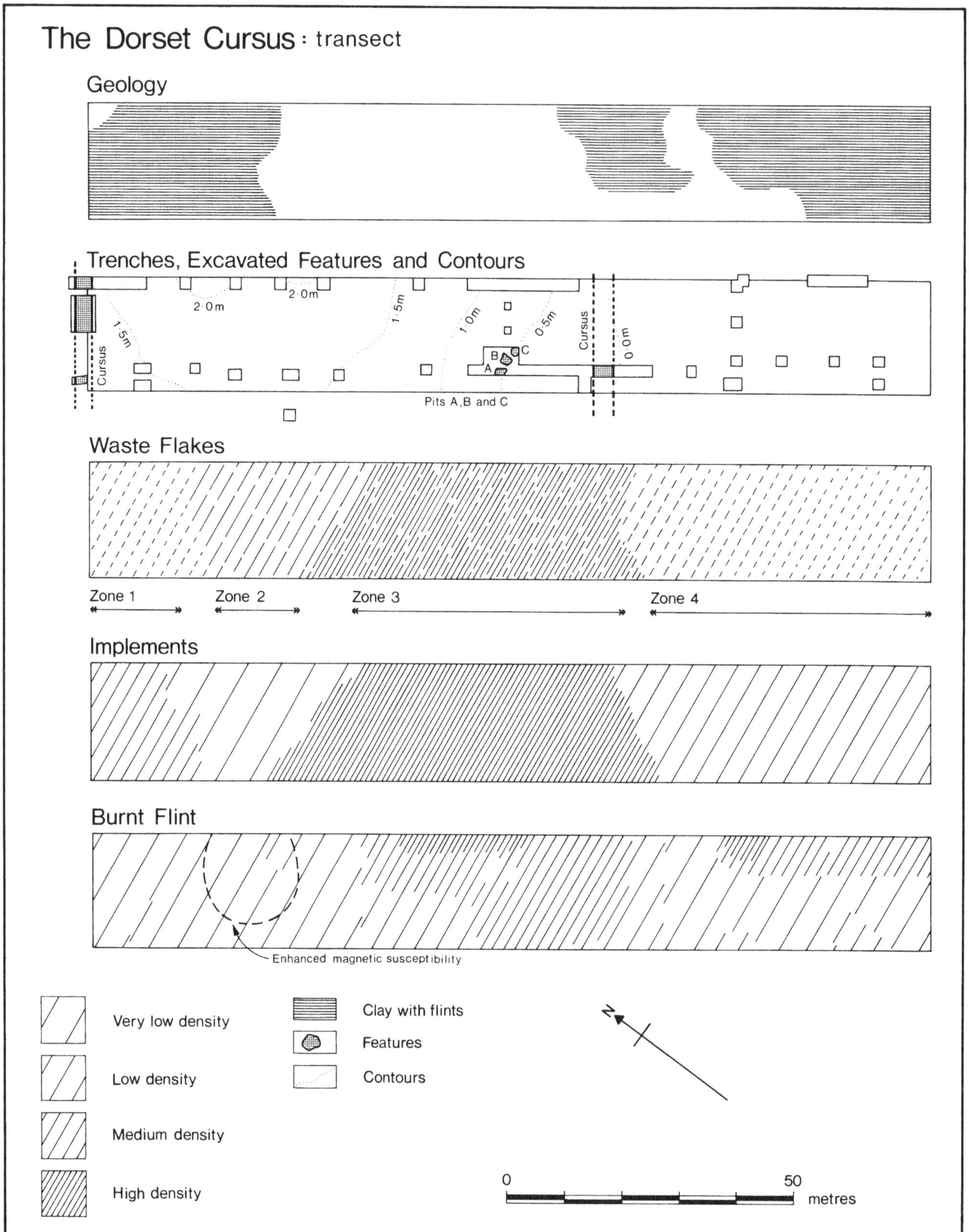

Fig. 3.8 The excavated transect across the Dorset Cursus in Chalkpit Field. The upper two drawings summarise the geology of the site, the topography, the positions of the excavated trenches and the locations of Neolithic features. The lower three drawings summarise the relative densities of excavated material in relation to the four zones described in the text

implements to flakes. Most of the implements were simple edge-retouched flakes, and these seem to have included a few residual pieces of Mesolithic date. Zone 4 included a deposit of clay with flints, which seems to have provided most of the raw material used on the site. The low proportion of regular implements, however, suggests that this zone had been used mainly for flint procurement. It is particularly striking that it should lie so near to the main occupation area on the site and that the division between the two should have been marked by the earthwork of the Cursus.

3.3.1.iv Discussion[1,2]

Now that we have an unbiased sample of archaeological material, our perception of the character of this site is somewhat changed. Special artefact types continue to appear, but it is easier to see the problem in perspective. The industry was made from nodules obtained on the site itself, even though better raw material was available nearby. At the same time, the character of the flintwork suggests that the site was used for an appreciable period, since it includes unfinished arrowheads as well as perfectly serviceable examples which had apparently been discarded. The polished axe flakes also suggest that tools were used for long enough to need repairing, and a number of artefacts exhibit signs of heavy wear. Similar concentrations of scrapers, borers and fabricators are found on sites with evidence of structures, and there seems little to separate this industry from excavated groups for which a domestic role is accepted.

On the other hand, these results also stress the individual character of this site. At least two artefact types, the polished knife and the macehead, are known from burials of this period (cf. Manby 1974, 86–90 and 92–104), whilst the small sample of animal bones has other unusual features. They seem to include a rather high proportion of wild animals for this period and certain body parts may have been intentionally selected for deposition in the Cursus ditch. The sample is extremely small, but its individual character is only emphasised by the discovery of human bones in the same deposit as the main group of pottery.

The excavation was designed to highlight any spatial patterning in the distribution of cultural material across the Cursus. In this it was largely successful. Even though Zone 4, with its greater evidence of 'industrial' activity, was in a part of the site with a deposit of clay with flints, the very low proportion of regular implements there suggests that the existing boundary of the Cursus separated an area of domestic activity inside the monument from one with more evidence of flint procurement outside it (Fig. 3.8). In short, the Cursus retained enough importance during the Later Neolithic to have attracted a rather distinctive settlement, and to have influenced the way in which activities inside it were organised.

3.3.2 The Grooved Ware-associated site at Firtree Field[5,1]

Before the evidence from Chalkpit Field can be studied in a wider context, we must introduce another excavated site. This lies on a low rise in the Upper Chalk about 130 m north-west of the Dorset Cursus (Fig. 3.6). Although the site was identified by a surface artefact scatter, much of the Neolithic material had been masked by flintwork originating in a Middle Bronze Age enclosure. The more diagnostic Neolithic items included four flaked axes, two picks, a Y-shaped tool and five transverse arrowheads. Neolithic activity should also account for some of the scrapers, fabricators and borers, but these types are recorded in both periods.

In this case excavation was determined by the chance discovery of the Bronze Age enclosure, and this governed its extent and the decision to remove the ploughsoil by machine (see pp. 183–200). It also meant that some of the Neolithic features had been damaged by later occupation. Even so, it was possible to recognise two clusters of Neolithic pits, plus one outlier, and an area of stakeholes which do not conform to the Bronze Age settlement plan (Fig. 3.9). The northern cluster of pits was excavated entirely, as was the single outlier, but the southern cluster, which was cut by the Bronze Age enclosure ditch, probably extended outside the excavated area. A further pit, 6A, had been cut away by the enclosure ditch and its contents were found as residual material in the filling of the latter feature.

3.3.2.i The excavated features[5,1,8]

Sixteen Neolithic pits were excavated (Figs. 3.9 and 3.10). One pit, Pit 26, was cut by a later feature which is interpreted as a treehole, whilst Pit 11A cut through a similar feature, which was also cut by the Bronze Age enclosure ditch. Pit 24 also impinged on a possible treehole, but their chronological relationship was ambiguous. In addition, Pit 25B seems to have been a treehole but cut through Pit 25A and was itself cut by Pit 25C, suggesting that a lengthy sequence is involved. The northern group of pits contained seven features, densely distributed over an area measuring 8 m by 3 m. The other group covered at least 200 m^2 but its southern and eastern limits were not defined. The pits were generally circular or oval in plan, with maximum dimensions between 0.7 and 1.35 m,

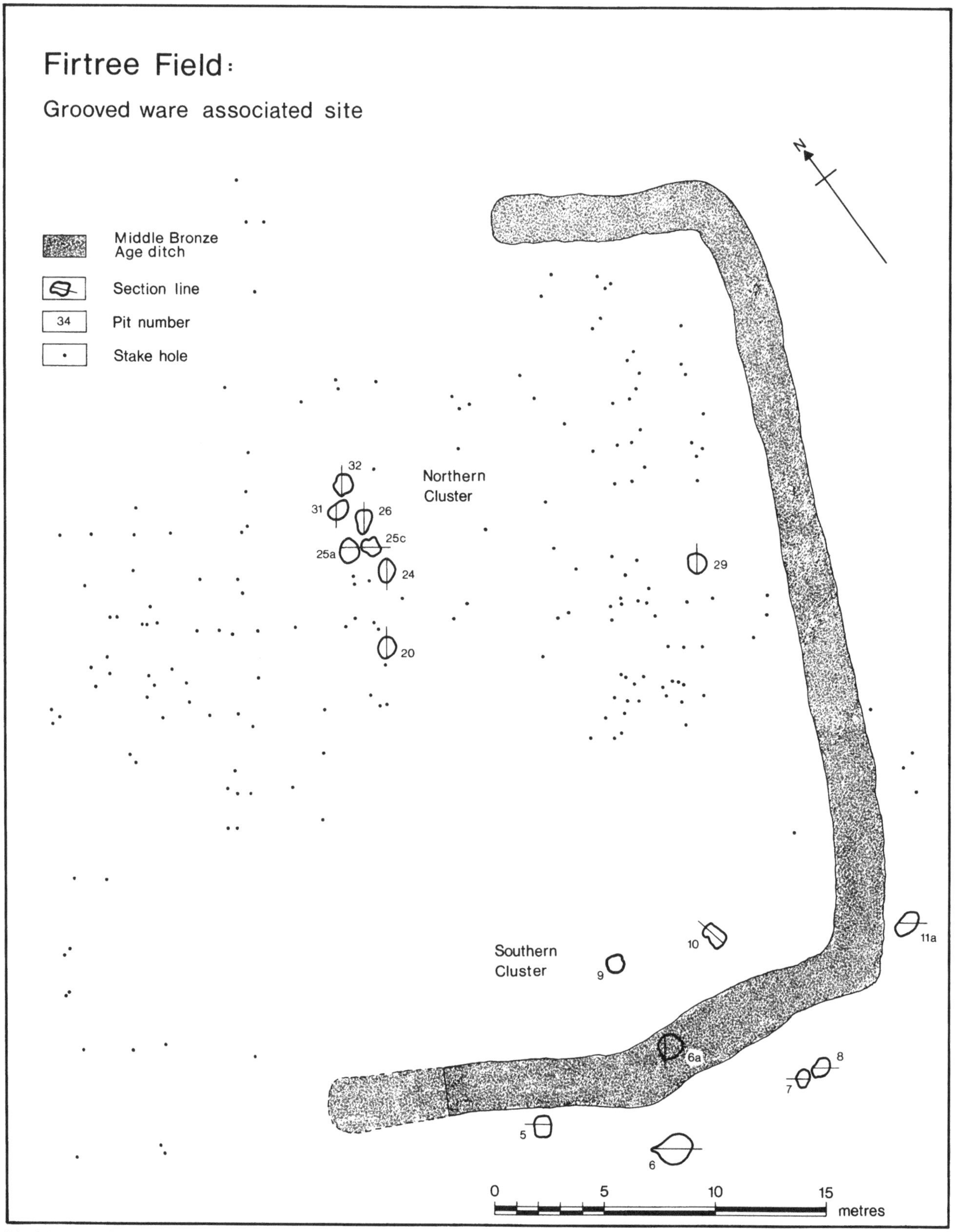

Fig. 3.9 Plan of the Later Neolithic site in Firtree Field, showing the positions of the excavated pits and stakeholes in relation to the Middle Bronze Age enclosure ditch

and were between 0.09 and 0.68 m deep in the natural chalk. These pits had four characteristic profiles:

A. Steep sides and flat or rounded bottoms
B. Shallow scoop
C. Shallow sides and flat bottom
D. Asymmetrical profile, shallowly shelving

In addition, the pits had three characteristic types of filling:

i. Asymmetrical filling including chalk rubble and dark humic material
ii. Patches and pockets of chalk rubble and dark humus
iii. Homogeneous dark earth

In some cases the pits had been disturbed during the Bronze Age and cannot be classified. The forms and fillings are listed in Tables 3.5 and 3.6, together with their contents, and the sections are illustrated in Fig. 3.10. The interpretation of this evidence is discussed below, but at this stage it is worth highlighting two further characteristics of these features. First, there are a few striking variations between the contents of the different types of pit. Type A contains all the arrowheads and polished flint implements on the site; it also contains a series of deposits associated with use of fresh chalk flint to be described below. Types A and B contain all the finds of 'boars' tusks' (pig incisors), and Types B and D contain the only finds of shells. Two of the three finds of Peterborough Ware were in pits with type iii fillings, as were the finds of arrowheads and polished implements. In addition, nearby pits tended to share the same form and the same type of filling.

Secondly, several of the pits contained what seemed to be rather formal deposits. In the southern group, Pit 7 contained two 'boars' tusks', one found beside a scraper and a complete Group VII axe, whilst Pit 8 contained a large quantity of antler. Pit 11A had a still more complex sequence, with an ox skull on its base, covering an antler. Higher in the filling of this pit were two more red deer antlers, whilst elsewhere in this feature a 'boar's tusk' and a roe deer antler were found together. There were fewer deposits in the northern group of pits, but Pit 24 contained an antler pick and a single tine, whilst Pit 6 included a large slab of pottery, which seemed to have been placed in its filling with the decorated surface uppermost. The other complex deposit was a group of six antlers on the base of Pit 32, which also contained a 'boar's tusk'. Lastly, the outlying Pit 29 contained a striking association between a pig mandible and a stone axe.

It is also clear from Andrew Brown's analysis of the flintwork that further distinctions can be made at the level of the individual context within these pits. The argument will be pursued in detail in the companion volume, but already it is apparent that two types of lithic raw material – small nodules of gravel flint and fresh or slightly weathered nodules of chalk flint – were being used on the site and were being worked down in quite different ways. The rarity of refitting material suggests that both groups were being introduced from middens or other deposits. The contexts with 'fresh' raw material tend to be associated with pigs' jaws, 'boars' tusks', cattle skulls, antler picks and rakes, whilst those with gravel flint are found with other body parts, such as vertebrae and long-bone fragments. The contexts containing 'fresh' raw material can also include axes, arrowheads or serrated flakes, as well as decorated sherds of Grooved Ware. Those with gravel flint are mainly associated with undecorated pottery. These two types of context are equally divided between the two groups of pits and the outlier, 29, but where there is a sequence of deposits, in Pits 6, 24 and 26, the gravel flint assemblage is secondary to groups associated with fresh raw material.

In addition to pits, excavation revealed a series of stakeholes. These were limited to roughly half the excavated area, despite favourable conditions for their survival and recognition elsewhere (Fig. 3.9). Where the stakeholes were 'box sectioned', they tapered to a point and had been set vertically into the chalk to depths of between 0.10 and 0.15 m. Their chronology can never be certain, but they occur in the same area as a series of Bronze Age buildings. Their distribution makes no sense at all in relation to these later structures (cf. Fig. 5.27, p. 185), but focuses on the area between the northern group of Neolithic pits and the outlier, Pit 29. There are too many stakeholes for obvious patterning to be recognised, but to the west of the latter feature it may be possible to pick out a series of fairly uniform arcs of stakeholes, on a diameter of about 3 m.

It seems likely, then, that the stakeholes belong to the same period as the pits. Moreover, there are indications that the two clusters of pits might have been in use at the same time. Sherds from Pits 6 and 25A, in the southern and northern clusters respectively, seem likely to belong to the same vessel, whilst samples of antler from one feature in each of these groups have given very similar radiocarbon dates: 2190 ± 60 bc for Pit 11a (BM 2406) and 2130 ± 50 bc for Pit 32 (BM 2407). The types and filling of the pits in both groups are also similar, apart from a greater proportion of type iii fillings in the northern cluster.

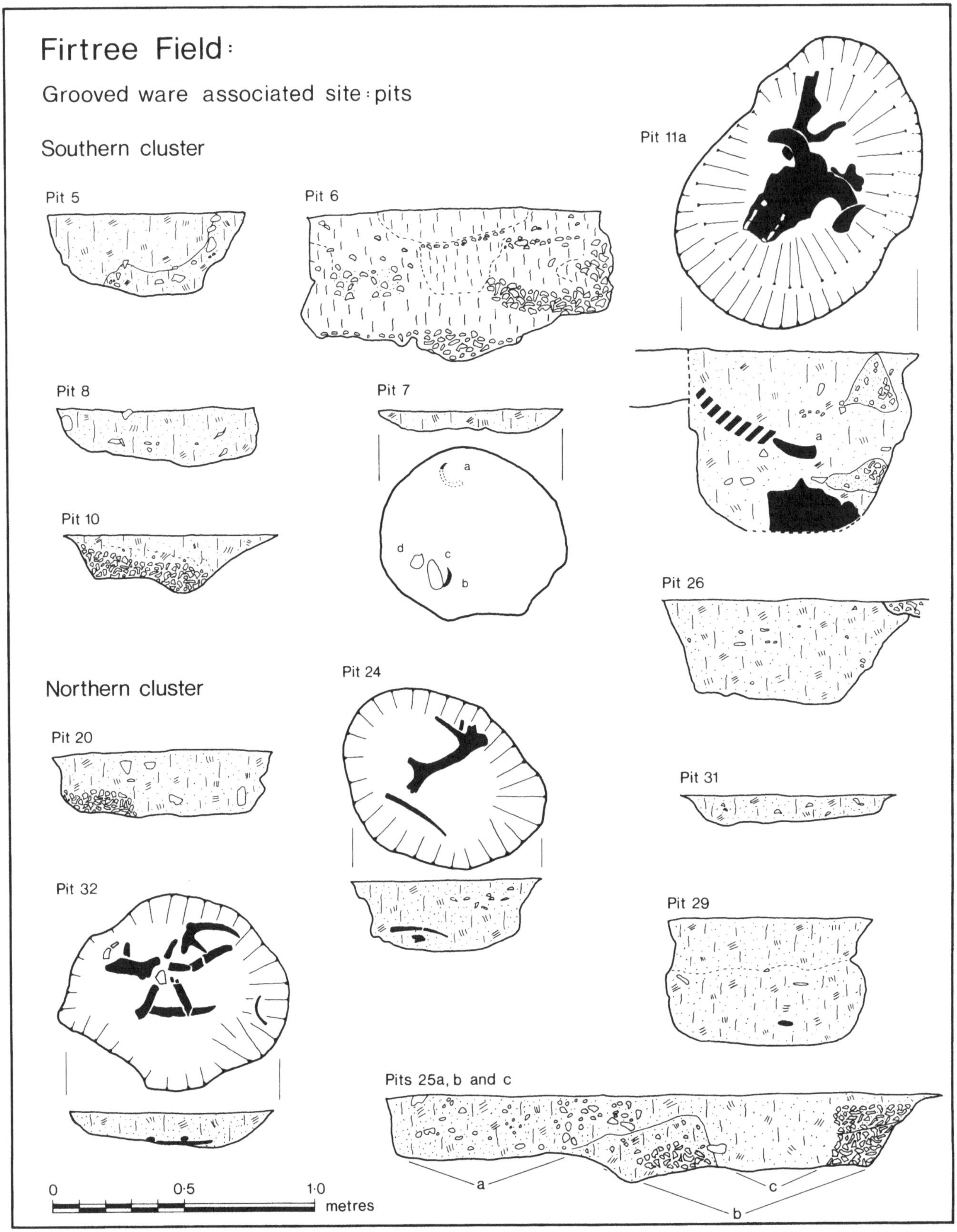

Fig. 3.10 Sections of the Later Neolithic pits in Firtree Field, with outline plans showing the layout of the principal deposits. Major finds of bone and antler are shown in black. The hatched area in the section of Pit 11a is a later disturbance. In the plan of Pit 7, (a) and (b) represent 'boars' tusk' blades, (c) represents an axe and (d) represents a flint scraper

Table 3.5. *The form, filling and contents of the Neolithic pits in Firtree Field*

	Pit type	Filling type	Minimum number of vessels	Flakes and cores	Flint/stone implements or utilised flakes	Animals represented	Antler
South Cluster							
5	A	i	1 G	79	8	p, c	–
6	A	i	2 G	45	2	p, c	–
7	B	UC	1 G	18	6	p, c	–
8	D	iii	1 G	162	11	p, c, s/g	1 red deer
9	A	UC	–	61	2	p	–
10	C	i	1 G; 1 P	13	3	c	–
11A	A	ii	1 G	66	4	p, c, red deer, roe deer, b	3 red deer 1 roe deer
North Cluster							
20	A	iii	4 G	47	3	p, c	–
24	A	iii	10 G	90	8	p, c, s/g	2 red deer
25A	A	iii	7 G; 1 P	60	4	p, c	–
25B	C	ii	5 G; 1 P	38	–	p, c	–
26	A	iii	2 G	63	–	s/g, red deer,	1 roe deer
31	B	i	1 G	18	–	–	–
32	B	i	4 G	185	4	p, c, s/g	6 red deer
Outlier							
29	A	iii	2 G	422	41	p, c, red deer	–

G = Grooved Ware
P = Peterborough Ware

p = pig; c = cattle;
s/g = sheep/goat;
b = bear

UC = unclassified

3.3.2.ii Spatial analysis: the pits and the Cursus[1]

Although neither group of pits is far from the Cursus, it was obvious, even during excavation, that the greater variety of archaeological material was in the southern cluster, which was located rather nearer to that monument, and also in the isolated Pit 29. At a more subjective level, this also seemed to apply to the character of the deposits found inside the pits, which appeared to be more complex at the southern end of the excavated area. By contrast, the pits with the less complicated fillings were generally in the area with the stakeholes. Both patterns are crosscut by the distinction between contexts associated with chalk flint and those containing inferior raw material, but these are equally distributed between the two areas. In this case, the major contrast was between the upper and lower fillings of some of these features.

Our subjective observations were only reinforced during post-excavation analysis, and in this section we consider to what extent they can be demonstrated for the excavated material as a whole. With that information in mind, we can also consider the basic interpretation of this site, and in particular its credentials as an area of *domestic* activity.

We need to make two basic comparisons: between the contents of the two clusters of pits, and between these and the finds from the one outlier, Pit 29. This discussion proceeds in three stages. First, the most common items on the site are considered. Next we consider the distributions of the less frequent types of artefact and, lastly, we offer an overview of the spatial patterning as a whole.

The first level of comparison concerns the most frequent classes of material and for this reason there are sufficient items for these figures to be presented as means and standard deviations. At this stage we are concerned with the relative frequency of flint debitage, flint implements and pottery (Table 3.7).

Already it is clear that Pit 29 stands out from the others, although the southern pit group has more flint implements and the northern group contains more pottery and includes more broken pieces of each vessel. (There are two exceptions to the latter pattern, Pits 8 and 26, with only one and two vessels respectively.) Only the outlier, Pit 29, contains Woodlands-style Grooved Ware.

Where the total amount of material is smaller, it seems to be more informative to consider the contents of each cluster together, again comparing these with the evidence from Pit 29 (Table 3.8). Most of this analysis is concerned with the details of the flint industry, but in addition we

Table 3.6. *Further details of the excavated material from the Neolithic pits in Firtree Field*

	South cluster							North cluster							Outlier
	5	6	7	8	9	10	11A	20	24	25A	25B	26	31	32	29
Flint axe	–	–	–	–	–	1	–	–	–	–	–	–	–	–	–
Stone axe	2	–	1	–	–	–	1	–	–	–	–	–	–	–	2
Axe roughout	–	–	–	–	–	–	–	–	–	–	–	–	–	–	1
Arrowhead	–	–	–	–	–	–	–	–	1ob	–	–	–	–	–	2ch
Scraper	3	1	2	4	1	1	3	3	5	2	–	–	–	2	8
Borer	–	1	–	–	–	–	–	–	–	–	–	–	–	–	10
Knife	–	–	–	2	–	–	–	–	–	–	–	–	–	–	–
Burin	–	–	–	–	–	–	–	–	–	–	–	–	–	–	?1
Saw	2	–	–	1	–	–	–	–	–	–	–	–	–	1	5
Waisted implement	–	–	1	–	–	–	–	–	–	–	–	–	–	–	–
Chopping tool	–	–	–	–	–	–	–	–	1	–	–	–	–	–	1
Hammerstone	–	–	2	4	–	–	–	–	–	–	–	–	–	–	–
Edge-polished knife	–	–	–	–	–	–	–	–	–	–	–	–	–	–	1
Edge-polished flake	–	–	–	–	–	–	–	–	–	2	–	–	–	–	10
Utilised flake	1	–	–	–	1	–	–	–	–	–	–	–	–	–	8
Notched flake	–	–	–	–	–	–	–	–	–	–	–	–	–	–	2
'Boars' tusks'	1	–	1	–	–	–	1	–	–	–	–	–	–	1	1
Haematite fragment	1?	–	–	–	–	–	–	–	–	–	–	–	–	–	–
Sarsen fragment	–	8	1	–	2	–	–	3	9	–	–	1	–	1	6
Sandstone fragment	–	–	–	5	2	–	–	–	1	–	–	–	–	–	–
Marcasite fragment	–	1	–	–	–	–	–	–	–	–	–	–	–	–	1
Banded flint pebble	1	–	–	–	–	–	–	–	–	–	–	–	–	–	–
Limestone pebble	–	–	–	–	–	1	–	–	–	–	–	–	–	–	–
Chalk fossil	–	–	–	–	–	–	1	–	1	–	–	–	–	–	1
Marine shells	–	–	–	P	–	–	–	–	–	–	–	–	–	P	–

ob: oblique.
ch: chisel.
P: present.

Table 3.7. *The relative frequency of worked flint and pottery in the pit group at Firtree Field*

	Southern pit group	Northern pit group	Pit 29
Flakes and spalls per pit	57 ± 41	70 ± 48	408
Implements per pit	4.0 ± 2.1	2.0 ± 1.7	21
Minimum number of vessels per pit	1.1 ± 0.4	4.4 ± 2.8	2
Sherds per vessel by individual pit	2.2 ± 0.7 (omitting Pit 8)	2.8 ± 0.9 (omitting Pit 26)	26.5
Peterborough styles	Fengate	Fengate; Mortlake	–
Grooved Ware styles	Clacton; Durrington Walls	Durrington Walls	Woodlands

include deposits of 'boars' tusks' and antler, and pits yielding carbonised cereals.

Again Pit 29 stands out from the others, although it shows the same evidence of flint knapping as the contents of the nearest pit cluster. Generally speaking, individual implement types are more abundant in Pit 29 and also in the southern group of pits, although this is not true of arrowheads. The same applies to the edge-polished flakes, whose distinctive appearance seems to be the result of heavy use (Andrew Brown pers. comm.). More striking is the evidence for greater flint processing from the fills of the northern group of pits. This part of the site also produced more evidence of carbonised cereals. Animal bone shows less spatial patterning, with only

Table 3.8. *The distribution of different categories of archaeological material among the pit groups at Firtree Field*

	Southern pit group	Northern pit group	Pit 29
Cores and irregular lumps: flakes	1:9.1	1:34.8	1:29
Regular cores: flakes	1:28	1:81.3	1:67
Scrapers	15	12	8
Axes and axe fragments	5	–	2
Saws	3	1	5
Utilised flakes	2	1	8
Arrowheads	–	1	2
Edge-polished flakes	–	2	10
'Boars' tusk' deposits	3	1	1
Antler deposits	3	2	–
Pottery slabs	1	–	–
Pits with carbonised cereals	2	4	+
Number of pits considered	7	7	1

Table 3.9. *The range of contents of the pit group at Firtree Field*

	Southern pit group	Northern pit group	Pit 29
Range of raw materials per pit	6 ± 1.6	5 ± 1.8	10
Range of separate categories per pit	9 ± 1.8	7 ± 3.2	20

small numbers of identifiable specimens in each group of pits. The exceptions to this pattern are Pit 29 again, and Pit 11A in the southern group, which is the one feature dominated by cattle bones. It also contained one unusual item – the ulna of a bear.

Lastly, we can carry out a more elaborate analysis of the nature of these pits. First, it has been observed that the number of different raw materials represented in Grooved Ware pits is greatest when they are found close to major monuments (Bradley 1984, 52). Given the proximity of the Cursus, we can take this approach to the finds from Firtree Field. A related approach is to consider the number of different categories of material in these pits, from lumps of sarsen to entire axes. Both these methods highlight the important position of Pit 29 and the greater variety of contents in the southern group of pits (Table 3.9).

Secondly, we can consider the distribution of what were identified as 'formal' deposits during the excavation

Table 3.10. *The distribution of pits containing 'boars' tusks' or formal deposits at Firtree Field*

	Southern pit group	Northern pit group	Pit 29
Pits with formal deposits	3	3	+
Pits with 'boars' tusks'	3	1	+

of these pits. We can also consider the distribution of the one type of object whose special significance seems to be demonstrated by its occurrence with human burials – 'boars' tusks', more properly pig incisors, which seem to have been treated as artefacts. To some extent the emphasis falls on the southern group of pits and certainly on Pit 29 (Table 3.10).

A final approach is to compare the contents of these pits with occupation layers on other sites: to what extent are we entitled to suggest that material had been deliberately selected for burial in these pits? We can consider two kinds of excavated evidence: flintwork and animal bones. The first type of analysis is suggested by work in eastern England which has drawn attention to a series of Grooved Ware pits which include such a high number of finished implements that their contents might result from intentional selection (Cleal 1984, 148). This approach requires careful discussion.

It is essential to identify the character of Later Neolithic occupation levels before we can tell whether the contents of individual pits are really anomalous. Clearly, there are limitations on that approach. Pottery cannot be considered, because it survives better in subsoil features than it does on the surface. For this reason our calculations must be restricted to flintwork. Again, assemblages must be selected for study which come from ground surfaces and are not biased by the contents of pits and ditches. Since so few suitable deposits have been published in detail, we must accept that the available sample will be small and cannot be limited to sites associated with Grooved Ware. Lastly, we have to make two further selections and omit sites which for other reasons may have played a specialised role in the settlement pattern, or which are so much larger than the collections being studied here that comparisons might be misleading. In the first case, this means that 'limited activity sites' cannot be studied. In the second case it means that collections of less than 1,000 flints are most relevant.

With these qualifications, it is possible to study the composition of the flint assemblage on nine sites where the material has been collected from what were interpreted as middens or occupation layers. Those used are:

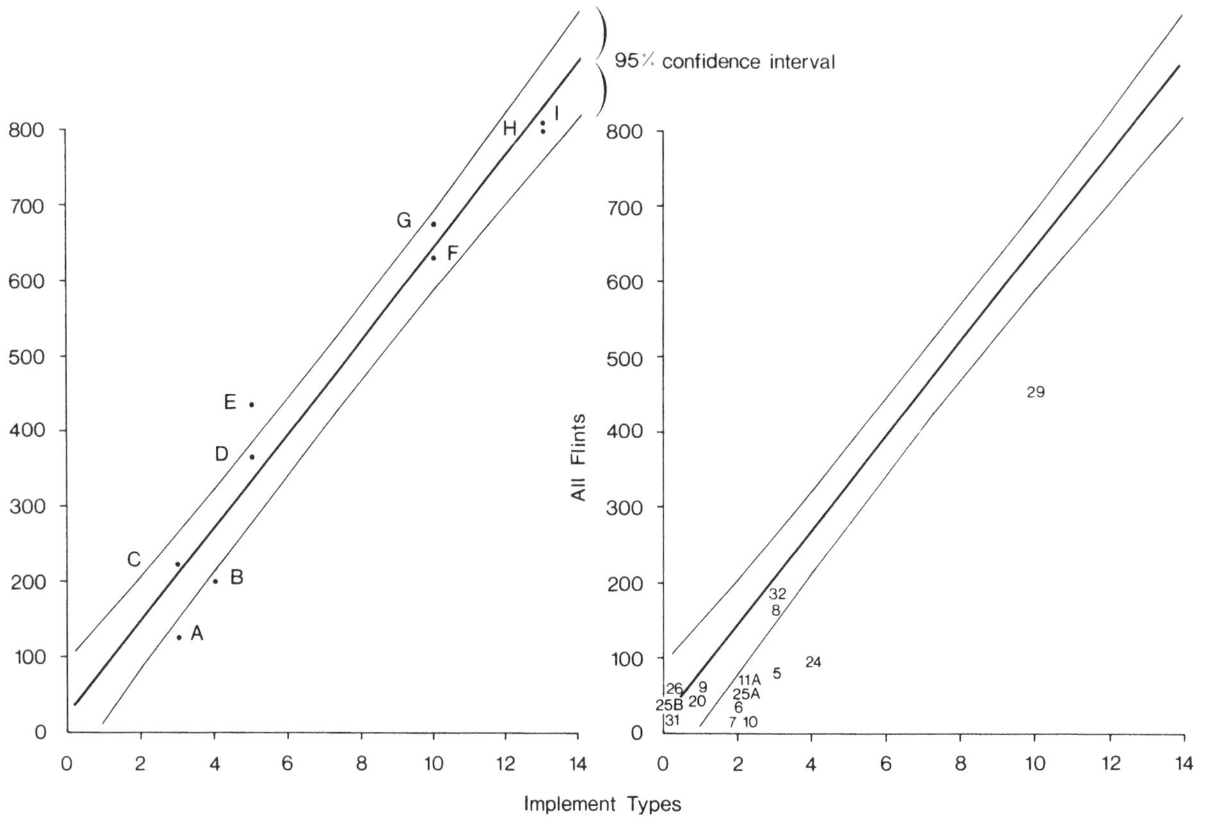

Fig. 3.11 (Left) The relationship between the number of implement types and the total size of the flint industry from a sample of nine excavated deposits which do not come from pits. The regression line and the 95 per cent confidence band are shown. Key – A: Swarkestone; B: Rudston Wold, East Reservoir Field 5; C: North Carnaby Temple, Field 3, site 3; D: Downton (Peterborough Ware site); E: North Carnaby Temple, Field 3, site 4; F: Willington; G: Trelystan; H: Downton (Beaker site) and I: Ecton. (Right) The excavated pits in Firtree Field in relation to the same regression line and confidence band

(A) Swarkestone (Greenfield 1960, 19–23); (B) Rudston Wold, East Reservoir Field 5 (Manby 1974, 20–2); (C) North Carnaby Temple Field 3, site 3 (*ibid.*, 52–61); (D) Downton, Peterborough Ware site (Rahtz 1962, 134–41); (E) North Carnaby Temple Field 3, site 4 (Manby 1974, 52–61); (F) Willington (Wheeler 1979, 133–44); (G) Trelystan (Britnell 1982, 173–83); (H) Downton, Beaker site (Rahtz 1962, 134–41); and (I) Ecton (Moore, Williams and Boddington 1975, 19–26). The total number of worked flints is plotted against the range of functionally different types, omitting irregular retouched pieces or utilised flakes, whose presence is not always recorded. There is a linear relationship between the two sets of figures (Fig. 3.11). This suggests that a remarkably consistent relationship may be found on sites which had not undergone intentional selection. Figure 3.11 also plots the 95 per cent confidence band.

It is instructive to plot the contents of the Down Farm pits on the same basis. This suggests that seven of the pits do not differ in this respect from the contents of occupation layers on Later Neolithic settlements; their contents may be drawn directly from the spread of refuse about the occupied area. On the other hand, six other pits fall outside the 95 per cent confidence band, and here it does seem that implements are over-represented. In such cases the contents of the pits could have undergone intentional selection. Only one of these pits was in the northern cluster, but four were in the southern

Table 3.11. *The distribution of anomalous features within the pit group at Firtree Field*

	Southern pit group	Northern pit group	Pit 29
Point scores for number of anomalies as percentage of possible maximum	48	24	100
Number of pits with anomalous features	6 (86% of total)	3 (43% of total)	+

group. In order of magnitude the greatest anomalies were: Pits 6, 7, 5, 10, 24 and the outlier, Pit 29. One member of each group, Pit 11A and Pit 25A, was a borderline case and is not considered further.

The second approach concerns the animal bones. This is discussed in detail by Legge in the companion volume. He comments on two striking features of this assemblage: the unusually low proportion of small unidentifiable fragments, together with the evidence that some of the bones had been gnawed by dogs. The survival of different body parts is very much what one would expect of an assemblage which had been exposed for some time before its burial. On the other hand, Legge considers that once that material was collected up for deposition in the pits, whole or relatively undamaged bones were deliberately selected. This is entirely consistent with some of the more striking patterns observed during excavation.

The major features considered here – the over-representation of implement types, the presence of 'boars' tusks' and the field evidence of formal deposition – are perhaps the best indications that some of the pits were used for specialised purposes. There are two ways of summarising this analysis (Table 3.11). Each of these features can be used in a scoring system by which any one pit can achieve a maximum score of 3. Alternatively, we can consider the distribution of the pits with any one or more of these features. In each case, Pit 29 stands out, together with the southern group of pits.

3.3.2.iii The interpretation of the excavated features[1]

If the contents of the different pits show such striking contrasts, it may be wrong to structure our discussion around mutually exclusive interpretations of the site. The continuing debate over 'domestic' versus 'ceremonial' interpretations of monuments like Durrington Walls emphasises the sterility of this approach (cf. Richards and Thomas 1984). 'Ritual' is a form of action; archaeological sites may be among the places where such actions took place, but this does not mean that they were necessarily dedicated to their performance. Rituals can form part of everyday life, and even if particular sites witnessed the structured deposition of artefacts or animal bones, that is no basis for categorising those sites as a whole.

In some respects we can compare this site with the site in Chalkpit Field, which we have already interpreted as a settlement. Again there is evidence of flint knapping, mostly from the northern pit cluster, but in this case the raw material was introduced from elsewhere and the actual location of these pits could have been selected for other reasons. There is only limited evidence for the production of objects at this site, and there were only two of the specialised cores thought to have been used for making arrowheads. There is little evidence for the maintenance of equipment: by contrast with Chalkpit Field, there was only one borer, and only one pit contained polished axe flakes. Other borers found in the ploughsoil could belong to the Bronze Age use of the site; the same applies to finds of fabricators. Because of the mixing of two lithic industries in the ploughsoil, it is hard to make direct comparisons, but it seems possible that use of this site may have been more specialised or less sustained than occupation in Chalkpit Field.

Stakeholes would not have survived in the unfavourable subsoil of the latter site, but work in Firtree Field did record a series of these features, confined to the area around the northern group of pits. Similar clusters of stakeholes are known on a range of sites in Wessex associated with Peterborough Ware, Grooved Ware and Beakers. These include Winterbourne Dauntsey (Stone 1934), King Barrow Ridge (Richards 1984, 183), Hengistbury Head (Chadburn in Cunliffe 1987, 65–6), Easton Down (Stone 1933) and Snail Down (Annable 1958, 8). In three cases arcs of stakeholes have been identified, surrounding pits or shallow hollows, and at Easton Down, the most extensively excavated of these sites, rings about 3 m in diameter seem to be the norm (Stone 1933). Again, this suggests that the evidence from Down Farm conforms to a wider pattern.

Other features of this site recall the evidence from henge monuments: the range of contents of the pits and the formality with which some of them were filled. The accumulations of antler resemble those at Durrington Walls (Wainwright and Longworth 1971, 22) and Maumbury Rings (Bradley 1975, 18–22; Bradley and Thomas 1984), and the distinctive distributions of different types of artefact and animal bone mirror the spatial patterning identified inside Durrington, Mount Pleasant, Woodhenge (Richards and Thomas 1984) and Maumbury (Bradley 1975; Bradley and Thomas 1984). If we consider these patterns as the residue of ritual actions, this does not mean that they must have taken place on what we call 'ritual sites'. Such deposits are not confined to these enclosures: indeed it is a characteristic of the Grooved Ware assemblage that some of the most varied collections of material are found *outside* such earthworks (see Bradley 1984, 52). Some of the closest parallels for the Down Farm Grooved Ware pits are in the area close to Woodhenge, where the positions of the Ratfyn pits had actually been marked by flint cairns (Stone 1935). Until recently these deposits were viewed in isolation, but the work of the Stonehenge Environs Project has shown that even the most distinctive pit groups could be located near to unexceptional artefact scatters (Richards 1984, 183). We are not dealing with a 'ritual landscape' here.

There is obviously a wide range of variation amongst Grooved Ware artefact assemblages, and this is complicated by the degree of formality with which some of them were deposited. There may be most evidence of structured deposition inside major monuments, but this does not allow us to treat such sites in isolation. If anything, Grooved Ware deposits show a gradient of decreasing complexity with distance from such sites (Bradley 1984, 52), but this *runs straight across* the boundaries of these enclosures. On a smaller scale such patterns may be observed in artefact scatters interpreted as settlement refuse. The work of the Stonehenge Environs Project suggests that on some sites we may find seemingly mundane deposits at the heart of the occupied area and more complex accumulations at or beyond its edges (Richards 1984, 183). This would be consistent with some of the spatial patterning observed in Firtree Field. There the more straightforward deposits are furthest from the Cursus and are found in part of the site where there is evidence of domestic activities and possibly of stake-built structures. Formal deposits are more common in the pits closer to the Cursus, but the most complex of all comes from an isolated feature on the edge of the site. On a still broader scale, these patterns are echoed in the evidence of surface flintwork, which includes a distinctive group of more elaborate artefacts in the area around the Cursus. It is to this wider, regional picture that we now return.

3.4 The evidence of earthwork monuments

3.4.1 Introduction[1]

It seems likely that the influence of the Cursus extended beyond the distribution of settlement. Like similar features elsewhere, it appears to have attracted other monuments to it long after its earthwork was in disrepair. This is often treated as evidence of 'continuity', but such continuity must be carefully defined, and questions of cultural meaning must be kept quite separate from the more tangible issue of chronology. The major developments treated here are the emergence of a new tradition of funerary monuments – round barrows – first witnessed around the existing earthwork at Wor Barrow, and the construction of the specialised enclosures known as henge monuments. Besides providing an account of the important sequence at Wor Barrow, this section describes a recently excavated round barrow or ring ditch adjoining the Cursus at Down Farm, and the investigation of a nearby henge monument whose entrance is aligned on the Peterborough Ware domestic site in Chalkpit Field. In addition to discussing these excavated sites, we shall also comment on the evidence of air photography, which again suggests that the Cursus was a focus for monument building throughout the later third millennium.

3.4.2 Structural details of the round barrows: the Wor Barrow complex[1,6,3]

3.4.2.i Introduction

It is ironic that such a well-known site as Wor Barrow should conceal a sequence of burials running from the long barrow, discussed on pp. 38–43, to two Later Neolithic round barrows, Handley 26 and 27. The reason that this evidence is not widely known is that Pitt Rivers' report (*Excavations* IV, 58–142) does not document the ceramic sequence in detail, and this has to be reconstructed from the museum material. Moreover, whilst the plan of Handley 27 is well known (*ibid.*, Pl. 293), its relationship to Wor Barrow has been overlooked. At the same time, its neighbour, Handley 26, is well known for its Later Neolithic burial, but the character of this mound, and even its relationship to Wor Barrow, have not been appreciated, since no plan of the barrow is provided with the excavation report.

The crucial elements for a fuller understanding of this complex are the pottery sequence in the ditches of the three barrows and the relative positions of the mounds and their Neolithic burials. The latter are provided in Figure 3.12, which brings together the published plans of Wor Barrow and Handley Barrow 27, as well as an outline plan of Barrow 26 made from a three-dimensional model of the site after excavation. This shows that the three earthworks go together to form a small cemetery.

The ditch silts of Wor Barrow contain an important pottery sequence, the main elements of which can be reconstructed from the depths marked on the sherds

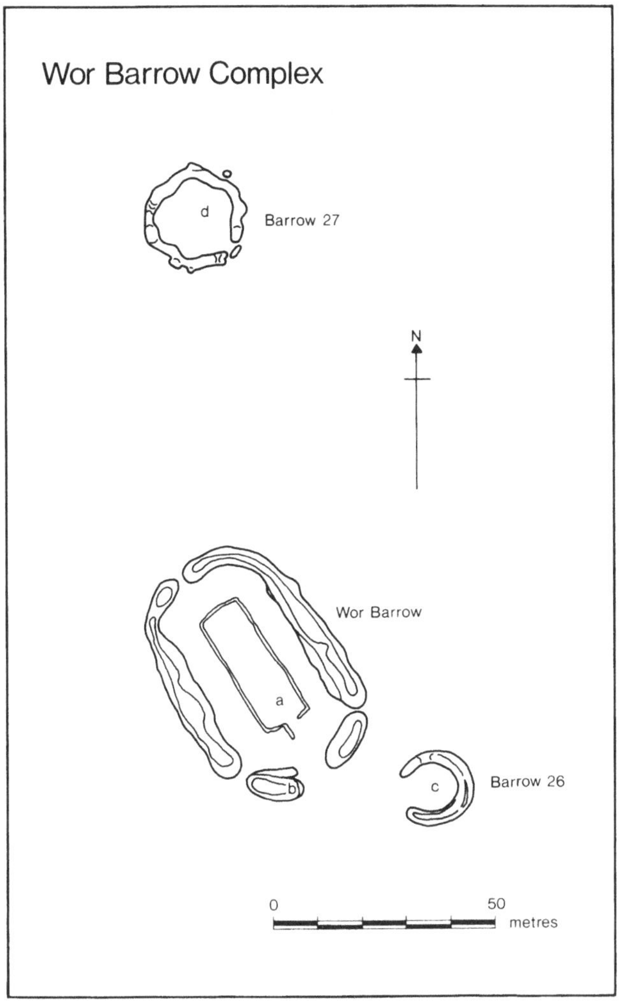

Fig. 3.12 Outline plan of Wor Barrow and Handley Barrows 26 and 27 (a, b, c and d represent human burials)

themselves. The lowest silts of the ditch contain plain bowls of Earlier Neolithic date. A general context is offered by the two dates quoted earlier (p. 43). Above these, but below any of the Peterborough Ware on the site, were two crouched skeletons, only one an adult, which had been buried together in the ditch silts against the west terminal of the entrance. These were associated with a relatively large lozenge-shaped arrowhead. The burials were fully articulated and both were identified as males. In these respects they recall some of the deposits beneath the long barrow itself. At a higher level in the long-barrow ditch were sherds of Ebbsfleet/Mortlake Ware, and higher still were pieces of Mortlake Ware. Beaker pottery also occurred in the upper silts, certain pieces at a considerable depth in the ditch. Reference to Pitt Rivers' site records, however, show that Roman graves had been excavated into the silts to about this depth, and it is possible that this material was intrusive.

3.4.2.ii Handley Barrow 26

Not much is known about the structure of this barrow. Before excavation it seems to have been 0.90 m high. This low mound was surrounded by a ditch 13 m in diameter, with a single causeway to the west, pointing towards the 'entrance' of Wor Barrow (Fig. 3.12). The ditch had a distinctive profile on the carpenter's model, suggesting that it had been recut at least once. The Neolithic burials are not shown, but Pitt Rivers' report indicates that two were found on the old land surface. At the centre of the mound was an unaccompanied inhumation, but a skeleton identified as male was found 2.5 m to the west, together with a belt slider. Mortlake Ware was found at the bottom of the barrow ditch, but examination of the museum material has also identified sherds of Collared Urn, apparently from the body of the mound, suggesting re-use of this barrow in the Early Bronze Age.

3.4.2.iii Handley Barrow 27 (Figs. 3.12 and 3.13)

Pitt Rivers published a full account of this barrow, accompanied by a plan (*Excavations* IV, 136–42), although changes in the depth of the ditch have been added from the carpenter's model. This barrow was about 0.85 m high at the time of excavation and was surrounded by a most irregular ditch, 17.5 m in diameter. It had a single entrance on the south-east, the same axis as the entrance of Wor Barrow. It had already been dug by Colt Hoare who had found that 'the interment(s) had been disturbed by the intersection of a boundary ditch' (1812, 242). Fragments of human bone, however, still survived. The ditch was excavated completely by Pitt Rivers. Although its upper levels had been disturbed and included medieval pottery, a sherd of Mortlake Ware was found in its lower filling. This had not been appreciated and the barrow has been assumed to date from the second millennium bc.

The irregular layout of the barrow ditch raises a number of problems, since it is clearly not of a single phase, but the General made no attempt to work out the sequence. In the absence of any section drawing, Figure 3.13 has been based on the published plan, with further details from the carpenter's model. This allows a number of separate elements to be isolated, but it cannot establish their relative chronology. First, the ditch was remarkably irregular and we can pick out the deepest segments from the others. These occur at roughly equal intervals around the barrow, except on the northern side. We can also look for sharp changes of depth in the base of the ditch and these provide a rather similar outline. Again the evidence appears to be confined mainly to

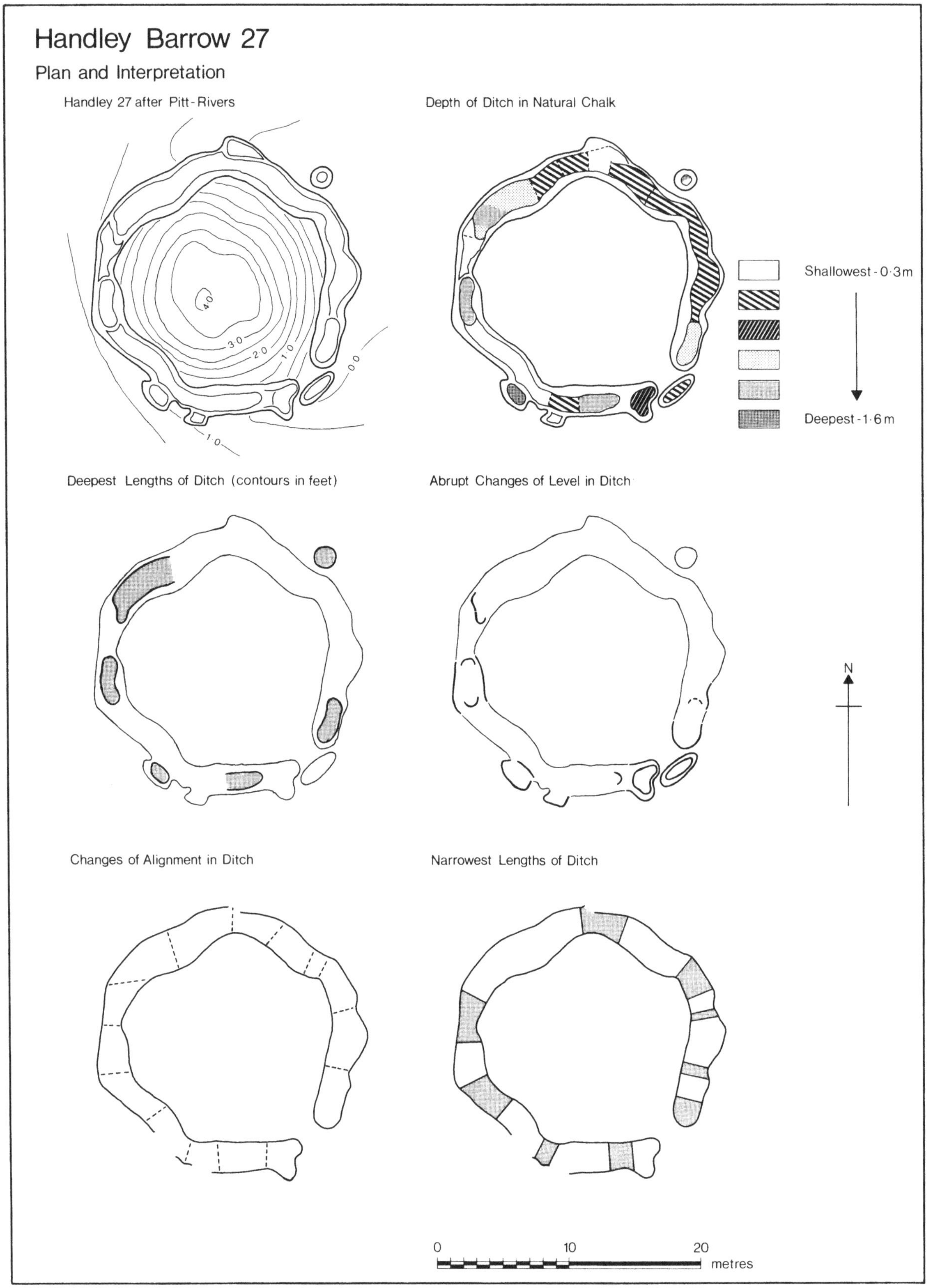

Fig. 3.13 Outline plans of Handley Barrow 27 (after Pitt Rivers 1893), supplemented by details from his three-dimensional model of the site after excavation

the southern half of the monument, whilst the shallower sections tend to occupy the northern part of the barrow. A third approach is to focus attention on the abrupt changes of direction shown by the ditch in Pitt Rivers' plan. Fourteen of these can be recognised and usually occur where the ditch is at its narrowest; the simplest explanation is that the ditch had originally been interrupted by causeways and that they were eventually removed. The General's plan also suggests that the ditch was broken by an entrance to the south-east, which was later blocked by a pit.

This analysis suggests that as many as three different layouts are represented on the site: a ring or partial ring of deeper segments up to 3 m long and 1.5 m deep; a causewayed ring ditch with at least nine ditch segments, most of them under 5 m long; and a shallow ring ditch which removed all but one of those causeways. There is no way of telling whether all these ditches contributed to a central mound, although we do know that a mound roughly a metre high existed at the time of Pitt Rivers' excavation.

3.4.2.iv Synthesis and discussion[1]

Having considered Wor Barrow and its neighbours separately, it is time to treat them as a group. The two round barrows are located towards either end of the long barrow (Fig. 3.12). Neither of their ditch causeways are aligned upon Wor Barrow exactly, but each faces in that general direction. Barrow 26 is inclined towards the end of Wor Barrow with the primary and secondary burials, but the axis of Barrow 27 skirts the northern edge of the mound. We have seen how Wor Barrow exhibits an important structural and ceramic sequence. It may be possible to link the other barrows into that scheme. Wor Barrow itself has two phases of Neolithic burials. As we saw in Chapter 1, the earlier burials reveal a mixture of traditional practice and innovation. The bodies were collected together in some form of mortuary structure, and some were placed there after they had lost their articulation; others are represented by complete skeletons. All the bodies were identified as males. The second group consists of the two burials on top of the primary filling of the ditch, one of them accompanied by an arrowhead. These were fully articulated and again both the burials were identified as male. Although this deposit has sometimes been treated as evidence of warfare, 'double' burials like this are recorded at Aldwincle (Jackson 1976), Ramsgate (Dunning 1966, 8–11) and Barrow Hills (Halpin and Bradley in prep.). In any event, it is rather unlikely that the same weapon was the cause of death in both cases, especially as the arrowhead was rather large and is better paralleled in other burials than on settlement sites (see Green 1980, 84–92).

It seems possible that these deposits already anticipate a new burial rite in this area, and so it is particularly striking to find a Later Neolithic mound so near to the eastern end of the long barrow. This was associated with Mortlake Ware, which also appears in the secondary filling of the ditch at Wor Barrow. By this stage, the burial rite and the form of the mound had changed. The two skeletons were articulated but were covered by a round barrow. One of the bodies was accompanied by a personal ornament. Towards the opposite end of Wor Barrow is another round barrow, but with a causewayed ditch which recalls the layout of the long barrow itself. The clustering of these three earthworks in such a small area can hardly be an accident. This sequence of monuments charts the latest stages of the long-barrow tradition and the development of a new type of funerary monument.

*3.4.3 **Structural details of the round barrows: the excavation of a Neolithic ring ditch in Firtree Field***[6,7]

3.4.3.i Introduction

The Neolithic ring ditch is located only 160 m from the Grooved Ware occupation site in the same field and just 130 m outside the Cursus, close to the scene of the 1982 excavation. It was not investigated as a Neolithic field monument. The site had been observed from the air, and in view of its close proximity to the Middle Bronze Age enclosure which overlies the Grooved Ware pits, it was thought that it could mark the site of a cremation cemetery associated with the Bronze Age settlement. In the event this did prove to be the case, but it became clear that the later prehistoric cemetery was making use of a very much older earthwork. With one exception, the structural features of the ring ditch are reported in this chapter. An account of the Middle Bronze Age use of this site appears in Chapter 5 (pp. 211–14).

3.4.3.ii The excavated features (Figs. 3.14 and 3.15)

The site was excavated almost completely in 1980 and what appeared from the air as a simple ring ditch proved to have had a complex sequence of use. The original ring ditch had been polygonal and at first may have been dug in segments about 3 m in length. It was 15 m in diameter, and thus was almost the same size as Handley Barrow 26. The primary filling (Fig. 3.15, 1. 23) was roughly symmetrical and was sealed by a buried soil (1. 17) before a more rapid phase of filling took place, marked by a rather stony layer which extended around

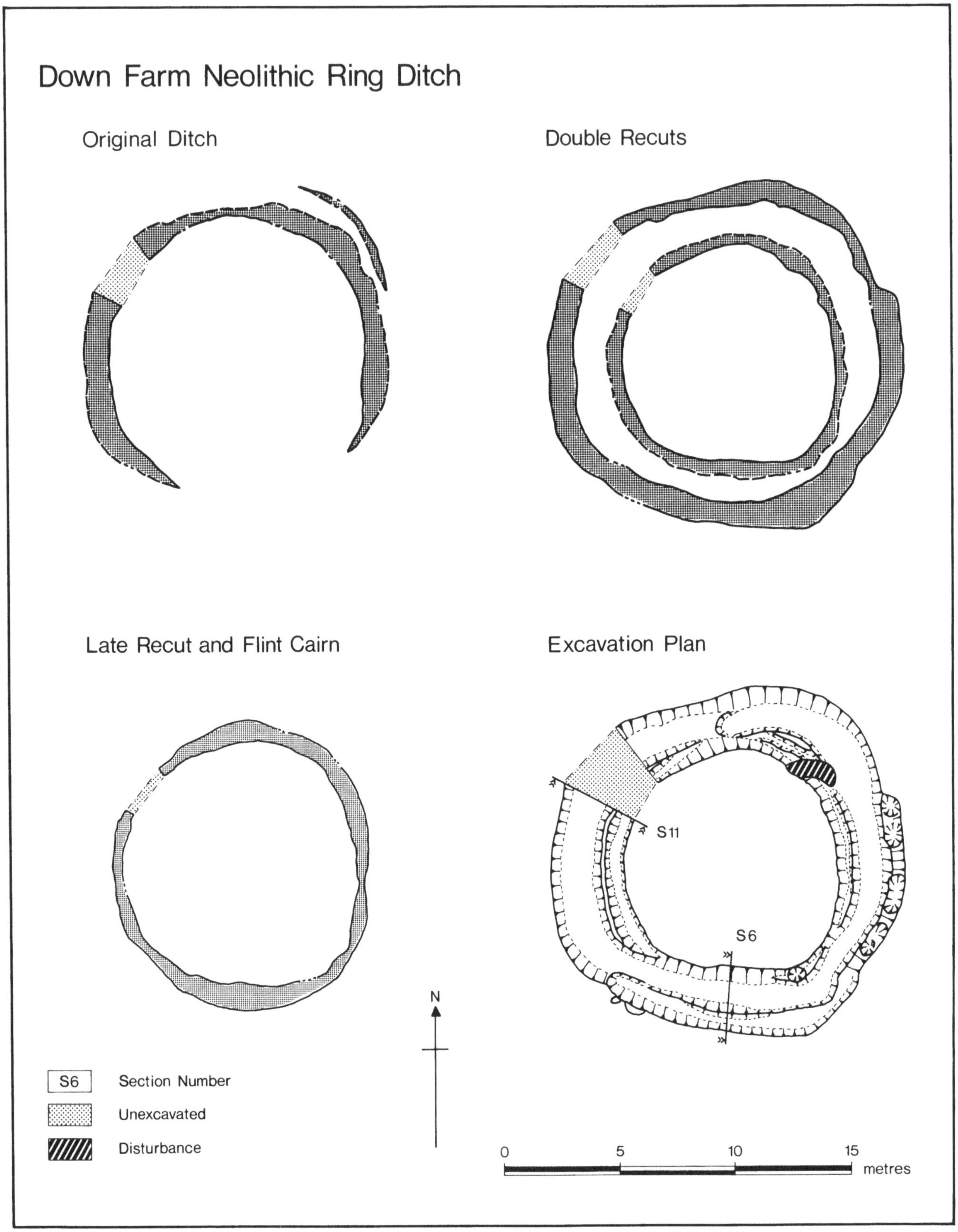

Fig. 3.14 The excavated ring ditch in Firtree Field, Down Farm, showing the successive layouts of the monument and the positions of the sections illustrated in Figure 3.15

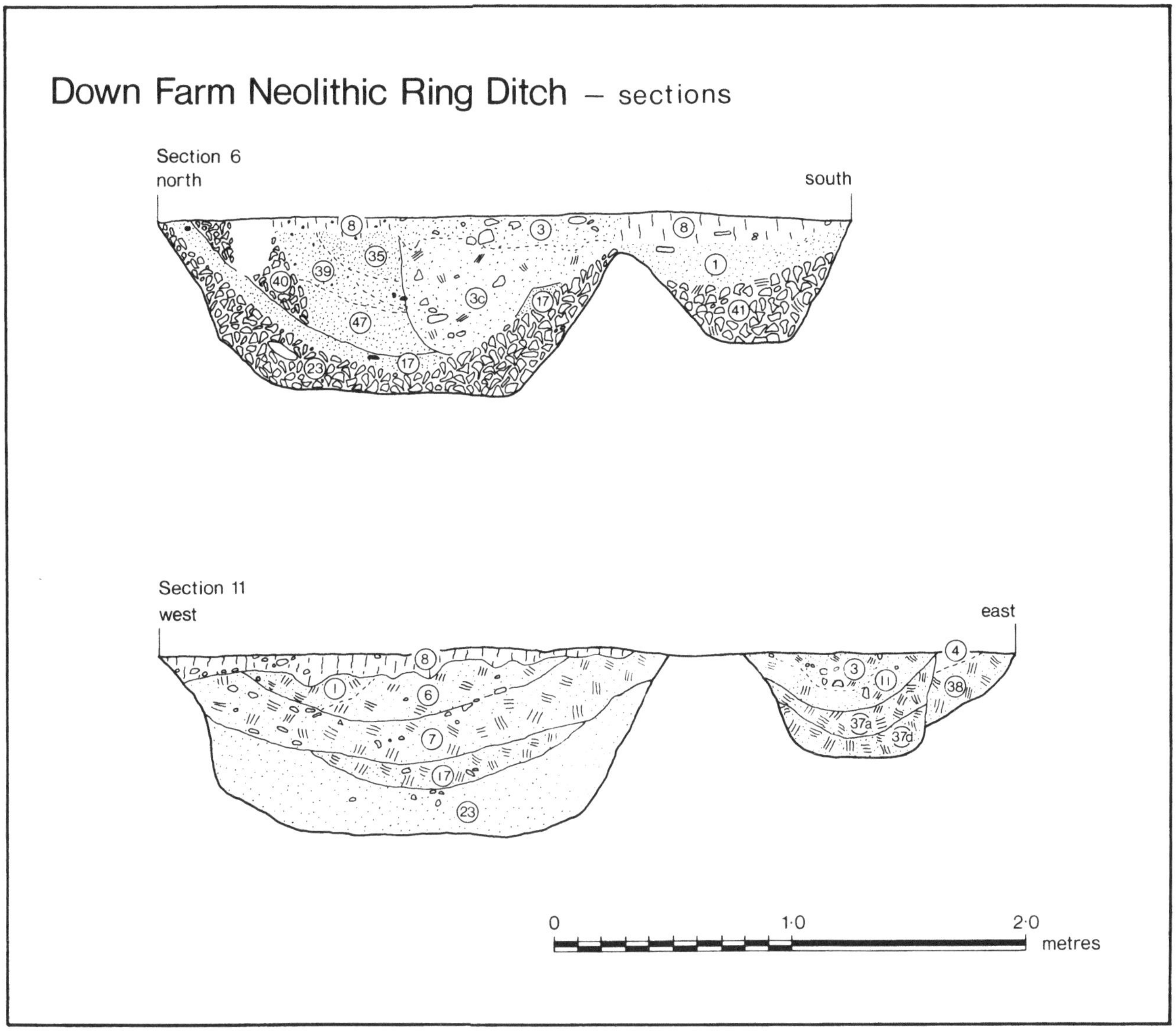

Fig. 3.15 Sections of the excavated ring ditch in Firtree Field, Down Farm

the entire circuit of the ditch (section 6, l. 47 and section 11, l. 7). This appears to have come from the interior, suggesting the former presence of a mound. After this deposit had stabilised, there was evidence for two roughly concentric recuts, the inner of which was dug through the filling of the original ditch (section 6, l. 3c). The primary and secondary fillings of both ditches again had a high stone content (section 6, layers 3c and 17; section 11, layers 3, 11, 37a and 37d). All three features were sealed by a layer of silt containing Middle Bronze Age pottery (l. 8), but the discovery of a quantity of Beaker ceramics and flintwork at this level might suggest that they had been deposited over the tops of the ditches and later disturbed. Despite this complex sequence of construction and reconstruction, no archaeological features were recorded inside the ring ditch and the only indication of a mound is the asymmetrical secondary filling of the earliest ditch.

3.4.3.iii Dating evidence[1,6]

There are several reasons for suggesting that this monument was of Neolithic date, apart from the possible *terminus ante quem* in the Beaker period. Apart from large quantities of fresh knapping debris, the only finds from stratified levels in the original ditch were two Y-shaped tools and a tranchet axe, all of which are matched in the Neolithic artefact scatters described earlier. There was also a lozenge arrowhead like the example accompanying the secondary burials at Wor Barrow. This example was found in a Bronze Age layer in the ring ditch. In addition, the ploughsoil over the monument included two pieces of Peterborough Ware, one a Fengate-style rim. More important, it is possible to correlate the molluscan sequence from the filling of the primary ditch with a sequence in the western ditch of the Cursus only 190 m away, which ran from the initial construction of the monument up to the Beaker period. If the basic equation can be accepted, it would suggest that the ring ditch was constructed well before the appearance of Beaker pottery on either site and whilst the secondary silts of the Cursus were first forming.

3.4.4 Structural details of the round barrows: the evidence of aerial photography[5]

The excavation of the ring ditch in Firtree Field provides an object lesson in the interpretation of air photographs: what seemed to be a single-phase monument dating from the Later Bronze Age in fact proved to have a history of construction and reconstruction beginning in the Neolithic period. We may be underestimating the frequency of Neolithic round barrows/ring ditches in the study area. For this reason it is worth noting that another four crop marks of similar form have been recognised close to the Cursus (Fig. 2.7, p. 38). On the other hand, equally striking parallels can be found among earthworks belonging to later periods, and it would be unwise to be too dogmatic.

3.4.5 General discussion of the round barrows[1,6]

The main result of this study has been the identification of a succession of monuments and burials in the Wor Barrow complex which may provide a regional sequence to set beside better-known sequences from other areas, in particular the important evidence from Aldwincle (Jackson 1976) and Duggleby Howe (Kinnes, Schadla-Hall, Chadwick and Dean 1983). This local sequence is also important for the way in which it is linked to a monument in the long-barrow tradition. As we suggested earlier, the burials in the ditch at Wor Barrow play a critical role. Both were apparently articulated males and were accompanied by a grave offering. This prefigures the rite of individual burial seen at Handley Barrow 26. The striking distribution of these sites and the ring ditch in Firtree Field also stresses the importance of the Cursus. The molluscan evidence from Firtree Field emphasises how short an interval may have separated the construction of these two types of monument. The ceramic sequence at Wor Barrow, combined with the radiocarbon dates from the ditch, carry the same implication. Further support comes from the Barrow Hills long barrow, just outside the Abingdon causewayed enclosure. We have already seen that this mound has features in common with both Thickthorn Down long barrow and Wor Barrow and that it has a radiocarbon date of 2550 ± 60 bc (BM 2392). Some indication of how rapidly the change of mortuary rite was accomplished is provided by the burials at this site, which consisted of two articulated skeletons with grave goods. One of the two skeletons, a male, had a belt slider like that from Handley Barrow 26, together with a large leaf-shaped arrowhead similar to the example from the secondary burials at Wor Barrow (Halpin and Bradley in prep.).

The sites considered here take very varied forms, but all have structural parallels in other areas (Fig. 3.16). At different stages in their history two of these earthworks – Handley Barrow 27 and the ring ditch in Firtree Field – may have been surrounded by a segmented ditch without a single sharply demarcated causeway. This is important since apparently similar sites are sometimes classified as hengiform *enclosures* (Wainwright 1969). One example is Dorchester on Thames Site 2, which had apparently been part of an alignment of monuments predating the cursus on that site (Bradley and Chambers 1988). In Cranborne Chase the survival of standing mounds into the last century means that we can reconstruct the form of the original monument without undue reliance on the details of the ditch silts.

The original ring ditch in Firtree Field was replaced by two concentric ditches, separated by a narrow baulk. This is strikingly similar to a series of rather more elaborate monuments in the Thames valley and the south Midlands. In view of the early date suggested for this example in Cranborne Chase, it is worth drawing attention to two much larger sites with this characteristic ground plan – Aldwincle phase 4 in Northamptonshire, where the ring ditch may replace a late long barrow and has a *terminus post quem* of 2610 ± 70 bc (Har 1411 – Jackson 1976); and Dorchester on Thames Site XI, which again predates the cursus on that site. A developed phase of this monument has provided two radiocarbon dates of 2370 ± 90 bc and 2370 ± 50 bc (BM 2440 and 2442 – Bradley and Chambers 1988).

The last type is represented by Handley Barrow 26 and by one phase of Handley Barrow 27. In each case the surrounding ditch is broken by a single causeway of varying width, orientated towards the south. On both sites there was clear evidence of a mound, and human remains were discovered. This is particularly important because once again these might have been identified as

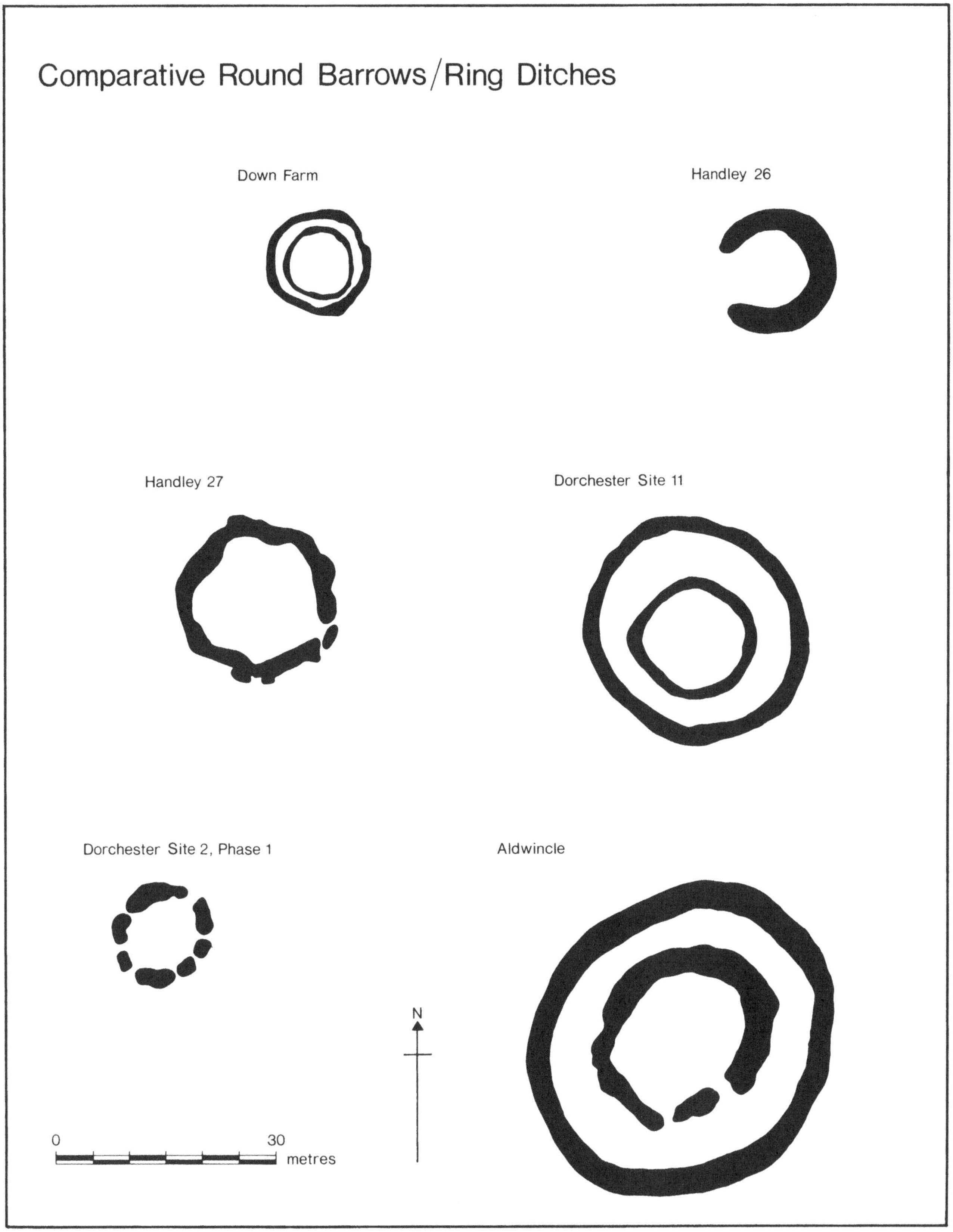

Fig. 3.16 Outline plans of the Neolithic ring ditches excavated in the study area in relation to comparable monuments cited in the text

small henge monuments if no trace of the internal mound had survived. This is more than a question of typology, as it bears directly on the functions of very different field monuments. Further light on this question comes from the excavation of the one bona fide henge monument identified close to the Cursus.

3.4.6 Henge monuments: the excavation on Wyke Down

3.4.6.i Introduction[1]

Compared with round barrows, henge monuments are not common in the study area, or in Cranborne Chase as a whole. Despite the presence of the Dorset Cursus, only one small monument of this type has been discovered, and the distribution of larger enclosures is limited to the valleys of two tributaries of the Avon (Fig. 3.17). It is sometimes supposed that there is a link between the round-barrow tradition and the use of Peterborough Ware and between henges and the use of Grooved Ware (Thorpe and Richards 1984). This cannot be analysed in such a limited geographical area, and in any case it may be due partly to chronological differences. Even so, it is striking that so much Peterborough Ware has been discovered around the Cursus, compared with finds of Grooved Ware. A similar contrast is seen between the pottery from the study area and the finds from the lowland basin. We have discussed the only Grooved Ware settlement to have been found in Cranborne Chase: now we turn to the excavation of a contemporary henge monument at Wyke Down. This is also associated with Grooved Ware, and radiocarbon dates suggest that the two sites were in use at the same time.

The difficulty of interpreting air photographs is illustrated by the excavation of the pit-circle henge at Wyke Down, since this showed from the air as an ordinary ring ditch. Work in the field commenced in the belief that it was a ploughed-out barrow, perhaps an outlier of a nearby cemetery (RCHM 1975, 21). In the event the site proved to be a single-entranced henge monument. It was located on level ground but aligned on a low hill (Chalkpit Field) where a Later Neolithic occupation site overlay the Dorset Cursus (Fig. 3.6, p. 70). It seems likely, however, that the henge monument postdates that settlement. Having considered the character of the excavated features and the phasing of the site, we shall show how the distributions of the associated artefacts lend emphasis to that alignment.

3.4.6.ii The excavated features[1,5]

The two main phases of the henge at Wyke Down are planned in Figure 3.18, and sections of a number of the excavated features are illustrated in Figure 3.19. In order to avoid burdening the text with excessive detail, much of the basic information on the site is presented there.

After the mechanical stripping of the ploughsoil, the ring ditch was revealed as a single-entranced, roughly circular enclosure, defined by a ring of twenty-six chalk-cut pits (Fig. 3.18). The outlines of these separate pits had not been visible from the air, as the baulks separating them had eroded away to a depth of between 0.10 and 0.70 m in the natural chalk. The enclosure was formed by four distinct arcs of pits, with an entrance 3 m wide. The long axis measured 19.5 m internally and the short axis measured 17 m. Where the two crossed, a shallower pit was excavated. With the exception of a 'double pit' at the entrance, all the pits were of roughly oval plan and shelved quite steeply to a depth of between 1.05 m and 2.00 m. The deepest pits were found close to the entrance and towards the back of the enclosure. Their changing depths are summarised in Figure 3.19. The central pit differed from the rest and was only 0.52 m deep. None of these pits was accompanied by ramps and there is no evidence that any of them held posts. Assuming that the material dug from these features had contributed to an unrevetted bank 2 m outside the ring of pits, it need have been no more than 2 m wide and 0.60 m high.

In some cases the pits had remained open long enough for a thin layer of earth to accumulate in the bottoms (Fig. 3.19, section II, 1. 6; section III, 1. 6; section V, 1. 6), but the main filling of each pit consisted of about 0.50 m of loose coarse chalk, apparently derived from the weathering of the sides (S. I, layers 5–7; S. II, 1. 5; S. III, 1. 5; S. IV, 1. 5; S. V, 1. 5). Observations made at the time of excavation suggest that such an accumulation could have formed during one winter. The lower part of this layer contained occasional lenses of humus, which may have resulted from fallen turves (S. I, 1. 6). A sample of red-deer antler from the primary silt of Pit I gave a radiocarbon date of 2090 ± 90 bc (BM 2395).

Once this coarse rubble had formed in the lower parts of the pits, there is evidence for a change in the character of the filling. The later silts consist of a fairly fine chalk wash, occasionally laminated by further lenses of humus (S. I, ls. 4 and 4a; S. II, 1. 4; S. III, 1. 4; S. IV, 1. 4). There is only limited evidence of humus at the junction of the primary and secondary filling of the pits and no real sign of a period of stabilisation. The entire process may have happened extremely fast. The density of chalk fragments in the secondary silts varied from one pit to another, but there is no evidence of collapsed bank material, and the silts seem to have entered the pits from all sides.

These chalk silts were cut by a series of shallow pock-

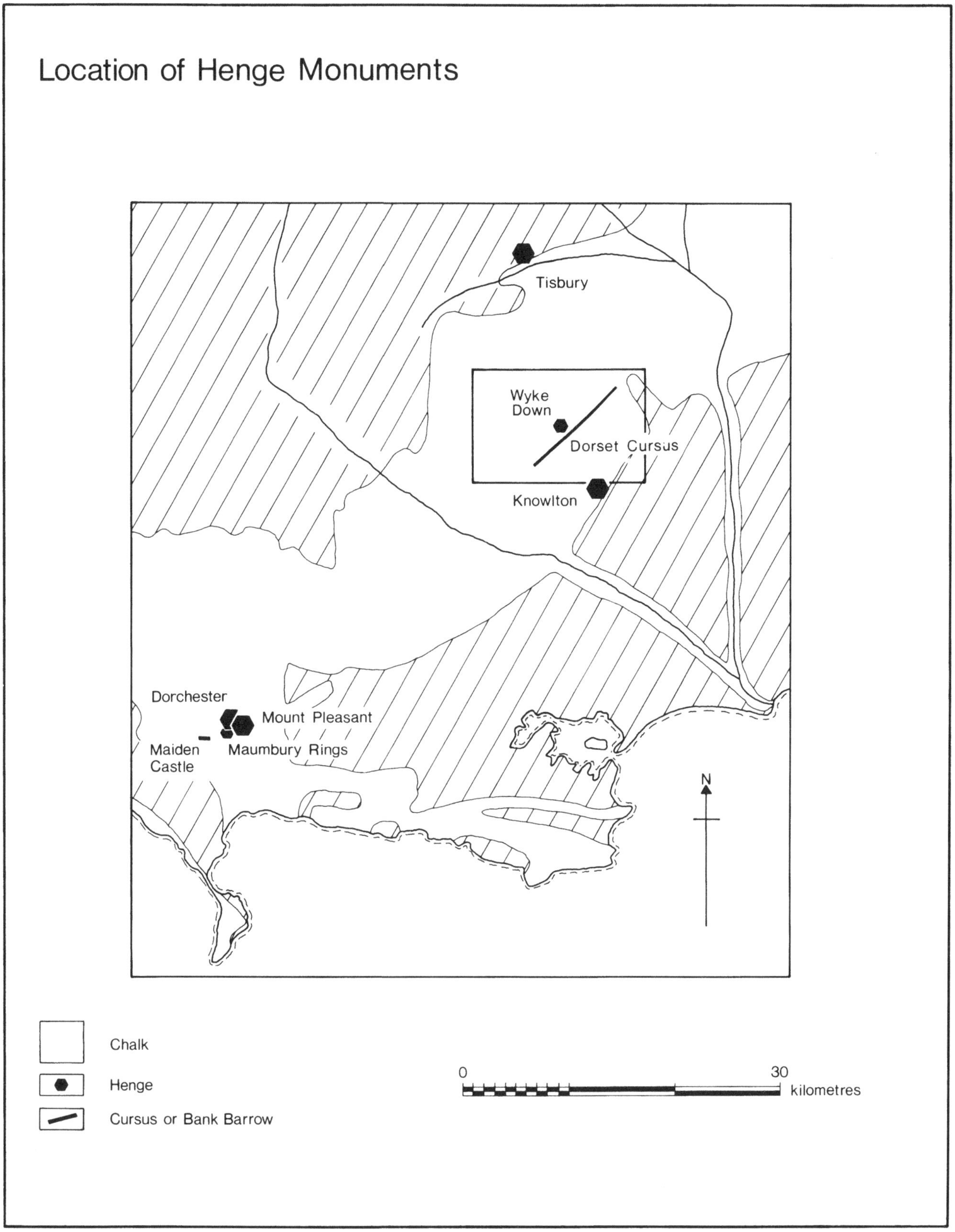

Fig. 3.17 The distribution of henge monuments in southern Wessex, highlighting the position of the study area

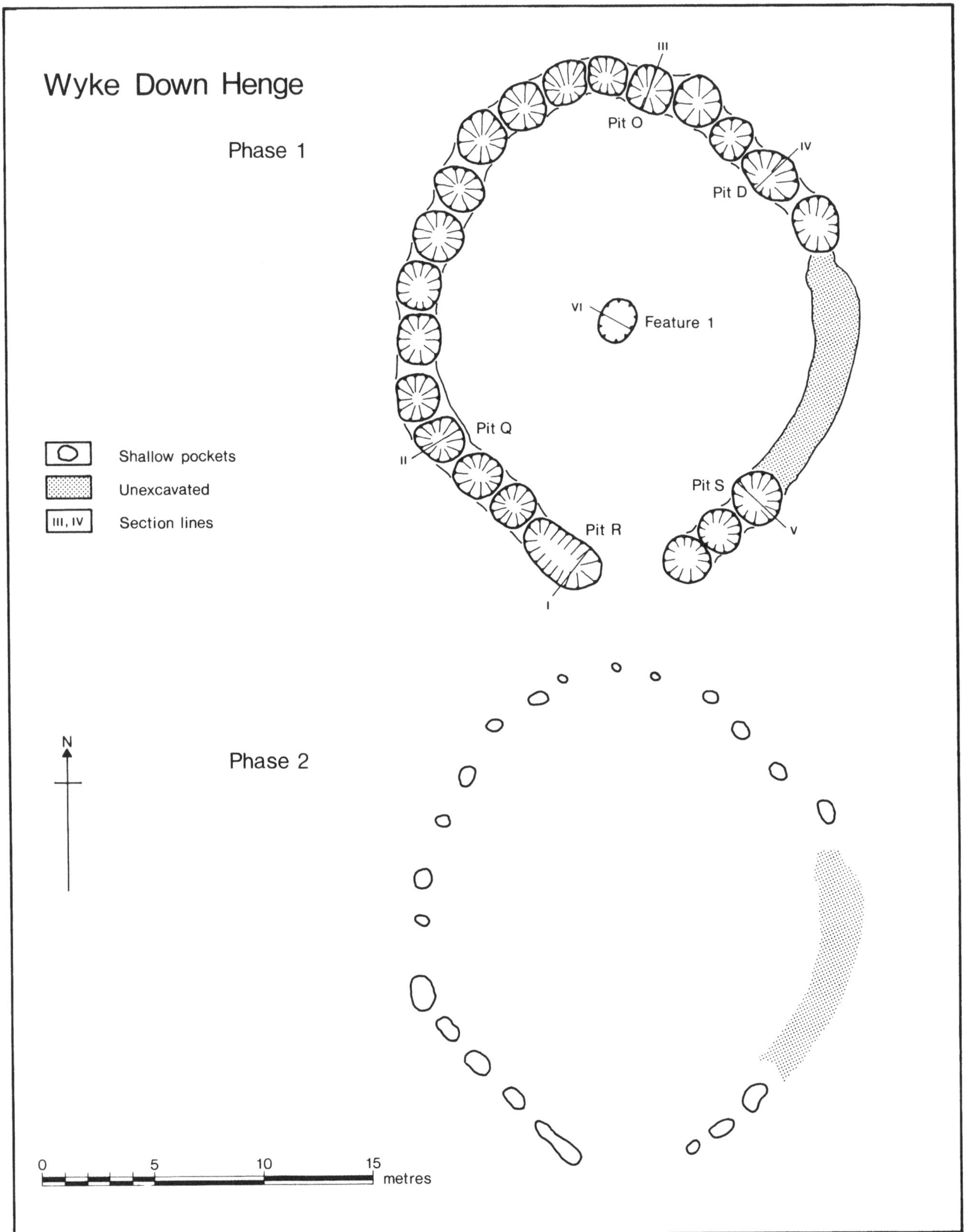

Fig. 3.18 (Upper) The major excavated features of the Wyke Down henge monument, showing the positions of the sections illustrated in Figure 3.19 (Note that the central pit is a later addition, dating from the Early Bronze Age.) (Lower) The positions of the secondary recuts in the upper levels of the pits

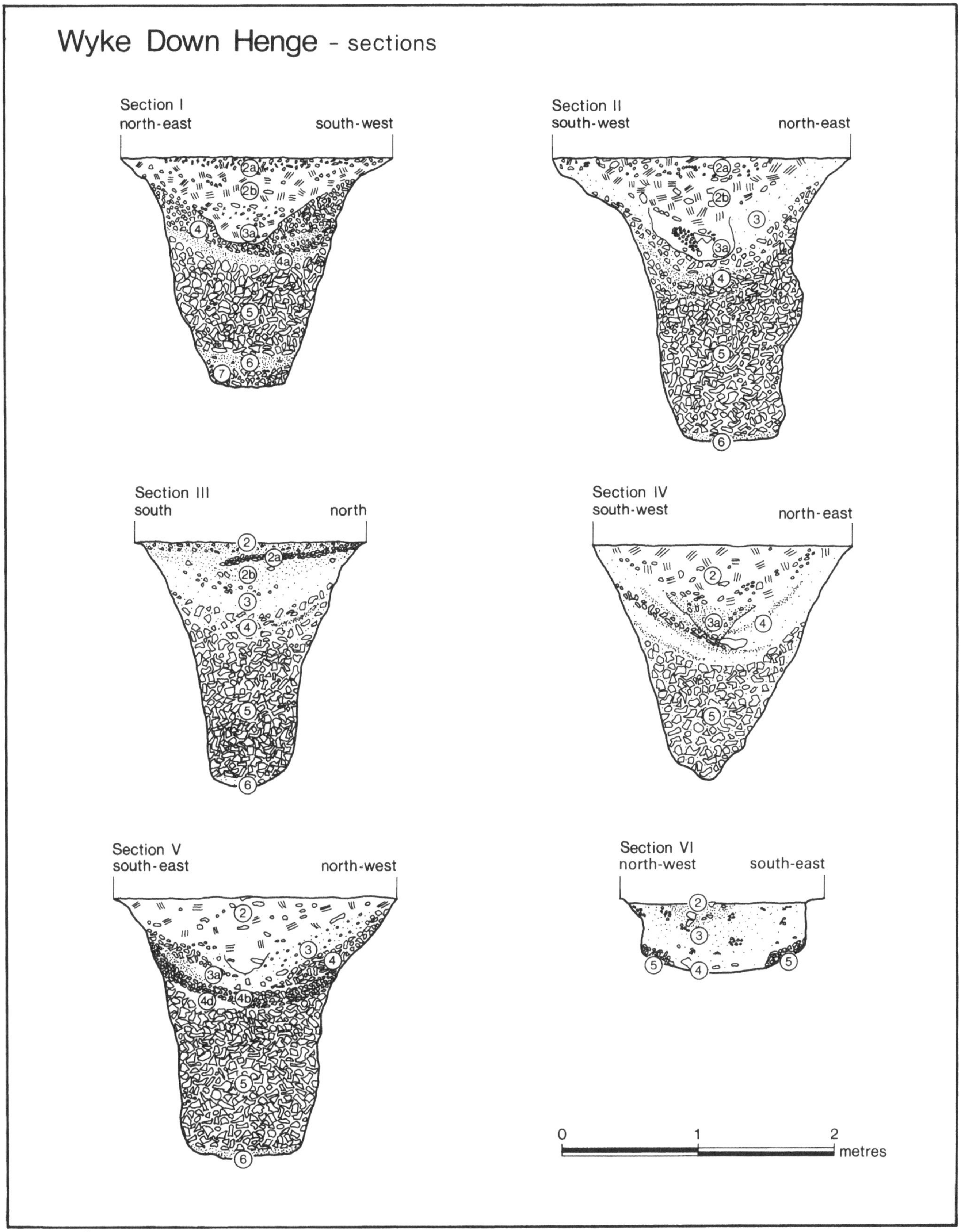

Fig. 3.19 Sections of excavated features belonging to the Wyke Down henge monument

ets, located over roughly the centres of the existing pits (Figs. 3.18 and 3.19, S. I, 1. 3a; S. II, 1. 3a; S. IV, 1. 3a). These were generally oval or circular in outline and were smaller in the area opposite the entrance to the enclosure. These pockets had a shallow U or V profile. Depths were between 0.16 m and 0.56 m. The central pit, however, was not recut. These features were too irregular to have held uprights. They had a rather clayey filling, sometimes containing pockets or runs of charcoal and a quantity of flint nodules. In addition, they included animal bones which had been packed into their filling. Pit Q near the entrance included a human skull fragment in the recut, whilst Pit R, which flanks the entrance itself, contained a minor scatter of cremated bone at this level. Two of the recut features provided samples for radiocarbon dating. Charcoal of oak heartwood from the recut feature in Pit I gives a date of 2190 ± 80 bc (BM 2396). Charcoal of three other species (alder over ten years old, hazel over ten years old and buckthorn up to twenty-five years old) taken from the recut in the filling of Pit K provides a second date of 2200 ± 50 bc (BM 2397).

After the recuts had been filled, the pits silted over naturally, and were sealed by layers of clayey loam containing many flint nodules (Fig. 3.19, S. I, ls. 2a and b; S II, ls. 2a and b; S. III, ls. 2, 2a and b; S. IV, 1. 2; S. V, 1. 2). These were eventually covered by the modern ploughsoil.

Little need be said about the central feature. This was much shallower than the other pits at Wyke Down and seems to have silted up gradually. It had not been recut (Fig. 3.19 section VI). A sample of animal bone from the lower filling of this pit provided a date of 1510 ± 90 bc (BM 2394). This places the pit in the period in which a nearby barrow cemetery was probably in use and indicates that it was a secondary addition to the monument.

3.4.6.iii The excavated material and its distribution[1,3,4,5,8]

Artefacts and animal bones were found in each of the three main stratigraphic divisions of the site – at the bottom of the pits and in their primary fillings; inside the later recuts; and in the silts which masked these features. The distribution of finds from each of these units is mapped in Figures 3.20, 3.22 and 3.23. In addition to providing insights into the date and character of the monument, the detailed distribution of the material from each phase emphasises the alignment of the enclosure. The finds from the primary phase are mapped in Figure 3.20. Five distributions can be considered, two of which emphasise the long axis of the enclosure. Finds of used and unused antler were confined to the area by the entrance of the monument and were restricted to the bottoms of the pits and to the lowest part of the primary silts (Fig. 3.20). They included a pick and a possible rake. Much the same applies to the distribution of the six carved chalk objects, four of which were found at the bottom of pits towards the causeway, whilst a further example came from the bottom of a pit directly opposite the entrance. A sixth chalk object was found close to the entrance, but on the surface of the primary silts (Fig. 3.21). To some extent similar spatial patterning is shown by the animal bones from the lower filling of the pits. They include one group found in pits on either side of the entrance. These were the only features to contain deer, ovicaprid and pig bones. A smaller group occurs towards the back of the enclosure, but was not located opposite the entrance. The distribution of flintwork is less informative. Most of the debitage came from the very bottoms of the pits and seems to have resulted from flint knapping on the site itself. The material is extremely widespread but is mainly confined to the western half of the enclosure. This is mirrored by the distribution of implements, which do not seem to have been made on the site (Andrew Brown pers. comm.). These show little spatial patterning, but it is striking that an arrowhead was found at the bottom of both pits flanking the entrance.

The secondary recuts contain more finds, and from the way in which they had been packed into these features it is clear that they had been placed there deliberately. Virtually all the distributions focus on the entrance to the monument (Fig. 3.22). Most striking, perhaps, was the distribution of pottery, all of which belonged to the Grooved Ware tradition. The number of separate vessels was greatest around the entrance, and parts of the same vessel were found in features on either side of the causeway. The pottery with the most complex decoration was found in this area (cf. Fig. 3.23). The three deposits of human bone were also concentrated in this part of the site. Two of these, a cremation and a human skull fragment, came from features not far from the entrance, whilst the upper part of the secondary silts in Pit S, just east of the entrance, included a compact mass of ashy soil which might have been deposited in a bag. This also included minute amounts of cremated bone. The distribution of animal bones, however, is less compact, although the greatest number of identifiable pieces was found close to the entrance. The only deer bone and three of the four pig bones came from this part of the site. Lastly, the evidence of the flintwork is broadly consistent with the other spatial patterns. The density of unretouched material is greatest around the causeway, and the distribution of the few retouched pieces is concentrated in this area even more strongly. Most of these

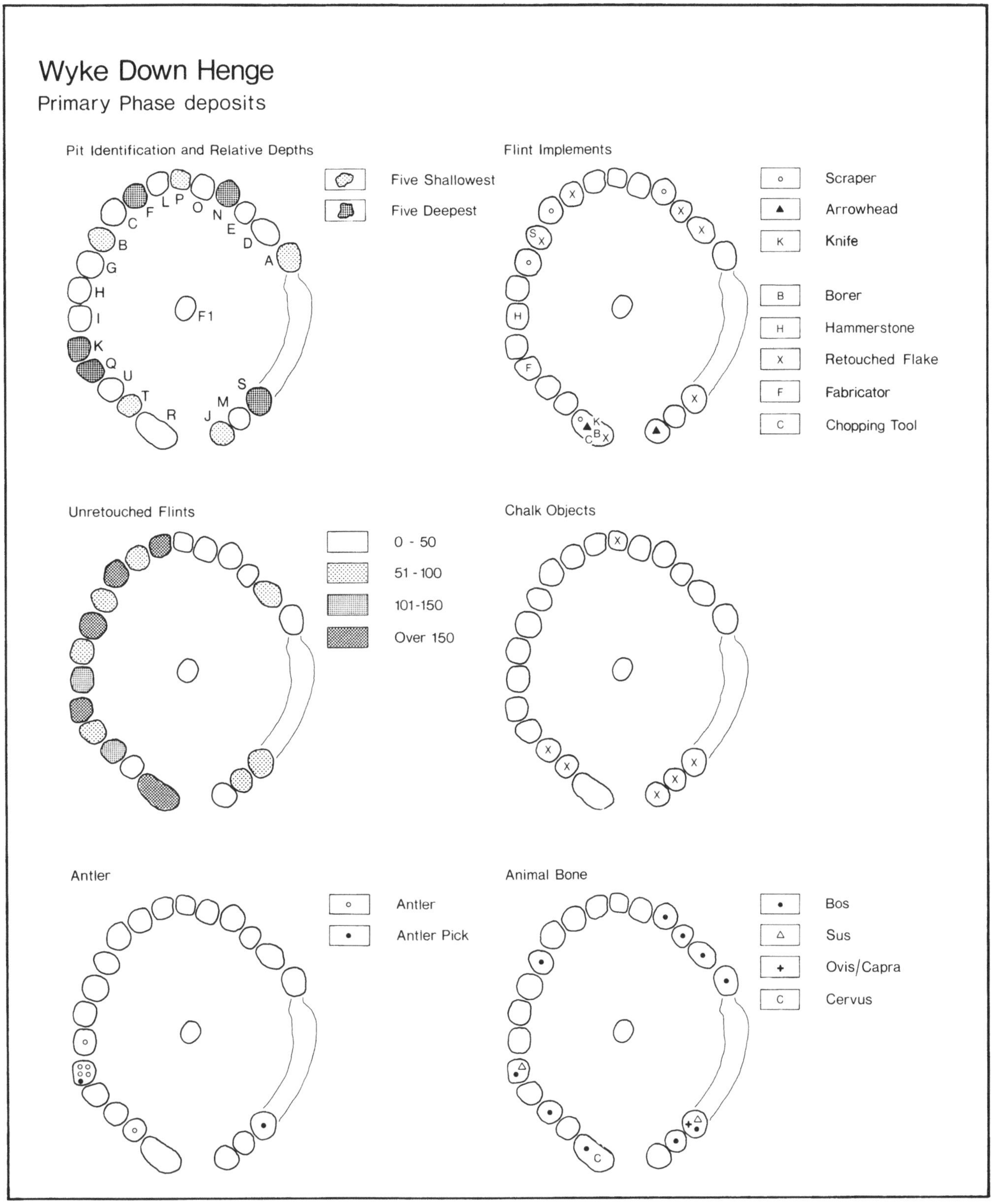

Fig. 3.20 Outline plans of the Wyke Down henge monument, showing the distribution of deposits belonging to the primary phase

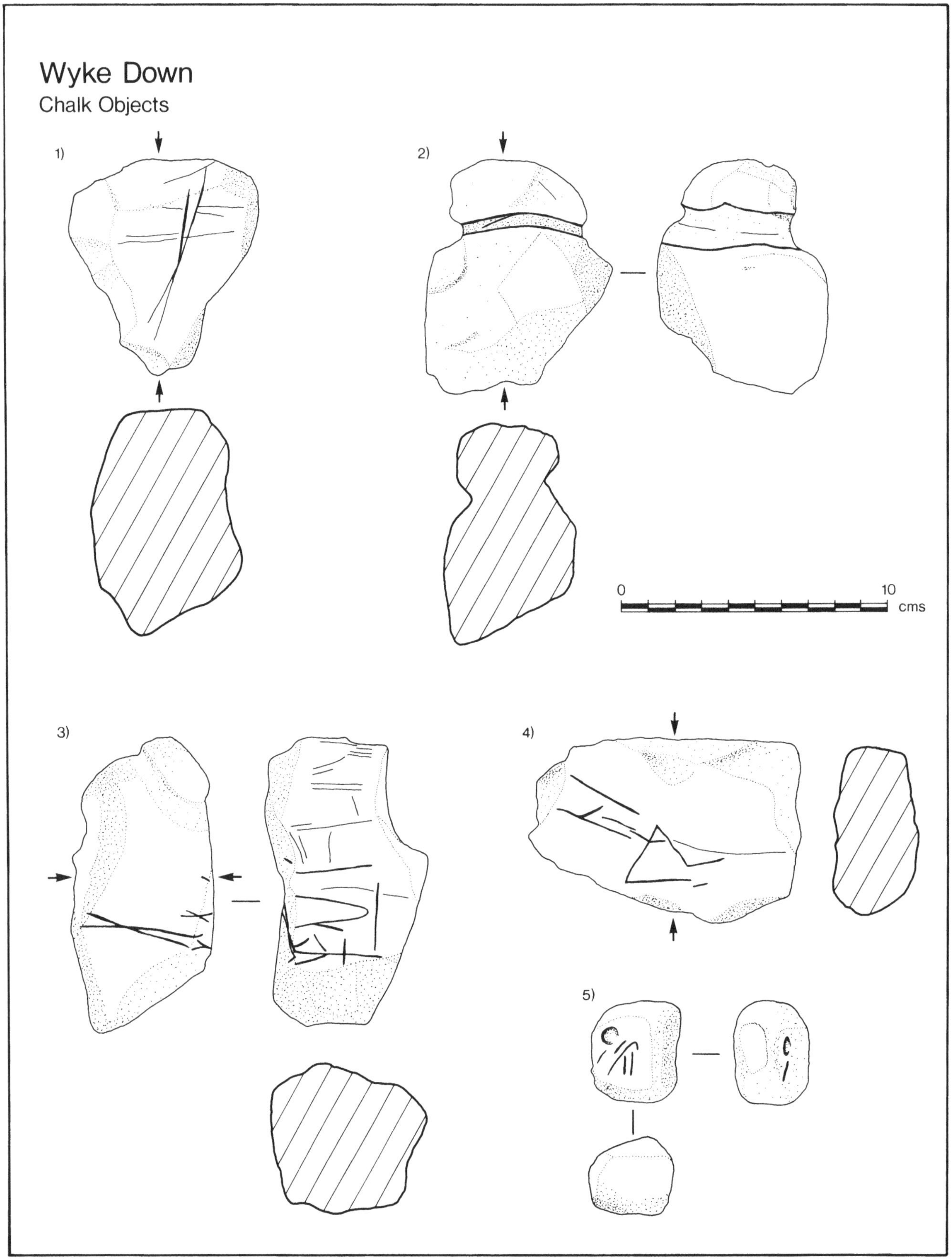

Fig. 3.21 Carved chalk objects from the primary levels of the Wyke Down henge monument

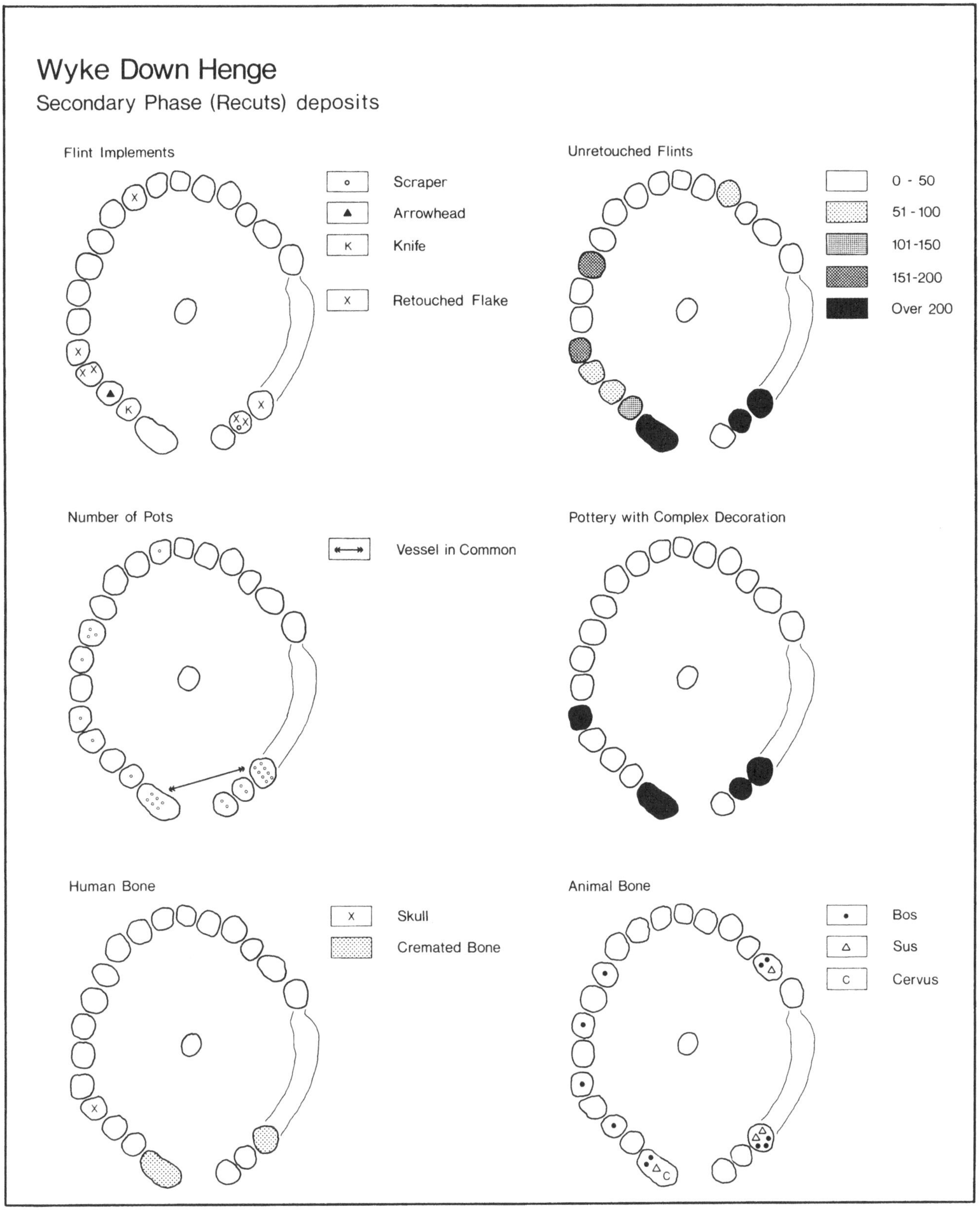

Fig. 3.22 Outline plans of the Wyke Down henge monument, showing the distribution of deposits in the secondary recuts

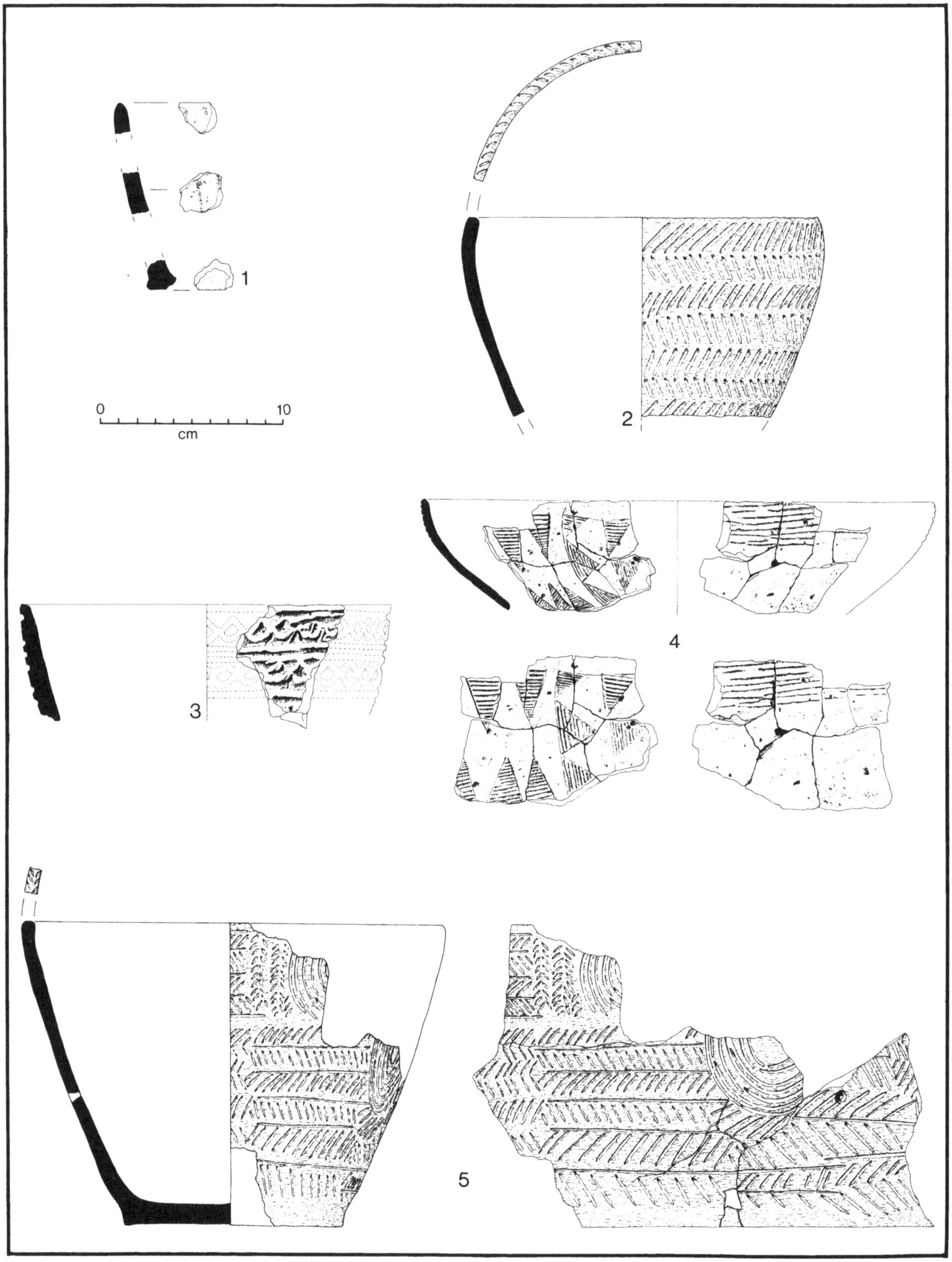

Fig. 3.23 Selected sherds of Grooved Ware from the Wyke Down henge monument, illustrating the distinction between simple and complex decoration

were simply retouched flakes, but again an arrowhead was found close to the entrance to the monument. Whilst a number of these distributions share the same basic configuration, it is worth adding that there is little evidence of consistent associations between different types of material.

Since it is likely that the silts sealing these recut features accumulated only gradually, there is no reason to expect the same degree of spatial patterning to be found in the final phase. On the other hand, the precise placing of the central pit shows that the outlines of the earlier earthwork were still visible during the mid-second millennium bc. Few of the distributions have any clear focus (Fig. 3.24), but the largest amounts of flintwork still came from the area near to the entrance. More importantly, Pit R, against the entrance causeway, contained part of a flint axe and a complete Group VIII stone axe. The other implement types were more widely distributed. Almost all the finds of animal bone came from the back of the enclosure and only two bones were found at the entrance. Some indication of the period over which these deposits were forming is provided by sherds of Late-Style Beaker and Collared Urn, both found towards the rear of the enclosure. These could be contemporary with the use of the nearby barrow cemetery.

3.4.6.iv Discussion[1]

The Wyke Down henge monument has affinities with sites in neighbouring areas. To the north its closest parallels are at Dorchester on Thames (Atkinson, Piggott and Sandars 1951), and to the south its nearest counterpart is the more massive earthwork at Maumbury Rings (Bradley 1975). The chalk-cut shafts at Maumbury supply much the best comparison with the Wyke Down monument, as does a similar monument at Sutton Veney in south Wiltshire (Fig. 3.25). This observation is particularly important as these two sites still survive as earthworks. They show that pit-circle henges are preeminently *enclosures* and may be different from causewayed ring ditches, which can be the sites of mounds. Reassessment of the well-known monuments at Dorchester on Thames lends weight to this distinction and even suggests that enclosures of this kind may be later in date than the Neolithic ring ditches on that site (Bradley and Holgate 1984, 123–6; Bradley and Chambers 1988).

Again we depart from conventional wisdom in considering the function of this monument. It has been customary to treat pit-circle henges as collective cremation cemeteries and to stress their links with other funerary monuments of Neolithic date (Atkinson, Piggott and Sandars 1951, 73–80; Kinnes 1979; 67–9). This seems very doubtful, for work at a number of sites has emphasised how often the human cremations were placed in features that were secondary to the original design. This is the case at Wyke Down, and on the type site at Dorchester on Thames where cremations were actually placed in the hollows left by the posts of a timber circle which had been destroyed by fire (Bradley and Chambers 1988). The other finds from the recuts at Wyke Down show that such cremations formed only a small part of a much wider series of deposits. In this case they are outnumbered by groups of animal bone and decorated pottery. Again at Stonehenge 1 the human cremations take their place alongside a more complex series of placed deposits, including a macehead, Grooved Ware and antlers (Burl 1987, Fig. 8). Like those at Wyke Down, their distribution emphasises the entrance(s) to the site. The Aubrey Holes of Stonehenge 1 have also been described as a cremation cemetery (Atkinson 1956, 13–14), but the human remains found in the higher levels of the Neolithic shafts at Maumbury Rings were not cremations at all but scattered pieces of excarnated bone (Bradley 1975, 35–6).

The human remains at Wyke Down belong to a broader series of deliberate deposits, which are also in evidence at other Wessex henges, particularly Durrington Walls, Mount Pleasant (Richards and Thomas 1984) and Maumbury Rings (Bradley 1975; Bradley and Thomas 1984). Indeed, the distribution of antlers and carved chalk objects at Wyke Down is very similar to those at Maumbury Rings and Stonehenge 1. In the same way, Rosamund Cleal stresses how the distribution of Grooved Ware in the Southern Circle at Durrington (Wainwright and Longworth 1971) resembles its distribution at Wyke Down, with sherds from the same vessels concentrated around the entrance and an emphasis on pieces with internal decoration or circular motifs (Fig. 3.26). The pottery from the two sites is very similar indeed, and in both cases the distribution of arrowheads provides additional evidence of patterned deposition. Dr Cleal also suggests a link with Woodhenge, where vessels with circular motifs are again concentrated around the entrance to the monument (Cunnington 1929).

At Wyke Down we can find similar evidence at another level, for there are signs that the character of the different deposits changed during the stratigraphic sequence (Table 3.12), another observation which can be matched at Maumbury Rings (Bradley 1975, 18–22). At Wyke Down it is clear that carved chalk objects were limited to the primary levels of the monument, and the same applies not only to the antler picks but also to pieces of antler which may not have been used. At the same time, the Grooved Ware was confined to the secondary

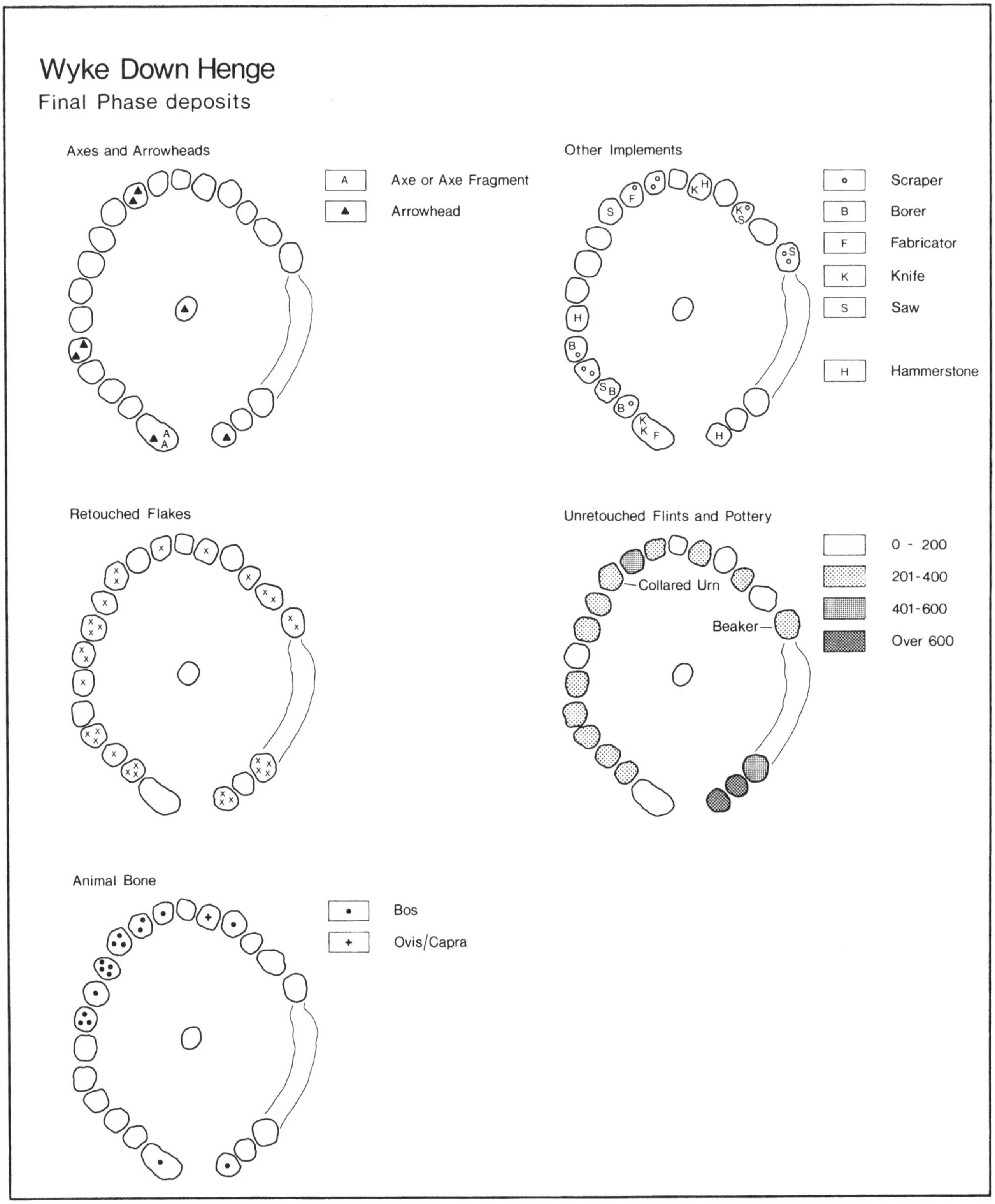

Fig. 3.24 Outline plans of the Wyke Down henge monument, showing the distribution of deposits post-dating the secondary recuts

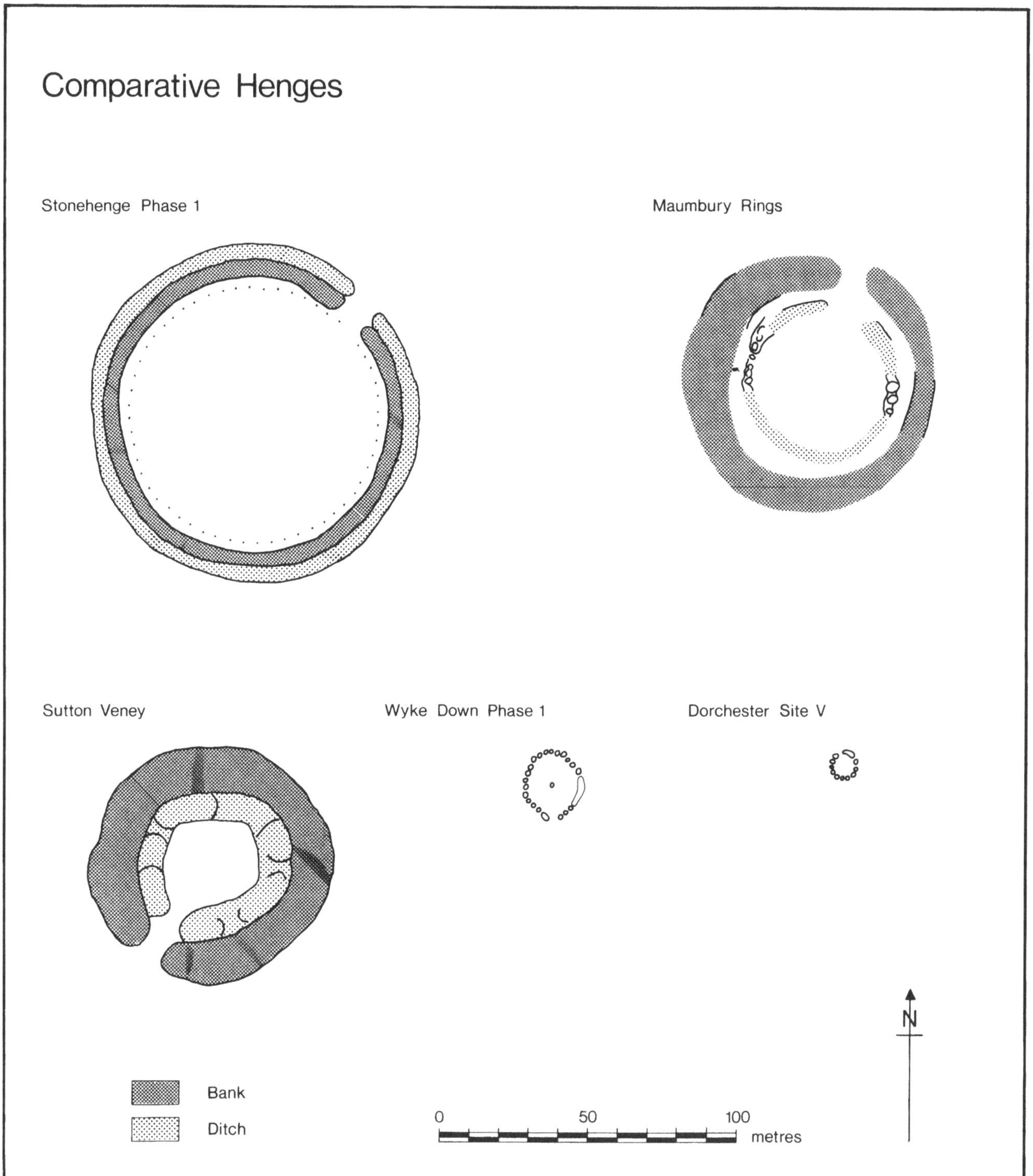

Fig. 3.25 Outline plan of the Wyke Down henge monument in relation to other sites discussed in the text

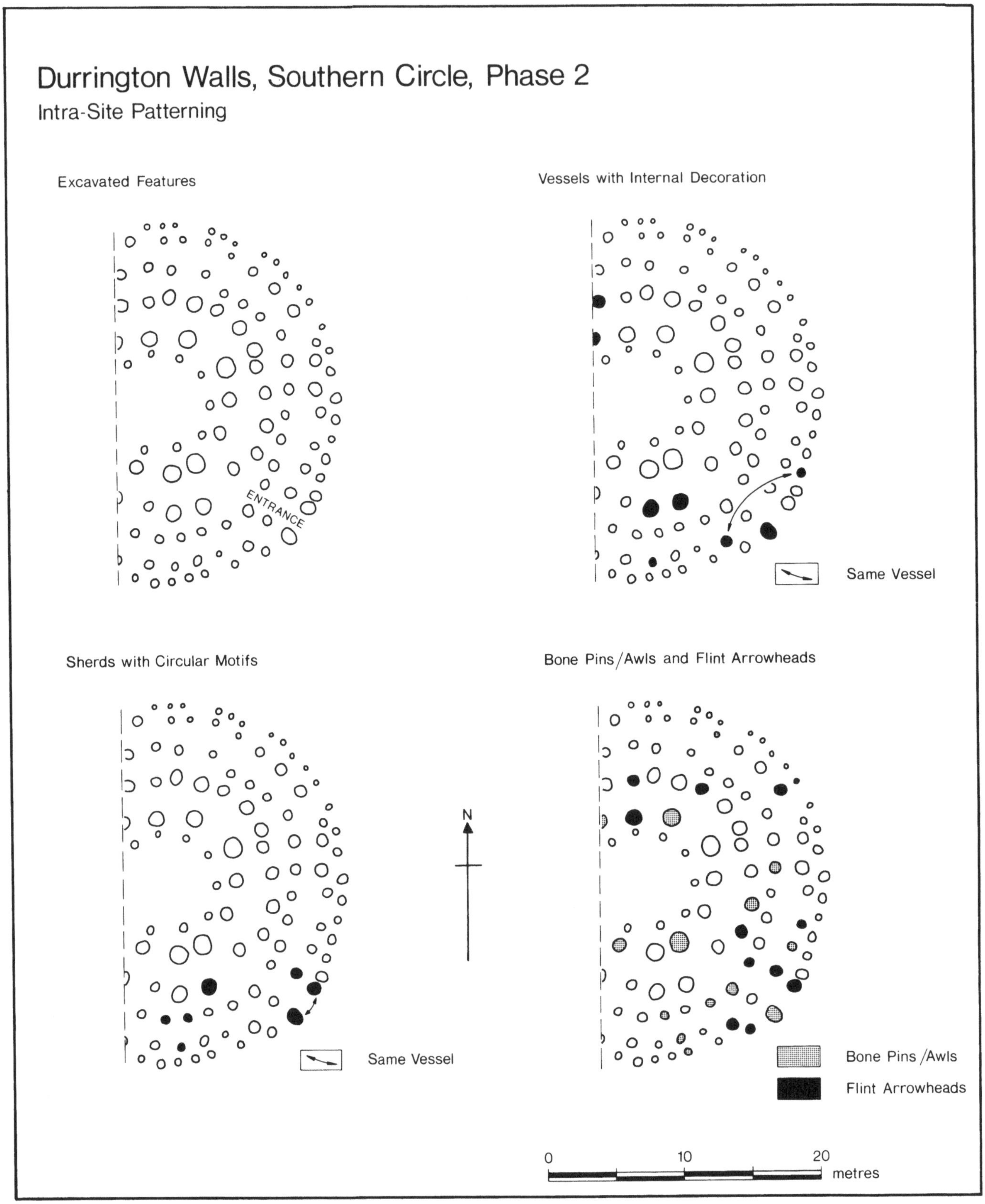

Fig. 3.26 Intra-site patterning in Phase 2 of the Southern Circle at Durrington Walls

Table 3.12. *The contrasting contents of the primary and secondary deposits in the Wyke Down henge monument*

	Primary levels	Secondary recuts
Minimum number of vessels	–	25
Carved chalk objects	6	–
Antler picks	2	–
Other finds of antler	6	–
Animals represented	cattle, pig, sheep/goat red deer	cattle, pig, red deer
Human bone (cremated)	–	2 groups
Human bone (unburnt)	–	1 skull
Scrapers	4	1
Knives	1	1
Arrowheads	2	1
Borers	1	–
Hammerstones	1	–
Fabricators	1	–
Chopping tools	1	–
Retouched flakes	6	7

recuts.

In addition, we must consider the relationship of this monument to three other sites: the Peterborough settlement in Chalkpit Field; the Grooved Ware settlement in Firtree Field and the earthwork of the Cursus.

The alignment of the henge was obviously felt to be important since it was emphasised by the location of a series of deliberate deposits, which focus on the long axis of the enclosure. That emphasis was most apparent in the earliest phase. The earthwork is aligned exactly on the low hilltop occupied by both the Dorset Cursus and the Peterborough site in Chalkpit Field (Fig. 3.6, p. 70). This is unlikely to be fortuitous, as this was the only place where the interior of the Cursus is known to have been reused. On the other hand, that site may no longer have been occupied by this stage. An alternative is that it was the earthwork of the Cursus that was important, for at this point it runs along the top of a Pleistocene river cliff and would have been unusually conspicuous.

We also have to consider the relationship between the two Grooved Ware sites, which are located on the same side of the Cursus, 870 m apart (Fig. 3.6, p. 70). This is easier because the radiocarbon dates suggest that they could have been used at the same time. In both cases material was being deposited in the ground after it had accumulated elsewhere. The flint implements at Wyke Down may not have been made from the nodules tested on the site, since there is a relatively small quantity of tertiary flaking debris in the pits (Andrew Brown pers. comm.). Similarly, a few of the animal bones showed signs of gnawing by dogs, and the rarity of unidentifiable fragments suggests that once again bones were being deliberately selected for burial (A. J. Legge pers. comm.).

Equally striking are the *differences* between the finds from these two sites, for they may reflect detailed differences in the activities taking place there. These are summarised in Table 3.13.

A final comment on these deposits may be in order. In our earlier discussion we stressed the degree of formality behind the filling of some of the pits in Firtree Field. This seems to be borne out by the overlap between the contents of these two sites and the limited number of elements which are restricted to the henge. Carved chalk objects are known quite widely in Wessex – in fact there may be a roughly contemporary example from Stonehenge (Burl 1987, 98) – but it is more striking that human remains should appear in this list. Human long bones were found in the secondary filling of the Cursus ditch not far away, and the Cursus itself, however ancient its fabric, seems to have been associated with the celebration of the dead. That earthwork had influenced the siting and even the character of later settlements. Now its position in the landscape may have had a similar influence over the creation of new forms of monument.

Just as the settlement evidence makes little sense until it is viewed against a wider background, the evidence from Wyke Down is difficult to interpret unless it is seen in relation to two other sites: the Knowlton complex on the south-eastern edge of the study area (RCHM 1975, 113–15), and Tisbury, in the Vale of Wardour, 18 km away (Colt Hoare 1812, 251). Neither has been excavated.

The Wyke Down henge is situated close to the source of the River Allen, which runs within 200 m of the monuments at Knowlton, 5 km downstream. The main features of the Knowlton group are four henge monuments, which are between seven and ninety times the size of the Wyke Down enclosure. These are accompanied by an outsize circular mound. The closest counterparts to these enclosures are the great henges at Mount Pleasant, Durrington Walls and Marden, with which they share their distinctive lowland situation (Wainwright 1979b, 232–7). The latter sites have been shown by excavation to belong to the period around 2000 bc and were associated with Grooved Ware. The large mound at Knowlton also has its counterparts at other major monuments in Wessex: the bank at Mount Pleasant is buried beneath the mound of Conquer Barrow (*ibid.* 65–8) and the Marden enclosure once contained an outsize circular mound, the Hatfield Barrow (Wainwright 1971, 182–3). An even better-known site of this date is Silbury Hill (Atkinson 1970).

Table 3.13. *Contrasts between the contents of the henge monument at Wyke Down and those of the contemporary occupation site in Firtree Field*

	Wyke Down henge monument (primary levels and recuts only)	Firtree Field Grooved Ware pits
Features restricted to the henge monument:	Carved chalk objects	–
	Human remains	–
Features restricted to the Grooved Ware pits:	–	Saws
	–	Edge-polished flakes
	–	'Boars' tusks'
Items more common in the Grooved Ware pits:	–	Axes
Qualitative differences:	More complex ceramic decoration	–
	Durrington Walls style Grooved Ware dominant	Durrington Walls, Clacton and Woodlands styles of Grooved Ware represented
	Cattle bones dominant	Pig bones dominant, except in Pit 11a

Much less is known about the monument at Tisbury, the exact location of which has been lost. This seems to have been a fairly considerable earthwork and again it was situated on or near the bottom of an important river valley. It is also known that this enclosure had contained a stone circle and a central setting of stones, possibly a 'cove' (Colt Hoare 1812, 251). Comparable features are found at four major sites in Wessex: Mount Pleasant, Stonehenge, the Sanctuary and Avebury. Two of these, Mount Pleasant and Avebury, also contain coves (Wainwright 1979b, 230–2). Where there is any definite dating evidence, stone settings appear to be a secondary feature developing in the early second millennium bc (*ibid.* 232).

The evidence of both sites contrasts with the situation in the study area. The henge monuments just described seem to have been much larger than the example at Wyke Down and were probably later in date. Their characteristic siting is a further point of contrast, for the positions of both Tisbury and Knowlton seem to be influenced by the proximity of rivers (Fig. 3.17, p. 93), whilst the siting of the Wyke Down monument at the source of the River Allen seems to have been affected at least as strongly by the location of the Cursus.

3.5 Synthesis[1]

In Chapter 2 we argued that the creation of the Cursus complex marks a vitally important horizon in the development of the study area. It enhances a major division in the pattern of contemporary land use and may well have been created as the first large-scale settlement of the upland chalk took place. Once established, the Cursus complex was omnipresent in the lives of those who used this area, whether as agricultural land or for its raw material. The political geography of the Earlier Neolithic retained its hold over the population, and it seems possible that it was through activities in and around that monument that the continuity of society was maintained. The focusing of so much activity on the Cursus complex went on long after its earthworks were in disrepair and left behind it a series of striking manifestations in the archaeological record.

We have been able to trace two major areas of activity and to observe important contrasts between them. We have seen how the proximity of the Cursus complex is reflected in the character of the lithic evidence, with the more specialised assemblages around the earlier monuments. Although it now seems likely that many of the findspots mark settlement areas, the two excavated sites possess a complex spatial structure, and some of the artefacts in them had been buried with a certain formality. Although the collections differ considerably in their details, it is striking how far the spatial patterning evident in the archaeological record emphasises the importance of the Cursus.

The identification of structured deposition in the excavated sites at Down Farm is particularly important here, since this seems to have taken place within the context of other, everyday activities. This does not turn these into 'ritual sites'; rather, the indications of formal behaviour within a domestic setting may emphasise how important such behaviour may have been in structuring social relations. The repeated, everyday character of such activities could have played a larger part than we suppose in emphasising the distinctions on which the political system rested. Indeed, it is particularly revealing that only one special-purpose *enclosure*, the Wyke Down henge monument, has been identified in this area. Even the orientation of this earthwork may reflect the long-standing importance of an *occupation site* where such practices had once taken place. This point is made in a different way by the substantial overlap between the contents of the pit circle on Wyke Down and the range of material from the contemporary site in Firtree Field (Table 3.13)

At the same time, the actual character of the monuments built around the Cursus proves to be very revealing. The most common are the round barrows, which are found very close to that monument and in direct relationship to one of the latest long barrows. This is important for two reasons. It is surely significant that early individual burials should be found so near to a monument belonging to a long-established tradition. At the same time, the choice is striking, since Wor Barrow is one of the sites where an unusually restricted section of the population was represented. Given the haphazard sampling of round barrows which has taken place in Cranborne Chase, it seems likely that more Neolithic examples will come to light, and quite possible that some will prove to be still earlier in date than those considered here. At present, however, it seems as if the process of exclusion embodied in the very layout of the Cursus continued with the burial of a small number of individuals in round barrows close to it.

This emphasis on the dead and on the crucial importance of the past is surely seen in other aspects of Later Neolithic activity. Not only did a domestic site associated with Peterborough Ware become established inside the Cursus: the west ditch of that monument itself contained human bones, together with a polished knife of a type found in contemporary burials. Even the wild cattle bones may be significant, since these are a special feature of deposits found under long barrows, where occasionally they take the place of human remains (Thorpe 1984, 51). A local example may be at Thickthorn Down long barrow, where they were found in a ditch terminal and on the old land surface (Drew and Piggott 1936, 93). During the Later Neolithic period, further animal bones were deposited around this barrow, together with Peterborough Ware.

The two Grooved Ware sites may have a rather similar emphasis. One of the most distinctive features of the pits in Firtree Field is the discovery of so many deposits of 'boars' tusks'. These are not found in the contemporary henge monument and are most unusual in southern England. They are, however, among the most distinctive of the *grave goods* found in Later Neolithic individual burials (see Kinnes, 1979, 51–3), and their deposition so near to the Cursus may represent a reference to such associations. The same might also be true of the deposits of human bone found close to the entrance of the henge, and in particular to the unburnt human skull fragment. Similar finds from Maumbury Rings were viewed as evidence of excarnation (Bradley 1975, 35–6), a practice found widely on Earlier Neolithic sites.

We must not neglect the question of chronological development. It has been possible to trace the emergence of a local tradition of individual burial in the Wor Barrow complex, but we have also drawn attention to contrasts between the excavated occupation sites in the Cursus complex. There seems to be far more evidence of structured deposition in the Grooved Ware site than in the site associated with Peterborough Ware, and at Firtree Field this practice apparently extended to a much wider range of items. This is a contrast of degree and not one of kind, yet the same development may be suggested by the construction of the Wyke Down henge, aligned on the site of the Peterborough settlement inside the Cursus. This is perhaps the first evidence from southern Wessex for the creation of distinctive enclosures where the formal deposition of artefacts and animal bones took place. Previously, it seems, such practices were to be found in settlements. It is obvious that the situation changed rapidly, and within a century or so of the building of the Wyke Down enclosure the massive henge monuments of Wessex were being constructed (Wainwright 1979b, 232–7). Again we should not suppose that they were divorced entirely from the pattern of settlement – they could perfectly well have been inhabited on a permanent basis. What matters is that such enclosures mark such a rapid and dramatic development. We have already argued that the range of items in use in the Grooved Ware sites was much wider than it had been in earlier periods. In addition, some of the finds consist of exotic material, and some of the pottery carries designs whose basic elements were developed in far-distant areas. To some extent this emphasis on the exotic may have grown at the expense of the local continuities revealed in activity around the Cursus. This development may account for the change in political geography marked by the growth of the Knowlton complex. Similar changes of location can be charted in other parts of Wessex (Bradley 1975, 37), and, generally speaking, they seem to have involved the establishment of important new centres along the main rivers discharging into the English Channel. It may be too simple to suggest that this happened in order to make more use of long-distance exchange networks, but in local terms this could be one factor in the rise of Hengistbury Head. There may be links between the ceramics and flintwork found in Cranborne Chase and the Hampshire Basin, just as there are close similarities between artefacts found at Wyke Down, Hengistbury and Durrington Walls (cf. Gardiner in Cunliffe 1987, 332–3).

We can relate this local change to a fairly rapid diminution in the amount of evidence for domestic activity in the study area, compared with the coastal region around Christchurch and Bournemouth (Fig. 4.2, p. 112). Similarly, molluscan analysis shows less evidence for a sustained impact on the landscape than there is in the area around Stonehenge (Roy Entwistle pers. comm.). Such evidence belongs properly to the second millennium bc and will be considered in detail in the next chapter. In the light of this discussion, it is worth observing that some of the newly established henges still seem to have expressed links with longstanding developments in their hinterland. Despite the shift of emphasis away from the Cursus complex, one of the monuments at Knowlton is the largest round barrow in Dorset (RCHM 1975, 116). On analogy with other groups of monuments in Wessex, this should be of Later Neolithic date. The Great Barrow at Knowlton may be said to belong to the end of one long-lived system and the very beginning of another.

Notes

1 Richard Bradley
2 Julie Gardiner
3 Rosamund Cleal
4 A. J. Legge
5 Martin Green
6 Mark Bowden
7 Barry Lewis
8 Andrew Brown

4. THE EARLY BRONZE AGE

4.1 Introduction[1,2]

The rather traditional division drawn here between the Late Neolithic and Early Bronze Age is simply one of convenience. It allows us to focus upon the development of round barrows, the construction of which show an essential continuity with developments during the previous period. However, henge monuments are no longer constructed in our area, and the barrows evidence a monumentality with an almost exclusive emphasis upon the dead. It is the changing emphasis in the practices associated with monumentality which is the issue here, rather than a simple technological division in the artefact sequence (Fig. 4.1).

Burgess has suggested a series of period divisions for the second millennium bc (Table 4.1) in which his Mount Pleasant Period (*c.* 2150–1700 bc) sees the introduction of copper, and then the full adoption of bronze metallurgy (metal Stages I–IV), along with most of the 'steps' of Beaker development (n.d. [1980]; 1980, 71; 1986). Although there remain considerable doubts about the detail of the Beaker chronology in Britain (see Longworth in Wainwright 1979b, 90), it seems most likely that the main currency of this material pre-dates 1700 bc. The Beaker and early metal finds from the region are discussed below and, although sparsely represented, they are likely to have been contemporary with the final history of the Wyke Down henge. It is also probable that they fall within the period of use of the Knowlton henges.

Our main concern in this chapter is that period which conforms with Burgess' Overton and Bedd Branwen Periods (*c.* 1700–1250 bc). It embraces the main use of Collared Urns and Food Vessels and the early development of Deverel-Rimbury ceramics. Less can be said about the finds of flintwork because so few diagnostic types were in use at that period. With the continuing dearth of radiocarbon dates, metalwork remains the main guide to the chronology of the period, although its occurrence is effectively limited to the burial record.

We will begin by considering the range of artefacts represented, and the way they relate to specific depositional contexts. We will then go on to consider those contexts in more detail. Towards the end of Chapter 3, we observed that the largest monuments were now being built on the lower ground outside the study area. The Early Bronze Age appears to witness a similar shift of emphasis in the settlement pattern. Once again the evidence of specialised monuments overshadows the more limited traces of domestic activity. Diagnostic flint artefacts are few, and much of the pottery comes from the secondary silts of earlier monuments and need not be the result of occupation (Fig. 4.4). Subsoil features are limited to a few pits, only one group of which has been excavated in recent years.

Although monuments seemingly cover a restricted range of activity, their actual frequency cannot be overestimated. The evidence is extended by one excavation reported here, that of a cremation cemetery at Down Farm. Continuity with earlier practices was maintained, for not only does the general distribution of round barrows follow the line of the Dorset Cursus; the detailed arrangement of deposits in the excavated cemetery appears to have been influenced by the position of that monument.

4.2 The artefact sequences

4.2.1 Introduction[1]

The artefacts discussed here are those recovered from two rather broad types of context. Domestic material has come mainly from the surface debris recovered in fieldwalking, or as the residual remains incorporated in later monuments. The second category, that of mortuary deposits, appears more specific. Obviously both contexts encompass a wider range of different practices, in which a selection of artefacts will have been made. In discussing this material we must remain sensitive to the complex processes at work which gave rise to our artefact assemblages. These extend from the selection of material within a particular social domain, to the chronological development of artefact types.

4.2.2 *The flint industries in the study area*[3]

The Beaker/Early Bronze Age phase in Cranborne Chase is marked by a shift in emphasis, and this is clearly registered by the lithic material. In contrast to the large quantity of third-millennium flintwork, there is little that can be assigned to this period. This is most clear from the distribution of arrowheads (Fig. 4.2). It has not been possible to locate any distinctive 'Beaker' industries in the study area, although this may not be a true reflection

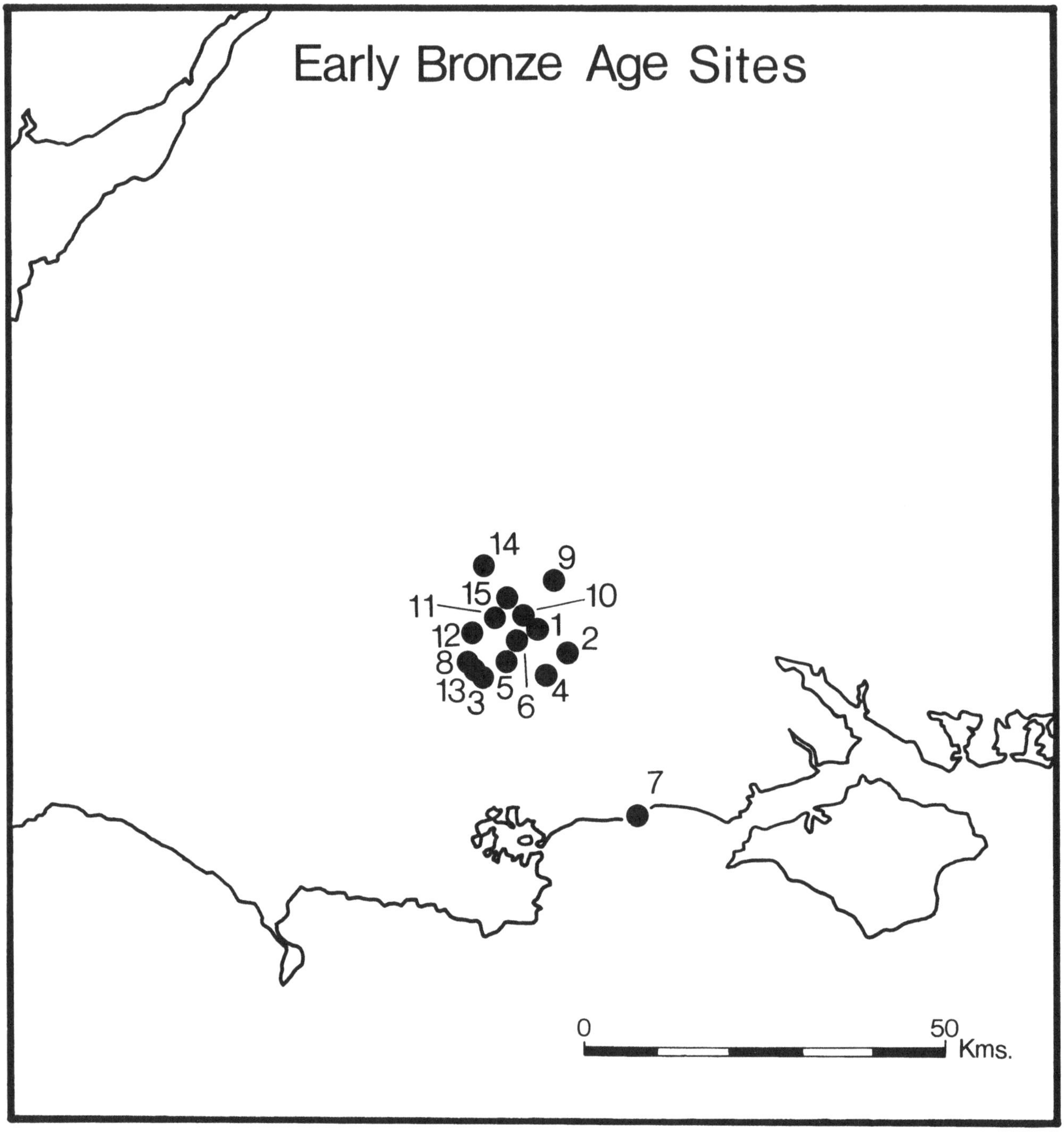

Fig. 4.1 The distribution of Early Bronze Age sites which are considered in this chapter. Key: 1 Bottlebush; 2 Boveridge House; 3 Crichel Down; 4 Edmondsham; 5 Firtree Field (Down Farm); 6 Handley Hill; 7 Hengistbury; 8 Launceston Down; 9 Martin Down; 10 Oakley Down; 11 Scrubbity Coppice; 12 South Lodge; 13 Thickthorn Down; 14 Woodlands Down; 15 Woodminton Down

Table 4.1. *Outline chronology for the early stages of metalworking (after Burgess n.d. [1980], 1980, 1986)*

Period	Suggested chronology	Metal stages	Ceramics
Mount Pleasant	*c.* 2150–1700 bc	I–V	Grooved Ware Peterborough Ware Beaker Steps 1–6
Overton (Includes Fargo and Bush Barrow Phases)	*c.* 1700–1450 bc	IV–VI	Beaker Steps 5–6 Collared Urns Food Vessels (Deverel-Rimbury)
Bedd Branwen (Includes Aldbourne-Edmondsham Phase)	*c* 1450–1250 bc	VII	Collared Urns Cordoned Urns Enlarged Food Vessels Deverel-Rimbury

of the situation, since groups of domestic ceramics do occur. Unfortunately, these groups were generally found in areas which are now under permanent grassland, so that surface collection has been impossible.

A small amount of 'Beaker' flintwork was recovered from one surface scatter at Donhead. This site is located on greensand on the edge of the Vale of Wardour and is one of only two major flint scatters to have been discovered off the chalk; a recent survey of the Vale failed to find any comparable material (Gingell and Harding 1983). The 'Beaker' element in this collection is small, however, consisting of a barbed and tanged arrowhead, a series of tiny 'thumb-nail' scrapers and a flint dagger, although two plano-convex knives and a polished flint macehead may also belong with this group.

The lack of actual flint industries is matched by the paucity of barbed and tanged and related arrowheads. Only ten barbed and tanged, and one tanged example have been recovered, together with fourteen triangular arrowheads. By contrast, the Bournemouth area has produced almost 250 of these 'late' forms, including 216 barbed and tanged arrowheads (Fig. 4.2).

Again the evidence from Bournemouth is far from complete (Fig. 4.3). Calkin (1951) records the distribution simply of arrowhead types and pottery, but a number of assemblages of 'Beaker' lithic material have been identified by the present author. As in the study area, discrete Beaker assemblages do not seem to occur but are mixed with Later Neolithic flintwork. Thumbnail scrapers, barbed and tanged arrowheads and a variety of finely worked pieces, such as some of the plano-convex knives, are present in at least seven places. A number of closely spaced stray finds, including some very fine barbed and tanged arrowheads, a late polished axe and a flint dagger, suggest another focus of Beaker activity. It seems that all but two of these concentrations of lithic material are in areas which have also produced Beaker pottery.

It seems obvious that the incidence of second-millennium flintwork on the coastal plain indicates a higher level of activity than in Cranborne Chase (see Gardiner in Cunliffe 1987, 333–5). As in the Later Neolithic period, there is a particular concentration of finds in the vicinity of Hengistbury Head. These distinctive patterns are underlined when we compare them with the evidence of contemporary pottery.

4.2.3 *The ceramic sequence*[1,4]

The classes of ceramic material traditionally assigned to this period are well known: Beakers, Collared Urns and Food Vessels. Brief comment must, however, be made on the way such material is normally assessed. The different ceramic traditions are defined in terms of vessel form and decorative style. These classifications are the products of an earlier, cultural archaeology, where types were defined by attribute clusters. Such types were treated as the building blocks with which a particular cultural universe could be constructed. Each universe supposedly found archaeological representation in recurrent patterns of association. Beaker grave assemblages are a case in point.

The demise of cultural archaeology has left these classificatory approaches as relics, stranded within our contemporary archaeological methodology. However, reform of the position is not easily achieved because more recent approaches have separated the analysis of *style* from that of *function*, depriving us of any clear foundation upon which to rethink the analysis of the former (Shanks and Tilley 1987). The distinction is unwarranted, for style is not a cultural gloss overlying the functionally adaptive role of the artefact (Gould 1980). Instead style

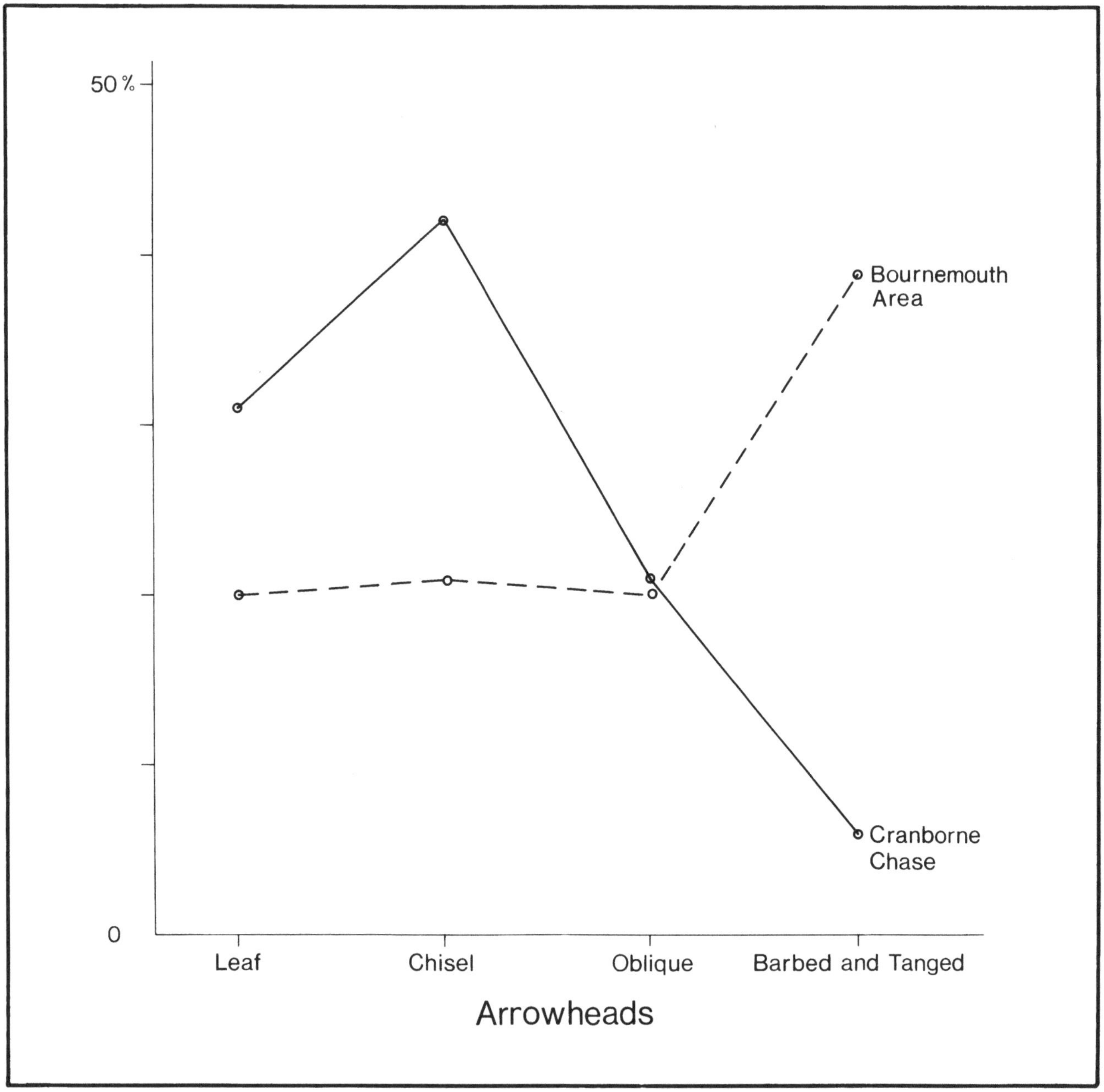

Fig. 4.2 The occurrence (as a percentage) of different classes of flint arrowhead in Cranborne Chase and the Bournemouth area

is one means by which people ordered and understood the world, allowing them to act meaningfully. Style therefore encompasses function.

This position rejects an analysis of style which treats decoration as the accumulation of individual traits and differs from studies based upon laborious schemes of trait comparanda. In its place a number of recent studies have, with varying degrees of success, embarked upon the analysis of design structure. These include the ethnoarchaeological work of Hardin (1983), who has established the way an underlying set of formal design problems are resolved, using a range of decorative styles. She shows how the surface of the vessel may be divided into a hierarchy of spatial configurations, each of which receives a major design element. Other workers, concentrating upon the Neolithic ceramic traditions of northern Europe, have attempted to show that different forms of decoration, structured through the use of different 'design grammars', are drawn into different roles in their use as a medium for communicative action (Braithwaite

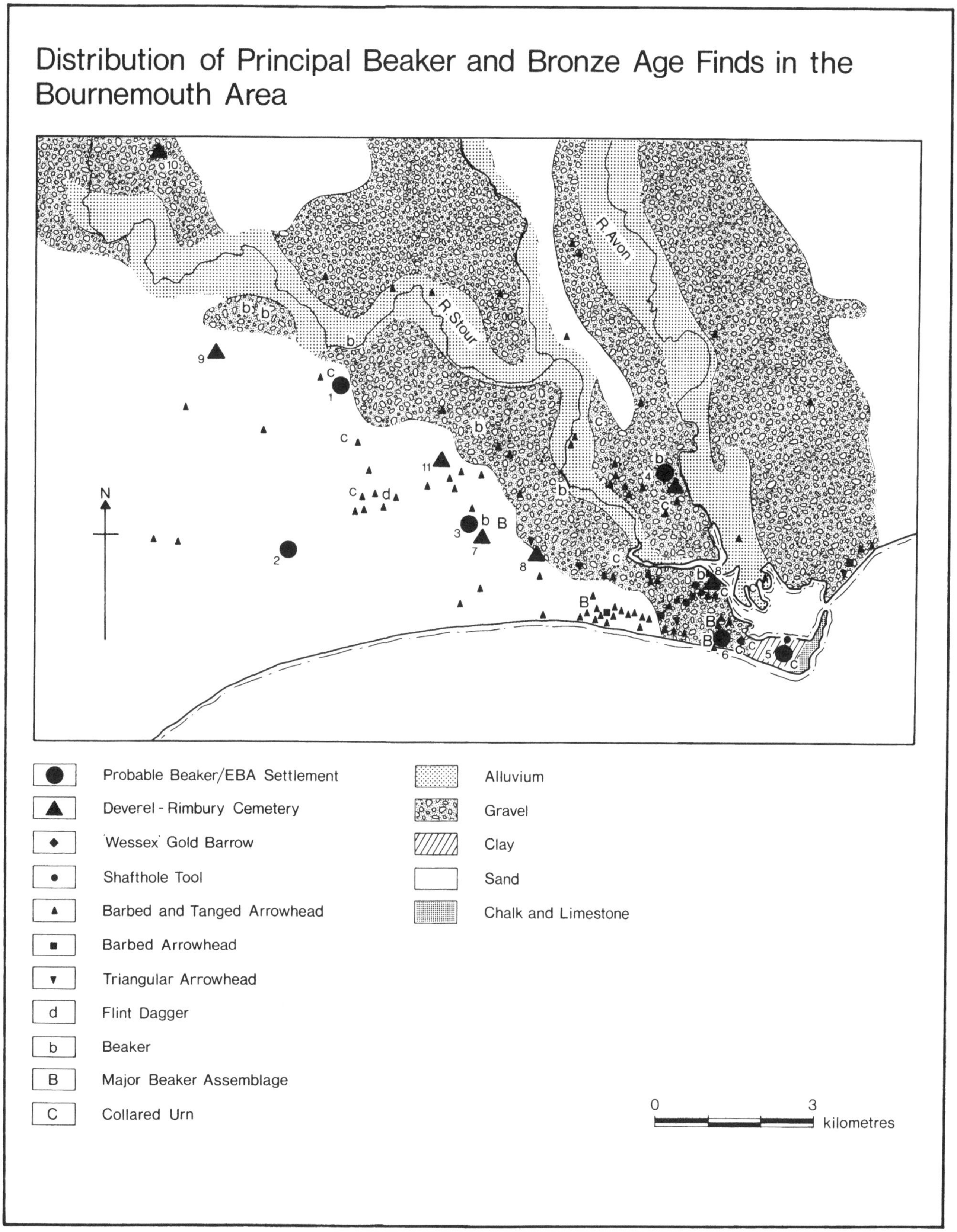

Fig. 4.3 The distribution of Beaker and Early Bronze Age artefacts, settlements and cemeteries around the confluence of the Rivers Avon and Stour. Key: 1 Redhill Common; 2 Talbot Woods; 3 Thistlebarrow; 4 Latch Farm; 5 Hengistbury Head; 6 Whitepits (South Field); 7 King's Park; 8 Pokesdown Cemetery; 9 Kinson Urnfield; 10 Stapehill Urnfield; 11 Haddon Hill

1984; Hodder 1982; Richards and Thomas 1984; Tilley 1984).

One way in which the structuring of material design may work is around sets of opposition and between patterns of inclusion and exclusion. Consequently studies of single ceramic traditions are poorly placed to examine the way oppositional groupings may have operated to create different, but contemporary, traditions. An example is the way Peterborough and Grooved Ware traditions arose in the Late Neolithic from the use of different fabrics, design structures and decorative techniques (and ultimately depositional practices), establishing each tradition in relation to the other. Against this emergent duality of traditional ceramic design traditions in the Late Neolithic must be set the early introduction of Beakers. The early steps in the development of this particular tradition are also distinctive in fabric, vessel form and design. Their use as a basic element in certain grave assemblages further distinguishes them from contemporary traditions. The earliest use of these vessels in grave rituals may be illustrated by the examples from Rushmore Barrow 20, the inhumation grave at Rotherley (*Excavations* II, 19 and 50), and two of the secondary inhumations in the Thickthorn Down long barrow (Drew and Piggott 1936, Figs. 1 and 2).

It is generally accepted that changes in Beaker form and design occurred during the history of the tradition, although the proposed sequence is based entirely upon the analysis of a few grave associations (Lanting and van der Waals 1972; Case 1977; Burgess n.d. [1980]). Indeed, many of the elements of this sequence may have continued in contemporary usage after 1700 bc (Longworth in Wainwright 1979b, 90), indicating not a simple evolution of types but an increasing diversity of styles. In the light of this we might expect an increasing diversity in the contexts of deposition to occur over the same period. Certainly the nature of the grave assemblages appears to change (Case 1977), and Whittle (1981) has argued that the inclusion of Beaker-type vessels amongst domestic assemblages is a late development in the tradition. Late grave assemblages are less well represented in the study area, although there is a spread of domestic material.

Within the non-grave assemblages a minimum of 130 separate vessels have been identified among the excavated material, of which two can be attributed to Case's Early Style, two to his Middle Style and two to his Late Beaker Style (see Case 1977). The remaining 124 belong to either Middle or Late Style vessels. The Early group has been found at only two sites and Middle Style at three. Two sites contain vessels in Case's Late Style, but pottery which might belong to either Middle or Late Style Beakers has been recorded from twenty-two separate locations; some of these are so close together, however, that the number of findspots can probably be reduced to fourteen. The distribution of Beaker pottery is summarised in Figure 4.4. This does not include finds from burials. Although much of the pottery was found near the Cursus, there are more outliers to the general distribution than was the case with Peterborough or Grooved Wares.

This material comes from four kinds of context. At least three of the sites contained pits. These are discussed below. On another eight sites, Beaker pottery appears in the upper levels of monuments established during the Neolithic period: Thickthorn Down long barrow (cf. Figs. 2.11 and 4.6), Wor Barrow, Handley Barrows 26 and 27, the ring ditch in Firtree Field, the Wyke Down henge and the Dorset Cursus. In another four cases Beaker pottery appears as residual material on monuments of later date. In addition, unstratified pieces of Beaker pottery were found in the excavation of seven other sites.

Because so much of this material appears to be residual in character, very little can be said about its association. As mentioned in the previous chapter, it is possible that some of this material was in use alongside Peterborough Ware, but none of the contexts of this material is entirely satisfactory. By contrast, there are no cases in which Beaker pottery has been found with Grooved Ware. Moreover, none of the Beaker pit groups described in the following section contain any other style of ceramic.

Beaker pottery is almost equally abundant in the coastal basin, where it is known from fourteen separate findspots (see Gardiner in Cunliffe 1987, 333). The precise context of this material is rarely recorded. A point of interest is that the identifiable material seems to include a slightly higher proportion of vessels in Case's Early and Middle Styles, compared with finds from the study area.

The decline in use of Beakers at grave rituals, and the possibility that these ceramic styles were drawn into a wider range of non-funerary activity, is one of the features of Burgess's Overton Period (*c.* 1700–1450 bc) (Burgess 1980, 79ff.). Many writers have noted the way that the inclusion of ceramic vessels within mortuary contexts changes during the Early Bronze Age. O'Connor's discussion of the metalwork (below) bears this out, for it is notable that associations between metalwork and ceramics from the study area become almost non-existent around the time of Stage V metalworking and Late Beakers. This indicates two things. One is the emergence of a series of inhumation graves where ceramic associa-

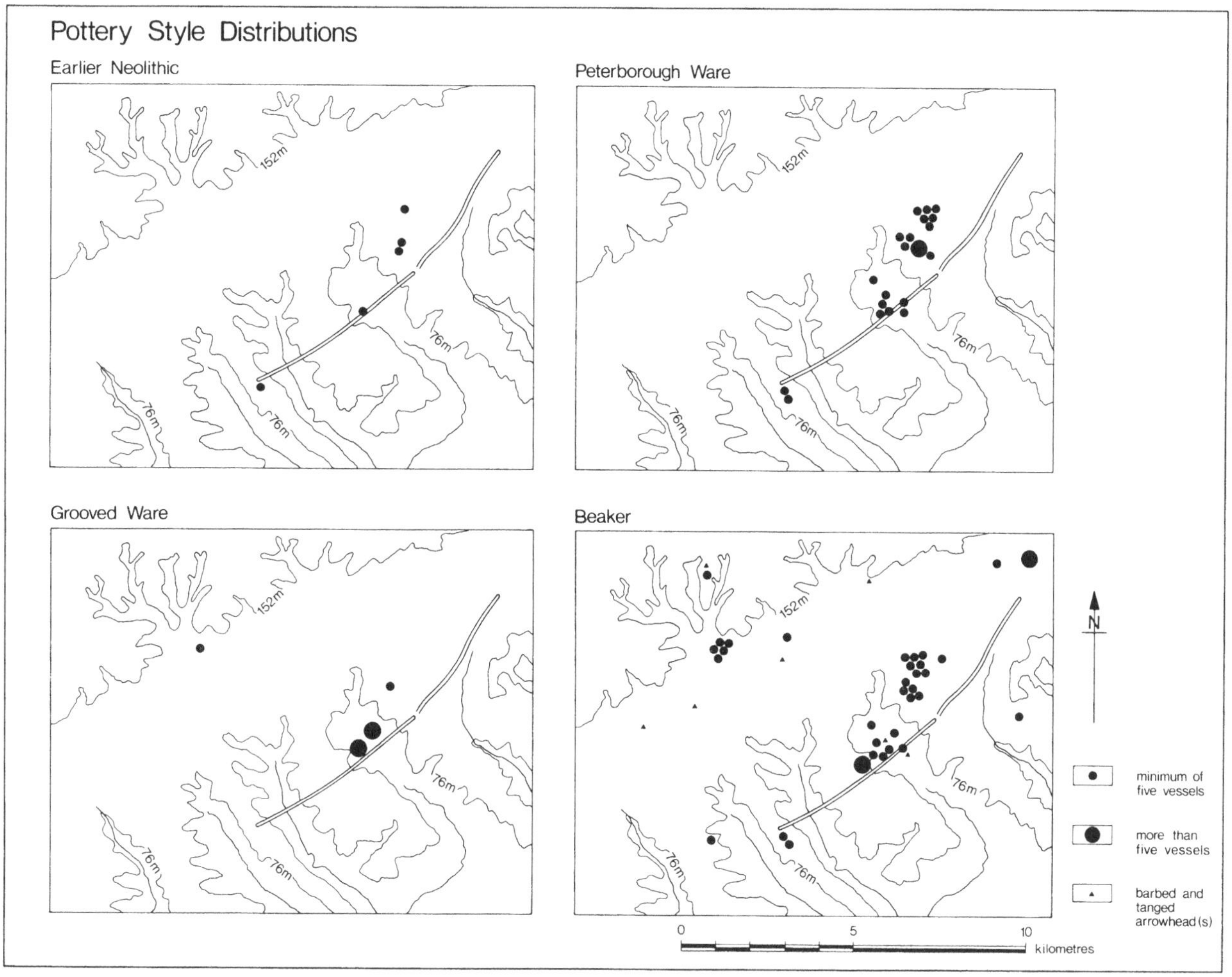

Fig. 4.4 The distribution of Neolithic and Early Bronze Age ceramic styles in relation to the Dorset Cursus

tions are rare, and where those which do occur are unrepresentative of the more common ceramic traditions. These inhumation graves commence with metal associations of Stage VI, where the corpse is occasionally richly adorned, and which, in the past, have been assigned to the Wessex Culture. Dating for the beginning of this series is difficult but Burgess places it between 1700 and 1450 bc (Burgess 1980, 108). Around this time cremation itself becomes an increasingly widespread funerary rite. This in turn involves drawing a new range of ceramic vessels into grave deposits, particularly the Collared Urn. Classic examples of such deposits come from the barrow cemetery in Scrubbity Coppice (*Excavations* II, 42). Other associations with these deposits are few, reflecting, as will be argued below, more the structure of the funerary ritual than the status of the deceased, but again there is a range of cremation deposits where a different selection of material is assigned to the grave, often excluding the use of an urn. Traditionally these graves belong to the late Wessex Culture, which includes the example of Edmondsham G2 with its date of 1119 ± 45 bc (BM 708).

The particular nature of the Early Bronze Age grave assemblages is emphasised by the scarcity of Collared Urn sherds amongst early domestic assemblages. It would be wrong to interpret this simply in chronological terms. Indeed, just as in the Late Neolithic, so in this period different but contemporary traditions may arise from the different categorisation of raw materials (use or non-use of flint filler), design structures and techniques (use or non-use of cord and finger-tip impressions) to generate the Collared Urn and Deverel-Rimbury traditions. It is more than likely that both modes of ceramic production were contemporaneous for part at least of the Early Bronze Age (Barrett 1976). They are distinct in style and in archaeological contexts because the different social practices which drew upon these elements of the cultural repertoire resulted in different depositional practices.

Calkin (1962) drew attention to the finds of Deverel-Rimbury material from the lower reaches of the Stour and Avon, around Christchurch harbour. It may be that the chronology of this material extends back into the Early Bronze Age, representing an additional element of the activity in the lowland basin. No Deverel-Rimbury material is recorded on the southern side of the harbour, around the important barrow cemetery on Hengistbury Head (Gardiner in Cunliffe 1987, 47).

Although very broad developments can therefore be traced in the use of ceramics within the funerary traditions of the Early Bronze Age it must be stressed again that these developments do not mark a sequence of cultural norms. Instead they arise from the increasingly complex mechanisms of categorisation which appear to have been involved in the funerary rituals at this time, and in which ceramic design played its part. At each step in the cycle of production, exchange, use and deposition, choices would have been made concerning how society and the natural world were to be ordered and thus given meaning. The monitoring of that meaning would guide and structure further action. Thus a consistent tradition, such as that identified by Longworth for Collared Urns (1984), is not the product of the regular application of cultural norms, but the routine ordering of the available options in social practice. It is changes in such practices which give rise to new artefact types or new depositional contexts.

4.2.4 The metalwork[5]

The finds of metalwork from the study area are dominated by material recovered from mortuary contexts. The details of recovery and association are often sketchy, but an overview of these finds is important for two reasons. It tells us much about the range of choices made in the employment of artefacts in the funerary rituals, as well as offering some form of chronological control over our understanding of the history of this mortuary activity.

The earliest metal objects from Cranborne Chase appear to be the double-pointed awls from Thickthorn long barrow and Launceston Down G8. Such awls mark the beginning of metalworking in Britain with Stage II metalwork and Step 2 Beakers (Burgess 1980, 72–3), a point illustrated by the Thickthorn burial (Lanting and van der Waals 1972, Fig.1; Burgess 1980, 71; n.d. [1980], Figs. 1, 2, 5: 2–3). The Thickthorn Down awl has been described variously as of both bronze and copper. The Launceston Down awl was analysed and tin detected 'in analytical quantity' (Piggott and Piggott 1944, 77). The associated Beaker of plastic rusticated ware belongs to Clarke's S4 group (1970, 43, 480 no. 203, 554); though it is not identified in the Lanting-van der Waals scheme, Rosamund Cleal (*in litt.*) attributes this vessel to Step 5. According to Burgess, Steps 5 and 6 overlap, with Step 5 associated with Stages IV and V (n.d. [1980], 211, Fig. 3). Launceston Down may be contemporary with the primary grave at West Overton G6b (Smith and Simpson 1966, 129, Figs. 3, 5) with its double-pointed awl and Step 6 Beaker. However, bronze was already known in Stage II (Burgess 1980, 73), so a Stage III date may be possible for the Launceston Down awl.

The status of the lost 'halberd' from Blandford is uncertain. Halberds belong to Stages III and IV (Burgess n.d. [1980], 209); English finds are rare and there appear to be none from Wessex (Ó Ríordáin 1936, 276, 312, Fig. 54), only the later halberd-pendants (Gerloff 1975, 201, 222–3; Burgess 1980, 111, 114).

While double-pointed awls were still current in burials of the Bush Barrow group (Burgess 1980, 104), the single-pointed form became more common in the contemporary Stage VI metalworking (*ibid.*, 115). Although the Beaker from Oakley Down G9 is lost (Clarke 1970, 480 no. 206), this is said to be a 'typical, if unusually rich, late beaker grave' (Burgess 1980, 110), with barbed and tanged flint arrowheads of Green Low type (Green 1980, 133; Gerloff 1975, 56). Case uses Oakley Down G9 to exemplify the appearance of single-pointed awls in his Late Beaker phase (1977, 83). The associated dagger, with its long broad blade, is related to the East Kennet variant of Gerloff's Milston type (1975, 57), but the trapezoid butt with four rivets is compared also to continental Locham forms (*ibid.*) This later dating would align the dagger with the Arreton, late Wessex, phase after the disappearance of Beakers, so it more probably belongs amongst the flat blades with plug rivets characteristic of Stage VI (Burgess 1980, 114).

The lost dagger from Oakley Down G4 was found with a shale bead and four-footed handled cup (Annable and Simpson 1964, no. 463). If the early Wessex date for the burial is accepted (Grinsell 1982, 19), then the dagger also probably belonged to Stage VI.

Two daggers found in foundation digging at Boveridge House have recently been attributed to two separate burials (Grinsell 1959, 104; 1982, 19). The first dagger is a large example of the Winterbourne Came variant of Gerloff's Armorico-British form C, which Burgess places between the Bush Barrow and Camerton-Snowshill groups. This variant is related to both Camerton-Snowshill series and weapons of the Early to Middle Bronze Age transition on the Continent (Gerloff 1975, 84–5, 97–8). It is, therefore, tantalising that the second dagger in this doubtful association is of the Snowshill type, belonging to Stage VII (Burgess 1980, 124).

The primary burial in Edmondsham G2, with perforated whetstone, bone tweezers and bone pin, is eponymous for the second phase of Wessex burials, the Aldbourne-Edmondsham group (Burgess 1980, 104). Its dagger belongs to the Camerton type, like Snowshill, characteristic of Stage VII (*ibid.*, 124). The burial has a radiocarbon date of 1119 ± 45 bc (BM 708). Oakley Down G20 also produced a Camerton weapon and a pointed bone tool, not a pin as stated by Annable and Simpson (1964, no. 350).

There are two knife-daggers which are related to both phases of the Wessex grave series from Cranborne Chase. The unassociated Charlton find cannot be dated more closely than Stages VI or VII. The second find comes from the primary cremation in the north-western tump of the twin disc barrow Oakley Down G8, accompanied by an awl, amber beads and amber space-plates, all lost. An Aldbourne cup from the south-eastern primary cremation (Annable and Simpson 1964, no. 433) survives, but another awl and beads of amber, faience and shale are lost. Gerloff regards these two finds as a single deposit of the second Wessex phase (1975, 127–8, 168, 198–9, 207, App. 7,7). Grinsell treats the two burials separately (1959, 170; 1982, 19).

Bottlebush G33a produced a primary cremation with a bulb-headed pin similar to the pin in the Camerton burial (Gerloff 1975, 127). The presence of beads of amber and 'glass', presumably faience (but see Guido *et al.* 1984), relates this burial to the Aldbourne series (*ibid.*, 206, n. 3, 207). The awl from Oakley Down Farm was found with 'four green glass beads, all with four segments', so this may be another Aldbourne burial.

Woodminton Down G5 produced a single pointed awl with a secondary series Collared Urn (Longworth 1984, no. 1664). This awl is similar to that from Oakley Down G24 accompanying a primary urned cremation (Parke 1953, 41 n. 3). The three awls from the Down Farm pond barrow are noted below (p. 132). An awl accompanied an inhumation from Pitt Rivers' barrow 23 on Handley Hill and another awl came from the silt of the causeway of saucer barrow G4, south of Winklebury (*Excavations* II, Pl. CXLIX).

The Arreton axe from Woodlands Down is among the few from Dorset and Wiltshire, in contrast with the concentration of contemporary Camerton-Snowshill daggers in the area (Burgess and Cowen 1972, 178, Figs. 6–7).

On the basis of these finds it is clear that variations did occur in the way metalwork was incorporated in the grave assemblages of the Early Bronze Age. Awls were deposited intermittently throughout the period with both inhumations and cremations, but daggers only appeared in the study area as part of Stage VI metalworking. It was during Stages VI and VII metalworking that the most varied grave assemblages were deposited, at the same time as the more simple deposits of cremated bone associated with Collared Urns.

4.3 The domestic sites: the results of excavation[2,1]

Apart from isolated scatters of pottery, whose interpretation is often ambiguous, more complex deposits with Beaker pottery have been discovered on four sites in the study area, two by General Pitt Rivers, and the others during our own fieldwork.

4.3.1 Handley Hill and Martin Down

Pitt Rivers' sites can be summarised very briefly, since they were never recorded in detail. First, there is Beaker pottery from pits on Handley Hill (*Excavations* IV, 49–56). As mentioned earlier, it is no longer possible to reconstitute the groups of artefacts found in these features, which contain material extending from the Earlier Neolithic to the Beaker ceramic phase. It seems possible, however, that the Beaker material was associated with some Peterborough Ware considered on p. 69. Further discussion of its context does not seem warranted.

The second site discovered by the General was beneath the Middle Bronze Age enclosure at Martin Down, not far from the northern terminal of the Cursus (*Excavations* IV, 185–214). This is represented mainly by sherds from the ditch and bank of the later enclosure, and by others from beneath its earthwork. In addition, a group of three pits was recognised inside the later enclosure. Two of these, 7 m apart, contained Beaker pottery, whilst a third pit, 8 m away, seems to have lacked any artefacts. Few of the worked flints from Martin Down survive, but examination of the museum collection does reveal a small selection of implements which closely resemble the 'Beaker' flintwork described by Julie Gardiner. They consist of a chert knife or scraper, and eleven flake scrapers. Where they retain a provenance they seem to have occurred throughout the excavated area. In addition, there are two finds for which Peterborough Ware associations might be more appropriate: a chisel arrowhead made of Portland chert, and a Y-shaped tool found on the surface nearby.

4.3.2 South Lodge Camp

The more recently excavated sites were also chance finds, perhaps emphasising how poor a showing material of this date makes in the surface record. At South Lodge Camp a flint scatter and a group of Beaker pottery sherds were found during sample excavation of a Middle Bronze Age cemetery, whilst at Firtree Field a group of Beaker pits close to the Cursus had been cut by features of a pond barrow dating to the later second millennium bc.

The excavated material from South Lodge Camp came from the excavation of the Barrow Pleck cemetery, described in detail in Chapter 5. It seems to have been distributed mainly between Barrows 4 and 18, both of which had been excavated by Pitt Rivers, and a nearby mound which had been levelled in the last century (Fig. 5.3). The museum material reveals that Barrow 4 included residual sherds of Grooved Ware and Barrow 18 contained small sherds of Late Style Beaker. Excavation in between these three barrows was intended to search for secondary cremations, but also produced a large amount of worked flint. At one point this material was also found in the upper levels of a periglacial feature, where it was associated with Late Style Beaker pottery. This material was apparently undisturbed and the sherds and some of the flakes could be reassembled. It seems likely that they had been deposited on a land surface and owed their protection to slumping within the natural feature; the same process has been observed in excavations carried out by the Stonehenge Environs Project (Julian Richards pers. comm.). The extent of the artefact scatter remains in doubt. The worked flints in the deposit with Beaker pottery are not very different from Middle Bronze Age material stratified on the same site, and the layout of the excavation did not lend itself to defining the distribution of this early material with much confidence. With these provisos, however, the material may have extended across an area of at least 600 m^2 with a mean density of about eleven flints per m^2. The distribution of flintwork was notably uneven, however, with the three highest densities towards the edge of the area sampled by excavation (Fig. 5.26).

The location of this material raises one interesting possibility, for the 'feature' containing the Beaker pottery was beneath a lynchet (F) which is known to predate some of the Middle Bronze Age barrows on the site (Fig. 5.3). This earthwork is on a different alignment from the remainder of the field system around South Lodge Camp and to some extent this flint scatter respects its position, being found mainly in the unploughed area to its east. Such tenuous evidence may provide one clue to the location of the agricultural settlements of this phase.

Unfortunately the excavated material is rather uninformative. The implements consist mainly of scrapers and retouched flakes. It must be emphasised, however, that only four retouched flakes and a possible knife were *stratified* with Beaker pottery, and the remainder could include later material.

4.3.3 Firtree Field[6.2]

The other recently excavated site was located just west of the Dorset Cursus and had been cut by a later pond barrow. The filling of this feature contained a considerable amount of residual Beaker pottery and large quantities of worked flint, some of which may be of similar origin. To confuse matters still further, this monument had been ploughed out during the Middle Bronze Age. More pottery of Beaker date, accompanied by a small quantity of undiagnostic flintwork, was found in a buried soil sealing the western ditch of the Cursus 60 m from this site (Fig. 2.13: 1982 section, 1.3 lower), and in the upper filling of the Neolithic ring ditch 165 m to the west (Fig. 3.15: 1.8). The latter material had been completely disturbed during later use of that site but included a series of small flake scrapers like those from the pond barrow. These observations serve to illustrate the wide distribution of this material on a site where fieldwork failed to identify a clear-cut surface scatter.

The creation of the pond barrow had impinged on a compact group of up to ten small pits, three of which could be shown, stratigraphically, to belong to the earlier feature (Fig. 4.5). They were distributed over an area of about 250 m^2, although they could have extended beyond the western limit of the excavation. The fillings of the pits were strikingly similar, with chalk rubble towards the base and a series of natural silts in the higher levels. Feature 31 had a distinct lens of ash in its filling. No postholes or stakeholes were identified in their vicinity.

The contents of these pits confirm that they pre-date the pond barrow, which belongs to the mid-second millennium bc. Quantities of Beaker pottery were discovered in two pits, with smaller amounts in four others. Four of the pits also contained flint implements, perhaps of earlier second millennium date (scrapers, knives and a saw), whilst a fifth contained utilised flakes. The amount of flintwork was small, but four of the pits contained a sufficient number of flakes to give the impression that they belonged to the same basic industry. The contents of three of these pits call for comment. Feature 22 contained the remains of a fragmentary Beaker vessel, which had a complete bowl placed inside its rim, whilst part of a Food Vessel was found in the very top of Feature 24. In addition a pig's jaw and a struck flake seemed to have been placed together on the bottom of Feature 23; it seems possible that once again the proximity of

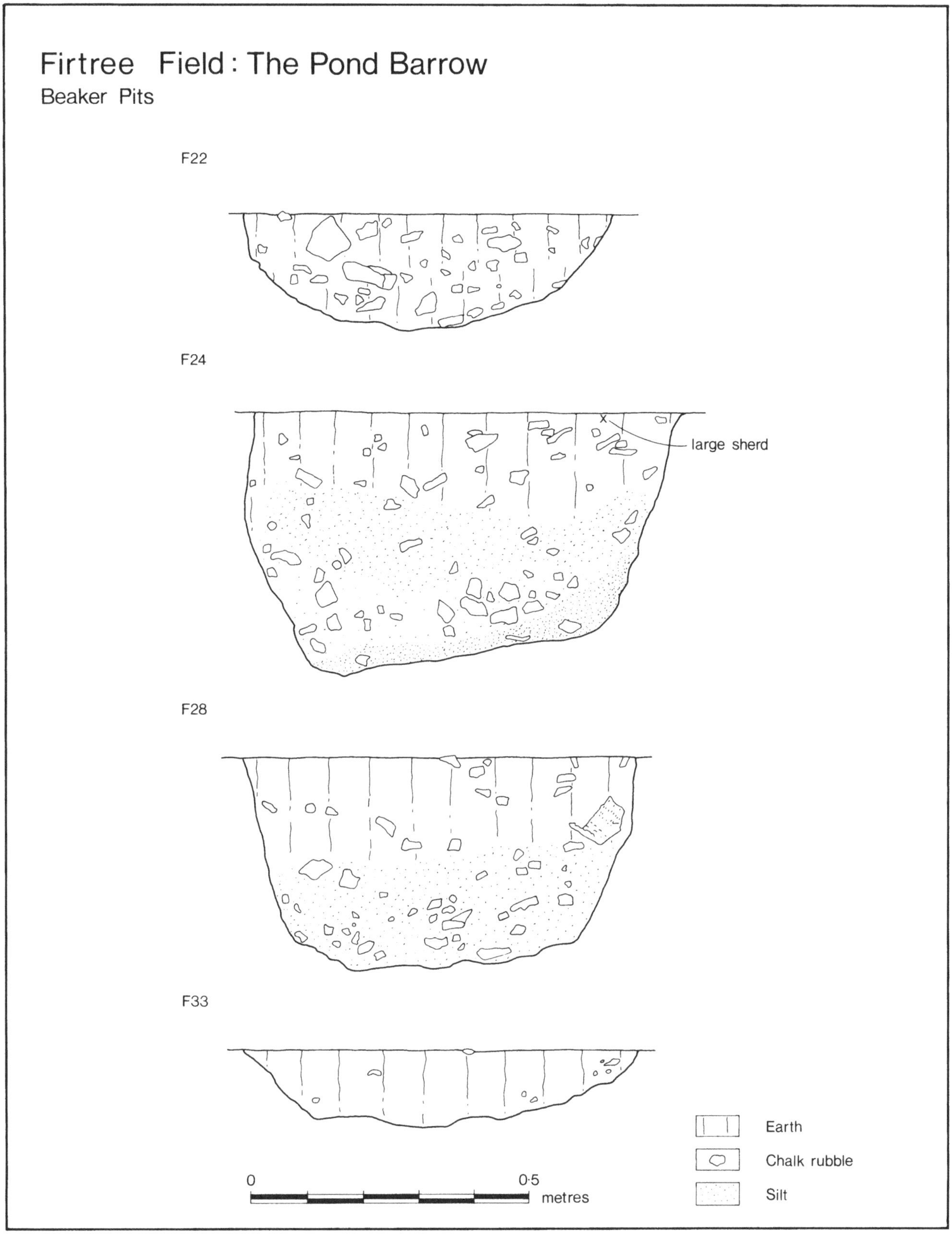

Fig. 4.5 Sections of four of the Beaker pits pre-dating the pond barrow in Firtree Field, Down Farm

the Cursus was reflected by rather formal deposits in what otherwise seems to be a domestic site. There is a radiocarbon date of 1920 ± 50 bc (BM 2325) from oak heartwood in the middle filling of Feature 31. A second date of 1950 ± 120 bc (BM 2191R) comes from oak heartwood from the middle filling of Feature 28, one of those containing Beaker pottery.

Since these pits were cut by the later pond barrow, it may be worth considering the residual material occurring within its filling. This included an appreciable number of Beaker sherds of similar character to those from the pits and from the Cursus ditch, as well as a large amount of worked flint. Much of this material was of very similar character to the finds from the Beaker pits. Although little weight can be placed on this evidence, 91 per cent of the regular implements from this context were scrapers; two other finds consisted of edge-retouched knives for which a similar date seems possible.

If this material was related to the Beaker occupation, such a high proportion of scrapers would link it with a series of excavated industries found in rather specialised environments in other parts of the country (Bradley 1978, 57 and 59). Some of these areas might have been used seasonally, or for very short periods. We cannot place much weight on this comparison, but, taken at face value, it reinforces the suggestion that already use of the study area was becoming less intensive.

4.3.4 Conclusion[1]

The problem confronting an analysis of this 'domestic' material is partly the way our knowledge is constrained by the relative visibility of certain classes of evidence. Discussion of the Early Bronze Age, where settlement evidence is often difficult to locate, is normally dominated by a concern with the more visible mortuary deposits, but different classes of deposit (settlement finds or mortuary deposits) do not result from entirely isolated areas of human experience. Certainly their separation results from scheduling regions of time and space, whereby different aspects of social experience were ordered, but it is the overall pattern of that ordering which constitutes the totality of social life. We cannot therefore write separate histories of settlement or of burial simply because those are the deposits available to us. Instead the challenge is to understand, within the limits of the available evidence, the interrelationship of those scheduled areas of social experience. It is in these terms that we must now turn to analyse the mortuary deposits, and to place them within the wider context of the routine practices of settlement and agricultural activity.

4.4 Mortuary archaeology

4.4.1 Introduction[1]

Mortuary practices constitute one major, recognisable, activity associated with the monuments of the Neolithic and Bronze Age on Cranborne Chase. These monuments, and the finds recovered from them, dominate our understanding of this period. The nature of mortuary activities also changed during the Middle–Late Bronze Age and the Iron Age. So widespread are these earlier remains, and so important are the changes in mortuary practices during the prehistoric period, that a general comment on the interpretation of this material now seems necessary (see Barrett 1988a).

Saxe (1970) and Binford (1971) argued that mortuary variability reflects the degree of organisational complexity in the social system. The suggested reason for this is that the treatment of the corpse depended upon marking out a selection of the *social identities* achieved by that individual in life. The number of identities available for selection within the system clearly increases with its complexity. The human energy expended in the act of burial is also supposedly proportional to the size of the group with responsibilities to that individual. It is as if individuals remained active participants in their own funerals, achieving similar levels of social discourse in death to those achieved in life.

There are numerous problems in this approach. If the organisation of the social system is reflected in the organisation of burial then, whilst analysis of the burial record can 'reveal' the form of the social system, it can tell us nothing in turn about the origins, nor the reproduction, of that system. If mortuary data are used to explain social conditions, then the explanations are necessarily tautologous. They describe functional 'needs' which emerge with the social system, to be satisfied by the mortuary rites. Examples are the 'needs' of segmentary groups to establish territorial markers – and thus facilitate segmentation (Renfrew 1976) – or the 'needs' of corporate groups to control critical resources – and thus maintain a corporate identity (Chapman 1981).

If the archaeology of death is to have any analytical power, we must be able to observe the way mortuary practices intervened in an overall cycle of social reproduction. By social reproduction I mean the reproduction of the entire system, in both its material and its human aspects. We should not assume that the social roles once held by the deceased determine burial rituals. Instead, we must turn our attention to the living, to understand their actions, played out around the corpse and the grave. The dead are not active participants in their own funeral, but the corpse does present a symbolic medium by which, for example, the decay of the flesh may evoke the transition from life to death. Burial rituals are the means by which the living renegotiate relations of obligation, affinity and inheritance. They do this as they negotiate their relations with their dead and their ancestors. Death precipitates the requirement for such a negotiation, and the body provides a potent symbol upon which such a discourse between the living may be projected.

Woodburn has observed that hunter–gatherers with simple death beliefs 'are those with ... immediate return rather than delayed return economies, social organisations and values' (Woodburn 1982, 205). In other words, immediate-return systems are characterised by Woodburn as having a minimum investment in 'long lasting artefacts or in long enduring debts, obligations or other binding commitments to other humans, affines, contractual partners or members of bonded corporate groups, however they are recruited' (*ibid.*). He argues that such immediate-return systems do not provide 'fertile ground for the ideological elaboration of death beliefs and practices in general' (Woodburn 1982, 208). However, if mortuary rituals are concerned in the restructuring of debts, obligations and affinities, then a correlation between social complexity and mortuary complexity is hardly surprising. What is more to the point is the way mortuary practices, and the material symbolism employed, contribute to the reproduction of certain social and material conditions. Mortuary rituals are a form of social practice. However, we cannot employ a reductionist logic which sees the entire essence of the social system mapped out in this single practice.

I want to make a series of analytical distinctions concerning mortuary practices which are of relevance for archaeological analysis. I will then attempt to use these to explore the origins and the changing nature of the Early Bronze Age material recovered from Cranborne Chase, and to set the scene for the Middle Bronze Age activity which we will discuss in the next chapter.

Let us begin by distinguishing between *funerary rituals* and *ancestor rituals* (Barrett 1988a; cf. Kinnes 1975). I take the former to concern the rites of passage which structure the transference of an individual from life to death. In such rituals the idea of a transition, or movement, as discussed by Van Gennep (1960) and Turner (1969), is central to the activities of the mourners and the treatment of the corpse. Ancestor rituals, on the other hand, draw the symbolic presence of ancestors into the world of the living. Here a wide range of symbolism, which may include the physical remains of such ancestors, will be used to evoke their presence. However, whilst a transition in social and cultural states may be involved in ancestor rituals, a transition between the living and the dead need not occur.

Obviously there are links between these two types of ritual. Funerary rituals produce ancestral remains, and the form of the funeral, including the symbolism and architecture associated with it, structures the resulting form those ancestral remains take and partly determines the way such remains are approached in the future. Ancestors may also appear to be present at the time of burial, and ancestor rites may pave the way for, and thus help to structure, the burial rites (cf. Bloch 1971). Leach (1976, 83) has also pointed out that the path by which the dead reach the ancestors is likely to be the same path by which the ancestors may approach the living. The point which needs stressing is that whilst both types of ritual are distinct, both may employ human remains. This means that the archaeological recovery of human remains cannot simply imply *burial*.

My second set of distinctions concerns the funerary rites themselves. Here it is necessary to distinguish between *inhumation*, *secondary burial* and *cremation*. In Van Gennep's threefold division of the rites of passage we find a sequence running from the rites of separation to the rites of liminality, and ending with the rites of incorporation. The threefold sequence arises from the creation of two categories (alive:dead) which, whilst appearing stable and unambiguous, are transgressed by death itself. Funerals involve the transference of an individual between these categories, a transference which involves passing through a *liminal* stage 'betwixt and between' the normally accepted stability. As such the liminal stage appears ambiguous and dangerous because it is here that these stable categories appear to dissolve. The first and last stages are periods in which the limits of cultural stability are set, and the liminal stage is the period of cultural transformation. In funerary rites the liminal phase may be marked by carrying and storing the corpse away from the living community, and the actual decay of the body may, in some cases, be taken as indicating the cultural transformation which is occurring. Turner argues that in rites associated with the actual movement of an individual from one state to another the rituals of liminality will be of central importance. He has also demonstrated that each stage in the sequence may be marked by different symbolic procedures.

Archaeologists do not observe the entire sequence of a funeral. At the same time the parts of the sequence which are observed vary according to the form of the funeral ritual. Inhumation rites, as we tend to understand them, are structured in such a way that the liminal period ends with placing the body in the grave. The body is thereby received in death, and the mourners returned to the wider community. In this case it is possible to envisage that some of the symbolic materials used to structure the liminal period may be carried over into the grave. This possibility must distinguish the archaeological remains of inhumation from those of secondary burial and cremation.

Hertz (1960) demonstrated that secondary burial involved a clear spatial and temporal separation between the rites of liminality and the rites which close the sequence for the deceased and the mourners. By secondary burial I do not mean the construction of a satellite grave in or next to an earlier burial deposit. Instead the term, as applied here, concerns a particular form of funerary ritual. The body may have been stored or buried before the bones, recovered and cleaned, receive their final burial. Here the separation is clear enough for the symbols of liminality to receive little or no representation amongst the archaeological deposits accompanying the final burial. Thus the term *secondary burial* as used here refers to the form of the burial ritual (such as excarnation) and not, as in common archaeological usage, to the sequence of interment in a barrow.

Cremation may similarly 'distance' the close of the ritual process from its earlier stages, for with cremation liminality may end with the conflagration of the pyre. However, the incorporation of the cremated remains, if they are buried or scattered, is temporally and spatially separate from these earlier rites to such a degree that the archaeological record may fail to record the symbolism of the liminal phase.

The methodological implications of these observations prevents us from comparing the grave furnishings of inhumations with those of contemporary cremations. They are not indicators of relative 'wealth' or 'social status', for we are not comparing like with like. Indeed, it seems that many of the grave goods associated with inhumation burial in the Bronze Age are the ornaments of dress with which the corpse was decorated for its journey from life to death (Barrett 1985, 104).

The distinction between inhumation, secondary burial and cremation, establishes a different temporal and spatial distance between the living and the dead during these rites. In the former there is a very direct transition for the corpse from liminality into the world of the dead, and the point of that transition is physically marked by the grave. Cremation and secondary burial produce a greater temporal and spatial distance between the living and the dead, and the point of transition may be defined with less geographical precision.

All these distinctions have analytical implications for our understanding of archaeological material. One final point must now be made. This concerns mortuary monuments themselves. Here I would wish to reserve the term *funerary monument* strictly for those monuments which are constructed during the funerary process. It is possible to demonstrate that a large number of our mortuary monuments do not conform to this specific definition, and terms such as 'burial mound' are often misleading (Kinnes 1975, 17).

I have been concerned to argue that our attention must focus more upon the actions of the mourners than upon the apparent status of the corpse. This is because it is the mourners' actions which affect the treatment of the corpse, and those actions structure future relations between the living, and between the living and the dead. Such actions reproduce certain social relations of authority and obligation, and result in the inheritance of certain property or status rights amongst the living. Our concern now is not to identify particular ranks and statuses but to investigate how certain social practices were maintained. Those practices may have maintained or challenged a particular authority, and I am concerned to develop archaeological procedures which will allow us to identify the reproduction or the transformation of such an authoritative discourse (Barrett 1987). Authority allows control to be established over people and materials. As such, the symbols of authority have to be mobilised at the moment social obligations are established, perhaps at a funeral itself, and the acceptance of that dominant authority marks the beginning of the fulfilment of the obligation.

4.4.2 Ancestor and funerary rituals: the Neolithic/Early Bronze Age transition[1]

We may now turn to examine some of the mortuary structures from Cranborne Chase. The Later Neolithic/Early Bronze Age is traditionally depicted as a period of change. New mortuary customs appear to accompany the first use of metal (but see Burgess and Shennan, 1976; Kinnes 1979). Whilst the change in mortuary customs was once explained in the cultural-historical terms of 'Beaker invasions', recent emphasis has been placed upon tracing an apparent social transformation. Renfrew's arguments concerning the emergence of 'ranked' societies in the Early Bronze Age are well known and depend largely upon his interpretation of the mortuary evidence (Renfrew 1973 and 1986). Renfrew suggests that the occurrence of inhumation graves with a variety of grave goods depicts, in the terms of Saxe and Binford, a greater differentiation in social status amongst the living. I have already touched upon the problems inherent in such an argument.

Let us assume instead that the paths which the dead are made to take in funerary ritual structure the relationship which is perceived to exist between descendants and the other world of ancestors and gods. The projection of that ordered relationship in a funerary ritual is partly the means by which relations between the living are restructured. Ritual concerns establish a particular discursive knowledge about the world which, at the crisis of death, is likely to set out the lines, obligations and rights of inheritance. It follows that the cultural mechanisms of the funerary ritual, determining the way the corpse is treated or the way the funerary architecture and the ancestral deposits are approached, produce relations of distance or immediacy between descendants and this 'other world'. It is necessary to get beneath the techniques used to build paths of access between the living and the dead. These are the strategies employed by the living which result in certain kinds of social authority being maintained or challenged. Different paths will be available at any particular moment, although they will all have to accommodate the material conditions which had resulted from earlier actions. Certain paths, direct or indirect, may come to dominate the funerary practices of a particular period.

The mortuary remains from the Cranborne Chase area can be viewed in terms of either funerary or ancestral rituals, a distinction which clarifies the transformation in practices which seems to originate in the Later Neolithic. In the case of funerary rituals we must examine the temporal and spatial distance established between the bereaved and either an ancestral line or a more generalised group of ancestors.

Wor Barrow has already been described (p. 38), as has the series of mortuary deposits placed around it (p. 84). Within the mortuary area of Wor Barrow a number of skeletal remains were recovered. These are recorded as the disarticulated remains of three males, and the articulated remains of a further three individuals, again males. Some caution may be needed here, both in the nineteenth-century sexing of the skeletal remains, and in the identification of articulated remains (cf. Ashbee 1966, 10). However, taking the record at face value, we may now distinguish between the articulated and disarticulated remains. Whilst we do not know the sequence of deposition, it seems likely that the rituals of inhumation burial (the articulated skeletons) were either combined with rituals of secondary burial, or with ancestral rites. The latter are represented by the deposits of disarticulated remains. This means that the mourners' actions, connected with the recently deceased, also achieved some direct access to these ancestral resources. These bone deposits, lying on the old ground surface, were then covered by a 2.3 ft (0.70 m) high mound, which may reasonably be accepted as a burial structure.

It seems likely that the final sequence of mound construction was itself complex (p. 38 – cf. Kinnes 1981; Vyner 1985), although the supporting evidence is limited. The massive construction of the Wor Barrow mound was not linked with acts of burial, and the long-barrow mound on Thickthorn Down covers no human remains, an observation which need no longer surprise us. The entire monumental construction of long barrows and the Cursus within which they are integrated was not for the burial of the dead, even if it does then become the focus for such activity.

A further important distinction between the primary structures and the final mound is possible. This concerns the different levels of social participation in, and social effects of, such building projects. The original mortuary deposits, collected to satisfy the demands of burial and other rituals, lay within a relatively small, possibly embanked area. Few people could have been involved in constructing such deposits. The initial burial mound also appears to have been a relatively small affair, again demanding only a limited participation in its construction. On the other hand, the building projects which raised the final mound at Wor Barrow, the Cursus and the associated mounds is of quite a different order. These are projects which would have lasted for a number of seasons and drawn upon the labour of a number of communities.

The importance of this distinction in terms of social participation is not to argue that it represents an evolutionary step in the scale of social complexity (Renfrew 1973), nor does it imply that the final project was instigated by some autocratic authority. But it does tell us something about the claimed 'ideological' role of the primary deposits (Shanks and Tilley 1982). If human skeletal deposits and ancestral remains are being used to map ideas of social order in an ideological way, because they work to preserve rather than transform the structure of social relations, they can hardly be claimed to achieve it by imposing this order upon the consciousness of the entire community. Most of that community was probably excluded from ever seeing these rites. It seems more likely that we are observing the ritual construction of order by some elite, drawn from the community by prior claims of ritual purity, and the resulting deposits simply reassert the ritual competence of that elite (cf. Abercrombie, Hill and Turner 1980). By way of contrast, it is with the monumental construction of the Cursus and long mounds that we now find the wider community involved, constructing the earthworks which would have dominated the organisation of their landscape.

We can now consider the extent to which the Later

Neolithic did witness a change in the nature of mortuary rituals and examine the significance of these changes. Most writers would now see the period marking a steady trend towards single-grave inhumation beneath round barrows, and a number of attempts have been made to establish the chronology of this development (Burgess and Shennan 1976; Kinnes 1979). This change, no longer tied to a Beaker cultural horizon, cannot simply be regarded as a change from 'communal' to 'individual' burial. Instead, what we see is the emergence of archaeological deposits which are more directly the result of burial rituals. These stand in contrast to earlier deposits which were largely formed around the activities of ancestral rites. These are therefore changes in burial and ancestral rituals, and these changes are linked in a rather more complex way to the archaeological deposits than has normally been allowed.

After the ditches of the Wor Barrow had begun to silt, two inhumations, again both recorded as male, an adult and child, took place in the eastern terminal of the ditch at the northern end of the mound. Around this time further burials seem to have taken place, but this time immediately beyond, though close to the limits of, the mound of Wor Barrow. These deposits were found beneath Barrows 26 and 27, each barrow being surrounded by a penannular ditch (Fig. 3.12 and p. 84).

Each deposit beneath the mounds of Barrows 26 and 27 may represent the direct deposition of a corpse at the end of a funeral rite. There is no extensive preparation of the ground which is archaeologically visible. The earlier mound still provided the direct focus for the funerary rites but the deposits were now isolated within an enclosing penannular ditch. Other inhumations were placed in the Wor Barrow ditch.

At Thickthorn Down burials were inserted into the barrow mound itself (Fig. 2.10). One, that of a child, was accompanied by additional skeletal fragments of a female. Another burial also had additional bones deposited with it, whilst a third inhumation was accompanied by a Beaker and an awl (Drew and Piggott 1936). At a date probably before these funerary and ancestral deposits were placed in the mound two chalk phalli were buried in the barrow ditch along with the pottery and animal bone already mapped (Fig. 2.11).

At the end of the third millennium bc we observe, archaeologically, the emergence of funerary deposits in the strict sense, and it is the existence of monuments associated with these deposits which now comes to play an active part in the organisation of the contemporary landscape. The changes are complex, and ancestral remains may still be drawn into other ritual practices, such as the small deposit of cremated bone placed in the top of two of the silted pits within the Wyke Down henge, and the deposition of a human skull.

4.4.3 Early Bronze Age mortuary archaeology[1]

The non-uniform distribution of Bronze Age round barrows has long been recognised (Atkinson 1972). Concentrations and cemetery clusters of mounds cannot be explained simply in terms of differential survival (Fig. 4.6). Fleming demonstrated very clearly the nature of these distributions for the Wessex uplands (Fleming 1971). He notes that, overall, there is a low density of mounds on Cranborne Chase, with a very small proportion of bell- and disc-barrows (Fleming 1971, 154). These 'special types' of mound structure are defined by the form of the mound in the last stage of its development. In contrast to this overall pattern for Cranborne Chase, and in the centre of the region, there lie the complex nucleated cemeteries on Oakley Down, an area of high barrow density comparable to the concentrations of mounds known from the Dorset Ridgeway.

The development of these monuments on Cranborne Chase took place throughout the first half of the second millennium. Its origins, as we have seen, lay in the end of the third millennium with the emergence of a distinct set of burial rites. Our understanding of the detailed development of these mortuary rites is hampered by the variable quality of the excavation record. The main investigation of the Oakley Down cemetery (Plate 1) was by Colt Hoare and Cunnington, who left us with little account of the internal structure of the mounds themselves (Colt Hoare 1812). However, a clearer understanding of the way these funerary rites were executed, and the subsequent acts which took place around the resulting deposits, can be gained from the excavations of barrows on Crichel and Launceston Downs (Piggott and Piggott 1944; Green, Lynch and White 1982) (Fig. 4.6).

The Piggotts excavated a number of low mounds on Crichel Down. Amongst these is a series, seemingly dated to the Early Bronze Age, where graves had been dug to receive inhumations. Some of them are accompanied by beakers and in one, Barrow 17, the inhumation was also accompanied by an awl. Out of the five early graves four appear to have been subsequently reopened. Some of the bodies were disturbed, perhaps with the removal of skeletal fragments, and in one case a cremation was dug into the edge of the grave.

The earliest deposits from Crichel Down include the Beaker burials. These were covered by low, or negligible mounds, a pattern repeated for three deposits recovered by Pitt Rivers (*Excavations* II, 19–20, 50 and Pl. XCII; *Excavations* IV, 14 and Pl. 265). Pitt Rivers also noted

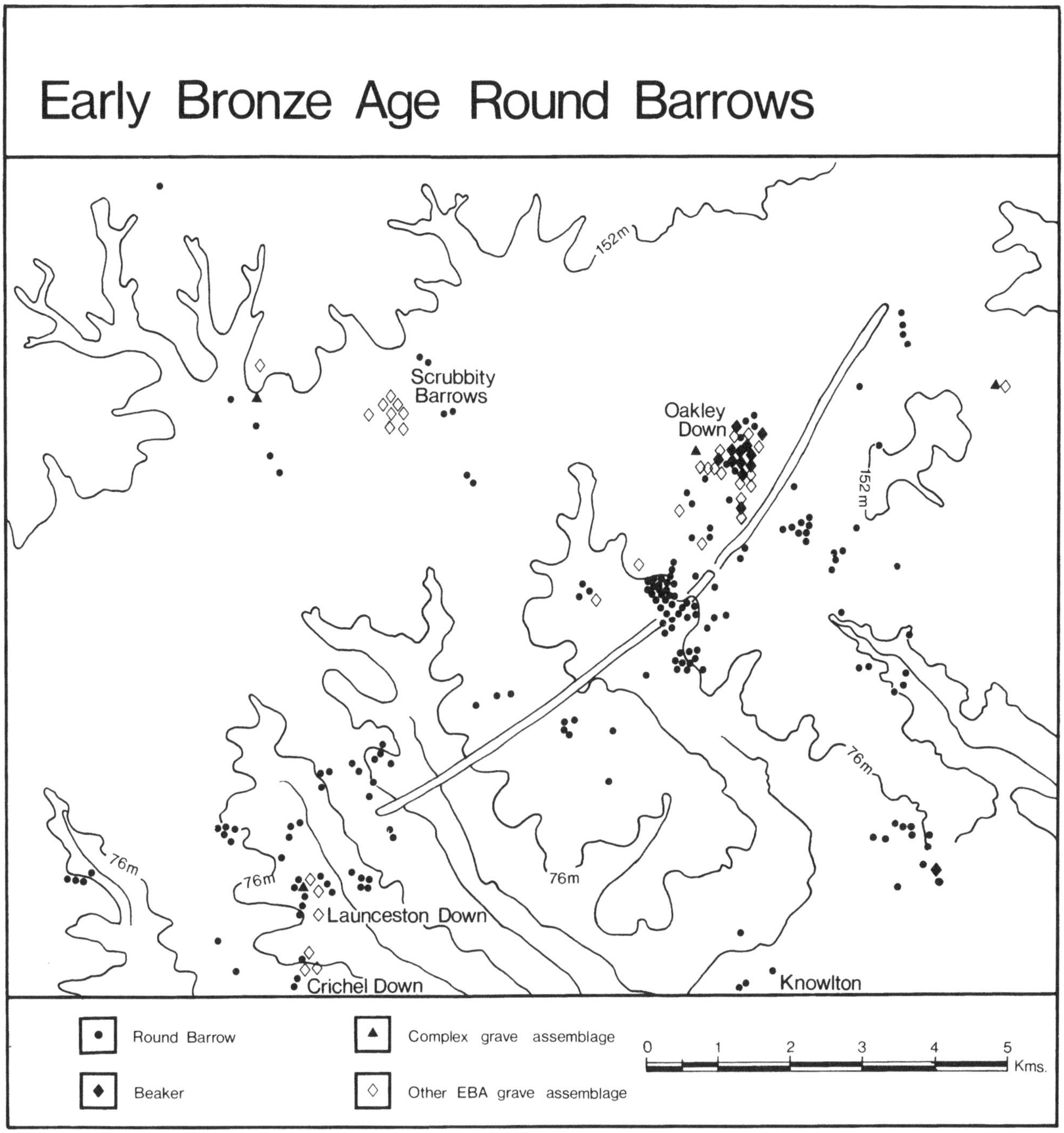

Fig. 4.6 The distribution of Beaker and Early Bronze Age burials and round barrows in the study area

the possibility that one of these burials had been disturbed in antiquity.

In each of these cases a single focal point is defined by a central grave sealed beneath a low mound, often encircled by a circular or penannular ditch. The burial ritual could thus culminate in a conscious and precise transformation of the local topography by fixing a new position within the landscape. Future mortuary observances were therefore presented with an increasingly wide range of reference points with which to fix, in turn, the position of additional deposits. The complexity of this process of spatial reordering is indicated by the use of earlier monuments, such as the burials deposited in the top of the Thickthorn Down long barrow already dis-

Plate 1 Oakley Down barrow cemetery from the south-east. The excavated remains of Wor Barrow can be seen (top left) whilst the Roman road which cuts one side of a disc barrow lies in the foreground

cussed (Drew and Piggott 1936, 80), or the reopening of graves for the insertion of additional material clearly witnessed on Crichel Down and in the case of the Thickthorn Down graves.

The development of the funerary practices which accompanied the building of more elaborate mound structures is best illustrated by Green's excavations on Launceston Down (Fig. 4.7). These concentrated on two larger mounds (Long Crichel 5 and 7). The primary deposits beneath each were once again placed in deep, chalk dug graves, although the two primary deposits differed. In Barrow 5 the funeral deposited a male corpse, along with a Beaker, in the grave. In Barrow 7 the funeral resulted in the body of a young female being placed in the grave along with some bones of an adult male. Immediately above this corpse the body of a four-year-old child was also placed in the grave. Both graves were infilled and a low mound was built over them (Fig. 4.7: 1 and 2). As with the Crichel Down examples, the mounds were then dug through and the graves seem to have been re-excavated (Fig. 4.7: 3). A sequence of further deposits was added, firstly inhumations, and then in the case of Barrow 5 cremations were also placed into the upper fill of the grave.

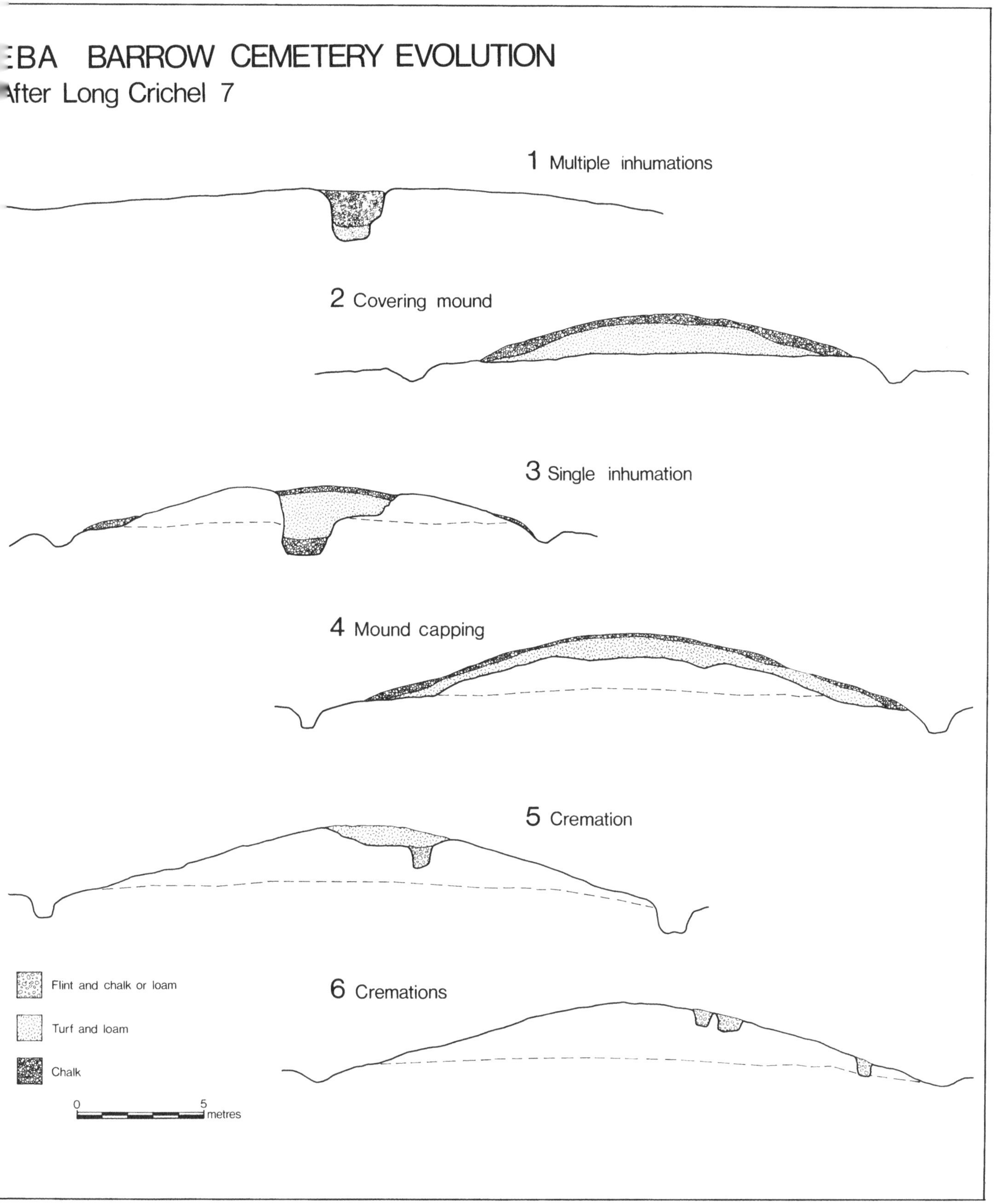

Fig. 4.7 A model of Early Bronze Age barrow evolution, based on Long Crichel 7, showing a sequence of dug graves and mound capping, terminating in the deposition of cremations on the margins of the mound

The primary deposits therefore conform to the pattern of a central grave which was periodically reopened. However, these two larger mounds also display a series of structural developments which typify the development of Early Bronze Age mortuary structures (Fig. 4.7).

In Barrow 5 further burials were spatially distinguished from those in the central grave. Two graves were dug between the central grave and the surrounding barrow ditch, and one of these was itself later reopened. Above both funerary mounds larger chalk barrows were then erected. These mounds effectively distanced any later activity from the earlier deposits, and the building of the enlarged mounds cannot be associated with any particular funerary ritual. This distancing of later activity from the earlier graves which contained the founding deposits of each particular cemetery was further effected by the addition of cremations to the edge and top of the enlarged mounds. The positions of the funeral pyres have not been recorded, and the place at which each corpse was thus transformed is no longer marked by an earlier grave. The construction of mounds, and their potential use as platforms upon which some aspects of the funerary ritual could be executed and into which burial deposits could be dug, further extended the range of ordering possible between the burial deposits. Not only may burials now have been placed above the ground surface, but others could continue to be deposited on the edge of the mound (particularly in the ditch) or in the ground surface beyond. The enlargement and capping of a barrow may have been activity organised separately from funerary rituals, and indeed may have represented a continuation of the earthwork-building obligations which are so well attested in the earlier period. By this later period, however, even these activities were fragmented around the foci of individual cemetery clusters.

If some barrows did function as platforms, then we might envisage the ground surface as one datum about which funerary deposits could be arranged. The initial graves were cut down below that datum, whilst activity on the mound was elevated above it. But such arrangements highlight in turn the importance of those deposits placed in shallow excavations within the ground surface itself. These may include not only burials in the ditches and immediately beyond the margins of the mound but also the 'flat' cremation cemeteries such as the 'Launceston sepulchralia' (Warne 1866). The use of the mound as a platform above the ground surface also finds its counterpart in the sunken surface of the Down Farm pond barrow, and it is to this monument that we must now turn.

4.4.4 Excavation of the Down Farm pond barrow[6,2,1]

Lying 35 m north of the cursus (NGR: SU 00061454), the Down Farm pond barrow was first recorded as a shallow, circular feature containing dark humic soil (Green 1981 and 1982). Excavations in 1981–82 revealed a shallow, scooped surface cut down into the chalk to a surviving depth of 0.32 m at its deepest point and with an overall diameter of just under 20 m (Figs. 4.8 and 4.9). Pits which contained Beaker sherds appear to have been truncated by the digging of the dish, which at its edges cut some 0.20–0.25 m into the natural chalk. The details of these pits have already been noted (p. 118).

It is difficult to ascertain the ultimate destination of the spoil derived from quarrying the 'pond'. Making no allowance for the effects of later erosion, a minimum of 71 m^3 of chalk would have been excavated. Although no trace of external bank remained and no protected surface was recorded from around the 'pond', there is some indication that this material was deposited around the rim of the excavated area. This depends upon the observation that the lower filling of the hollow had entered from the exterior. This consisted of dark-brown topsoil with a few chalk lumps and contained mainly Beaker pottery. Two clusters of deposits lay in the area which such a bank might have occupied. Allowing for a berm a metre wide, such a bank may have been 3 m wide and 0.75 m high.

The excavation of the surface had revealed a large chalk fossil which had been left in place. The surface of the 'pond' seems to have become the focus for a long history of activity, which can be described in terms of the following seven groups of deposits (Fig. 4.9):

1. A setting of four postholes from near the centre of the barrow. The largest (PH 8) contained the sherds of a small and incomplete Food Vessel. A radiocarbon date of 1500 ± 50 bc (BM 2327) was obtained for charcoal from young wood of *Fraxinus* from this feature. Charcoal from young wood of *Rhamnus* type from another of these features (PH 10) gave a date of 1440 ± 150 bc (BM 2192R). All four of the posts had been removed (e.g. PH9 Fig. 4.10), and the upper filling of two of the sockets included fragmentary sherds of Beaker and Deverel-Rimbury fabrics.

2. On the base of the hollow, towards its western edge, was a small knapping cluster measuring some 0.25 m across (Fig. 4.8). Like some of the surrounding pits, excavation of the hollow had exposed a number of workable nodules.

3. A smaller cluster of inhumation and cremation burials lay within and beyond the eastern margin of the

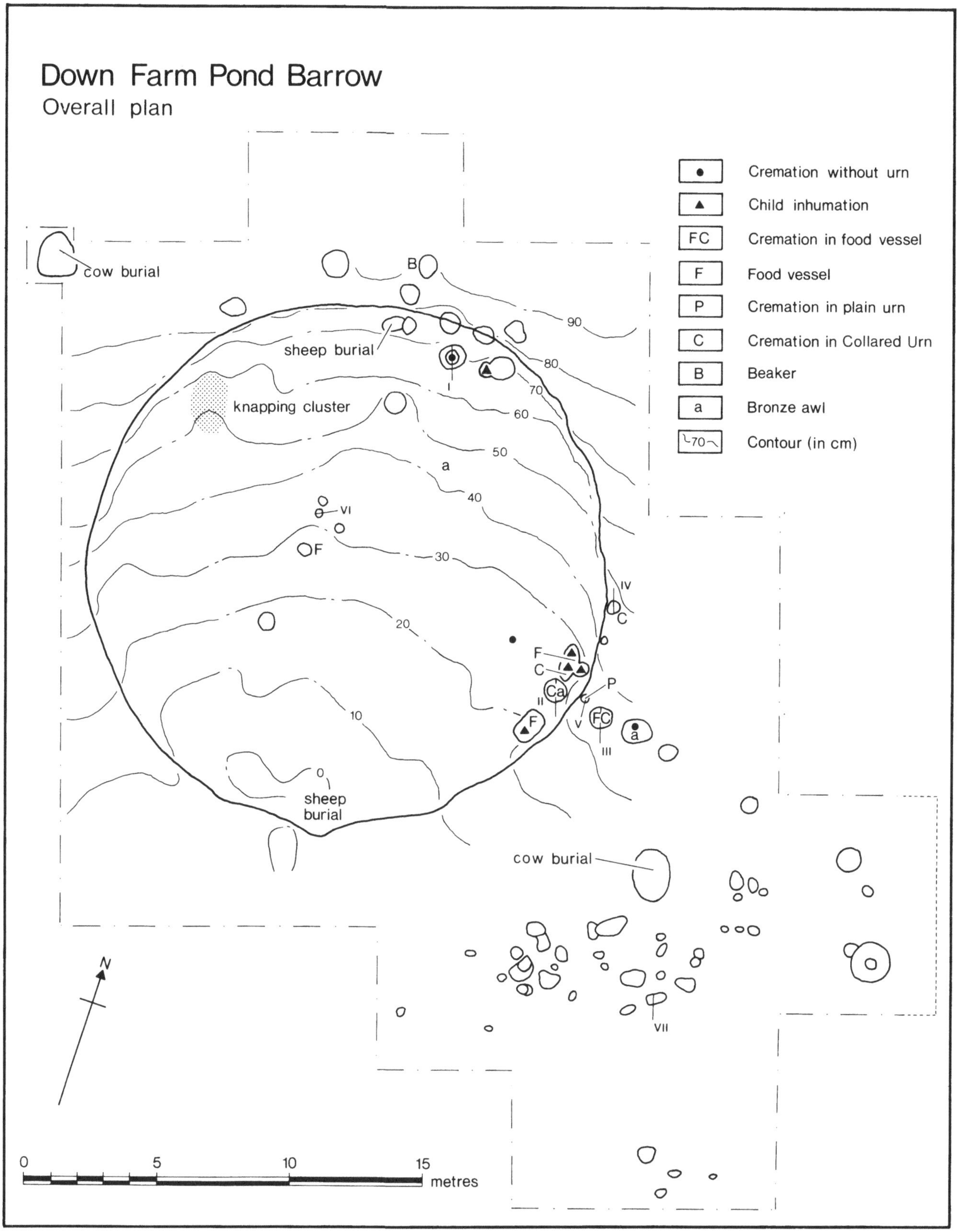

Fig. 4.8 The excavated features of the pond barrow in Firtree Field, Down Farm. The contours show the chalk hollow *after* excavation

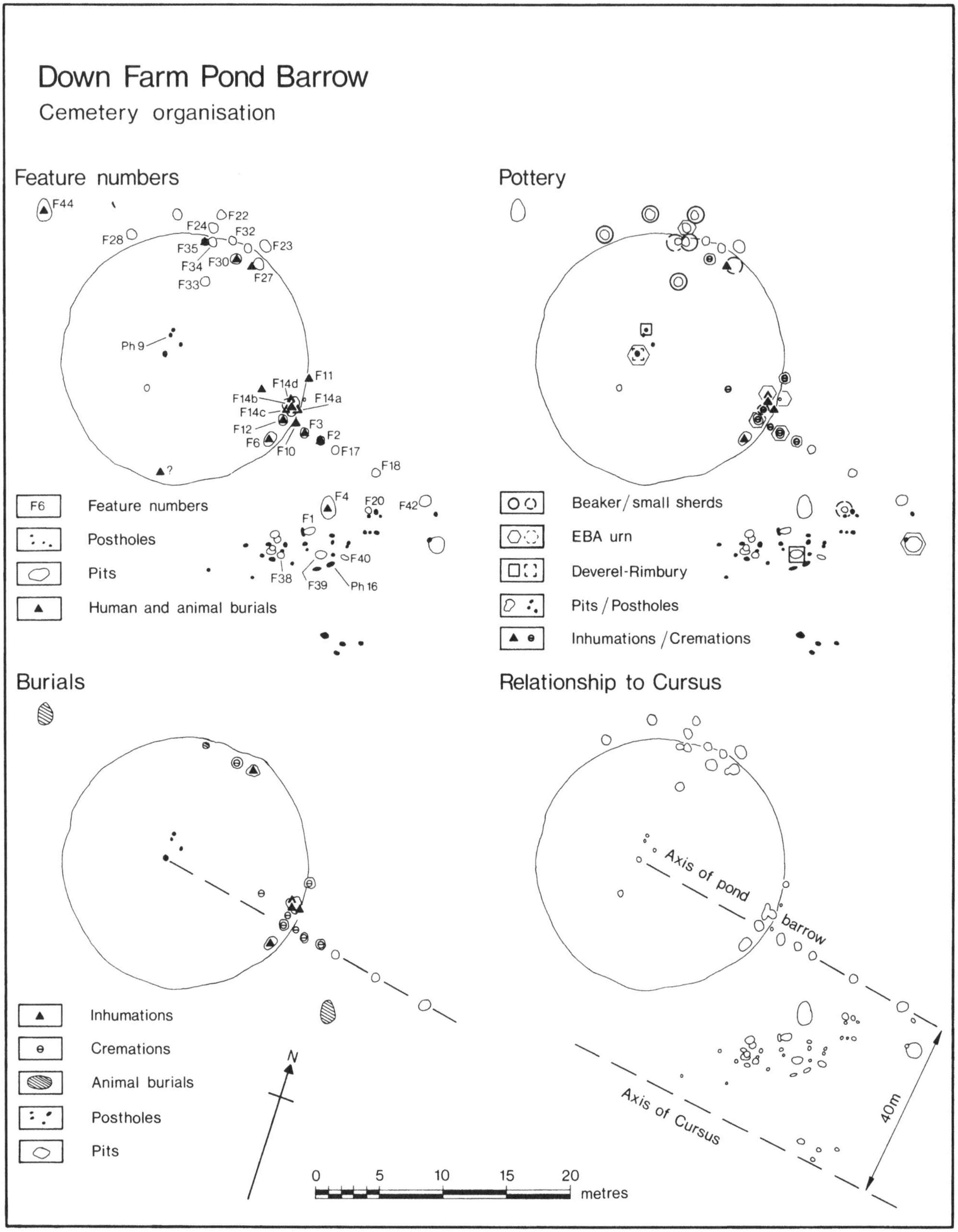

Fig. 4.9 The distribution of deposits around the pond barrow in Firtree Field, Down Farm

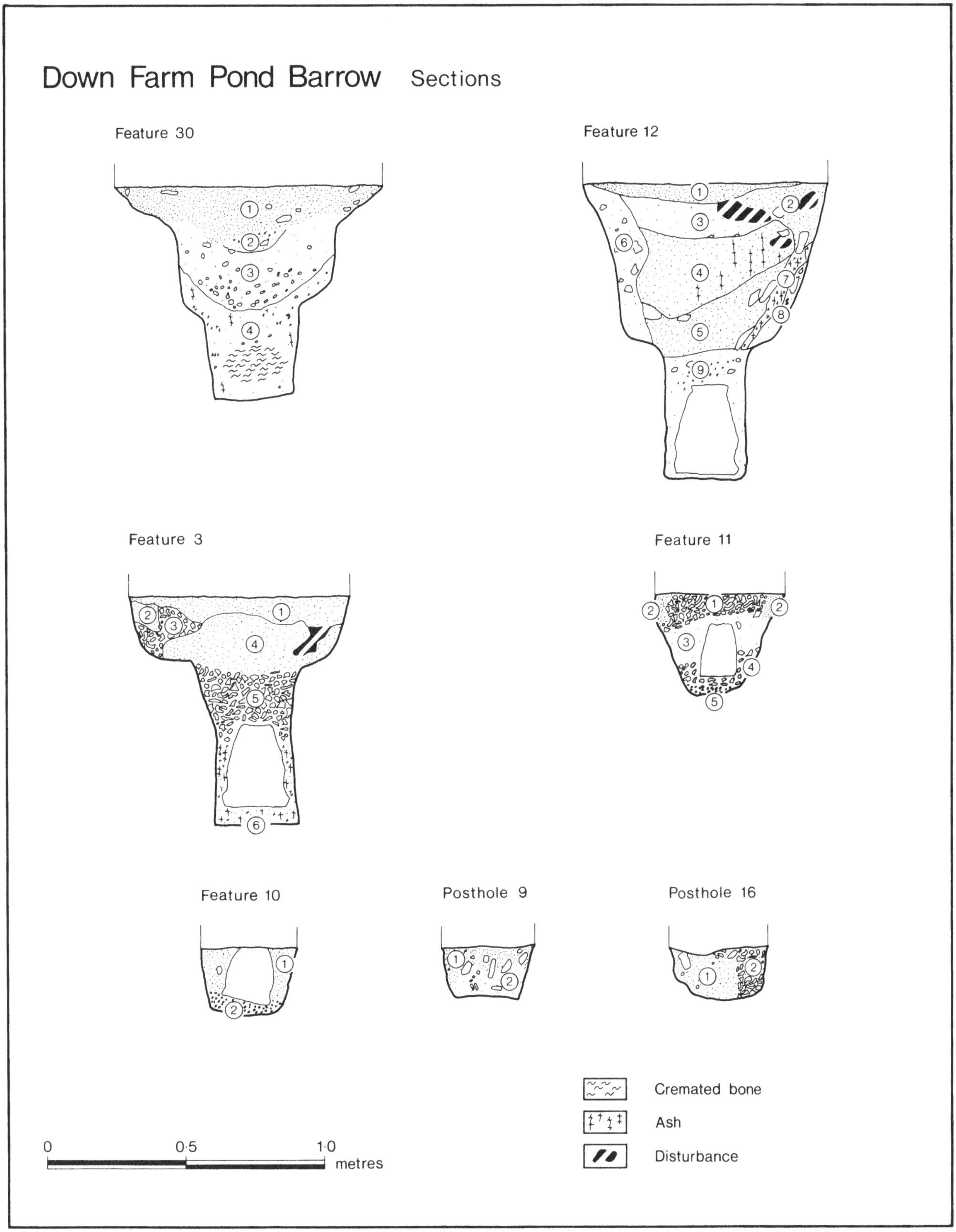

Fig. 4.10 Sections of selected features in the pond barrow cemetery

barrow. Leading away from these, and in line with one of the centre posts (PH 8) and three cremations (F14c, F3, F2), were three pits (F17, F18, F42). Each had similar characteristics and profiles, and this line of pits ran parallel to the axis of the cursus some 40 m to the south (Fig. 4.9). They were between 0.70 and 0.85 m in diameter at the top, with sharply cut sides and between 0.32 and 0.40 m deep. F18 could have been re-cut, but more likely it contained a substantial post-pipe. F17 and F42 had silted up, possibly after an upright had been retrieved. In all three cases the features were plugged by a deposit of chalk rubble. A few poorly executed flint flakes, similar to examples from the central postholes, were all that was recovered from these features. Excavation was sufficiently extensive to show that the line had not extended further to the east.

4.4.4.i The burials and their contexts (human bone identified by Juliet Rogers)

F2 (Fig. 4.10): A flat-bottomed pit, 0.72 m diameter at the top and 0.60 m diameter at the base, 0.30 m deep. It was refilled, seemingly in one operation, with chalk rubble. Some fragments of cremated bone occurred in this rubble near the base but the cremated remains were mainly in one compact deposit extending from 0.15 m from the bottom of the pit. These were the remains of an adult and infant. Among the bones was a bronze awl. Charcoal of oak heartwood from the bottom of the pit gave a date of 1670 ± 110 bc (BM 2189R).

F3 (Fig. 4.10): A 'double' pit comprising an upper bowl 0.63 m in diameter and 0.27 m deep with a lower pit 0.28 m in diameter and 0.80 m deep. An inverted enlarged Food Vessel, containing a cremation, had been placed in the lower pit, its rim resting on a black ashy soil which had also been tipped around the vessel, leaving the base of the pot exposed. The ashy layer was then capped with chalk and rubble, whilst the upper pit seems to have silted up naturally. The cremation contained the bones of a single adult. Charcoal of oak more than fifteen years old from the lower filling gave a date of 1620 ± 40 bc (BM 2326).

F6 (Fig. 4.11): An oval grave, 1.24 m long, 0.78 m wide and with an overall depth of 0.68 m. This contained, within a limited area, the fragmented and partly extended skeleton of an infant aged between eighteen months and two years. It is likely that this child was suffering or had suffered some nutritional disturbance. A Food Vessel had been placed over the legs, and the grave filled with large chalk rubble. A series of rounded flint nodules was in the filling at the level of the body, whilst its upper filling contained part of a saddle quern.

F10 (Fig. 4.10): A shallow circular pit on the edge of the hollow, 0.35 m in diameter at the top, 0.25 m at the base and 0.22 m deep. An inverted plain Food Vessel Urn was set on a layer of burnt silt 0.01 m above the bottom of the pit. This contained the cremated remains of an adult and an infant aged between five and seven years. The pit was then filled with a fine brown earth. The bottom of the pot had been lost to the plough.

F11 (Fig. 4.10): A circular pit with shelving sides on the edge of the hollow, 0.45 m in diameter at the top, 0.20 m at the base and 0.35 m deep. On the bottom of the pit was a layer of burnt silt, and above this was an inverted Collared Urn containing the cremated remains of an infant between three and five years old. The pit had been infilled with alternating layers of chalk rubble and finer chalk wash, as if there had been intervals in the filling when the upper part of the feature remained open.

F12 (Fig. 4.10): A 'double' pit, the upper part being a deep bowl 0.87 m in diameter at the top and 0.55 m deep. The lower pit was 0.31 m in diameter, and the entire feature reached a depth of 1.05 m. An inverted Collared Urn had been placed directly on the base of the pit in a layer of fine silt. There was a small quantity of cremated bone also on the base of the pit, representing an adult. The main deposit of cremated remains from within the urn was of another adult. Underneath the urn were two bone awls and a bronze awl, together with a struck flint flake. There was some charcoal just above the base of the urn. The upper part of the feature seems to have filled in with natural silt, indicating that it might have been open for some time. Charcoal from young wood at the bottom of the feature gave a date of 1550 ± 130 bc (BM 2190R).

F14 (Fig. 4.11): This complex feature lay just within the rim of the 'pond' (Fig. 4.9). It consisted of four separate cuts (F14a–d), although all shared the same filling of chalk rubble. They must have been in use at the same time, and all the indications are that they should be regarded as a contemporary group. F14b–d formed one cutting 1.44 m by 0.50 m; the maximum depth was 0.62 m. F14a was a circular pit to the east of this cutting.

F14a was between 0.6 m and 0.7 m wide and up to 0.72 m deep. It contained the fragmentary and abraded inhumed remains of an infant of about six months.

F14b was an area of the pit containing the fragmented, but possibly complete, inhumed remains of a two to four month-old infant. It is possible that this burial and 14a had both been disturbed by animals. Above the inhumation in the grave filling were urn sherds of uncertain character.

F14c was a slightly dished area on the bottom of the

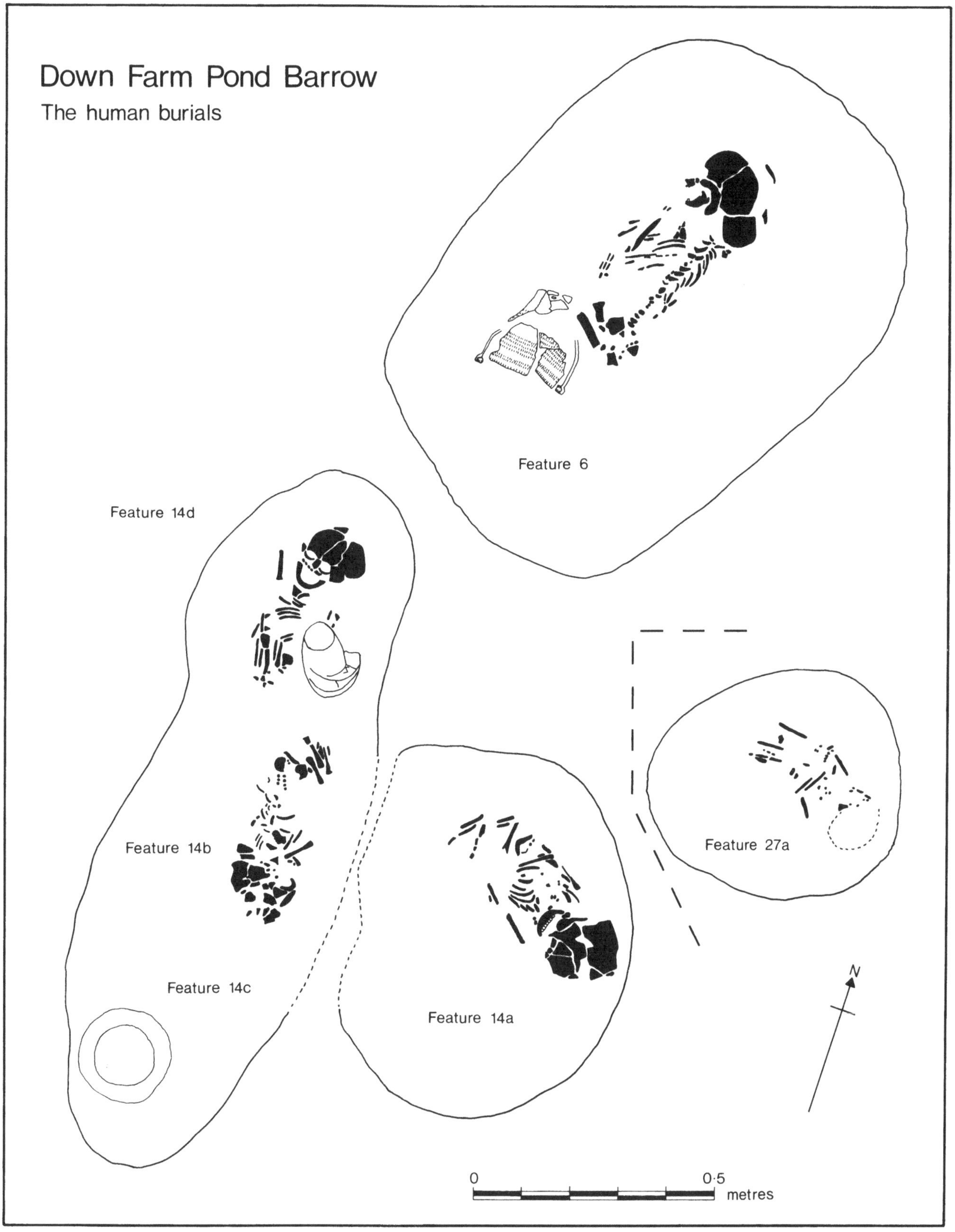

Fig. 4.11 Plans of the human inhumation graves in the pond barrow cemetery

main cut, on which stood an inverted Collared Urn. This contained the cremation of a single adult; some cremated bone from outside the urn seems to be from the same individual.

F14d was a rather deeper, scooped area in which lay the fragmentary, but complete inhumation of an infant of between two and three months. A Food Vessel was placed above this corpse when the grave was being infilled.

All these features shared a common filling of chalk rubble, which contained a further two sherds of pottery. All the burials may have taken place at more or less the same time and the only evidence for later disturbance was the animal burrowing.

Inner fill: An unurned cremation of a single adult lay in a compact area some 0.20 m across on the bottom of the eastern side of the hollow.

4.4.4.ii The animal burials[7]

4. Three animal burials, two of cattle and one of a sheep, were recorded at the periphery of the monument. During the study of the bones one further burial, excavated at the margin of the barrow and in the lower deposits within the 'pond', was identified. This consisted of a partial sheep skeleton, placed diametrically opposite the other sheep burial. Lines drawn to bisect each pair of cattle and sheep burials intersect at the centre of the barrow.

F4 (Fig. 4.12): 6 m outside the south-eastern margin of the barrow, this cow was placed on its left side in a 0.28 m-deep pit. Both front limbs were flexed in a natural position and the hind limbs fully extended. The skull was damaged as a result of its comparatively superficial burial. The cow was of considerable age with the M_3 well worn on the third cusp, although the skeleton showed little sign of bone pathology. The pit had been filled initially with chalk rubble, but a hollow had formed above this containing a finer humic filling.

F44 (Fig. 4.12): 6 m outside the north-western margin of the barrow this cow was also placed on its left side in an oval pit 0.38 m deep. The pit was somewhat shorter than the animal, so that the neck was twisted, and the head turned backwards over the cow's thorax. The front and back legs were all moderately flexed, those on the left side more so than the right. The mandible again shows that the cow was fully adult, though rather younger than the specimen F4. The pit had been infilled with chalk rubble, and humus had again accumulated in the hollow above this filling.

F35 (Fig. 4.12): Less than 1.0 m within the northern lip of the barrow was a sheep burial placed in a small oval pit 0.25 m deep. Most of the bones had suffered from a degree of erosion since burial. The animal was placed in the pit on its belly, with hind legs extended forwards on either side of the body. The head was sharply twisted round to the left side. The pit was only just large enough for the carcase, as a consequence of which the anterior part of the skeleton was very mixed. The bones of the front limbs were the worst preserved, but appear to have been flexed below the thoracic region of the sheep.

Although badly crushed, sufficient remained of the cranium to show that the sheep was of a horned breed. The small size of the horn core shows that the sheep was female. The limb bones and most vertebrae appear fully fused.

The pit had been filled with humus and a little chalk rubble.

Inner fill (Fig. 4.8): Contained in the inner fill of the pond barrow immediately against its southern lip, was part of the skeleton of a second sheep, though rather poorly preserved. Cranial and horn fragments showed that the burial was of a female sheep. The animal was quite old when buried.

5. A second cluster of deposits, including some containing Beaker material, lay on the northern margins of the barrow (Figs. 4.8 and 4.9).

F27a (Fig. 4.11): A grave pit, which impinged upon an earlier feature, and contained the partial and fragmentary remains of an infant inhumation aged between birth and two months. The surviving bones retained their articulation.

F30 (Fig. 4.10): A 'double' pit with an upper bowl, below which was cut a cylindrical pit 0.32 m in diameter and 0.75 m deep. The lower pit contained a cremation which was not accompanied by an urn. The remains were of a single adult. The fill of the lower pit was of a loose grey silt containing charcoal in the lower half; the cremation formed a compact mass 0.05 m above the floor of the pit and was overlain by chalk rubble. The upper bowl had a humic filling containing a distinct pocket of charcoal but with no further human remains. Charcoal from young wood of *Creatagus* type from the upper bowl gave a date of 1540 ± 130 bc (BM 2324R).

Other features in this area appear to predate the barrow and have been described above (pp. 118–20).

6. A cluster of features to the east and south of the cow burial in F4 (Figs. 4.8 and 4.9) does not appear to conform to any particularly coherent pattern. With the exception of three fairly shallow scoops (F1, 20 and 38), the other pits in this area were irregular and had generally shelving profiles. With a maximum diameter of 1.0 m and depths of up to 0.30 m, all were filled with

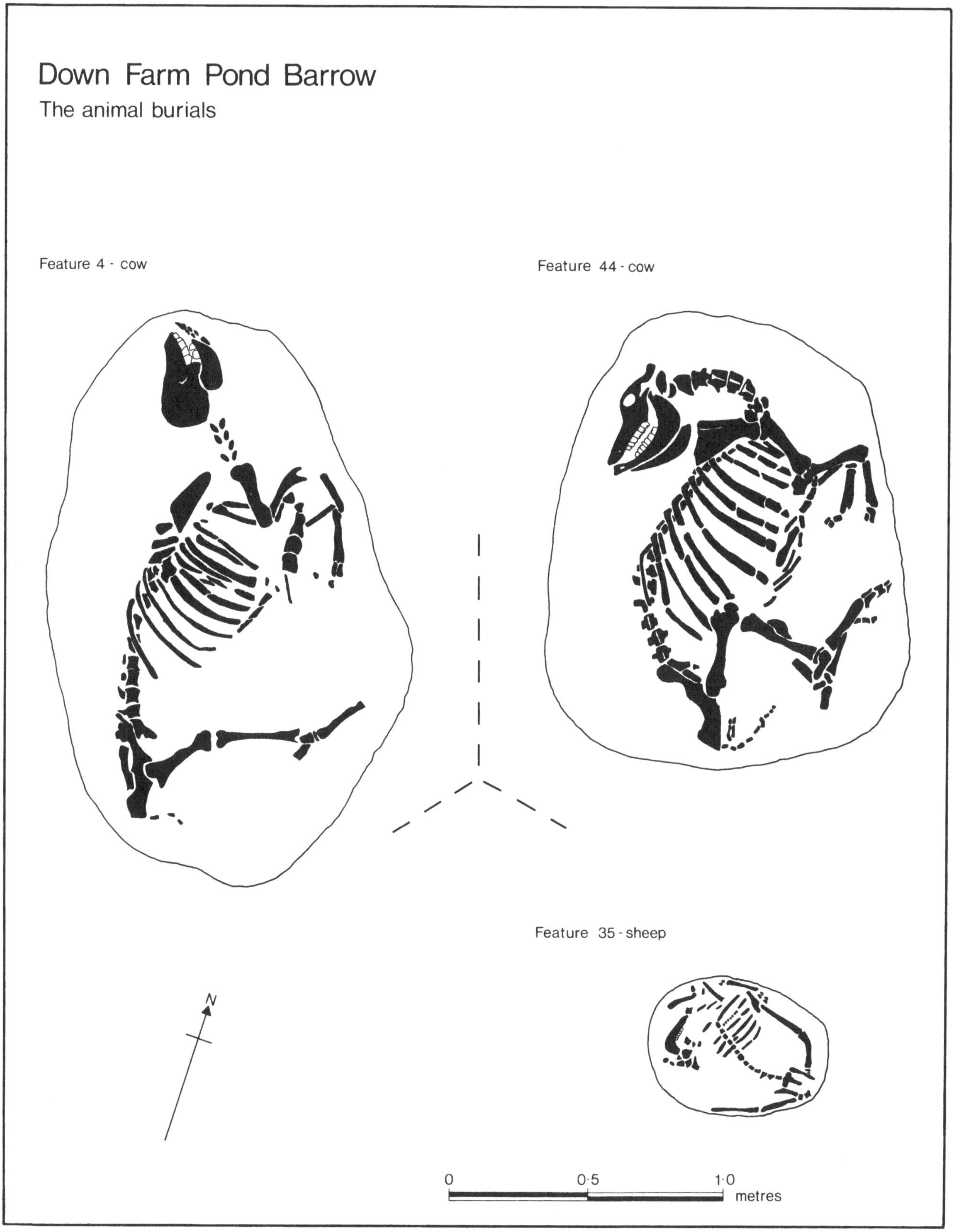

Fig. 4.12 Plans of the animal burials in the pond barrow cemetery

chalk rubble containing a large number of flint nodules, interspersed with more humic silt. In the case of F39 and F40, the pits were practically packed with large flints. There were no flint implements from this part of the site and the lithic debitage, although sparse, seemed less regular than the finds from the Beaker pits. It was dominated by nodular fragments and by cortical flakes, suggesting that the area functioned as a quarry for raw material. Comparison with other industries from the study area suggests that these finds are later in date than those from the Beaker pits.

This area also produced some twenty-six postholes, the majority of which occupied an area 11 m by 3 m, with four outliers on the edge of the excavation towards the Cursus. Only three of these features retained post-pipes (including PH16, Fig. 4.10). The small quantity of flintwork from these posts has the same character as the finds from the pits. A well-preserved *Bos* long bone from PH 12 has given a date of 500 ± 110 bc (BM 2416).

7. We have already noted that the primary infilling of the pond appears to have entered the feature from the exterior and may represent the erosion of the bank. The secondary filling, towards the centre of the hollowed area, consisted of brown earth with a number of flint nodules. This contained mainly Deverel-Rimbury and later pottery and a bronze awl. There were worked flints in both layers. The upper filling appears to represent ploughing taking place over the monument during the Middle Bronze Age. The sheep skeleton buried within the fill of the pond itself appears to have been hit by this ploughing.

The pottery[1,4]

In all some 397 sherds of prehistoric pottery were recovered from the infill of the pond, unassociated with any particular focus of deposition. Amongst these were twenty-nine identifiable sherds of Beaker pottery. In addition to this material 100 sherds of Roman pottery were also recovered. The high proportion of sherds belonging to Deverel-Rimbury ceramics indicates the accumulation of a Middle Bronze Age ploughsoil.

The animal bones[7]

The fill of the 'pond' contained twenty-two bones, one jaw and nineteen loose teeth of cattle, with a few specimens from sheep and pig. None of the bones appeared to be in association, and their date cannot be determined.

4.4.4.iii Discussion[1,2]

There are a number of specific points which can be made about the Down Farm pond barrow. Although the form of the monument is unusual, its general affinities are clear. Within Wessex there are distinctive pond barrows recorded close to major Early Bronze Age cemeteries. These take the form of embanked hollows, generally rather deeper than the eroded monument at Down Farm. Only four examples of these sites, including Down Farm, have been excavated to modern standards (Fig. 4.13). At Winterbourne Steepleton, Dorset, the site consisted of an embanked hollow only 10.6 m in diameter. Here all the burials were cremations associated with Food Vessels and Collared Urns. They were found inside the hollowed area, some sealed by a flint pavement, although hardly any excavation was done outside this area where more burials may have existed (Atkinson, Brailsford and Wakefield 1951). The third site is the pond barrow on Snail Down, Wiltshire. This was a slight depression *c.* 12 m in diameter with a bank that was *c.* 2.4 m wide and 0.2 m thick. The bank surrounded a stake-built enclosure containing three pits. Two were basin-shaped, with chips of burnt bone. The third, near the centre, was another of our double pits, with an upper fill of loam and a small amount of cremated bone in the lower (Annable 1958, 16). Nearby was a saucer barrow, which covered two more double pits. Cremations were in the lower pits and the upper fills were of 'earth which incorporated food refuse and domestic pottery' (Thomas and Thomas 1955, 134–7). The final site has been excavated only recently. This is in the massive cemetery at Radley in the Upper Thames Valley, a complex long recognised as resembling cemeteries in Wessex (Leeds 1938). Here a deeper circular hollow containing two cremations was again flanked by two groups of inhumation burials, mainly female and children, and associated with Food Vessels. These probably lay beneath a bank derived from the central feature. Work on the publication of this site is still in progress and no radiocarbon dates are so far available.

The pond barrow presumably represents a floor or surface upon and around which a variety of activities may have been undertaken. These may find only limited representation amongst the archaeological deposits, which are themselves dominated by mortuary remains. The selection of this place as a focal point may not have arisen fortuitously. Earlier Neolithic pottery occurs at this point along the Cursus and Beaker activity is represented on the site. These mortuary rites may thus have been integrated within older and more complex routines by which this part of the landscape was occupied. Some-

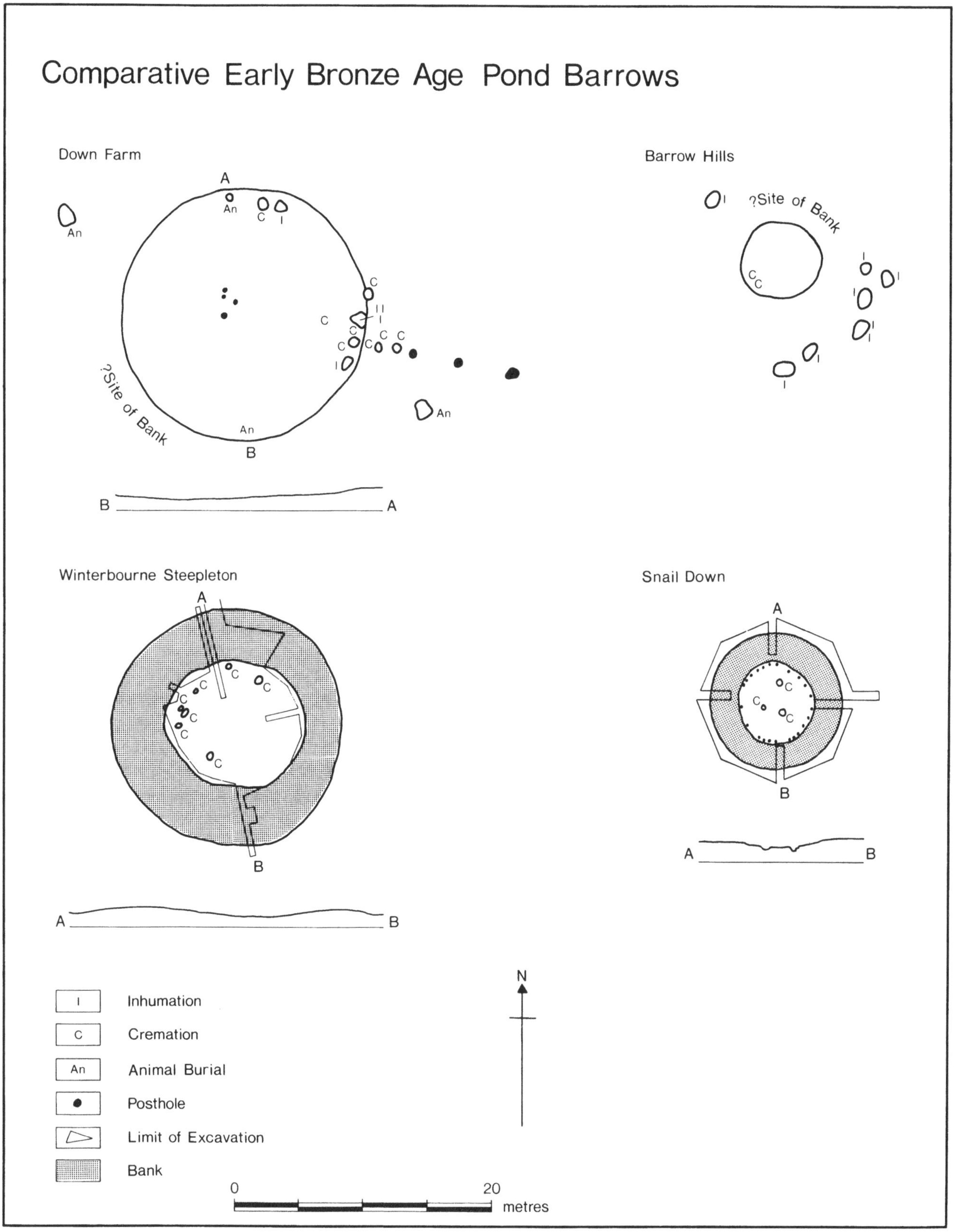

Fig. 4.13 Plans of the excavated pond barrows in southern Britain

thing of the quality of that routine occupancy of this particular place is given by the archaeological deposits themselves. It is by the regular orientation of the people who approached, entered and left this floor area that the ordered distribution of archaeological deposits arose. Those orientations in people's actions gave rise to, and may in turn have been guided by, the arrangement of pits (or posts?) and cremations which ran from beyond the eastern edge of the pond towards the post placed close to its centre. This line is almost exactly parallel to the axis of the Dorset Cursus, which lay 40 m south of the centre of the barrow. And the symmetry of the animal burials, themselves on a similar if slightly different axis, has already been noted. The routine by which this area was occupied is surely exemplified by the way cremation pit F11 was infilled intermittently and the form of the 'double' cremation pits (F3, F12 and F30), which remained only partly infilled, presenting a likely focus for later offerings. These are paralleled at Shrewton Barrow 25 (Green and Rollo-Smith 1984). It is notable that the human burials are dominated by the remains of infants. Of the small number of adults, no single adult deposit is accompanied by a Food Vessel, although Food Vessels are the dominant ceramic form from the cemetery. It is likely that the pond barrow is only one locale within a wider, contemporary cemetery complex, the overall use of which maintained particular categories amongst the dead. However, such routines of veneration were ultimately forgotten as ploughing encroached upon the barrow and its centre began to infill with an accumulating ploughsoil during the Middle Bronze Age. The chronology, given by the radiocarbon dates, indicates burial activity originating here in the mid-seventeenth century bc and terminating by the fifteenth century bc.

4.5 Conclusion[1]

The Early Bronze Age is normally painted as a period of change, not only in terms of new metalworking technologies but also in terms of social organisation. Indeed the two themes are now often linked, the development of an early metalworking 'florescence' resulting from social processes, not simply technological achievement (Renfrew 1986). Such processes have been measured in terms of two archaeological variables. First, the scale of monument building in an area such as Wessex was taken to indicate the growth of centralised authority, capable of drawing upon increasingly greater reserves of labour (Renfrew 1973). Secondly, the Early Bronze Age mortuary deposits were seen to reflect more complex systems of ranking and individual status emerging at the end of the Neolithic (Shennan 1982).

The first of these arguments is open to challenge, both on the basis of the labour estimates (Startin and Bradley 1981) and the actual chronology of the monuments. Our study of the Dorset Cursus, for example, has shown its construction to be earlier than previously assumed. It is clear from this monument and from the complex of earthworks at Hambledon that quite massive constructional programmes were under way in the early third millennium bc. The basis of the second argument has already been questioned above. It is now necessary to look at this period, not in terms of increased hierarchy or centralisation within the social system, but as arising from a transformation in social practices.

Death is not contained within a predictable temporal framework, unless it is the product of regularised warfare or sacrifice. It intervenes haphazardly, and whilst the funerary ritual may, through long and complex processes of secondary burial, re-establish a temporal harmony with other areas of social experience, it is none the less instigated at uncontrollable moments of time.

The complex nature of Neolithic monumentality on Cranborne Chase has already been discussed. The construction of the Cursus and its attendant mounds and that of the later henge complexes are likely to have been projects executed in the tempo of routine, seasonal demands for labour. Indeed, the use of these various monuments for ritual observance, or their engagement in everyday activities, are also likely to have been patterned by the daily and seasonal demands of agricultural production. Restricted areas of settlement and ritual activity along the line of the Cursus, at Chalkpit Field and Firtree Field, have been described above. The crisis of death may always have cut across more regular routines, but now, in Later Neolithic and Early Bronze Age, grave digging and the markers around them began to reorder this landscape at the behest of such temporal irregularity; if the instigation of death rituals was irregular, the spatial arrangements demanded by some of the funerary rituals was precise. Each deposit contributed to the elaborate topography of the burial ground. Thus earlier graves were sometimes reopened, or they acted as reference points for later deposits.

The traditional routines of agriculture would have been continued and would themselves have encountered this new topography of death. Here some changes may also have occurred during this period, for the indications are that the main weight of the settlement activity lay away from the uplands of the Chase and on the lower ground towards the coast.

We have seen that many of the earliest graves lay beneath low mounds in areas which may have been reserved by an encircling ditch. Additional graves may have been placed within this enclosed space, or dug directly into the earlier grave pit. Many such deposits lay along the line of the Cursus, between the line of the Cursus and Wor Barrow in the Oakley Down cemetery, or to the south-west in the cemeteries on Launceston and Crichel Downs. These funerary deposits accumulated at a time when the ditches of the Cursus were silted and need no longer have represented a significant barrier, and they indicate a rescheduling of at least some aspects of the ritual observances which had previously taken place along the line of the Cursus. This, for example, is indicated by the siting of the pond barrow.

The funerary rites incorporated certain artefacts within the grave filling. These may have been items of dress affixed to the corpse, such as the dagger, or placed around the corpse, such as the beaker. They may also include the symbolic paraphernalia of mourning discarded at the grave side. Some of these artefacts appear new and exotic, including early metal finds and the distinctive beakers. However, it is in the very nature of these deposits that we do not have a comparable understanding of how such material circulated and was used away from the funerary rites. There is, however, a distinct period, corresponding roughly to metalwork Stage VI, sometime after 1600 bc, when this symbolism became highly elaborate. The rituals involved were largely restricted to the area around the Cursus and the Oakley Down cemetery in particular (Fig. 4.6), and the resultant grave assemblages have in the past been assigned to the 'Wessex Culture' (Piggott 1938).

Most of the early graves may have lain beneath low mounds, including the cremation placed beneath the low 'tumps' of disc barrows and Colt Hoare's scant records of central, presumably primary, cairns beneath some of the larger of the Oakley Down barrows. The enlargement and construction of the larger turf and chalk barrows need not be connected directly with funerary rituals, as the occurrence of some 'empty' mounds testifies. In fact we lack clear evidence regarding the organisation of labour involved in the building of the turf- and chalk-capped bell and bowl barrows, and little is known of the overall chronology of the process. Such mounds effectively sealed the primary deposits from any further access, and their possible use as platforms has already been noted. The physical distance established between the earliest deposits and later activity is accompanied by an increased use of the ditches and marginal area around the mound for deposition and by a more widespread adoption of cremation. Obviously cremation had been used throughout the Early Bronze Age, and away from the Cursus, in a cemetery such as Scrubbity Coppice (*Excavations* II, 32ff.), it appears to have been the general rite. But its more widespread adoption has long been recognised as a feature of the later half of the period, and with it we find the increasing employment of the major urn forms in the closing stages of the funerary ritual (Burgess 1980, 79). The Down Farm pond barrow illustrates clearly the degree of order maintained in the recurrent deposition of these marginal deposits.

There is no single 'burial tradition' for the Early Bronze Age, as Petersen has clearly demonstrated (Petersen 1972). Instead, strategies of architectural construction, funeral-rite and spatial location, and the scheduling of time itself, were all used to structure the distance between the living and the dead, between inheritors and ancestors. Thus, at the end of the third millennium bc, funerary strategies began to display new formal characteristics resulting from an increased concern with the classification of the dead and the denial of an undifferentiated body of ancestors. That classification was constructed in terms of spatial order, through rituals instigated at the moment of an individual's death. This all implies a restructuring in the rights of inheritance amongst the living, and thus a change in practices of social reproduction. Those changes may have been profound, indeed they may have arisen in other aspects of life, including the organisation of kinship (and thus settlement), the obligations of agricultural labour and the working of the land. It seems likely that it was within these changes that the foundations for the major transformation represented by the Middle Bronze Age settlement evidence were laid.

Notes

1 John C. Barrett
2 Richard Bradley
3 Julie Gardiner
4 Rosamund Cleal
5 Brendan O'Connor
6 Martin Green
7 A. J. Legge

PART II
THE LIVING AND THE DEAD

Section these dwellings, expose the
life of a people.
W. H. Auden: *The Dog Beneath the Skin*

5. THE MIDDLE BRONZE AGE

5.1 Introduction[1]

It is during the Middle Bronze Age in southern Britain that archaeological field evidence for settlement and cultivation becomes readily available for study. This evidence comprises earthwork enclosures and lynchet systems. Childe regarded the apparent changes in agricultural practices indicated by these field remains as representative of an 'agricultural revolution'. He evoked a comparison between an earlier state where the 'warrior-herdsman's wife' had 'tilled a little wheat and barley with the hoe', with the emergence of 'villages of a size and permanence hitherto unprecedented in Britain' and their accompanying field systems (Childe 1947, 186–9).

The distinction between a prehistoric archaeology dominated by burial and ceremonial monuments, and one dominated by settlement sites and the earthwork remains of cultivation is still drawn today (Bradley 1984, 160). The explanation for the apparent transformation needs careful consideration. At base, this distinction is partly a matter of archaeological visibility. Settlements and cultivation have occurred in all the periods since the Neolithic, and whilst writers such as Childe and Curwen regarded Neolithic and Early Bronze Age settlement to be of a non-permanent and shifting character associated with a heavily pastoral economy (Childe 1947; Curwen 1938), this view is at least questioned, if not totally rejected today. We must be certain of the processes which render settlement and agriculture so visible in our later prehistory and then set about explaining those processes. This will be the main theme of this chapter.

Settlements become visible by virtue of the earthwork enclosures which surround some of them. These mark out the settlement as an earthwork, or give coherence to the otherwise slight traces on an aerial photograph. This use of enclosure around smaller settlement nuclei, first recorded during the Middle Bronze Age, continues with considerable variation and elaboration throughout our later prehistory. Before this, earthwork enclosures are more usually associated with the larger ceremonial monuments. If some of the settlement nuclei of the earlier period had also been enclosed, they would surely have been recognised by now. It is this consistent lack of enclosure which renders the archaeological visibility of the earlier settlement so low. But there is an additional point. The survival of so much of the settlement record to which Childe and Curwen referred is itself a reflection of the abandonment of areas of upland and thus their preservation from later activity.

Field systems are recognisable by virtue of the lynchets formed on hillslopes (Bowen 1961). Whilst the date of most of these systems on the chalk downland of southern Britain is difficult to establish, it remains true that their appearance and initial development seems to occur during the Bronze Age. Their recognition as field remains can again be partly explained by their occurrence on areas of downland which have not seen intensive arable exploitation since their desertion in prehistory or during the Romano-British period. It is also true that any period of arable activity is likely to remove or substantially transform the field remains of earlier agricultural practices. However, it is becoming increasingly difficult to assert that extensive lynchet systems of the Neolithic lie ploughed out on the chalk downlands of southern Britain. We have also noted in the preceding chapter that more evidence for Early Bronze Age settlement comes from the Hampshire Basin than from the uplands. This is not to deny the existence of earlier, and at times extensive, arable activity but to raise the possibility that such activity did not leave the kind of lynchet systems which we associate with later prehistory (Barrett 1989).

Another change must now also be noted. As we examine the archaeological literature of the southern British Later Bronze Age and the Iron Age, we find that the term ritual drops out of use almost entirely. No longer are archaeologists embarrassed, or so it seems, by ritual enclosures, ritual deposits or, indeed, complex mortuary rituals. Instead we find a considerable amount of detail on economic activities. We should pause, however, before rushing headlong into an interpretation of this period as one determined by 'rational' economic strategies. Such is the strength of empiricism in archaeology that we never explain why things do not occur. When we are lucky enough to be dealing with a period which produces an extensive burial record, a considerable amount of time is spent discussing the nature of mortuary rituals. However, since all societies have such rituals, should we not also consider those rituals which, after their execution, have left little or no archaeological traces, and where the disposal of the body or cremated remains is not associated with grave digging or the erection of monuments? A change in burial practices certainly occurred during the Middle Bronze Age. We have already discussed the way in which human remains were incorporated within various monumental structures during the Neolithic and Early Bronze Age. During the Middle Bronze Age cremation became the predominant rite, and whilst the ashes were buried, the degree of monumental construction associated with that rite decreased. By the end of the Bronze Age burial and monumentality can no longer be observed with any clarity in the archaeological record. This feature of mortuary rituals must also be discussed, not ignored because we do not find graves. Similarly, the apparent lack of other 'ritual' activity needs more careful consideration. We will argue here that such activity seems to have disappeared, not because it was no longer central to the daily life of these communities, but because we do not recognise it. That failure of recognition is because rituals were at that time played out around the settlement sites and the cycles of agricultural reproduction. The archaeological remains of these rituals have, all too easily, been confined to 'economic' activity in the minds of contemporary archaeologists (Barrett 1988b and 1989).

We have presented some contrasts in the archaeological record between the Neolithic and Early Bronze Age on one hand and the Middle–Late Bronze Age and Iron Age on the other. We have been deliberately imprecise over chronology. This discussion must now turn to the precision of an empirical investigation of material relevant to these themes from our study area on Cranborne Chase.

The changes in settlement form, agricultural practices and burial rites are traditionally assigned to the 'Deverel-Rimbury Culture'. This 'culture' is defined around a particular ceramic repertoire, although the details of that repertoire display marked regional variation (Ellison 1980a). The problems inherent in working within the analytical framework of cultural archaeology have already been discussed. Our concern is not therefore to establish a more precise definition of the 'Deverel-Rimbury Culture' which can then be applied beyond the area of our study. Instead, we are interested in the way particular kinds of settlement, agricultural and burial practices arose in central Wessex during the Bronze Age. The generations of people who developed these new activities used, amongst other things, a limited and relatively uninspiring range of ceramic vessels. Similar vessels are found quite widely across southern Britain and they belong to the urn traditions of the Bronze Age; let us not over-generalise on the basis of a common ceramic tradition.

This chapter is concerned with the excavation of two settlements and two cemeteries and the reanalysis of a further two settlements and one cemetery. It is to these that we must now turn.

5.2 The excavations: South Lodge enclosure, cemetery and field system[1,2]

5.2.1 Introduction

These Bronze Age monuments lie within Rushmore Park, just inside the south lodge gates (NGR: SY 953174). The earthworks lie on a westerly facing hillslope, overlooking the junction of two dry valleys (Figs. 5.1 and 5.2).

The whole area saw extensive survey and excavation at the end of the nineteenth century (*Excavations* II and IV) and the field evidence was reconsidered by Toms (1925). We will discuss the nature of the nineteenth-century excavations when describing our own work on these sites. Toms' survey also needs consideration here. He was an assistant to Pitt Rivers before moving to Brighton Museum (Holleyman 1987), and what his survey achieved, in a remarkably perceptive piece of field observation, was to demonstrate a link between the enclosure and barrows which had been excavated in the nineteenth century and the lynchets of a field system, the full extent of which had not previously been recognised. Crucial to Toms' argument was the observation that one lynchet ran up to, and was apparently cut by, the enclosure ditch, whilst a second lynchet appeared not only to be cut by the ditch but also to survive, preserved within the eastern entrance into the enclosure. This entrance had remained unexcavated in the nineteenth century. Toms therefore suggested that the enclosure overlay the field lynchets.

The result of Pitt Rivers' excavations and Toms' survey was that we had available the publication of an enclosure which had produced a considerable number of artefacts, including a small group of bronzes, a nearby barrow cemetery where the cremations were accompanied with pottery of exactly similar form to that recovered from the enclosure, and a field system which appeared to predate the enclosure.

Such a group of monuments seemed to offer the possibility of investigating more closely the emergence of our enclosed and cultivated landscapes of the late second millennium BC. At the same time there were problems with the published interpretations, in particular the uncertain nature of the enclosure (Piggott 1973, 396–7). The nineteenth-century excavations found no definite structural remains in the interior, despite the considerable numbers of artefacts. Our excavations and museum researches were designed to clarify this particular problem, to confirm Toms' observations and to undertake a full analysis of the artefacts and surviving bone materials.

The recent excavations will be described, beginning with the lynchet system, and then proceeding to the enclosure and barrow cemetery. The original numbering of each mound in the barrow cemetery will be maintained. The numbers used by Pitt Rivers are part of a running series of designations applied to all the mounds investigated at Rushmore (*Excavations* II).

Something must be said about the problems of returning to a site previously excavated in the nineteenth century. These earlier excavations took place between 1880 and 1893, the barrow cemetery being investigated in 1880 and 1883, and the enclosure during the early summer of 1893. Our knowledge of this work derives from the published accounts, the museum archive and our own fieldwork. The quality of the nineteenth-century record varies over the thirteen years during which these excavations took place.

Pitt Rivers was able to observe Bronze Age earthworks which had lain protected from later agricultural erosion, although he believed that the one field lynchet he recognised (Fig. 5.3, lynchet C) was Roman in date. There is no evidence of Iron Age or medieval settlement within the immediate vicinity of these sites, whilst Roman activity is only witnessed by a small scatter of pottery from the enclosure and its ditch.

Whilst similar unploughed landscapes existed until quite recently in parts of Wessex (C. M. Piggott, 1942), Pitt Rivers' excavations here, at the Angle Ditch, and at Martin Down (*Excavations* IV, 185 ff.) represent the most extensive and most detailed on any such enclosure in Wessex before it had suffered plough erosion. Today the South Lodge enclosure must represent the only unploughed Deverel-Rimbury enclosure known on the Wessex chalk.

The nineteenth-century excavations were extensive. The entire ditch silts of the enclosure were removed, and much of the surrounding rampart and interior was also excavated. The barrow mounds were dug extensively,

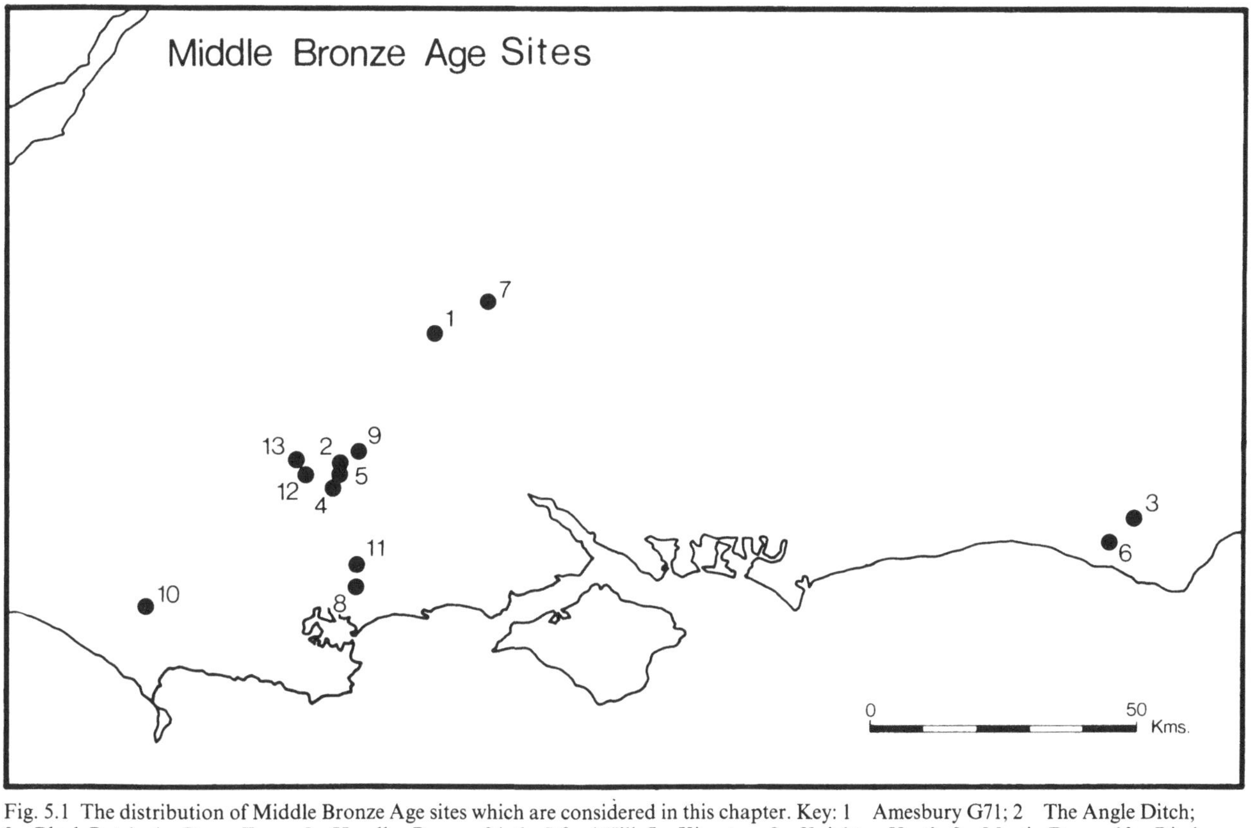

Fig. 5.1 The distribution of Middle Bronze Age sites which are considered in this chapter. Key: 1 Amesbury G71; 2 The Angle Ditch; 3 Black Patch; 4 Down Farm; 5 Handley Barrow 24; 6 Itford Hill; 7 Kimpton; 8 Knighton Heath; 9 Martin Down; 10 Rimbury; 11 Simons Ground; 12 South Lodge; 13 Tinkley Down

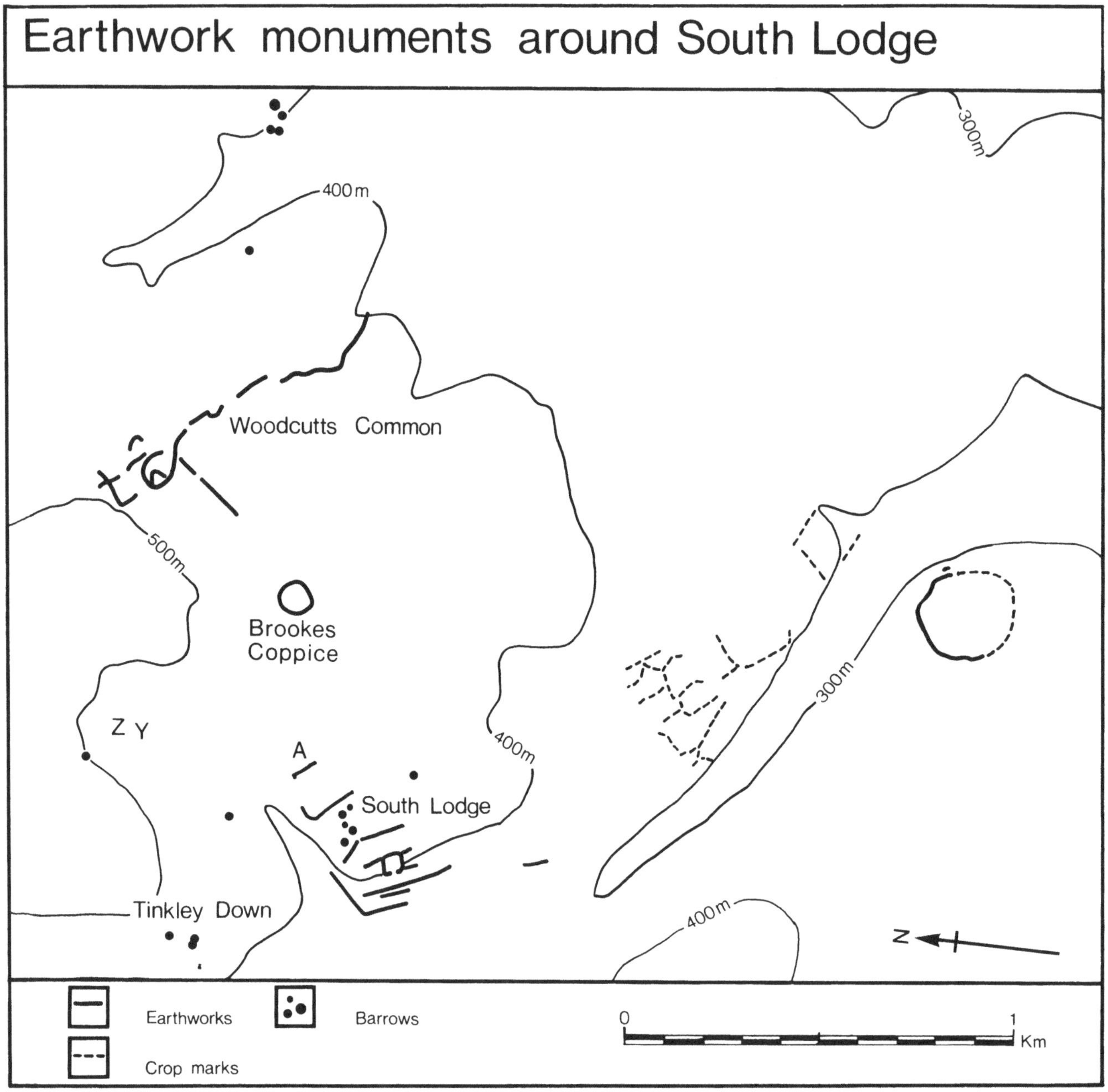

Fig. 5.2 The distribution of earthwork monuments, including enclosures, barrows and field lynchets, in the area of South Lodge, Rushmore. Key: A Easternmost surviving lynchet of the South Lodge field system; Y and Z Flint scatters

along with most of the ditch fills. The earthworks which Toms recorded in 1924, and which we observed in 1977, were a nineteenth-century enclosure, nineteenth-century barrow mounds, and a Bronze Age lynchet system. Our own excavations have therefore included a large element of historical archaeology, with the removal of overlying nineteenth-century deposits before the Bronze Age features could be investigated. Figure 5.3 shows the full extent of our excavations.

5.2.2 *The field lynchets*

The lynchets survive in the area immediately around the barrows and enclosure extending to the north-east, north and west of these monuments. They terminate along the line of the dry valley, the last surviving lynchet (A) to

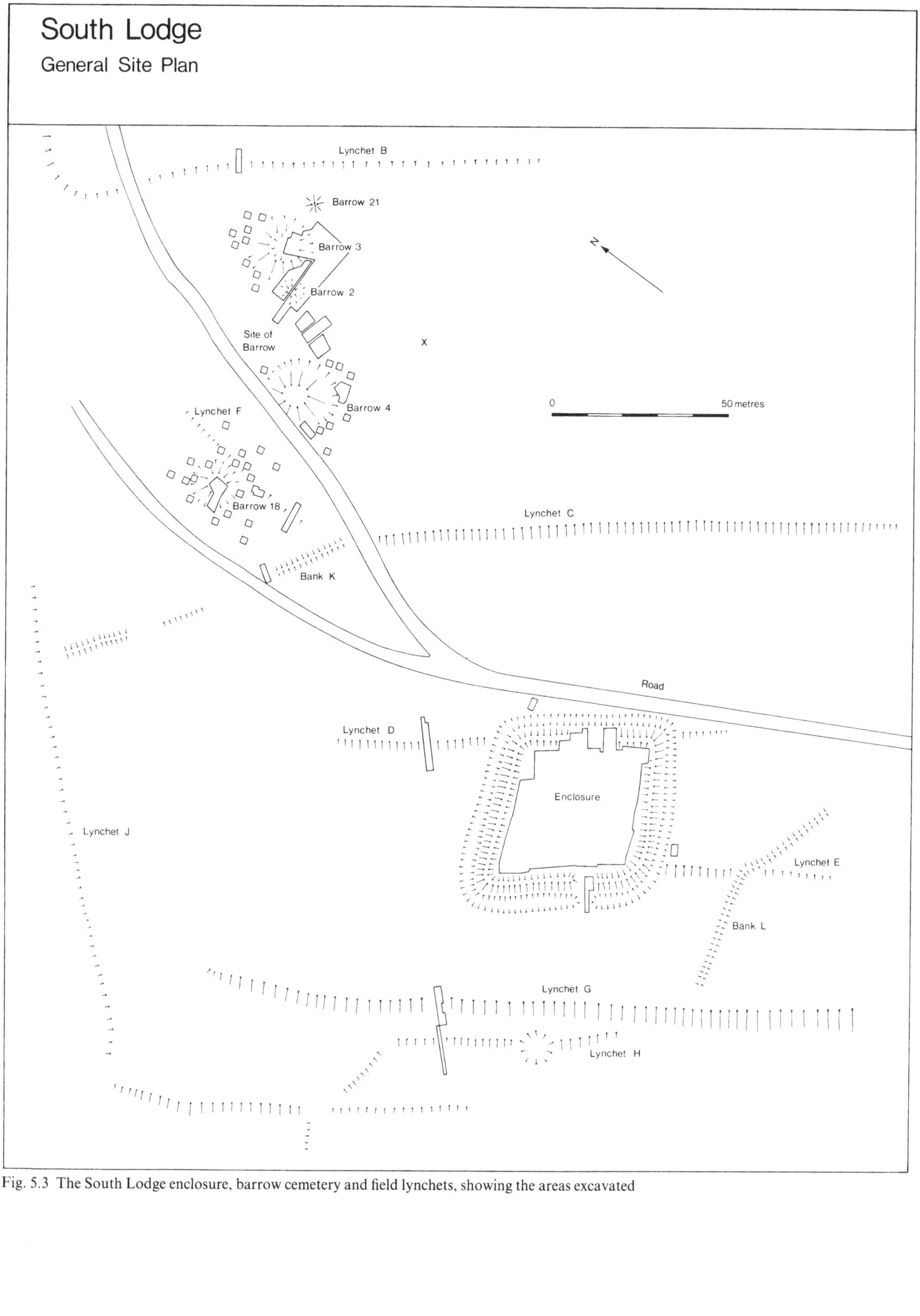

Fig. 5.3 The South Lodge enclosure, barrow cemetery and field lynchets, showing the areas excavated

the north-east being some 125 m away from Barrow 3 (Fig. 5.2). The full extent of the lynchets is difficult to determine. The eastern margins of the system are obscured by thick woodland, but, as may be expected, the lynchets die away as they reach the plateau of the hill to the north and east. To the south, beyond the boundaries of the park, the land has been recently cultivated. Lynchets can be glimpsed in the low light in this area, and a single surviving line of lynchet has also been recorded (Fig. 5.2). Aerial photographs reveal lynchets further to the south-east, although there is also an Iron Age enclosure in this area (Fig. 5.2).

There are no traces of lynchets on the western slopes of the dry valley. We therefore appear to be looking at the margins of a field system which ended above a dry valley. The system may have extended to the south but its survival as earthworks is limited to the confines of Rushmore Park.

Lynchets A, B, C and E are evenly spaced down the hillside, whilst D lies halfway between C and E. Lynchets A and B each turn along the line of the valley, whilst C may also be continued along the line of lynchet F (for an alternative reading see below). To the west of the enclosure there is a short length of double lynchet way, G and H, the distance between E and G being similar to that between D and E. Lynchet J lies along the northern margins of the system, above the dry valley.

Two low banks of flint, K and L, also occur amongst the lynchets. One bank, L, clearly overlies lynchet E, whilst K is aligned on the northern end of lynchet C. Any junction between K and C has been destroyed by the carriageway to Rushmore (Fig. 5.3).

It is now important for us to establish the chronological link between the fields and the other monuments.

5. 2.2.i *The fields and the cemetery*

Lynchets exist around the cemetery, and one lies between the main group of barrows and Barrow 18. Excavations of barrow mounds 18, 3 and 21 revealed that the earlier excavators had removed the entire mound and buried soil. No direct relationship between cultivation and mound construction could therefore be observed. There is, however, some indirect evidence as to the sequence of this activity.

Lynchets D and F were sectioned (Figs. 5.3 and 5.4) by two 2 m-wide trenches. In the former a positive lynchet some 0.4 m deep occurs but no corresponding negative lynchet cutting into the bedrock to the west of this accumulation could be observed (Fig. 5.4:1). In the case of lynchet F no convincing positive lynchet was located in the eastern half of the trench, but the soil here was not completely worm-sorted, and the lower horizon contained flint and angular chalk fragments. To the west the bedrock was clearly scarped in the form of a negative lynchet (Fig. 5.4:2).

These sections indicate that no cultivation had taken place to the west of lynchet B at this point. This would allow the barrows built here either to have been planned, under construction, or actually to be in existence at the time cultivation took place to the east. If the barrows had been later than this cultivation, we might expect ploughing to have extended to the plot lying to the west of the lynchet.

The formation of lynchet F is more complex. The negative lynchet to the west of its line must imply cultivation here before the construction of Barrow 18. If B and F were contemporaneous, then this clearly makes Barrow 18 later than the rest of the cemetery. However, the line of F does not conform to that of the other lynchets on this slope. It is also possible that a ploughsoil lies to the east of this line, even allowing that no well-developed lynchet occurs here. Indeed, it is noticeable that a different soil profile occurred on the uphill side of F than was located in a similar position in lynchets B, C, D, E and G. Today lynchet F is the slightest of all the field remains. Based upon these observations, we would suggest that F represents a phase of cultivation earlier in date than that which formed the main lynchet system. Such activity may be connected with Beaker pottery and flintwork found to the east of the lynchet (p. 117). This cultivation had ceased before the cemetery was constructed, but appears to have commenced again while the cemetery was being developed. This primary phase of cultivation may also have resulted in the formation of a positive lynchet immediately to the east of Barrow 4, which was located in the soil survey (Fig. 5.3:X; Fisher 1983, Fig. 4:M). This is not to be seen as an earthwork and may have been ploughed over by the later activity.

The later phase of cultivation established lynchets A, B, C, D, G, H and J on a different axis from the first phase, and with a plot of land containing the cemetery remaining unploughed. This second phase of cultivation ploughed away the earlier lynchets, although a worm-sorted ploughsoil was preserved at F, protected by the barrow cemetery.

We must now turn to the low flint bank, K. Upon excavation, this bank appeared to represent a dense spread of flint, which included some struck flakes and cores. Two sherds of Deverel-Rimbury pottery were also recovered. Whilst some of this material appears to be knapping debris, most of the flint is likely to derive from field clearance during cultivation. There is no clear formation of a positive lynchet in the section, and only the

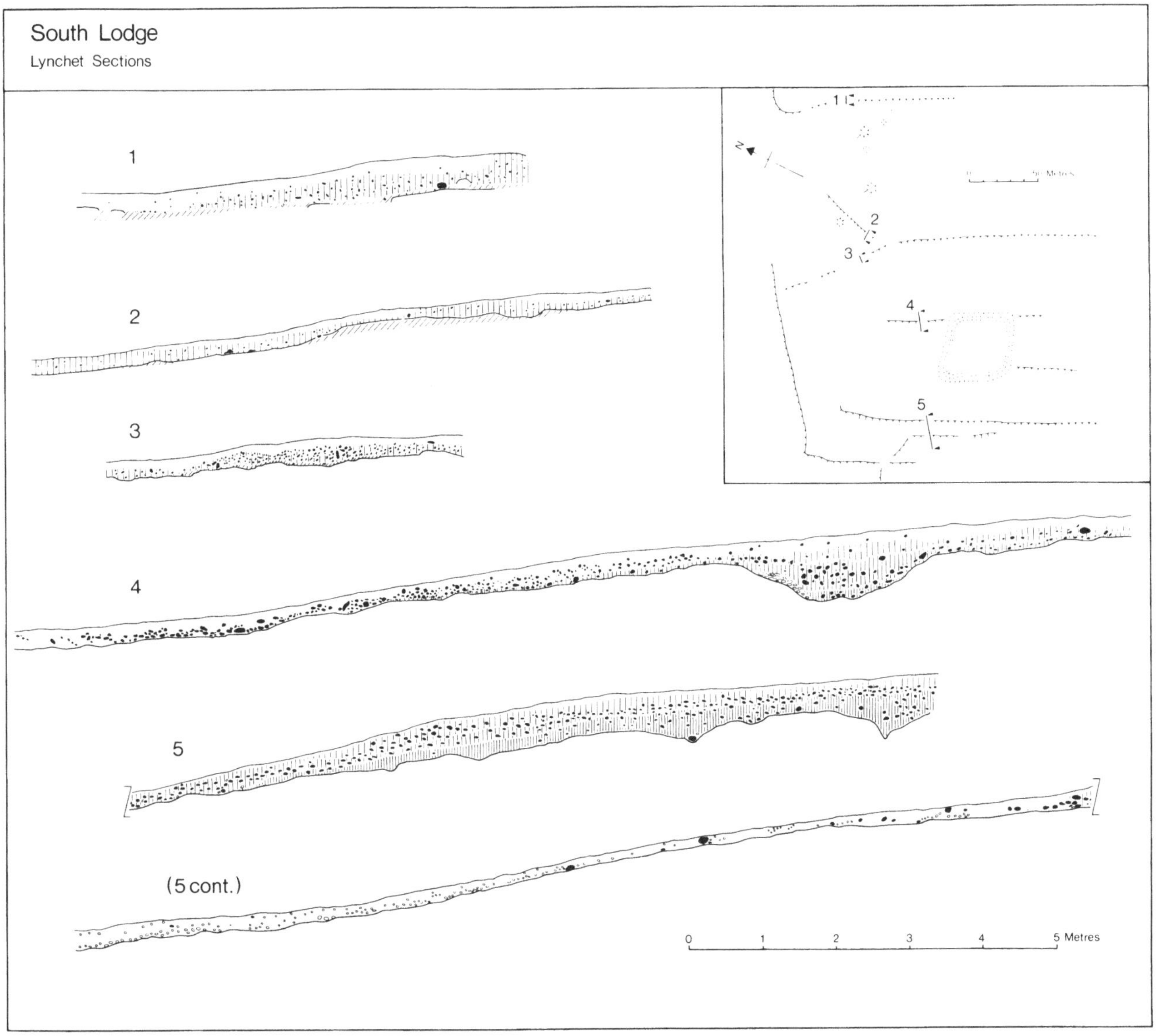

Fig. 5.4 Sections through the South Lodge field lynchets. For position and orientation of sections see inset

slightest trace of a negative scarp to the west (Fig. 5.4:3). If this bank is agricultural in origin, it could be connected with the main lynchet development, as well as delimiting the western extent of the land dedicated to the cemetery.

5.2.2.ii The fields and the enclosure

Toms' argument that the construction of the enclosure post-dated the development of the lynchets rested upon two observations: (1) Lynchets D and E run directly up to the edge of the ditch as it had been excavated in the nineteenth century, implying that the ditch had been cut through these lynchets. (2) The entrance causeway on the west of the site displayed the scarp of a lynchet within it. This represented a continuation of E, which does not extend beyond the north-western corner of the enclosure.

Our excavations on the eastern side of the enclosure confirmed that lynchet D was to be found here, and that it had been truncated by the digging of the enclosure ditch. Excavations in the western entrance confirmed the existence of lynchet E here.

Today the enclosure is a nineteenth-century earthwork. The entire length of the enclosure bank had been removed in the nineteenth century, with the exception of an 18 m length on the eastern side. The bank was then rebuilt. Our own excavations included two large sections through the nineteenth-century earthwork on this eastern side (Figs. 5.3 and 5.5). At the base of the

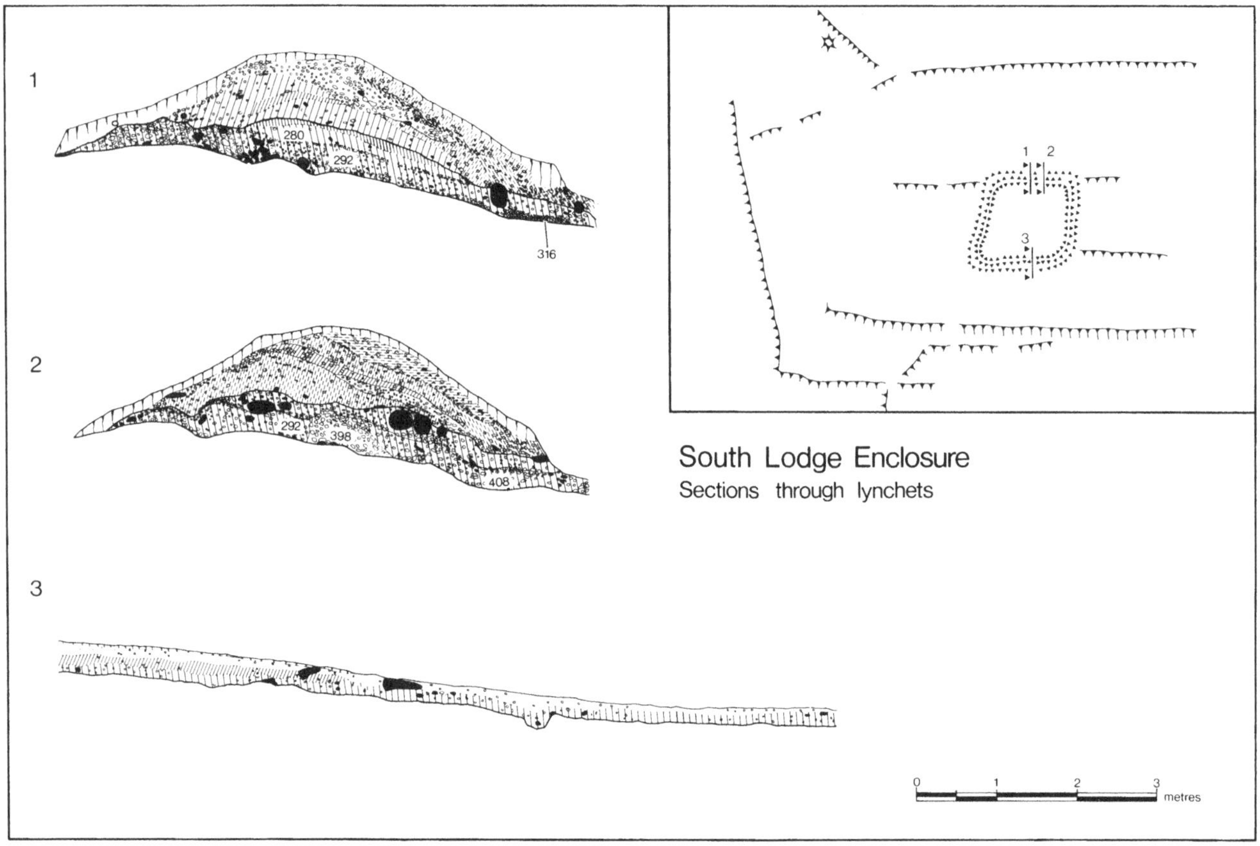

Fig. 5.5 Sections through the eastern bank (1 and 2) and the western entrance (3) of the South Lodge enclosure. The former reveal the Bronze Age field lynchet buried beneath nineteenth-century upcast, the latter a surviving lynchet in the entrance

exposed sections lay a Bronze Age ploughsoil. This is the remnant of a positive lynchet, with a well-developed negative lynchet to the west. This soil is sealed by a turf line, and above this lies the upcast of the nineteenth-century earthwork, made up of chalk rubble and humic silts. It is not intended to discuss the nineteenth-century earthwork here; what must be stressed is that nowhere in this length of bank was the upcast of a Bronze Age *rampart* located.

The negative lynchet is a slight scarp cut into the slope of the coombe rock. It was marked by a concentration of weathered and fractured chalk lumps (Fig. 5.5: A316) and flint nodules (A408). Along the scarp a small gully (Fig. 5.9: A053 & A313) was located. This uneven feature contained a large number of flint nodules and some struck flakes and may be a hedge line. The chalk surface under the positive lynchet was uneven, with a number of probable tree hollows.

Over this weathered and mechanically eroded scarp lay a ploughsoil (Fig. 5.5: A292 & A280). It contained small, angular fragments of chalk and flint and was partly worm-sorted, with a higher concentration of stone and chalk lumps in the lower half of the profile. A large amount of this flint was burnt and a number of struck flakes also occurred. In our southern section a concentration of flint nodules lay scattered along the line of the lynchet and buried within the ploughsoil. This must represent a rickle of field clearance which had eventually been buried in an encroaching lynchet.

The formation of this positive lynchet was truncated (if ploughing had not already ceased) by the digging of the enclosure ditch. This ditch cuts through the lynchet at the north-eastern and south-eastern corners of the enclosure.

If, as is likely, the enclosure lies across the corner of a field defined by lynchets D and E, then some evidence for that field corner may be expected to have survived. There is a slightly different formation noticeable in the negative lynchet at the northern and southern ends of our bank sections. The northern profile seems sharper than that to the south. In the centre of the enclosure a very slight east–west scarp was recorded in some places, which might have resulted from the differential mechanical erosion of the chalk between the two field plots.

Lynchet E was sectioned within the confines of the enclosure by a trench which ran through the entrance causeway (Figs. 5.3 and 5.5:3). Pitt Rivers' original contour survey of the enclosure makes it clear that, whilst a lynchet does appear here, as Toms noticed, it had been eroded, presumably by the use of that entrance (*Excavations* IV, Pl. 234, reproduced here as Fig. 5.6). Our section demonstrated the existence of a positive lynchet in this entrance, represented by a 0.35 m of soil accumulation (Fig. 5.5:3). The soil of this positive lynchet contained some flint flakes and pottery.

Our excavations thus confirmed Toms' observations. This leads to another observation. Lynchets D and E run directly against the edge of the enclosure ditch as it had been excavated in the nineteenth century. If cultivation had continued to lead to the further development of these lynchets, we would expect the lynchets beyond the enclosure to have changed alignment so as to avoid the ditch. This does not happen. At the same time the scale of lynchet D is no greater beyond the enclosure than it is under the enclosure bank. We must conclude that cultivation did not continue in the immediate vicinity of the enclosure after the ditch had been cut.

5.2.2.iii Additional sections

Further sections were cut through the lynchets outside the enclosure. Lynchet D was sectioned north of the enclosure, and the double lynchet-way G–H to the north-west (Figs. 5.3 and 5.4:4 and 5). In both cases positive lynchets of argillic brown earths were recorded (Fisher 1983) with a negative lynchet of humic rendzina. At G–H these two features were separated by a slightly eroded trackway. Below the positive lynchet D, a broad and irregular hollow was located, cutting down into the coombe rock. This was 2.5 m wide and reached a depth of 0.5 m. A similar feature was also recorded on the scarp of the positive lynchet at G, although this feature was far more irregular and its edges were difficult to trace. Attempts to trace these features as ditches proved unsuccessful, and they are best interpreted as solution hollows or ancient tree holes. The problem of such features is one to which we shall return when discussing the interior of the enclosure.

5.2.2.iv Later activity

If the enclosure ditch and the barrow cemetery partly or wholly post-date the main lynchet development, two other features may also be later than these lynchets.

The first is the second bank of flints, L, lying to the south-east of the enclosure (Fig. 5.3). This clearly overlies lynchet E. The second is a large pit excavated in the nineteenth century immediately west of the enclosure. No relationship between the pit in its original state and lynchet H is recorded. It is always possible that the lynchet ran, unnoticed, down into the weathered top of this pit. Otherwise the pit is later and cut H. It was *c.* 2 m deep and contained a human pelvic bone and a Neolithic polished axe fragment in its middle fills and Bronze Age and Roman pottery in the upper fills (*Excavations* IV, 42, Pl. 243). This feature is treated as a single Neolithic 'flat grave' by Kinnes (1979, 126).

5.2.2.v Summary

Three points must be emphasised:

1 Cultivation represented by the lynchets and clearance material has a long and complex history. Earlier lynchets may have been amongst the features ploughed out by that phase of ploughing which produced the lynchets visible today.
2 During this history of cultivation two different sets of earthworks were constructed on the edge of this field system, a barrow cemetery and a ditched enclosure.
3 After the ditch of the enclosure had been dug, cultivation appears to have ceased in its immediate vicinity.

5.2.3 Early domestic occupation

Cultivation presupposes domestic settlement in the vicinity. We have said nothing about the date at which cultivation may have started, simply because we have so little evidence. The main lynchet system formed during or after the development of a barrow cemetery, which we will assign for the moment simply to the Middle Bronze Age. The possibility of earlier cultivation has already been noted. The snail fauna recovered from lynchets D and E and from the ditch and quarry scoop around Barrow 4 all contain a high proportion of shade-loving species. This might indicate that during barrow construction, and during cultivation, the environment was not entirely open. The earlier artefacts recovered from the area, including Later Neolithic sherds from Barrow 4, Beaker sherds from a pit near Barrow 18 and from the enclosure itself, may represent the traces of earlier settlement (p. 117).

A local, open settlement is therefore presumably associated with the final phase of agricultural activity and the early development of the barrow cemetery. Settlement debris in the form of pottery and struck flints does occur in the lynchets. Fieldwalking by Stephen Ford in an area to the north-east of the site of the enclosure

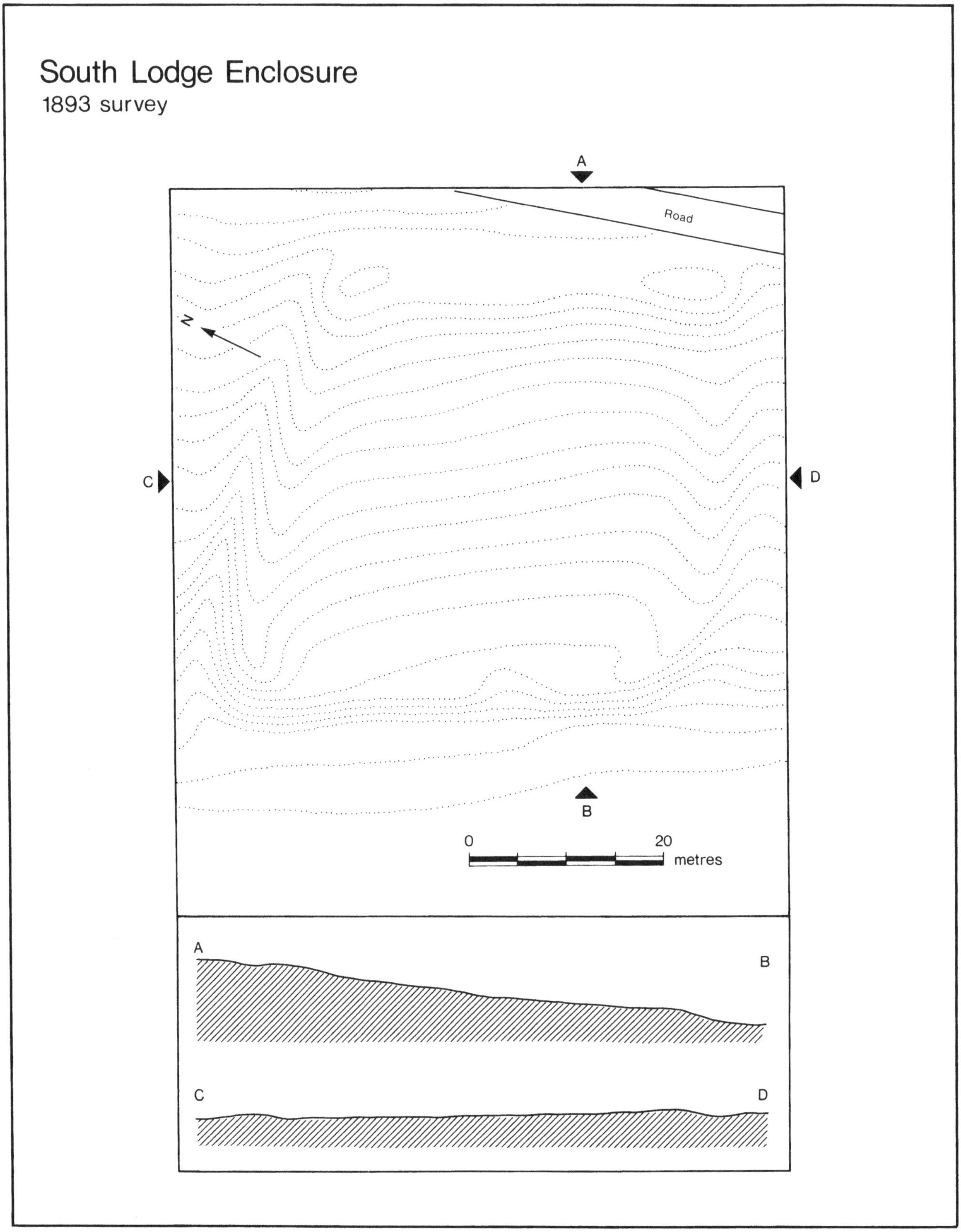

Fig. 5.6 The nineteenth-century contour survey of the South Lodge enclosure prior to excavation (contours at 0.12 m)

recovered an overall scatter of flints. The material is not particularly diagnostic but two concentrations of material are identifiable (Fig. 5.2: Y and Z). Again this is a problem of archaeological visibility. Unless buildings were placed on substantial platforms, or were constructed out of stone, open settlements are going to be difficult to recognise. It is not until enclosure, late in the sequence here, that we are able to focus upon one element of the settlement system. The open settlement either lies in an area uninvestigated by excavation, or it is represented amongst some of the structural features found within the later enclosure. It is to the enclosure that we must now return.

5.2.4 The enclosure

As we have seen, the enclosure had been extensively excavated in the nineteenth century. The ditch silts were removed entirely, and most of the bank and interior were cleared.

The enclosure will be discussed in terms of the main structural elements found within it, followed by a description of the distribution of the artefacts. This descriptive material will be drawn together in a synthesis at the end of the South Lodge section of this chapter (p. 181).

There are two sources of information concerning the original appearance of the earthwork, the nineteenth-century accounts and the results of our own excavations.

Pitt Rivers records a ¾ acre (0.3 hectare) enclosure obscured by a thick hazel 'nut-wood' coppice. It was clear that the enclosure had been little disturbed, with the exception of the slight truncation of the south-eastern corner of the ditch by the Rushmore carriageway. The first published survey appears in *Excavations* II, Pl. 80, where the enclosure, Barrows 2, 3, 4, 18 and 21, and lynchet C are all represented. This plan depicts an irregular, rectilinear enclosure bank with a single break in the south-eastern corner. The outer lip of the surrounding ditch was traced for almost the entire circuit of the enclosure, only to be obscured by the carriageway.

A clearer idea of the earthwork's original appearance can be gained from the second published survey and from two scale models of the enclosure now preserved in Salisbury museum. The second plan is a contour survey (*Excavations* IV, Pl. 234), and this is reproduced here along with two cross-sections taken from it (Fig. 5.6). This makes clear that the enclosure was originally defined by a very slight bank and the silted top of the ditch. We discuss the nature of this bank below. The bank was truncated in the south-eastern corner, and at the mid-point of its western side, the latter corresponding with a causeway in the ditch. Today a more substantial nineteenth-century earthwork occupies the site of the Bronze Age enclosure; the two are compared in Fig. 5.7.

5.2.4.i The ditch

Our understanding of the ditch depends entirely upon the nineteenth-century accounts. Today it is represented by an eroding feature, 4.5–5.0 m wide, with a single causeway on the western side of the enclosure.

The nineteenth-century excavations began with six 10-ft (3.05 m)-wide sections cut through the rampart and ditch (Fig. 5.8), and then proceeded to clear the silts from the entire length of the ditch. Pitt Rivers' description is therefore important: 'The Ditch was of an average width of 9.5 feet [2.9 m] at the top, and a depth about 6.6 feet [2.01 m], and was of nearly uniform dimensions all round. The lower 3 feet [0.91 m] of the silting consisted entirely of chalk rubble, above which the mould began, and got thicker towards the top. ... [It had a] smooth flat bottom, about 1 foot [0.30 m] wide all round ... the sides ... were unusually abrupt, being at an angle of 60°' (*Excavations* IV, 5). The preserved plane-table survey of the site depicts seventeen schematic sections taken along the length of the ditch. These support the description of a uniform ditch and the sharp profile. The only published profile is an 'average' of all these sections (*Excavations* IV, Pl. 237). This sharp and uniform profile is significant and is a point to which we must return. It is sufficient to note here that, although Pitt Rivers regarded the fill of the ditch as a natural silt, the excavated profile is steeper than we would expect from a chalk-cut ditch which had silted naturally. This point can be supported by both the experimental results from Overton Down (Jewell and Dimbleby 1968) and by the broad profile of the ditch today, which has silted naturally over the last century.

No drawn sections are available from the ditch silts. The assertion that the lower 3 ft (0.91 m) of ditch silts were chalk rubble is supported by one photograph (*Excavations* IV, Pl. 235, Fig. 2), although another indicates that more variable deposits amongst these lower silts might also have been encountered in some places (*Excavations* IV, Pl. 235, Fig. 1).

We will return to consider the finds from the ditch silts below.

5.2.4.ii The bank

Before the nineteenth-century excavations had removed or buried it, the bank rose barely 0.5 m above the level of the interior. Always a slight feature, its definition

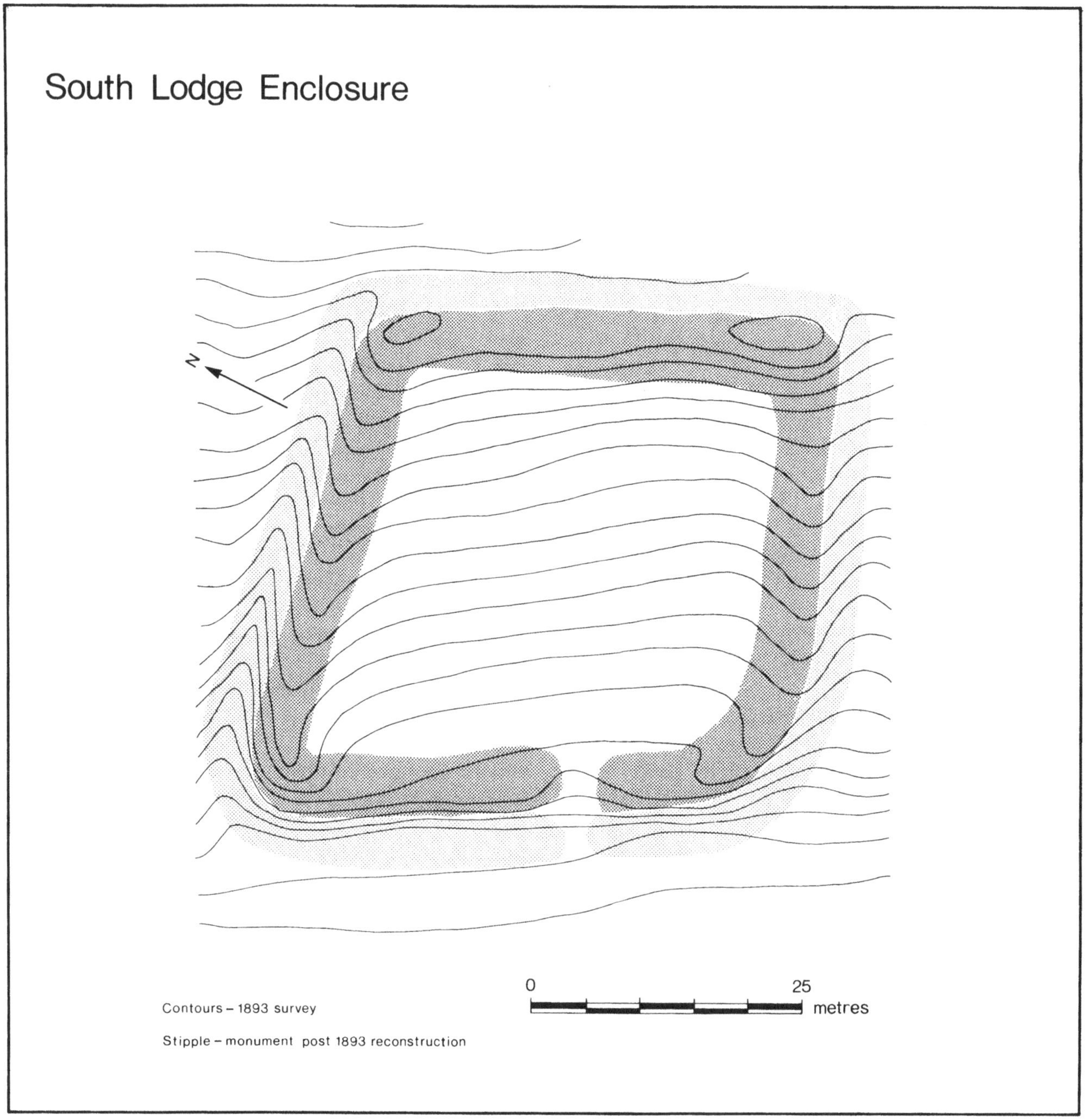

Fig. 5.7 The extent of the present earthwork of the South Lodge enclosure projected onto the nineteenth-century contour survey (contours at 0.12 m)

would have depended more upon the scarp which dropped from the crest of the bank into the top of the external ditch than any rise from the interior of the enclosure to the bank top. As with the ditch, Pitt Rivers was more concerned to record the nature of the finds recovered and their absolute depth than any structural detail. This emphasis upon 'finds depth' derives from a concern to establish a secure date for the enclosure. It results in a text quite unconcerned with the structural nature of the earthwork, but instead with the comparative depth of each class of artefact within the broad contextual divisions of 'interior', 'rampart' and 'ditch'. The distinction drawn between 'rampart' and 'interior' is, however, arbitrary, depending as it does not upon stratigraphic context but upon the limits of the bank as it was observed as a surface undulation.

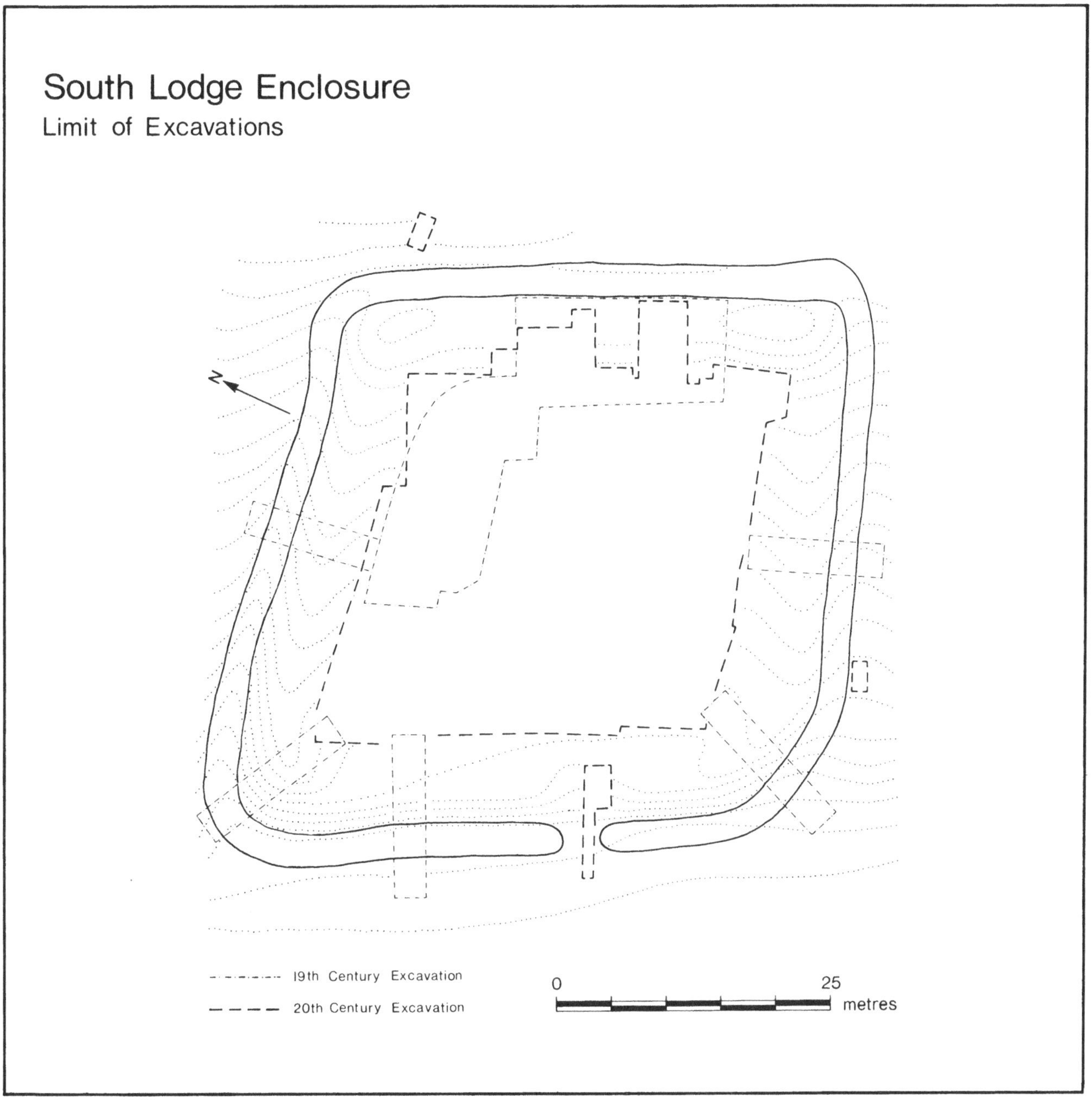

Fig. 5.8 The overall extent of the areas excavated in the two programmes of work undertaken at the South Lodge enclosure

It was only on the eastern side of the enclosure, and in the western entrance, that any of the original bank remained available for investigation below the nineteenth-century earthwork. We have documented our own work on these bank sections above and have demonstrated that below the nineteenth-century upcast the Bronze Age 'bank' is represented by the ploughsoil of lynchets D and E. Nowhere in these particular sections could we locate an upcast bank of soil and chalk rubble which might have derived from the ditch. We may draw the following conclusions about the bank:

1 It is a very slight earthwork over its entire length.
2 On the east and west of the enclosure it is made up of a positive lynchet and the cut scarp of the ditch.
3 On the east and west there is no additional material, nor is there a fence-line or palisade.
4 The northern and southern arms of the bank are pre-

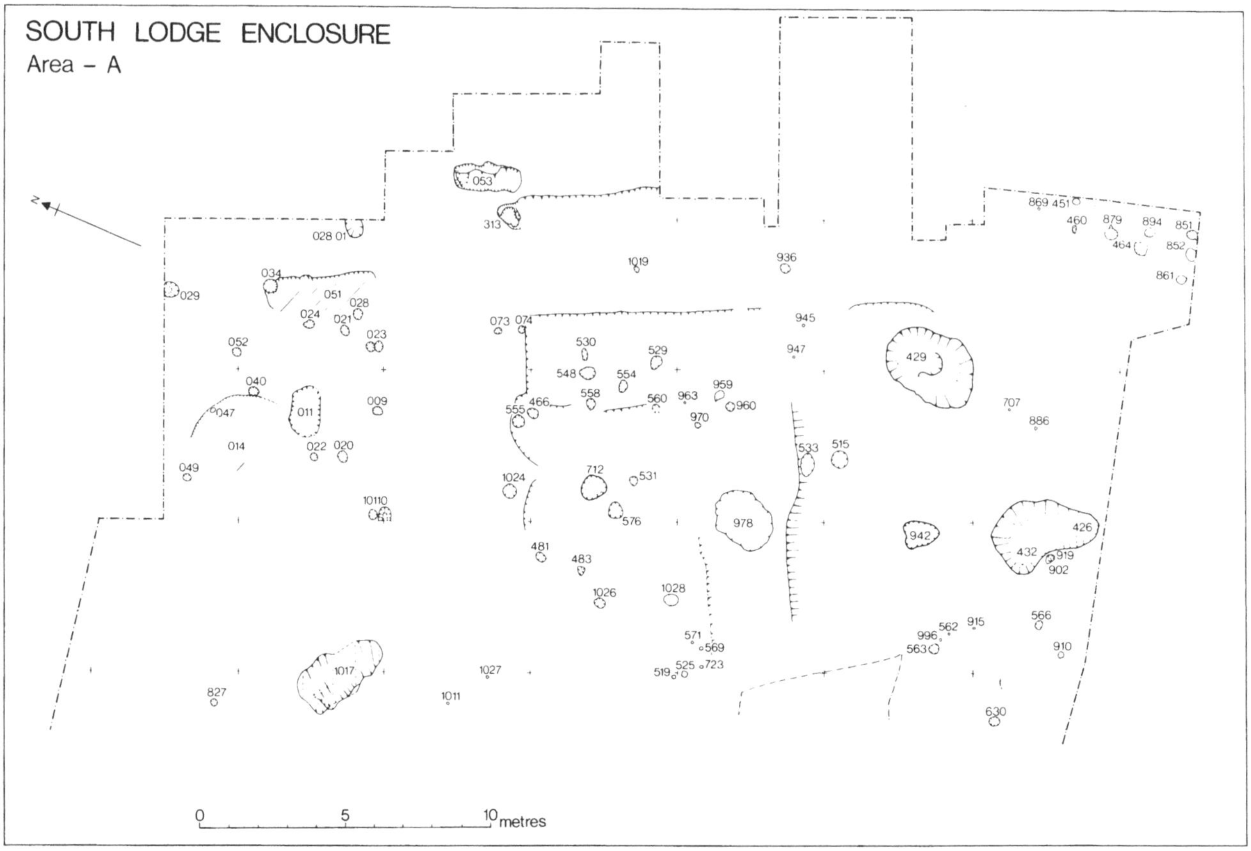

Fig. 5.9 All excavated features (Bronze Age and later) in the eastern half of the South Lodge enclosure

sumably upcast, and the slight mounding observable in the north-eastern and south-eastern corners of the enclosure in the contour survey may be this upcast overriding the lynchet.

5.2.4.iii The entrance(s)

The western entrance of the enclosure was unexcavated by Pitt Rivers, and has now been only partially investigated. A 2.0 m-wide causeway in the ditch corresponds with an eroded hollowing in lynchet E. This erosion has not entirely removed the lynchet. Toms recorded it, and we were also able to observe and section this feature. No gate structure, and no terminal of an enclosing fence, were recorded in the area of our excavations.

The 1888 survey revealed a second break in the south-eastern corner of the enclosure bank and does not record the western entrance. This feature can also be observed in the contour survey published ten years later. This break did not correspond to any recognised causeway through the ditch, and the evidence for the break was dug away by Pitt Rivers.

5.2.4.iv The interior

The interior of the enclosure was excavated in five seasons between 1977 and 1981. The excavation procedure was largely determined by what we knew of the nineteenth-century excavation programme. This had resulted in the clearance of most of the interior, with the exception of a small area in the north-eastern corner of the site, and a strip of ground immediately within the eastern bank (Fig. 5.8).

In 1977, 70 m^2 of what remained of the unexcavated interior was hand-excavated, with the purpose of locating any structural remains which would indicate that other features might have been missed by the earlier excavators. We also began the investigation of the unexcavated bank. Structural remains were located, and in the following year the eastern half of the enclosure was partially machine-stripped (designated area A: Fig. 5.9). The area stripped, and the total area of the interior eventually investigated, was limited by the extent of the nineteenth-century bank around the site, which had encroached upon the interior, and which we did not wish to remove. The machine-stripping of A was also halted well above

Table 5.1. *South Lodge enclosure, Structure 1 posthole grades*

Postholes	A024	A021	A023	A009	A020	A022	A040	A052
Grades	1	1	1	2	2	1	1	2

the level of the coombe rock because we did not understand the nineteenth-century procedure of excavation and backfilling, and we therefore could not date the many complex deposits we encountered. After further extensive hand excavation we were finally able to identify the full extent of nineteenth-century backfill, and to identify some of the 2.0–2.5 m wide trenches which had been dug across the site in the nineteenth century. Using this technique, we presumed that the soil had been moved from one trench to the next, and that no extensive area of the interior was ever clear at any one time. A very similar procedure is known to have been used by the General's former assistant, St George Gray, in his extensive excavations at Meare (Coles 1987, 10–11).

Once the nature of the deposits and the nineteenth-century excavation strategy had been determined, the western half of the enclosure was machine-stripped down to the Coombe Rock (area F: Fig. 5.11), the surface of which was hand cleaned.

We will discuss the built structures identified within the interior and then describe the overall distribution of artefacts recovered by ourselves and by Pitt Rivers. Although a sequence of building activity may be expected within the interior, in fact we have very little evidence from which to construct it.

The postholes identified in our excavations were graded subjectively on a scale from 1 to 3, where grade 1 was the most and grade 3 the least definite feature. This grading was necessary simply because of the highly variable quality of the bedrock, which was transversed by a series of periglacial features and solution hollows.

Terrace A was identified as an arc cut against the eastern slope of the chalk (Fig. 5.9). Lying in the unexcavated area, it had a fill of brown clay soil below which lay a small area of eroded or trampled chalk and an area of flint cobbling (A014). Two postholes lay on the line of the terrace arc (A047, A049).

Terrace B was a straight scarp cut against the slope of the hill (Fig. 5.9). Again the fill was of a brown clay soil. Although the chalk-cut scarp was slight, it could be observed in section cutting back into the lynchet ploughsoil of the bank to a depth of 0.50 m. A scatter of flint nodules lay along the back of the terrace. And immediately to the west a 1.0 m band of trampled or eroded chalk was observed (A051). The scarp was cut by a single posthole (A034).

Structure 1 is defined by an irregular cluster of postholes, which were isolated by eye and also by a programme of nearest-neighbour analysis (Bradley and Small 1985). In plan this cluster partly overlies the extent of Terraces A and B. The posthole cluster includes a roughly circular arrangement with a diameter of *c.* 4.5 m (Table 5.1).

If this was a small circular building, its outer wall line would have lain beyond this circle of posts which would have defined the inner roof supports (Avery and Close-Brooks 1969; Musson 1970). It would be difficult to argue for more than a single period of construction for the building, although A052, A028 and A023 may be single replacements. Terrace B may have been the terrace cut for this building, but the area of floor erosion associated with the terrace does not lie within the post circle, as happens in other buildings of similar date (Burstow and Holleyman 1957; Musson 1970). Indeed postholes A024 and A028 would seem to cut that eroded surface. The plan of the building does not conform to the arc of Terrace A, and A040 seems to have been cut by, or to have cut, this terrace.

Within the area of the building was a single pit, A011. This was observed to cut down through the clay fill of the terrace itself and into the underlying chalk. The upper fill contained a cluster of flint nodules, and at the bottom of the pit and against its northern edge lay the bones of the left half of the carcase of a small cow (p. 167). The pit was relatively shallow, and seems unlikely to have been filled in this way when the building was still in use. However, it was not observed cutting through the upper fill of the terraces.

Structure 2 lay to the south in the area previously excavated. The surface of the Coombe Rock was slightly terraced by the nineteenth-century trenching in the area of this structure (Fig. 5.9), and one posthole of this building (A466) had been excavated and recorded at that time (*Excavations* IV, Pl. 234:P). Again, nearest-neighbour analysis isolates a cluster of postholes in the area of this building, and these include a clear circular arrangement (Fig. 5.9 and Table 5.2).

These postholes are quite evenly spaced, *c.* 2.5 m apart, but with a 6.5 m break between A1028 and A960. A959 and A960 are taken to be replacements and A466 may also have represented a replacement. None of the postholes displayed any evidence for surviving post-pipes. With the exception of the replacements noted, there was no evidence for the substantial rebuilding of this struc-

Table 5.2. *South Lodge enclosure, Structure 2 posthole grades*

Postholes	A1028	A1026	A481	A1024	A466	A555	A548	A529	A959	A960
Grades	1	2	2	2	/	2	2	1	2	2

ture. Charcoal recovered from A529 gave the dates: 1290 ± 120 bc and 1160 ± 110 bc (BM 1921R-2R).

It is difficult to orientate this building. Again we must assume the post-ring represents the inner roof supports of a large roundhouse. There is, however, no clear evidence for a forward-projecting porch, unless A485 is included in the ring; this would account for the forward displacement of A1026 and A1028, which face towards the western entrance through the enclosure. The only marked break in the spacing of the post-ring is between A1028 and A960. If this marks an entrance then it faces in the traditional southerly direction, but is not orientated towards the entrance of the enclosure. There is an additional complication: 'pit' A978 lay directly in the area of the gap in the post-ring. As with a number of similar features discussed below, this 'pit' had been dug out in the nineteenth century and we know nothing of its original contents. It may have been humanly dug, or a natural solution hollow. If it was of Bronze Age origin it is unlikely to have been dug in the entrance during the use of the building (cf. Drewett 1982, Fig. 5, Hut 1), and if it were contemporary with the building, is likely to have lain under the roof eaves. However, if it were earlier than the building (and it must have been earlier than a pottery spread which Pitt Rivers records partly overlying it, discussed below), then a posthole may have been set into the top of it, all trace of which would have been removed in the nineteenth century.

This structure is situated on a very slight terrace. Pitt Rivers' contour survey failed to reveal this as a surface feature, and his surveyor's eye for detail was good enough to pick out the low mound of a midden situated on the southern side of the building. Although the surface is truncated in this area by Pitt Rivers' own excavations, our contour survey does reveal the vestiges of the terrace upon which this building was set (Fig. 5.10).

Posthole clusters 3 and 4 are two further groups of postholes isolated by the programme of nearest-neighbour analysis (Bradley and Small 1985). Both lie towards the margins of the excavated area. Cluster 3 lies around a large 'pit' and a concentration of pottery was recovered in the nineteenth century from the surface of the chalk between F092 and F103 (Fig. 5.11). These postholes do not present any particularly coherent plan. If a building did stand here, it lay almost immediately within the entrance, some 13.0 m from the ditch terminals. Alternatively, such a structure may have pre-dated the enclosure.

Cluster 4 lay in the south-eastern corner of the site, and may clearly have continued beyond the area excavated. This building (if that is what it is) lay in the area of the break recorded in the enclosure bank in the nineteenth century (Fig. 5.9). Those excavations had removed the evidence for the bank in this area, but had not cleared down to the chalk. A residual spread of clay soil was located in the area of these postholes, and this contained flints and pottery sherds (A890 and A894).

The other postholes and stakeholes within the enclosure do not present any clear pattern, although their distribution appears to be confined to the southern side of the site. In the south-western corner there is a possible line of stakeholes (Fig. 5.11) to the east of a 'pit' excavated in the nineteenth century. Apart from this no fence line can be traced anywhere within the enclosure.

Pits within the enclosure pose a particular problem. In the form in which they were observed most were the product of nineteenth-century excavation. Pitt Rivers' account of his excavations is important on this point:

> There were no pits in this Camp, such as are common in all the residences of the Romanized Britons. A hole, P . . . evenly cut, 2 feet [0.61 m] in diameter and 2 feet 6 inches [0.76 m] deep, was found, but nothing except fine mixed earth and two pieces of decayed wood were found in it. Numerous soft places in the chalk – which are the *bête noire* of the excavator in a chalk soil – had to be conscientiously cleared out, but without finding anything that appeared to be artificial, except the small hole above mentioned and a pit 10.5 feet [3.2 m] long, and 5.3 feet [1.6 m] wide, Q . . . which might have been a grave, but had no bones in it'. (*Excavations* IV, 12)

Pitt Rivers thus distinguishes between natural and artificial features cut into the chalk of the enclosure, and comments upon the existence of artificial pits on other occupation sites on the chalk. It is not clear how he makes the distinction. Of the two artificial features he accepted, one, P, can be identified as a possible posthole associated with Structure 2 (A466), the other is our pit F024. The location of the other 'soft patches' was recorded on a plane-table survey but never published. Using that survey, we can locate all those features in

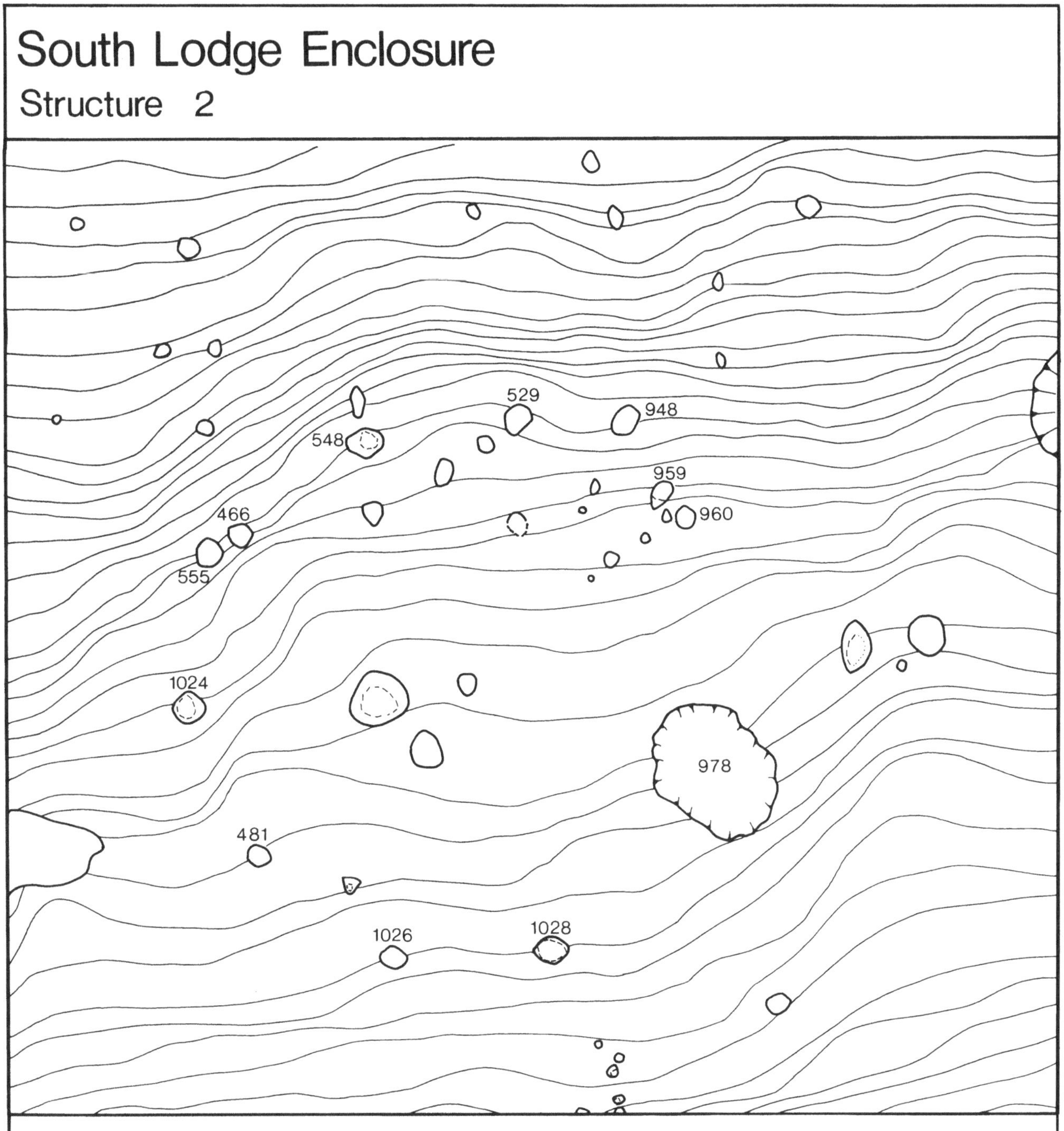

Fig. 5.10 Contour survey (at 0.02 m intervals) of the chalk surface in the area of Structure 2 in the South Lodge enclosure (contours at 0.005 m

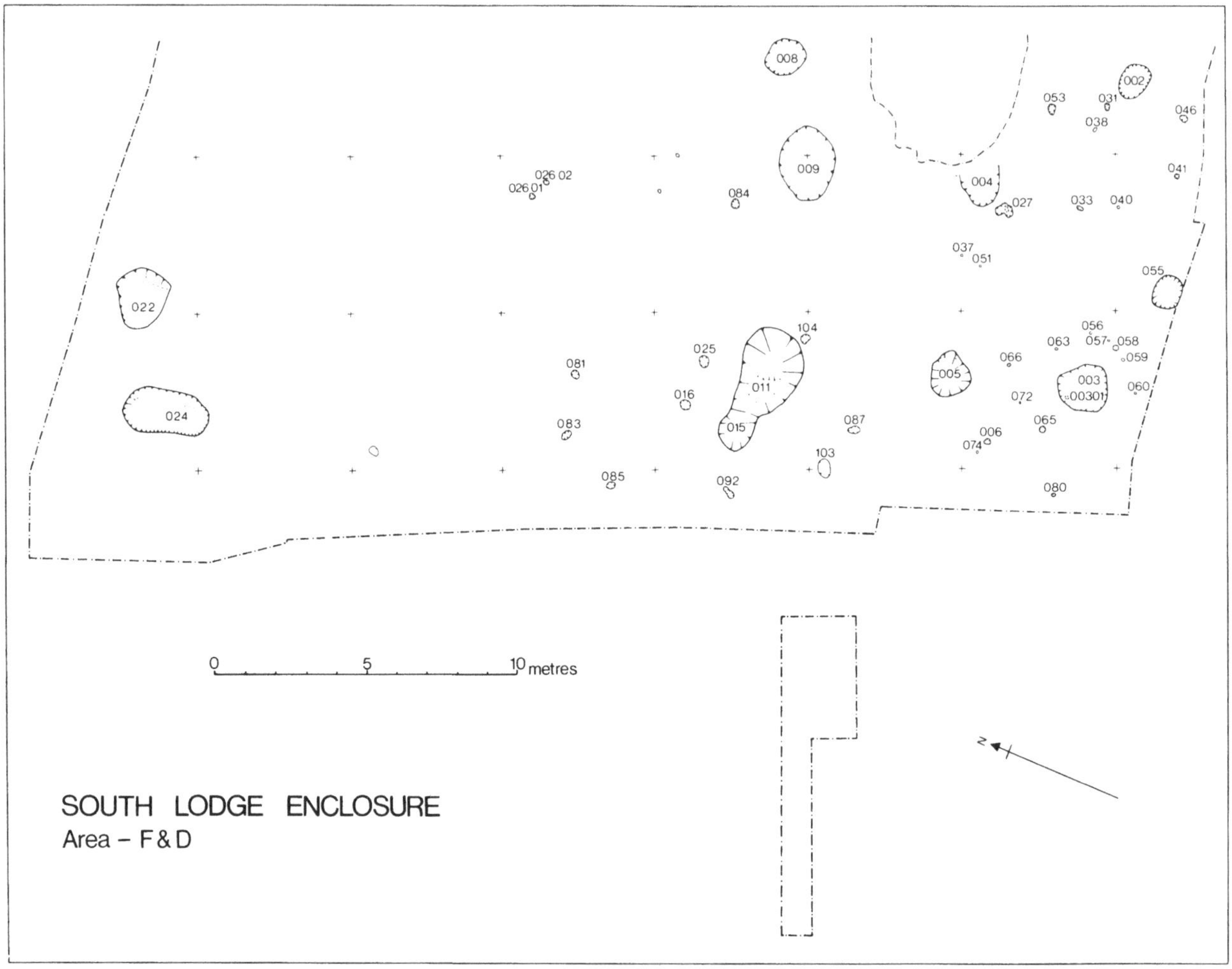

Fig. 5.11 All excavated features (Bronze Age and later) in the western half of the South Lodge enclosure

our own excavations. They are A978, A429, A426/432, F008, F009, F004, F002, F003, F005, F011 and F024 (Figs. 5.9 and 5.11). The question is now to decide whether we accept Pitt Rivers' judgement on these.

Our excavations recovered not only Pitt Rivers' excavated features but also a number of other, unexcavated features. These may be divided between tree holes of uncertain date and Bronze Age features.

Seven tree holes were identified. They were irregular in shape, with diameters greater than 1.0 m, and were filled with a soft chalky wash. Of the remaining features two, F022 and F055, had fills directly comparable to those pits which had been dug and backfilled in the nineteenth century. We must suppose that they were also excavated then, but went unrecorded.

The remaining pits are A011 and A1017. The former has already been discussed (p. 157), being a Bronze Age pit dug into the floor area occupied by Structure 1. A1017 is more difficult to interpret. It was a very uneven feature, 0.6 m at its deepest point, with no clearly defined cut edges. The orange clay fill contained some burnt flints and charcoal on the northern edge of the feature; these occurred to a depth of 0.5 m. A large mound of burnt flints lay immediately to the north of this feature but did not overlie it. This may be a solution hollow into which a small Bronze Age feature had been dug. However, the whole feature may represent a tree hollow, formed at a date later than the burnt mound, into which some of that material had fallen.

These results make clear the problems in interpreting 'soft places in the chalk', with only one of the features excavated by ourselves being an obvious Bronze Age pit. Pitt Rivers records the existence of eleven other 'soft places' listed above, to which we would also add F022 and F055. Of these, the backfill of A429 and A426/432 contained a considerable amount of loose chalk rubble and flint nodules, presumably the result of overdigging these features in the nineteenth century. All the remaining pits also contained some chalk rubble amongst the loose soil, again presumably resulting from the over-cutting of these features. The only real variation in the fills is with A978, the pit within the floor area of Structure 2. Although loose chalk rubble again occurred in this fill, the base of the pit appeared weathered and was overlain by a humic and chalk wash.

Given these results we can only urge caution in the interpretation of these features. If any were artificial then we may note that most of the pits lie in the western half of the enclosure away from Structures 1 and 2. All are likely to have been over-cut, two very substantially, in the nineteenth century. The very even A024 is presumably artificial, as was originally suggested. A good case could also be made for A978 being a Bronze Age pit within Structure 2.

The burnt mound lay almost entirely within the area of the interior left unexcavated in the nineteenth century (Fig. 5.12). Pitt Rivers' trenching may have begun to encroach upon its western edge, but it would seem that here, in the vicinity of what is today a large tree, excavation was superficial and that the chalk was not reached. The main concentration of the burnt flints extended *c.* 4 m east–west and *c.* 7.5 m north–south. The northern limit was concealed by the nineteenth-century enclosure bank (but see below). The layer of burnt flints was between 0.10 m and 0.15 m thick. There was no substantial trace of burning within or around the mound.

The mound was probably one of the earliest features on the site. No features, with the exception of a possible posthole, A829, lay beneath it. The burnt flint layer sealed a stone-free soil, which in turn overlay the Coombe Rock. This soil had clearly not been ploughed immediately prior to the accumulation of the flints. We have already noted that the western lynchet, E, does not extend beyond the north-western corner of the enclosure, implying that the enclosure ditch incorporated part of an uncultivated plot. It would seem likely that this uncultivated area continued beneath the burnt mound. Our excavations did not extend beyond the enclosure ditch to the north, but burnt flints can be observed on the surface just beyond the enclosure at this point. It is quite possible that the burnt mound originated during an unenclosed phase of settlement activity and that the ditch cut through, or along its northern edge.

5.2.4.v The finds

This discussion will consider the artefacts recovered during both campaigns of excavation and the single deposit of animal bones found in 1977. The recovery rates of material in these different excavations will have varied, and between 1977 and 1981 Bronze Age artefacts were recovered from both Bronze Age and nineteenth-century deposits.

The recording of the material has also varied. The nineteenth-century record of recovery for bronze, worked bone, pottery and quern fragments seems to have been good. We recovered few sherds of pottery and no worked bone or Bronze Age metalwork from the re-excavated areas of backfill. However, the record concerning the context of recovery of animal bone is more schematic (*Excavations* IV, 39) and the nineteenth-century recovery of flint was low, being directed almost entirely at the collection of regular tool types.

The contexts of the nineteenth-century finds are recorded in the published account (*Excavations* IV, 16–42, Pls. 234–42), and the museum archive. The latter includes notations attached to the finds and two plans. One of these is a large plane-table survey of the site, which is annotated, the second a smaller-scale plan recording the find spots of pottery. This pottery record is not an original field plan and may have been produced schematically from the plane-table survey and additional notes (Fig. 5.13). All these plans display variation in detail.

Bronzes. All the Bronze Age metalwork was recovered from the enclosure ditch in the nineteenth century (Fig. 5.13). The stratigraphic contexts are not known in any detail; all we have are generalised statements of depth and ditch fill (*Excavations* IV, 16–26, Pls. 234–8).

A razor and an awl were recovered on, or close to, the bottom of the ditch. The razor lay in the north-eastern corner and the awl in the opposite south-western corner of the enclosure ditch.

Three other objects, another razor, a bracelet and a bunch of bronze wire which 'appears to have been plaited in a strand' lay within about 5 m of one another at the northern end of the eastern ditch. They also occurred at a similar level, recorded as 3 ft (0.9 m) below the surface 'at the bottom of the mixed silting'.

Finally a side-looped spearhead occurred high in the ditch, 0.9 ft (0.27 m) below the surface in the 'surface mould'. It lay in the southern ditch near the south-eastern corner, close to a break in the enclosure bank.

The recent excavations did, however, produce one find which seems connected with metalworking. This is a probable clay mould fragment, representing an inner valve component, the concave surface of which could represent a socketed object such as a spear shaft. This came from the topsoil over the area of Terrace B.

Metalwork: chronology and affinities[3] Of the two razors the smaller came from on the bottom of the ditch

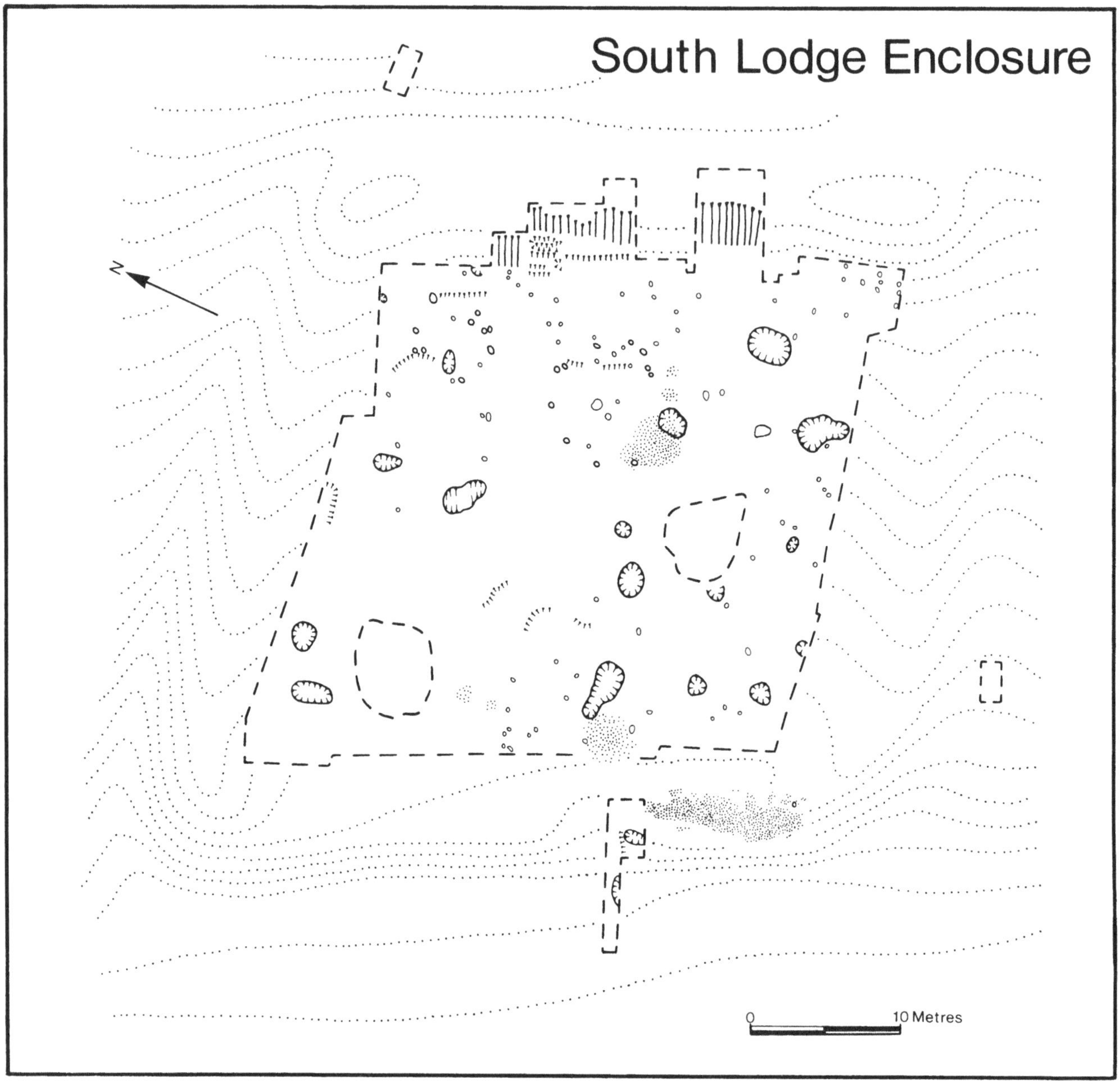

Fig. 5.12 Overall plan of Bronze Age features within the South Lodge enclosure, with the main surface distribution of pottery sherds recorded by Pitt Rivers

(*Excavations* IV, Pls. 237 and 238:3). Burgess has dated the two razors to separate chronological phases: the smaller explicitly to metalworking Stages VII and VIII, the second, and larger razor to Stage IX (1980, 134, 204, Fig. 3:14). He attributes the first to Class Ia, which is Butler and Smith's Class IA, razors with short tang and single rivet-hole (1956, 29). In passing, it should be noted that Butler and Smith suggested that the angular shoulders of this South Lodge razor were more characteristic of Class II (*ibid.*, 33 n. 34). Burgess places the appearance of Class Ia razors late in Stage VI and their development in Stage VII (1980, 115 and 124).

Jockenhovel places the first South Lodge razor among his 'double-edged razors with long-oval blade and tang' (1980, 40:81, 37 and 42). This places it alongside razors of Class IB, which Butler and Smith characterised by the long narrow tang (1956, 29), and thus apart from examples with broad perforated tang. Jockenhovel's examples with long-oval blade and tang have a wider range of ceramic associations than those with broad per-

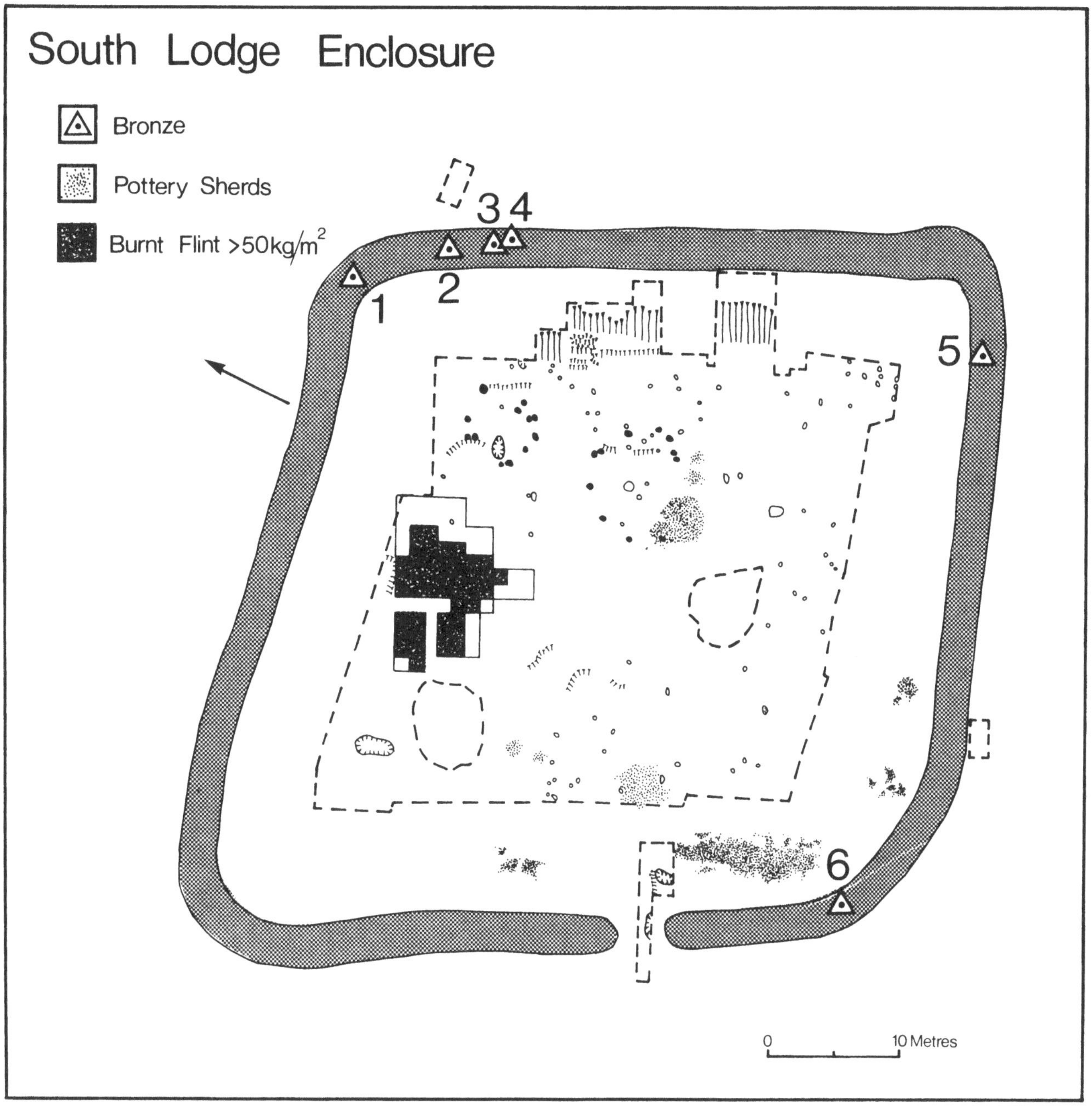

Fig. 5.13 Plan of the South Lodge enclosure, showing the main post-built structures, the burnt mound and the distribution of pottery and bronze finds recorded by Pitt Rivers

forated tang. These associations embrace: Food Vessels, Pygmy Cups, Cordoned Urns, Collared Urns, Cornish Urns and Biconical Urns, and also battle-axes (Jockenhovel 1980, 46–9).

Associations of early razors with chronologically diagnostic bronzes are scarce. Burgess illustrates the occurrence of Class Ib razors in his Stage VI by the example from Bryn Crug, Caernarvonshire, whose dating relies on the continental parallels of its trilobate-headed pin in the Lochham phase (Burgess 1980, 124, Fig. 3:11,8; Gerloff 1975, 121). The razor, perhaps of British origin, in the Sogel burial from Drouwen, Drenthe, Netherlands, is of similar date (Jockenhovel 1980, 39:68, 49 n. 49; O'Connor 1980, 342:75). Jockenhovel regards the hoard finds, Glentrool, Kirkcudbrightshire, and Chailloue, Orne, as residual; both are dated to the Penard phase (1980, nos. 80 and 94, 49).

Class I razors appear to be typologically heterogeneous, not surprisingly, given the worn or damaged condition of many examples. They may have been current during five of Burgess's metalworking stages, VI to X. The awl found just above the bottom of the ditch in its southern corner does not assist the dating (*Excavations* IV, Pl. 238:2). It is more slender than the usual single-pointed form and square in section, with its point broken. It lacks the marked distinction between the rectangular-sectioned tang and round-sectioned point characteristic of single-pointed awls.

The second, notched, razor belongs to Piggott's original Class II (1946, 138:41). Burgess implies a Taunton date for this example, although he does not include notched razors among metalwork characteristic of this phase and has previously placed them in the Penard phase (Burgess 1980, 134; 1974, 205). Burgess illustrates this razor alongside one from the Rosnoen hoard, Finistère, and another from the Thames at Richmond (Burgess 1969, Fig. 4:7 and 9). Both belong to Jockenhovel's Henon type (1980, 58–61, nos. 137 and 151). That from Richmond is the only British example of this type characteristic of *Bronze final* I in northern France. This single import, or local Henon variant, seems insufficient to restrict the appearance of notched razors in Britain to the Penard phase. Jockenhovel places the South Lodge example beside that from the Taunton hoard, Somerset, whilst identifying the second razor from the Glentrool hoard also as a notched razor. Again the varied form and damaged condition of these razors caution against close dating derived from the metalworking sequence.

A find relevant to the South Lodge material is the razor from amongst the homogeneous group of bronzes from the settlement site of Black Patch, Alciston, Sussex (Drewett 1982, 361, Fig. 29:1). Although damaged, this razor has a roughly rectangular blade and possible remains of a notch. The razor came from pit 3 in hut 3 and grain from this pit has been given a date of 1070 ± 70 bc (HAR 2940). The Black Patch example is slightly larger than the South Lodge notched razor. Two single-pointed awls and a broad double-edged tanged knife were found in the same building (Drewett 1982, Fig. 29:2 and 6–7).

A stone mould from near Ballymena, Co. Antrim, combines matrices for oval-bladed and notched razors, indicating that the two examples from South Lodge could be contemporary (Piggott 1946, 141, Fig. 10; Jockenhovel 1980, 53, nos. 120–1).

The form of the ribbed bracelet, from the same depth in the ditch as the notched razor, is part of the Taunton phase 'ornament horizon' and was probably derived from French examples of *Bronze moyen* date (O'Connor 1980, 85–6).

Table 5.3. *South Lodge enclosure, distribution of pottery sherds recorded in the nineteenth century*

	'Interior'	'Bank'	'Ditch'
Bronze Age	435	851	251
Roman	16	1	91

The bronze wire from a similar depth in the ditch is also a characteristic component of the 'ornament horizon' (Smith 1959, 146; Rowlands 1976, 92–3). Slender wire occurs, for example, in hoards from Monkswood and Taunton, Somerset (Inv. Arch. GB42, 10–11; 43, 13), although this appears to be thicker than the South Lodge wire.

Finally the side-looped spearhead from high in the ditch (*Excavations* IV, Pl. 238:1) has 'string' loops and an angular midrib, characteristic of Rowlands' group 2 (1976, 52). Hoard finds suggest a Taunton date for these spearheads, but this is probably not exclusive.

Worked bone Only three pieces of worked bone are recorded from the site, all of which were recovered in the earlier excavations (*Excavations* IV, 16 and 26, Pls. 234, 237 and 238). Two bone awls were found in the area behind the western bank and south of the entrance. Another pointed and perforated artefact came from the mid-point of the eastern ditch, 3 ft (0.91 m) from the surface.

The pottery[1] The pottery analysis established a fabric sequence for the later prehistoric material from Cranborne Chase and is presented in the companion volume. A total of twenty-four fabrics was identified, and these are referred to simply by fabric number in the analysis presented here. In the case of the South Lodge material a record of all the contextual information from the nineteenth-century archive was also established and the maximum dimension of each sherd was recorded.

Using the full nineteenth-century record and the material recovered between 1977 and 1981, we can make the following assertions about the pottery distribution.

(1) The published nineteenth-century account is misleading. Most of the pottery is recorded as from the 'rampart' (*Excavations* IV, Pl. 237), but the unpublished plan shows that a high proportion of this material was recovered from the back of the western lynchet bank, to the south of the entrance (Fig. 5.13).

(2) Most of the Bronze Age pottery comes from the enclosure rather than the ditch. This is in marked contrast to the Roman material, which clearly accumulated in the upper hollow of the infilled ditch (Table 5.3).

(3) The marked concentrations of pottery within the

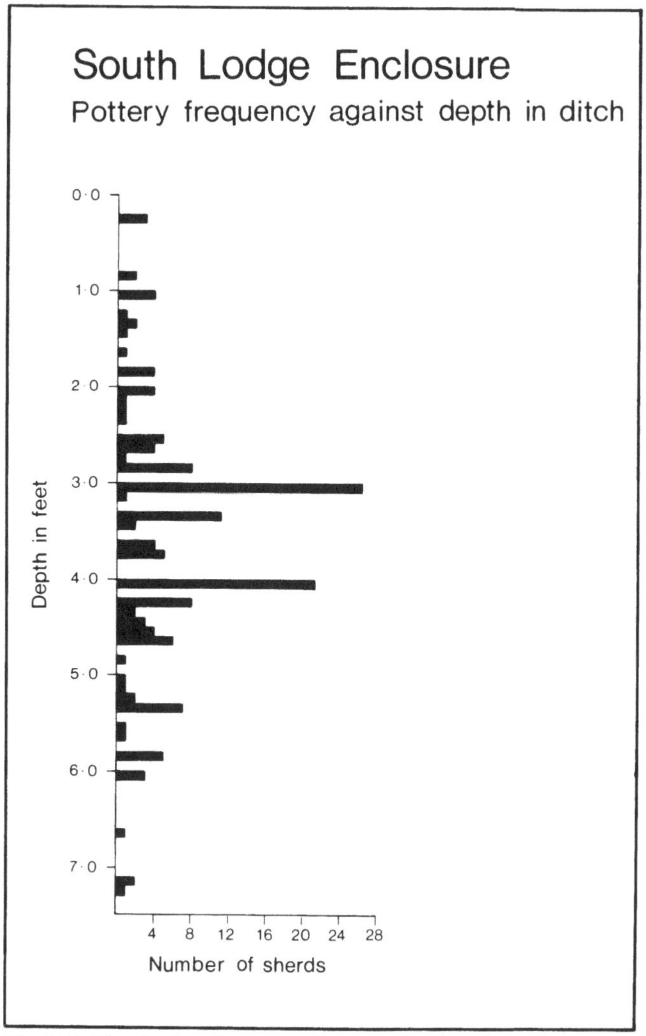

Fig. 5.14 The absolute frequency of pottery sherds at the various depths in the South Lodge enclosure ditch

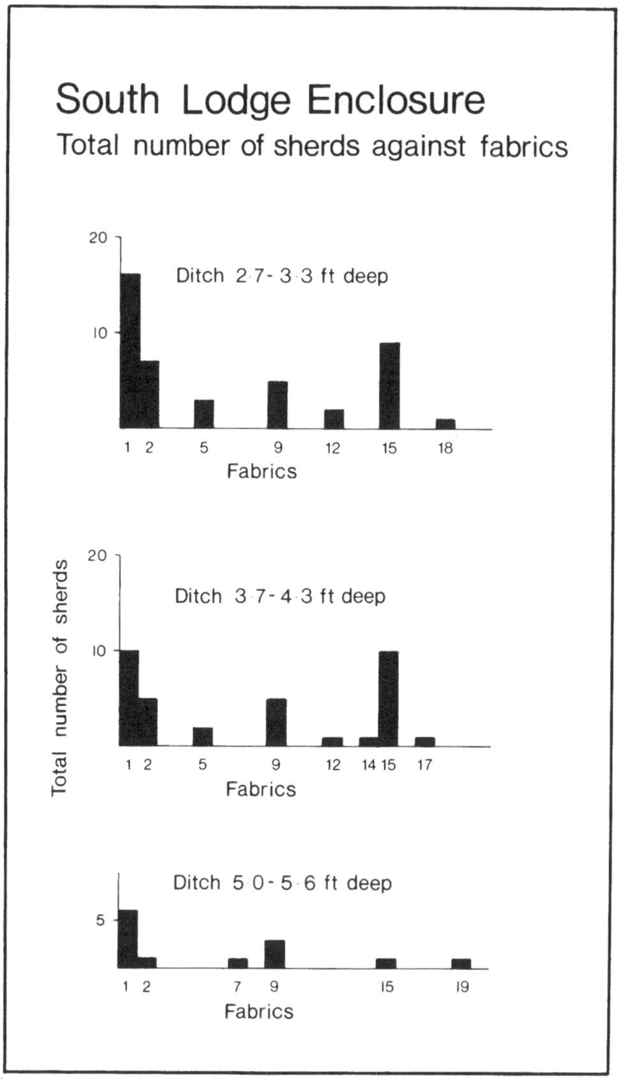

Fig. 5.15 Comparative frequency of pottery fabrics from three levels within the South Lodge enclosure ditch

enclosure (Fig. 5.13) are not reflected in the ditch deposits: the southern terminal of the ditch, for example, has relatively little pottery, whilst it is here, behind the rampart, that one of the major sherd concentrations occurs.

(4) Most of the pottery from within the ditch comes from depths recorded between 2.5 ft (0.76 m) and 4.5 ft (1.37 m) (Fig. 5.14). There is no major variation in the range of fabrics recovered throughout the ditch stratigraphy, as demonstrated here by comparing material from 5.0–5.6 ft (1.50–1.71 m), 3.7–4.3 ft (1.13–1.31 m) and 2.7–3.3 ft (0.82–1.01 m) (Fig. 5.15).

(5) Within the enclosure some distinction can be made between the pottery recorded from the 'internal rise' within Structure 2, the sherds from the south-western corner of the enclosure, and those recovered by us in the southern section through the lynchet (D004) (i.e. behind the south-western rampart terminal). Firstly, the range of fabrics differs, with two fabrics (3 and 4) being unrepresented amongst the rampart material (and, incidentally, amongst the ditch assemblage) (Fig. 5.16). Secondly, the overall sizes of the sherds differ (Fig. 5.17). Comparison of sherds belonging to the coarse fabric 1, for example, indicates that the larger sherds occurred in the deposit at the south-western corner of the site.

A range of the pottery forms is illustrated here (Fig. 5.18). In all some 1,650 Bronze Age sherds were recovered from all contexts around the enclosure, not in itself a large amount of pottery. They represent a range of large storage and cooking vessels, the main distinctions being between the coarser Bucket Urn with fingertip-decorated strips and cordons around the rim and

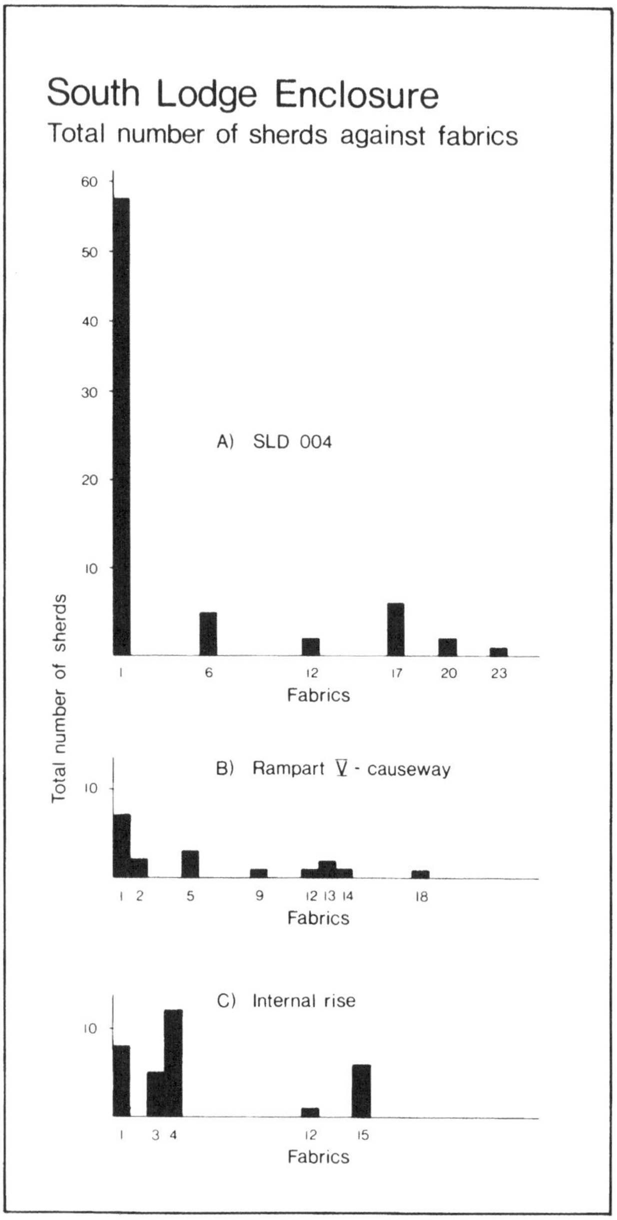

Fig. 5.16 Comparative frequency of pottery fabrics from three contexts within the South Lodge enclosure

girth of the vessel, and Barrel Urns, which have distinctive fabrics, thin body walls and slight fingertip-decorated strips built into the body of the vessel. Some of these cordons run vertically down the wall of the pot. The third vessel class is defined by a different form, a globular body, and decorative techniques which avoid the use of fingertip impressions, using instead slight rilling or fluting around the body of the vessel.

This threefold division amongst such domestic assemblages has long been recognised (Calkin 1962) and remains unchallenged by the South Lodge pottery. The degree of nineteenth-century labelling associated with the material, and the small size of the overall assemblage, precludes a more detailed analysis of the distribution of the various ceramic types within the enclosure.

One notable find is the almost complete Barrel Urn found 'on the bottom' of the eastern arm of the enclosure ditch (*Excavations* IV, 240).

Stone

Sandstone: Pitt Rivers records the discovery of two fragments of saddle quern (*Excavations* IV, 37). One was found 'in the body of the rampart' on the southern side of the enclosure in the eastern half of the bank. The second lay amongst the pottery of the 'internal rise' on the floor of Structure 2.

Flint[2]: Pitt Rivers' recovery of flint was low and confined almost entirely to implements. Large quantities of struck flakes thus remained in the backfill from his trenching. There are therefore two levels of recovery of flint from the enclosure: those areas excavated for the first time between 1977 and 1981, and the material collected from nineteenth-century backfill, which was hand dug, over the eastern half of the site.

In the areas excavated for the first time a number of observations can be made (Figs. 5.19–21).

(1) A small concentration of scrapers occurs outside the limits of Structure 1, whilst cores cluster to the west of the structure, only two being found within the post-ring itself. The density of flint flakes in this part of the site is low, the only concentration being from Pit A011 cutting the floor of the building.

(2) Slight concentrations of flakes are found beyond the limits of the building to the east and west. Terrace A also has a minor concentration of flintwork, including some cores and scrapers. Burnt flints, which also respect Structure 1, spread over Terrace A, building up towards the edge of the burnt mound to the west.

(3) In the unexcavated length of eastern lynchet/rampart a concentration of flakes was recovered to the east of Structure 2. To the south of this lay a concentration of burnt flint and cores.

In examining the material recovered from nineteenth-century backfill we might attempt to search for broad distinctions in the distribution, on the assumption that, whilst the material will obviously have been displaced by excavation, the techniques of trenching will have blurred rather than have eradicated totally the original distributions. Again we stress that we are only able to examine the material from the eastern half of the enclosure. The distribution of the material has been studied

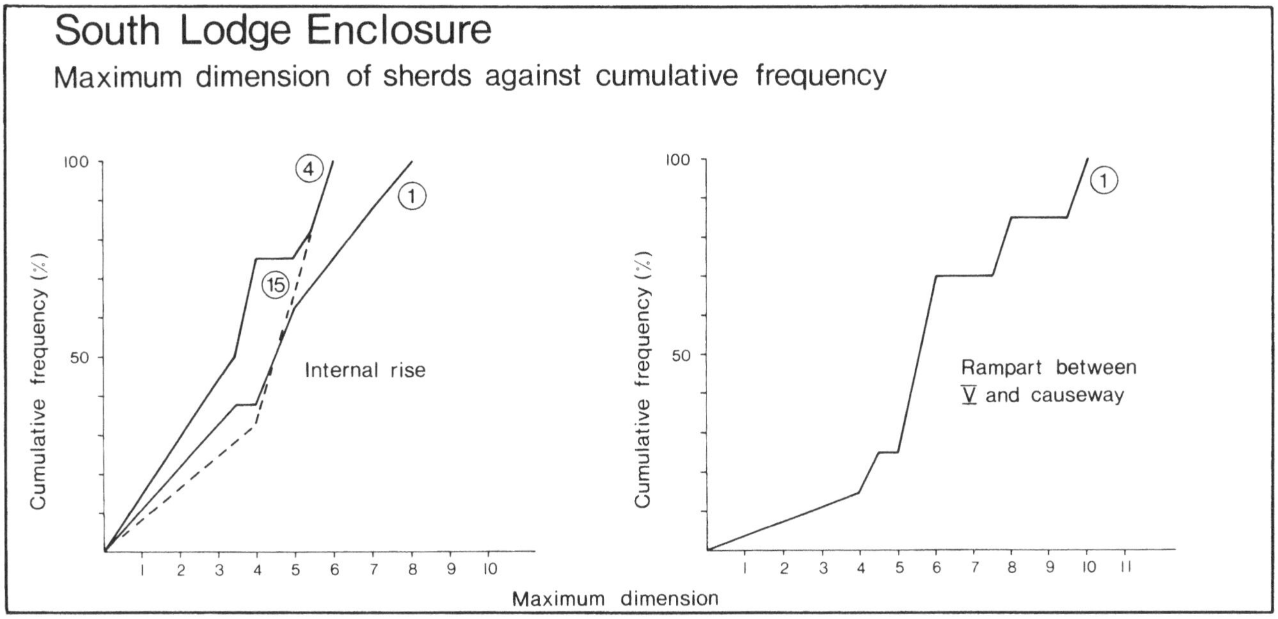

Fig. 5.17 The cumulative frequency of sherd sizes from the surface deposits within Structure 2 and from behind the eastern enclosure bank. Note that sherds of fabric 1 are larger in the latter deposit (sherd size in mm)

on the basis of a 5 m grid and the mean density of flakes calculated on this basis (Fig. 5.20).

Most of the material comes from the vicinity of Structure 1 and the eastern half edge of the area, falling away rapidly towards the centre of the site. The highest concentration of worked flint comes from the area of Structure 1.

Some general comments on the entire body of the material may now be possible:

(1) Concentrations of cores are found around Structure 1, also the inner, southern limits of the eastern bank and to the west of the burnt mound. Pitt Rivers records another concentration of cores to the south of the entrance causeway on the inner edge of the bank (*Excavations* IV, 28).

(2) Most implements were regularly retouched. The distribution of this material respects Structure 1, with nearly all the regular implements to the west and the expedient tools to the east of the building. A similar division is present among the small collection of implements recovered by Pitt Rivers from the eastern ditch of the enclosure. Another concentration of implement finds comes from the south-eastern edge of the enclosure around posthole cluster 4.

(3) The two fabricators came from the edge of Structure 2 in the area previously excavated.

Animal bone: a possible cow burial[4] The bones from A011 are rather poorly preserved, and have suffered considerable damage during the period of burial. Given their very fragile state, there is also some degree of excavation damage. All the bones are from a small cow; the metatarsal dimensions indicate an animal of similar size to the two animals buried around the Down Farm pond barrow.

The bones are from the left side of the body, with the exception of a few vertebrae fragments, and both right and left lower M_3. One possibility would be that the pit had contained a complete cow burial, placed upon its left side, with the more exposed upper parts becoming severely eroded to the point of dissolution. However likely this might seem, the representation of body parts supports an alternative explanation. When cattle or other mammals are buried whole (as at the Down Farm pond barrow) it is likely that limb extremities would lie at the same level; the carcase would most naturally lie on one or other side, and while bones such as the uppermost scapula or innominate might suffer differential exposure to erosion, the left and right feet would be more equally buried. In the South Lodge case, *only* the lower left limb bones were found. It would therefore appear that only the left side was buried. The bones do not show signs of breaking due to butchery; though most are damaged, parts of both articulations usually survive. The presence of a few damaged vertebrae, right and left lower third molars and some rib fragments suggests that the right front and hind limbs were removed before the remainder of the carcase was buried.

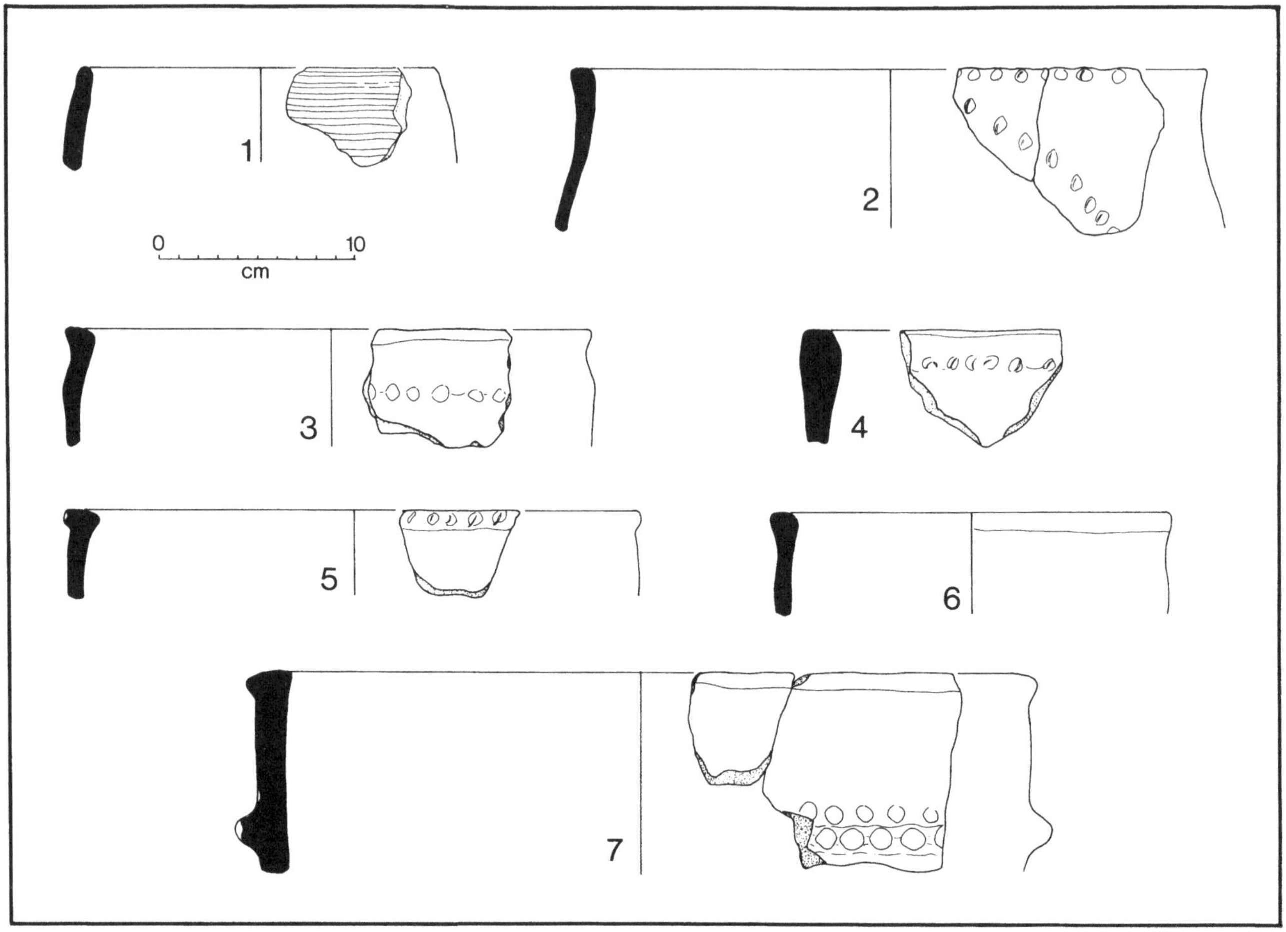

Fig. 5.18 Selection of pottery sherds from the South Lodge enclosure

5.2.5 The barrow cemetery

5.2.5.i Introduction

Between 1880 and 1883, five round-barrow mounds were excavated on an area of land known as Barrow Pleck (BP) lying some 100 m north-east of the South Lodge enclosure, Rushmore (Fig. 5.3). Pitt Rivers' original numbering of the mounds (2, 3, 4, 18, 21 cf. Grinsell 1957, 156) is retained here (*Excavations* II, 1 ff.). Pitt Rivers records the existence of a further, unnumbered, mound which had been 'destroyed for the sake of the materials' (*Excavations* II, 2) before his arrival at Rushmore.

Our own excavation had two primary objectives. First, we wished to reinvestigate the mounds of Barrows 3 and 18 in the hope that the mound structure had survived. This would give information on their construction, the nature of any buried soil, and on any burial deposits which might have been missed by the earlier excavators. Secondly, we planned to investigate the area around the mounds in the hope of tracing satellite deposits. In the event none of the mound structures and no buried soils survived the nineteenth-century excavation.

The sampling strategy was designed to locate any additional groups of cremations which might have been buried beyond the outer edges of the barrow ditches. A number of such deposits are known from elsewhere (Ellison 1980a), and we used this information to determine the required sample size. A 5 per cent sample of the ground extending 10 m beyond the outer lip of each barrow ditch was examined by a random series of 2 m squares. The location of these squares was determined by a central point fixed by two randomly generated coordinates. The first was a compass bearing selected between 1 and 360° and taken from the centre of the mound, the second was a distance between 1 and 10 m measured from the outer edge of the ditch. The sampling procedure was devised by Stephen Cogbill.

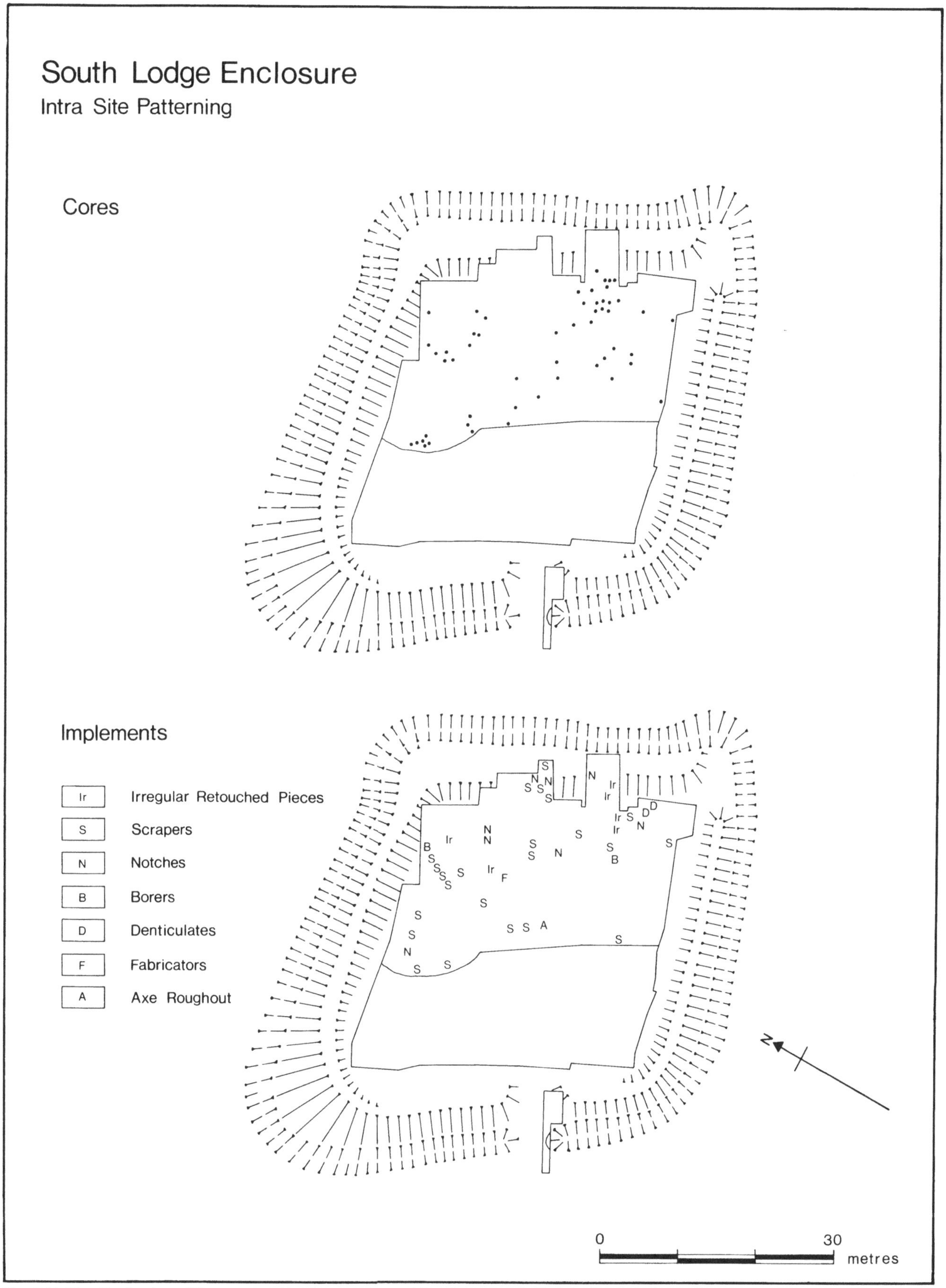

Fig. 5.19 The distribution of flint cores and implements from within the eastern half of the South Lodge enclosure

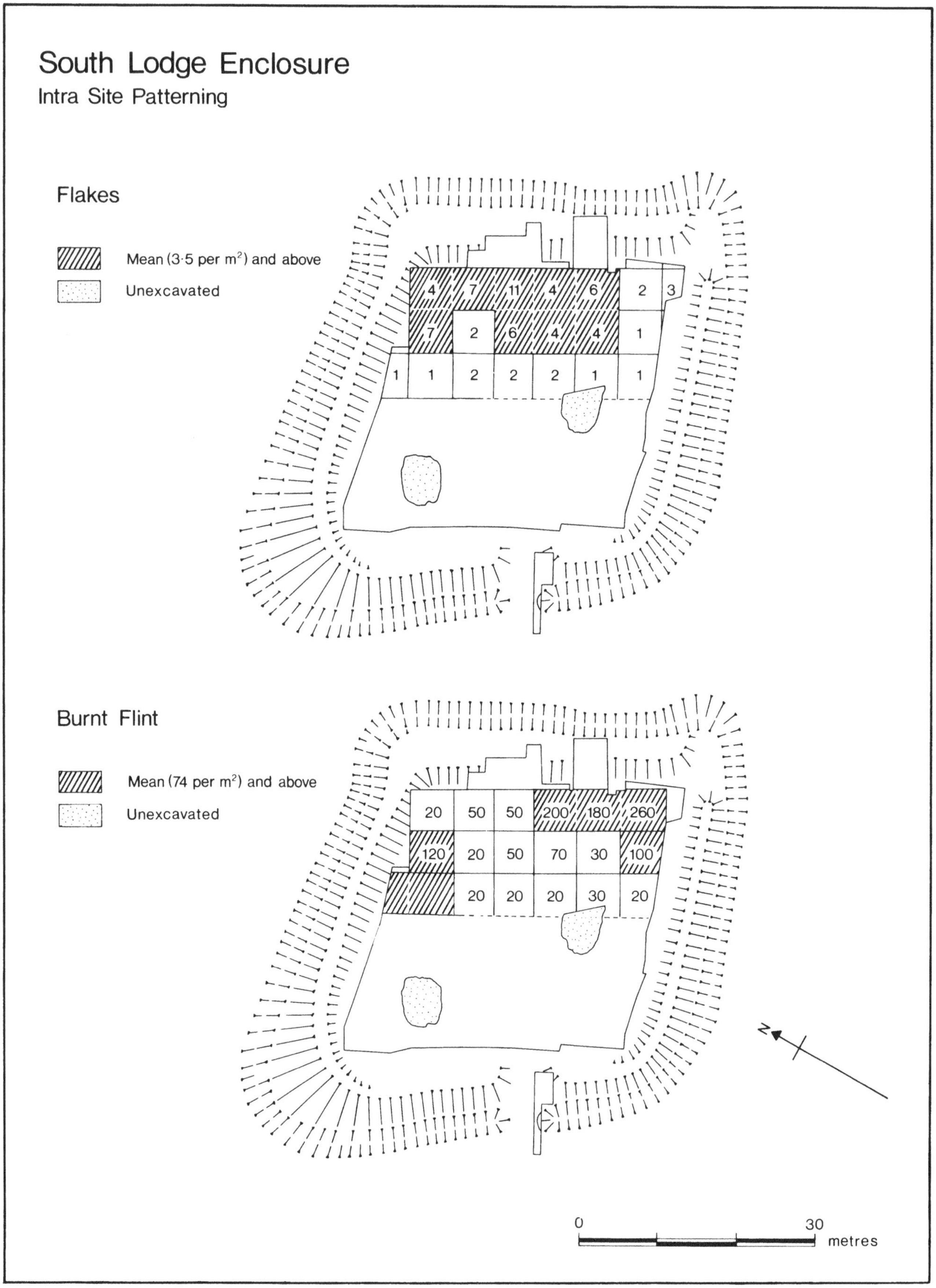

Fig. 5.20 The distribution of flint flakes and burnt flint from the eastern half of the South Lodge enclosure

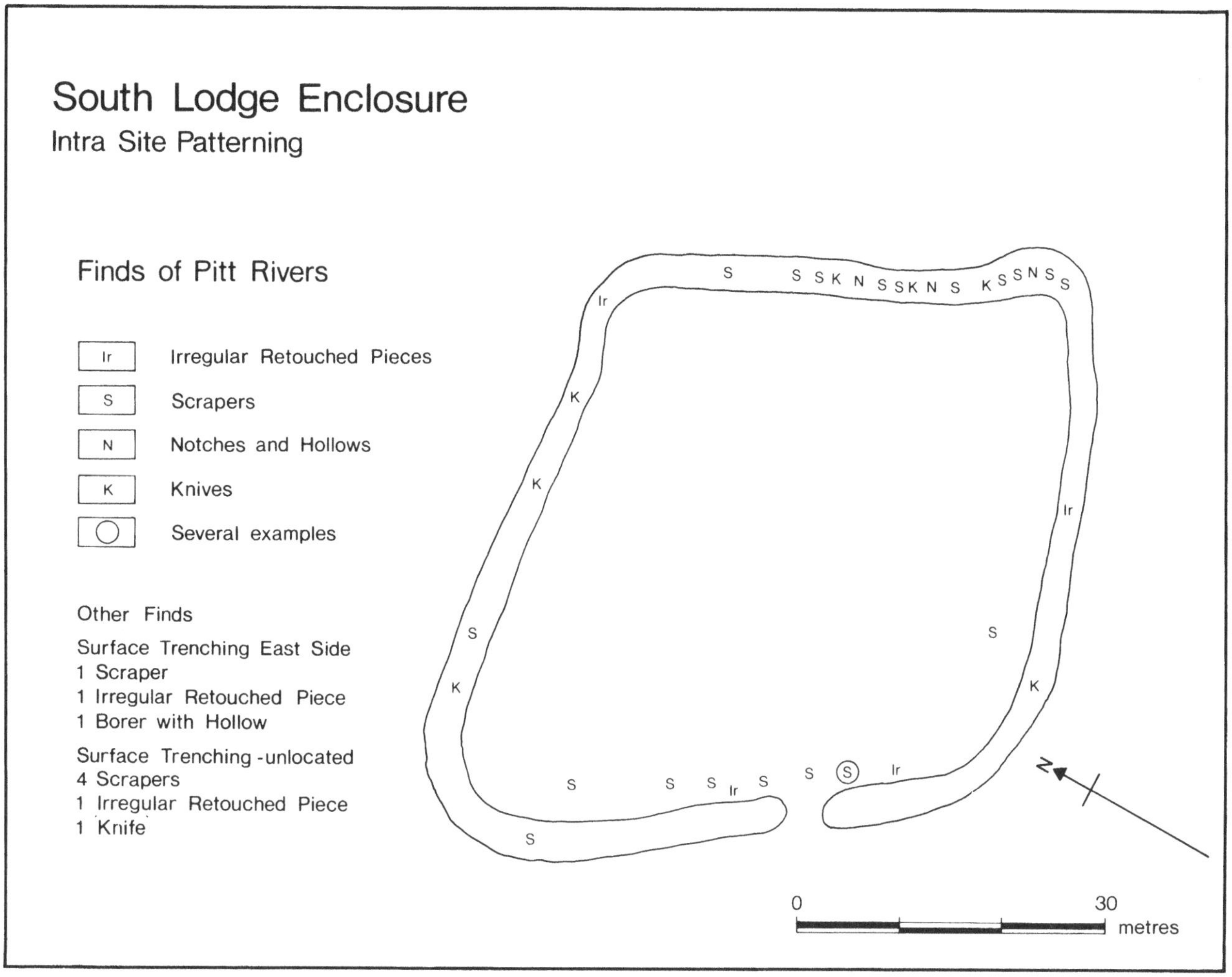

Fig. 5.21 The distribution of flint tools recorded by Pitt Rivers from the South Lodge enclosure

5.2.5.ii Barrows 2, 3 and 21 (Human bone identified by Juliet Rogers)

Before the original excavations, the ditches around these and the other mounds were not visible on the surface (*Excavations* II, 28 ff.). These three mounds cluster at the north-eastern extremity of the cemetery, and excavation had totally removed each of the mounds and most of the ditch fill around Barrow 3.

Barrow 3 originally stood to a height of 4.5 ft (1.37 m). It was surrounded by a chalk-cut ditch, with a maximum overall diameter to the outer lip of 17 m. After excavation, the mound had been restored around a concrete plinth, built into the southern part of the mound, which marked the position of the nine cremations which had been discovered (Fig. 5.22 and Plate 2). Barrows 2 and 21 were smaller, Barrow 2 was 1.5 ft (0.46 m) high and Barrow 21 had only a 'very slight elevation above the natural surface' (*Excavations* II, 20). Single cremations were recovered from within each of these mounds, and in the case of Barrow 2 the position was again marked by a small concrete plinth. We do not know whether a similar practice was followed in the case of Barrow 21.

The re-excavation of this cemetery involved cutting a section back into the nineteenth-century mound of Barrow 3 around the area which produced the original cremations. An area to the south of the barrow was also excavated, involving the removal of the nineteenth-century mound of Barrow 2 and the excavation of its previously undiscovered ditch. Barrow 21 was not available for excavation, being covered in dense undergrowth behind the park fence.

This part of the cemetery appears to have developed with one major and two secondary foci, although we know little about the original mound structures which

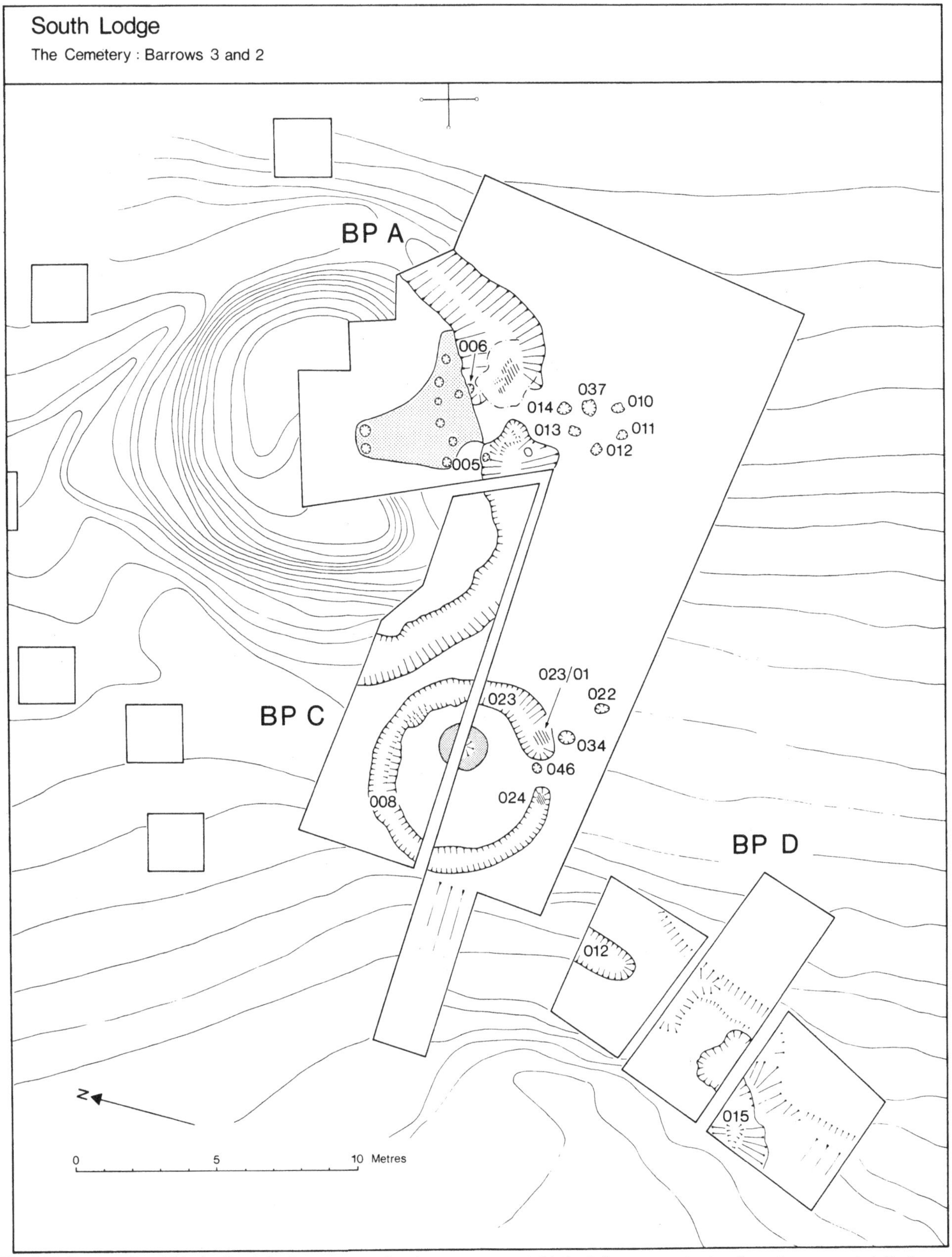

Fig. 5.22 Barrows 2 and 3 in the South Lodge cemetery, showing areas excavated (stippled areas are nineteenth-century concreted display plinths) (contours at 0.1 m)

Plate 2 Re-excavation of the restored mound of South Lodge Barrow 3, viewed from the south. This shows the nineteenth-century concrete display plinths which marked the location of pits containing deposits of cremated bone

formed these foci. This apparently simple arrangement in fact facilitated a complex set of choices in the spatial ordering of the burial deposits by the use of the areas within the mounds, the ditches, the ditch causeways and the level ground beyond the ditches.

(1) Within or beneath the mound of Barrow 3, nine deposits of cremated bone had been placed in 'round basin-shaped holes, cut in the chalk floor' (*Excavations* II, 29). Two of these were central to the area of the mound, whilst the other seven lay on the south-eastern edge (Fig. 5.22). (For details of these deposits see *Excavations* II, 11; the material no longer survives in the museum collections.)

One of the central deposits was accompanied by fragments of urn, the other was not. Of the remaining cremations excavated by Pitt Rivers, four were also accompanied by deposits of pottery. In all cases no complete urn is represented and a mixture of urn sherds occurred in the same deposits (*Excavations* II, Pl. 86:10 and 12).

(2) The ditch silt had been almost totally removed, but traces of an upper ditch fill did survive in part of the western terminal. The ditch was a fairly irregular feature some 1.5 m wide but expanding towards the terminals on either side of a single, southern causeway. Its depth averaged 0.60 m. In the western terminal, against the edge of the barrow mound, traces of the original ditch fill still survived. A chalky silt (BPA 020) was overlain by a dense concentration of flint nodules within a clay matrix (BPA 064). By analogy with the deposits around the ditches of Barrows 2 and 18, these flints were a deliberate deposit of material which may have been placed in a recut along the top of the ditch. Dug into this, and packed around with flints, was a cremation deposit (BPA 005). The cremated bone was of a single adult contained within a Bucket Urn. This urn had neither rim nor base. A radiocarbon date of 1060 ± 120 bc (BM 1917R) was obtained for this deposit.

Fragments of cremation and a few urn sherds from the nineteenth-century backfill imply that other cremations may also have been placed in the ditch. The only other recorded find from the ditch is a small fragment of a twisted bronze neckring (*Excavations* II, Pl. 86:5).

(3) Pitt Rivers recovered a single cremation from the centre of the causeway, but it is not known whether this was accompanied by pottery sherds.

Cutting into the eastern edge of the causeway, and the top of the ditch terminal, was the grave of a single inhumation, orientated north-west–south-east, crouched and lying on its left side (Fig. 5.22) (*Excavations* II, 11). The bones from this burial no longer survive amongst the museum collections.

(4) A small group of cremations had been buried immediately beyond the causeway outside the mound (Figs. 5.22 and 5.23). These were:

(a) BPA010: a pit 0.4 m wide and 0.2 m deep, containing the cremation of at least a single individual and sherds of a Bucket Urn. A radiocarbon date of 950 ± 150 bc (BM 1918R) was obtained for this deposit.
(b) BPA011: a few Bucket Urn sherds overlay the top of a pit 0.4 m wide and 0.2 m deep, containing burnt flint and the cremated bones of at least one adult. No pottery came from within the pit itself. A radiocarbon date of 1190 ± 120 bc (BM 1919R) was obtained for this deposit.
(c) BPA012: a pit 0.5 m wide and 0.15 m deep, which contained some burnt flint and the cremation of at least one adult.
(d) BPA013: a pit 0.4 m wide and 0.2 m deep, containing part of a Bucket Urn, a sherd of another vessel and some unidentifiable cremated bone.
(e) BPA014: a pit 0.5 m wide and 0.15 m deep containing the cremation of at least one adult at the bottom of the feature, over which had been placed the base of a Globular Urn, burnt flint and further cremated bone. A radiocarbon date of 1010 ± 120 bc (BM 2024R) was obtained for this deposit.
(f) BPA037: a pit 0.5 m wide and 0.1 m deep, containing a small deposit of unidentifiable cremated bone, a few sherds of pottery and some burnt flint.

The mound of Barrow 2 was totally removed in the nineteenth century and then restored around a small concrete plinth which marked the findspot of a single cremation. Our own excavations removed most of the restored mound and examined the ditch and an area beyond the barrow (Fig. 5.22).

(1) The single cremation from within the mound is recorded as coming from a 2 ft (0.61 m) wide 'basin shaped hole cut in the solid chalk ... no pottery or charcoal, but several flint flakes were found' with this cremation (*Excavations* II, 29). To the south of the modern plinth lay a shallow, curving trench cut into the top of the chalk. The fill was loose chalk mixed with a little charcoal and a few flecks of cremated bone. This feature certainly seems to have resulted from the nineteenth-century excavations and it may indicate that additional cremated material was disturbed without being recognised.

(2) The ditch around Barrow 2 was not located by Pitt Rivers. It had an overall diameter of 7.0 m and was on average 1.0 m wide and 0.6 m deep. There was a single 1.0 m wide causeway and the eastern ditch terminal had been dug with a slight expansion, although this may be the result of a re-cutting (below). The ditch of Barrow 2 was cut close to, but did not intercut, that of Barrow 3. It seems likely that Barrow 2 was the later structure.

The ditch contained a primary chalk filling (BPA031 and 065), which was cut away at the top of the ditch to contain a brown clay soil densely packed with flint nodules (BPA023 and 063, BPC008). Into this secondary deposit, and probably contemporary with it, were placed two cremations:

(a) BPA024: the cremation of at least one adult in the western terminal of the ditch. In its upper fill, burnt flint and cremated bone were found together, overlying the main concentration of cremated bone. No other material was associated with this deposit.

(b) BPA02301: the cremation of at least one adult overlain by a dense concentration of flint nodules. Amongst the cremated bone lay the contorted tip of a bronze spearhead. Towards the bottom of the deposit a dense concentration of charcoal was recovered. A very small fragment of pottery was also recovered from this feature. Two radiocarbon dates were obtained for this deposit: 940 ± 120 bc (BM 1920R) and 950 ± 110 bc (BM 2023R).

(3) A 1.0 m wide causeway separated the ditch terminals; BPA046 was a 0.4 m wide shallow scoop dug slightly off-centre into that causeway, containing the cremation of at least one juvenile aged between four and five years, mixed with some charcoal.

(4) Beyond the limits of the ditch and to the east of the causeway lay one further cremation and a possible posthole (Fig. 5.23):

(a) BPA034: a pit 0.5 m wide and 0.2 m deep, containing the cremation of at least one adult.
(b) BPA022: a 0.2 m deep posthole.

The sample squares excavated in the available areas around Barrows 2 and 3 failed to reveal any further burial deposits.

5.2.5.iii Barrow 4

Pitt Rivers records Barrow 4 as being the largest mound in the cemetery, standing 8.5 ft (2.59 m) high, with a diameter of 40 ft (12.19 m). Pitt Rivers had a trench driven in from the southern side of the mound to expose a large area at the centre of the mound (*Excavations* II, 11–12, Pl. 81). Here a complex group of deposits was recorded cutting into the chalk. A 'basin shaped' pit 2.75

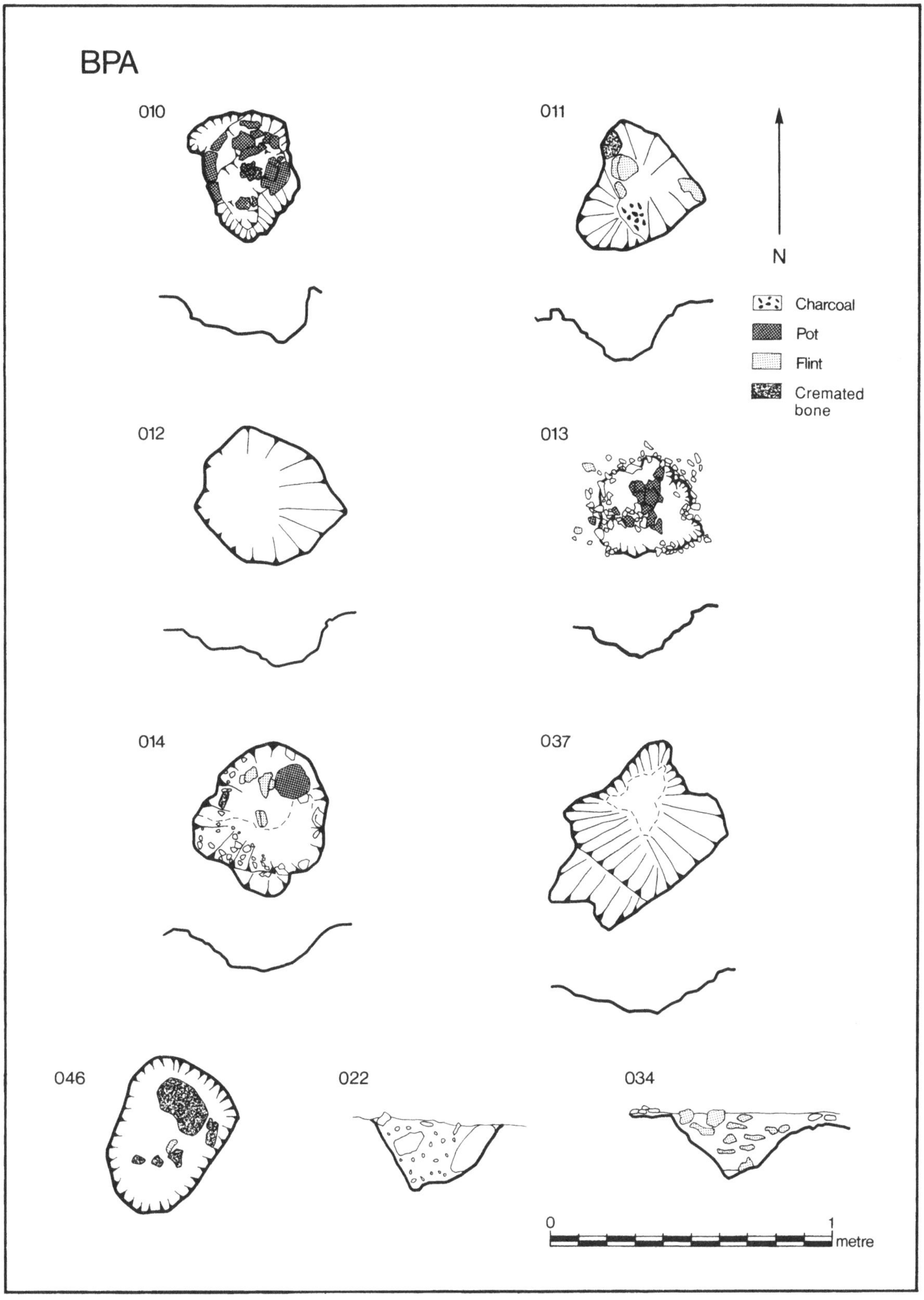

Fig. 5.23 Plans and sections of Bronze Age features around Barrows 2 and 3

ft (0.84 m) deep was found in the centre of the mound but no deposit was recorded. Three 'stakeholes' were observed to the west, south and cutting (?) the northern edge of the pit. To the south-west of the pit, presumably on the natural chalk, lay a cremation, whilst the lower part of a Barrel Urn was found 'standing' on the chalk 7 ft (2.13 m) to the east of the pit. No deposit was recorded from the urn. Animal bones were recovered 'west of the centre' of the mound.

No details of mound stratigraphy are recorded; consequently it is difficult to interpret these deposits. It is possible, for example, that the cremation and the Barrel Urn were dug into the barrow or into a smaller primary mound from above rather than being buried beneath such a structure. We certainly have evidence that the mound had a complex structural history (below). A small sherd of Later Neolithic pottery came from the material of this barrow (*Excavations* II, Pl. 86).

As restored, Barrow 4 is substantial (Fig. 5.24) and re-excavation of this mound was not attempted. Pitt Rivers records that the ditch was totally excavated, except for the section which ran under the road. BPG was dug against the road and over the line of the ditch to recover any of these unexcavated ditch deposits.

The remaining excavations around the barrow were in the form of 2 m sample squares. One of these uncovered a large, chalk-cut pit, and BPH was dug to investigate this feature.

1. BPG. Unexcavated ditch deposits were recovered in the area of this trench. The eroded profile of the ditch was 2.5 m wide at the top and 0.9 m deep (Fig. 5.25). Primary deposits of a fine chalk wash (BPG00202) were overlain, and may have been cut into by, a deposit of brown clay soil containing a high concentration of flint nodules (BPG00203). On the northern edge of the trench a chalk lens lying within this upper deposit presumably represents material eroding from the barrow. The flint deposit is similar to the upper deposits recorded in the ditches of Barrows 2 and 3 (above) and Barrow 18 (below).

2. BPH. This large, chalk-cut pit lay just beyond the outer lip of the barrow ditch. Most of the pit was excavated. The feature measured 3.5 m north–south by at least 4.5 m east–west and around 0.9 m deep (Figs. 5.24 and 5.25). The basal deposits were the result of natural chalk erosion (BPH00103 and 00102), overlain by a soil containing small stone and chalk particles, interpreted as a ploughsoil (BPH00101).

3. The proposed sequence for the ditch and quarry pit is as follows:

(1) A primary mound was constructed partly or wholly from material derived from the ditch. The ditch then began to silt.

(2) The mound was capped by chalk derived from a single quarry pit. The pit began to silt but then formed a catchment for ploughsoil deriving from cultivation in the immediate vicinity of the mound.

(3) The upper line of the barrow ditch was redefined around the time that the same thing was happening to other barrow ditches in the cemetery. This redefinition involved re-cutting and the addition of a flint cairn in the top of the ditch.

5.2.5.iv *The snail fauna from BPG and BPH*[5,6]

The analyses indicate that the ditch and quarry silts accumulated in a predominantly shaded environment. There is very little variation between the samples. The barrow ditch is characterised by large quantities of *Discus rotundatus, Carychium tridentatum* and the *Zonitidae*. The quarry ditch also has large numbers of *D. rotundatus* and *Zonitidae* but *C. tridentatum* is only present in small numbers and there are slightly higher proportions of *Pomatias elegans*. Taken together, these factors suggest that, in the case of the quarry pit, the surface was looser, the vegetation cover less complete, and the situation drier than in the ditch. This may reflect the later clearance of the quarry pit at the time of cultivation.

5.2.5.v *The destroyed mound*

Pitt Rivers places this unnumbered mound to the north of Barrow 4 and west of Barrow 2 (*Excavations* II, Pl. 80). The mound is still recorded, lying between the two surviving mounds on the Ordnance Survey 1:2500 sheet (ST 9517). The ground in this area was observed to have been disturbed, and three trenches (BPD) (Fig. 5.22) were dug across a well-defined north–south scarp. It was intended that this excavation should reveal any ditch associated with the destroyed mound.

The excavation revealed a series of heavily disturbed deposits, mainly derived from nineteenth-century quarrying. A water pipe also ran through this area. Below these disturbances the Coombe Rock had been cut into a series of irregular hollows, containing a quantity of worked flint. BPD015 appeared to represent the fill of a very irregularly dug ditch swinging south-west out of the excavated area. BPD012 was more regular, a short, shallow length of ditch terminating in the area excavated and running north. At most this feature penetrated 0.4 m into the bedrock and it was not found in BPA. Neither of these features seems a particularly likely candidate for a barrow ditch.

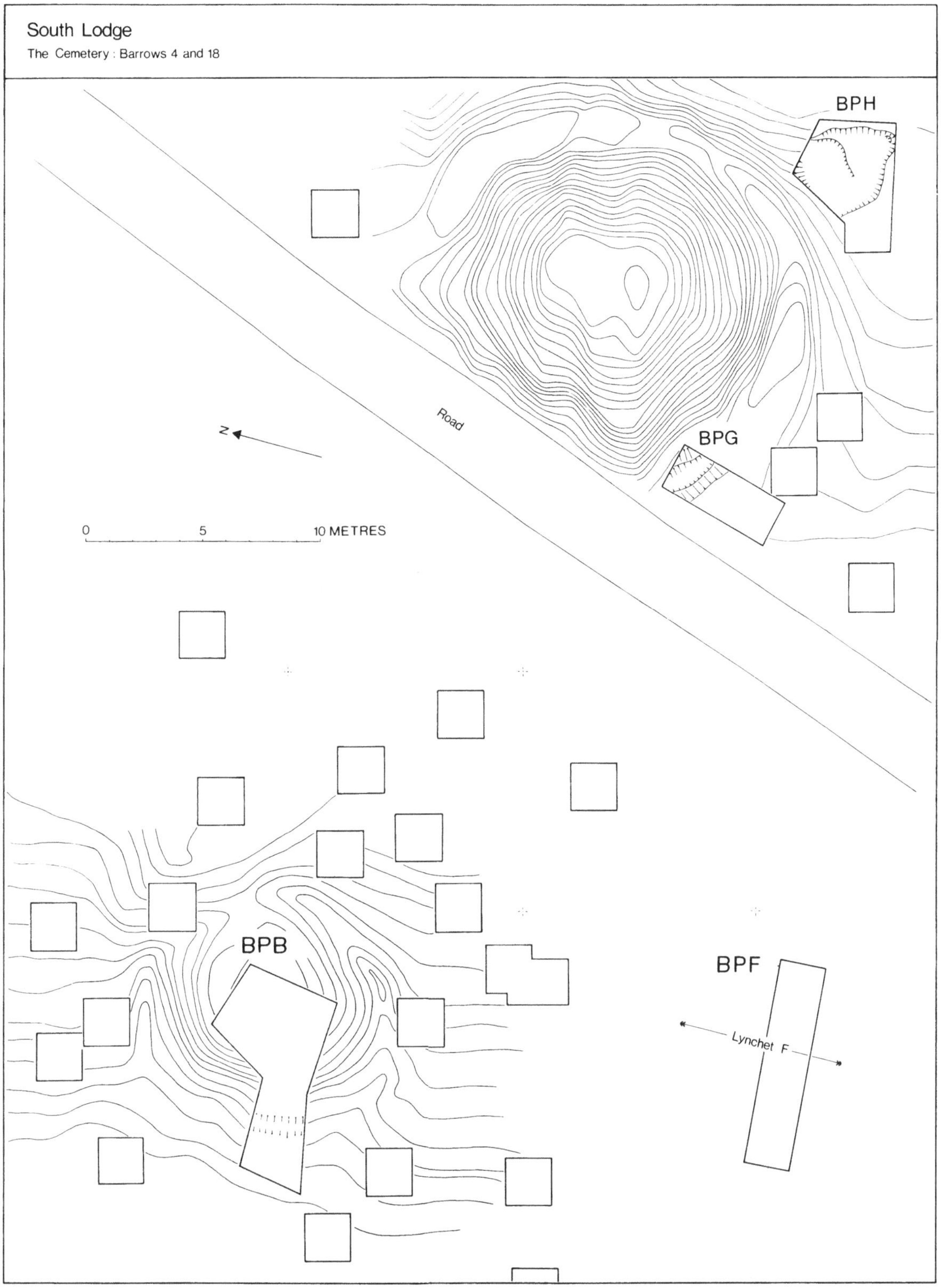

Fig. 5.24 Barrows 4 and 18 in the South Lodge cemetery, showing areas excavated (contours at 0.1 m)

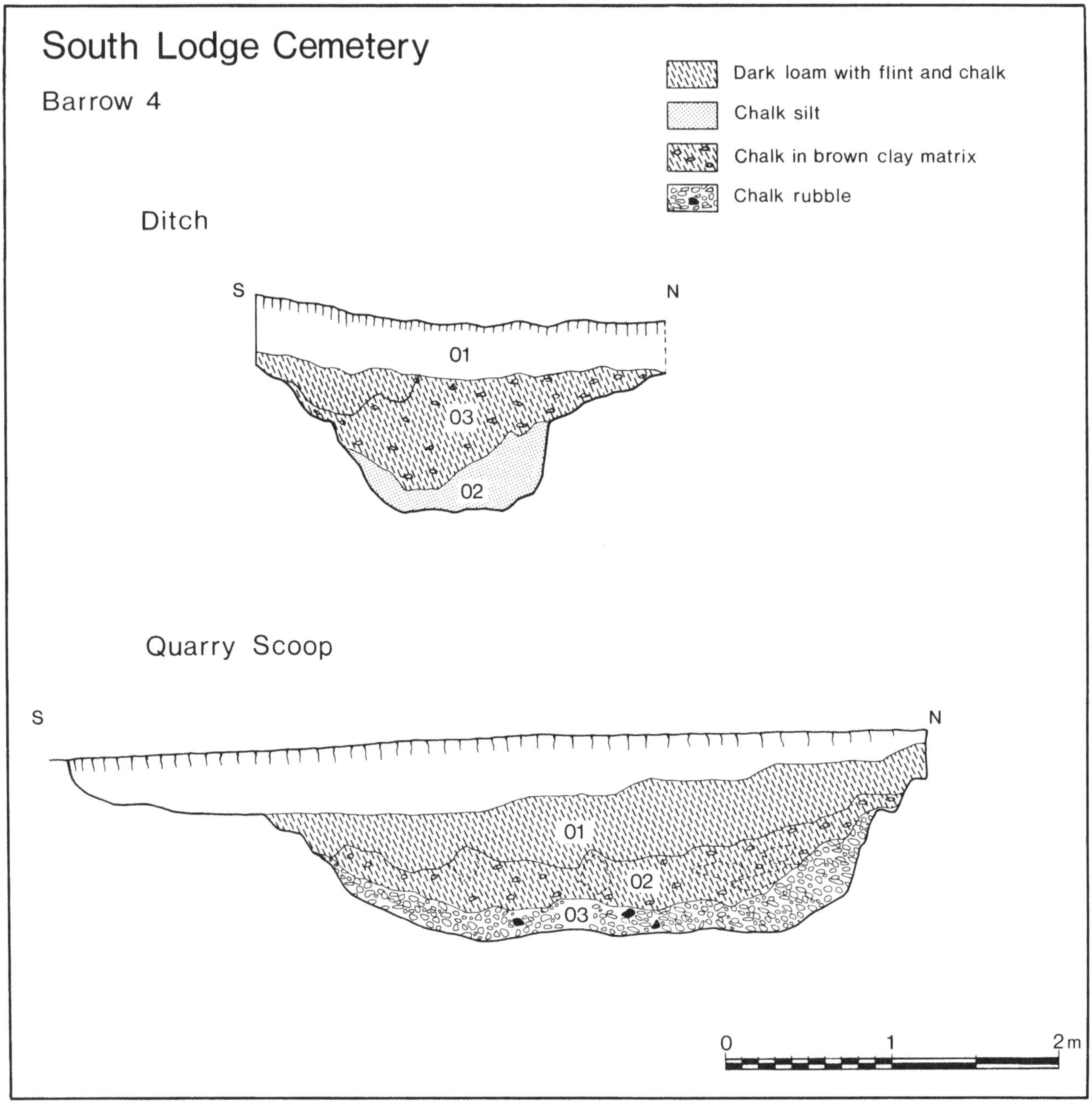

Fig. 5.25 Sections through the Barrow 4 ditch and the quarry pit

5.2.5.vi Barrow 18

This barrow is recorded as having an overall diameter of 30 ft (9.14 m), but was of such slight elevation that it went unnoticed in the first programme of barrow excavations in 1880.

The excavation of 1883 totally removed the mound, along with almost the entire circuit of the ditch, the only section remaining being protected by a growing tree. No burial deposits were recovered and the original records are schematic (*Excavations* II, 19 and 30). The mound produced two flint scrapers and 104 struck flakes along with eight pottery sherds, five of which were of 'superior quality'.

BPB was cut into the nineteenth-century mound and extended out over the area of the unexcavated ditch (Fig. 5.24). Here this section of ditch was clearly visible as a surface feature. Our aim was to investigate the buried ground surface beneath the mound (in case a primary deposit had been missed) and to section the ditch. The remaining area around the mound was sampled by a series of 2 m squares.

The excavation of the mound confirmed that its present structure was of nineteenth-century origin. Within this a small terracotta vase had been placed containing, amongst other things, a Pitt Rivers medallion (Barrett, Bradley, Bowden and Mead 1983, Pls. xxv and xxvi a). It is this medallion, not the published account, which gives the true date of the original excavation as 1883. No primary deposit was recovered from beneath the mound.

A 2.5 m length of unexcavated ditch was exposed. This relatively slight feature was 0.8 m wide and 0.25 m deep. Once again primary silts were overlain by a densc deposit of flint nodules. In the upper layers these nodules were unbroken, but the lower levels contained more shattered flint. The flints were embedded in a brown clay.

5.2.5.vii Additional finds

Metalwork affinities[3] The broken tip of the spearhead from the ditch of Barrow 2 is bent back just above the break, the edges are badly damaged and the point completely eroded. However, where the original surface survives, there appears to be no sign of wear or resharpening, suggesting that the object had been little used before breakage. There is a pronounced angular midrib along the whole surviving length of the fragment. The blade edges are slightly bevelled.

The angular midrib is characteristic of side-looped spearheads of Rowlands' group 2 and of basal-looped spearheads of his groups 1 and 2 (Rowlands 1976, 52, 58; Ehrenberg 1977, 7, 10). Comparison of the Barrow Pleck fragment with complete spearheads shows that it is too small and slender to belong to a basal-looped spearhead. It appears to be from a small side-looped spearhead with narrow, 'string' loops (Rowlands 1976, Pl. 38:1230–1370). When we set it beside the complete example of this form from the enclosure, 125 mm long and somewhat resharpened, the Barrow Pleck fragment appears to be from a smaller spearhead. Side-looped spearheads less than 120 mm long are not uncommon (Rowlands 1976, 52, Fig. 2) and there is a nearby example from Berwick Down. Two radiocarbon dates come from material associated with this find: 940 ± 120 bc and 950 ± 110 bc (BM 1920R and BM 2023R).

A human skeleton from Tormarton, Gloucestershire, has, embedded in it, the tips of two spearheads which are assigned by Rowlands to his side-looped group 2 (Knight, Browne and Grinsell 1972; Rowlands 1976, 55 and 192). This, along with the find of a basal-looped spearhead in a human pelvis from Dorchester, Oxfordshire (Ehrenberg 1977, 22, 37:54, Fig. 15 and Pl. I), raises the question of whether the Barrow Pleck example came from the body whose cremation was deposited in the barrow ditch. If so, it would appear to have been removed from the body before cremation as it did not pass through the fire, or had certainly not been heated over 675°C. The Tormarton skeleton has produced a radiocarbon date of 977 ± 90 bc (BM 542), in close agreement with the Barrow Pleck dates.

The other bronze fragment from the ditch of Barrow 3 (*Excavations* II, Pl. 86:5) has been ascribed to a neck-ring and may plausibly be given a Taunton date (Burgess 1976, 90; Rowlands 1976, 205). However, comparable fragments of twisted bronze come from the primary cremation in a probable bell barrow on Easton Down, north-east of Winchester, accompanied by a knife-dagger and three amber beads (Fasham 1982, 32 and Fig. 12: M1, M2–3 and S1–3). Gerloff assigns this form of knife-dagger with a broad mid-rib to the later Wessex phase (1975, 170). Also, some bronze pins from Wessex burials have twisted shafts (Gerloff 1975, 111). Four fragments of spirally twisted wire *c.* 250 mm thick were found with pottery within the Handley Barrow 24 cemetery (below).

The flint[2] Barrow Pleck contained an appreciable quantity of worked flint, whose distribution can be reconstructed from the contents of the sample squares (Fig. 5.26). The largest concentrations of material were: east of Barrow 18; south and east of Barrow 4; south of Barrows 2 and 3 and north of Barrow 3. We have seen that the first group included Beaker pottery (p. 117) and have suggested that this early activity accounts for much of the material between that mound and our BPD.

The Middle Bronze Age deposits contained four small groups of stratified flintwork, although these were similar in character to the material associated with Beaker pottery. They came from: the top and bottom of the ditch of Barrow 2; the ploughwash filling the quarry pit outside Barrow 4; and the uppermost filling of the ditch of Barrow 18. The finds from BPD are of uncertain date but have most in common with the earlier material. There is little to connect these *in situ* deposits with the general spread of flintwork. The areas with most material are not closely linked to the distribution of finds in the barrow ditches, and the latter do not seem to have spread beyond their parent features. The one exception was to the south of Barrow 3, and here a limited group of implements was also found, immediately alongside the cremations.

It seems as if flint nodules exposed during barrow

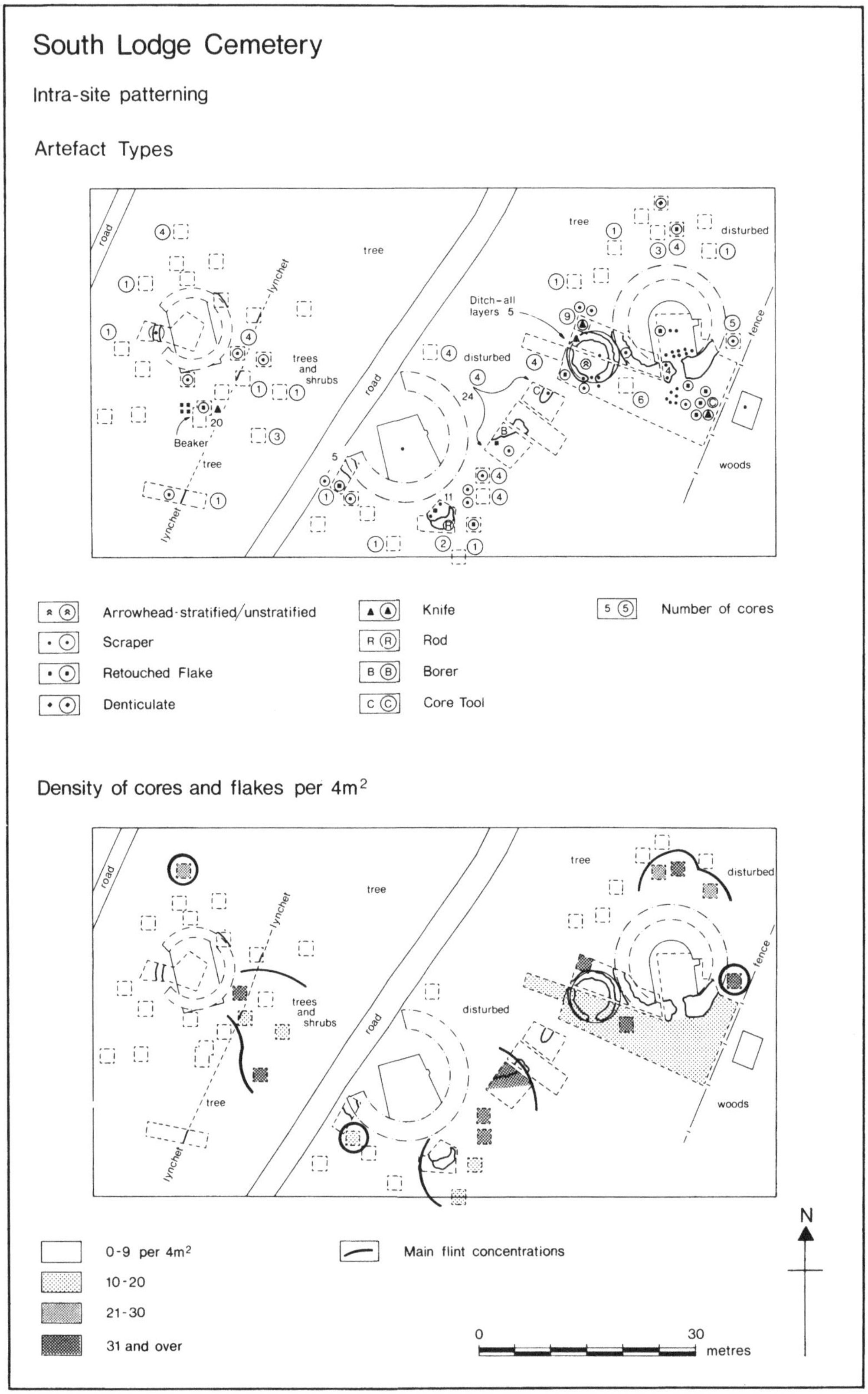

Fig. 5.26 The distribution of flint artefacts (above) and flakes and cores (below) within the South Lodge cemetery

building were being worked *in situ*. The distribution of cores and flakes is summarised in Fig. 5.26. Except in two small areas (to the north of Barrow 3 and in the ditch of Barrow 4) between 14 per cent and 17 per cent of the flakes retained more than two-thirds of their cortex, and with the exception of the finds from the quarry pit, the stratified flintwork also showed a consistent ratio of cores to flakes. The figure was from 1:17.5 for finds from the ditch of Barrow 2 to 1:12.8 in the area around Barrows 2 and 3. For comparison, the figure for the eastern half of the enclosure was 1:16.6. In the Beaker deposit at Barrow Pleck, however, the equivalent ratio was 1:7.3. The density of flintwork close to the Beaker material was 11 per m^2, but south of Barrows 2 and 3 it was only 2 per m^2. The equivalent figure for the enclosure was 3.5 per m^2.

Lastly, the implements at Barrow Pleck show a certain patterning. Regular tools were more frequent close to the Beaker deposit and expedient tools were more common in the vicinity of the later Barrow 3. This is consistent with what is known about the chronological development of Bronze Age flint industries (Ford, Bradley, Hawkes and Fisher 1984). It is also thought that distinctive implements became less common through time. Close to the Beaker deposit and Barrow 18, the ratio of implements to flakes is 1:30; on BPD it is 1:25. By contrast, it is 1:51 south of Barrows 2 and 3 and 1:52 in the area to their north. The equivalent ratio at the enclosure is 1:59.

Undoubtedly, this material is mixed, but it seems likely that during the Middle Bronze Age activity took place mainly around Barrows 2 and 3 and was directed towards working nodules exposed in the ditches of these monuments. The few implements near to the main group of cremations may be of the same date. This material is very like that in the eastern half of the enclosure, but occurs at a significantly lower density than the flintwork from that site.

5.2.6 South Lodge: the chronological sequence[1,2]

This section is concerned simply with the relative sequence of activity recognised in the area of the enclosure and barrow cemetery at South Lodge, Rushmore. The wider implications of this sequence will be discussed at the end of this chapter.

The excavations allow us to examine a long history of activity within the vicinity of these monuments, and to say something about the organisation of that activity. This is made possible by the survival of surface stratigraphy, details of which were recovered by Pitt Rivers and ourselves. We thus avoid some of the problems which confront the excavation of plough-eroded sites, where surface stratigraphy is missing and where chronological sequences depend upon intercutting features, internal sequences of artefact types or radiocarbon dates (see our discussion of the Down Farm enclosure below). In connection with this, it is also worth recalling that most of the artefacts came from surface deposits within the enclosure, whilst a very different range of material was recovered from the surrounding ditch. This single observation will have major implications for the analysis of material recovered entirely from dug features on an eroded settlement site.

The sequence may be clarified by considering it in terms of four phases of activity. The first of these has been discussed in the preceding chapter and it is difficult to identify. The earliest ceramics are two sherds of Grooved Ware incorporated in the mound of Barrow 4, and Beaker material which came from the area of the enclosure and from near Barrow 18. An element of the flint assemblage from Barrow Pleck is likely to be early in date. It is difficult to place this material in any precise settlement context. The available evidence would indicate that the main weight of settlement activity at this time lay on the lowlands of the Hampshire Basin. Obviously this does not preclude settlement and cultivation on the uplands, and on Pentridge Hill a bell barrow is recorded as lying within possibly earlier cultivation lynchets (RCHM 1975, 57 no. 25). We have argued that lynchet F belongs to an early phase of cultivation on the hillside. The nearest Beaker burial is Barrow 20, some 700 m away (*Excavations* II, 26 and Pl. 77). Early Bronze Age mounds are also known in Scrubbity Coppice nearby, some of which produced cremations associated with Collared Urns (*Excavations* II, 42 ff.). None of the mounds on Barrow Pleck are demonstrably Early Bronze Age. The destroyed mound itself remains undated although the flint assemblage from the disturbed ground to the east may be early, and Barrow 4 is larger than the remaining mounds and was, seemingly, of a more complex build. We have already noted the possibility that the Barrel Urn from the latter barrow may have been inserted into an already existing mound.

The second phase of settlement and agriculture may simply emerge from this earlier activity. A field system runs along the slope of the dry valley, ending as a staggered line running south-west to north-east. This is partly defined by the break in the slope of the valley but may have also been determined by the existence of one or two early barrow mounds on Barrow Pleck. Contemporary settlement still seems to have been unenclosed. Worked flint and some pottery sherds come from the lynchets, and two clusters of postholes within the area of the later enclosure may have belonged to an earlier, open phase of settlement. However, it is impossible to link these post clusters directly with the history of cultivation, and the clusters need not be contemporary with each other.

Of the other structural details recovered from within the enclosure, neither Terrace A nor Terrace B need be contemporary with the enclosure. Terrace B certainly cuts the soils of the negative lynchet of D, but both terraces may be overlain by Structure 1, which we would assign to the enclosed phase.

There is therefore good evidence for a quite complex sequence of cultivation and settlement within this small area of the field system, with some buildings and platforms being established at the head of earlier cultivation plots. The flint scatters recorded by Stephen Ford may also indicate further clusters of settlement to the north of the excavated areas (p. 151). In the area of the enclosure activity seems to cluster around the margins of the cultivated land. Immediately to the west of Terrace B, on uncultivated soil, a burnt mound began to accumulate, and although that mound was ultimately incorporated within the enclosure, and presumably continued to develop at that time, it may have been of earlier origin and have been cut through on its north side by the ditch.

All these observations emphasise that the enclosure ditch, our third phase, is late in the history of the settlement. That ditch cuts round the northern margins of two field plots and encloses most of the area occupied by the burnt mound. There is one clear entrance causeway to the west. The ditch is clearly later than lynchets D and E and it is important to stress that no lynchet accumulation can be associated with the enclosure itself. The only possible agricultural activity later than the main lynchet system is the flint bank L.

The ditch was cut into the chalk but, around the east and west of the enclosure at least, the excavated material was not thrown up in the form of a bank. The slight banks defining the northern and southern margins of the site are presumably upcast, an idea supported by a single reference from Pitt Rivers to an 'old land surface' (*Excavations* IV, 41), but this cannot account for all the material derived from the ditch. Given the uniformly sharp profile of the ditch recorded by Pitt Rivers, we would suggest that the ditch was partly backfilled almost immediately after excavation. This idea is supported by the nature of some of the finds recovered from the ditch. A small scatter of pottery does come from its lower fill, but the distribution and range of material differs from that recovered within the interior. However, in the case of the flints, the distribution of recorded finds from the ditch does echo the distribution of material within the eastern half of the enclosure. Amongst the pottery from the ditch is a near-complete Barrel Urn found by Pitt Rivers. The survival of this vessel is difficult to understand. Indeed Mark Bowden has drawn our attention to a letter from Greenwell to Pitt Rivers discussing this very point (Salisbury Museum, dated 10.5.1893). Greenwell writes: 'there is not much difficulty in imagining how such a vessel got into the ditch, but how it remained there unbroken is not easy to account for'. Large sections of urn were seemingly deposited in the ditch of the Down Farm enclosure, but these were eroded to a largely uniform sherd size (below, p. 200). The difference would be explained if the South Lodge urn was covered over rapidly whilst the Down Farm material lay in an open and eroding ditch. This possible infilling of the South Lodge ditch is of further interest when the metalwork from the site is considered. All the metal comes from the ditch and it occurs in three horizons. At the bottom of the ditch lay one of the razors and the awl, in the north-east and south-west corners respectively. Mid-way up the ditch and along its eastern arm came the second group of metal, the arm-ring, 'wire' and second razor. The spearhead was very high in the ditch silts in the south-eastern corner of the site. The first two deposits are likely to have been deliberate and associated with some backfilling of the ditch.

The ditch thus marked out an area of activity, without establishing a substantial bank. No fence line or gate structures are associated with this enclosure. Structure 2 lies centrally within the upper half of the enclosure and seems aligned on the western entrance. It is likely that this building and the subsidiary Structure 1 were contemporary with the enclosure. Although the wall lines of the two buildings would have been close, they need not have overlapped. Indeed, these two buildings would conform to the structural unit identified by Ellison (1980b) on other, contemporary, sites.

The range of artefacts recovered from the interior is almost entirely limited to stone and pottery. In considering the distribution of this material we must make allowances, firstly for the long history of activity which had already taken place in this area, and secondly for changes in the organisation of those activities that focused upon the enclosure. A single set of behavioural parameters will not explain the distribution of all this material. The problem is rather similar to that recently discussed by Binford (1982), where he points out that 'site assemblages' represent a palimpsest of depositional acts, each situated in different systemic contexts.

Some of the flints recovered from the eastern part of the enclosure may derive from the earlier phases of activity. The main deposit of pottery, lying in the south-west corner of the enclosure, is presumably contemporary with it.

The second deposit of pottery, recorded by Pitt Rivers immediately within the entrance, is, however, less easy to explain. The enclosure may not have had a very long history of use, the main indicator of this being the entrance, where lynchet E, although slightly eroded, remains clearly visible. Heavy traffic through that entrance would surely have caused more severe erosion. Two deposits of material within the enclosure are presumably connected with a fourth and final phase of activity leading to abandonment. These are the cattle bones buried in a shallow pit dug through the floor of Structure 1 and the mound of pottery sherds, with a quernstone placed on the top, found within Structure 2. Less certainly connected with the latest use of the enclosure is the possible break in the bank in the south-east corner. The ditch here was not observed as a clear surface feature by Pitt Rivers, and a case could be made for some bank material having been pulled down into that ditch. It is at this point that the bronze spearhead was recovered from high in the ditch silts.

Given this complex, four-phase sequence of activity, it is unfortunate that the history of the cemetery and settlement cannot be more precisely linked. The question of broad contemporaneity is not in doubt, the pottery from both areas is closely comparable and stratigraphic relationships with the field system support this view.

We have suggested that the cemetery had a lengthy history, beginning by at least the second phase of open settlement. The re-excavated barrows themselves display a sequence of development. Both Barrows 2 and 21 are likely to be later than Barrow 3, and the area defined by these mounds, and their ditches, accommodated a quite complex cemetery. Cremations were placed beneath the mounds, within the ditches and beyond the causeways. Further distinctions also occur; pottery only accompanies the cremations within and around Barrow 3, and the two pieces of bronze from the cemetery come from the ditches of Barrows 2 and 3. An inhumation was also placed at the junction of the ditch and causeway of Barrow 3. The importance of the ditches for defining the barrows, and therefore different areas within the cemetery, is further emphasised by the recutting and deliberate deposition of flint, some of it worked, in the top of all the ditches. The cemetery was therefore structured around a series of choices as to how and where the cremated remains were to be deposited, choices made at a late stage of the funerary ritual. This point is examined in more detail in relation to Handley Barrow 24 (below, p. 214). It is tempting to suggest that Barrow 18 is the last construction within the cemetery. It represents an outlier of the group as a whole and was never developed as a cemetery focus.

The only radiocarbon dates from the enclosure, 1290 ± 120 bc and 1160 ± 110 bc (BM 1921R-2R), derive from charcoal in one of the postholes belonging to Structure 2, possibly representing the remains of large structural timbers. All the other dates are from the cemetery. Three dates, 1190 ± 120 bc, 1010 ± 120 bc and 950 ± 150 bc (BM1919R, 2024R and 1918R) are for deposits placed beyond the ditch of Barrow 3. Two deposits which had been cut into the upper fills of the barrow ditches also produced dates: 1060 ± 120 bc (BM 1917R) for a cremation outside Barrow 3, and the two dates of 950 ± 110 bc and 940 ± 120 bc (BM 2023R and 1920R) for the cremation associated with the tip of a spearhead from Barrow 2. All these dates presumably relate to the later history of activity and could indicate abandonment sometime around the tenth century bc.

Of the bronzes from the enclosure ditch all, with the exception of the side-looped spearhead, are likely to have been deposited over a relatively short period of time. We need not, therefore, place too much weight upon the detail of the stratigraphic sequence (Barrett 1976, 291; Burgess 1980, 134) and we can assign this ditch assemblage to the third phase of our settlement sequence. The two pieces of metalwork from the cemetery, one from late deposits in the ditch of Barrow 2, seem broadly contemporary with the material from the enclosure ditch. O'Connor's study of these finds shows that the assemblage as a whole would lie within the Taunton metalworking tradition of southern Britain, equivalent to Burgess's metalworking Stage IX. This Stage falls within Burgess's Knighton Heath period (*c.* 1250–1050 bc), and in absolute terms he dates the Taunton tradition to the fourteenth and thirteenth centuries BC (Burgess and Coombs 1979, iv).

5.3 The excavations: Down Farm enclosure and cemetery[7,2,1]

5.3.1 Introduction

The enclosure was discovered by accident during the laying of a water pipe (NGR SU 002148) and was excavated between 1977 and 1979. It occupied a low plateau of Upper Chalk and had been under cultivation at least since the Iron Age. No trace of the enclosure was visible from the air and the only surface indication was a poorly defined flint scatter. Subsequent analysis has shown that this scatter contained a mixture of Later Neolithic and Middle Bronze Age material. After the enclosure ditch had been noticed, the entire site was excavated following the removal of the ploughsoil by machine. It overlay the Grooved Ware pits described above (p. 75) and a series of tree holes of uncertain date. The internal features were excavated completely and the ditch was fully excavated, except for a length of 5 m at the southern terminal (Fig. 5.27).

The site lay in an area with abundant evidence of Deverel-Rimbury activity, and the excavation of the enclosure must be considered together with two other pieces of work. Sectioning the Dorset Cursus 240 m from the enclosure indicated that its earthwork may have been reused as a field boundary during this period. It is clear that the pond barrow adjoining the Cursus was also ploughed over during this phase of activity. In addition, excavation of the Neolithic ring ditch, 130 m to the southwest of the Bronze Age enclosure showed that it had been reused as a cemetery. On the evidence of the pottery the settlement and the burials should be broadly contemporary.

5.3.2 The enclosure

5.3.2.i Stratigraphic information

The enclosure contained five, possibly six, circular timber Structures (A–E), a possible four-post structure which overlapped Structure E, a long rectangular building (F), eight pits, a possible water hole, up to five lengths of internal fence, a palisaded enclosure and a chalk-cut ditch reinforcing the palisade for roughly half the perimeter. In addition, an enigmatic chalk-cut gully or channel (F14) crosses the positions of the outer palisade and one of the house structures, providing evidence of the sequence (Fig. 5.27). Before these structural features are discussed in detail it is useful to outline the principles by which the structural sequence has been identified.

1. *Direct relationships* exist only when one feature can be shown to have cut another. This applies to two circular Structures, A and B.

One posthole of A is cut by a posthole belonging to the outer palisade. Another post-socket belonging to Structure A is cut by one post of a short length of fence running parallel to the enclosure ditch.

The channel (F14) cuts two of the inner ring of postholes designated to Structure B, and the channel is itself cut by another posthole of the palisade.

2. *Structural relationships* are of various kinds. First, there are those cases in which the orthodox reconstruction of the circular buildings, with an outer wall flush with the porch, would mean that different structures would have overlapped the same ground space. This applies to the relationship between B and C, which on this basis cannot be contemporary. It also applies to Structure A and the perimeter palisade; the latter runs up to the inner ring of postholes of Structure A, and the posthole in the centre of that structure probably belongs to the palisade rather than with the building.

Structure E presents several problems. It overlaps the position of the long building (F) which lies on the eastern side of the settlement. Since the pits (F30) which would have been located beneath the eaves of E were refilled with fresh chalk, as were some of the post-sockets, it seems very likely that Structure E had been levelled before the long building was constructed. The long building comprises an array of internal postholes, but these contained post-pipes whereas the posts of the main ring of E had been removed. It seems likely that two different buildings were represented here. Other postholes in this area may belong to yet another building and the most plausible explanation is that a four-post structure lay within the ground area also occupied by Structure F.

Lastly, at least two of the fences impinge on the likely area occupied by E and F.

3. *Posthole dimensions* are useful in trying to isolate the positions of the different structures (Table 5.4), but in two cases they may shed light on the sequence itself. The postholes of the outer palisade are remarkably uniform, except where they lie alongside the ditch, where they are smaller in diameter and significantly shallower. This suggests that they may have been set in the tail of a pre-existing bank. The same applies to Structure F, where the posts of the eastern wall are significantly shallower than the posts of its western counterpart.

4. *The ditch stratigraphy* is extremely straightforward, but since no trace of the bank remained above ground it is hard to relate this evidence to the sequence of internal buildings. There are two exceptions, however. The only length in which there is convincing evidence that an internal bank had fallen back into the ditch is near Structure A, whose porch postholes were filled with fresh chalk rubble. Given the volume of upcast material deposited in this area, it is inconceivable that the bank could have skirted a standing structure.

There is also clear evidence for the sequence of midden deposits within the filling of the ditch comprising bone, pottery, flint and charcoal, and these change position steadily through time. The first deposits are concentrated in the southern and eastern sections of the ditch. Subsequently the midden distribution extended along the full length of the enclosure ditch, but those in its upper filling were confined to just two areas: between the northern terminal and the northern end of the rectangular building; and to just beyond its southern end. This might sug-

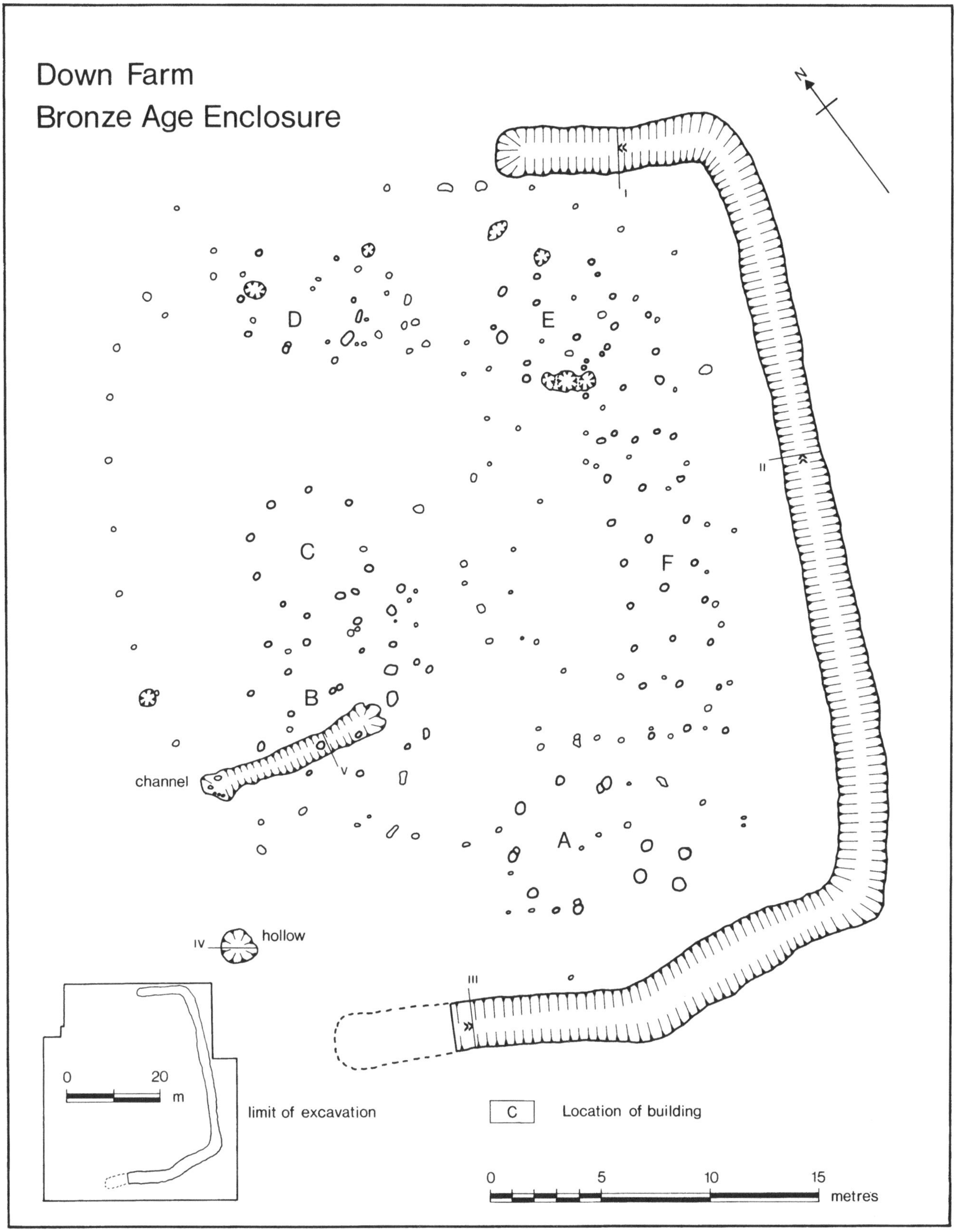

Fig. 5.27 The Down Farm enclosure, showing all Bronze Age features

Table 5.4. *Down Farm enclosure, posthole dimensions in the circular structures*

	Mean diameter of postholes (m)	Diameter of post-pipes (m)
Phase 1:		
Structure A	0.42	0.25–0.30
Structure B		
(inner ring)	0.27	–
(outer ring)	0.26	0.10–0.15
Phase 2:		
Structure C	0.26	0.15–0.25
Structure D	0.18	–
Structure E	0.23	–

gest that a major section of the enclosure ditch had become inaccessible from within the enclosure during the period in which the rectangular building was in use.

5. *Summary.* Taken together, these arguments suggest a basic sequence with at least two main elements: (1) the building of at least two structures, A and B, before the construction of the enclosure and their abandonment before the palisade was built; (2) the construction of a rectangular building after that of the enclosure in a late phase of the occupation, during which it replaced Structure E.

Further refinements of this sequence must await detailed presentation of the evidence.

5.3.2.ii The structural sequence (Fig. 5.28)

Phase 1. We have argued that the two groups of postholes assigned to Structure A and the inner ring of Structure B must pre-date the enclosure. Both structures share a similar axis and they are the only elements of the site to have been constructed entirely from fairly large posts. Posts attributed to later phases are significantly smaller (Table 5.4).

The two buildings are on an axis running exactly parallel to nearby Celtic fields identified by the Royal Commission and at right angles to the Cursus, which was certainly reused as a field boundary during this phase.

It seems likely that Structures A and B belong to a period of unenclosed settlement and were integral with a system of contemporary field boundaries.

Structure A (Fig. 5.29) consisted of a circle of eight postholes 5.5 m in diameter, with a further two large postholes forming a projecting porch. The two postholes at the inner end of this porch were as large as their counterparts. Only four of the postholes showed any traces of post-pipes, which were between 0.25 and 0.30 m in diameter. This applied to the row of four sockets opposite the porch. The central posthole was much slighter and falls outside the dimensions for this building but within the range recorded for the perimeter palisade. A similarly sized posthole impinged on the regular outline to the north of the porch, whilst another structural element of the building was cut by a shallower posthole on the line of the palisade. Four slighter postholes, forming a line running parallel to the ditch, ran up to the main ring of uprights and one appears to cut a posthole belonging to this building.

Following the discussion by Avery and Close-Brooks (1969), Musson (1970) and Guilbert (1981), it seems likely that the outer wall of this house would have been flush with the porch, giving a diameter of 10 m. A few unassigned postholes are close to this projected line.

Structure B (Fig. 5.30) presents more fundamental problems of interpretation. It consists of two roughly, but not exactly, concentric rings of postholes, *c.* 5 m and 7.5 m in diameter. Both end in larger postholes, defining an entrance facing south-east. Two postholes of the inner ring were truncated by a shallow channel or gully (F14) 1.5 m wide and up to 0.13 m deep, containing Deverel-Rimbury pottery. This did not impinge on the outer post-ring. Although these two post-settings were approximately concentric, the relationship is not exact and the axis of their respective entrances differs by about 10°.

The inner ring is composed of eight postholes, plus one in the centre. The entrance posts are larger than the others and are offset from the rest of the circle by 0.25 m.

The outer ring was made up of eleven postholes arranged symmetrically around the axis of the porch, with a possible twelfth on the same line. Again there was one central posthole. This time the entrance projected from the main arc by 0.5 m. It consisted of a large posthole and an elongated posthole which had probably held two posts. There were no post-pipes. The remaining postholes formed a fairly coherent group in terms of size, and again the centre post was of a similar size. Three of the postholes contained pipes between 0.10 and 0.15 m in diameter. These were amongst the smallest and shallowest postholes and it may be that other more substantial timbers had been retrieved.

At the time of excavation the two post-rings were treated as a small round house in its own fenced enclosure, but this interpretation is unsatisfactory for four reasons. The postholes attributed to the 'fence' are of the same general size as those belonging to the internal building and are much more substantial than those belonging to any of the freestanding fences on the site. In any case, following the accepted reconstruction of

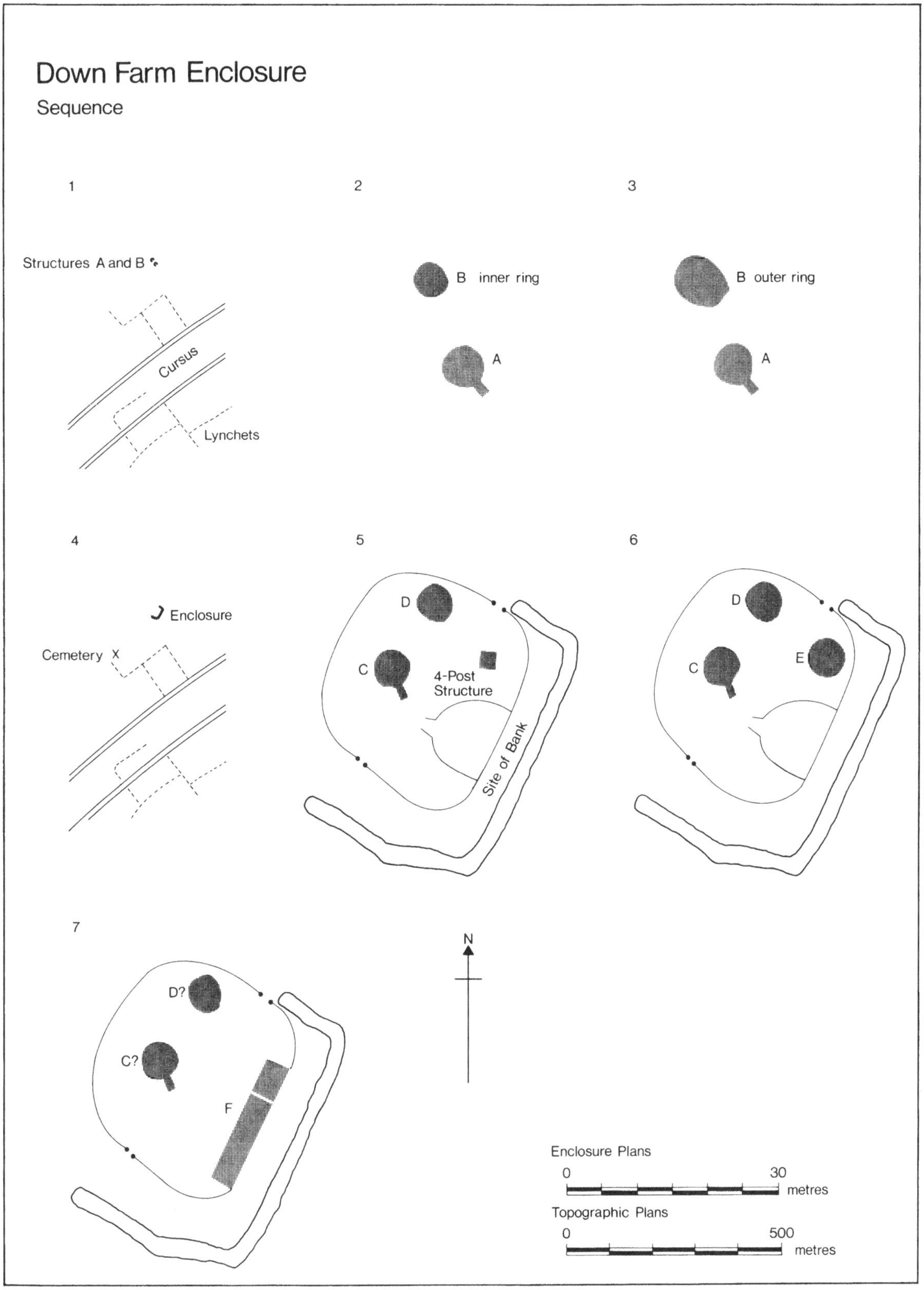

Fig. 5.28 The Down Farm Bronze Age settlement and cemetery in relation to the Cursus and field system (1 and 4) and the suggested architectural sequence for the settlement

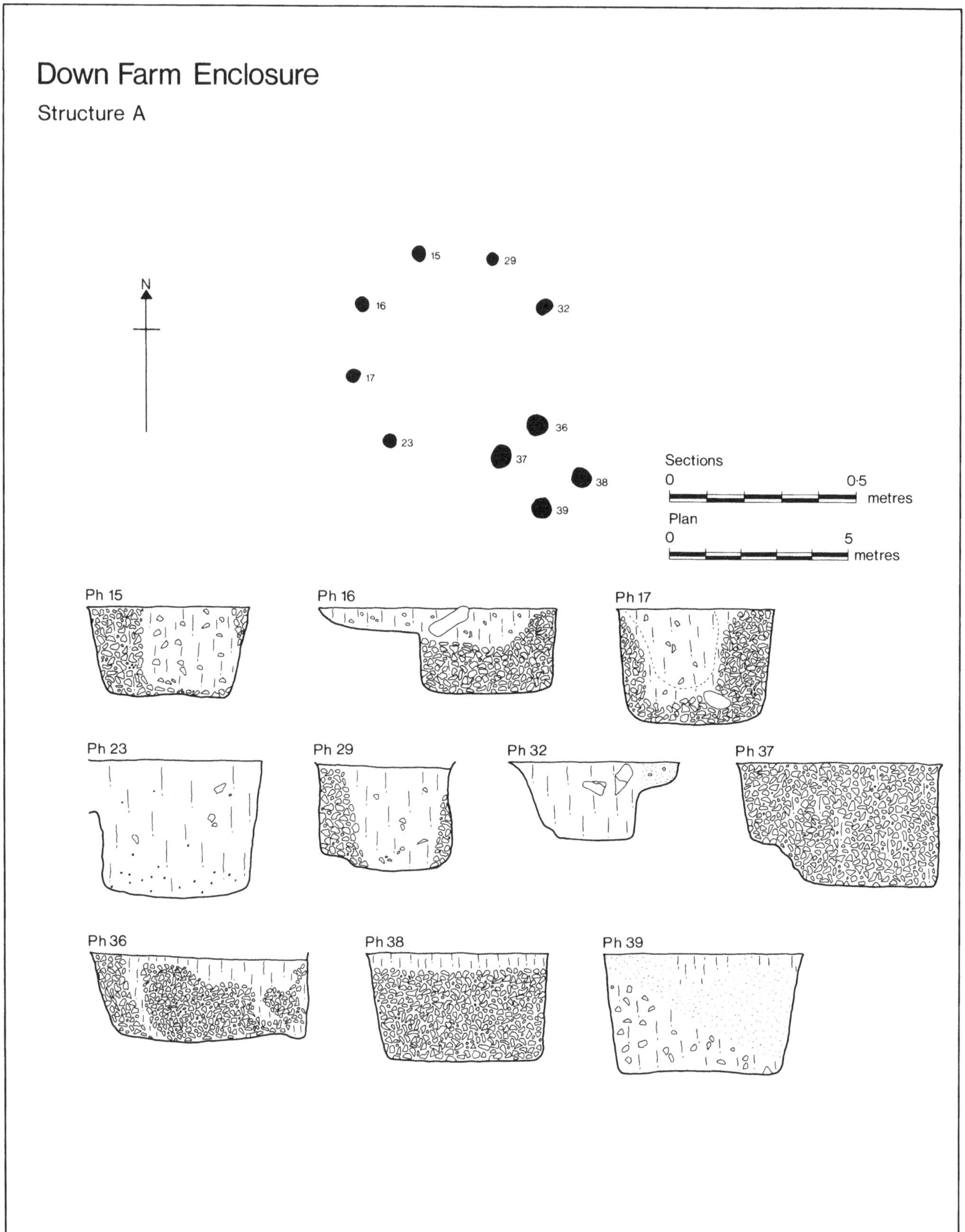

Fig. 5.29 Plan and sections of the postholes of Structure A, Down Farm enclosure

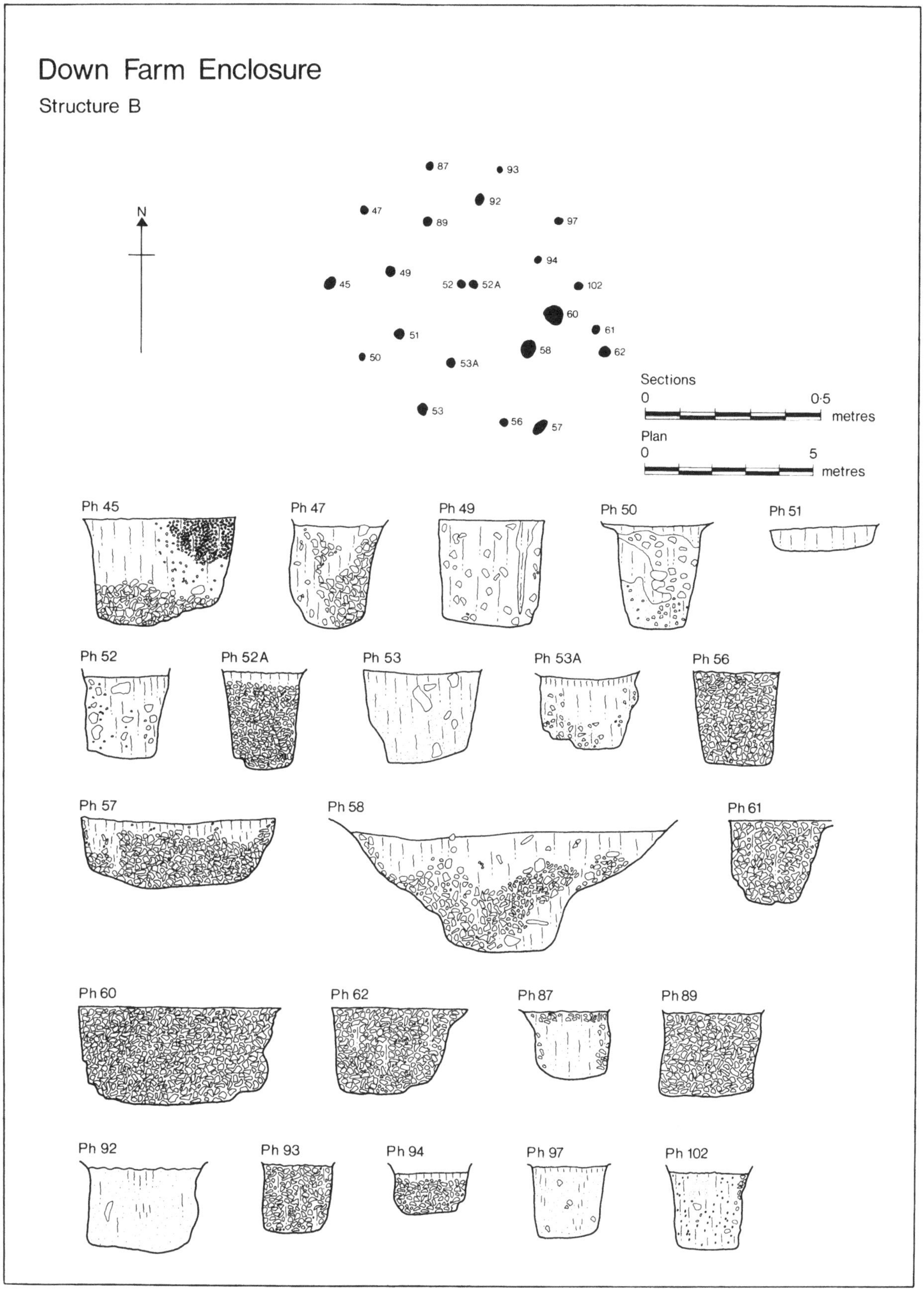

Fig. 5.30 Plan and sections of the postholes of Structure B, Down Farm enclosure

these buildings, the eaves would almost certainly impinge upon these posts. On the other hand, the marked difference of axis between the two circles makes it difficult to take them together as a double-ring round house. Moreover, the ground plan of the larger post-ring conforms to Guilbert's (1981) Sussex style of Bronze Age round house, in which the post layout is symmetrical, with a single post directly opposite the porch; in this type of building the porch itself should not project far from the main post circle. In addition, there should be a wider gap between the porch posts and the main post-ring than there is between the uprights towards the rear of the building. It is unlikely that such a sophisticated design is a fence, when it is supposed to contain a building of simpler design.

If these were two separate buildings, what was their sequence? The inner ring pre-dates the enclosure, as does Structure A, which is also of fairly massive construction, but does this mean that the outer post-ring is a later replacement? The survival of post-pipes is probably decisive here. Unless these particular posts had been cut off at ground level, which seems unlikely, it would be more logical for the posts of the outer ring which remained bedded in the ground to have belonged to the later structure.

Finally, it must be noted that, if the final phase of B were contemporary with the enclosure, its porch would have blocked direct access between the two gates.

Pit F13 impinged upon the position of the phase 2 palisade. However, the relationship between the two was not clear in excavation. The pit was roughly circular, 0.80 m in diameter and 0.65 m deep (Fig. 5.31). It had a flat bottom and almost vertical sides and had been filled in by two distinct layers of chalk fragments and one of humus. It resembles other pits in the enclosure but contained fewer artefacts.

Phase 2. If our interpretation is correct, the enclosure is later than Structures A and B and its construction may have involved a shift of about 50° in the axis of the site. Change is possibly reflected by the molluscan evidence for shaded conditions in the main fills of the ditch, in contrast to the more open environment evidenced from its primary fill and from the Deverel-Rimbury ploughsoil over the western Cursus ditch. The ditch and the palisade will be described first, followed by the internal buildings and the other features.

The enclosure ditch ran for 70 m, of which 5 m were not examined. The ditch follows a little under half the circuit defined by the palisade (Fig. 5.28). Both ditch terminals correspond quite closely to the probable gates in the palisade.

The ditch was not particularly substantial, being between 0.9 and 1.2 m in depth and between 1.7 and 2.2 m wide (Fig. 5.32). The ditch was of only one phase, except for a length of 12 m towards the north-eastern corner, where it might have been preceded by a more sharply cut, segmented earthwork. In the south-eastern corner the primary silts had been removed for a distance of 9 m. The ditch was generally deepest around the southern half of the site. Its filling showed a broadly consistent sequence; a series of silts at the bottom was overlain by the first of a series of three successive middens, marked by a quantity of cultural material in layers of soil with a high charcoal content (Fig. 5.33). There is a date of 1000 ± 100 bc (BM 1851R) for this deposit. Another short period of silting followed and in the south-eastern corner of the enclosure up to five dog skulls, one cow skull and other bones were deposited in these silts. After this silting the second midden accumulated, from which a date of 950 ± 160 bc (BM 1850R) was obtained. The ditch sides then appear to have stabilised and further weathered material derived from the bank. The last midden was confined to the northern ditch terminal and overlay these silts. Unlike its predecessors, it contained fairly few artefacts and consisted almost entirely of burnt flints. Associated charcoal gave dates of: 1210 ± 40 bc (which is the mean of four dates from one original charcoal sample BM 1852N1–1852N4), 1030 ± 50 bc (BM 1853N) and 1030 ± 50 bc (BM 2577). In addition there is one recalculated date of 1080 ± 110 bc (BM 1854R).

Later layers in the ditch probably result from subsequent agriculture.

For the most part the bank is evidenced by a strip of empty ground roughly 4 m wide on the inside of the enclosure. In one limited area, towards the southern ditch terminal, there is evidence for the collapse of fresh bank material at an early stage in the sequence.

The perimeter palisade consisted of approximately thirty-four postholes enclosing an area of 750 m^2. The posts were set at intervals averaging 2.5 m, the only gap being in a badly weathered area on the northern side, where two postholes seem to be missing (Figs. 5.27 and 5.28). The postholes can be divided into two groups. Those found beyond the limits of the bank were between 0.20 m and 0.34 m in diameter, and between 0.04 m and 0.12 m deep. Where the palisade and bank overlapped, postholes were between 0.16 m and 0.23 m in diameter and between 0.04 m and 0.12 m deep. Only three postholes, all clear of the bank, retained any post-pipes. These were among the largest and deepest set and may have been more difficult to retrieve.

At two points on opposite sides of the circuit the spacing of the posts narrowed to 1.0 m and 1.5 m, and in each case one of the posts flanking that gap had been

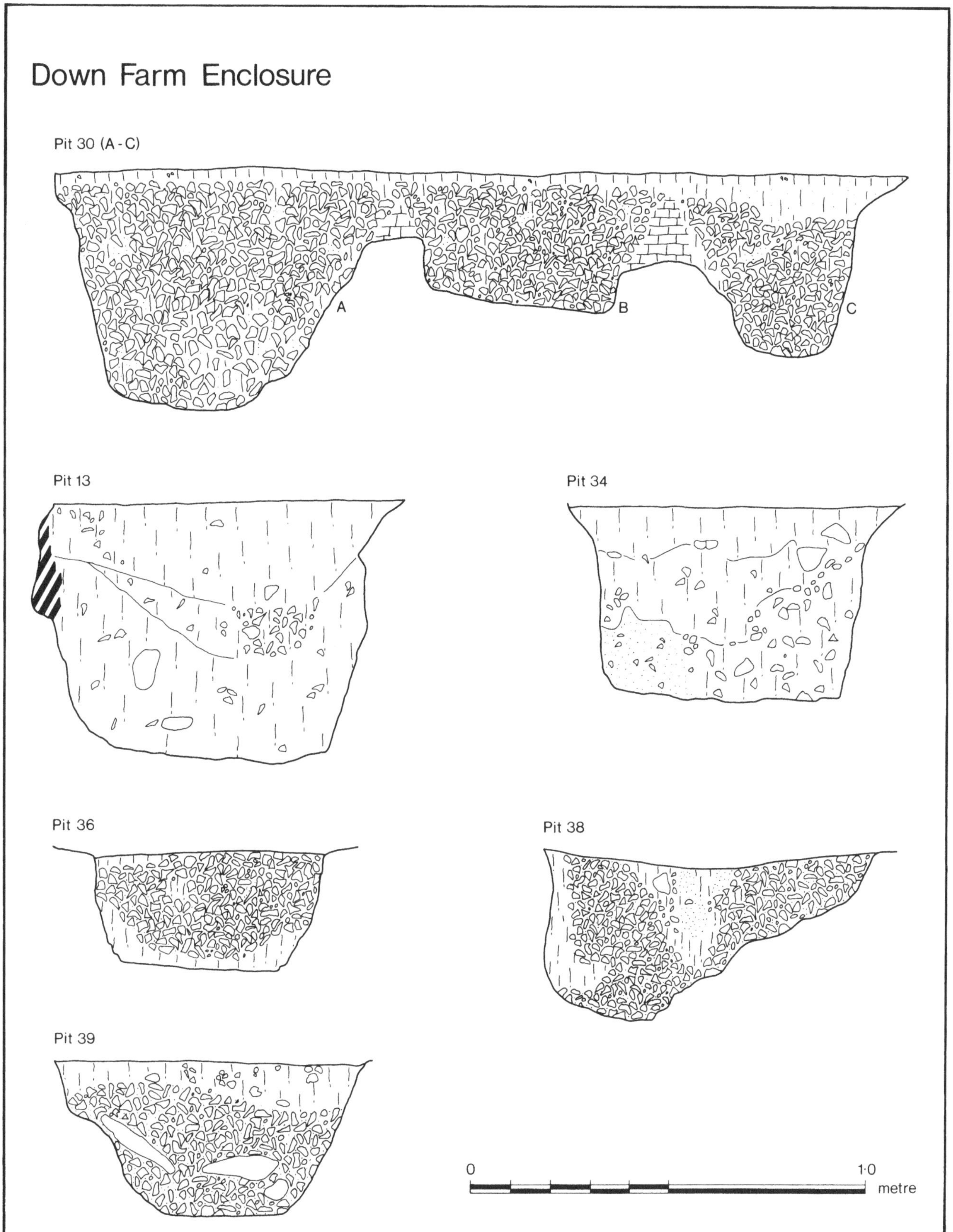

Fig. 5.31 Sections of Bronze Age pits associated with the Down Farm enclosure

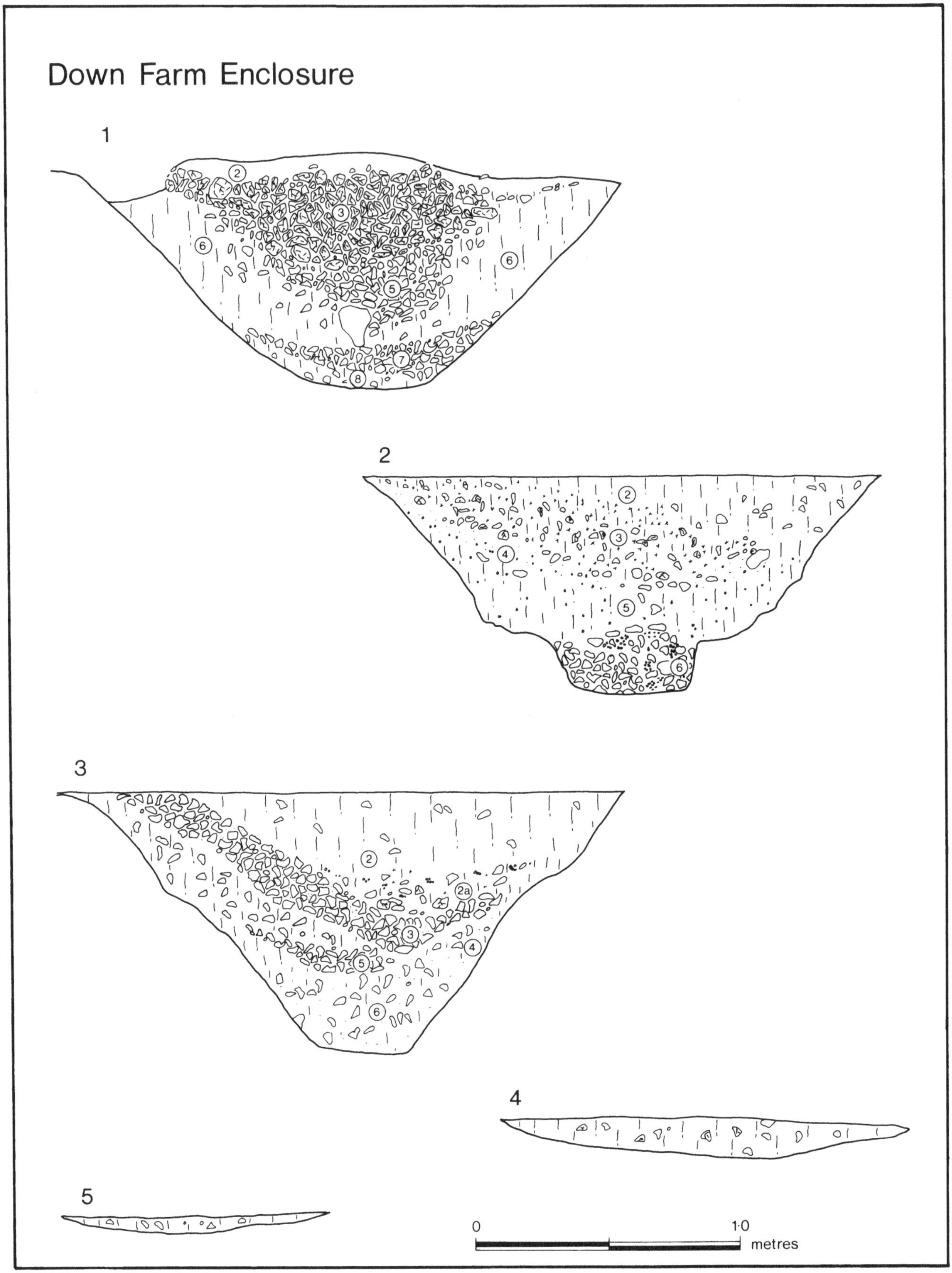

Fig. 5.32 Sections through the ditch (1–3), ? pond (4) and 'channel' (5) at the Down Farm enclosure

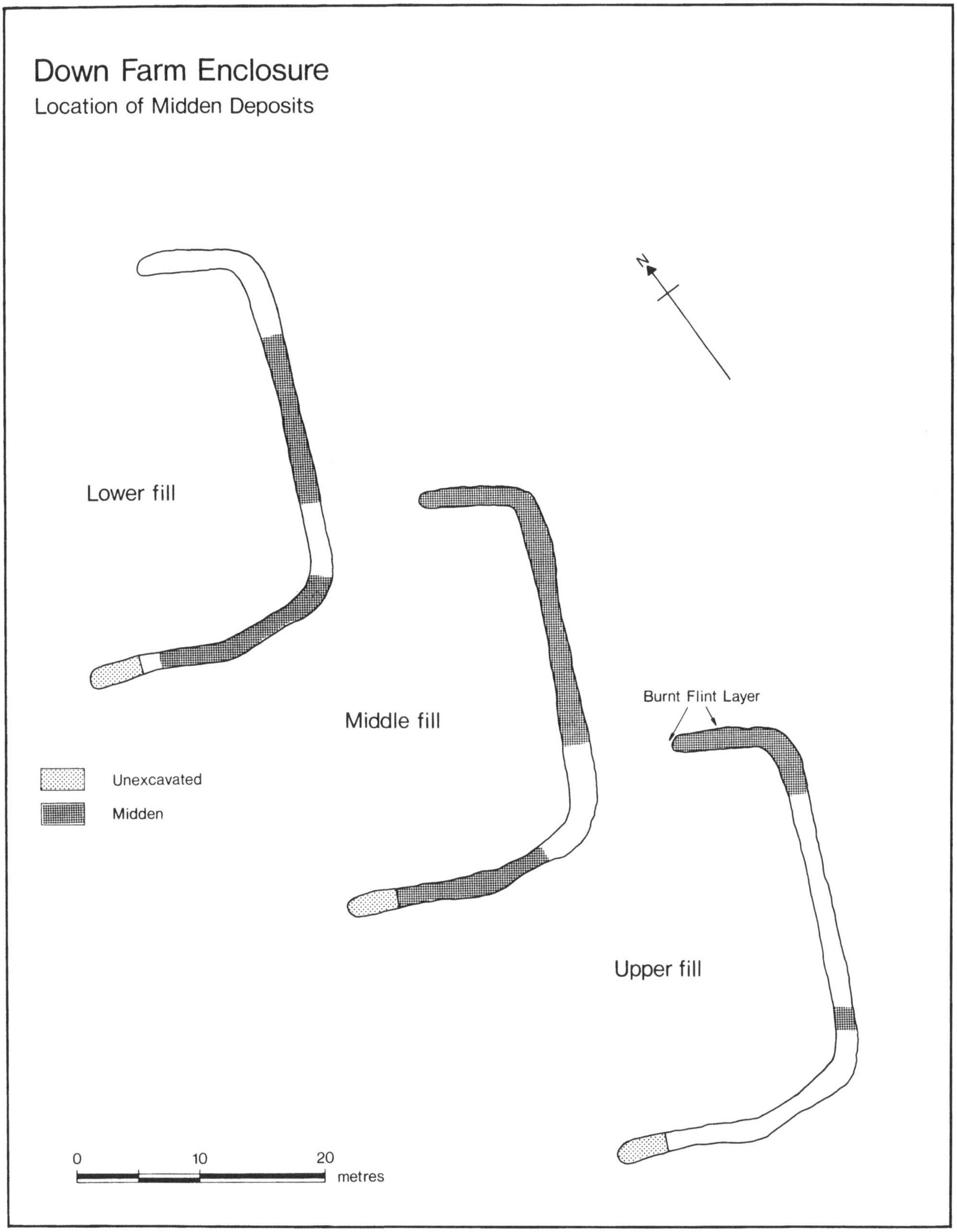

Fig. 5.33 The main concentration of midden material as it occurred in the three levels of ditch fill at the Down Farm enclosure

replaced. These seem likely to have been gates. The wider north-eastern gap was marked by two exceptionally large, deep postholes, whilst those marking the south-western break were of the same proportions as their neighbours.

The relationship between this fence and certain of the other structures has already been considered. It seems to post-date Structure A and cuts F14, which itself post-dates the inner ring of posts comprising Structure B. It impinges upon pit F13, but their chronological relationship is uncertain. It must have abutted the outer wall of Structure D, but postholes in this area seem not to have survived erosion. Lastly, the likely course of the palisade towards the south-eastern corner of the enclosure overlaps the corner of rectangular Structure F, and it seems unlikely that the two were in use together.

Structure C (Fig. 5.34) consists of a circle of ten posts, 5.5 m in diameter with a projecting porch 2.0 m deep. The posts are regularly spaced, except in the area of the inner porch. Apart from the porch posts, which are larger, the postholes are between 0.23 m and 0.29 m in diameter and between 0.11 m and 0.18 m deep. The three largest postholes contained traces of uprights 0.15 m to 0.25 m in diameter. These were the only post-pipes to survive from this structure, suggesting that all but the larger posts had been retrieved.

Adopting the view that the outer wall would have been flush with the porch, the original diameter would have been 9 m, and the structure would have impinged upon both phases of Structure B. Structure C, unlike B, allowed direct access between the gates through the palisade. It was also built on the same alignment as Structure D.

Structure D (Fig. 5.35) (published as E in Barrett *et al.* 1981) consisted of a ring of seven postholes with a diameter of 5 m. Two porch postholes projected 0.5 m from the circle on the same axis as Structure C. There were no post-pipes in the postholes of the main ring and the porch consisted of two oval pits, roughly concentric with the post-ring. Each was wider towards the entrance passage, and each may have held two, or even three, posts, although no trace of these survived. If the outer wall had been continuous with this porch, it might have met the line of the palisade fairly precisely. Two postholes do exist on its projected perimeter. In that case the full diameter of Structure D would have been 6.5 m.

Structure D enclosed one pit, F34, within the main post-ring, and another, F36, was just outside the projected line of the outer wall. F34 was a vertical-sided oval pit 0.95 m long and 0.50 m deep, with a flat bottom. It had been deliberately filled, with chalk rubble in the lower levels and fairly unmixed topsoil higher up. F36 was circular, 0.57 m in diameter and 0.28 m deep, with steeply shelving sides and a flat bottom. It had been refilled with chalk rubble (Fig. 5.31).

Structure E (Fig. 5.36) (published as D in Barrett *et al.* 1981) lay in a part of the site more difficult to summarise as it may contain the plans of up to three overlapping structures. The simplest to recognise, Structure E, is virtually the double of D, which it faced across the route between the entrances of the enclosure. The two buildings were of the same size but slightly different construction. Structure E consists of a 5 m diameter ring of eight postholes, plus two possible replacement posts. The porch projects from this circle by 0.50 m, giving an overall diameter for the building of 6.5 m. As in Structures A and B, the posts at the rear of the building were much closer together than the others. There were no post-pipes and many of the postholes contained large amounts of chalk. The porch was defined by two oval pits, each roughly on the same axis as the main ring of posts. No post-pipes survived, but in one case it was clear that the feature had been a double posthole, with the shallower posthole on the inside. The base of its counterpart sloped as if it had been used in the same way. The depths of the two clear postholes were 0.18 m and 0.25 m, whilst those of the others ranged from 0.17 m to 0.25 m.

The wall of the house would have enclosed one pit, F39, to the north and a line of three others, F30, to the south. A further pit, F38, lay just outside the building, between the wall and the north-western gate. F39 was circular, 0.75 m in diameter with a steep, rounded profile 0.38 m deep (Fig. 5.31). It had been refilled almost to the top with chalk rubble. The same applies to the row of pits, F30. All were roughly circular with diameters of 0.75 m, 0.60 m and 0.55 m and depths of 0.55 m, 0.33 m and 0.45 m respectively. All were steep-sided and fairly flat-bottomed, and they seem to have been used and refilled together. In this case the chalk rubble was tightly packed. F38 had a gradually shelving profile and flat bottom. It was 0.40 m deep with a maximum diameter of 1.0 m and was again filled with chalk rubble (Fig. 5.31).

Other features in the area of Structure E give more problems. The whole area contains a marked concentration of postholes. Apart from those which can be attributed to Structure F, the main post-ring of E encloses a further five postholes, whilst there are another three in the area contained by the likely position of an outer wall. A few of these may belong to this wall. The postholes inside the main ring retained post-pipes, unlike the post-ring of E. They may therefore belong to a different phase of building. The most satisfactory reconstruction uses a group of postholes of very similar size,

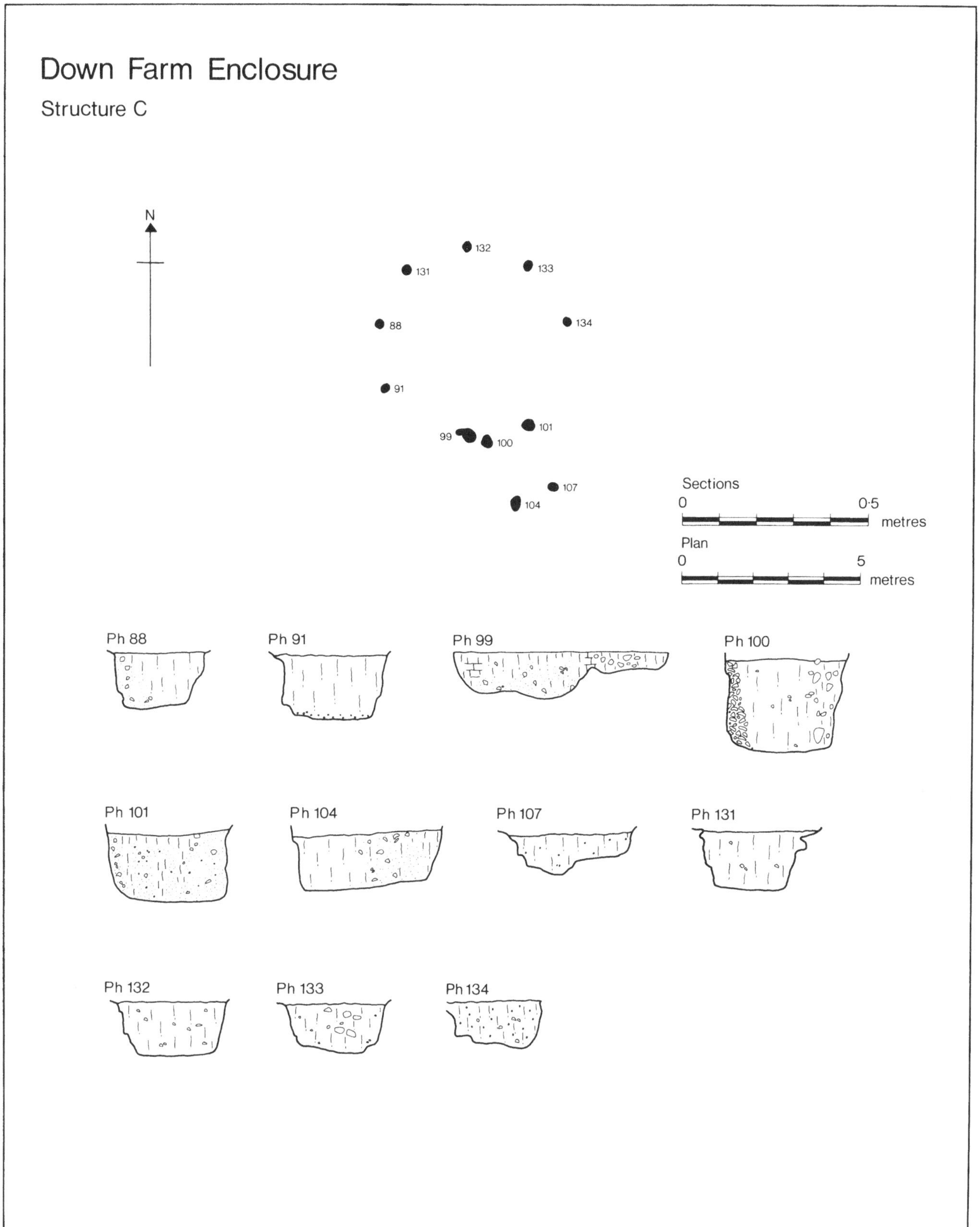

Fig. 5.34 Plan and sections of the postholes of Structure C, Down Farm enclosure

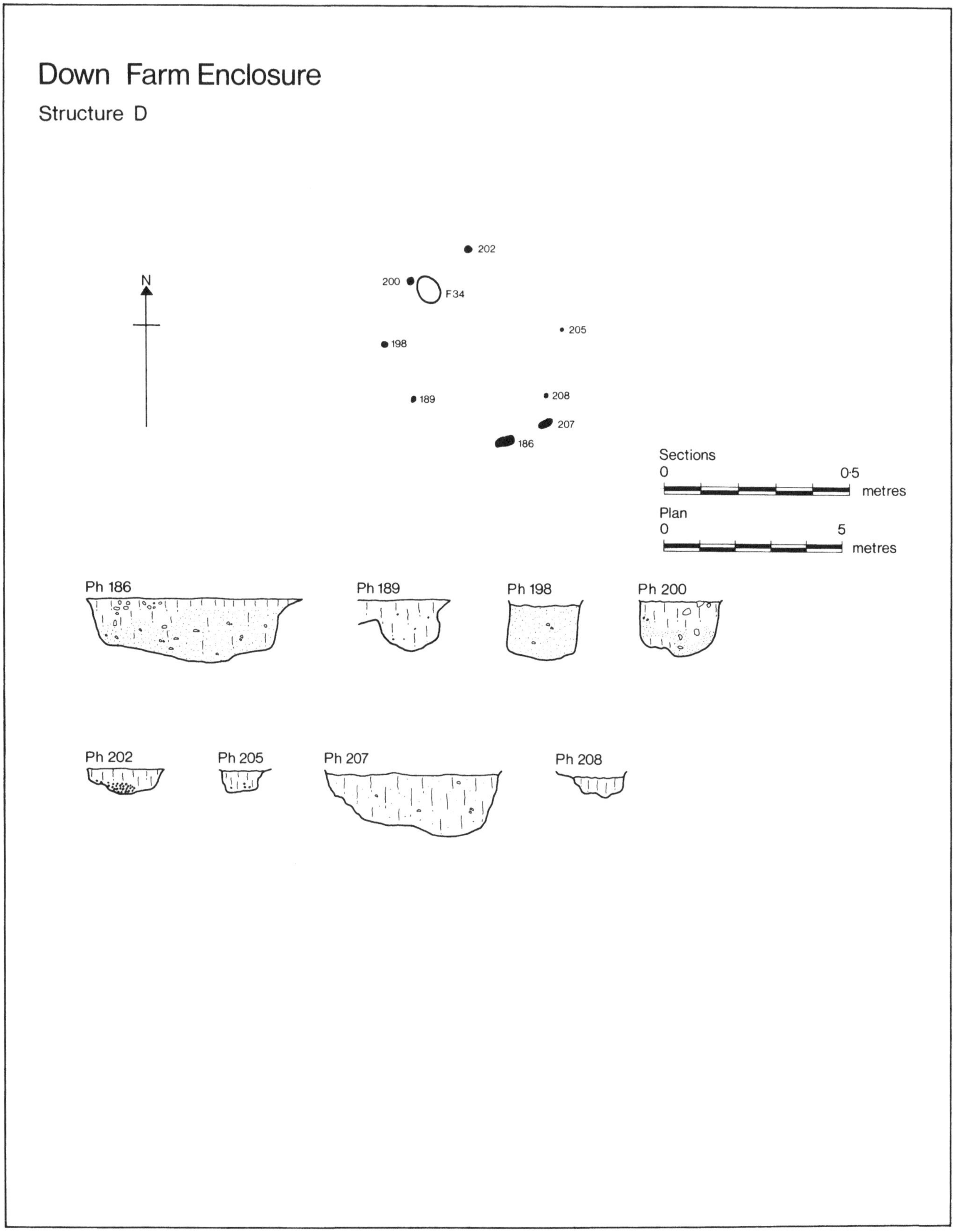

Fig. 5.35 Plan and sections of the postholes of Structure D, Down Farm enclosure

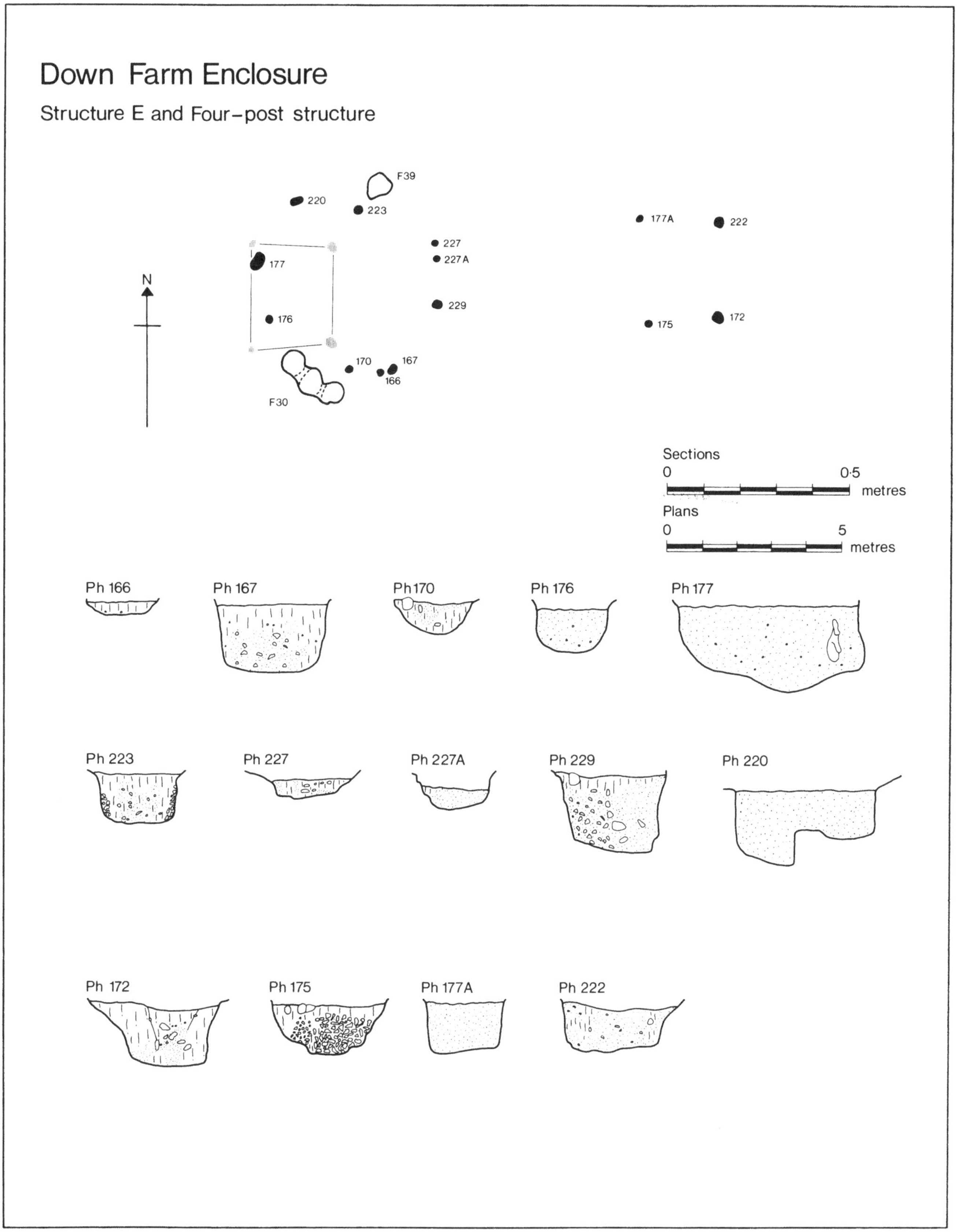

Fig. 5.36 Plan and sections of the postholes of Structure E and four-post structure, Down Farm enclosure

between 0.21 m and 0.31 m in diameter and 0.31 m and 0.19 m in depth, two of which contained post-pipes 0.10 m to 0.15 m in diameter, giving a regular four-post building 2.75 m by 2.25 m (Fig. 5.36). This is aligned almost directly on the gate of the enclosure.

Fence lines. Apart from the perimeter fences already described, we can consider five other alignments of postholes inside the enclosure:

(a) Posts in the vicinity of Structure A. These comprise two alignments. The most convincing runs parallel to the southern ditch of the enclosure and its end post cuts one of the inner ring of postholes belonging to this building. The postholes cover a wide range of diameters but are much the same depth. They form a convincing unit and may be associated with the bank. The second alignment runs outward from the perimeter palisade to the corner of the enclosure ditch. This alignment points at the section of the ditch which contained a major deposit of animal bones, an association which may have been intentional.

(b) Post alignment possibly associated with Structure D. This includes postholes of different sizes, which are part of a larger group of features, but some may form an arc of fence screening the approach to the building.

(c) Post alignment possibly associated with Structure E. This seems to mark the southern edge of the route between the two gates of the enclosure, running directly up to the porch of this building. However, the spacing of these postholes is rather irregular and again this group comprises features of very different diameters.

(d) A fenced yard opposite Structure B. This was composed of a quartet of postholes and a wide arc of other posts. We suggest that this may have been a fenced yard approached by a gate (Fig. 5.28). The suggested gate posts are much larger than the other postholes, which cover a limited size range rather similar to the perimeter palisade. Apart from the gate posts, these postholes are between 0.15 m and 0.24 m in diameter and between 0.05 m and 0.17 m deep. Both gate postholes and six other postholes in this fence retain pipes. This fence seems to overlap Structure F and cannot be contemporary with it.

A possible water hole lay just outside the southern edge of the enclosure. This consisted of an even hollow, 1.5 m in diameter and 0.20 m deep, with a filling of chalky rubble mixed with humus. Although it has the same profile as ponds of this period, it is substantially smaller, and as well as worked and burnt flints it included a sherd of Roman pottery (section: Fig. 5.32, 4).

Phase 3. This phase is connected with the construction of the long building, Structure F. This followed the eastern edge of the enclosure, overlapping the position of Structure E and possibly part of the palisade at the south-eastern corner. Its construction may have occasioned the deliberate packing of the pits in E, which may also explain the rather chalky fill of that building's postholes. It has already been suggested that this building post-dates the enclosure bank. It also overlaps the position of the fenced yard.

Structure F (Fig. 5.37) is 18 m long and 3.5 m wide and consists of three roughly parallel rows of postholes following the long axis. The centre and eastern rows are practically straight, whilst the western row has an irregular outline and divides into three lengths of about 6 m, each of which runs in a slight arc. This side may be offset from the others. There seems to be evidence for only one clear entrance to this building, towards the northern end, where two postholes were found only 1.25 m apart. On the eastern side they are marked by a similar pair at the same spacing. This possible entrance is located at roughly the midpoint of a partitioned area defined by a line of postholes running across the width of the building. The placing of the postholes might suggest that they had supported a plank wall. This end 'compartment' has a ground area of 17.5 m^2. It will be seen that the major postholes in this part of the site are rather smaller than the others.

The sizes of the three rows of posts vary considerably. The postholes of the centre row are generally the deepest, whilst the depths of the postholes in the side walls differ markedly. The structural postholes around the 'compartment' at the northern end of the building have a range of diameters between 0.18 m and 0.26 m, compared with 0.22 m and 0.32 m in the remaining part. Depths also vary. In the whole building only two postholes contained post-pipes and these were the largest.

It is hard to work out the character of this building. Whilst the northern end does make an acceptable rectangular unit, in the remainder of the structure the placing of the posts in the three rows, whilst fairly regular, takes no regard of their location in the adjacent line. This would not affect their ability to carry horizontal beams, but does result in a forest of uprights which would make the southern two-thirds of the building very difficult to use. We shall return to this problem later.

There seem to be clear indications that the southern end of the building continued as a fence. The constituent postholes are of very similar diameter and with one exception are of much the same depth.

The channel, F14, was 8.5 m long and up to 1.5 m wide. It had a rounded profile and was between 0.06 m and 0.14 m deep, sloping down slightly from the south-west to north-east. The filling was of chalky rubble, mixed with humus. Its date is uncertain; it runs across

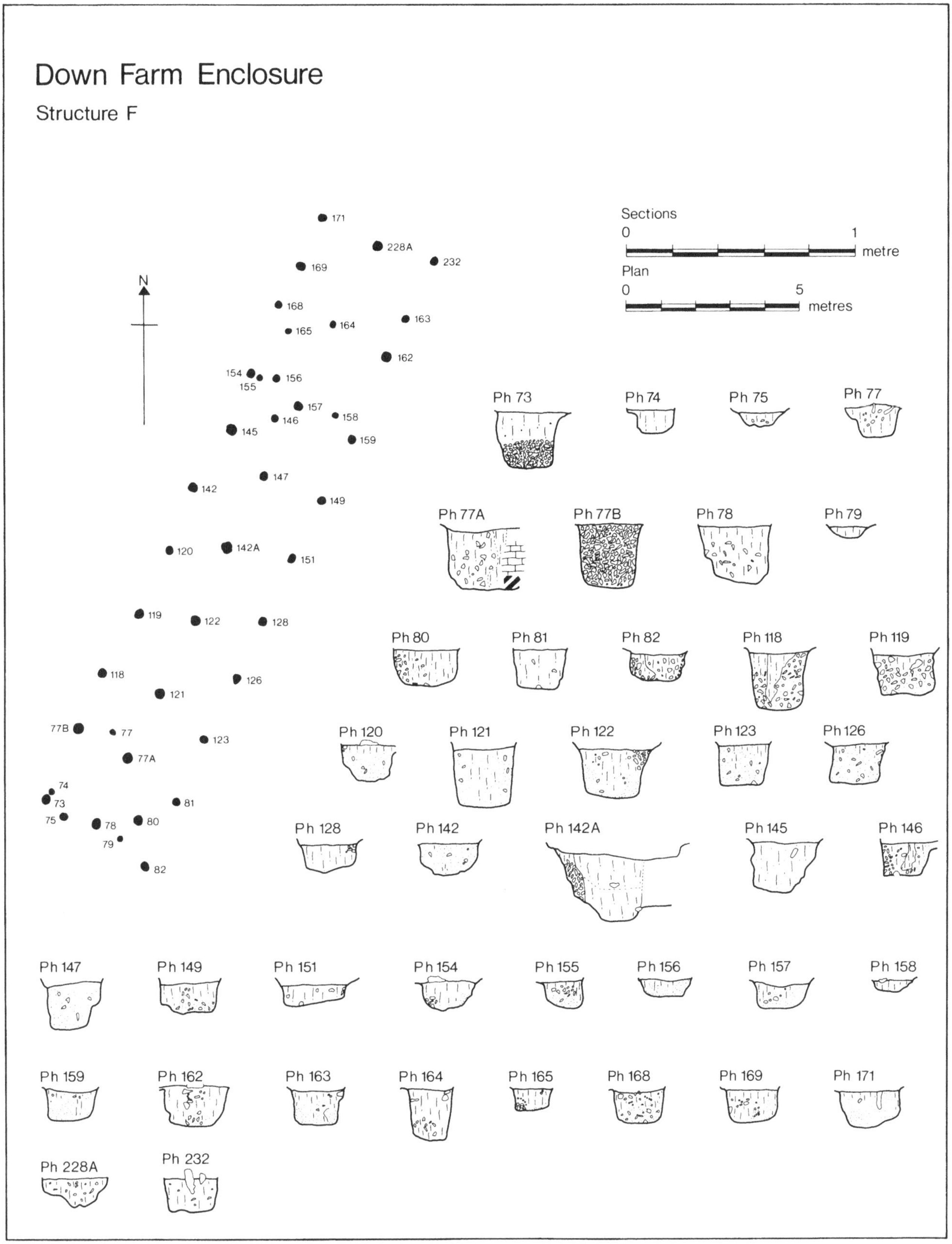

Fig. 5.37 Plan and sections of the postholes of Structure F, Down Farm enclosure

the position of Structure B and the perimeter palisade and contained substantial fragments of a Barrel Urn. In some ways it resembles a hollowed track, but this would not explain its abrupt beginning and end (section: Fig. 5.32, 5).

5.3.2.iii *The finds*

Pottery[1] No attempt was made at the systematic recovery of pottery from the topsoil, and it is unlikely that much material would have survived plough erosion. The material recovered from the interior is therefore restricted, coming from postholes and pits. In all, this amounts to some 106 sherds. The much larger quantity of pottery, some 1,837 sherds in all, was recovered from the ditch silts. The size of this assemblage is greater than that recorded by Pitt Rivers from the ditches of South Lodge Camp, Martin Down or the Angle Ditch, and it is important to remember that Pitt Rivers' excavations at South Lodge and Martin Down indicate that the greatest quantities of pottery from each of these sites came from surface deposits within the enclosures. At Down Farm neither surface midden deposits nor floor deposits within the houses (cf. Drewett 1982) survived.

Within the interior, pottery was recovered from some postholes belonging to each structure, the channel F14 and from one pit, F34. Obviously sherds from the various postholes could have been deposited amongst the packing or have been incorporated within the feature when the post was withdrawn or the structure collapsed.

The ditch was excavated in a series of running sections, starting at the northern terminal and working along the ditch to within 5 m of the southern terminal. The material recorded in these sections was also grouped into five relatively arbitrary ditch segments (Fig. 5.38) and the pottery analysis is presented here with reference to these segments. The pottery distribution around the ditch does not necessarily conform with the distribution of the other midden material. In this discussion use has been made of the more detailed archive record.

The ditch sequence has already been described. A lower midden deposit overlay primary silts, which themselves derived from the weathered sides of the ditch. 467 sherds of pottery were recovered from this lower deposit, although their distribution along the ditch was not uniform (Fig. 5.38). It is clear that major groups of sherds, from around the southern and northern terminals of the ditch, largely derived from the deposition of a few substantial, but incomplete, parts of single urns. Nearly all the sherds from these deposits are small, indicating that the ditch remained open, silting naturally, with the pottery breaking down in the process.

The occasional deposition of large portions of urn also took place, along with the accumulation of a scatter of smaller sherds, in the main eastern arm of the ditch. Here fewer sherds than at the terminals are recorded, but a wider range of fabrics is represented.

The second midden deposit lay above another layer of silt. Most of the pottery from the ditch comes from this second deposit, 1,245 sherds in all. The majority of this material came from the southern arm of the ditch (Fig. 5.38). Again, it seems likely that the deposition of large portions of single vessels and the accumulation of already-eroded sherd material combined to form these deposits. Subsequent erosion of the larger vessel fragments within the ditch makes it difficult to distinguish between these two processes simply on the basis of sherd size.

Further silting, this time partly derived from collapsing bank material, overlies this second midden and is, in turn, overlain by the final midden deposit. This produced the radiocarbon dates of 1210 ± 40 bc (BM 1852N1-N4), 1030 ± 50 bc (BM 1853N), 1030 ± 50 bc (BM 2577) and 1080 ± 110 bc (BM 1854R). The final deposit is of a different character; it is mainly composed of burnt flint, with only 125 sherds of pottery. Most of the burnt flint comes from the northern length of the ditch, and the pottery itself lies along the eastern and northern arms of the ditch, with hardly any material now entering the southern part of the ditch. The deposition of large fragments of urn no longer seems to occur in this phase.

A range of vessels from the site is illustrated in Fig. 5.39.

Flint[2]

1. Deposits in the ditch. The distribution of middens in the enclosure ditch is closely matched by that of the 6,278 flakes and cores and 242 implements. The lower filling of the ditch contained 1,137 flakes and cores and seventy-five implements, whose distribution corresponds quite closely to the position of the midden deposits, with the highest density of flint around the southern corner of the enclosure. Its middle filling was more prolific and contained 4,234 flakes and cores, and 137 implements. Again, these covered the same general areas as the middens, with the highest density of finds to either side of the southern corner of the enclosure. There were noticeably fewer artefacts towards the end of the western arm of the ditch and to either side of its northern angle. Finally, the latest levels of the ditch contained a much lower quantity of finds, with 907 flakes and cores and only thirty implements. These were evenly distributed.

2. Evidence of activities. The flintwork provides two kinds of evidence. The stratigraphy offers limited evi-

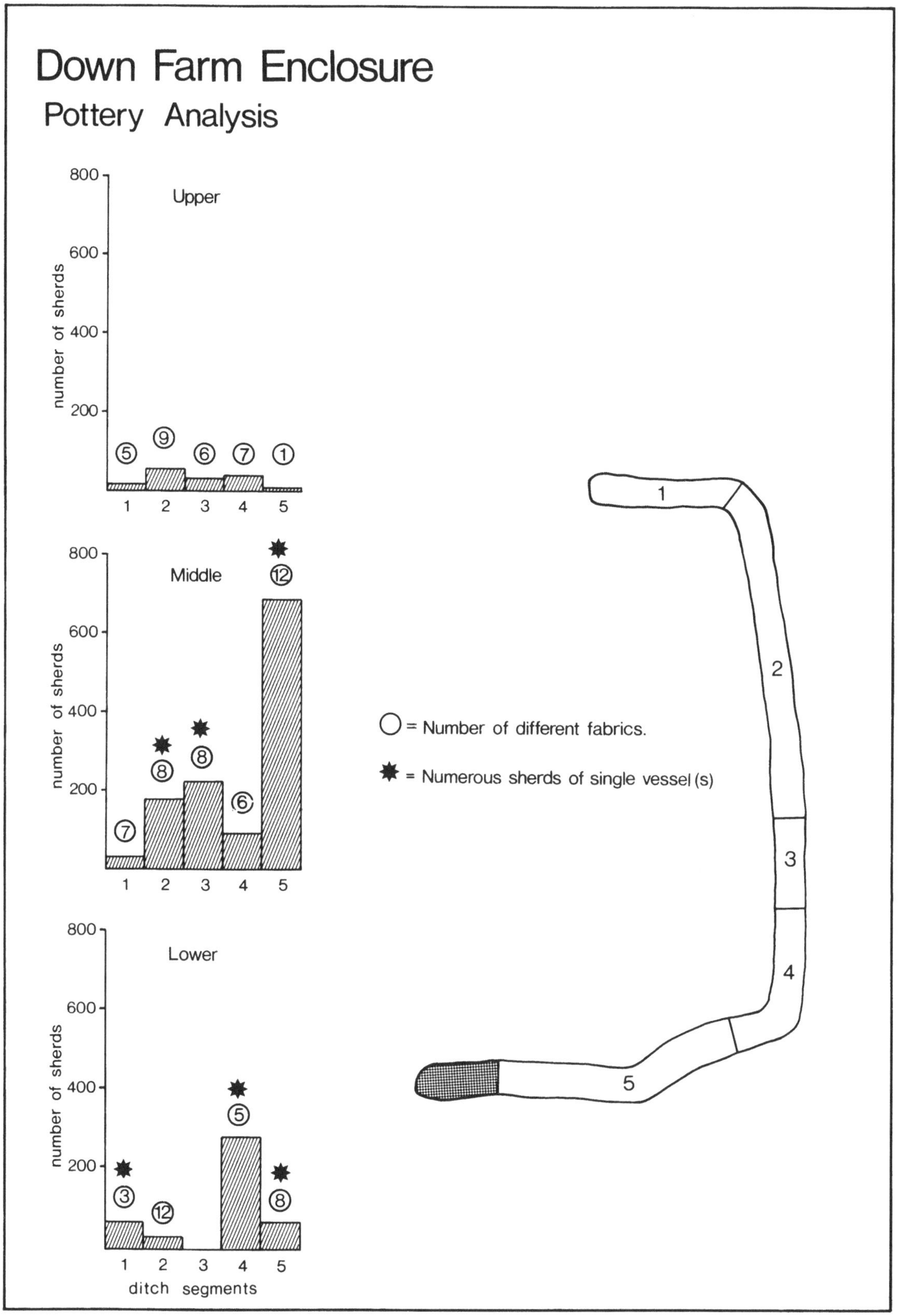

Fig. 5.38 Pottery sherds from the three levels of ditch fill at Down Farm enclosure, showing the number of sherds and fabrics occurring within five segments of the ditch

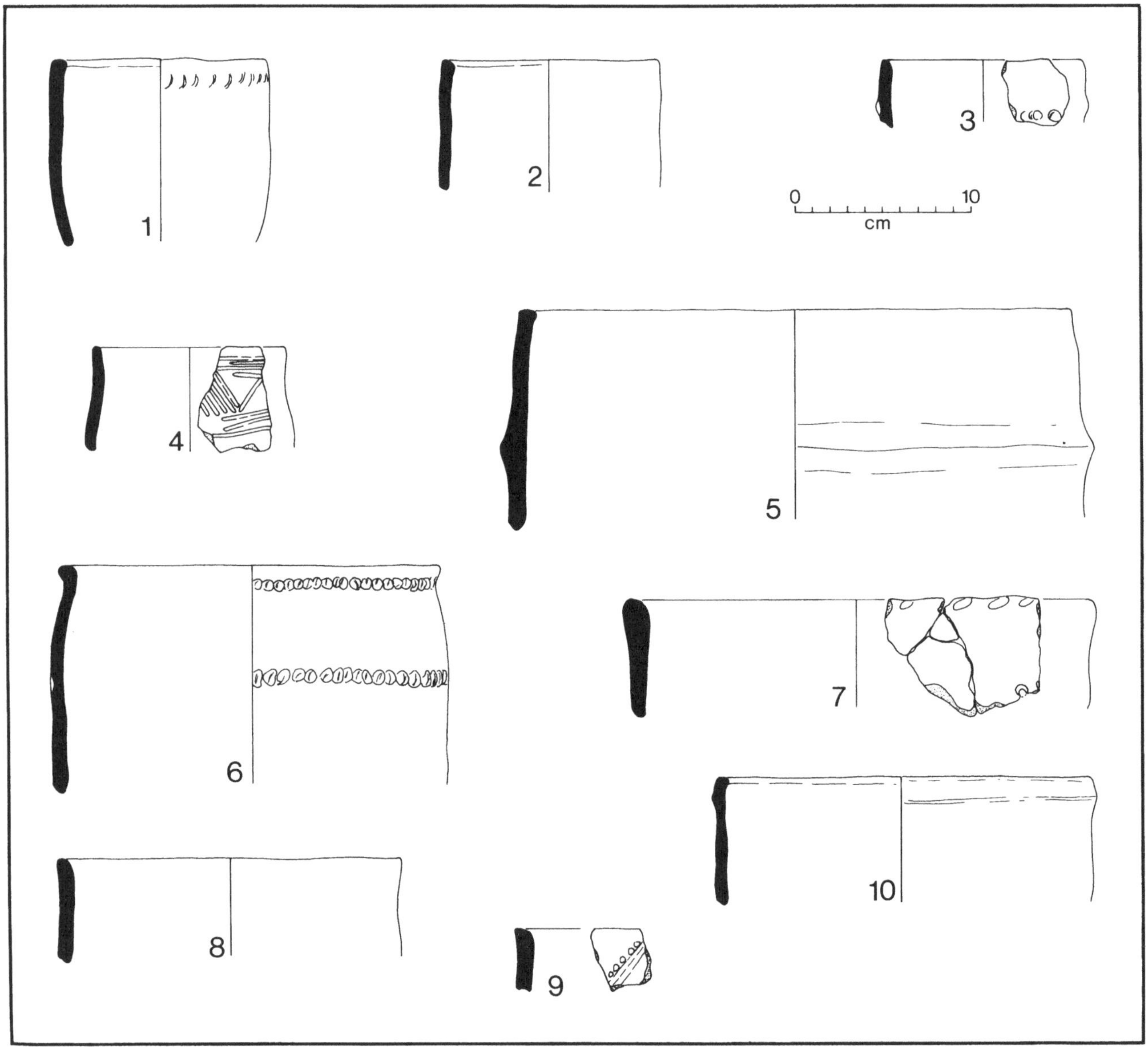

Fig. 5.39 Selection of pottery sherds from the Down Farm enclosure

dence of *chronological* patterning. There was a fall in the proportions of retouched flakes and pounders/hammerstones. The latter may have been used for working fresh flint nodules, exposed when the ditch was dug, and became less common as the ratio of cores to flakes changed. Perhaps raw material was in shorter supply, so that nodules were used more extensively (Table 5.5).

During the same sequence there was an increase in the deposition of flint scrapers, from 49 per cent in the lower filling and 59 per cent in the middle filling to 70 per cent in the top layers of the ditch. To some extent these percentages are affected by the changing proportion of pounders/hammerstones. When the latter are left out of the calculation, the figures become 65 per cent, 64 per cent and 81 per cent respectively. There may therefore still be evidence for some change in the activities taking place.

Table 5.5. *Down Farm enclosure: the nature of the worked flint from the ditch deposits*

	% retouched flakes	% pounders/ hammerstones	Cores: flakes
Lower filling	24	25	1:7
Middle filling	20	8	1:12
Upper filling	15	14	1:21

The flintwork from the ditch shows little detailed *spatial* patterning. In its lower filling the major evidence of flint knapping comes from the areas with the densest distribution of artefacts. It also includes finds of pounders and hammerstones. Apart from that, a small group of scrapers was found in the northern arm of the enclosure ditch. The middle filling shows a similar pattern: flint knapping is best evidenced in the areas with most of the finds, although scrapers are still concentrated in the northern arm of the ditch. Two of the three rods/fabricators were in the northern corner of the enclosure, and three of the four borers were deposited near to its southern corner. There was no real spatial patterning in the top levels of the ditch.

In addition, a few flint artefacts were recovered from subsoil features inside the enclosure. Cores were found in postholes belonging to Structure B and the perimeter fence. One feature in the outer post-ring of Structure B contained four cores, perhaps suggesting a significant episode of flintworking in this area. Scrapers came from postholes belonging to Structures A, B and the perimeter fence, and there was one fabricator from a posthole belonging to Structure A. Although the sample is very limited, it is striking that nearly all this material came from the southern part of the site and that some of it must have pre-dated the construction of the enclosure.

Loom weights In common with other sites on the Wessex chalk, the Down Farm enclosure contained very few loom weights. The only such evidence of textile production came from two postholes belonging to the outer ring of Structure B.

Worked bone A bone awl was found in the filling of a posthole belonging to Structure B.

Worked stone[8] A hundred rock fragments were recovered by excavation. Two types of stone are represented, mainly by small fragments. 78 per cent of the material consists of locally available sarsen, of which only five pieces – four rubbers and a whetstone – are known to have been utilised. The remaining 22 per cent consists of finds originating in local Cretaceous greensand beds. Of these, twelve pieces – ten rubbers and two flakes – show signs of use. The whetstone came from a posthole belonging to Structure E, whilst rubbers are recorded from features belonging to Structures A, B and D, as well as the entrance to the yard. A sarsen whetstone was also found in the ploughsoil overlying Structure A. The remaining artefacts came from the enclosure ditch. Those in its lowest levels were clustered around the south-eastern corner of the enclosure, although one sarsen rubber came from its north-eastern angle. In the secondary phase the distribution extended along the eastern side of the earthwork, with a concentration of sandstone fragments, including three rubbers, in its northern arm. Two further examples, one of sarsen and the other of sandstone, were found close to the south-eastern angle of the ditch. Very little stonework occurred in the uppermost levels of the ditch, but two rubbers, one of each raw material, were found in the eastern ditch of the enclosure, towards its junction with the northern arm. The growing number of grain rubbers in this part of the site matches the changing location of the middens and may reflect the wider structural sequence.

Animal bones[4] In order to express the simple abundance of bones by species from the enclosure ditch, all identified bone fragments have been counted. For the dental specimens only mandibles, part-mandibles and third milk teeth and permanent molars that are unlikely to come from broken mandibles are included. The numbers of bones and mandibles represented are given in Table 5.6.

The proportions of the species represented by the bones in the lower and middle ditch fills present a characteristic pattern for a Middle Bronze Age site; they are very similar to those found in Bronze Age domestic refuse at Grimes Graves, Norfolk (Legge 1981). Cattle (50 per cent and 55 per cent) are the commonest species with sheep (38 per cent and 39 per cent) second. Pigs are uncommon, and deer are rare. However, the mandibles give very different proportions, sheep (58 per cent and 73 per cent) becoming more common and cattle less so. Pigs are again infrequent (Fig. 5.40A). This variation can be best explained by severe attrition working upon the bones. Bone preservation is variable, with some specimens showing rather severe erosion, and the gnawing of bones by dogs was also common. Most bones are represented by shaft fragments, or shaft 'tubes' from which the articular ends have been gnawed or otherwise broken. This points to a severe incidence of gnawing by dogs, with many of the limb bones likely to be removed from the site or consumed entirely. By this means the smaller bones of sheep would suffer a higher degree of damage, and would more easily be reduced to undiagnostic fragments. On the other hand, the tooth rows of mandibles are resistant to dog attack, and these probably represent more exactly the original proportions in which the species were killed. It would thus appear that the Down Farm region was marked by a significantly higher proportion of sheep than was found at Grimes Graves.

The six cattle mandibles from the lower midden are

Table 5.6. *Down Farm enclosure: animal bone identifications from the ditch*

	Pig	Cattle	Sheep/goat	Red deer	Roe deer	Horse	Dog
Phase 1 bones	6	45	35	2	2	0	0
	6.8%	51.1%	38.6%	1.1%	2.2%	0	0
Phase 1 jaws	0	7	14	1	1	0	2
	0	28.0%	56.0%	4.0%	4.0%	0	8.0%
Phase 2 bones	4	102	72	3	0	0	3
	2.2%	55.4%	39.1%	1.6%	0	0	1.6%
Phase 2 jaws	2	7	33	1	0	1[1]	2
	4.4%	15.6%	73.3%	2.2%	0	0	4.4%
Phase 3 bones	0	17	1	1	0	0	0
Phase 3 jaws	0	1	1	1	0	3[1]	0

Horse: [1]indicates loose teeth only.

Fig. 5.40 Species identification (left) and sheep slaughter pattern (right) for animal bones from the Down Farm enclosure

reasonably intact and three are from cattle which were old at the time of death. In the middle ditch deposits, tooth rows are absent, and cattle are mainly represented by loose third milk molars; the bone from these young cattle has not survived. The very high ratio of sheep mandibles to bone fragments also demonstrates the extreme attrition of the bones. Yet the presence of animal skulls in the earlier two midden deposits should be set against this. The lower had skulls of two dogs, and right and left maxillas probably representing two more skulls, and the well-preserved skull of a cow. The middle deposit had parts of a further two dog skulls.

Sheep mandibles and certain isolated teeth from the ditch deposits are attributed to an age class based upon the tooth eruption and tooth-wear state following the method of Payne (1973). Eighteen specimens from the lower and thirty-eight from the middle fills could be classed by this method. The pattern of sheep slaughter shown can be compared with that at Grimes Graves (Fig. 5.40B), a site with excellent preservation (Legge 1981 and forthcoming). The enclosure ditch contains relatively few mandibles from very young sheep, though in the light of evidence of severe bone damage this observation must be regarded with caution. The eighteen mandibles from the lower fill include none from stage A, and two from stage B, while the middle fill has produced no mandibles at this or the earlier stages in the sample of thirty-eight.

At Grimes Graves 12.5 per cent of sheep mandibles from one sample indicate death by stage B (Legge 1981), and 16 per cent from the second sample (Legge forthcoming). It is possible that the rather harsh conditions at Down Farm have contributed to the low proportion of very young mandibles. The Down Farm mandibles also show rather lower rates of slaughter in stages D and E than at Grimes Graves, but by stage F the proportions are quite similar.

Nineteenth-century observations (Simonds 1854) indicate that the M_3 of sheep erupts at about eighteen months of age, and is in early wear shortly afterwards. From this, it would appear that about one half of the Down Farm sheep were killed before the age of two years; the pattern of slaughter, as at many other British prehistoric sites, appears to be directed towards the husbandry of sheep as a meat supply.

As shown above, cattle mandibles are less common than those of sheep in the ditch fill. If likely pairs are eliminated, and the largest number of right *or* left is counted, the total for lower and middle deposits is five young, possibly one sub-adult and three adult cattle. One third milk molar shows early wear, and comes from an animal of only one or two months of age. Three then show moderate wear in the third milk molar and eruption or initial wear on M_1, and were about four to six months old at death. The fifth specimen shows early wear on the M_2, and would be fifteen to eighteen months of age. A slightly damaged but unworn loose M_3 might also belong to this specimen. The adult specimens are from quite aged cattle; three specimens show late wear on the M_3 extending well down the bovine pillar (Grant 1982, 92: stage k), and one is beyond this (Grant's stage m). Although numbers of dental specimens are few, this distinction of age classes is also confirmed by maxilla fragments; unusually, bearing in mind the attrition that seems to have worked on the bone assemblages, these are as abundant as mandibles and lower teeth. It is possible to regard the distribution of age classes as indicating a concern with milk production in the cattle husbandry, as has been argued for Grimes Graves (Legge 1981). In view of the small sample numbers the parallel will be taken no further.

Carbonised plant remains[9] One hundred and four samples of soil, each approximately twenty-five litres in volume, were taken from features on the site and processed in the manner outlined in Jones (1978). Nineteen of these samples were from pits, the remainder from postholes. Five of the pit samples and eleven of the postholes produced between one and two seeds/fruits/tubers, and the remainder produced none.

Details of this material are presented in the companion volume. Of the eleven cereal grains three can be further identified as wheat, and six as barley. Dorsal ridging, characteristic of hulled barley, is discernible on one of these grains. There was also a fragment of carbonised cereal straw in one of the pits.

A sparse data-set such as this is best viewed in conjunction with contemporary data elsewhere in southern Britain. This sparseness is in itself a feature which is shared by other data-sets from a number of pre-Iron Age sites, and which is in striking contrast to the regularly prolific nature of Iron Age carbonised assemblages from sites such as Ashville, Danebury and the nearby Gussage All Saints (Evans and Jones 1979; Jones 1978 and 1984b). I have suggested elsewhere that a widespread shift in the nature of carbonised plant assemblages through time, from being made up of a sparse miscellany of edible food plants, to comprising a plentiful range of grains, weeds and chaff, reflects a change in the organisation of agriculture and its relationship to on-site behaviour (Jones 1984a and 1984c).

An interesting comparison may be drawn between Down Farm and two other Bronze Age sites in southern Britain, the broadly contemporary Black Patch in Sussex and the Late Bronze Age sites at Springfield Barnes in Essex (Hinton in Drewett 1982; Murphy forthcoming). The material from Black Patch and Springfield Barnes compares better with the 'typical' assemblages of the Iron Age than with the assemblage from Down Farm.

5.3.2.iv Down Farm enclosure: the chronological sequence[1,2,7]

The history of the Down Farm enclosure has been presented here in terms of a three-phase structural sequence. This undoubtedly masks discontinuities in the history of human settlement, just as it may fragment the essentially continuous processes of building and rebuilding as the structures were replaced and maintained. This discussion must therefore extend our understanding of the history of occupation beyond a simple statement of sequence.

Structures A and B, lying on a common axis, are likely to be contemporary and to pre-date the enclosure ditch. The area of excavation was determined by the extent of the enclosure itself, but we can be sure that no other circular buildings, pre-dating the enclosure, lie within the immediate vicinity (i.e. within 10 m) of A and B.

Structure A, with its four-post porch, had a floor area of 64 m^2, whilst Structure B had a simpler, shallow entrance and, even in its enlarged form, a smaller floor area of 44 m^2. The postholes of A were the more substantial of the two buildings. Neither building contained pits. The recognisable structural differences between the two buildings may imply that they were used differently, and some slight support for this comes from the artefacts recovered from the postholes. Loomweight fragments were recovered from the outer ring of B and cores were also associated with this building, other examples coming from a posthole of A.

These two buildings can be compared with the pattern of paired structures recognised by Ellison in her study of contemporary settlement plans (Ellison 1980b). She suggests that such associated buildings represent residential and ancillary buildings. The only other post-built structure which could also belong to a phase of open settlement is the four-poster. Assigned to the enclosed settlement on the grounds that it is aligned on the north-eastern entrance through the palisade, it none the less occupies the ground space also occupied by Structure E and aligns awkwardly with F. Thus it may not have been contemporary with these buildings, nor can it have been demolished immediately before their construction, as two of its posts appear to have decayed *in situ*.

The pre-enclosure phase therefore represents two circular buildings which may have been part of a wider scatter of settlement amongst a contemporary field system. Both circular buildings then appear to have been abandoned. Whilst the first phase of B was demolished for the construction of the larger outer ring of posts, these posts were not themselves withdrawn. Some of the posts of Structure A were also left in place. No radiocarbon dates are available for this open settlement.

Following upon a break in occupation, the complex sequence of activity relating to the enclosure itself begins. Some indication of the date of this enclosure is given by the radiocarbon dates of 1000 ± 110 bc (BM.1851R) and 950 ± 160 bc (BM 1850R) for the lower and middle midden deposits contained within the ditch. The detail of the building sequence which gave rise to the phase 2 plan is difficult to establish (Fig. 5.41). The ditch and bank certainly seem to precede the palisade. The ditch cuts across the south-eastern alignment maintained by Structure B and, with the palisade, reorientates the path of access through the site onto a north-eastern–south-western line. Partially ditched enclosures are known elsewhere, the most obvious example being the Angle Ditch (*Excavations* IV, Pl. 248) (Fig. 5.47). The use of fencing to augment partially embanked areas is also attested in Sussex (Burstow and Holleyman 1957; Drewett 1982), where the banks do not derive from ditches, and at Easton Lane, Hampshire (Fasham pers. comm.), where a fenced enclosure butted up against an existing boundary ditch.

Within the fenced enclosure, Structures C, D and E all appear to respect the main line of access through the site between the two gateways. Once again a division between a major structure and ancillary buildings can be identified on the basis of the floor areas and structural details. Structure C is the larger building, with more substantial posts and the more complex porch. This building faced south-east towards the entrance of the fenced 'yard'. Structures D and E are smaller and almost direct replicas of each other. They have a more 'shallow' porch passage, the 'slotted' foundations of which are a feature of other Wessex sites, represented at Shearplace Hill (Rahtz and ApSimon 1962) and Bishops Cannings (Gingell 1980). Each building also has storage pits, which are restricted to this part of the site, beneath the eaves. This practice is well represented elsewhere, particularly in Sussex (Burstow and Holleyman 1957; Drewett 1982) but also, seemingly, at South Lodge Camp. Both buildings face each other across the north-eastern–south-western route through the site, and it is possible that both were partly fenced off from the rest of the enclosure. There is no evidence regarding their sequence of construction, unless E replaced a four-poster which belonged to this enclosed phase of settlement.

Simply upon the basis of the plan, we appear to have a quite complex level of organisation within the enclosure. It is unfortunate, to say the least, that no surface deposits of artefacts or animal bones had survived, but

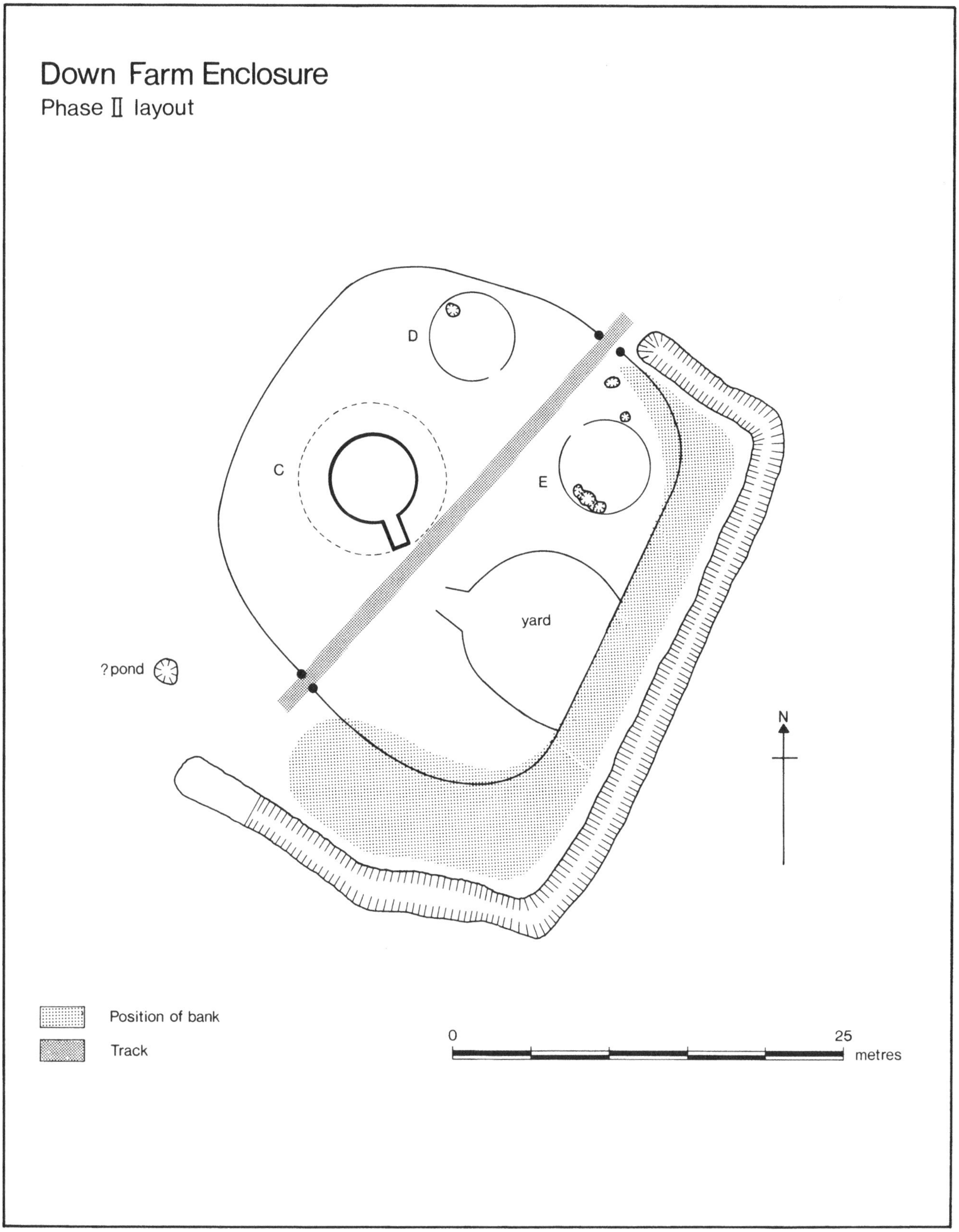

Fig. 5.41 Schematic representation of the organisation of the second phase of the Down Farm enclosure

further indications of settlement activity are available from the enclosure ditch. The attrition on the animal bones and the nature of the pottery sherds indicate material accumulating within an open and eroding ditch. The north-eastern terminal ends just clear of the larger of the two entrances through the palisade; the south-western terminal runs across the front of the second gate. It is near the south-western terminal that the possible pond is located. Large pieces of pottery were deposited in both terminals during the first two phases of midden deposition, but it was the south-western terminal which received by far the larger amount of material. In the south-eastern corner of the ditch another deliberate deposit of material was a group of animal skulls and other bones, which accumulated during the second phase of silting. The combined barrier of the fence and bank would have prevented anything but the most limited drift of settlement debris into the eastern arm of the ditch.

This settlement organisation clearly differs from the seemingly simple arrangement known from some Sussex sites where buildings are situated along the 'back' of embanked and fenced enclosures, with small yards, some containing ponds, in front of the buildings. Such an arrangement is also recognisable at Shearplace Hill, Dorset (Rahtz and ApSimon 1962) and in the final development of South Lodge enclosure (Fig. 5.42). Putting aside the little-understood plan of Thorny Down (Stone 1941), the best comparison for Down Farm may be the poorly recorded enclosure at Cock Hill in central Sussex (Ratcliffe-Densham 1961). Like Down Farm, Cock Hill consisted of a partially ditched enclosure, this time with an external bank. The remaining part of the circuit seems to have been made up by a fence, which continued on top of the bank itself, as at Down Farm. Inside the enclosure there may have been two pairs of structures facing one another, whilst there are also hints of internal fence lines, perhaps defining something like the yard area at Down Farm. Again this was entered through a four-post gateway.

Whatever the details of the organisation of the enclosure, the erection of the rectangular building F marks a clear reorganisation of that settlement. This need not mark a break in occupation since Structure E, which occupied part of the area of F, was demolished and the pits in this area packed with chalk. Structure D was demolished at the end of its life, but this act cannot be connected with the erection of F. The position of F overrides the line of the palisade on the eastern edge of the site and part of the fenced yard. Both must either have been at least partially demolished or have collapsed. There is also evidence for a continuity in some of the spatial parameters of the site.

One interpretation of F would be to see it as a specialised agricultural facility, perhaps a barn with a closed chamber for storage at one end. The alternative is to see it as a *long house*, with a living area at one end and a storage-cum-working area making up the remainder of the building. Given the degree of settlement reorganisation which may have been heralded by the erection of this structure, the second suggestion is perhaps the more plausible. This is supported by a comparison between the floor areas of C and F. It has often been suggested that the internal area of Bronze Age round houses can be divided into a 'living area', defined by the main post-ring, and a more specialised zone used partly for storage, between the main roof supports and the outer wall. The northern part of F has a floor area of 17.5 m^2, which is also the area enclosed by the main post-ring in Structure C. The remaining part of F encloses 45.5 m^2, whilst the area between the roof supports of C and the projected line of the outer wall is 44.1 m^2. Phosphate analysis over the surface occupied by F maintains the distinction between the two parts of the building. The northern chamber gave levels between two and four times as high as that over the remainder of the building. A further indication of continuity in spatial organisation is the way the northern compartment occupies the position of the earlier Structure E, whilst the remainder of the building lies in the area of the earlier yard.

It is hard to find parallels for F. It is not unique in this period, for smaller rectangular buildings, possibly houses, have been found at the Dorset site of Poundbury (Sparey Green 1987), but its closest parallel is on the recently excavated site at Easton Lane, Winchester (Fasham pers. comm.), where once again the building follows one side of a fenced enclosure (Fig. 5.43). So far it is not apparent how that building had been used, and the site also included round houses. The Easton Lane building is smaller but more regular than the Down Farm example. No radiocarbon dates for this structure are available yet. The only buildings of broadly similar size are of rather later date and are found in the first hillfort at Crickley Hill, where there are structural indications that they were long houses (Dixon 1976). These were built on much the same scale as Structure F but were very much more regular in plan. The earliest date for Crickley Hill is not much later than 640 $\pm$ 60 bc (HAR 392). It should be stressed that the building bears little resemblance to contemporary buildings on the Continent.

The reorganisation of the enclosure implied by the construction of F is a point to which we shall return in the following chapter. However, one further observation

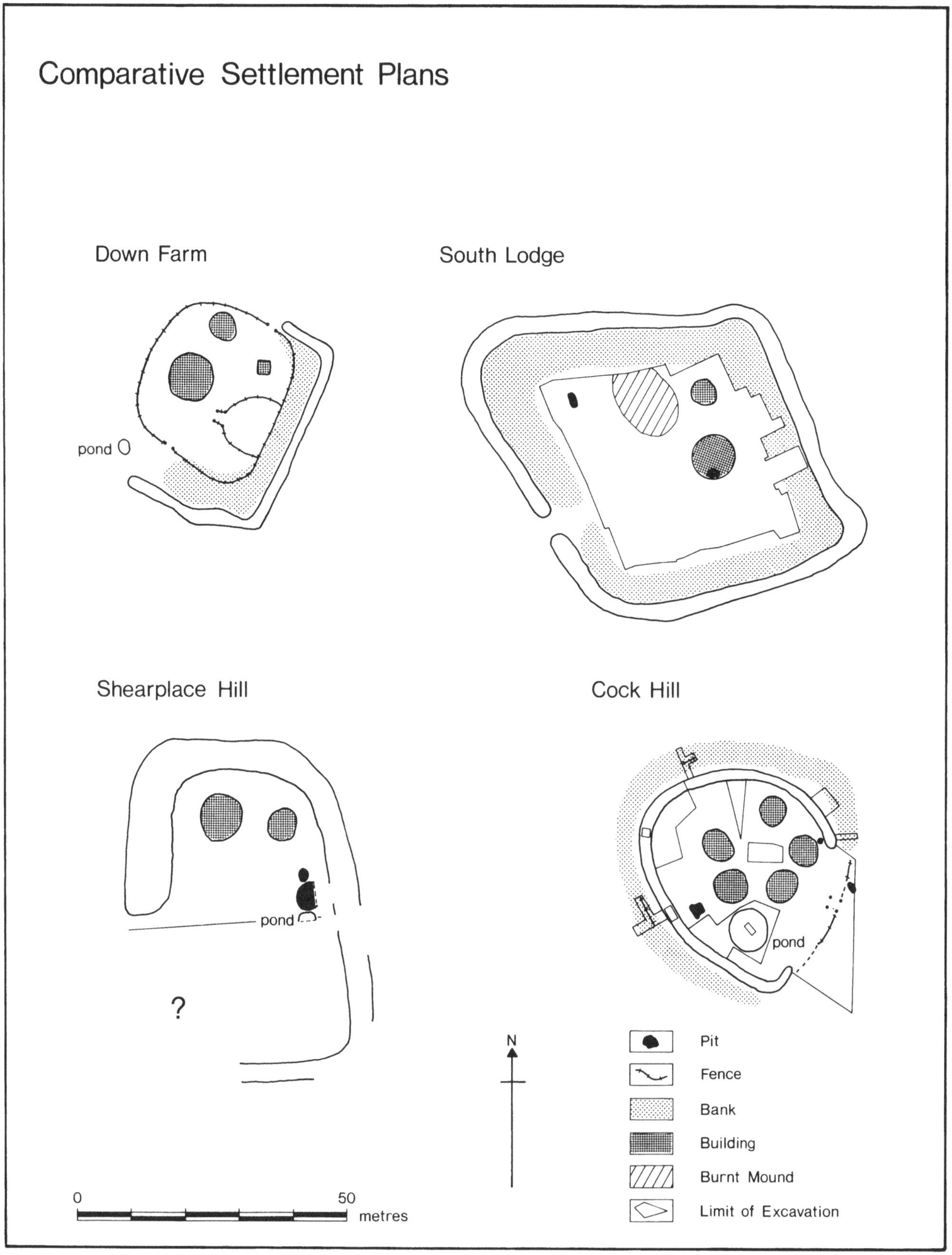

Fig. 5.42 Comparative Middle Bronze Age settlement plans from southern Britain

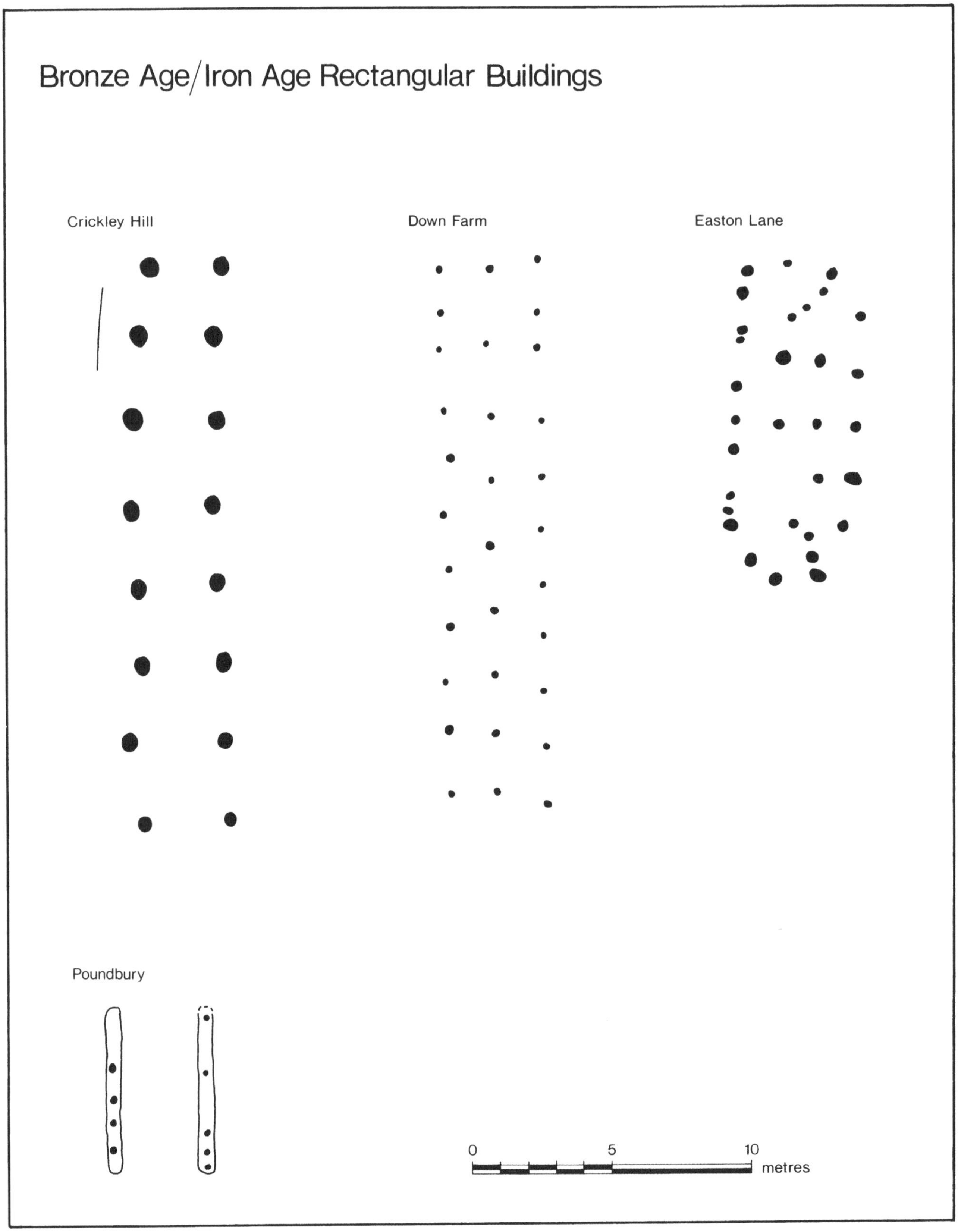

Fig. 5.43 Rectangular buildings from southern Britain

on this theme needs to be made. The final ditch fill displays a change in the processes of deposition. These deposits are composed mainly of burnt stone, but they, and what little pottery there is, lie at the opposite end of the ditch from most of the earlier deposits. The relatively early dates of 1210 ± 40 bc (BM 1852N1-N4), 1030 ± 50 bc (BM 1853N), 1030 ± 50 bc (BM 2577) and 1080 ± 110 bc (BM 1854R) from this context could all indicate a derivation from structural timbers.

5.3.3 Down Farm ring ditch cemetery[5,11,1,2,10]

This monument, excavated in 1980, has already been described in terms of its construction in the Later Neolithic and the deposition of Beaker pottery over the infilled ditches (p. 87). Lying 145 m from the enclosure, the ring ditch was first disturbed by ploughing and then reused in the Middle Bronze Age as a focal point for a small cemetery.

It seems that at this stage the ditch was again recut. The new earthwork was little more than a slot, from 0.42 to 1.10 m wide and 0.15 m deep. It had a homogeneous filling, but in places this included small dumps of material, often flints, as if it had been deliberately refilled (Fig. 3.15: 1.6). It was sealed by a dense deposit of flint nodules, which ran right round the earthwork (Fig. 3.15: 1.8). This may represent the last stage in the refilling of the ditch (Fig. 5.44). The flint packing contained Deverel-Rimbury pottery, worked flint and small pieces of cremated bone, all of which were concentrated on the south-eastern side of the monument. In addition there was Beaker pottery in this layer, and also in the main filling of the ditch. The date of all this activity is difficult to ascertain. Two radiocarbon dates were obtained, one from oak heartwood from the upper part of the recut ditch of 1320 ± 120 bc (BM 2177R), the other also from oak heartwood from the flint packing of 1290 ± 120 bc (BM 2178R).

The flint packing was cut by five of a series of twenty shallow holes, possibly for posts. The others were outside the earthwork or had been cut from a high level in the ditch, although their filling was so similar to its uppermost layer that their exact stratigraphic context is uncertain. They do not form a coherent layout, and at least one of the features may be better understood as a marker for the group of crouched burials described below. The human burial deposits took three forms:

1. The cremations, which had been very badly disturbed by the plough. Very little of these deposits remained in position, although they formed a compact group to the south and south-east of the earthwork.

The burials (Human bone identified by Juliet Rogers)
The amount of cremated bone recovered from these deposits was small, ranging in weight from 2 to 930 g.

C1. A single adult with two animal-bone fragments and sherds of a globular urn. This cut the uppermost filling of the ditch.
C2. An individual of indeterminate age and sex, accompanied by a small group of Bucket Urn sherds.
C3. Sherds of Bucket Urn but no cremated bone.
C4. A single adult.
C5. An individual of indeterminate age and sex.
C6. An adult and juvenile between six and nine years of age, accompanied by a small group of Globular Urn sherds. Charcoal from this deposit has produced the radiocarbon date of 1080 ± 110 bc (BM 2180R).
C7. An adult and juvenile between three and seven years of age.
C8. A single adult accompanied by the base of a Bucket Urn.
C9. A single adult accompanied by a small group of Bucket Urn sherds.
C10. Indeterminate fragments of cremated bone with the upper part of a Globular Urn.
C10A. A single adult. This deposit was cut into the uppermost filling of the ditch.
C11. Indeterminate fragments of cremated bone.
C12. Possibly a single adult accompanied by sherds of Bucket Urn. Charcoal from this deposit gave the radiocarbon date of 1010 ± 100 bc (BM 2179R).

2. A group of five inhumations, four of which lay to the south-west of the monument away from the cluster of cremations (Figs. 5.44 and 5.45).

Three of these formed a compact group, with a posthole, perhaps a marker, at its centre.

The burials (Human bone identified by Juliet Rogers)
F16. A complete adult male crouched inhumation aged twenty-five to thirty-five years. This burial cut the uppermost filling of the ditch, but was outside the area of the flint packing.
F25. This badly disturbed grave contained the fragmented and partial remains of a child aged three to five years. The grave cut through the uppermost filling of the ditch and the inner re-cut, but its relationship to the flint cairn was ambiguous.
F105. The fragmentary remains of a single adult extended inhumation. This grave lay outside the

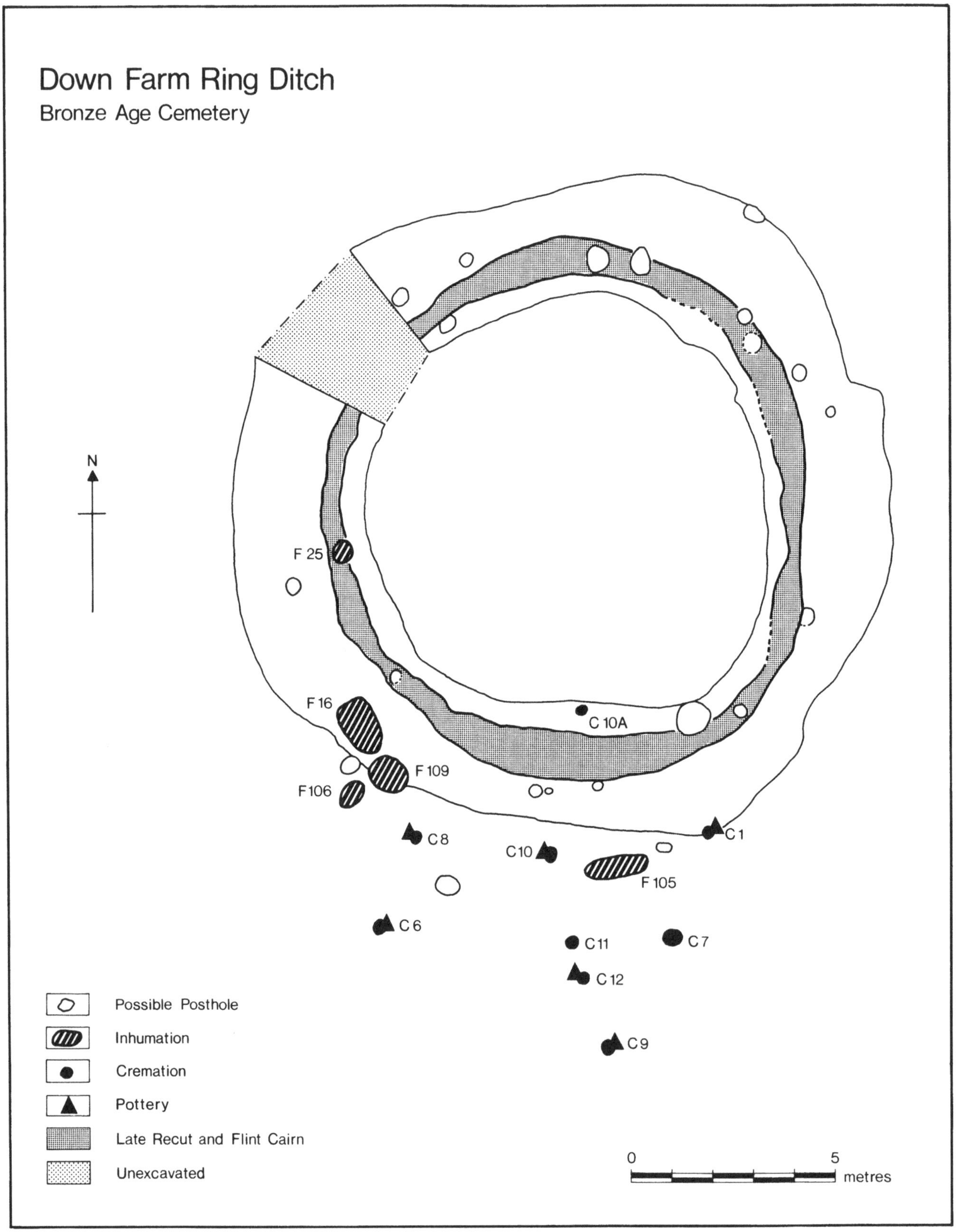

Fig. 5.44 Plan of the Middle Bronze Age cemetery at Down Farm, which developed on the southern edge of the earlier ring ditch

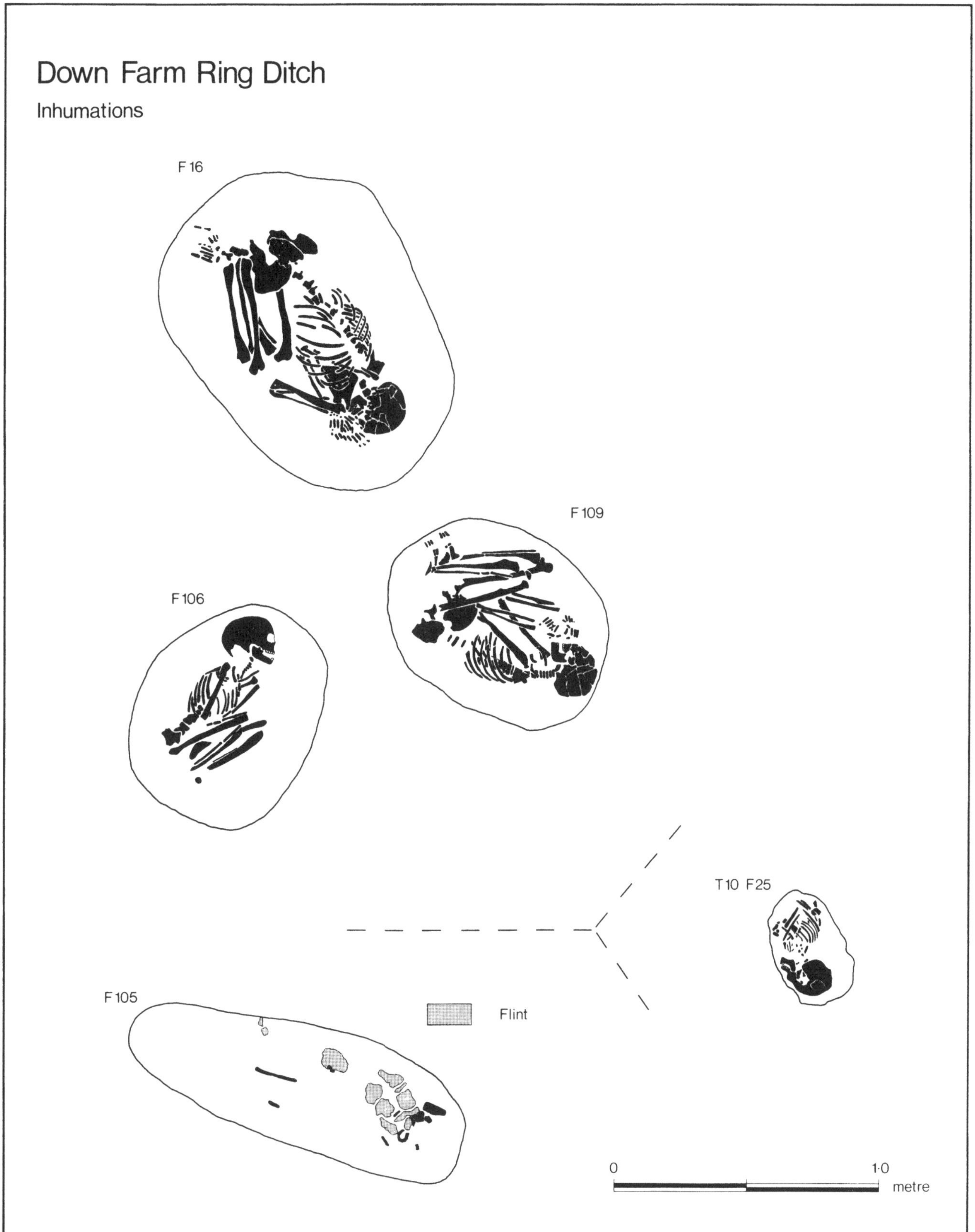

Fig. 5.45 Plan of the inhumation burials from the Middle Bronze Age cemetery, Down Farm

ring ditch and was the one inhumation to lie in the same area of the cemetery as the cremations.

F106. The crouched inhumation of a juvenile aged ten to twelve years. The body was accompanied by shell beads.

F109. A complete adult female crouched inhumation of unknown age.

3. Finally, there was a group of eleven unburnt human bones scattered over the northern portion of the ring ditch. Two of the bones came from the filling of features identified as possible postholes, whilst the others were in the uppermost filling of the ditch. Juliet Rogers identifies these as the remains of two adults and one infant.

Metalwork. A bronze, spiral ring came from the base of the ploughsoil over the southern sector of the ring ditch. This is comparable to the finds from Black Patch, Sussex (Drewett 1982, Fig. 29: 3 and 4), and such rings would belong within the Taunton metalworking traditions of the Middle Bronze Age (Smith 1959, 151 ff.).

5.3.3.i Discussion

Although the site had been badly disturbed, it presents several features of wider interest. The flint packing of the latest ring ditch is distinctive and has been recognised in the ditches of three of the mounds at South Lodge, Barrow Pleck (p. 168). There were no postholes in the recently excavated ditches of those mounds, but these features find a striking parallel in the cemetery barrow at Itford Hill in Sussex, which also had a shallow flint-packed ditch (Holden 1972).

The cremations are a well-known feature of Middle Bronze Age cemeteries and the associated ceramics would allow this cemetery to be contemporary with the occupation of the enclosure. Two of the cremation deposits produced radiocarbon dates around the eleventh century bc. Inhumations would be a more unusual feature at this date, and we might start by distinguishing between the *crouched* inhumations, all of which lie in an area of the cemetery away from the cremations, and the single extended inhumation which lies amongst the cremations. The latter would be best paralleled amongst the Anglo-Saxon cemeteries of Cranborne Chase and south Wiltshire. Stratigraphically, three of the crouched inhumations belong to a late stage in the development of the ring ditch and the whole group may well be contemporary with the cremations. At Barrow Pleck we have seen how a crouched inhumation was buried in the causeway of Barrow 3 (p. 173), and at Amesbury G71 both urned and crouched burials occurred in the same stratigraphic context on the south-eastern side of the mound; with one exception the two groups had a complementary distribution, as they do at Down Farm (Christie 1967). In this context we should note that inhumations are also recorded from amongst the cremations at the eponymous site of Rimbury (Grinsell 1959, 142; Weymouth barrow G34).

Lastly, the scatter of human bones from the northern part of the ring ditch anticipates the distinctive practices recognised on Iron Age sites. Indeed, isolated human bones like those here are already known from Late Bronze Age settlement sites like Potterne, Wallingford and Runnymede Bridge (Gingell and Lawson 1985; Thomas, Robinson, Barrett and Wilson 1986, 193; Longley 1980, 79).

5.4 The Pitt Rivers archive

5.4.1 Introduction[1]

We now return to the archive of the nineteenth-century excavations which investigated three further Middle Bronze Age sites in our study area. These are Handley Barrow 24, the Martin Down enclosure and the Angle Ditch. It is not intended to repeat the substantial information contained in the original reports (*Excavations* IV), nor to attempt a reinterpretation based simply upon those published accounts. But our more recent excavations have raised issues which warrant a reworking of part of the substantial museum archive.

5.4.2 Handley Barrow 24[1]

This small, low mound lay within 44 m of the neighbouring Early Bronze Age Barrow 23. It was surrounded by a penannular ditch some 7 m in diameter. The ditch was shallow with an average depth of less than 1 m. The single causeway lay to the south-west (Fig. 5.46).

The problems of identifying any pre-mound activity and of dating the barrow itself are connected. Little mound material appears to have survived, there being about 0.3 m recorded between the top of the mound and the chalk. Only one, very general, section through the mound is published (*Excavations* IV, Pl. 295).

When the mound was removed three 'cavities' were identified, 'in the body of the mound' (*Excavations* IV, 147). These appear to have cut down into the chalk and Pitt Rivers identified two of them as empty graves. These contained chalk rubble and produced a single small ox bone and a sherd of flint gritted pottery. From above one of these features a further eight 'coarse' sherds were recorded. Whilst all these could be Bronze Age material, a single earlier sherd is also recorded, an unabraded rim

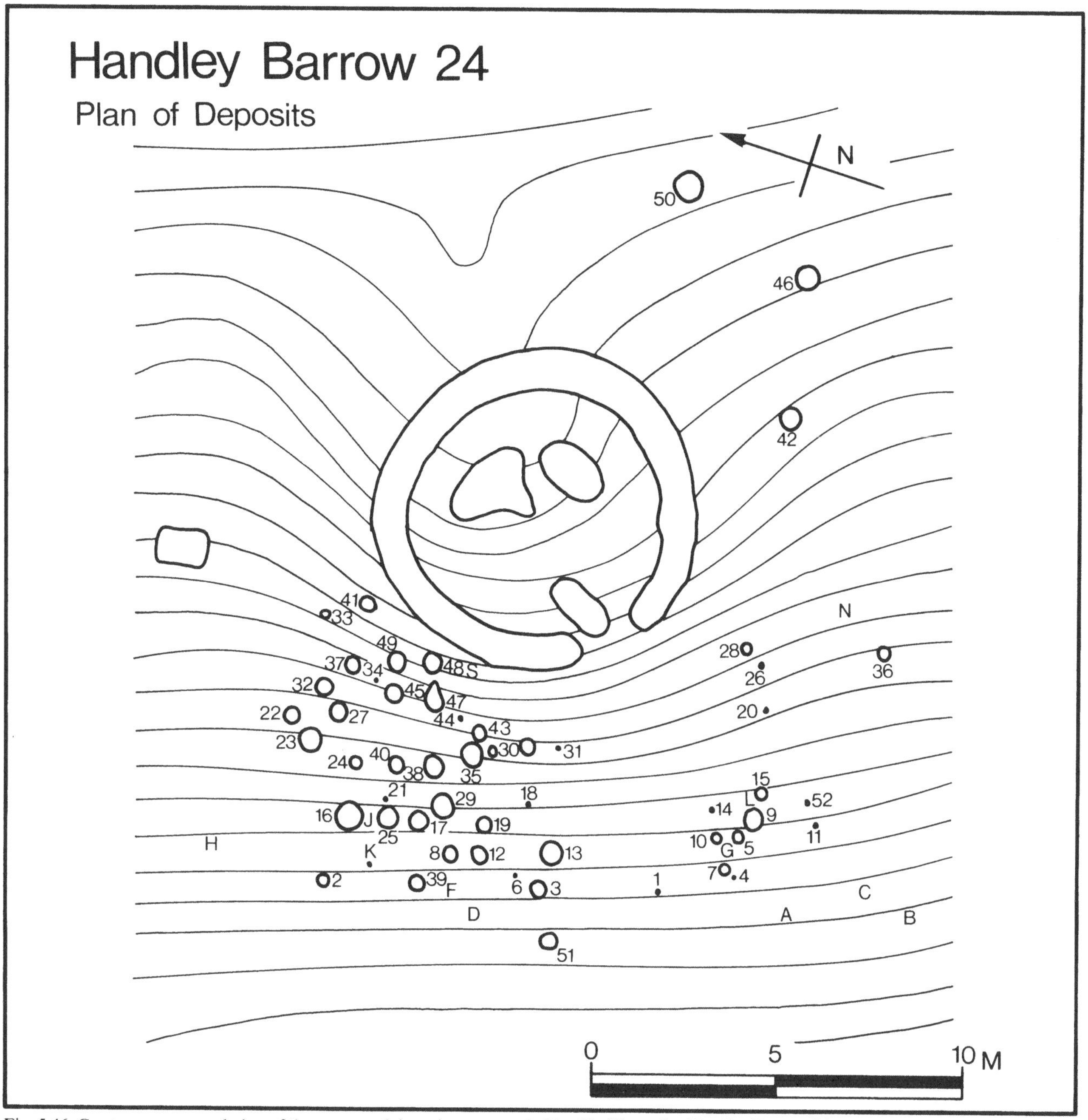

Fig. 5.46 Contour survey and plan of the excavated deposits, as recorded by Pitt Rivers for Handley Barrow 24 (contours at 0.061 m)

sherd of Later Neolithic Mortlake ware from beneath the mound on the 'chalk floor' (*Excavations* IV, 163 and Pl. 298:8). No material at all was recovered from the ditch.

In diameter the barrow is smaller than Barrows 3, 4 and 18 on Barrow Pleck at South Lodge, being closer in size to Barrow 2. It is comparable in size to the Deverel-Rimbury barrows from Simons Ground, Dorset (White 1982), and also with Late Neolithic mounds in the study area. The evidence is not secure, but the construction of the mound itself certainly could fall within the same general period as the cremations which came to be placed around it.

The mound becomes the focus for activity defined mainly, but not entirely, by deposits of cremated bone and pottery which were buried beyond the outer lip of the ditch. The cremations were originally numbered 1 to 52 (Fig. 5.46), whilst pottery deposits unaccompanied by cremated bone were designated A to H, J to O and S. One of the latter (F) also included fragments of a twisted bronze ornament. To the north of the barrow a rectangular pit 1.3 ft (0.40 m) deep was recorded and interpreted as an 'empty grave'.

Our understanding of these deposits, based upon the original published account, is significantly enhanced by the museum collections. Nearly all the collected material survives and most is still contained in the original finds bags within which it was stored immediately after excavation. These have been described elsewhere (Burleigh, Bradley, Barrett and Kinnes 1982). This archive has allowed a high degree of confidence in our ability to assign material to particular funerary deposits. The museum collections include charcoal samples from which radiocarbon dates were originally obtained for six separate deposits (Burleigh, Bradley, Barrett and Kinnes 1982). All these fall within the British Museum date series which is in error and it has not proved possible to revise these data. However, a further, reliable, determination of 1150 ± 50 bc (BM 1648N) has been obtained for charcoal found in deposit 38, where cremated bone representing both an adult and an infant was found in and around an upright urn. Little of this vessel survives today.

Although the original account contains a fairly full description of the pottery from the cemetery, at that time no work was possible on the cremated bone. All the available material has now been analysed by Juliet Rogers and is discussed here.

5.4.2.i The cremated bone[10]

Fifty-two bags of cremated bone were available for examination. Details of the analysis appear in Tables 5.7 and 5.8. The amount of bone in each cremation was very variable, ranging from 0.5 g to 1,085 g, and the number of fragments from one to *c.* 1,100. Most of the fragments were small: the mean size was usually between 20 mm and 25 mm, and ranged from 3 mm to 94 mm. Most fragments were calcined and were a greyish-white colour, although a few were dark grey or almost black. In some cremations there were occasional fragments of non-calcined bone and in cremation 42 most of the bone was non-calcined. The fragments of bone in this cremation were also larger than those of the other cremations.

Only from the material inside the urn of cremation 38 was there evidence for more than one person, where one fragment amongst the adult cranial material indicates the probable presence of an infant.

Age (Table 5.7) was assessed by the stage of eruption or formation of teeth (Brothwell 1973) and by epiphyseal fusion (Genoves 1969b). The fusion of cranial sutures, although not an accurate method of ageing, was used, as was the thickness of the long-bone cortex. Sex (Table 5.7) was established, where possible, from the morphology of the pelvis or skull (Genoves 1969a).

Cranial fragments were recognised in all cremations with identifiable fragments except cremation 2. Femoral fragments were the next most frequently occurring bone. The frequency of occurrence of these two types may be because they are more easily recognised as separate entities. With this in mind, there does not appear to be a particular pattern of bone type inclusion for age and sex, although the difficulty of precise ageing and sexing may obscure any pattern.

In six cremations animal bones were recognised (Table 5.8); all were unburnt.

It seems likely that all cremations, except 42, had been well burnt and crushed. They varied a good deal in the amount of bone included, ranging from a few fragments to over a kilogram of bone, but in no instance was a whole skeleton represented. There was no apparent selection of bone in these token collections of cremated remains. No pathological change or other abnormality was seen.

5.4.2.ii The organisation of the cemetery[1]

With the publication of Knighton Heath (Petersen 1981), Kimpton (Dacre and Ellison 1981) and Simons Ground (White 1982), along with our own work at South Lodge (Barrow Pleck) and the Down Farm ring ditch, greatly increased amounts of data are now available for Deverel-Rimbury-type burials. The organisation of such cemeteries has been discussed by Ellison (1980a and in White 1982, 59). Amongst the considerable variety in cemetery form identified, Ellison has been able to demonstrate that a number are made up of clusters of cremation deposits. These clusters vary in the number of deposits, but most contain between five and twenty burials and 'there is no correlation between age and sex determinations and the style of the containing vessels, and neither is there any spatial patterning of age or sex groups' (Ellison 1981a, 124). Ellison accepts that multiple clusters may reflect the chronological development of a cemetery (cf. Dacre and Ellison 1981), although she also suggests that the clusters may represent 'kin-groups'. These two suggestions are contradictory, unless we are observing discontinuous kinship history in a single cemetery. All in all, whilst there is considerable variation in cemetery layout, the level of 'organisation' represented in the patterning of deposits is limited. The approach which has been followed in dealing with this type of cem-

Table 5.7. *Handley Barrow 24: age and sex determinations on cremated bone*

Deposit	Age	Sex
1	Indet.	Indet.
2	Adult	Indet.
3	Adult	Indet.
4	Adult	Indet.
5	Indet.	Indet.
6	Adult	Indet.
7	Adult	Indet.
8	Adult	?Male
9	Adult	Indet.
10	Adult	Indet.
11	Adult	Indet.
12	?Adult	Indet.
13	Adult	Indet.
14	Adult	Indet.
15	Adult	Indet.
16	Adult	Indet.
17		
Inside urn	Adult	Indet.
Outside urn	Adult	Indet.
18	Adult	Indet.
19	?Adult	Indet.
20	Adult	Indet.
21	Indet.	Indet.
22	Non-adult	Indet.
23	Adult	Indet.
24	Indet.	Indet.
25	Adult	Female
26	Indet.	Indet.
27	Adult	Female
28	Immature	Indet.
29	Adult	Indet.
31	Adult	Male
32	Adult	Indet.
33	Indet.	Indet.
34	Adult	Indet.
35	Adult	Male
37	Adult	Indet.
38		
Inside urn	Adult & Infant	Indet.
Outside urn	Indet.	Indet.
40	Adult	Indet.
41	Adult	Indet.
42	Adult	Female
44	Indet.	Indet.
45	Adult	Indet.
46	Adult	Indet.
48		
Inside urn	Young Adult	Female
Outside urn	Indet.	Indet.
49	12–14 yrs	Indet.
51	Adult	Indet.

etery has been to search for clusters of association (e.g. age, gender, vessel type, position in cemetery). Such clusters have not been located; instead the various attributes appear to cross-cut associations.

To understand how this arises we must again move away from treating cemeteries as a blueprint for social organisation. The cemetery, with its mound, is simply an area of ground where, at the end of a complex cremation ritual, deposits of human bone were brought and interred. Each burial was structured around a series of choices. These were drawn from and maintained a particular cultural/symbolic system, and were established in relation to the architecture of the monument itself. It is notable that deposits do not intercut, and salvage excavation on the site after ploughing led Martin Green to observe the existence of a posthole, probably indicating the use of marker posts. It is possible at Handley 24 (and elsewhere for that matter) to reconstruct something of this process of cultural choice, set out here as Table 5.8. The structure of these choices may be outlined as follows:

1. The selection of material. This concerns the decision to include or exclude either human bone or charcoal (presumably from the pyre). Juliet Rogers has already noted that the selection of the bone itself involved the retrieval of only part of the more easily recognisable remains.
2. Orientation of the deposit towards the mound. Although we do not know the direction(s) from which the mound was approached we can specify three broad foci for deposition at Handley 24: west, east and centre. This choice may then have been followed by the decision whether or not to dig a chalk-cut pit.
3. The final set of choices concerns the nature of the material placed in the ground, including the type of ceramic deposit and the inclusion, if any, of additional material. In only one case does this involve the inclusion of any bronze, with the burial of fragments of twisted bronze.

Presented in this way we can observe that, for most deposits, each step in the funerary sequence from the pyre to the grave does not determine the choices made in the following step. Thus, although the sequence in each case is complex and employs an elaborate symbolic universe, the cumulative pattern of deposits does not reveal a set of clustered associations. There are, however, some important exceptions.

Deposits without human bone also tend to be without charcoal. They may therefore have little to do with activities around the pyre. They also tend to be placed towards the edge of the other deposits, away from the mound. Deposit 42 is one of only three placed to the east of the mound, and is one of only two definitely inverted

Table 5.8. *Handley 24: cemetery organisation*

STEP 1

Selection of material

- **Charcoal**
  2, 3, 4, 5, 8, 13, 16, 17, 18, 19, 24? 32, (36) 38, 40, 43, 48
- **No Charcoal**
  1, 6, 7, 9, 10, 11, 12, 14, 15, 20, 21, 22, 23, 25, 26, 27, 28, 29, 30, 31, 33, 34, 35, 37, 39, 41, 42, 44, 45 46, 47, 49, 50, 51, 52, (A) (B) (C) (D) (E) (F) (G) (H) (J) (K) (L) (N) (O) (S)

○ = No human bone

STEP 2 (Approach to mound)

Relation of deposit to mound

- **West**
  2, 3, 6, 8, 12, 13, 16, 17, 18, 19, 21, 22, 23, 24, 25, 27, 29, 30, 31, 32, 33, 34, 35, 37, 38, 39, 40, 41, 43, 44, 45, 47, 48, 49, 51, D, E, F, H, J, K, O, S
- **Centre**
  1, 4, 5, 7, 9, 10, 14, 15, 20, 26, 28, 36, 52, A, B, C, G, L, N
- **East**
  42, 46, 50

STEP 3 (Action at mound 1: preparation)

Excavation of Chalk cut pit

- **Yes**
  2, 3, 5, 7, 8, 9, 10, 12, 13, 15, 16, 17, 19, 22, 23, 24, 25, 27, 28, 29, 30, 32, 33, 35, 36, 37, 38, 39, 40, 41, 42, 43, 45, 46, 47, 48, 49, 50, 51
- **No**
  1, 4, 6, 11, 14, 18, 20, 21, 26, 31, 34, 44, 52, A, B, C, D, E, F, G, H, J, K, L, N, O, S

STEP 4 (Action at mound 2: deposition)

Pottery *with* cremation

- **Urn complete**
  [23] ▽26 29, 43, 45
  - **Inverted**
    14 △42 *
  - **Upright**
    (8) 10, 12, 15 ▽16 [17] [21] (27) 30 32, 33 [35] 37 △38 39 (40) 46
  - 48
- **Urn sherds**
  11, 19 △(20) 24 25, 34, 44, ▽50
- **Two vessels**
  18 ▽(22) 49
  - **Upright**
    (9)
- **assemblage**
  2, 3, 4, 5, 7, △13 31, 47, 51, 52
- **No pottery associated**
  1, 28, 36, 41

Pottery deposits without bone

- **With charcoal**
  (36)
- **Urn sherds**
  A, B, C, D, G, H, J, K, L N, S
- **Mixed sherd assemblage**
  E [F] O

○ Sandstone fragments
△ Unburnt animal bone
□ Additional sherds
▽ Flint flake
* Bone tweezers
□ Bronze object

urns. Juliet Rogers notes that most of the bone here is also differently treated; it is not calcined and is not as heavily crushed as in the other deposits. The bone tweezers are a unique association from the site and the urn is the only Collared Urn in the cemetery. This particular vessel belongs to Longworth's secondary series of Collared Urns (Longworth 1984, 186); the latest extent for the chronology of such vessels is uncertain. There seems no reason to doubt that this deposit is part of, but marked off from, the rest of the cemetery. The one valid radiocarbon determination of 1150 ± 50 bc (BM 1648N) for another deposit within the cemetery would also be of an acceptable order for a vessel late in the Collared Urn series.

5.4.3 The Angle Ditch and Martin Down enclosures[1]

5.4.3.i The nature of the record

The Angle Ditch was discovered and excavated as part of the investigation of the archaeological remains on Handley Hill in late October 1893, the South Lodge enclosure having been dug that summer. The Martin Down enclosure was excavated between November 1895 and March 1896. Both were published in *Excavations* IV in 1898. Different recovery rates are likely to have operated on the different sites with changes in labourers and supervisors. For example, Toms supervised the Martin Down excavation. Certainly the quality of the archive records varies, the labelling on the Angle Ditch pottery is not full and a fair proportion of it is now damaged and illegible. On the other hand, the Martin Down record is remarkable. Nearly every sherd carried a printed label with additional written information about the context of recovery. It is all the more unfortunate that the field plans for the site do not survive. Given our understanding of the South Lodge archive, there seems little doubt that these would have carried considerably more information than is contained in the final report. This suspicion is supported by the cross-referencing to the site plan noted on the finds labels. We are left with a degree of uncertainty regarding the precise location of the areas excavated in the interior, which are recorded in terms of the four cardinal points and the lengths of ditch recorded as north-east, south-east, south-west and north-west. However, the published sections do provide some hint as to which ditches are being referred to (*Excavations* IV, Pl. 307) (Fig. 5.47).

5.4.3.ii The nature and history of the enclosures

The Angle Ditch was not recognised as a surface feature. It represents a 68.60 m length of ditch, which appears to run around one corner of an earlier field plot (*Excavations* IV, Pl. 248; Toms 1925) (Fig. 5.44). The ditch averaged some 2.0 m in depth and no rampart was recorded as a surface feature or in excavation. The eastern side of the area partly enclosed by this ditch is cut by an apparently later, linear feature.

The Martin Down enclosure (Fig. 5.47) was recognisable as an earthwork. It covers a larger area (0.81 hectares) than any of the enclosures so far discussed. Indeed the site has been assigned to a separate class of larger enclosures in the southern British Middle Bronze Age, alongside Ogbourne Down West, Wiltshire and Rams Hill, Berkshire (Piggott 1942; Bradley and Ellison 1975; Ellison 1980b). The Martin Down enclosure comprises three uneven lengths of ditch, which average just under some 3.00 m in depth and an upcast rampart, the chalk rubble of which is referred to on the finds labels. The wide causeways between the butt ends of these ditches and the lack of observable structural details within the enclosure, led Pitt Rivers to suggest that the site was a cattle enclosure. Like South Lodge, it may have been inserted into a pre-existing field system.

Although neither site, despite extensive surface trenching, revealed any post-built structures, our work at the South Lodge enclosure would indicate that such buildings probably did exist. The location of these enclosure ditches amongst seemingly earlier lynchet systems, and our own observations at South Lodge and Down Farm, also indicate that the enclosure ditches may be late in a long and complex history of settlement.

This idea is supported by the distribution of ceramics at Martin Down. If we compare the fabrics in the small but discrete assemblages from (1) two 'Beaker' pits within the enclosure, (2) the old land surface beneath the rampart, (3) the lower, (4) middle and (5) upper ditch fills (Fig. 5.48), then we see a sequence in the fabrics represented. This runs from Beaker to Deverel-Rimbury traditions, with the addition (not considered here) of Roman pottery in the upper ditch fill. Of particular importance is the material from the sealed old land surface. Recorded from beneath all lengths of the rampart, this surface represents a very clear horizon (*Excavations* IV, Pl. 306). It indicates the existence of grassland prior to the construction of the enclosure. Lying on, or buried within, that turf is a wide range of fabrics, including Beaker material and sherds of Deverel-Rimbury urns. The complex, but little-understood, history of activity on the site prior to the construction of the enclosure therefore includes the use of Deverel-Rimbury pottery.

The published sections indicate that the ditches of both enclosures had similarly sharp profiles, comparable to that of the South Lodge enclosure. Again we might sus-

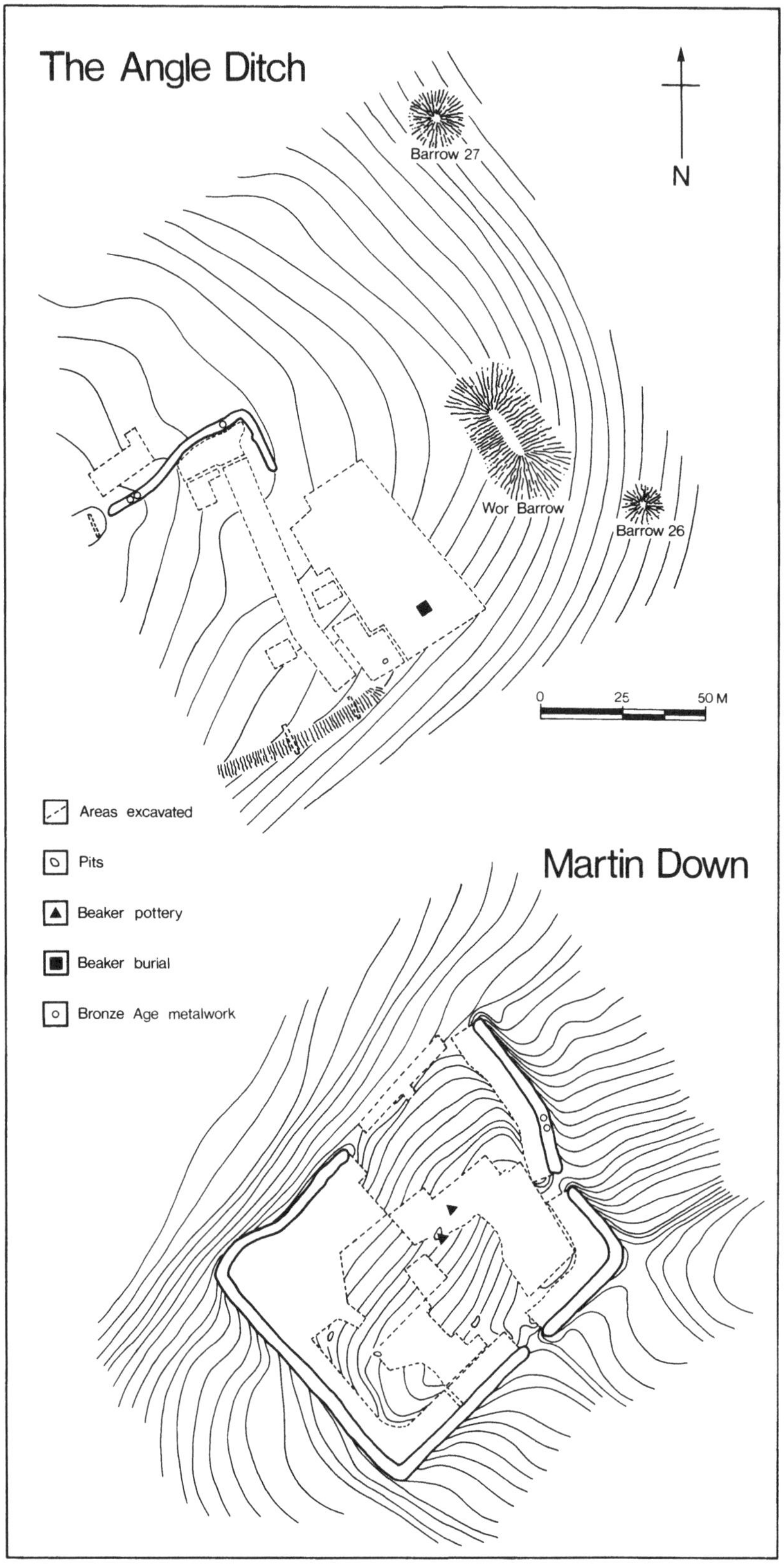

Fig. 5.47 The Middle Bronze Age enclosures of the Angle Ditch and Martin Down, as recorded by Pitt Rivers (contours at 0.15 m)

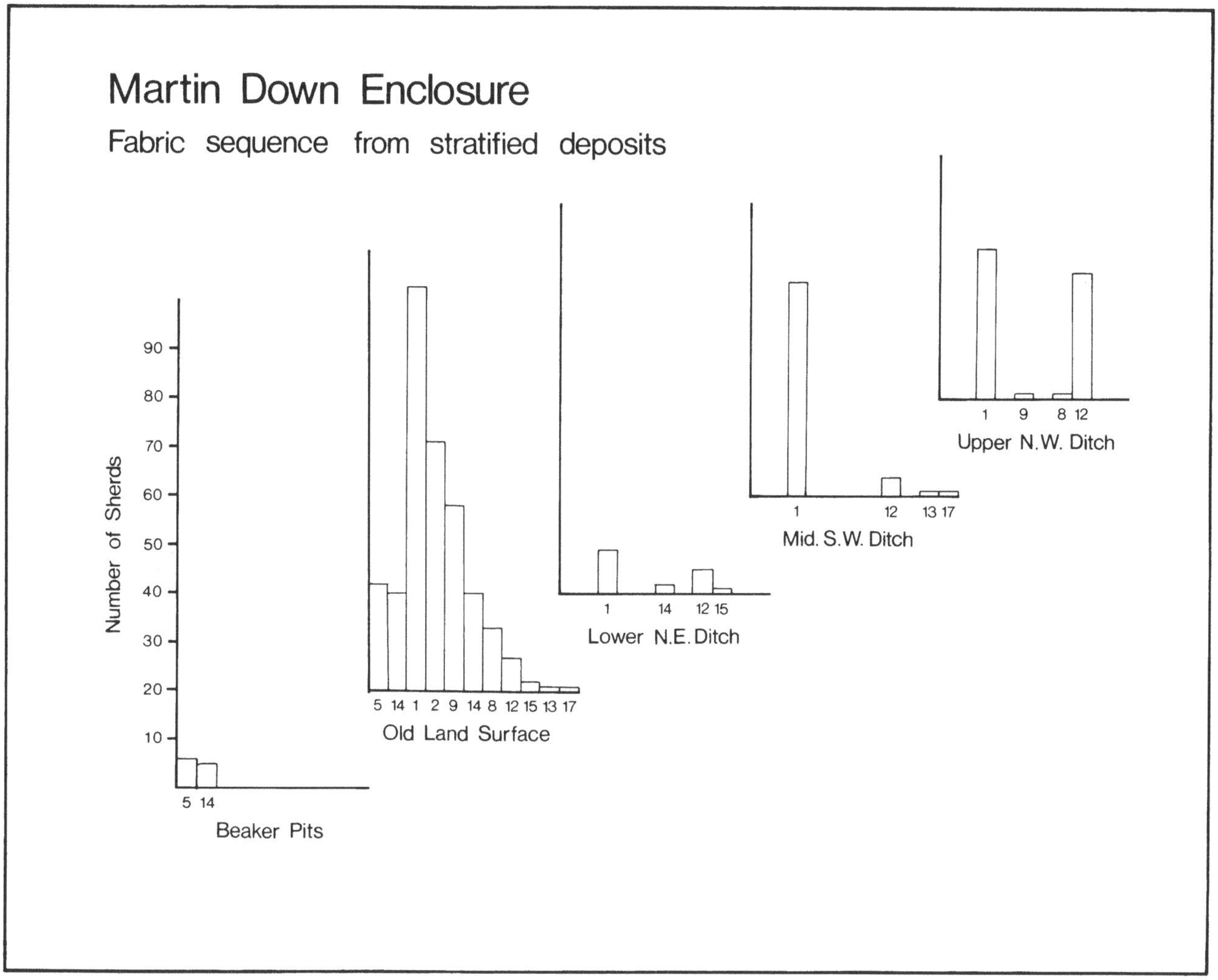

Fig. 5.48 The pottery fabric sequence at Martin Down, based upon five different stratigraphic contexts

pect that the infilling of these features had been rapid, a product of natural erosion and the deliberate dumping of material. Pitt Rivers records both ditch fills in terms of a three-fold division: lower 'chalk rubble'; middle 'mixed fill'; and upper 'mould'. At the Angle Ditch the rapid accumulation of the lower 'rubble' is illustrated by the unweathered sides at the bottom of the ditch, which still preserved axe marks (*Excavations* IV, 104). On both sites most of the Bronze Age pottery lay in the middle ditch fills, in contrast with the worked flint and burnt flint, most of which is recorded from the upper fill. This pattern recalls our own observations at the Down Farm enclosure. Animal bone, mainly of sheep and cattle, occurred at all levels. In the Angle Ditch the basal 'rubble' contained most of the sherds of a single urn, a saddle quern and the fragmentary remains of a bronze razor, awl and palstave (*Excavations* IV, Pls. 262 and 263). Some human skeletal fragments were recovered from the middle fill.

Our understanding of the nature of the ditch deposits is greater for the Martin Down enclosure. In some ways these seem comparable to the material already described from Down Farm; distinct clusters of pottery sherds occur around the ditch, some at least representing the fragmentation of large portions of single vessels. Only one such cluster occurs in the lower 'rubble', from the 'north-eastern' section of the ditch; the others lie in the 'mixed silting', and seem to concentrate around the 'south-western' and 'south-eastern' lengths of ditch. Finally, there is a relatively large deposit of sherds in the upper 'mould' of the north-eastern and north-western lengths of ditch.

As at South Lodge and at the Angle Ditch, the Bronze Age metalwork from Martin Down, an awl and a razor, was found in the lower 'rubble' (*Excavations* IV, 188, 198–9, Pls. 307 and 311:5 and 6). They lay close together in the 'north-eastern' length of ditch about 5 ft (1.52 m) below the surface. No pottery is recorded from this position. An undiagnostic bronze ring was also recovered from the 'mixed silting'.

One final point must be made. The surface deposits within the Martin Down enclosure produced more Bronze Age pottery than was recovered from the ditch silts (533 sherds compared to 355 sherds). Most of this material (212 sherds) is recorded as having come from the 'western' quadrant of the enclosure. At the Angle Ditch extensive surface trenching also recovered pottery and flint in variable quantities over the area investigated, with a distinct concentration of finds in area P (Fig. 5.47).

5.5 Middle Bronze Age chronology[1,3]

This is not the place for a global assessment of the southern British chronology; our concern is to outline the extent to which we can define a 'Middle Bronze Age' in our study area, before turning to consider the historical processes which may have given rise to this phenomenon.

Details of the available radiocarbon dates have been given above. All the material used to obtain these data could have resulted from the later phases of activity in a long sequence of settlement, which we have been able to trace in some detail at South Lodge and Down Farm. On the whole these dates concentrate within the period 1200–950 bc (± 100). The enclosed settlement sites are therefore a *final* manifestation of a long sequence of settlement activity. From the ditches of those enclosures Pitt Rivers recovered a number of metalwork finds. Those from the South Lodge enclosure have already been discussed and placed generally within the Taunton metalworking tradition. This is the same tradition to which the small piece of twisted bronze from Handley Barrow 24 is also usually assigned, and also where the spiral ring from the Down Farm ring ditch would belong. Of the remaining material the finds from the Martin Down enclosure lack precise chronological detail. One fragment is usually identified as a razor (Piggott 1946, 125, 137:33), and Jockenhovel places it among fragments of early razor forms (1980, 42:100). However, it is not certain that this is a razor rather than, say, a fragment of a knife. The second bronze, a fine single-pointed awl, cannot be confined to any particular stage in the Middle–Late Bronze Age metalworking sequence.

The Angle Ditch finds are more diagnostic. The broken palstave has been assigned to the transitional type of Penard date (Burgess 1980, 145, 204; Smith 1959, 185 n.1) The substance of this group of palstaves has yet to be defined for southern Britain and many supposed candidates (Schmidt and Burgess 1981, 155) have been assigned by one of us to the looped Norman type of the Taunton phase (O'Connor 1980, 49 and 1984, 60). The typological position of the Angle Ditch palstave appears to be uncertain (O'Connor 1980 49); it is small and slender compared with the looped narrow-bladed axes in the Taunton phase palstave hoards from southern England. In the absence of a comprehensive study of looped palstaves in southern Britain, this example could be assigned to metalworking Stage X.

Of the other bronzes, one is the broken point of an awl, similar to the Martin Down example. Finally there is a fragment of a razor, apparently broken in half. The swept-back blade probably had a narrow notch and a small circular perforation outlined by a rib; another rib flanked the centre of the blade. Jockenhovel classifies this blade among a group of fragmentary razors (1980, 135:455), although perhaps a place could be found for it in his Feltwell type (*ibid.* 67–70 esp. Taf. 11:177–80). Although associated finds are comparatively few in preceding phases, hoard finds provide little evidence of associations before the Ewart Park phase for these razors (*ibid.* 1980, 67–70; Needham 1980, 19–20). However, on the basis of museum inspection it is clear that the Bronze Age pottery from the Angle Ditch all belongs to the Deverel-Rimbury tradition and does not include typologically later forms as has been suggested (Barrett 1976, 295).

One final definite metalwork association must be mentioned. Some burials on Launceston Down were disturbed by trenches dug in World War I, exposing three Deverel-Rimbury urns (Piggott and Piggott 1944, 50–1, 60–1). One of these contained a blade fragment of a small spearhead (*ibid.*, Fig. 6). This has a rounded midrib, suggesting that it belongs to a side-looped spearhead of group 1 (Rowlands 1976, 52).

All the indicators, radiocarbon dates and associated metalwork, place the mature phase of the settlement and cemetery sequences discussed here within Burgess's Knighton Heath period *c.* 1250–1050 bc (1980, 131). The chronological integrity of the Middle Bronze Age is thus defined by the developed and enclosed phase of settlement on the chalk. It emerges at the end of the traditional 'Wessex' barrow cemeteries; Edmondsham G2, for example, has produced dates of 1527 ± 52 bc (BM 709) for pyre material and 1119 ± 45 bc (BM 708) for charred human bone associated with a dagger. The suggested termination of activities which define this period lies in the tenth century bc.

5.6 Synthesis[1]

This chapter opened with a summary of the changes which have long appeared to define a break in the archaeology of the Bronze Age. They include the emergence of enclosed settlements with associated field systems, and a shift in the nature of mortuary practices. It is now necessary to understand how these empirical changes resulted from already existing historical conditions. For this reason our discussion must embrace the earlier centuries of the Bronze Age, for it is from here that the practices which built the settlements and cultivated the hillsides arose.

Throughout our discussion of the earlier material, contrasts have been drawn between the uplands of Cranborne Chase and the lowland basin around Christchurch Harbour to the south-east. These distinctions are recognisable in the pattern of artefact deposition and in the position of the surviving monuments. In particular, the Cursus and its associated long mounds established a line above the watershed of those valleys draining from the uplands into the coastal basin. It is within this landscape that people moved, a movement which, like all those movements that we encounter in the pre-industrial world, is likely to have been structured around the seasons of agricultural reproduction and the cycles of animal migration. It is within this temporal framework that certain groups will have crossed the line of the Cursus to exploit the uplands. This does not suppose that the uplands were occupied only on a seasonal basis but that greater numbers of people would have been found on the hills in the spring and early summer whilst the main weight of settlement activity seems to have been in the lowlands.

The Cursus complex seems to mark a boundary within this seasonal landscape. Its construction, along with the long mounds, would have arisen within the seasonal allocation of labour by the communities in this region, and would have given a more pronounced physical definition of these migrations.

The Late Neolithic and Early Bronze Age is one of the most complex periods in British prehistory. The period contains a considerable diversity in monuments, artefacts and depositional contexts, but similarities exist in all these data between widely dispersed geographical regions. It is in this period that the way in which time and space were allocated to particular social practices may have begun to undergo a series of profound changes. These involved the renegotiation of particular forms of authority, giving access to various temporally and spatially distributed resources. The Cursus and long mounds were one obvious, physical, medium through which change could have been negotiated. But the Wyke Down enclosure with its complex deposits and the beginning of inhumation burial in graves surrounded by ring ditches, indicate a different ordering of time and a restructuring of the landscape. This point can be best explained by reference to the early inhumation burials.

Death may precipitate a crisis in identifying rights of inheritance, and in controlling an uncertain transition between the cultural values of life and death. The importance of inhumation is that the ritual, precipitated by an individual's death, fixes the point and moment of that transition at a particular place in the landscape. The rituals imbued the landscape with a new meaning, explicitly defined over the brief period of the burial ritual, and implicitly understood by those who passed between these burial grounds during the cycles of agricultural production. The period of the burial ritual needs stressing, for in the case of the early articulated inhumations the timescale was brief. This was not the recurrent exploitation of ancestral remains, and the symbolism surrounding the corpse (the grave goods) would have been observed for only a short period of time by a limited number of people. This point affects arguments which suggest such items are 'prestige goods' and the *means* of achieving social standing. If that were the case, they would have been of limited effect when used in grave rituals. How does such a technology of social prestige work? It is perhaps more likely that the grave goods simply reasserted the statuses and obligations which were claimed from the individual by the living, and that each burial reflected a short-lived and localised political aim.

A strategy concerned with inheritance, connected with an occasionally high level of investment in the burial symbolism, is a strategy concerned with the future claims of the living. Thus, whilst ancestor rituals, which appear to be associated with the primary phases of some of the Earlier Neolithic monuments, might emphasise the almost timeless authority of the past, the burial rituals which emerge at the end of the third millennium bc recognise the passing of political authority from one life to another. These rites now appear separated from ancestral rituals, although the recurrent reopening of earlier graves could demonstrate a genealogical concern extending across more than one generation. The monumental form of the upland landscape was, therefore, transformed in the early second millennium almost entirely as a result of mortuary rituals. The place of burial for part of the population became increasingly elaborate. The design of the monuments and the spatial allocation of deposits enabled a more complex classification of the dead, and thus the living.

We have little understanding of how else the uplands were being used in the Early Bronze Age. Gardiner has been able to show that flint assemblages of the period appear to have been non-existent, although the identification on typological grounds of late Beaker assemblages is itself difficult. Our knowledge of the contemporary flint assemblages may therefore be affected by poor typological resolution. Beaker ceramics do occur, including the late Beaker grave finds and the recurrent Beaker material beneath the later settlements. However, all the evidence indicates a greater weight of settlement in the lowland basin. The ritual reordering of the landscape need not in itself have affected the way in which the uplands were used, but if we accept the idea that certain practices of inheritance and social obligation were being reworked at the end of the third and into the early second millennium, this must have implications for the way the routine practices of an agricultural cycle were maintained.

This point is important, for we are now in a position to consider the nature of the Deverel-Rimbury material on Cranborne Chase. As we saw at the beginning of this chapter, Deverel-Rimbury settlement has been taken to represent a transformation in agricultural practices, an 'agricultural revolution' on the chalk. We can use the results of our own fieldwork on Cranborne Chase to make two suggestions. First, although it does indeed represent a change in agricultural practices running throughout much of our later prehistory, it cannot be understood other than in the historical context of the Early Bronze Age. Secondly, the Deverel-Rimbury material is the cumulative result of historical processes. It has to be understood in terms of dynamic cycles of reproduction and not as a single system. Indeed, the most obvious elements of Deverel-Rimbury material in our area and elsewhere are the final period of land use and settlement, preserved simply because parts of the landscape were largely abandoned by the end of the second millennium BC.

The characteristics of Deverel-Rimbury material, which seem to distinguish it from what goes before, are the appearance of enclosed settlements, domestic ceramics associated with cremation cemeteries and the occurrence of field systems. An adequate explanation has to demonstrate how these elements were welded together by a coherent strategy of social reproduction.

Burial strategies concern the political implication of an individual's death, and the future of inherited status. Early Bronze Age burial ritual was partly structured by using a vertical axis above and below the ground surface. Some barrows came to act as raised platforms. That ground surface can also be taken to be represented by the boundary around the barrow cemetery. Deverel-Rimbury burial, normally by cremation, is often placed directly into the ground surface. It can occur in three locations: beneath a low mound; in the ground beyond a barrow structure, as in the case of Handley 24; or in the ditches and on the edge of earlier mounds. We also have examples of cremations seemingly placed in unbounded cemeteries. The other notable feature of these cemeteries is the use of domestic vessels, often broken and simply represented by the arrangement of sherds around the cremation. No longer do we find ceramic forms which appear to be restricted to cemetery use, like the pottery from the Down Farm pond barrow.

These burial patterns do not present a new set of cultural norms: they represent alternative strategies in burial, which used and transformed pre-existing practices. There seems no doubt that Deverel-Rimbury ceramics have a long history pre-dating their inclusion in cemeteries on the chalk uplands of southern Britain. Again, assumptions of cultural archaeology have confused the date of particular contextual assemblages with the chronology of the various elements which make up those assemblages. We do not possess a full chronology for all types of cremation cemetery from Cranborne Chase, but the dates from Handley 24, South Lodge and Down Farm, and the metal association from the cemetery at South Lodge, all indicate that cemeteries using small, specifically constructed mounds were in use before 1000 bc (1200 BC).

At the time this cemetery organisation emerged, a range of settlements begin to appear which are themselves enclosed. Indeed, it is this which renders them archaeologically visible. It is also clear that these enclosures are late in a longer sequence of development. At Down Farm two of the buildings within the area of the enclosure are likely to be related to an unenclosed phase, and at South Lodge two posthole structures seem unrelated to the enclosure. At the latter site the enclosure is also later than the field system. We have already suggested that the use of the enclosure is short-lived. The Martin Down enclosure also post-dates settlement and probable cultivation in the immediate area.

The nature of these enclosures is variable, in terms of the size of the area enclosed, and the means of enclosure, with the partial ditching of Down Farm, Martin Down and the Angle Ditch and the totally ditched enclosure at South Lodge. There is also variation in the internal organisation of the structures. The enclosures presumably represent areas of settlement, but such settlements are not self-reproducing, either materially or biologically. Only Down Farm has produced evidence of a structure which might be capable of maintaining the large storage requirement of seed grain, or perhaps for the penning of stock. But, as is true of other chalk upland settlements of this date, such as those in Sussex, the storage of grain and animal penning are not generally identifiable components of these sites. Martin Jones has pointed out that large-scale on-site processing of grain is also not attested at Down Farm. In the case of Sussex, the enclosures are not ditched but embanked with soil scraped up from the surface, and with fences completing the enclosure. Here the enclosure defines the area immediately around the house structures, with only a limited yard area beyond.

In the case of the Cranborne Chase enclosures and the Sussex sites, the enclosure defines a particular area of buildings. It is more than likely that unenclosed settlements occurred in the contemporary landscape. On the opposite side of the valley, west of South Lodge, another small group of barrows on Tinkley Down, which produced cremations, may indicate further Deverel-Rimbury settlement in this area (*Excavations* II, 13, Fig. 5.2). Enclosure redefined the landscape, isolating particular settlement foci, where previous distinctions had been on the basis of distance between buildings and the walls of the buildings themselves (cf. Hingley 1984). The material recovered from the ditches of the Cranborne Chase enclosures may include some deliberate deposits, and we have suggested that the basal deposits of metal and an urn in the ditch at South Lodge were placed there before the ditch was partially backfilled. Such deposits would previously have been expected to accompany the ashes of the dead. Now the concern is with enclosing particular areas of activity associated with the living. At the same time burials were placed at or beyond the limits of enclosure (see Barrett 1988b).

Within the South Lodge enclosure, in the area in front of the buildings, the one major structural component was the accumulation of a burnt mound. Large amounts of burnt stone were also placed in the top of the ditch at Down Farm. No cereal grains were recovered from either deposit. If these enclosures contained a residential space, they also contained areas of food preparation and service. The technology of food storage and cooking presumably included the large Bucket, Barrel and Globular Urns found on the enclosures and also employed in the burial rituals.

The enclosures, which had been established by the eleventh century bc, are situated amongst the lynchets of field systems. In the case of the South Lodge enclosure, the ditches cut field lynchets, which, in the immediate vicinity of the site at least, were no longer developing. These lynchets do not imply that it was only now that plough agriculture was adopted, as Childe and Curwen had once assumed. We have clear evidence elsewhere for traction ploughing back into the Neolithic. However, they do imply that ploughing was, for a few seasons at least, confined to the same regular plots of land, and that the regularity of the cultivated plots extended over quite large tracts of the countryside.

An investigation of the temporal and spatial cycles of social reproduction has to comprehend the material conditions which were drawn upon in those social practices. The Early Bronze Age burials indicate an increasing concern with particular lines of inheritance: death generates moments of political crisis and conflict. The rituals of burial fix a particular order amongst the dead as part of the future strategies of the living. The monuments associated with these rituals became increasingly elaborate as the procedures of ordering death developed. These monuments also structured the landscape within which the routines of agricultural practice took place and across which people moved.

The contrast with Deverel-Rimbury material is that the dominant structure of the landscape was now given by the actions of the living in relation to daily procedures of agricultural reproduction, and in the case of South Lodge the fields almost seem to *contain* the cemetery. In the design of the cemeteries, barrows may well have been retained as a dominant architectural feature, but where earlier mounds are used burials were placed on the periphery or in the ditches, and where new mounds were constructed they were built over some cremations, with other cremations placed around them. A cemetery such as that at South Lodge almost appears a miniaturisation of earlier barrow cemeteries. Cemeteries were also placed near to settlement sites. We have noticed this relationship at South Lodge and Down Farm, and Handley Barrow 24 may also pair with the Angle Ditch (Bradley 1981).

Many (but not necessarily all) of the enclosed settlements are areas restricted to residential space, food preparation and service, in contrast to the more extensive foci we meet in the Late Bronze Age and Iron Age. Thus, whilst daily routines were once undertaken on the chalk uplands with reference to monuments concerned with the political implications of death, the crisis of death now appears to have been controlled within the routine, and at times perhaps ritualised, procedures of biological reproduction. The dead were even accompanied to the grave by the vessels used to store and cook food. How was such a transformation achieved? If an emphasis upon future political strategies arose with the more precise and problematic procedures of inheritance, this could in turn establish a political authority over future human and agricultural reproduction. This itself would have concerned the structuring of gender relations, inheritance and, with it, modes of agricultural reproduction (Barrett

1988b), but it would also have turned the products of agricultural labour and the cycles of reproduction into resources of an explicit, dominant ideology.

Notes

1 John C. Barrett
2 Richard Bradley
3 Brendan O'Connor
4 A. J. Legge
5 M. Bowden
6 S. Butcher
7 Martin Green
8 Jameson Wooders
9 Martin Jones
10 Juliet Rogers
11 Barry Lewis

6. THE LATE BRONZE AGE AND IRON AGE

6.1 Introduction[1]

It is now more than twenty years since the origin of the British Iron Age was debated in terms of either invasion or indigenous development. Hawkes (1959) established a subtle temporal and spatial classification of the British material, which mapped its suggested continental origins and indigenous development. However, the general application of the 'Invasion Hypothesis' was soon challenged (Clark 1966), and the specific treatment of the British Iron Age in these terms was criticised in detail by Hodson (1960 and 1964). Both Hodson and Hawkes accepted the basic premise, that analysis depended upon matching cultural traits over time and space. By this means Hodson established the claim that the British Iron Age contained a core of cultural traits (the 'Woodbury Culture'), whose origins lay within the indigenous Bronze Age.

Not only did both writers accept that a 'cultural' analysis was the valid framework within which to work; they also operated within the terms of national archaeologies. It is from this perspective that movement of peoples between (say) Wessex and East Anglia may be presented as an 'indigenous' process, whilst movement between the Pays de Calais and Kent was an 'invasion'. Neither set of assumptions stands particularly close scrutiny today.

Our study of Cranborne Chase has been regionally based. This has not assumed that the region defines the spatial extent of some closed social system. Our treatment of the region has been to take it as a relatively arbitrary area of topography, within which certain social practices were executed, and through which we may examine the history of those practices. Such practices contributed towards local systems of social reproduction. These systems were not closed, thus maintaining the larger geographical conditions of which they were a part. In these terms an assessment of 'indigenous' or 'foreign' elements within the Iron Age is obsolete.

We may now be in a position to consider the Late Bronze Age, which sees, on the one hand, a dislocation in the local pattern of settlement and, on the other, a change in metal technology which, within a century, had affected Central and Western Europe.

In the most influential model recently presented for the period, Rowlands (1980) specifies the type of kinship systems which we might expect, on the basis of linguistic, historical and archaeological evidence, to have been established during the period. These kinship systems, Rowlands argues, structured the basic political units of social reproduction. Amongst their characteristics was a tendency to establish distant alliance networks. These networks, which would have carried marriage partners, gifts and the payment of marriage obligations, could have resulted in the circulation of a specific set of exotic and prestigious items. Such items, and the alliances by which they were procured, would have increased local political prestige by the use of exotic material in local gift exchanges and ritual display.

The implications of this model are two-fold. Firstly, the articulation of the different spheres of exchange takes place through political institutions which were themselves structured by kinship. Local agricultural production may be converted into political prestige (through feasting for example), but such relatively unstable differences in rank would only become secured through kinship alliances. These local alliances may have allowed the accumulation of such local products as hides or textiles, which could, in turn, have entered a sphere of prestige exchange, again secured through marriage alliances. By these means exotic items would have entered the local system and would have increased the authority of local elites. Thus economic processes are embedded in social/political relations and take the form of gift exchanges and social debt payments. These are not the kind of commodity exchanges where different commodities are bartered or traded (cf. Gregory 1982), and whilst the model does not preclude the existence of such exchanges, they have no major role to play in the processes of social reproduction.

Secondly, growth in such systems is to be expected and is seen as expansion in the scale of political authority, a process which Friedman and Rowlands (1977) term 'evolution'. The alliance and gift-exchange networks are therefore inherently competitive. However, the limits of growth are determined by local ecological conditions *and* by the conditions of the wider system, over which local productive cycles have no control. Both these determinants, when combined with the political demands of growth, may result in cycles of evolution and devolution.

This model confronts the issues raised by Kristiansen's earlier study of the Danish Bronze Age, where he links strategies of local agricultural production to the rate at which bronzes could have been procured from Central Europe to be 'consumed' through the ritual demands of local burial customs (Kristiansen 1978). The elegance of Rowlands' model is that it allows us to consider how the history of political structures was determined by both local and regional conditions, and the way in which certain items such as weaponry may have had an essential role in social reproduction. That elegance, however, should not blind us to the highly generalised nature of the model, where specific details of local cases still need to be established (cf. Barrett and Needham 1988). It should not be taken as a general solution to the problems of the period, but as one suggestion which demands careful consideration.

It is a logical requirement that an assessment of this model cannot take place in its own terms. However, the previous chapter has outlined one set of analytical procedures derived independently of Rowlands' model. These avoid identifying archaeological evidence with a particular form of social organisation and instead attempt to understand the routine social practices maintained within given material conditions. This moves us, necessarily, away from discussing social totalities, such as are specified by Rowlands, towards an analysis of particular modes of social action. We are now interested in discovering how forms of authority and authoritative knowledge were reproduced through these practices, the kinds of resources these practices sought to control, and the time–space matrix which they occupied. From this perspective we should be able to assess not only Rowlands' model, but the extent to which we understand the processes behind our Iron Age settlement patterns.

6.2 Chronology[1,2]

The current chronological framework for the Late Bronze Age and Iron Age of southern Britain draws upon diverse and not necessarily comparable classes of data. After the seventh century BC, metalwork no longer plays a central part in chronological analysis and the period is no longer defined in terms of metalworking traditions. The radiocarbon chronology also becomes increasingly difficult to use because of the 'plateau' effect now recognised on the tree-ring correction curves (Stuiver and Pearson 1986; Pearson and Stuiver 1986). It is ceramics which, as in the past, continue to offer the most widely used framework for chronological analysis. It has now proved possible to construct a chronological sequence for the Late Bronze Age (Barrett 1980), and deeply stratified sequences of material recovered from hillfort ramparts and occupation deposits have been employed to refine sequences of ceramic development (Alcock 1980; Cunliffe 1984). The Danebury scheme of ceramic phases is of central importance for the southern British Iron Age. Here, stratified assemblages have been linked to a long radiocarbon chronology, although doubts have been expressed regarding the way absolute dates have been assigned to these ceramic phases (Haselgrove 1986, 364). It is not until the beginning of the first century BC that the arrival of datable continental imports along the southern coast of Britain offers some renewed precision in the dating of archaeological deposits.

The case established in the previous chapter was that the acceptable radiocarbon dates and the metalwork associations indicate that the Middle Bronze Age settlements and cemeteries need date no later than the eleventh century bc or the Taunton industrial phase. With the exception of the occasional finds of Roman material, this dating evidence represents the last phase of activity on those sites.

The lack of any later metal associations, and the notable absence of Late Bronze Age ceramic assemblages from the study area, must indicate some shift in the location and the organisation of settlement in the first half of the first millennium bc, as well as a change in certain depositional practices. The latter is most clearly indicated by the finds of Late Bronze Age metalwork, details of which are given in the accompanying volume. None of this material, dating from the Penard phase onward, appears to have come from any certainly identifiable settlement or burial contexts. Admittedly the finds are not numerous, but the limited contextual information would support our contention that the Late Bronze Age was a period of change.

The sequence of Iron Age settlement which emerges after this hiatus is discussed below. The origins of this settlement pattern are not clear. We have few early ceramic assemblages, but as we have seen in the case of the Middle Bronze Age settlements, it is the earliest periods of activity which lie so effectively hidden beneath the later monuments.

6.3 Later first millennium settlement morphology[3]

Our understanding of the development of the Iron Age settlement patterns on Cranborne Chase can now draw upon the substantial body of fieldwork and excavation which has taken place since Hawkes' reassessment of

Pitt Rivers' excavations published over forty years ago (Hawkes and Piggott 1947).

The study area is bounded on the west and east by the valleys of the Stour and Avon, both of which give access to the coast at Hengistbury Head (Fig. 6.1). The northern limit is marked by the chalk escarpment south of the river Ebble, whilst further east the line of the Bokerley Dyke/Grims Ditch complex runs to the edge of the Avon valley opposite Downton. The Bokerley Dyke/Grims Ditch complex marks the southern limit of the main Wessex linear ditch system, which is itself likely to be the product of a long and complex development in the organisation of land divisions in the area (Bowen 1978; RCHME forthcoming). It is also the southern limit of the main distribution of many of the ceramic styles which typify the mid–late first millennium in south Wessex, such as haematite-coated scratch-cordoned bowls and the mainstream saucepan pot tradition (Cunliffe 1984, Figs. 6.21, 6.22 and 6.24). This pattern reflects an earlier situation. Two of Ellison's Deverel-Rimbury style zones divide around the line of the Bokerley Dyke/Grims Ditch complex (Ellison 1980a), and our own neutron activation analysis distinguishes between the Middle Bronze Age pottery from Martin Down and that from sites to the south-west.

As if to underline the division between the two areas, large multivallate hillforts are conspicuous by their absence, only occurring on the extremities of the study area at Hod Hill and Hambledon Hill to the west, Badbury to the south, Castle Ditches to the north and Castle Ditches Whitsbury to the east. The latter is also at the eastern end of the Bokerley Dyke/Grim's Ditch complex (Fig. 6.1). To the north on the escarpment lies the univallate and possibly unfinished hillfort of Winklebury (*Excavations* II, 233; Feachem 1971).

Within the Chase there are two small (under 2 ha) univallate enclosures, Penbury Knoll and Mistleberry, both probably unfinished (RCHME 1975). To the west is a further *c*. 2 ha enclosure at Bussey Stool (RCHME 1972, 96). Although defended, this is not a true hillfort and may represent a separate class of monument. This class would also include Sixpenny Handley (RCHME 1975, 69–70), a univallate 6 ha enclosure from which late Iron Age and Romano-British material has been recovered by Martin Green (Fig. 6.2).

Within the core of the study area (Fig. 6.2) something in excess of seventy enclosed settlements are known from an area of 190 km^2. Most are recorded by aerial photography and are undated. The general morphology of the sites does, however, indicate dates within the latter half of the first millennium BC and the first century AD.

A few of these sites have been excavated, with large-scale excavations at Rotherley (*Excavations* II), Woodcutts (*Excavations* I), Berwick Down, Tollard Royal (Wainwright 1968) and Gussage All Saints (Wainwright 1979a). Only the latter site clearly had an origin in the early to mid-Iron Age; the remainder are mainly a development of the century before the Roman conquest.

Beyond the study area early Iron Age activity has been recorded at Pimperne, where a large timber round house was set within a 6 ha enclosure (Harding and Blake 1963; RCHME 1972, 54). Within the study area small-scale salvage excavation has been conducted on the mid to late Iron Age enclosure at Martin (Catherall, Barnett and McClean 1983), the late Iron Age and Romano-British enclosures at Oakley Down and Farnham (PDNHAS vols. 71, 72 and 73; Green pers. comm.) and the late Iron Age settlement complex and linear ditch system at Great Ditch Banks, Bower Chalk (Rahtz, forthcoming).

All this settlement activity is established within an ordered agricultural landscape. Extensive field systems covering many hectares are known (RCHME 1972, 1975 and forthcoming), along with possible areas of reserved pasture defined by ditch systems. The most extensive of these, covering some 700 ha, is between Gussage Hill and Thickthorn Down (below), with a further example known from Tarrant Launceston Down (RCHME 1972, 106 and forthcoming). Such large tracts of land devoid of signs of agriculture have led to suggestions of specialised stock rearing, possibly of horses, involving a seasonal round-up of animals (Wainwright 1979a, 189).

Two recently excavated sites clearly indicate a more mixed economy in the Iron Age. During the lengthy occupation of Gussage All Saints, barley gives way to wheat and legumes as the dominant crops (Evans and Jones 1979, 173). On-site crop processing is clearly evident from large storage pits and numerous querns (Wainwright 1979a, 87–9). Faunal remains show that sheep dominate the record, followed by cattle and pig. Bones of red deer, roe deer, hare and wild fowl are also recorded. Bone combs and loom-weights indicate woollen textile production (Wainwright 1979a, 101 and 116–18).

Berwick Down, Tollard Royal originated in the first century BC. Both barley and wheat were present, whilst the faunal remains differed from Gussage All Saints in that cattle dominated the record, followed by horse, sheep and pig (Wainwright 1968, 146). The bone assemblages from both sites display butchery marks.

The majority of quernstones from Gussage All Saints are of lower greensand (Wainwright 1979a, 190). The nearest stone source is some 16 km to the west, at Child Okeford, at the foot of the Hambledon Hill. A further outcrop 35 km to the north-west lies in the Vale of War-

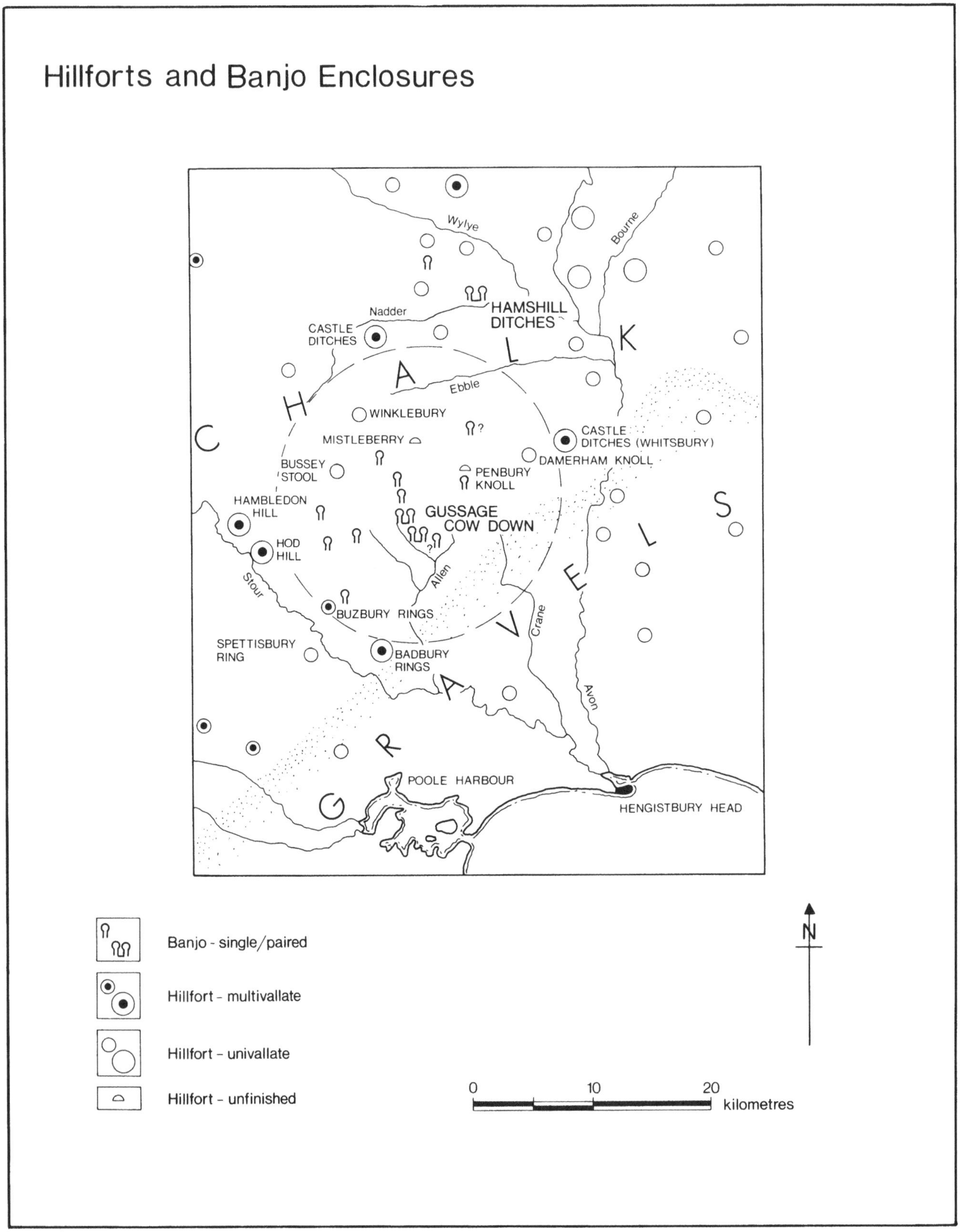

Fig. 6.1 Hillforts and banjo enclosures in central-southern Wessex, indicating the occurrence of multivallate hillforts outside the area of Cranborne Chase

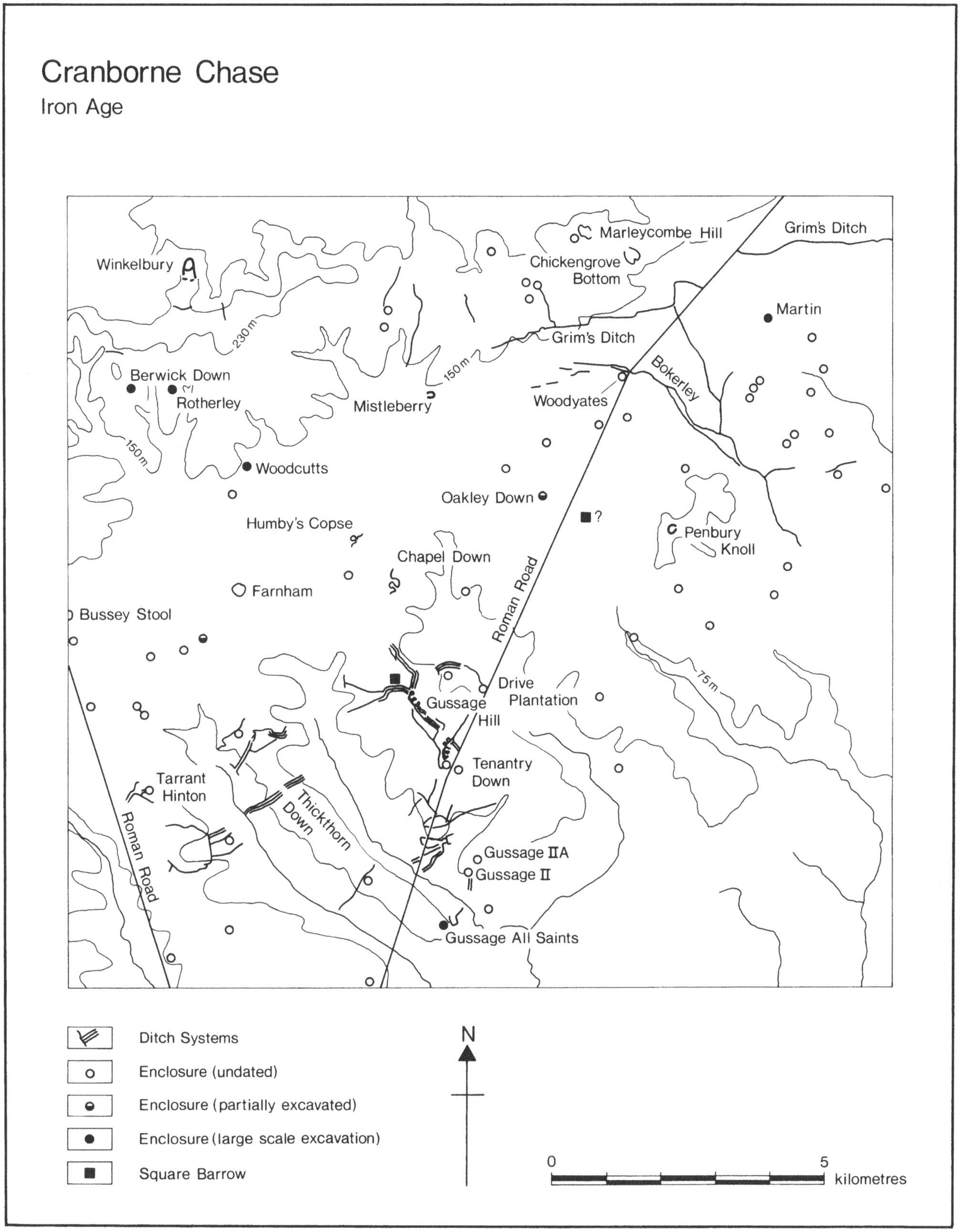

Fig. 6.2 The distribution of Iron Age monuments in Cranborne Chase

Table 6.1. *Iron Age surface finds recorded from the study area*

			Coins			Fibulae			Other finds		
Site	NGR	Site type	Coin type	Qty	Reference	Qty	Type/date	Reference	Type	Date	Reference
Berwick Down	ST 9419	Encl.	–	–	–	1	E—M 1st cent. AD	Wainwright 1968	–	–	–
Chapel Down	ST 9816	Banjo	Mack 317 AR Amorican	3 1	M.G.[1]	2	E—M 1st cent. AD	M.G.	–	–	–
Damerham	SU 1016	?	'British B'	1	Allen 1961	–	–	–	–	–	–
Drive Plantation	SU 0014	Encl.	–	–	–	1	Mid 1st cent. AD	M.G.	Pascaul 1 amphora	1st cent. BC	M.G.
Farnham	ST 9912	?	Mack 317	27	Allen 1961	–	–	–	–	–	–
Gussage All Saints	ST 9910	Encl.	–	–	–	12	1: La Tène I 11: 1st cent. BC—1st cent. AD	Wainwright 1979	Dressel 1 amphorae + Arretine	1st cent. BC	Wainwright 1979
Gussage St Michael	ST 9811	?Sett.	Mack 317	1	M.G.	1	La Tène I	M.G.	Æ toggle Æ bucket mount	1st cent. BC	M.G.
Gussage Cow Down North	ST 9914	Banjo pair	Mack 317	5	M.G.	9	2: La Tène I 7: E—M 1st cent. AD	M.G.	–	–	–
Gussage Cow Down South	ST 9913	Banjo pair	–	–	–	1	E—M 1st cent. AD	M.G.	–	–	–
Harley Down	SU 0012	?Banjo	Mack 317	3	M.G.	1	E—M 1st cent. AD	M.G.	Æ terret FE bridle link	1st cent. BC	M.G.
Hinton Bushes	ST 9110	Sett.	–	–	–	2	E—M 1st cent. AD	M.G.	–	–	–
Home Field	ST 9914	?	–	–	–	1	E—M 1st cent. AD	M.G.	–	–	–
Jack's Hedge Corner	SU 0414	Sett.	–	–	–	1	E—M 1st cent. AD	M.G.	–	–	–
Monkton Drove	SU 0214	Encl?	Mack 317	4	M.G.	3	E—M 1st cent. AD	M.G.	–	–	–
More Crichel	ST 9908	?	Mack 317	1	Allen 1961	–	–	–	–	–	–
Oakley Down	SU 0117	Encl.	Mack 317 Mack 321	3 1	M.G.	3	E—M 1st cent. AD	M.G.	–	–	–
Rotherley	ST 9419	Encl.	Mack 317	2	Pitt Rivers 1888	2	E—M 1st cent. AD	Pitt Rivers 1888	Gallo—Belgic imports	1st cent. BC—1st cent. AD	Pitt Rivers 1888
Tarrant Crawford	ST 9203	?	Mack 317	1	Allen 1961	–	–	–	–	–	–
Tarrant Gunville	ST 9212	?	Mack 317 British B	2 1	Allen 1961	–	–	–	–	–	–
Tenantry Down	SU 0112	?Sett.	Mack 317	5	M.G.	1	L 1st cent. BC—E 1st cent. AD	M.G.	Dressel 1A amphora	1st cent. BC	M.G.
Tollard Royal	ST 9417	?	Mack 317	*c.*20	Allen 1961	–	–	–	–	–	–
Woodcutts	ST 9618	Encl.	Mack 317	4	Pitt Rivers 1867	1	La Tène I	Pitt Rivers 1887			

[1]Collection of Martin Green, Down Farm, Sixpenny Handley

dour. The Child Okeford source might indicate some form of relationship between the Cranborne Chase settlements and the hillforts at Hod Hill and Hambledon Hill. Other stone present at Gussage All Saints includes Dartmoor granite, Purbeck limestone, Bembridge limestone (Isle of Wight) and Tertiary gritstone, probably from the Hampshire Basin (Wainwright 1979a, 190).

Networks of longer-distance contact are also clearly evident, especially by the late Iron Age. Fibulae are present in growing numbers from the La Tène I–III, and the advent of coinage during the first century BC is abundantly reflected in the study area (Table 6.1). Larger deposits of metalwork appear at Hod Hill (Brailsford 1962; Richmond 1968) and Spettisbury Rings (Gresham 1939). The latter deposit may be associated with the advance of the Roman army under Vespasian, probably in AD 44. Other exotic material such as Roman amphorae probably entered the area via Hengistbury Head and Poole Harbour.

6.3.1 The Gussage Hill/Thickthorn Down complex[3]

The Gussage Hill complex of enclosures, settlements and multiple ditch systems is at the heart of the study area (Fig. 6.3).They are situated on a chalk ridge at about 110 m OD, defined by the River Allen and Gussage

Brook. Activity is centred around two banjo complexes at either end of the hill. This type of enclosure is named after its distinctive shape. The north-western pair had long been known (Colt Hoare 1821, 31–3), but interest was renewed following the series of aerial photographs taken by O.G.S. Crawford (Crawford and Keiller 1928, Pls. XV and XVI). The most recent assessment (RCHME 1975) has been followed by continuing aerial reconnaissance which has revealed a further pair of banjos some 900 m to the south-east (NGR: ST 9913).

Both banjo complexes are closely comparable, each being an average of 0.3 ha in area, defined by a ditch with an external bank. (On the south-east pair, no standing earthworks survive, but the distribution of pits within each enclosure makes the former existence of an external bank a virtual certainty: Fig. 6.4.)

Related to these banjo groups are a series of multiple ditch systems of varying complexity. Although these clearly represent a major investment of labour and resources, the surviving sections rarely exceed *c.* 1.5 m in height. They can range from a single ditch and bank to a series of lengths, sometimes interrupted, comprising up to three ditches and banks (Fig. 6.3; RCHME 1975, plan opp. 24: A–B and C–D).

In addition to defining blocks to the north and west of Gussage Hill, these systems are linked to the line of the Neolithic Cursus, and immediately downslope, to the north-east, enough of the Cursus survived to influence the layout of the field system.

On approaching the south-eastern complex, the linking ditch deviates to respect the ditch forming an enclosure behind the banjos and terminates against a small (*c.* 25 ha) irregular enclosure with a short funnel entrance reminiscent of a banjo. This entrance funnel points directly at the ditch to the rear of the banjos. No break is visible in this ditch, suggesting that the single enclosure is either not contemporary with the banjo complex (which seems unlikely as the main linear feeding into it clearly respects the banjo), or that it reflects a different function or status for the main complex. Some 200 m east of this enclosure, on Harley Down, a further enclosure, probably of banjo type, has its entrance funnel partly overlain by a Roman road, the Ackling Dyke.

At the foot of Gussage Hill a further isolated length of multiple and single ditch system is known from aerial observation. Similar in character to the ditches on the hilltop, this stretch is closed at its western end by the northern ditch turning through 90°, with the southern two ditches abutting it. There is no hint of any continuation up to Gussage Hill. Within the angle defined by the ditch turning through right angles, and aligned on it, is a 'tombstone'-shaped enclosure. Recent fieldwork and excavation by Martin Green in the immediate vicinity of this enclosure has recovered pottery, probably of Early Iron Age date. Contemporary pottery is associated with evidence for cultivation across the Cursus in Chalkpit Field. (Fig. 3.6).

As the multiple ditches approach the line of the Cursus, the northern pair stop. From this point the line is continued eastwards by a single ditch, which stops just short of the Drive Plantation enclosure ditch, suggesting the former presence of an external bank. The enclosure is partly overlain by the Ackling Dyke.

North and east of the Gussage Hill earthworks aerial photography reveals an extensive field system, the line of which, as it runs downslope to the north-east, is clearly influenced by the line of the Cursus. This system respects the banjo complexes and multiple ditch systems, and does not reappear on the south-western side of the hill. This zone, devoid of any trace of former field systems, extends across the valley of the Gussage Brook, over and beyond Thickthorn Down. On Thickthorn Down itself a multiple ditch system, comparable to that on Gussage Hill, appears for a distance of *c.* 1.25 km. For part of its length the system re-uses the northern line of the Cursus, and with a minor dog-leg at the Cursus terminal, continues the line downslope to the brook south-west of the Down. This system is clearly intended to cut off the spur to the south-east from the main body of the chalk. Just under 1 km to the north-west, a further ditch system ranging from single to triple ditch performs a similar function, beyond which, to the north and south-west, field systems can be traced on aerial photographs.

When all the multiple systems described here are considered, along with the intermittent and complex ditches and large enclosures underlying the Ackling Dyke 1 km north-west of the Gussage All Saints enclosure complex (Fig. 6.2), an extensive tract of land, free of field systems and encompassing 700 ha, is revealed (Bowen in Wainwright 1979a, 181). Along the south-eastern edge of this block is a further series of enclosures, including the totally excavated site of Gussage All Saints (Wainwright 1979a) (Fig. 6.4:g). Of the other enclosures, Gussage IIA displays certain morphological traits worthy of further discussion (Bowen in Wainwright 1979a). The ditch, which encloses some 1.5 ha, is markedly sinuous except on the east, where a regular and tapering wedge-shaped entrance is flanked by a triple ditch façade (Fig. 6.4:e). Such an arrangement clearly emphasises the importance of the approach from that direction. The air photographs would suggest that the main enclosure was slight (perhaps little more than a boundary), all effort being expended on the entrance and its flanks. In addition, pits can be seen within the enclosure, as well as immedi-

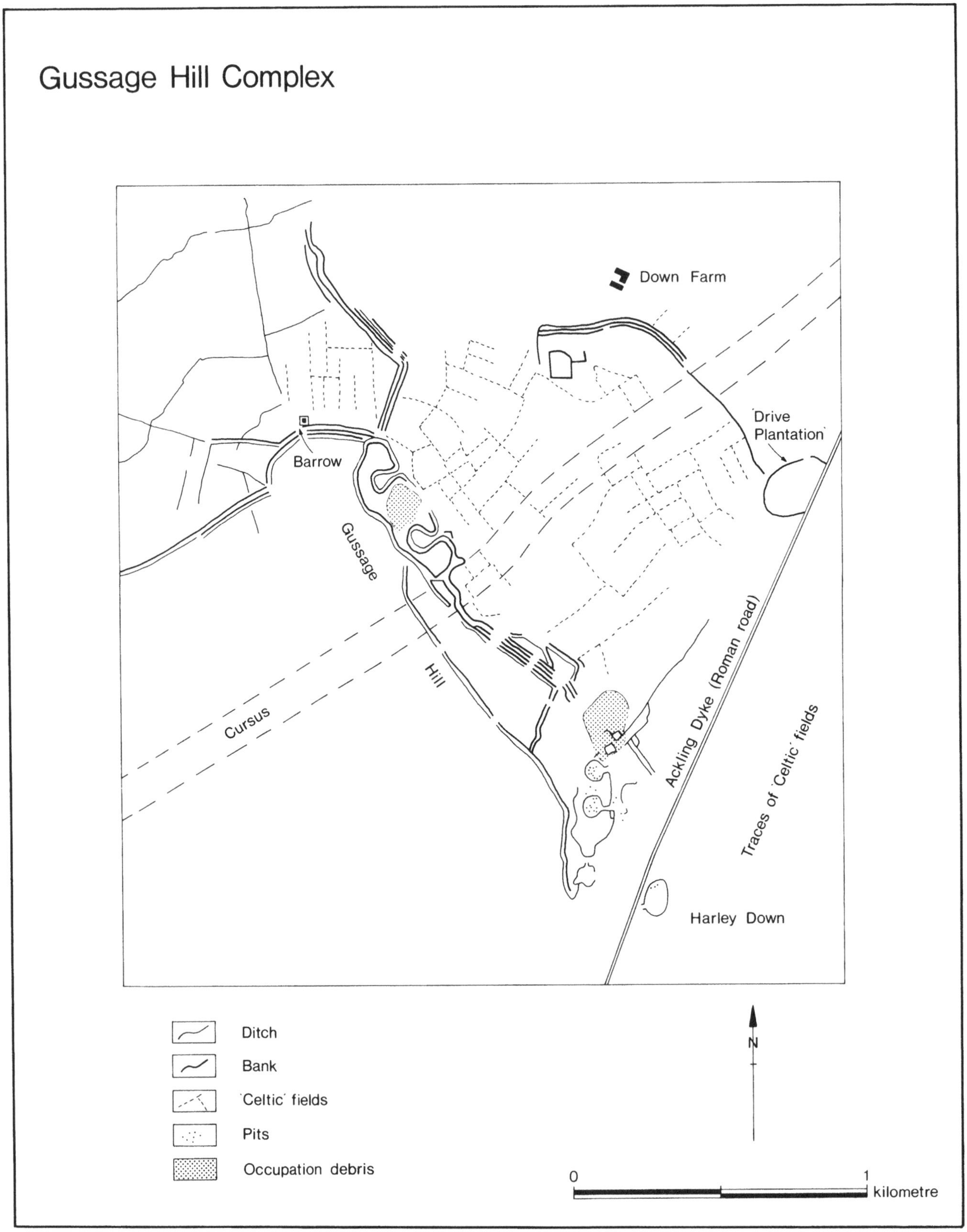

Fig. 6.3 The complex of Iron Age earthworks on Gussage Hill, overlying the line of the Cursus

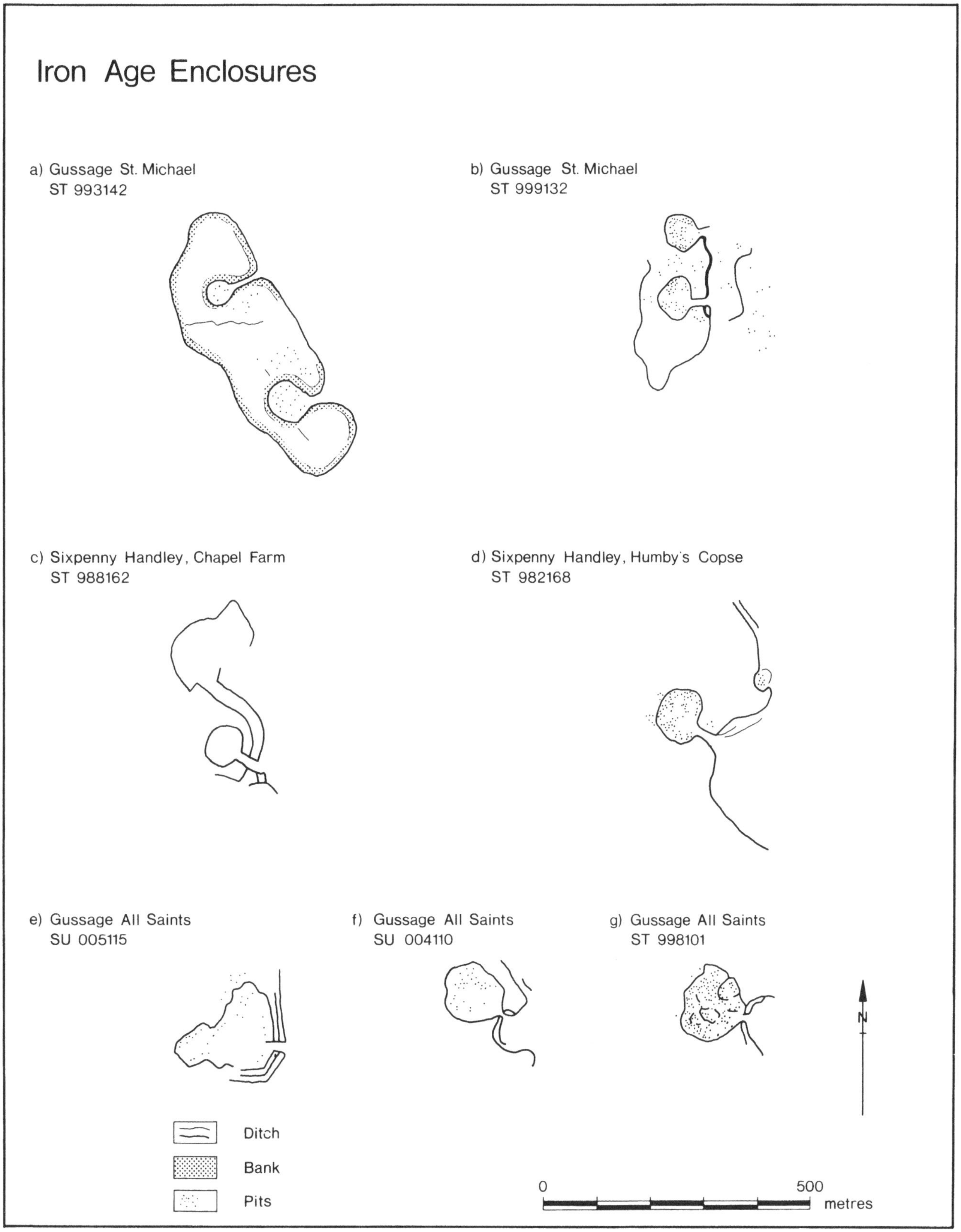

Fig. 6.4 Comparative plans of Iron Age enclosures in Cranborne Chase including banjo (a–d) and 'Little Woodbury type' enclosures (e–g)

ately to the north, indicating a possible phase of open settlement. The nature of the entrance ditches invites comparison with the multiple systems on Gussage Hill and Thickthorn Down. As far as this author is aware, no parallels exist for this enclosure type elsewhere in the study area. With the exception of Gussage All Saints, none of the enclosures related to the Gussage Hill/Thickthorn Down complex has been excavated.

Small-scale work elsewhere in the area has led to the identification of a square-ditched barrow, late Iron Age in date and possibly robbed in antiquity, immediately adjacent to the western multiple ditches on Gussage Hill (Fig. 6.3; White 1970). That such a barrow, the contents of which can only be guessed at, should be located close to the north-western banjo complex is a matter of some interest. Comparisons should be made with a small barrow at Hurstbourne Tarrant, Hants., which covered a rich La Tène III cremation close to the Blagdon Copse banjo enclosure (Hawkes and Dunning 1931; Stead 1968). Funerary monuments of the late Iron Age are rare in the south of England (Whimster 1981). The presence of such barrows close to banjo complexes may therefore be significant indicators of the special activities which occasionally took place at these locations.

The multiple ditch system has only been examined on Thickthorn Down, where the few finds which were made (a Beaker sherd from the old land surface and two medieval sherds from the upper levels of the ditch) led to the original suggestion that the earthwork was Roman in date (Harding 1960, 112–13).

Total excavation of the Gussage All Saints enclosure revealed three main phases of activity, ranging from the first half of the first millennium BC to the later first century AD (Wainwright 1979a, 186). The first two phases, defined by a 1.2 ha enclosure with ditched 'antennae' flanking the entrance, are overlain by a third phase of small enclosures. Particular interest was generated by the recovery of metalworking debris from a phase II pit, with mould fragments from the production of horse harnesses dominating the assemblages (Spratling in Wainwright 1979a). Two radiocarbon dates of 70 ± 70 bc (Q 1206) and 150 ± 65 bc (Q 1207) were obtained from material in the pit fill. The third phase sees small amounts of material imported from the Roman world appearing, including Terra Rubra, Dressel I amphorae and one sherd of 'Arretine' sigillata. No Durotrigian or other pre-Roman coins were found.

Despite the lack of excavation elsewhere in the Gussage Hill/Thickthorn Down block, thanks to fieldwalking by Martin Green, we do have a growing body of surface finds from other enclosures and locations in the region. Details of this material appear in the accompanying volume and are summarised in Table 6.1 and Fig. 6.5.

In addition to the material recovered by Martin Green, a further Durotrigian coin is known from Gussage St Michael village (Allen 1961, appendix II), and a sherd of haematite-coated furrowed bowl is recorded from Gussage Hill just to the north-west of the banjo complex (PDNHAS 73, 115). Iron Age activity clearly spans the entire period, as evidenced by the Gussage All Saints excavation, the two La Tène fibulae (Table 6.1) and the sherd of furrowed bowl.

Although further systematic field collection and sample excavation is clearly desirable, the current record underlines the particular importance of the area in the century before the Roman invasion of AD 43. The distribution of finds of this period indicates that the banjo enclosure complexes and multiple ditch systems were in use at this date.

6.4 Synthesis[1,3]

Deverel-Rimbury burial and settlement evidence on the chalk has been discussed in the previous chapter in terms of a transformation of the dominant modes of social authority. This seems to have involved focusing upon human and agricultural reproduction as a dominant symbolism, laying particular emphasis upon fertility. It has been our further contention that this transformation is understandable, arising as it does from the Early Bronze Age concern with inheritance and with the political crises precipitated by death.

The form of the settlement architecture, cemeteries and cultivation plots has been presented as a material representation of the cultural primacy given to biological reproduction. This is the dominant cultural value around which the authority of age and gender relations would have been structured. The settlements themselves, rather than cemeteries or separate non-domestic enclosures, now seem to become the stage for political conflict. They have a long history and some achieve an almost monumental form. It is from this position that we must consider the origins of the settlement record of the mid to late first millennium BC.

Deverel-Rimbury sites in both Wessex and Sussex represent a particular residential area and nothing more. We see no reason why we should go further and suggest that these sites are self-sustaining units of economic production and consumption (*contra* Drewett 1982). Thus the labour of agricultural reproduction and the resources required for those reproductive cycles (land, animals and grain) were likely to have been drawn from, and controlled by, inhabitants belonging to a number of separate

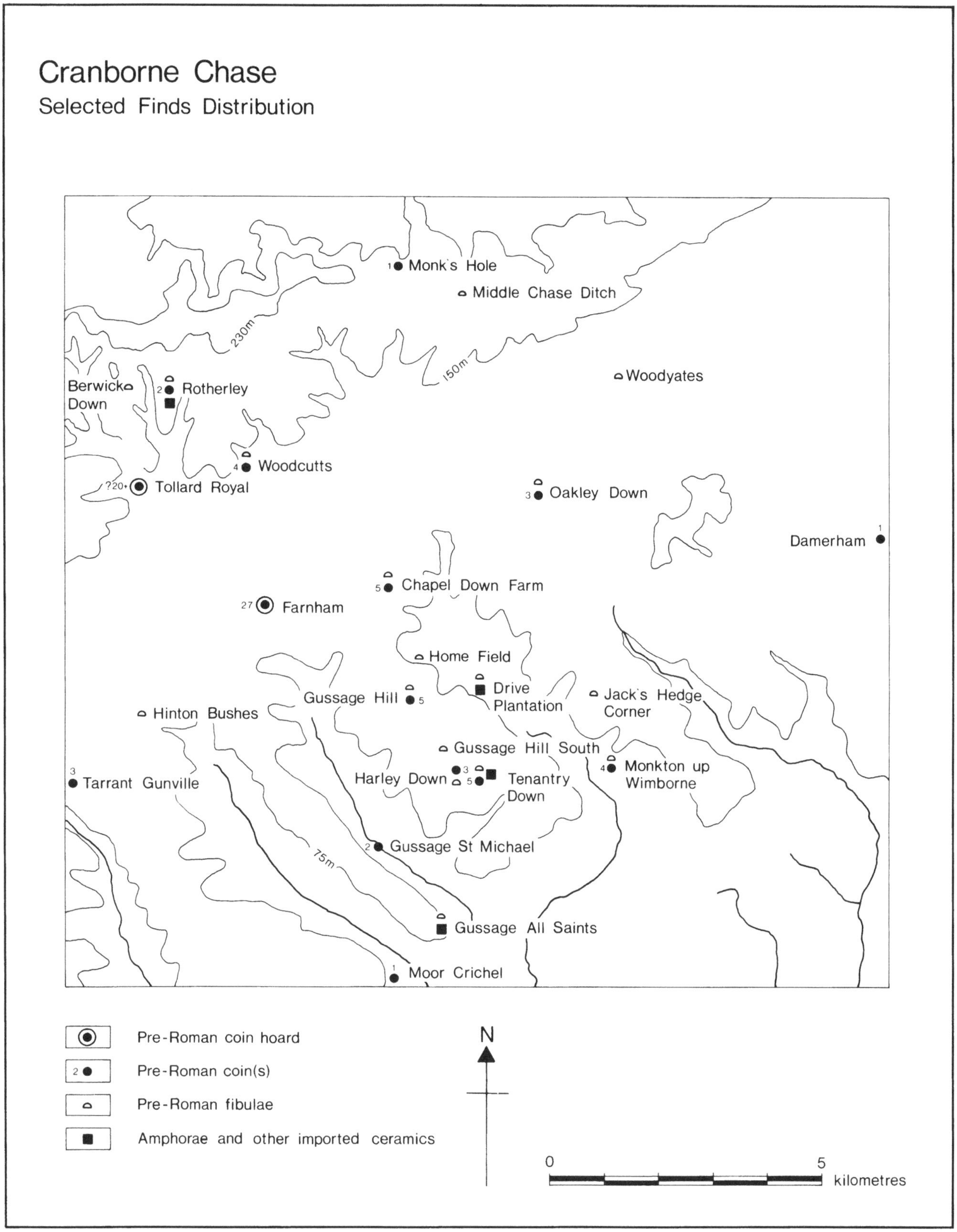

Fig. 6.5 The distribution of selected late Iron Age finds from Cranborne Chase

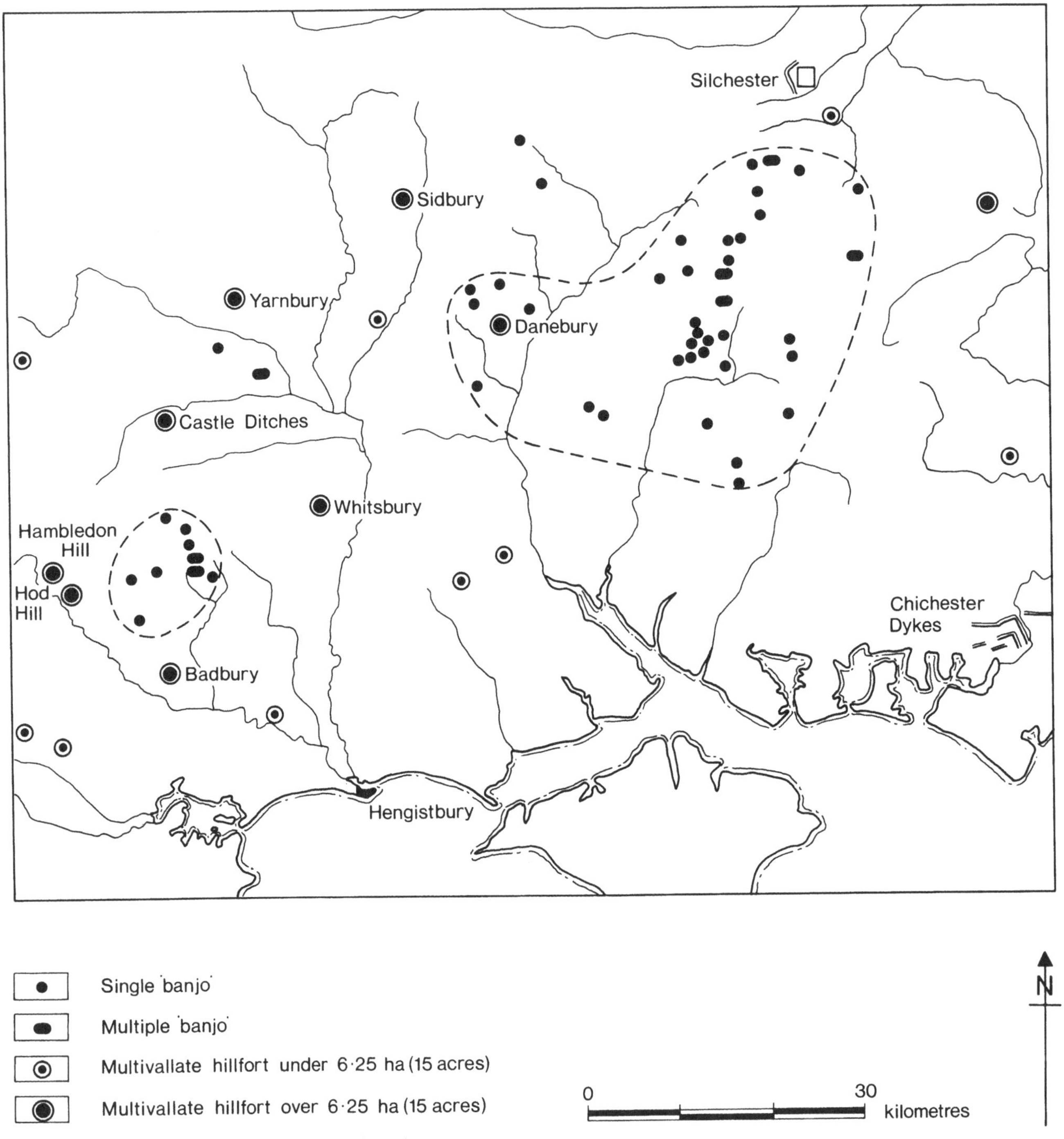

Fig. 6.6 Multivallate hillforts, 'Oppida' and Banjo enclosures

settlement foci. We have no clue as to how frequently people may have moved between these sites, but the labour demands would obviously have varied around the cycle of the agricultural year. These activities were culturally loaded. Agricultural production was not simply a response to ecological conditions; the organisation of labour and the distribution and consumption of the products of that labour were means by which the structures of age and gender were established.

The architecture of the settlement site structured the daily routines, not simply by the isolation of one residential group from another, but through the entire internal organisation of the settlement (see Moore 1986). Such organisation is marked by the arrangement and use of the buildings and the various fenced divisions encountered within some of the enclosures. We must also recognise the place of personal dress, and the preparation and service of food, as symbolic codes employed in these localised routines (Barrett 1988b). Alongside such practices we might expect moments of ritual display connected with life crises and the passing of the agricultural seasons. It is noticeable that, by the Late Bronze Age, the monumentality associated with funerary rites has disappeared completely. Indeed, the extension of agriculture since the Middle Bronze Age had begun to erode some of the earlier monuments. If our assertion is correct concerning the role of the settlement site in the mechanisms of social discourse, we might expect such rituals to focus increasingly upon the settlements themselves. Indeed, the occurrence of human burials within earlier grain storage pits, well represented for example at Gussage All Saints (Wainwright 1979a, 32), is a regular feature of the Wessex Iron Age (Whimster 1981, 5). These burial rites remind us of the symmetry Bloch and Parry have suggested might often exist between rituals of death and ideas of fertility and rebirth (1982).

Archaeologists have been slow to understand the importance of the preparation and consumption of food as a means of social discourse, both as routine daily activity and as ritualised and competitive feasting. We need to distinguish between the storage and preparation of agricultural resources on the one hand, and the preparation and consumption of food on the other. The latter is a transformation of the former. Within the South Lodge enclosure a large burnt mound, presumably connected with the baking of meat, lay in a prominent position within the enclosure. In Sussex it is also possible, at Itford Hill, to identify a single enclosure associated with cooking (Burslow and Holleyman 1957, Fig. 5, enclosure II). We have also noted the large deposit of burnt flint in the upper fill of the Down Farm enclosure ditch. However, on these and other similar sites large bone deposits were not recovered.

If these Middle Bronze Age settlements are not single units of economic reproduction, then their abandonment need not be represented as a sequence of ecological disasters. On the contrary, abandonment and the establishment of the later settlement record may be part of the same process. We would therefore suggest that the underlying theme is the renegotiation of age and gender status and of local political alliances based upon kinship. We have argued that these social relations (and thus their renegotiation) will have been established through the organisation of agricultural labour, the control of agricultural forces, and the organisation of domestic space. Martin Jones (p. 205), for example, has recognised a long-term change in the working practices connected with harvesting between the Middle Bronze Age and the Iron Age.

It is noticeable that the domestic space of the Deverel-Rimbury settlements changes during their history. In Sussex, Ellison has shown the chronological depth implied by the Itford Hill plan, and a lengthy chronology for the Black Patch complex also seems likely (Ellison 1980a; Drewett 1982). At South Lodge the enclosure is late in the history of settlement, but the most dramatic example of reorganisation is the rectangular building at Down Farm. This contains a floor area comparable with the larger round house, but the rectangular plan must have involved a radical reorganisation of that domestic space. If these settlements are neither socially nor economically autonomous, their abandonment may reflect the growing momentum of settlement reorganisation.

The result is a break in the settlement sequence as we currently understand it, with settlements reappearing on a number of new locations by the seventh century BC. As O'Connor's work makes clear, this break appears to be matched by a change in the depositional contexts of Late Bronze Age metalwork. In terms of Rowlands' model there are three ways in which metal may enter and circulate within a regional system. Firstly, this may happen through barter, where no lasting obligation is established between transactors and heterogeneous things are exchanged at an agreed level of value (see Gregory 1982, 47). Secondly, there are gift exchanges, where obligations, established as the gift is accepted, are fulfilled when the equivalent of the gift is returned. This establishes a 'relation of equality between homogeneous things at a different point of time' (Gregory 1982, 47). Gift exchange often seems to result in a balanced reciprocity over a period of time, but it can also become competitive through the ritual consumption of gifts, resulting in a sustained position of political authority (Gregory 1982; Bradley 1982 and 1984). In this form of gift-giving, the gift plays a part in the establishment of political authority; it establishes a debt which must be repaid. The third form of circulation would also seem to fall within Gregory's category of gifts, but here the gift circulates as a secondary, debt repayment to an authority already established by some other means.

Archaeologists do not observe circulation but deposition, and the link between the two processes is not direct but complex (Bradley 1984; Needham 1988; Thomas 1988). It is quite possible to envisage a cycle of reciprocal gift-giving which is unattested archaeologically. Most of the Middle–Late Bronze Age metal finds are the result of small-scale deposition. This includes the Middle Bronze Age ornament finds in a few hoards, burials and some settlements, and the Late Bronze Age finds dominated by single finds of spearheads and by finds of axes in isolation or in hoards. There are no major weapon hoards and sword fragments are few. This localised pattern of deposition within Wessex is part of the regionally varied strategies of deposition which have been discussed by Thomas (1988).

If some metal artefacts (such as swords) were circulating as gifts, there might be no evidence of it in the archaeological record. However, if that strategy of gift-giving took on an element of competitive display, being drawn more centrally within the processes of political growth, we should expect to find some evidence of the ritualised consumption of metal in weapon hoards or in graves. This does not seem to occur. It is difficult not to conclude that the small votive deposits extend only to the display of social and cultural distinctions, which were structured through the divisions of labour associated with agricultural reproduction.

This argument implies that the mechanisms of social reproduction do not conform to Rowlands' model. This is not to suggest that the model may not have greater application elsewhere. What it does imply is that the major social distinctions of age, gender and various kinship and lineage ranks, were structured through cycles of agricultural labour and drew upon the symbolism of fertility. What competitive display we can observe seems connected with feasting. The circulation of 'prestige' items may have occurred, but that process never developed into a competitive strategy for establishing social rank.

If metal entered the region by means of barter and reciprocal gift-giving or moved into the area with people themselves, it was not central to strategies of social reproduction. For the same reasons the arrival of iron may simply have been determined by conditions established beyond our study area. These changes affecting the supplies of material would not have generated a major change in the social processes already at work in Wessex.

The settlements which had emerged by the seventh century BC, often in new locations, include enclosures which are generally larger than those which we have been considering so far. They sometimes contain very large round houses with a greater range of agricultural storage facilities, where the storage pits are now dug outside the houses. The double enclosures at Pimperne, one of which contained a large 20 m diameter round house, provide an example of these developments in the study area (Harding 1974, Fig. 2 and Pl. III). Many of these newly established sites continued as settlement foci for considerable periods, such as the enclosure of Old Down Farm, Hants. (Davis 1981). An inter-site level of reorganisation may also be linked with the continuing development of linear boundary systems, although their distribution is restricted to the northern part of our study area. We have commented elsewhere upon the problems in dating these earthworks (Barrett and Bradley 1980, 191), but they do imply some reorganisation of landholding, and by the latter half of the Iron Age Bowen is prepared to accept the emergence of large-scale stock movement on the uplands (in Wainwright 1979a, 181).

The overall sequence of Iron Age settlement remains imperfectly understood and it is not until the late Iron Age that we observe the major earthwork complex on Gussage Hill. In southern and eastern England, single and multiple ditch systems defining large tracts of land, often on the boundary between major changes in soil types, or rivers and coastal havens (i.e. Silchester, Verulamium and Camulodunum) are characteristic of major administrative and political centres or 'oppida'. Gussage Hill could now be seen as a similar centre for the eastern part of the area thought to be occupied by the pre-conquest Durotriges. The complex is close to the boundary of the chalk uplands with the sands and gravels of the coastal plain (Fig. 6.1), whilst the valleys of the Allen, Crane and Stour give access to Hengistbury Head.

The 'banjo syndrome' (Perry 1966) has been the subject of much discussion over the last two decades (Perry 1966 and 1970; Cunliffe 1978a; Hingley 1984). Interpretations have ranged from stock enclosures to mixed farming complexes. On the central Wessex chalkland, where the majority of such sites have been recognised, two groups can be identified. The larger covers eastern and central Hampshire and includes the only recently excavated examples: Blagdon Copse (Stead 1968), Micheldever Wood (Monk and Fasham 1980) and Bramdean (Perry 1972, 1982 and 1986). Apart from the latter, these excavations have been primarily concerned with the enclosure only, although these sites are demonstrably associated with ditched tracks. The available evidence indicates a date range spanning the last three centuries of the first millennium BC.

The second group, smaller and more homogeneous in morphological terms, is located in the north of Cranborne Chase and the Dorset/Wiltshire border. Its northern limit is marked by Hamshill Ditches, on the chalk ridge between the Wylye and Nadder. This is the only paired banjo complex to survive intact and, like the Gussage Hill complexes, is clearly associated with multiple ditch systems defining a larger settlement area (Bonney and Moore 1967; Cunliffe 1973).

A common feature of both groups is their location

in areas where 'developed' multivallate hillforts are rare. In addition, these areas may also have a series of distinctive late Iron Age burials. These are the barrow burials at Hurstbourne Tarrant close to the Blagdon Copse banjo (Hawkes and Dunning 1931), Gussage Hill (White 1970) and a series of relatively rich cremations, probably in flat graves, distributed between Winchester, Basingstoke and Alton, which continued to be deposited into the Roman period (Millett 1986, 80–3).

The presence of these distinct groups tends to argue against a purely stock-farming interpretation for the banjos, especially when they occur in pairs associated with multiple ditch systems. Indeed, at Hamshill Ditches the preservation is such that the funnel entrances survive and seem to have been metalled with flint nodules. Such a feature argues against the easy movement of unshod animals.

The emergence of these complexes within the late Iron Age landscape may be partly explained with reference to two further phenomena: the quantity and quality of surface finds (especially coins) and the relationship between banjo enclosures and Roman villas (Palmer 1984, Figs. 18 and 20). Much Roman material, including building debris, painted wall plaster, fibulae and pottery spanning the first to fourth centuries AD, is present on Gussage Hill (PDNHAS 1969, 139; RCHME 1975, 24; M. Green pers. comm.). At Hamshill Ditches an extensive nucleated Roman settlement developed immediately to the east of the banjo complex (Bonney and Moore 1967).

A recent survey of Iron Age coinage has led to the identification of a group of silver quarter staters (categorised as Mack 321), possibly related to the main Durotrigian coinage tradition (Selwood 1984, 200). The coins form a discrete group centred on the Dorset/Hampshire border and Avon valley, leading Selwood to propose the existence of a 'sub-Durotrigian' bloc (Selwood 1984, Fig. 13:11).

The northernmost distribution of Mack 321 does not go beyond the Wylye Valley, a suggested boundary of the Durotriges (Cunliffe 1973, 435). Hamshill Ditches, the northernmost banjo complex in the study area, is situated on the ridge defined by the rivers Wylye and Nadder. If the emergence of this territory in the late Iron Age is accepted, the position of the Gussage Hill complex, at the heart of the bloc and with easy access to a major emporium at Hengistbury Head, is clearly important.

It should be noted that examples of Mack 321 occur at Hengistbury (Cunliffe 1987, 141) and a small but significant group of amphorae sherds occurs in our study area. An American coin, possibly of Coriosolites, is known from the Chapel Down Farm banjo at Sixpenny Handley, and a further example of a Mack 321 has been found on Oakley Down (Table 6.1).

These finds may now be placed within a more general understanding of late Iron Age coinage within southern Britain. Of particular relevance is a series of inscribed issues, predominantly silver, attributed to those tribes surrounding the south-eastern Trinovantes and Catuvellaunii. All these issues bear two personal names, including the Iceni CANS-DVRO, ALE-SCA, and Coritani AVN-AST, ESVP-ASV and VEP-CORF (for full lists see Allen 1961, App. II; Cunliffe 1978a, 80). The Dubonnic coinage includes issues, probably contemporary, with a mutually exclusive distribution, inscribed CORIO and BODVOC respectively (Selwood 1984, Fig. 13:2).

Two interpretations for this dual element may be offered. One is that the formula includes the names of 'moneyers' responsible for issuing the coinage, the other and more favoured is that these are names of 'dual magistrates' elected or appointed as tribal leaders for a set period (Cunliffe 1978a, 80). A similar feature is noted on Gallic coins, where the practice is seen as marking a stage in the tribes' political development from a single authority to a more oligarchic society overseen by elected rulers or magistrates (Nash 1976, 125–9).

The political interpretation of the dual-name coinage is attractive. Can such a system be suggested in areas where inscribed coins are lacking? Durotrigian coinage is also based on a silver standard, although weights vary greatly between the regions. Apart from two issues inscribed CRAB, none carry legends (Allen 1961, 245). We have accepted the case for a distinct 'sub-Durotrigian' bloc with the Gussage Hill complex at its centre. Its dominant position during the late Iron Age is also suggested by surface finds and by the barrow burial. The paired banjo complexes, integrated with the ditch systems, may therefore have an added significance as indicative of some dual form of authority. Here we may have residences of magistrates or centres where ceremonies connected with a dual administration were enacted.

The northern complex at Hamshill Ditches may indicate the complexity of these social hierarchies, and the single banjos may be further elements of the residential hierarchy within this political system. Surface finds suggest that all are contemporaneous. The settlement complex on Woodcutts Common may be reinterpreted as including a banjo in its initial phase. Finds from the site include four Durotrigian coins, pre-Roman fibulae, and pottery similar in form to imports or copies of imports originating in Amorica/Normandy, and present in large numbers at Hengistbury Head (*Excavations* II,

Pl. XXXV:7; Cunliffe and Brown in Cunliffe 1987, 310). Such finds are best dated from the mid-first century BC to the Roman conquest, a date range remarkably close to that for surface finds from other sites in the area. Although there remain problems in the detail of the dating evidence, it may be that the Cranborne Chase banjos lie in a more restricted chronological horizon than has been suggested for morphologically similar sites in Hampshire (Cunliffe 1978a, 165).

In the late Iron Age Cranborne Chase may have seen the emergence of a distinct 'sub-Durotrigian' political entity. This political structure did not involve the construction of hillforts but focused instead upon the Gussage Hill complex of banjos and multiple ditch systems, a complex whose function may have been akin to the oppida of south-eastern England, with an outlying centre at Hamshill Ditches. The political authority which maintained this structure may now have arisen in part through the import of exotica and finally through the direct patronage of the Roman military and provincial administration itself. The extension of political control through these means would not have displaced the traditional modes of authority but have incorporated them within larger systems of political reproduction. The land continued to be worked, and the often-recognised evidence for rural continuity need come as no surprise. Elsewhere in Wessex it has been possible to show that medieval land boundaries may have pagan Saxon, Roman or even Iron Age antecedents (Bonney 1972). This is the physical manifestation of the continuity of resources, traditional rights and of working practices. We have suggested that a dual system of political inheritance may have operated during the Iron Age, and J.T. Smith has suggested that some villa plans in Britain and Gaul also reflect dual systems of land tenure. One example is the villa at Rockbourne, to the east of the study area. Here the plan seems to represent two domestic units with an additional cluster of communal buildings (Smith 1978, 168 and Fig. 56).

Throughout this entire study our theme has been the way monuments arose and operated within particular arenas of social practice. There can be no neat conclusion to such a narrative. The architecture of the Romano-British landscape operated upon the remnants of four thousand years of prehistory and was in many ways a product of that prehistory. But, as with every other age, it also created its own monumentality. Today the most striking element of this is the massive earthwork of the Ackling Dyke, the road between Old Sarum and Badbury Rings (RCHME 1975, xxxi). This roadway, which, in terms of its scale, must also have operated as a land boundary, cuts the Dorset Cursus as it crosses Wyke Down and then the barrow cemetery on Oakley Down. In the eighteenth century William Stukely recognised the stratigraphic relationship established between the Roman and Bronze Age earthworks. Pitt Rivers' excavations in the nineteenth century, on monuments such as these, extended the foundations of an empirically sound understanding of the past. Our own work is offered as a contribution to this continuing endeavour.

Notes

1 John C. Barrett
2 Brendan O'Connor
3 Mark Corney

I

I traversed a dominion
Whose spokesmen spake out strong
Their purpose and opinion
Through pulpit, press and song.
I scarce had means to note there
A large-eyed few, and dumb,
Who thought not as those thought there
That stirred the heat and hum.

II

When, grown a Shade, beholding
That land in lifetime trode,
To learn if its unfolding
Fulfilled its clamoured code,
I saw, in web unbroken,
Its history outwrought
Not as the loud had spoken,
But as the mute had thought.

Thomas Hardy: 'Mute Opinion'

REFERENCES

Abbreviations

Excavations I = Pitt Rivers, A. L. F., 1887. *Excavations in Cranborne Chase* Vol. I. Privately printed.

Excavations II = Pitt Rivers, A. L. F., 1888. *Excavations in Cranborne Chase* Vol. II. Privately printed.

Excavations III = Pitt Rivers, A. L. F., 1892. *Excavations in Cranborne Chase* Vol. III. Privately printed.

Excavations IV = Pitt Rivers, A. L. F., 1898. *Excavations in Cranborne Chase* Vol. IV. Privately printed.

Inv. Arch. = *Inventaria Archaeologia*

PDNHAS = *Proceedings of the Dorset Natural History and Archaeological Society*

RCHM = Royal Commission on Historic Monuments (England)

Abercrombie, N., S. Hill and B. S. Turner, 1980. *The Dominant Ideology Thesis*, London: Allen & Unwin.

Alcock, L., 1980. The Cadbury Castle sequence in the first millennium BC, *Bulletin of the Board of Celtic Studies*, 28, 656–718.

Allen, D. F., 1961. The origins of coinage in Britain: a reappraisal, in S. S. Frere (ed.) *Problems of the Iron Age in Southern Britain*, pp. 97–308, London: University Institute of Archaeology Occasional Paper 11.

Ambers, J., K. Matthews and S. Bowman, 1987. British Museum natural radiocarbon measurements XX, *Radiocarbon*, 29(2), 177–96.

Annable, F. K., 1958. Excavation and fieldwork in Wiltshire: 1957, *Wiltshire Archaeological and Natural History Magazine*, 57, 2–17.

Annable, F. K. and D. D. A. Simpson, 1964. *Guide Catalogue of the Neolithic and Bronze Age Collections in Devizes Museum*, Devizes: Devizes Museum.

Arnold, J., M. Green, B. Lewis and R. Bradley, 1988. The Mesolithic of Cranborne Chase, *Proceedings of the Dorset Natural History and Archaeological Society*, 110, 117–25.

Ashbee, P., 1966. The Fussell's Lodge long barrow excavations 1957, *Archaeologia*, 100, 1–80.

1984. *The Earthen Long Barrow in Britain*, 2nd edn, Norwich : Geo Books.

Ashbee, P., I. Smith and J. Evans, 1979. Excavations of three long barrows near Avebury, Wiltshire, *Proceedings of the Prehistoric Society*, 45, 207–300.

Atkinson, R. J. C., 1955. The Dorset Cursus, *Antiquity*, 29, 4–9.

1956. *Stonehenge*, London: Hamish Hamilton.

1965. Wayland's Smithy, *Antiquity*, 39, 126–33.

1970. Silbury Hill 1969–70, *Antiquity*, 44, 313–14.

1972. Burial and population in the British Bronze Age, in F. Lynch and C. Burgess (eds.) *Prehistoric Man in Wales and the West*, pp. 107–16, Bath: Adams and Dart.

Atkinson, R. J. C., J. W. Brailsford and H. G. Wakefield, 1951. A pond barrow at Winterbourne Steapleton, Dorset, *Archaeological Journal*, 108, 1–24.

Atkinson, R. J. C., C. M. Piggott and N. K. Sandars, 1951. *Excavations at Dorchester, Oxon.*, Oxford: Ashmolean Museum.

Avery, M. and J. Close-Brooks, 1969. Shearplace Hill, Sydling St. Nicholas, Dorset, House A: a suggested re-interpretation, *Proceedings of the Prehistoric Society*, 35, 345–51.

Barker, G. and D. Webley, 1978. Causewayed camps and Early Neolithic economies in central southern England, *Proceedings of the Prehistoric Society*, 44, 161–86.

Barker, P., 1977. *Techniques of Archaeological Excavation*, London: Batsford.

Barrett, J. C., 1976. Deverel-Rimbury: problems of chronology and interpretation, in C. Burgess and R. Miket (eds.) *Settlement and Economy in the Third and Second Millennia BC*, pp. 289–307, Oxford: British Archaeological Reports, BAR 33.

1980. The pottery of the later Bronze Age in lowland England, *Proceedings of the Prehistoric Society*, 46, 297–319.

1985. Hoards and related metalwork, in D. V. Clarke, T. G. Cowie and A. Foxon (eds.) *Symbols of Power*, pp. 95–106, Edinburgh: HMSO.

1987. Fields of Discourse: reconstituting a social archaeology, *Critique of Anthropology*, 7(3), 5–16.

1988a. The living, the dead and the ancestors: Neolithic and Early Bronze Age mortuary practices, in J. C. Barrett and I. Kinnes (eds.) *The Archaeology of Context in the Neolithic and Early Bronze Age: Recent Trends*, pp. 30–41, Sheffield: Sheffield Academic Press.

1988b. Food, gender and metal: questions of social reproduction, in M. L. Sørensen and R. Thomas (eds.) *The Bronze Age–Iron Age Transition in Europe: Aspects of Continuity and Change in European Societies c. 1200 to 500 BC*, pp. 304–20, Oxford: British Archaeological Reports.

1989. Time and tradition: the rituals of everyday life, in H.-A. Nordstrom and A. Knape (eds.) *Bronze Age Studies*

Proceedings of the British-Scandinavian Bronze Age Colloquium, Stockholm: National Museum.
Barrett, J. C. and R. Bradley (eds.) 1980. *Settlement and Society in the British Later Bronze Age*, Oxford: British Archaeological Reports, BAR 83.
in prep. *Papers in the Prehistoric Archaeology of Cranborne Chase*, Oxford: Oxbow Books.
Barrett, J. C., R. Bradley, M. Bowden and R. Mead, 1983. South Lodge after Pitt Rivers, *Antiquity*, 57, 193–204.
Barrett, J. C., R. Bradley, M. Green and B. Lewis, 1981. The earlier prehistoric settlement of Cranborne Chase: the first results of current fieldwork, *Antiquaries Journal*, 61, 203–37.
Barrett, J. C. and S. P. Needham, 1988. Production, circulation and exchange: problems in the interpretation of Bronze Age metalwork, in J. C. Barrett and I. Kinnes (eds.) *The Archaeology of Context in the Neolithic and Early Bronze Age: Recent Trends*, pp. 127–40, Sheffield: Sheffield Academic Press.
Bell, M., 1983. Valley sediments as evidence of prehistoric land-use on the South Downs, *Proceedings of the Prehistoric Society*, 49, 119–50.
Binford, L. R., 1971. Mortuary practices: their study and potential, in J. A. Brown (ed.) *Approaches to the Social Dimension of Mortuary Practices*, Memoir of the Society for American Archaeology, No. 25.
1982. The archaeology of place, *Journal of Anthropological Archaeology*, 1, 5–31.
Bloch, M., 1971. *Placing the Dead*, London: Seminar Press.
1985. From cognition to ideology, in R. Fardon (ed.) *Power and Knowledge: Anthropological and Sociological Approaches*, pp. 21–48, Edinburgh: Scottish Academic Press.
Bloch, M. and J. Parry, 1982. *Death and the Regeneration of Life*, Cambridge: Cambridge University Press.
Bonney, D., 1968. Iron Age and Romano-British settlement sites in Wiltshire: some geographical considerations, *Wiltshire Archaeological and Natural History Magazine*, 63, 27–38.
1972. Early boundaries in Wessex, in P. J. Fowler (ed.) *Archaeology and the Landscape*, pp. 168–86, London: John Baker.
Bonney, D. J. and C. N. Moore, 1967. Hamshill Ditches, *Wiltshire Archaeological and Natural History Magazine*, 62, 118–21.
Bowen, H. C., 1961. *Ancient Fields*, London: British Association for the Advancement of Science.
1978. 'Celtic' fields and 'ranch' boundaries in Wessex, in S. Limbrey and J. G. Evans (eds.) *The Effect of Man on the Landscape: the Highland Zone*, pp. 115–23, London: Council for British Archaeology Research Report 21.
Bowman, S. G. E. and J. C. Ambers, 1988. Past and present: the identification of an error in, and the present status of, radiocarbon dating at the British Museum, in H. T. Waterbolk (ed.) *Proceedings of the Second International Symposium on Archaeology and C-14*, Strasbourg: PACT.
Bradley, R., 1973. Two notebooks of General Pitt Rivers, *Antiquity*, 47, 47–50.
1975. Maumbury Rings, Dorchester – the excavations of 1908–13, *Archaeologia*, 105, 1–97.
1978. *The Prehistoric Settlement of Britain*, London: Routledge & Kegan Paul.
1981. 'Various styles of urn' – cemeteries and settlement in southern England, in R. Chapman, I. Kinnes and K. Randsborg (eds.) *The Archaeology of Death*, pp. 93–104, Cambridge: Cambridge University Press.
1982. The destruction of wealth in later prehistory, *Man*, 17, 108–22.
1983a. Archaeology, evolution and the public good: the intellectual development of General Pitt Rivers, *Archaeological Journal*, 140, 1–9.
1983b. The bank barrows and related monuments of Dorset in the light of recent fieldwork, *Proceedings of the Dorset Natural History and Archaeological Society*, 105, 15–20.
1984. *The Social Foundations of Prehistoric Britain*, Harlow: Longman.
1985. *Consumption, Change and the Archaeological Record*, Edinburgh: Department of Archaeology Occasional Papers 13.
1986. A reinterpretation of the Abingdon causewayed enclosure, *Oxoniensia*, 51, 183–7.
1987a. Flint technology and the character of Neolithic settlement, in A. Brown and M. Edmonds (eds.) *Lithic Analysis and Later British Prehistory*, pp. 181–5, Oxford: British Archaeological Reports, BAR 162.
1987b. Radiocarbon and the cursus problem, in J. Gowlett and R. Hedges (eds.) *Archaeological Results of Accelerator Dating*, pp. 139–41, Oxford: Oxford University Committee for Archaeology Monograph 11.
1987c. A field method for investigating the spatial structure of lithic scatters, in A. Brown and M. Edmonds (eds.) *Lithic Analysis and Later British Prehistory*, pp. 39–47, Oxford: British Archaeological Reports, BAR 162.
Bradley, R. and R. Chambers, 1988. A new study of the cursus complex at Dorchester on Thames, *Oxford Journal of Archaeology*, 7, 271–89.
Bradley, R. and A. Ellison, 1975. *Rams Hill*, Oxford: British Archaeological Reports, BAR 19.
Bradley, R. and R. Entwistle, 1985. Thickthorn Down long barrow – a new assessment, *Proceedings of the Dorset Natural History and Archaeological Society*, 107, 174–6.
Bradley, R. and C. Hart, 1983. Prehistoric settlement in the Peak District during the third and second millennia BC: a preliminary analysis in the light of recent fieldwork, *Proceedings of the Prehistoric Society*, 49, 177–93.
Bradley, R. and R. Holgate, 1984. The Neolithic sequence in the upper Thames valley, in R. Bradley and J. Gardiner (eds.) *Neolithic Studies*, pp. 107–34, Oxford: British Archaeological Reports BAR 133.
Bradley, R. and C. Small, 1985. Looking for circular structures in post hole distributions: quantitative analysis

of two settlements from Bronze Age England, *Journal of Archaeological Science*, 12, 285–97.
Bradley, R. and J. Thomas, 1984. Some new information on the henge monument at Maumbury Rings, Dorchester, *Proceedings of the Dorset Natural History and Archaeological Society*, 104, 132–4.
Brailsford, J. W., 1962. *Hod Hill I; Antiquities from Hod Hill in the Durden Collection*, London: British Museum.
Braithwaite, M., 1984. Ritual and prestige in the prehistory of Wessex *c.* 2200–1400 BC: a new dimension to the archaeological evidence, in D. Miller and C. Tilley (eds.) *Ideology, Power and Prehistory*, pp. 93–110, Cambridge: Cambridge University Press.
Britnell, W., 1982. The excavation of two round barrows at Trelystan, Powys, *Proceedings of the Prehistoric Society*, 48, 133–201.
Brothwell, D. R., 1973. *Digging Up Bones*, London: British Museum Natural History.
Burgess, C., 1969. The later Bronze Age in the British Isles and North-Western France, *Archaeological Journal*, 125, 1–45.
1974. The Bronze Age, in C. Renfrew (ed.) *British Prehistory*, pp. 165–232, London: Duckworth.
1976. Burials with metalwork of the later Bronze Age in Wales and beyond, in G. C. Boon and J. M. Lewis (eds.) *Welsh Antiquity*, pp. 81–104, Cardiff: University of Wales Press.
1980. *The Age of Stonehenge*, London: Dent.
n.d. [1980]. The background of early metalworking in Ireland and Britain, in M. Ryan (ed.) *The Origins of Metallurgy in Atlantic Europe*, pp. 207–14, Dublin: Proceedings of the Fifth Atlantic Colloquium 1978.
1986. 'Urnes of no small variety': Collared Urns reviewed, *Proceedings of the Prehistoric Society*, 52, 339–51.
Burgess, C. and D. Coombs, 1979. *Bronze Age Hoards: Some Finds Old and New*, Oxford: British Archaeological Reports, BAR 67.
Burgess, C. and J. D. Cowen, 1972. The Ebnal hoard and Early Bronze Age metal-working traditions, in F. Lynch and C. Burgess (eds.) *Prehistoric Man in Wales and the West*, pp. 167–81, Bath: Adams and Dart.
Burgess, C. and S. Shennan, 1976. The Beaker phenomenon: some suggestions, in C. Burgess and R. Miket (eds.) *Settlement and Economy in the Third and Second Millennia BC*, pp. 309–30, Oxford: British Archaeological Reports, BAR 33.
Burl, A., 1981. *Rites of the Gods*, London: Dent.
1987. *The Stonehenge People*, London: Dent.
Burleigh, R., J. Ambers and K. Matthews, 1982. British Museum natural radiocarbon measurements XV, *Radiocarbon*, 24(3), 262–90.
Burleigh, R., R. Bradley, J. C. Barrett and I. Kinnes, 1982. New radiocarbon dates from south Wessex, *Antiquity*, 56, 130–2.
Burstow, G. P. and G. A. Holleyman, 1957. The late Bronze Age settlement on Itford Hill Sussex, *Proceedings of the Prehistoric Society*, 23, 167–212.
Butler, J. J. and I. F. Smith, 1956. Razors, urns and the British Middle Bronze Age, *University of London Institute of Archaeology Twelfth Annual Report*, 20–52.
Calkin, J. B., 1951. The Bournemouth area in Neolithic and Bronze Age times, *Proceedings of the Dorset Natural History and Archaeological Society*, 73, 32–70.
1962. The Bournemouth area in the Middle and Late Bronze Age, with the 'Deverel-Rimbury' problem reconsidered, *Archaeological Journal*, 119, 1–65.
Care, V., 1979. The production and distribution of Mesolithic axes in Southern England, *Proceedings of the Prehistoric Society*, 45, 93–102.
1982. The collection and distribution of lithic raw materials during the Mesolithic and Neolithic periods in southern England, *Oxford Journal of Archaeology*, 1, 269–85.
Case, H., 1977. The Beaker culture in Britain and Ireland, in R. Mercer (ed.) *Beakers in Britain and Europe*, pp. 71–101, Oxford: British Archaeological Reports, BAR S26.
1982. The linear ditches and southern enclosure, North Stoke, in H. Case and A. Whittle (eds.) *Settlement Patterns in the Oxford Region*, pp. 60–75, London: Council for British Archaeology.
Catherall, P. D., M. Barnett and H. McClean, 1984. *The Southern Feeder; the Archaeology of a Gas Pipeline*, London: British Gas.
Catt, J., 1978. The contribution of loess to soils in lowland Britain, in S. Limbrey and J. Evans (eds.) *The Effect of Man on the Landscape: the Lowland Zone*, pp. 12–20, London: Council for British Archaeology.
Chapman, R., 1981. The emergence of formal disposal areas and the 'problem' of megalithic tombs in Europe, in R. Chapman, I. Kinnes and K. Randsborg (eds.) *The Archaeology of Death*, pp. 71–81, Cambridge: Cambridge University Press.
Childe, V. G., 1947. *Prehistoric Communities of the British Isles*, 2nd edn, London: Chambers.
1956. *Piecing Together the Past*, London: Routledge & Kegan Paul.
Childe, V. G. and I. F. Smith, 1954. The excavation of a Neolithic barrow on Whiteleaf Hill, Bucks., *Proceedings of the Prehistoric Society*, 20, 212–30.
Christie, P. M., 1963. The Stonehenge Cursus, *Wiltshire Archaeological and Natural History Magazine*, 58, 370–82.
1967. A barrow cemetery of the second millennium BC in Wiltshire, England, *Proceedings of the Prehistoric Society*, 33, 336–66.
Clark, J. G. D., 1966. The invasion hypothesis in British prehistory, *Antiquity*, 40, 172–89.
Clarke, D. L., 1970. *Beaker Pottery of Great Britain and Ireland*, Cambridge: Cambridge University Press.
Cleal, R., 1984. The later Neolithic in eastern England, in R. Bradley and J. Gardiner (eds.) *Neolithic Studies*, pp. 135–58, Oxford: British Archaeological Reports, BAR 133.
Coles, J. M., 1987. *Meare Village East: the Excavations of A.*

Bulleid and H. St. George Gray 1932–1952, Somerset Levels Papers 13.

Colt Hoare, R., 1812. *The Ancient History of South Wiltshire*, London: William Millar.

1819. *The Ancient History of North Wiltshire*, London: Lackington, Hughes, Harding, Mavor and Jones.

Cosgrove, D. E., 1984. *Social Formation and Symbolic Landscape*, London: Croom Helm.

Crawford, O. G. S. and A. Keiller, 1928. *Wessex from the Air*, Oxford: Oxford University Press.

Cunliffe, B., 1973. The late pre-Roman Iron Age, in E. Crittall (ed.) *A History of Wiltshire* Volume I pt.2, pp. 26–38, Oxford: Institute of Historical Research.

1978a. *Iron Age Communities in Britain*, London: Routledge & Kegan Paul.

1978b. *Hengistbury Head*, London: Elek.

1984. *Danebury: an Iron Age Hillfort in Hampshire*, London: Council for British Archaeology Research Report 52.

1987. *Hengistbury Head, Dorset*, Vol. 1, Oxford: University Committee for Archaeology Monograph 13.

Cunliffe, B. and D. Miles (eds.), 1984. *Aspects of the Iron Age in Central Southern Britain*, Oxford: University Committee for Archaeology Monograph 2.

Cunnington, M., 1929. *Woodhenge*, Devizes: George Simpson.

Curwen, E. C., 1938. The early development of agriculture in Britain, *Proceedings of the Prehistoric Society*, 4, 27–51.

1939. Blunted axe-like implements, *Proceedings of the Prehistoric Society*, 5, 196–201.

Dacre, M. and A. Ellison, 1981. A Bronze Age urn cemetery at Kimpton, Hampshire, *Proceedings of the Prehistoric Society*, 47, 147–203.

Davis, S. M., 1981. Excavations at Old Down Farm, Andover, Part II: Prehistoric and Roman, *Proceedings of the Hampshire Field Club*, 37, 81–163.

Dixon, P. 1976. Crickley Hill, 1969–1972, in D. W. Harding (ed.) *Hillforts: Later Prehistoric Earthworks in Britain and Ireland*, pp. 161–75 and 427–9, London: Academic Press.

Drew, C. and S. Piggott, 1936. The excavation of long barrow 163a on Thickthorn Down, Dorset, *Proceedings of the Prehistoric Society*, 2, 77–96.

Drewett, P., 1975. The excavation of an oval burial mound of the third millennium BC at Alfriston, East Sussex, 1974, *Proceedings of the Prehistoric Society*, 41, 119–52.

1982. Later Bronze Age downland economy and excavations at Black Patch, East Sussex, *Proceedings of the Prehistoric Society*, 48, 321–400.

Dunning, G., 1966. Neolithic occupation sites in east Kent, *Antiquaries Journal*, 46, 1–25.

Edmonds, M., 1987. Rocks and risk: problems with lithic procurement strategies, in A. Brown and M. Edmonds (eds.) *Lithic Analysis and Later British Prehistory*, pp. 155–79, Oxford: British Archaeological Reports, BAR 162.

Ehrenberg, M. R., 1977. *Bronze Age Spearheads from Berkshire, Buckinghamshire and Oxfordshire*, Oxford: British Archaeological Reports, BAR 34.

Ellison, A., 1980a. Deverel-Rimbury urn cemeteries: the evidence for social organisation, in J. C. Barrett and R. Bradley (eds.) *Settlement and Society in the British Later Bronze Age*, pp. 115–26, Oxford: British Archaeological Reports, BAR 83.

1980b. Settlements and regional exchange: a case study, in J. C. Barrett and R. Bradley (eds.) *Settlement and Society in the British Later Bronze Age*, pp. 127–40, Oxford: British Archaeological Reports, BAR 83.

Erasmus, C., 1965. Monument building: some field experiments, *Southwestern Journal of Anthropology*, 21, 277–301.

Evans, A. M. and M. K. Jones, 1979. The plant remains, in G. J. Wainwright, *Gussage All Saints: an Iron Age Settlement Site in Dorset*, pp. 172–5, London: HMSO.

Evans, J., 1972. *Land Snails in Archaeology*, London: Seminar Press.

1984. Stonehenge – the environment in the late Neolithic and Early Bronze Age, *Wiltshire Archaeological and Natural History Magazine*, 78, 7–30.

Fasham, P., 1982. The excavation of four ring-ditches in Central Hampshire, *Proceedings of the Hampshire Field Club*, 38, 19–56.

Feachem, R. W., 1971. Unfinished hillforts, in M. Jesson and D. Hill (eds.) *The Iron Age and its Hillforts*, pp. 19–39, Southampton: Department of Archaeology.

Fisher, P. F., 1983. Pedogenesis within the archaeological landscape at South Lodge Camp, Wiltshire, England, *Geoderma*, 29, 93–105.

Fleming, A., 1971. Territorial patterns in Bronze Age Wessex, *Proceedings of the Prehistoric Society*, 37, 138–66.

Foley, R., 1981. Off-site archaeology: an alternative approach for the short-sighted, in I. Hodder, G. Isaac and N. Hammond (eds.) *Pattern of the Past*, pp. 157–83, Cambridge: Cambridge University Press.

Ford, S., 1987a. Chronological and functional aspects of flint assemblages, in A. Brown and M. Edmonds (eds.) *Lithic Analysis and Later British Prehistory*, pp. 67–85, Oxford: British Archaeological Reports, BAR 162.

1987b. Flint scatters and prehistoric settlement patterns in South Oxfordshire and East Berkshire, in A. Brown and M. Edmonds (eds.) *Lithic Analysis and Later British Prehistory*, pp. 101–35, Oxford: British Archaeological Reports, BAR 162.

Ford, S., R. Bradley, J. Hawkes and P. Fisher, 1984. Flint-working in the metal age, *Oxford Journal of Archaeology*, 3, 157–73.

Fowler, P. 1971. Early prehistoric agriculture in western Europe: some archaeological evidence, in D. D. A. Simpson (ed.) *Economy and Settlement in Neolithic and Early Bronze Age Britain and Europe*, pp. 153–82, Leicester: Leicester University Press.

Friedman, J. and M. J. Rowlands, 1977. Notes towards an epigenetic model of the evolution of 'civilisation', in J. Friedman and M. J. Rowlands (eds.) *The Evolution of Social Systems*, pp. 201–76, London: Duckworth.

Gardiner, J., 1984. Lithic distributions and Neolithic settlement patterns in central southern England, in R. Bradley and J. Gardiner (eds.) *Neolithic Studies*, pp. 15–40, Oxford: British Archaeological Reports, BAR 133.
1985. Intra-site patterning in the flint assemblage from the Dorset Cursus, 1984, *Proceedings of the Dorset Natural History and Archaeological Society*, 105, 87–93.
1987. Tales of the unexpected: approaches to the assessment and interpretation of museum flint collections, in A. Brown and M. Edmonds (eds.) *Lithic Analysis and Later British Prehistory*, pp. 49–65, Oxford: British Archaeological Reports, BAR 162.
1988. *The Composition and Distribution of Neolithic Surface Flint Industries in Central Southern England*, PhD Thesis, University of Reading.

Genoves, S., 1969a. Sex determination in earlier man, in D. R. Brothwell and E. Higgs (eds.) *Science in Archaeology*, pp. 429–39, London: Thames and Hudson.
1969b. Estimation of age and mortality, in D. R. Brothwell and E. Higgs (eds.) *Science in Archaeology*, pp. 440–52, London: Thames and Hudson.

Gerloff, S., 1975. *The Early Bronze Age Daggers in Great Britain*, Munich: Prähistorische Bronzefunde VI/2.

Gingell, C., 1980. The Marlborough Downs in the Bronze Age: the first results of current research, in J. C. Barrett and R. Bradley (eds.) *Settlement and Society in the British Later Bronze Age*, pp. 209–22, Oxford: British Archaeological Reports, BAR 83.

Gingell, C. and P. Harding, 1983. A fieldwalking survey in the Vale of Wardour, *Wiltshire Archaeological and Natural History Magazine*, 77, 11–25.

Gingell, C. and A. J. Lawson, 1985. Excavations at Potterne, 1984, *Wiltshire Archaeological and Natural History Magazine*, 79, 101–8.

Godelier, M., 1986. *The Mental and the Material*, London: Verso.

Goody, J., 1961. Religion and ritual: the definitional problem, *British Journal of Sociology*, 12, 142–64.

Gordon, D. and C. Ellis, 1985. Species composition parameters and life tables: their application to detect environmental change in fossil land molluscan assemblages, in N. Fieller, D. Gilbertson and N. Ralph (eds.) *Palaeoenvironmental Investigations*, pp. 153–64, Oxford: British Archaeological Reports, BAR S258.

Gould, R. A., 1980. *Living Archaeology*, Cambridge: Cambridge University Press.

Grant, A., 1982. The use of tooth wear as a guide to the age of domestic ungulates, in R. Wilson, C. Grigson and S. Payne (eds.) *Ageing and Sexing Animal Bones from Archaeological Sites*, pp. 91–108, Oxford: British Archaeological Reports, BAR 109.

Green, C., F. Lynch and H. White, 1982. The excavation of two round barrows on Launceston Down, *Proceedings of the Dorset Natural History and Archaeological Society*, 104, 39–58.

Green, C. and S. Rollo-Smith, 1984. The excavation of eighteen round barrows near Shrewton, Wiltshire, *Proceedings of the Prehistoric Society*, 50, 99–120.

Green, H. S., 1980. *The Flint Arrowheads of the British Isles*, Oxford: British Archaeological Reports, BAR 75.

Green, M., 1981. Interim report on the excavation of an unrecorded pond barrow at Down Farm, Gussage St. Michael, *Proceedings of the Dorset Natural History and Archaeological Society*, 103, 117.
1982. Second and final interim report on the excavation of an unrecorded pond barrow at Down Farm, Gussage St. Michael, *Proceedings of the Dorset Natural History and Archaeological Society*, 104, 170–2.
1985. A burnt deposit at Blandford, *Proceedings of the Dorset Natural History and Archaeological Society*, 107, 153.

Greenfield, E., 1960. The excavation of Barrow 4 at Swarkestone, Derbyshire, *Derbyshire Archaeological Journal*, 80, 1–48.

Greenwell, W., 1877. *British Barrows*, Oxford: Clarendon Press.

Gregory, C. A., 1982. *Gifts and Commodities*, London: Academic Press.

Gresham, C. A., 1939. Spettisbury Rings, Dorset, *Archaeological Journal*, 96, 114–31.

Grinsell, L. V., 1957. Archaeological gazetteer, in R. B. Pugh and E. Crittall (eds.) *A History of Wiltshire*, Vol. Ipt.2, pp. 21–279, London: Institute of Historical Research, Victoria County Histories.
1959. *Dorset Barrows*, Dorchester: Dorset Natural History and Archaeological Society.
1982. *Dorset Barrows Supplement*, Dorchester: Dorset Natural History and Archaeological Society.

Guido, M., J. Henderson, M. Cable, J. Bayley and L. Biek, 1984. A Bronze Age glass bead from Wilsford, Wiltshire: barrow G42 in the Lake group, *Proceedings of the Prehistoric Society*, 50, 245–54.

Guilbert, G., 1981. Double-ring roundhouses, probable and possible, in prehistoric Britain, *Proceedings of the Prehistoric Society*, 47, 299–317.

Halpin, C. and R. Bradley, in prep. *The Neolithic and Bronze Age Cemetery at Barrow Hills, Radley, Oxfordshire*, Oxford: University Committee for Archaeology.

Hardin, M., 1983. The structure of Tarascan pottery painting, in D. Washburn (ed.) *Structure and Cognition in Art*, pp. 8–24, Cambridge: Cambridge University Press.

Harding, D. W., 1960. Excavation of multiple banks, Thickthorn Down, Dorset, *Proceedings of the Dorset Natural History and Archaeological Society*, 81, 110–13.
1974. *The Iron Age in Lowland Britain*, London: Routledge & Kegan Paul.

Harding, D. W. and I. M. Blake, 1963. An early Iron Age settlement in Dorset, *Antiquity*, 37, 63–4.

Haselgrove, C., 1986. An Iron Age community and its hillfort: the excavations at Danebury, Hampshire 1969–79. A review, *Archaeological Journal*, 143, 363–9.

Haskins, L. E., 1978. The vegetational history of south east Dorset, Southampton University: Ph.D. thesis.

Hawkes, C. F. C., 1959. The ABC of the British Iron Age, *Antiquity*, 33, 170–82.

Hawkes, C. F. C. and G. C. Dunning, 1931. The Belgae of Britain and Gaul, *Archaeological Journal*, 87, 150–335.

Hawkes, C. and S. Piggott, 1947. Britons, Romans and Saxons round Salisbury and in Cranborne Chase, *Archaeological Journal*, 104, 27–81.

Healy, F., 1987. Prediction or prejudice? The relationship between field survey and excavation, in A. Brown and M. Edmonds (eds.) *Lithic Analysis and Later British Prehistory*, pp. 9–17, Oxford: British Archaeological Reports, BAR 162.

Hertz, R., 1960. *Death and the Right Hand* (translated by R. and C. Needham), New York: Free Press.

Hingley, R., 1984. Towards social analysis in archaeology: Celtic society in the Iron Age of the upper Thames valley, in B. Cunliffe and D. Miles (eds.) *Aspects of the Iron Age in Central Southern Britain*, pp. 72–88, Oxford: University Committee for Archaeology Monograph 2.

Hingley, R. and D. Miles, 1984. Aspects of Iron Age settlement in the upper Thames valley, in B. Cunliffe and D. Miles (eds.) *Aspects of the Iron Age in Central Southern Britain*, pp. 52–71, Oxford: University Committee for Archaeology Monograph 2.

Hodder, I., 1982. Sequences of structural change in the Dutch Neolithic, in I. Hodder (ed.) *Symbolic and Structural Archaeology*, pp. 162–77, Cambridge: Cambridge University Press.

Hodson, F. R., 1960. Reflections on the ABC of the British Iron Age, *Antiquity*, 34, 138–40.

1964. Cultural groupings within the British pre-Roman Iron Age, *Proceedings of the Prehistoric Society*, 30, 99–110.

Holden, E. W., 1972. A Bronze Age cemetery-barrow on Itford Hill, Beddingham, Sussex, *Sussex Archaeological Collections*, 110, 70–117.

Holleyman, G., 1987. *Two Dorset Archaeologists in Sussex*. Privately printed.

Horsey, I. and K. Jarvis, 1984. The Stour Valley Gravels Project, *Proceedings of the Dorset Natural History and Archaeological Society*, 106, 114.

Jackson, D., 1976. The excavation of Neolithic and Bronze Age sites at Aldwincle, Northants, *Northamptonshire Archaeology*, 11, 12–70.

Jarvis, K., 1983. *Excavations in Christchurch 1969–1980*, Dorchester: Dorset Natural History and Archaeological Society.

Jessup, R., 1939. Further excavations at Julliberrie's Grave, Chilham, *Antiquaries Journal*, 19, 260–81.

Jewell, P. A. and G. W. Dimbleby, 1968. The experimental earthwork on Overton Down, Wiltshire, England: the first four years, *Proceedings of the Prehistoric Society*, 32, 313–42.

Jockenhovel, A., 1980. *Die Rasiermesser in Westeuropa*, Munich: Prähistorische Bronzefunde VIII/3.

Jones, M. K., 1978. The plant remains, in M. Parrington (ed.) *The Excavations of an Iron Age Settlement, Bronze Age Ring Ditches and Roman Features at Ashville Trading Estate, Abingdon, Oxfordshire 1974–76*, pp. 93–110, London: Council for British Archaeology.

1984a. The ecological and cultural implications of selected carbonised seed assemblages from southern Britain, Oxford University: D.Phil. thesis.

1984b. The plant remains, in B. Cunliffe, *Danebury: an Iron Age Hillfort in Hampshire*, pp. 483–95, London: Council for British Archaeology.

1984c. Regional patterns in crop production, in B. Cunliffe and D. Miles (eds.) *Aspects of the Iron Age in Central Southern Britain*, pp. 120–5, Oxford: University Committee for Archaeology.

Kinnes, I., 1975. Monumental function in British Neolithic burial practices, *World Archaeology*, 7, 16–29.

1979. *Round Barrows and Ring-Ditches in the British Neolithic*, London: British Museum Occasional Paper, No. 7.

1981. Dialogues with death, in R. Chapman, I. Kinnes and K. Randsborg (eds.) *The Archaeology of Death*, pp. 83–91, Cambridge: Cambridge University Press.

1984. Prehistoric sites in the Great Wold Valley, *Archaeological Journal*, 141, 36–7.

Kinnes, I., T. Schadla-Hall, P. Chadwick and P. Dean, 1983. Duggleby Howe reconsidered, *Archaeological Journal*, 140, 83–108.

Knight, R. W., C. Browne and L. V. Grinsell, 1972. Prehistoric skeletons from Tormarton, *Transactions of the Bristol and Gloucestershire Archaeology Society*, 91, 14–17.

Kristiansen, K., 1978. The consumption of wealth in Bronze Age Denmark. A study in the dynamics of economic process in tribal societies, in K. Kristiansen and C. Paludan-Müller (eds.) *New Directions in Scandinavian Archaeology*, pp. 158–90, Copenhagen: National Museum.

Lanting, J. N. and J. D. van der Waals, 1972. British Beakers as seen from the continent, *Helinium*, 12, 20–46.

Leach, E., 1976. *Culture and Communication*, Cambridge: Cambridge University Press.

Leeds, E. T., 1938. Further excavations in Barrow Hills Field, Radley, Berks, *Oxoniensia*, 3, 31–40.

Legge, A. J., 1981. The agricultural economy, in R. J. Mercer, *Grimes Graves Norfolk, Excavations 1971–72*, Vol. I, 79–103, London: HMSO.

forthcoming. *Animal Bones from the British Museum Excavations at Grimes Graves*, London: British Museum Fascicule Series.

Lewis, B. and R. Coleman, 1982. Pentridge Hill, Dorset: trial excavation, *Proceedings of the Dorset Natural History and Archaeological Society*, 104, 59–65.

Longley, D., 1980. *Runnymede Bridge 1976, Excavations on the Site of a Late Bronze Age Settlement*, Guildford: Surrey Archaeological Society Research Volume 6.

Longworth, I. H., 1984. *Collared Urns of the Bronze Age in*

Great Britain and Ireland, Cambridge: Cambridge University Press.
Manby, T., 1974. *Grooved Ware Sites in Yorkshire and the North of England*, Oxford: British Archaeological Reports, BAR 9.
Margary, I. D., 1973. *Roman Roads in Britain* (3rd edn).
Megaw, J. V. S. and D. D. A. Simpson, 1979. *Introduction to British Prehistory*, Leicester: Leicester University Press.
Mercer, R., 1980. *Hambledon Hill – A Neolithic Landscape*, Edinburgh: Edinburgh University Press.
Miller, D. and C. Tilley, 1984. *Ideology, Power and Prehistory*, Cambridge: Cambridge University Press.
Millett, M. M., 1986. An early Roman cemetery at Alton, Hampshire, *Proceedings of the Hampshire Field Club*, 42, 43–87.
Monk, M. and P. J. Fasham, 1980. Carbonised plant remains from two Iron Age sites in central Hampshire, *Proceedings of the Prehistoric Society*, 46, 321–44.
Moore, H., 1986. *Space, Text and Gender*, Cambridge: Cambridge University Press.
Moore, W. R. G., J. M. Williams and A. Boddington, 1975. A late Neolithic site at Ecton, Northampton, *Northamptonshire Archaeology*, 10, 3–30.
Morgan, F. de M., 1959. The excavation of a long barrow at Nutbane, Hants., *Proceedings of the Prehistoric Society*, 25, 15–51.
Murphy, P. J., forthcoming. The plant remains from Springfield Barnes, Essex.
Musson, C., 1970. House-plans and prehistory, *Current Archaeology*, 2, 267–75.
Nash, D., 1976. The growth of urban society in France, in B. Cunliffe and R. T. Rowley (eds.) *Oppida: the Beginnings of Urbanisation in Barbarian Europe*, pp. 95–133, Oxford: British Archaeological Reports, BAR S11.
Needham, S., 1980. The bronzes, in D. Longley, *Runnymede Bridge 1976: Excavations on the Site of a Late Bronze Age Settlement*, pp. 13–27, Guildford: Surrey Archaeological Society Research Volume 6.
1988. Selective deposition in the British Early Bronze Age, *World Archaeology*, 20, 229–48.
O'Connor, B., 1980. *Cross-Channel Relations in the Later Bronze Age*, Oxford: British Archaeological Reports, BAR S91.
1984. Review of Schmidt and Burgess 1981, *Scottish Archaeological Review*, 3, 58–62.
Olsson, I. U., 1983. Radiocarbon dating in the Arctic region, *Radiocarbon*, 25(2), 393–4.
Ó Ríordáin, S. P., 1936. The halberd in Bronze Age Europe, *Archaeologia*, 86, 195–321.
Palmer, R., 1984. *Danebury: an Aerial Photographic Interpretation of its Environs*, London: RCHM.
Parke, A. L., 1953. The excavation of a bell-barrow, Oakley Down, Wimborne St Giles, *Proceedings of the Dorset Natural History and Archaeological Society*, 75, 36–44.
Patrick, J., 1974. Midwinter sunrise at Newgrange, *Nature*, 249, 517–19.
Payne, S., 1973. Kill-off patterns in sheep and goat, *Anatolian Studies*, 23, 281–303.
Pearson, G. W., J. R. Pilcher, M. G. L. Baillie, D. M. Corbett and F. Qua, 1986. High-precision ^{14}C measurements of Irish oaks to show the natural ^{14}C variations from AD 1840–5210 BC, *Radiocarbon*, 28(2), 393–4.
Pearson, G. W. and M. Stuiver, 1986. High precision calibration of the radiocarbon time scale 500–2500 BC, *Radiocarbon*, 28(2B), 839–62.
Penny, A. and J. Wood, 1973. The Dorset Cursus complex – a Neolithic astronomical observatory? *Archaeological Journal*, 130, 44–76.
Perry, B. T., 1966. Some recent discoveries in Hampshire, in A. C. Thomas (ed.) *Rural Settlement in Roman Britain*, pp. 39–42, London: Council for British Archaeology Research Report 7.
1970. Iron Age enclosures and settlement on the Hampshire chalklands, *Archaeological Journal*, 126, 29–43.
1972. Excavations at Bramdean, Hampshire, 1965 and 1966, and a discussion of similar sites in southern England, *Proceedings of the Hampshire Field Club*, 29, 41–77.
1982. Excavations at Bramdean, 1973 to 1977, *Proceedings of the Hampshire Field Club*, 38, 57–74.
1986. Excavations at Bramdean, Hampshire, 1983 and 1984, with some further discussion of the 'banjo' syndrome, *Proceedings of the Hampshire Field Club*, 42, 35–42.
Petersen, F., 1972. Traditions of multiple burial in later Neolithic and Early Bronze Age England, *Archaeological Journal*, 129, 22–55.
1981. *The Excavation of a Bronze Age Cemetery on Knighton Heath, Dorset*, Oxford: British Archaeological Reports, BAR 98.
Pierpoint, S., 1980. *Social Patterns in Yorkshire Prehistory*, Oxford: British Archaeological Reports, BAR 74.
Piggott, C. M., 1942. Five late Bronze Age enclosures in north Wiltshire, *Proceedings of the Prehistoric Society*, 8, 48–61.
1946. The late Bronze Age razors of the British Isles, *Proceedings of the Prehistoric Society*, 12, 121–41.
Piggott, S., 1938. The early Bronze Age in Wessex, *Proceedings of the Prehistoric Society*, 4, 52–106.
1954. *The Neolithic Cultures of the British Isles*, Cambridge: Cambridge University Press.
1973. The final phase of bronze technology, in E. Crittall (ed.) *A History of Wiltshire* Vol. Ipt2, 376–407, Oxford: Institute of Historical Research, Victoria County Histories.
Piggott, S. and C. M. Piggott, 1944. Excavations of barrows on Crichel and Launceston Downs, Dorset, *Archaeologia*, 90, 47–80.
Preece, R., 1980. The biostratigraphy and dating of the tufa deposit at the Mesolithic site at Blackenwell, Dorset, England, *Journal of Archaeological Science*, 7, 345–62.
Pitts, M. and R. Jacobi, 1979. Some aspects of change in flaked stone industries of the Mesolithic and Neolithic in southern Britain, *Journal of Archaeological Science*, 6, 163–77.

Rahtz, P., 1962. Neolithic and Beaker sites at Downton, Wiltshire, *Wiltshire Archaeological and Natural History Magazine*, 58, 116–42.
forthcoming. Bowerchalke 1959: excavations at Great Ditch Banks and Middle Chase Ditch.
Rahtz, P. and A. M. ApSimon, 1962. Excavations at Shearplace Hill, Sydling St. Nicholas, Dorset, England, *Proceedings of the Prehistoric Society*, 28, 289–328.
Ratcliffe-Densham, H. and M. Ratcliffe-Densham, 1961. An anomalous earthwork of the late Bronze Age on Cock Hill, *Sussex Archaeological Collections*, 99, 78–101.
Renfrew, C., 1973. Monuments, mobilisation and social organisation in Neolithic Wessex, in C. Renfrew (ed.) *The Explanation of Culture Change*, pp. 539–58, London: Duckworth.
1976. Megaliths, territories and population, in S. J. de Laet (ed.) *Acculturation and Continuity in Atlantic Europe*, pp. 198–220, Bruges: Dissertationes Archaeologicae Gandenses, 16.
1977. Space, time and polity, in J. Friedman and M. J. Rowlands (eds.) *The Evolution of Social Systems*, pp. 89–112, London: Duckworth.
1986. Varna and the emergence of wealth in prehistoric Europe, in A. Appadurai (ed.) *The Social Life of Things*, pp. 141–68, Cambridge: Cambridge University Press.
Richards, C. and J. Thomas, 1984. Ritual activity and structured deposition in later Neolithic Wessex, in R. Bradley and J. Gardiner (eds.) *Neolithic Studies*, pp. 189–218, Oxford: British Archaeological Reports, BAR 133.
Richards, J., 1984. The development of the Neolithic landscape in the environs of Stonehenge, in R. Bradley and J. Gardiner (eds.) *Neolithic Studies*, pp. 177–87, Oxford: British Archaeological Reports, BAR 133.
Richmond, I., 1968. *Hod Hill*, Vol. 2, London: British Museum.
Rowlands, M. J., 1976. *The Production and Distribution of Metalwork in the Middle Bronze Age of Southern Britain*, Oxford: British Archaeological Reports, BAR 31.
1980. Kinship, alliance and exchange in the European Bronze Age, in J. C. Barrett and R. Bradley (eds.) *Settlement and Society in the British Later Bronze Age*, pp. 15–55, Oxford: British Archaeological Reports, BAR 83.
Royal Commission on Historical Monuments, 1970. *County of Dorset, Vol. 2: Southeast (Part 3)*, London: HMSO.
1972. *County of Dorset, Vol. 4: North*, London: HMSO.
1975. *County of Dorset, Vol. 5: East Dorset*, London: HMSO.
forthcoming. *Bokerley Dyke and the Pattern of Archaeological Features in its Vicinity*, London: HMSO.
Saville, A., 1981. *Grimes Graves, Norfolk, Excavations 1971–72*, Vol. 2: *The Flint Assemblage*, London: HMSO.
Saxe, A., 1970. *Social Dimensions of Mortuary Practices*, Michigan University: Ph.D. dissertation.
Schiffer, M., 1983. Toward the identification of formation processes, *American Antiquity*, 48, 675–706.
Schmidt, P. K. and C. Burgess, 1981. *The Axes of Scotland and Northern England*, Munich: Prähistorische Bronzefunde IX/7.
Schofield, A. J., 1987. Putting lithics to the test: non-site analysis and the Neolithic settlement of southern England, *Oxford Journal of Archaeology*, 6, 269–86.
Selwood, L., 1984. Tribal boundaries viewed from the perspective of numismatic evidence, in B. Cunliffe and D. Miles (eds.) *Aspects of the Iron Age in Central Southern Britain*, Oxford: University Committee on Archaeology Monograph 2.
Shanks, M. and C. Tilley, 1982. Ideology, symbolic power and ritual communication: a reinterpretation of Neolithic mortuary practices, in I. Hodder (ed.) *Symbolic and Structural Archaeology*, pp. 155–61, Cambridge: Cambridge University Press.
1987. *Reconstructing Archaeology: Theory and Practice*, Cambridge: Cambridge University Press.
Sharples, N., 1985. Individual and community: the changing role of megaliths in the Orcadian Neolithic, *Proceedings of the Prehistoric Society*, 51, 59–74.
Shennan, S., 1982. Ideology, change and the European early Bronze Age, in I. Hodder (ed.) *Symbolic and Structural Archaeology*, pp. 155–61, Cambridge: Cambridge University Press.
Simonds, 1854. *The Age of the Ox, Sheep and Pig*, London: W. S. Orr.
Smith, I. F. and D. D. A. Simpson, 1966. Excavation of a round barrow on Overton Hill, north Wiltshire, England, *Proceedings of the Prehistoric Society*, 32, 122–55.
Smith, J. T., 1978. Villas as a key to social structure, in M. Todd (ed.) *Studies in the Romano-British Villa*, pp. 149–85, Leicester: Leicester University Press.
Smith, M. A., 1959. Some Somerset hoards and their place in the Bronze Age of southern Britain, *Proceedings of the Prehistoric Society*, 25, 144–87.
Smith, R., 1984. The ecology of Neolithic farming systems as exemplified by the Avebury region of Wiltshire, *Proceedings of the Prehistoric Society*, 50, 99–120.
Sparey-Green, C., 1987. *Excavations at Poundbury, Vol. 1: The Settlements*, Dorchester: Dorset Natural History and Archaeological Society.
Startin, W., 1982. Prehistoric earthmoving, in H. Case and A. Whittle (eds.) *Settlement Patterns in the Oxford Region*, pp. 153–6, London: Council for British Archaeology.
Startin, W. and R. Bradley, 1981. Some notes on work organisation and society in prehistoric Wessex, in C. Ruggles and A. Whittle (eds.) *Astronomy and Society in Britain during the Period 4000–1500 BC*, pp. 289–96, Oxford: British Archaeological Reports, BAR 88.
Stead, I. M., 1968. Excavations in Blagdon Copse, Hurstborne Tarrant, Hampshire 1961, *Proceedings of the Hampshire Field Club*, 23, 81–9.
Stone, J. F. S., 1933. Excavations at Easton Down,

Winterslow 1931–1932, *Wiltshire Archaeological and Natural History Magazine*, 46, 225–42.

1934. Three 'Peterborough' dwelling pits and a doubly-stockaded Early Iron Age ditch at Winterbourne Dauntsey, *Wiltshire Archaeological and Natural History Magazine*, 46, 445–53.

1935. Some discoveries at Ratfyn, Amesbury and their bearing on the date of Woodhenge, *Wiltshire Archaeological and Natural History Magazine*, 47, 55–67.

1941. The Deverel-Rimbury settlement on Thorny Down, Winterbourne Gunner, S. Wilts., *Proceedings of the Prehistoric Society*, 7, 114–33.

Stuiver, M. and G. W. Pearson, 1986. High precision calibration of the radiocarbon time scale AD 1950–500 BC, *Radiocarbon*, 28 (2B), 805–38.

Sumner, H., 1913. *The Ancient Earthworks of Cranborne Chase*, London: Chiswick Press.

Thomas, J., 1986. Relations of Power: the Neolithic of central south-west England, Sheffield University: Ph.D. thesis.

Thomas, N. and C. Thomas, 1955. Excavations at Snail Down, Everleigh 1953 and 1955: an interim report, *Wiltshire Archaeological and Natural History Magazine*, 56, 127–48.

Thomas, R., 1988. The bronze–iron transition in southern England, in M. L. Sorensen and R. Thomas (eds.) *The Bronze Age–Iron Age Transition in Europe: Aspects of Continuity and Change in European Societies c. 1200–500 BC*, pp. 287–303, Oxford: British Archaeological Reports.

Thomas, R., M. Robinson, J. Barrett and B. Wilson, 1986. A late Bronze Age riverside settlement at Wallingford, Oxfordshire, *Archaeological Journal*, 143, 174–200.

Thompson, M. W., 1976. *Catalogue of the Correspondence and Papers of Augustus Henry Lane Fox Pitt Rivers*, London: Royal Commission on Historical Manuscripts.

Thorpe, I., 1984. Ritual, power and ideology: a reconstruction of earlier Neolithic rituals in Wessex, in R. Bradley and J. Gardiner (eds.) *Neolithic Studies*, pp. 41–60, Oxford: British Archaeological Reports, BAR 133.

Thorpe, I. and C. Richards, 1984. The decline of ritual authority and the introduction of beakers into Britain, in R. Bradley and J. Gardiner (eds.) *Neolithic Studies*, pp. 67–84, Oxford: British Archaeological Reports, BAR 133.

Tilley, C., 1984. Ideology and the legitimation of power in the middle Neolithic of southern Sweden, in D. Miller and C. Tilley (eds.) *Ideology, Power and Prehistory*, pp. 111–46, Cambridge: Cambridge University Press.

Tite, M. S., S. G. E. Bowman, J. C. Ambers and K. J. Matthews, 1987. Preliminary statement on an error in British Museum radiocarbon dates (BM-1700 to BM-2315), *Antiquity*, 61, 168.

1988. Preliminary statement on an error in British Museum radiocarbon dates (BM-1700 to BM2315), *Radiocarbon*, 30(1), 132.

Toms, H., 1925. Bronze Age or earlier lynchets, *Proceedings of the Dorset Natural History and Archaeological Society*, 46, 88–100.

Turner, V., 1967. *The Forest of Symbols*, London: Cornell University Press.

1969. *The Ritual Process*, New York: Cornell University Press.

Van Gennep, A., 1960. *The Rites of Passage*, Chicago: University of Chicago Press.

Vyner, B., 1985. Evidence for mortuary practices in the Neolithic burial mounds and cairns of northern Britain, *Scottish Archaeological Review*, 4, 11–16.

Wainwright, G., 1968. The excavation of a Durotrigian farmstead near Tollard Royal in Cranborne Chase, Southern England, *Proceedings of the Prehistoric Society*, 34, 102–47.

1969. A review of henge monuments in the light of recent research, *Proceedings of the Prehistoric Society*, 35, 112–33.

1971. The excavation of a Late Neolithic enclosure at Marden, Wiltshire, *Antiquaries Journal*, 51, 177–239.

1979a. *Gussage All Saints; an Iron Age Settlement in Dorset*, London: HMSO.

1979b. *Mount Pleasant, Dorset: Excavations 1970–1971*, London: Society of Antiquaries.

Wainwright, G. and I. Longworth, 1971. *Durrington Walls: Excavations 1966–1968*, London: Society of Antiquaries.

Warne, C., 1866. *The Celtic Tumuli of Dorset*. Privately printed.

Waton, P., 1982. Man's impact on the chalkland: some new pollen evidence, in M. Bell and S. Limbrey (eds.) *Archaeological Aspects of Woodland Ecology*, pp. 75–91, Oxford: British Archaeological Reports, BAR S146.

Wheeler, H., 1979. Excavation at Willington, Derbyshire, 1970–1972, *Derbyshire Archaeological Journal*, 99, 58–220.

Whimster, R. P., 1981. *Burial Practices in Iron Age Britain*, Oxford: British Archaeological Reports, BAR 90.

White, D. A., 1970. Excavation of an Iron Age round barrow near Handley, Dorset, 1969, *Antiquaries Journal*, 50, 26–36.

1982. *The Bronze Age Cremation Cemeteries at Simons Ground, Dorset*, Dorchester: Dorset Natural History and Archaeological Society Monograph 3.

Whittle, A., 1977. *The Earlier Neolithic of Southern Britain and its Continental Background*, Oxford: British Archaeological Reports, BAR S35.

1981. Later Neolithic society in Britain: a realignment, in A. W. R. Whittle, and C. L. N. Ruggles (eds.) *Astronomy and Society in Britain during the Period 4000–1500 BC*, pp. 297–342, Oxford: British Archaeological Reports, BAR 88.

Woodburn, J., 1982. Social dimensions of death in four African hunting and gathering societies, in M. Bloch and J. Parry (eds.) *Death and the Regeneration of Life*, pp. 87–210, Cambridge: Cambridge University Press.

INDEX

Compiled by James R. Smith

References to figures are given in italics.
References to tables are preceded by a 'T'.

Lightning Source UK Ltd.
Milton Keynes UK
UKOW06f2023130314

228071UK00001B/6/P

9 780521 109222